Microsoft® Official Academic Course

Configuring Windows 8.1
Exam 70-687

Craig Zacker

WILEY

Credits

VP & PUBLISHER	Don Fowley
EXECUTIVE EDITOR	John Kane
EXECUTIVE MARKETING MANAGER	Chris Ruel
MICROSOFT PRODUCT MANAGER	Keith Loeber of Microsoft Learning
EDITORIAL PROGRAM ASSISTANT	Allison Winkle
TECHNICAL EDITOR	Brian Svidergol
ASSISTANT MARKETING MANAGER	Debbie Martin
SENIOR PRODUCTION & MANUFACTURING MANAGER	Janis Soo
PRODUCTION EDITOR	Joyce Poh
CREATIVE DIRECTOR	Harry Nolan
COVER DESIGNER	Georgina Smith
SENIOR PRODUCT DESIGNER	Thomas Kulesa
CONTENT EDITOR	Wendy Ashenberg

This book was set in Garamond by Aptara, Inc. and printed and bound by Bind Rite Graphics. The covers were printed by Bind Rite Graphics.

Copyright © 2014 by John Wiley & Sons, Inc. All rights reserved.

No part of this publication may be reproduced, stored in a retrieval system or transmitted in any form or by any means, electronic, mechanical, photocopying, recording, scanning or otherwise, except as permitted under Sections 107 or 108 of the 1976 United States Copyright Act, without either the prior written permission of the Publisher, or authorization through payment of the appropriate per-copy fee to the Copyright Clearance Center, Inc. 222 Rosewood Drive, Danvers, MA 01923, (978) 750-8400, fax (978) 646-8600. Requests to the Publisher for permission should be addressed to the Permissions Department, John Wiley & Sons, Inc., 111 River Street, Hoboken, NJ 07030-5774, (201) 748-6011, fax (201) 748-6008. To order books or for customer service, please call 1-800-CALL WILEY (225-5945).

Microsoft, Active Directory, AppLocker, Bing, BitLocker, DreamSpark, Hyper-V, Internet Explorer, SQL Server, Visual Studio, Win32, Windows Azure, Windows, Windows PowerShell, Windows Server, and Windows Vista are either registered trademarks or trademarks of Microsoft Corporation in the United States and/or other countries. Other product and company names mentioned herein may be the trademarks of their respective owners.

The example companies, organizations, products, domain names, e-mail addresses, logos, people, places, and events depicted herein are fictitious. No association with any real company, organization, product, domain name, e-mail address, logo, person, place, or event is intended or should be inferred.

The book expresses the author's views and opinions. The information contained in this book is provided without any express, statutory, or implied warranties. Neither the authors, John Wiley & Sons, Inc., Microsoft corporation, nor their resellers or distributors will be held liable for any damages caused or alleged to be caused either directly or indirectly by this book.

ISBN 978-1-118-88275-7

The inside back cover will contain printing identification and country of origin if omitted from this page. In addition, if the ISBN on the back cover differs from the ISBN on this page, the one on the back cover is correct.

Printed in the United States of America

10 9 8 7 6 5 4

Welcome to the Microsoft Official Academic Course (MOAC) program for becoming a Microsoft Certified Solutions Associate for Windows 8.1. MOAC represents the collaboration between Microsoft Learning and John Wiley & Sons, Inc. Microsoft and Wiley teamed up to produce a series of textbooks that deliver compelling and innovative teaching solutions to instructors and superior learning experiences for students. Infused and informed by in-depth knowledge from the creators of Windows 8.1, and crafted by a publisher known worldwide for the pedagogical quality of its products, these textbooks maximize skills transfer in minimum time. Students are challenged to reach their potential by using their new technical skills as highly productive members of the workforce.

Because this knowledgebase comes directly from Microsoft, architect of Windows 8.1 and creator of the Microsoft Certified Solutions Associate exams, you are sure to receive the topical coverage that is most relevant to students' personal and professional success. Microsoft's direct participation not only assures you that MOAC textbook content is accurate and current; it also means that students will receive the best instruction possible to enable their success on certification exams and in the workplace.

■ The Microsoft Official Academic Course Program

The Microsoft Official Academic Course series is a complete program for instructors and institutions to prepare and deliver great courses on Microsoft software technologies. With MOAC, we recognize that because of the rapid pace of change in the technology and curriculum developed by Microsoft, there is an ongoing set of needs beyond classroom instruction tools for an instructor to be ready to teach the course. The MOAC program endeavors to provide solutions for all these needs in a systematic manner in order to ensure a successful and rewarding course experience for both instructor and student—including technical and curriculum training for instructor readiness with new software releases; the software itself for student use at home for building hands-on skills, assessment, and validation of skill development; and a great set of tools for delivering instruction in the classroom and lab. All are important to the smooth delivery of an interesting course on Microsoft software, and all are provided with the MOAC program. We think about the model below as a gauge for ensuring that we completely support you in your goal of teaching a great course. As you evaluate your instructional materials options, you may wish to use the model for comparison purposes with available products.

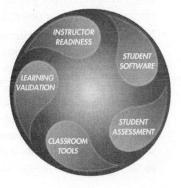

Illustrated Book Tour

▪ Textbook Organization

This textbook is organized in twenty-six lessons, with each lesson corresponding to a particular exam objective for the 70-687 Configuring Windows 8.1 exam. This MOAC textbook covers all the learning objectives for the 70-687 certification exam, which is the first of two exams needed in order to obtain a Microsoft Certified Solutions Associate (MCSA) certification. The exam objectives are highlighted throughout the textbook.

▪ Pedagogical Features

Many pedagogical features have been developed specifically for Microsoft Official Academic Course programs.

Presenting the extensive procedural information and technical concepts woven throughout the textbook raises challenges for the student and instructor alike. The Illustrated Book Tour that follows provides a guide to the rich features contributing to Microsoft Official Academic Course program's pedagogical plan. Following is a list of key features in each lesson designed to prepare students for success on the certification exams and in the workplace:

- Each lesson begins with an overview of the skills covered in the lesson. More than a standard list of learning objectives, the overview correlates skills to the certification exam objective.

- Illustrations: Screen images provide visual feedback as students work through the exercises. The images reinforce key concepts, provide visual clues about the steps, and allow students to check their progress.

- Key Terms: Important technical vocabulary is listed at the beginning of the lesson. When these terms are used later in the lesson, they appear in bold italic type and are defined.

- Engaging point-of-use reader aids, located throughout the lessons, tell students why this topic is relevant (*The Bottom Line*), provide students with helpful hints (*Take Note*), or show cross-references to where content is covered in greater detail (*X Ref*). Reader aids also provide additional relevant or background information that adds value to the lesson.

- Certification Ready features throughout the text signal students where a specific certification objective is covered. They provide students with a chance to check their understanding of that particular exam objective and, if necessary, review the section of the lesson where it is covered.

- Knowledge Assessments provide lesson-ending activities that test students' comprehension and retention of the material taught, presented using some of the question types that they'll see on the certification exam.

- An important supplement to this textbook is the accompanying lab work. Labs are available via a Lab Manual, and also by MOAC Labs Online. MOAC Labs Online provides students with the ability to work on the actual software simply by connecting through their Internet Explorer web browser. Either way, the labs use real-world scenarios to help students learn workplace skills associated with configuring Windows 8.1 in an enterprise environment.

■ Lesson Features

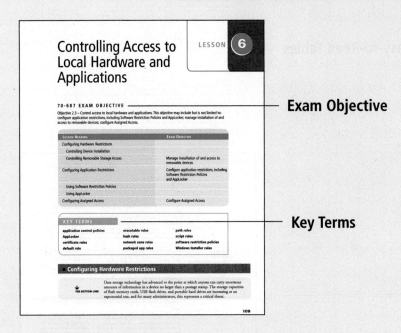

Exam Objective

Key Terms

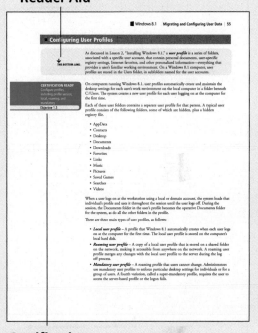

Bottom Line Reader Aid

Certification Ready Alert

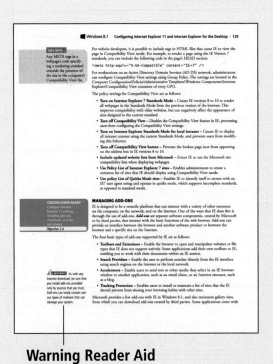

Warning Reader Aid

Easy-to-Read Tables

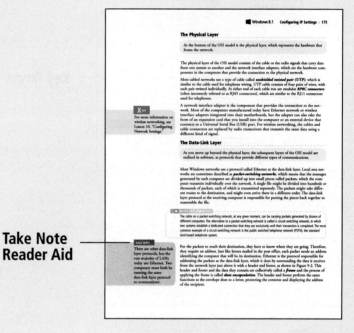

Take Note Reader Aid

Step-by-Step Exercises

Screen Images

Informative Diagrams

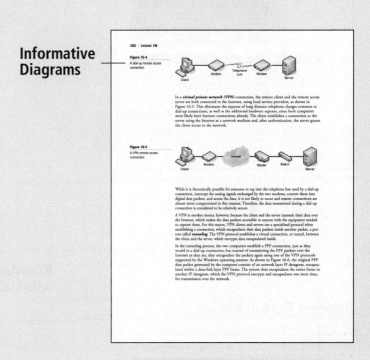

More Information Reader Aid

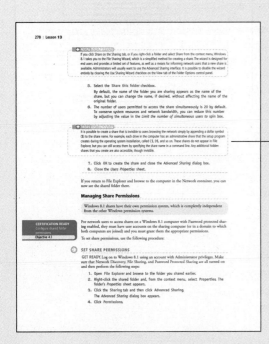

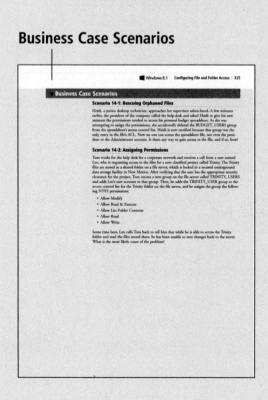

Business Case Scenarios

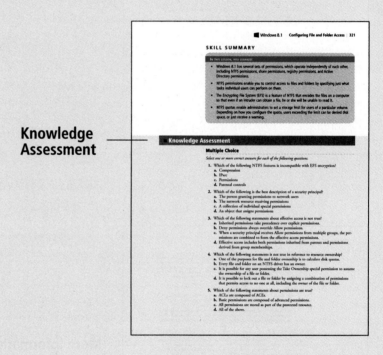

Skill Summary

Knowledge Assessment

Conventions and Features Used in This Book

This book uses particular fonts, symbols, and heading conventions to highlight important information or to call your attention to special steps. For more information about the features in each lesson, refer to the Illustrated Book Tour section.

CONVENTION	MEANING
↓ THE BOTTOM LINE	This feature provides a brief summary of the material to be covered in the section that follows.
CERTIFICATION READY	This feature signals the point in the text where a specific certification objective is covered. It provides you with a chance to check your understanding of that particular exam objective and, if necessary, review the section of the lesson where it is covered.
TAKE NOTE* ✚ MORE INFORMATION	Reader aids appear in shaded boxes found in your text. *Take Note and More Information* provide helpful hints related to particular tasks or topics.
⚠ WARNING	*Warning* points out instances when error or misuse could cause damage to the computer or network.
X REF	These *X Ref* notes provide pointers to information discussed elsewhere in the textbook or describe interesting features of Windows 8.1 that are not directly addressed in the current topic or exercise.
A ***shared printer*** can be used by many individuals on a network.	Key terms appear in bold italic.
cd\windows\system32\ServerMigrationTools	Commands that are to be typed are shown in a special font.
Click **Install Now**.	Any button on the screen you are supposed to click on or select will appear bold in blue.

Instructor Support Program

The Microsoft Official Academic Course programs are accompanied by a rich array of resources that incorporate the extensive textbook visuals to form a pedagogically cohesive package. These resources provide all the materials instructors need to deploy and deliver their courses. Resource information available at www.wiley.com/college/microsoft includes:

- **Instructor's Guide.** The Instructor's Guide contains solutions to all the textbook exercises as well as chapter summaries and lecture notes. The Instructor's Guide and Syllabi for various term lengths are available from the Instructor's Book Companion site.
- **Test Bank.** The Test Bank contains hundreds of questions organized by lesson in multiple-choice, best answer, build list, and essay formats and is available to download from the Instructor's Book Companion site. A complete answer key is provided.
- **PowerPoint Presentations.** A complete set of PowerPoint presentations is available on the Instructor's Book Companion site to enhance classroom presentations. Tailored to the text's topical coverage, these presentations are designed to convey key Windows 8.1 concepts addressed in the text.
- **Available Textbook Figures.** All figures from the text are on the Instructor's Book Companion site. By using these visuals in class discussions, you can help focus students' attention on key elements of Windows 8.1 and help them understand how to use it effectively in the workplace.
- **MOAC Labs Online.** MOAC Labs Online is a cloud-based environment that enables students to conduct exercises using real Microsoft products. These are not simulations but instead are live virtual machines where faculty and students can perform any activities they would on a local virtual machine. MOAC Labs Online relieves the need for local setup, configuration, and most troubleshooting tasks. This represents an opportunity to lower costs, eliminate the hassle of lab setup, and support and improve student access and portability. Contact your Wiley rep about including MOAC Labs Online with your course offering.
- **Lab Answer Keys.** Answer keys for review questions found in the lab manuals and MOAC Labs Online are available on the Instructor's Book Companion site.
- **Lab Worksheets.** The review questions found in the lab manuals and MOAC Labs Online are gathered in Microsoft Word documents for students to use. These are available on the Instructor's Book Companion site.

This page left intentionally blank.

Student Support Program

Book Companion Website (www.wiley.com/college/microsoft)

The students' book companion site for the MOAC series includes any resources, exercise files, and web links that will be used in conjunction with this course.

■ Microsoft Certification

Microsoft Certification has many benefits and enables you to keep your skills relevant, applicable, and competitive. In addition, Microsoft Certification is an industry standard that is recognized worldwide—which helps open doors to potential job opportunities. After you earn your Microsoft Certification, you have access to a number of benefits, which can be found on the Microsoft Certified Professional member site.

Microsoft Learning has reinvented the Microsoft Certification Program by building cloud-related skills validation into the industry's most recognized certification program. Microsoft Certified Solutions Expert (MCSE) and Microsoft Certified Solutions Developer (MCSD) are Microsoft's flagship certifications for professionals who want to lead their IT organization's journey to the cloud. These certifications recognize IT professionals with broad and deep skill sets across Microsoft solutions. The Microsoft Certified Solutions Associate (MCSA) is the certification for aspiring IT professionals and is also the prerequisite certification necessary to earn an MCSE. These new certifications integrate cloud-related and on-premise skills validation in order to support organizations and recognize individuals who have the skills required to be productive using Microsoft technologies.

On-premise or in the cloud, Microsoft training and certification empowers technology professionals to expand their skills and gain knowledge directly from the source. Securing these essential skills will allow you to grow your career and make yourself indispensable as the industry shifts to the cloud. Cloud computing ultimately enables IT to focus on more mission-critical activities, raising the bar of required expertise for IT professionals and developers. These reinvented certifications test on a deeper set of skills that map to real-world business context. Rather than testing only on a feature of a technology, Microsoft Certifications now validate more advanced skills and a deeper understanding of the platform.

Microsoft Certified Solutions Associate (MCSA)

The Microsoft Certified Solutions Associate (MCSA) certification is for students preparing to get their first jobs in Microsoft technology. Whether in the cloud or on-premise, this certification validates the core platform skills needed in an IT environment. The MCSA certifications are a requirement to achieve Microsoft's flagship Microsoft Certified Solutions Expert (MCSE) and Microsoft Certified Solutions Developer (MCSD) certifications.

The MCSA Windows 8.1 certification shows that you have the primary set of Windows 8.1 skills that are relevant across multiple solution areas in a business environment. Candidates for the 70-687 exam will show their knowledge in configuring and supporting Windows 8.1 computers, devices, users, and associated network and security resources. These networks are typically configured as a domain-based or peer-to-peer environment with access to the Internet and cloud services. These IT professional could be a consultant, full-time desktop support technician, or an IT generalist who administers Windows 8.1-based computers and devices as a portion of their broader technical responsibilities.

If you are a student new to IT who may not yet be ready for MCSA, the Microsoft Technology Associate (MTA) certification is an optional starting point that may be available through your institution.

You can learn more about the MCSA certification at the Microsoft Training & Certification website.

Preparing to Take an Exam

Unless you are a very experienced user, you will need to use test preparation materials to prepare to complete the test correctly and within the time allowed. The Microsoft Official Academic Course series is designed to prepare you with a strong knowledge of all exam topics, and with some additional review and practice on your own, you should feel confident in your ability to pass the appropriate exam.

After you decide which exam to take, review the list of objectives for the exam. You can easily identify tasks that are included in the objective list by locating the exam objective overview at the start of each lesson and the Certification Ready sidebars in the margin of the lessons in this book.

To register for the 70-687 exam, visit Microsoft Training & Certifications Registration webpage for directions. Keep in mind these following important items about the testing procedure:

- **What to expect.** Microsoft Certification testing labs typically have multiple workstations, which may or may not be occupied by other candidates. Test center administrators strive to provide a quiet and comfortable environment for all test takers.
- **Plan to arrive early.** It is recommended that you arrive at the test center at least 30 minutes before the test is scheduled to begin.
- **Bring your identification.** To take your exam, you must bring the identification (ID) that was specified when you registered for the exam. If you are unclear about which forms of ID are required, contact the exam sponsor identified in your registration information. Although requirements vary, you typically must show two valid forms of ID, one with a photo, both with your signature.

- **Leave personal items at home.** The only item allowed into the testing area is your identification, so leave any backpacks, laptops, briefcases, and other personal items at home. If you have items that cannot be left behind (such as purses), the testing center might have small lockers available for use.

- **Nondisclosure agreement.** At the testing center, Microsoft requires that you accept the terms of a nondisclosure agreement (NDA) and complete a brief demographic survey before taking your certification exam.

About the Author

Craig Zacker is an instructor, writer, editor, and networker whose computing experience began in the days of teletypes and paper tape. After making the move from minicomputers to PCs, he worked as a network administrator and PC support technician while operating a freelance desktop publishing business. After earning a Master's Degree in English and American Literature from New York University, Craig worked extensively on the integration of Microsoft Windows operating systems into existing internetworks, supported fleets of Windows workstations, and was employed as a technical writer, content provider, and webmaster for the online services group of a large software company. Since devoting himself to writing and editing full-time, Craig has authored or contributed to dozens of books on operating systems, networking topics, and PC hardware. He has also published articles with top industry publications, developed online training courses for the various firms, and authored the following Microsoft Official Academic Course (MOAC), Academic Learning Series (ALS), and Self-Paced Training Kit titles:

MOAC: Windows Server 2012, Installing and Configuring Windows Server (Exam 70-410)

MOAC: Installing and Configuring Windows Server 2012 R2 (Exam 70-410)

MOAC: Configuring Windows 8 (Exam 70-687)

MOAC: Windows Server 2008, Enterprise Administrator (Exam 70-647)

MOAC: Windows 7 Configuration (Exam 70-680)

MOAC: Windows Server Administrator (Exam 70-646)

MOAC: Configuring Windows Server 2008 Application Services (Exam 70-643)

MOAC: Configuring Microsoft Windows Vista (Exam 70-620)

MOAC: Implementing & Administering Security in a Windows Server 2003 Network (Exam 70-299)

MOAC: Managing & Maintaining a Microsoft Windows Server 2003 Environment (Exam 70-290)

ALS: Network+ Certification, Second, Third, and Fourth Editions

ALS: Planning & Maintaining a Windows Server 2003 Network Infrastructure (Exam 70-293)

ALS: Microsoft Windows 2000 Network Infrastructure Administration, Second Edition (2002)

MCSE Self-Paced Training Kit (Exam 70-293): Planning & Maintaining a Microsoft Windows Server 2003 Network Infrastructure (2003)

MCSA/MCSE Self-Paced Training Kit: Microsoft Windows 2000 Network Infrastructure Administration, Exam 70-216, Second Edition (2002)

MCSA Training Kit: Managing a Windows 2000 Network Environment (2002)

Network+ Certification Training Kit, First and Second Editions (2001)

Network+ Certification Readiness Review (2001)

About the Contributors

Ed Baker, Microsoft Certified Trainer (MCT), Microsoft Certified Solutions Associate (MCSA) and a Microsoft Certified Solutions Expert (MCSE), has 20 years of experience in the IT industry as a consultant, trainer, author, and project manager. Ed has experience in many of Microsoft's key technologies including Windows Server, Windows Client, Exchange Server, System Center, and SQL Server. Ed also teaches in Microsoft's IT Academy program in the United Kingdom. When not teaching or writing, you will no doubt find Ed either blogging (as a guest blogger for UK Technet and other IT sites) or riding his motorcycle.

Steven Fullmer, MCT, PMP, MBA, ITIL, MCTS/MCITP/MCSA, CTT+/A+, CDP/CCP, is a Staff Instructor for Interface Technical Training. He has more than 32 years of architecture and development experience in the supercomputer, financial, security, telecommunication, and Internet industries with Honeywell Large Computer Products, NEC Supercomputers, First Interstate Bank, Wells Fargo Bank, AG Communication Systems, and Lucent Technologies. Steven is an internationally published author including CIO.com, InformIT, Dr. Dobbs Journal, and One Planet Magazine.

Garrett Stevens is a Systems Software Specialist for Black Hills State University (BHSU). He currently designs, tests, implements, and manages solutions to efficiently meet and excel above the University's needs of virtualization, messaging, storage, backup, server operations, and client support. Garrett has earned the following certifications: Microsoft Certified Trainer (MCT), Microsoft Certified Solutions Associate (MCSA): Server 2012, MCSA: Server 2008, Microsoft Certified IT Professional (MCITP): Enterprise Administrator on Windows Server 2008, MCITP: Enterprise Messaging Administrator on Exchange 2010, and HP Accredited Platform Specialist. In his free time, Garrett enjoys spending time with his wife and children, hiking in the Black Hills, disk golf, writing, and trap shooting.

Richard Watson has over 20 years of industry experience in the technology and training fields. He has worked in the biotech, manufacturing, healthcare, and telecommunications industries as a Microsoft Certified Systems Engineer. Over the years, he has brought his real-world experience to the classroom by creating and teaching courses on network administration and security fundamentals. These courses were delivered to public universities, community colleges, and private businesses across the country. He is currently the President of Bridgehill Learning Solutions, LLC, which provides technical training/writing, content development, and content conversion services.

Acknowledgements

We thank the MOAC faculty and instructors who have assisted us in building the Microsoft Official Academic Course courseware. These elite educators have acted as our sounding board on key pedagogical and design decisions leading to the development of the MOAC courseware for future Information Technology workers. They have provided invaluable advice in the service of quality instructional materials, and we truly appreciate their dedication to technology education.

Brian Bridson, Baker College of Flint

David Chaulk, Baker College Online

Ron Handlon, Remington College—Tampa Campus

Katherine James, Seneca College of Applied Arts & Technology

Wen Liu, ITT Educational Services

Zeshan Sattar, Pearson in Practice

Jared Spencer, Westwood College Online

David Vallerga, MTI College

Bonny Willy, Ivy Tech State College

We also thank Microsoft Learning's Tim Sneath, Keith Loeber, Jim Clark, Anne Hamilton, Shelby Grieve, Erika Cravens Paul Schmitt, Martin DelRe, Julia Stasio, Josh Barnhill Heidi Johnson, and Neil Carter for their encouragement and support in making the Microsoft Official Academic Course programs the finest academic materials for mastering the newest Microsoft technologies for both students and instructors.

Brief Contents

Contents

Evaluating Hardware Readiness and Capability

70-687 EXAM OBJECTIVE

Objective 1.1 – Evaluate hardware readiness and compatibility. This objective may include but is not limited to: choose between an upgrade and a clean installation; determine which SKU to use, including Windows RT; determine requirements for particular features, including Hyper-V, Miracast display, pervasive device encryption, virtual smart cards, and Secure Boot.

LESSON HEADING	EXAM OBJECTIVE
Introducing Windows 8.1	
Using the Start Screen	
Using the Windows Desktop	
Accessing Configuration Settings	
Introducing Windows 8.1 Editions	Determine which SKU to use, including Windows RT
Understanding Windows 8.1 System Requirements	Determine requirements for particular features including Hyper-V, Miracast display, pervasive device encryption, virtual smart cards, and Secure Boot.
Selecting Installation Options	
Will the Hardware Support the New Operating System?	
Will the New Operating System Support the Existing Applications?	
Which Windows 8.1 Edition Should I Install?	
Which Processor Platform Should I Use?	
Should I Perform an Upgrade or a Clean Installation?	Choose between an upgrade or a clean installation
Do I Have to Install Multiple Languages?	
Running Windows 8.1 Upgrade Assistant	
Identifying Upgrade Paths	
Upgrading Windows 8.1 Editions	
Upgrading from Windows 8	
Upgrading from Windows 7	
Upgrading from Earlier Windows Versions	

KEY TERMS

apps   edge UI   multilingual user interface (MUI)

charms   in-place upgrade   Start screen

clean installation   live tiles   Upgrade Assistant

Introducing Windows 8.1

THE BOTTOM LINE

Windows 8 was a major release that represented a fundamental departure in Windows operating system design. The intention behind Windows 8 was to create a single operating system that can run on a variety of devices, including tablets and smartphones, as well as PCs. Windows 8.1 is an incremental upgrade that refines the innovations in Windows 8 and provides some additional capabilities.

For users, Windows 8 and Windows 8.1 provide a new way of looking at the software running on the computer. Many of the familiar Windows components are gone or substantially changed, and there are new ways of doing almost everything.

For IT specialists responsible for installing, configuring, and maintaining computers running Windows 8 and Windows 8.1 many of the familiar configuration tools are still there, such as Control Panel and Administrative Tools; you just have to become accustomed to accessing them in different ways.

Using the Start Screen

The first new element in Windows 8 and Windows 8.1 faced by users and support staff alike is the *Start screen*, which replaces the familiar Start menu from previous versions of Windows.

Designed to support both touch-based screens and the traditional mouse, the Start screen contains a series of tiles that provide access to the various operating system elements, as shown in Figure 1-1.

Figure 1-1

The Windows 8.1 Start screen

The resizable tiles are generally larger than the icons found on the Windows desktop, and unlike the static icons, they can contain dynamic content provided by the software they represent. For example, the tile for a Weather app can contain the temperature and other current weather conditions, while the Messaging tile can display part of your latest incoming email messages. Icons in Windows 8.1 that contain this type of dynamic content are called *live tiles*.

ACCESSING START SCREEN CONTROLS

The Start screen has no visible controls on it, initially, except for a circled arrow at the bottom left that scrolls the screen up to display icons for all of the apps installed on the computer. By touching the screen in specific ways or by mousing over certain areas designated as hot spots, you can navigate around the screen or make additional controls appear. For example, swiping a finger from right to left on a touch screen scrolls the Smart screen display to one side, displaying any tiles that were previously hidden. The mouse equivalent is a standard scroll bar.

However, when you swipe a finger from the right edge of a touch screen towards the center, a fly-out panel with icons on it called the *edge UI* appears, as shown in Figure 1-2. The mouse equivalent to this gesture is to place your cursor in the right-side top or bottom corner of the screen.

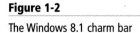

Figure 1-2

The Windows 8.1 charm bar

This UI (user interface) contains a series of buttons called *charms*, which provide access to common operating system functions, including the following:

- **Search** – Enables you to perform a system-wide search for apps, settings, or files, based on a word or phrase appearing in the element's name or in its content, as shown in Figure 1-3. You can also do this by typing a search term anywhere in the Start screen.
- **Share** – Provides access to the bidirectional sharing options for the currently selected app
- **Start** – Toggles between the Start screen and the Windows Desktop
- **Devices** – Provides quick access to hardware devices, such as printers, which you can use with the currently selected app
- **Settings** – Provides access to a Settings bar containing operating system controls specific to the current screen, as shown in Figure 1-4

Figure 1-3

The Windows 8.1 search bar

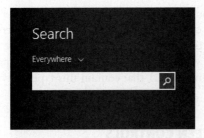

Figure 1-4

The Windows 8.1 settings bar

The same swiping gesture from the left edge of the screen, or mousing over the lower left corner and dragging up, displays a thumbnail bar containing your currently open apps, as shown in Figure 1-5.

Figure 1-5

The Windows 8.1 thumbnail bar

Swiping up from the bottom of the screen, or clicking the circled down arrow button Start screen displays an Apps screen full of small tiles representing all of the applications installed on the computer, as shown in Figure 1-6. This is the closest equivalent to the Start menu from Windows versions prior to Windows 8.

Figure 1-6

The Windows 8.1 Apps screen

MORE INFORMATION

The Windows 8.1 Start screen is the primary element of the user interface intended for use on tablets and smart-phones. All of the Start screen's features and capabilities are accessible using the mouse and the keyboard, but it is only with a touch screen that it takes on a certain ergonomic elegance. Operating a touch screen requires a familiarity with certain finger gestures, such as the following:

- **Tap** – Press a fingertip to the screen and release it. The function is identical to that of a mouse click.
- **Double-tap** – Press a fingertip to the screen twice in quick succession on the same spot. The function is identical to that of a double mouse click.
- **Press and hold** – Tap a point on the screen and press down for approximately two seconds. The function is the same as that of mousing over a designated spot and hovering.
- **Slide** – Press a point on the screen and draw your finger across it without pausing. The function is the same as clicking and dragging a mouse.
- **Swipe** – Draw a finger across the screen in the indicated direction.

The tiles on the Start screen are configurable in a number of ways. Users can move the tiles around, change their size and their groupings, and control whether they display live content. It is also possible to remove seldom-used tiles and add new tiles for applications, files, and shortcuts on the computer.

RUNNING START SCREEN APPS

The Windows 8.1 Start screen is not just a new way of launching your applications, however. The screen also provides a runtime environment called WinRT, which is designed to run a new class of software components called apps.

TAKE NOTE *

In the past, for many computer users, the term app was simply an abbreviation for the term application. Today, the term app is typically used to refer to a small, inexpensive program designed to perform a few specialized tasks. The term application is more commonly reserved for large, commercial, multipurpose software products.

Apps are programs that launch from the Start screen and run exclusively in the WinRT environment. Most of the tiles that appear on the default Windows 8.1 Start screen launch apps, and many others are available for purchase (or for free) through the Windows Store.

MORE INFORMATION

For more information on the Windows Store and on obtaining new apps, see Lesson 5, "Installing and Configuring Desktop Applications."

CLOSING START SCREEN APPS

One of the more frequent complaints made by new users of Windows 8.1 concerns the difficulty they have in closing applications. When you open an app on the Start menu, there are no window controls, such as the X button in the upper right corner.

Experienced Windows users are accustomed to closing unneeded applications, to free up system resources for other purposes. Windows 8.1 handles system memory in quite a different manner from previous Windows versions, however. When an application remains idle for a period of time, the operating system suspends it and reassigns its memory automatically, so there is really is no reason to close applications, from a performance standpoint.

However, having a thumbnail bar with a dozen or more open apps on it can be unwieldy, so users still might want to close their unused apps, which you can do in any of the following ways:

- On the thumbnail bar, drag a thumbnail to the bottom of the screen or right-click a thumbnail and select Close from the context menu,
- On a full screen app, tap or mouse over the top of the screen and, when the cursor changes to a hand, drag it down to the bottom of the screen.
- Press Alt+F4 on the keyboard.

Using the Windows Desktop

Although the Start screen appears by default when you boot a Windows 8.1 computer, the familiar Windows Desktop is still there, and it still functions in much the same way as pre Windows 8 versions.

To access the Desktop from the Start screen, you tap or click the bottom left Desktop. The Desktop appears, along with the standard Taskbar and the Recycle Bin icon. Users accustomed to launching applications from desktop icons or pinning them to the Taskbar can continue to do so. You cannot, however, run WinRT apps from the Desktop; they require the Start screen for their operating environment.

Once on the Desktop, you can return to the Start screen by mousing over the Start button on the left side of the Taskbar selecting the Start charm on the charm bar, or pressing the WinKey.

Many users and administrators have expressed a desire to boot Windows 8.1 directly to the desktop, bypassing the Start screen entirely, and while Windows 8 provides no such option, Windows 8.1 does. To do this, open the Taskbar and Navigation Properties sheet and, on the Navigation tab, select the *When I sign in or close all apps on a screen, go to the desktop instead of the Start* check box. There are also third-party utilities available that can do this, as well as restore the Windows 7-style Start menu.

Accessing Configuration Settings

For the IT professional working with Windows 8.1 for the first time, accessing the operating system's configuration settings will be a top priority.

As mentioned earlier, many of the familiar Windows configuration tools are still there in Windows 8.1; it's just a matter of finding them.

USING THE SETTINGS BARS

As mentioned earlier, clicking or tapping the Settings charm displays a Settings bar, the contents of which differs, depending on whether you are accessing it from the Start screen or the Desktop.

The Start screen version enables you to modify the behavior of the screen tiles, while the Desktop version provides access to the main Windows Control Panel and the Personalization and System control panels. Both versions also include tiles that provide access to network, audio, display, notifications, power, and keyboard settings. Finally, when you click Change PC Settings at the bottom of the bar, the PC Settings screen appears, with a multitude of configuration settings on separate pages, as shown in Figure 1-7.

TAKE NOTE*

Compared with Windows 8, Windows 8.1 includes many more of the most commonly used configuration controls on the PC Settings screen, as opposed to the standard Windows Control Panel.

Figure 1-7

The PC Settings screen

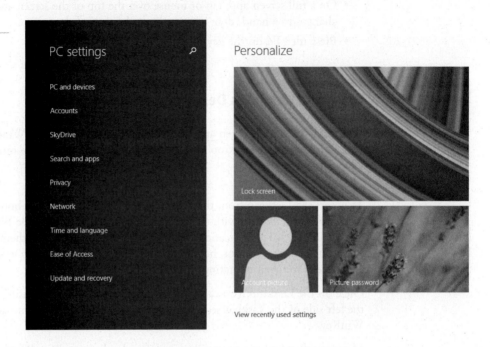

USING THE WINDOWS TOOLS MENU

When you right-click the Start button at the lower left corner of the desktop (also available on the Start screen by mousing over the lower left corner), or press the Win+X key combination, a Windows tools context menu appears that provides access to most of the tools an administrator is likely to need, including the following:

- Programs and Features
- Power Options
- Event Viewer
- System
- Device Manager
- Network Connections
- Disk Management
- Computer Management
- Command Prompt
- Command Prompt (Admin)
- Task Manager
- Control Panel
- File Explorer
- Search
- Run
- Shut down or sign out
- Desktop

TAKE NOTE *

To replace the Command Prompt shortcuts on the tools menu with Windows PowerShell shortcuts, open the Taskbar and Navigation Properties sheet and, on the Navigation tab, select the *Replace Command Prompt with Windows PowerShell in the menu when I right-click the lower-left corner or press Windows key+X* checkbox.

USING KEYBOARD SHORTCUTS

Because Windows 8.1 tends to hide administrative controls beneath multiple layers of user action, keyboard shortcuts–always a handy tool for Windows power users–are even more valuable. For any Windows 8.1 administrator, and many users as well, memorizing some of the more common key combinations is a worthwhile activity.

In addition to supporting the keyboard shortcuts from previous versions of Windows, Windows 8 and Windows 8.1 add several new ones, many of which use the Windows key, typically found between the Ctrl and Alt keys on most modern keyboards.

Some of the most useful Win key combinations in Windows 8.1 are as follows:

- **Win+X** – Displays the Windows tools menu, which contains links to the Event Viewer, Control Panel, Command Prompt, Task Manager, Device Manager, Computer Management, and File Explorer windows
- **Win+Tab** – Displays the task switcher
- **Win** – Displays the Start screen
- **Win+D** – Displays the Windows Desktop
- **Win+C** – Displays the charms bar
- **Win+Q** – Displays the everywhere search bar
- **Win+F** – Displays the files search bar
- **Win+H** – Displays the Share menu for the currently running app
- **Win+W** – Displays the settings search bar
- **Win+I** – Displays the Settings bar for the currently running app
- **Win+E** – Displays a File Explorer window
- **Win+R** – Displays the Run dialog box

▪ Introducing Windows 8.1 Editions

Windows 8.1 is available in multiple editions. Understanding the features and capabilities of each edition is crucial for technical specialists who must recommend a specific product for their users.

There are no less than six editions of Windows 7, but Microsoft has reduced that number down to four for Windows 8.1, one of which is a specialized version for tablets and other portable devices.

The four Windows 8.1 editions are as follows:

- **Windows RT** – Designed for OEM distribution on tablets and other devices using the low-power ARM processor platform, Windows RT can run WinRT apps, both prein-stalled and obtained from the Windows Store, but it cannot run traditional x86/x64 applications

- **Windows 8.1** – The base Windows 8.1 consumer product for PCs using x86 or x64 processors is designed for sale in retail channels and for original equipment manufacturer (OEM) distribution in new computers. The primary limitation of this edition is its inability to participate in an Active Directory Domain Services domain, making it unsuitable for use in any but the smallest business environments.

- **Windows 8.1 Pro** – The primary retail/OEM edition intended for small businesses, includes support for Active Directory Domain Services and Group Policy, as well as security features, such as BitLocker and BitLocker To Go, and the ability to host a Remote Desktop Connection.

- **Windows 8.1 Enterprise** – Available only through the Microsoft volume licensing programs, includes all of the features of Windows 8.1 Pro plus advanced options, such as AppLocker, BranchCache, and DirectAccess.

CERTIFICATION READY
Determine which SKU to use, including Windows RT.
Objective 1.1

Table 1-1 lists the operating system features and applications that are included in each of the Windows 8.1 editions.

Table 1-1

Feature Support in Windows 8.1 Editions

	WINDOWS 8.1 RT	WINDOWS 8.1	WINDOWS 8.1 PRO	WINDOWS 8.1 ENTERPRISE
Platform	ARM	X86/x64	X86/x64	X86/x64
Max Number of Processors	2	1	2	2
Licensing	OEM only	Retail / OEM	Retail / OEM	Volume only
AD DS Domain Support	No	No	Yes	Yes
AppLocker	No	No	No	Yes
Boot from VHD		No	Yes	Yes
BitLocker / BitLocker To Go	No	No	Yes	Yes
BranchCache	No	No	No	Yes
DirectAccess	No	No	No	Yes
Encrypting file System (EFS)	No	No	Yes	Yes
Group Policy	No	No	Yes	Yes
Hyper-V Client	No	No	Yes	Yes
Install x86/x64 desktop apps	No	Yes	Yes	Yes
Microsoft Office	Yes	No	No	No
Remote Desktop	Client only	Client only	Client and host	Client and host
Storage Spaces	No	Yes	Yes	Yes
Windows Media Player	No	Yes	Yes	Yes
Windows To Go	No	No	No	Yes

For the Windows 8.1, Windows 8.1 Pro, and Windows 8.1 Enterprise editions, you also have a choice between running the 32-bit or 64-bit version. The main difference between the two is the amount of system memory each can address.

Table 1-2 lists the differences between the two platforms.

Table 1-2

Differences Between
Windows 8.1 32-bit and 64-bit
Platforms

	32-BIT	64-BIT
Maximum addressable memory	4 GB	192 GB
Hyper-V support	No	Yes

■ Understanding Windows 8.1 System Requirements

THE BOTTOM LINE

Windows 8.1 has the same hardware requirements as Windows 7, making the upgrade process relatively painless. However, an upgrade to Windows 8.1 from Windows XP is likely to require hardware upgrades, and a thorough understanding of the Windows 8.1 system requirements is essential for the administrator.

Because the various Windows 8.1 workstation editions differ primarily in the number and type of applications and features included with each product, the basic minimum system requirements are the same for all of the editions. Table 1-3 shows the minimum hardware requirements for each of these designations.

Table 1-3

Minimum System Requirements
for Windows 8.1

	32-BIT (x86)	64-BIT (x64)
Processor speed	1 gigahertz (GHz) or faster	1 GHz or faster
System memory	1 gigabyte (GB)	2 GB
Available hard disk space	16 GB	20 GB
Graphics adapter	DirectX 9 graphics adapter with WDDM driver	DirectX 9 graphics adapter with WDDM driver

While the official system requirements that Microsoft provides are a useful starting point, they do not provide the whole picture. Upgrading to Windows 8.1 is a subject that is sure to be on the minds of many Windows users, ranging from home users with a single computer to corporate managers responsible for thousands of workstations. For these users, simply falling within the system requirements is not enough. They want to be sure that Windows 8.1 will be an improvement over their previous OS, and that requires them to consider the individual system components more carefully.

- **Processor** – Of the major computer components, the processor is likely to have the least effect on overall system performance. The 1 GHz processor called for in the Windows 8.1 system requirements is relatively outdated by today's desktop standards. Most of the PCs in use today have processors much faster than 1 GHz, and even computers that are four or five years old will most likely meet the required speeds. The benefits derived from a faster processor depend largely on the applications the computer is running. Hardcore gamers are the users most intent on wringing every last GHz from their systems, but for general computer use, the requirements are not so heavy. For the purposes of upgrading to Windows 8.1, it is probably not worthwhile to purchase a new computer just to get a faster processor. One possible exception to this rule is for laptops and other portable systems, in which the latest processors can provide extended battery life.

- **System memory** – The memory requirements of the Windows operating systems have risen precipitously in recent years. The 512 megabyte (MB) minimum required for a Vista Capable PC was pushing the lower limit, and often resulted in disappointing performance levels. Microsoft now treats the 1 GB minimum previously cited for a Windows Vista Premium Ready PC as the minimum for Windows 8.1. Memory is easy and inexpensive to upgrade, however; no other hardware upgrade will yield a more immediately detectable performance increase. The Windows 8.1 one GB memory minimum is barely sufficient for a general-purpose workstation, but memory-intensive applications such as video and image editing, as well as high-end games, will benefit from more. Be sure to check the system documentation to determine what memory upgrades are possible for your computers.

- **Hard disk** – Windows 8.1 requires much more hard disk space than earlier versions of Windows, but with the low prices and high capacities of today's hard disk drives, it is not difficult to meet or exceed the system requirements. For most users, the real disk space hog is not operating system files or even applications, but rather the collections of audio and video files that most users seem to accumulate. Another aspect to consider, however, is the performance level of the hard drive(s) in the computer. Drives that spin at 5400 RPM can lead to palpably poorer performance than drives running at 7200 RPM or faster. For even better performance, solid state drives (SSDs) with capacities of 256 GB and more are now available, providing fast access with no moving parts.

- **Screen resolution** – Windows Store applications require a minimum screen resolution of 1024x768. Below that, they fail to run. For snap functionality, the screen resolution must be at least 1366x768. The other main consideration regarding the display is touch screen capability. Windows 8.1 is fully operational using a standard display and a keyboard and mouse, but the operating system was designed with a touch screen in mind.

Another consideration for administrators is the Windows 8.1 applications and features that their computers will be running, some of which have their own special system requirements, such as the following.

CERTIFICATION READY
Determine requirements for particular features including Hyper-V, Miracast display, pervasive device encryption, virtual smart cards, Secure Boot
Objective 1.1

- **Hyper-V** – Windows 8.1 includes support for the Microsoft Hyper-V virtualization engine. However, to install and use Hyper-V, the computer must have appropriate hardware, including a 64-bit processor that supports hardware-assisted virtualization, such as Intel Virtualization Technology (Intel VT) or AMD Virtualization (AMD-V); a system BIOS that supports the virtualization hardware and on which the virtualization feature has been enabled; and hardware-enforced *Data Execution Prevention (DEP)*, which Intel refers to as eXecute Disable (XD) and AMD refers to as No eXecute (NS).

- **Miracast** – Miracast is a wireless display technology that enables you to send high-quality audio and video from a computer, tablet, or smartphone to a television, projector, or streaming media player, using an ad hoc Wi-Fi connection. Widows 8.1 includes support for Miracast, as long as the computer has suitable Wi-Fi hardware and appropriate drivers. The receiving device also requires a Miracast transceiver, which can be built-in or implemented as an external unit, plugged into a USB or HDMI port.

- **Pervasive device encryption** – Previously implemented only on Windows RT and Windows Phone, pervasive device encryption is enabled by default in all Windows 8.1 editions when the computer supports connected standby and meets the Windows

Hardware Certification Kit (HCK) requirements for TPM and SecureBoot on ConnectedStandby systems. When the system has the required hardware, Pervasive Device Encryption protects the hard disks automatically, preventing intruders from booting into another operating system or installing the disks into another computer and reading their contents. In addition to these requirements, administrators should consider that all encryption places an additional burden on the system processor.

• **Virtual smart cards** – Virtual smart cards emulate the functionality of physical smart cards and readers using the Trusted Platform Module (TPM) installed on many computer motherboards. Because the virtual smart card is built in to the computer, it cannot be lost or stolen by itself, and it provides comparable security to a physical smart card.

• **Secure Boot** – To support Secure Boot, a computer must have the Unified Extensible Firmware Interface (UEFI), which checks the digital integrity of the operating system's bootloader before it allows the OS to load. In addition, to run Windows 8.1, the system's firmware must enable Secure Boot by default, trust the Microsoft certification authority, and enable the user to add signatures to the UEFI database.

For businesses running hundreds or thousands of workstations, the cost of hardware upgrades can be enormous, so you should carefully consider the current state of your computers and what new hardware your organization will need to make a Windows 8 deployment practical and productive.

■ Selecting Installation Options

THE BOTTOM LINE

Before installing Windows 8.1, or any operating system, whether on a single computer or a fleet of machines, you must first answer a number of questions to determine what type of installation to perform.

Every Windows 8.1 installation should begin with a planning phase, which varies depending on the complexity of the installation you are contemplating. For standalone home users, installing Windows 8.1 might mean thinking about what data to preserve, determining whether the existing hardware will work with the new operating system (OS), and finally purchasing the right Windows 8.1 edition. For enterprise administrators responsible for hundreds or thousands of computers, an operating system deployment requires a huge amount of testing and preparation, and can represent a massive expense. However, the technicians supporting home users and enterprise technical specialists ask themselves essentially the same questions, just on a different scale.

The following sections examine some of the most important of these questions.

Will the Hardware Support the New Operating System?

Later in this lesson, you learn about the various Windows 8.1 editions and their hardware requirements. The first question to ask yourself when contemplating an operating system upgrade is whether the computer's current hardware can run the new software effectively.

In many cases, this question is not just a matter of whether the computer meets the Windows 8.1 minimum hardware requirements. After all, the user expects the new operating system to run better than the old one, not worse. If the computer does not meet the Windows 8.1 hardware specifications, you should consider a hardware upgrade.

For the home user, a hardware upgrade might mean purchasing and installing a new memory module or two, or perhaps a graphics adapter. Experienced users might install the hardware themselves, while less savvy users might have a professional do it. Either way, the cost and the time involved are relatively small.

However, to perform hardware upgrades like these, enterprise administrators must multiply the cost and the installation time by hundreds or thousands of workstations, and factor in other elements such as lost productivity and overtime costs. Therefore, as with all aspects of a large-scale deployment, administrators in an enterprise environment must plan and test carefully before even considering an upgrade to Windows 8.1. For example, you might want to perform a series of test installations on differently configured computers to determine exactly what hardware upgrade provides the best performance at the lowest cost.

Will the New Operating System Support the Existing Applications?

The second major consideration for a client contemplating a Windows 8.1 installation is whether the applications the client already owns will run on the new operating system. The last thing clients want to hear after the successful installation of a new operating system is that they need to purchase additional new software.

As with hardware upgrades, the prospect of upgrading or changing applications is far more daunting in the enterprise environment than for the home user. Home users typically run commercial, off-the-shelf applications, and prices for upgrades supporting new operating systems typically fall soon after the release of the OS.

At the enterprise level, however, you are more likely to find special-purpose or customized applications; these present greater difficulties. It might take time for developers to produce updates for special-purpose applications; for customized applications, it might be necessary to commission additional work from a programmer. Commercial applications can be extremely costly to upgrade, especially when you have to purchase hundreds or thousands of licenses.

In enterprise environments, application testing is as important as hardware testing. Even if an updated version of an application is available, you must test it carefully with the new operating system to ensure that it functions properly. The alternative could be the failure of a mission-critical application across the entire enterprise, resulting in extended down time and lost productivity.

To aid in evaluating and testing applications in the Windows 8.1 environment, Microsoft provides a free Application Compatibility Toolkit. For more information on using this and deploying applications on Windows 8.1, see Lesson 5, "Installing and Configuring Desktop Applications."

Which Windows 8.1 Edition Should I Install?

You should select a Windows 8.1 edition based on several factors, including the tasks the user will be performing and, of course, your budget.

For home and small business users, the choice between Windows 8.1 and Windows 8.1 Pro should be based primarily on networking requirements. If you are running an AD DS domain, then you must have Windows 8.1 Pro installed on your computers to join that domain.

Most enterprise installations require their workstations to log on to an Active Directory Domain Services domain, which eliminates the base Windows 8.1 edition as a possible choice because it lacks domain support. In most cases, the organization's relationship with Microsoft is the deciding factor in the choice between Windows 8.1 Pro and Enterprise. Windows 8.1 Pro is a retail product, available in stores everywhere, while Enterprise is only available directly from Microsoft as part of a volume license agreement.

In Windows 7, there was an Ultimate edition, which included the Windows Media Server application. Windows Media Server is now a separate application, available for an additional fee and installable on any edition except Windows RT.

Which Processor Platform Should I Use?

There was a time when a Windows desktop computer with 4 GB of memory was the state of the art.

Today, 4 GB is adequate for an average user's needs, but it is certainly not exceptional. Therefore, the 4 GB memory limitation imposed by the 32-bit processing platform can be a real handicap, especially when you consider that each successive Windows release is likely to have an increased memory recommendation.

It might be possible to save a little money by purchasing the 32-bit version of Windows 8.1, but if you have even the remotest thought of upgrading your computer's memory in the future, the 64-bit version is probably preferable.

Should I Perform an Upgrade or a Clean Installation?

The question of whether to install Windows 8.1 by performing an in-place upgrade or a clean installation depends on the amount and type of data stored on the computer, as well as the computer's current efficiency.

Obviously, new computers, or computers with new hard disk drives, require a ***clean installation***, in which you boot from the Windows 8.1 setup disk and create or select a blank partition where the operating system will reside. If the computer is currently running Windows 7, you must consider whether it is preferable to wipe out the existing operating system and install Windows 8.1 from scratch or perform an in–place upgrade to Windows 8.1 instead.

➕ MORE INFORMATION

You can perform an in-place upgrade to Windows 8.1 only on computers running Windows 7, Windows 8 or another edition of Windows 8.1. It is not possible to perform an in-place upgrade to Windows 8.1 from Windows Vista, Windows XP, Windows 2000, Windows Me, Windows 98, Windows 95, Windows NT, or Windows 3.1. For computers running these operating systems, you must perform a clean installation.

The primary advantage of performing a clean installation is that Windows 8.1 will achieve its best possible performance. Installing the operating system files on a blank disk means that the files will not be fragmented , improving disk performance. A clean installation ensures that the user retains the maximum amount of disk space for applications and data. Of course, a clean installation also erases all existing data, so you must be careful to back up everything that the user wants to retain.

CERTIFICATION READY
Choose between an upgrade or a clean installation
Objective 1.1

For home users, there is usually some data to preserve, such as image, audio, and video files, as well as data files for specific applications. Fortunately, writable CDs and DVDs, USB flash drives, and external hard drives make it relatively easy to back up a user's essential data. What can be more problematic in a case like this is the loss of important configuration settings, such as user names, passwords, and customized application templates. Be sure to preserve this type of information before wiping out a partition to perform a clean installation.

⚠️ **WARNING** If you decide to perform a clean installation of Windows 8.1 on a home user's computer, be sure to question the user carefully about all possible data that might need to be backed up first. Many less experienced users are unaware, for example, that accessing their email involves a server logon. Another technician might have set up the user name and password long ago, and all the user knows is to click the email icon.

Performing an *in-place upgrade* to Windows 8.1 means that whatever disk and registry clutter is present under the previous operating system will remain in place. Files might be extensively fragmented, even to the point of executing poorly, and outdated applications and data files could occupy significant amounts of disk space.

The advantage to performing an in-place upgrade is that all of the user's applications, data files, and configuration settings remain intact, but even this could be a problem. Upgrades can generate incompatibilities with drivers or applications that you must rectify before the computer can run properly.

In an enterprise environment, it is more typical for users to store their data files on servers, as opposed to local drives. Also, a properly maintained enterprise network should document all configuration settings and logon credentials. This minimizes the problem of potential data loss when performing a clean installation.

Clean installations are generally preferable in an enterprise environment because they ensure that all of the computers are running an identical system configuration. This eliminates many of the technical support problems that can occur when computers are running different configurations.

Do I Have to Install Multiple Languages?

Before Windows Vista, each language-specific version of a Windows operating system had to be developed, maintained, and distributed separately. Starting with Vista, however, and now with Windows 8.1, it is possible to install multiple language packs on a single computer so that individuals can work in multiple languages.

The main problems for multilingual users in the past have been the availability of the languages they need and the complex procedure for implementing multiple languages on a single computer. To use multiple languages on a Windows XP computer, you must begin with an installation of the English language Windows XP version. Then you install the *multilingual user interface (MUI)* pack and whatever additional language packs you need. Unfortunately, some of the language packs provide more complete support than others.

Windows 8.1 contains an MUI architecture that makes it easier to install multilingual support on a computer. In Windows 8.1, the binary code that makes up the operating system is entirely language-neutral. During the operating system installation process, the Setup program installs the operating system and then applies a language pack containing the information needed to provide the localized user interface.

Because the language packs for Windows 8.1 contain no binary code, they are interchangeable. Therefore, it is no longer necessary for technicians to consider localization issues before installing the operating system. You can change a Windows 8.1 installation from one language to another at any time, or install multiple language packs that utilize the same binary code.

➕ **MORE INFORMATION**

Because the Windows 8.1 binaries are language-neutral there is no need for language-specific service packs or other updates. Microsoft is therefore able to release each update in one generic version suitable for all Windows 8.1 computers around the world, regardless of the language they use.

Running Windows 8.1 Upgrade Assistant

THE BOTTOM LINE

All administrators should be familiar with the Windows 8.1 Upgrade Assistant application, as it is the surest way of determining whether a computer is capable of running Windows 8.1.

Upgrade Assistant is a Windows application that scans an individual computer's hardware and software to determine whether it is capable of running Windows 8.1 at peak efficiency.

To run Windows 8.1 Upgrade Assistant, perform the steps in the following section.

⊙ RUN UPGRADE ASSISTANT

GET READY. Before you run Upgrade Assistant, be sure to plug in and turn on any USB devices or other devices such as printers, external hard drives, or scanners that you regularly use with the PC you are evaluating. Then perform the following steps:

1. Open Internet Explorer or another Web browser and then browse to the *Buy Windows 8.1* page (try http://windows.microsoft.com/en-us/windows/buy).

   The Buy Windows 8.1 page appears, as shown in Figure 1-8.

Figure 1-8

The *Buy Windows 8.1* page

2. Click **Get Started**.

   The *Do you want to run or save Windows8-UpgradeAssistant.exe* bar appears at the bottom of the screen.

   An Internet Explorer – Security Warning message box appears, asking if you want to run the software.

3. Click **Run**.

   The Windows 8.1 Upgrade Assistant Wizard appears, displaying the *Here's what we found* page, as shown in Figure 1-9.

Figure 1-9

The *Here's what we found*
page in the Windows 8.1
Upgrade Assistant

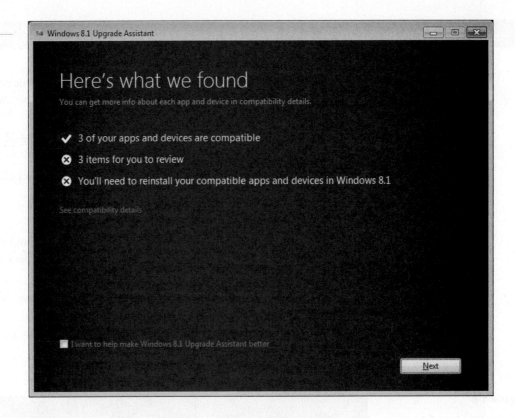

4. Examine the results and click Next.

The *Choose what to keep* page appears as shown in Figure 1-10.

Figure 1-10

The *Choose what to keep*
page in the Windows 8.1
Upgrade Assistant

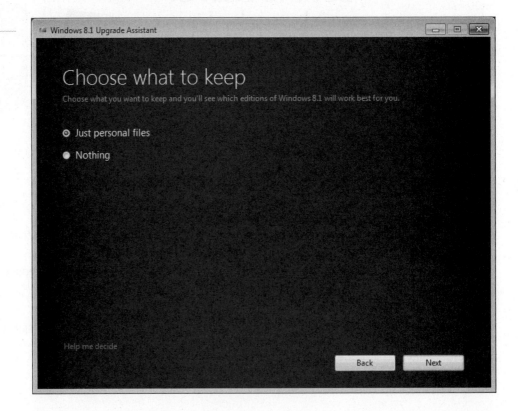

5. Select the option corresponding to the data you want to preserve from your existing installation and then click Next.

    A *Windows 8.1 for you* page appears listing the Windows editions available for immediate purchase.

6. Click Close.

The Windows 8.1 Upgrade Assistant is designed to provide retail users with immediate access to operating system upgrades. Enterprise customers using one of the Microsoft volume licensing programs should use their regular contact to discuss upgrades and pricing.

Identifying Upgrade Paths

 THE BOTTOM LINE   In some cases, the most convenient way to deploy Windows 8.1 on existing computers is to perform an upgrade from another operating system. However, there are a multitude of Windows versions, and not all of them support upgrades to Windows 8.1.

The term upgrade usually refers to an in-place upgrade, in which you install a new operating system over an old one, leaving some or all of the existing applications, configuration settings, and personal files intact. Windows 8.1 only supports in-place upgrades from Windows 7, Windows 8, and other editions of Windows 8.1, and the data types retained during the installation process vary.

Performing an in-place upgrade from Windows 7 to Windows 8.1 is a quick and convenient way to provide user with the new operating system without sacrificing the personal files that the users have built up over the years. If you choose to install Windows 8.1 to the partition that contains the old operating system, the Setup program renames the existing Windows folder to Windows.old, so that the old operating system is still recoverable.

For computers running versions earlier than Windows 7, no in-place upgrade is possible; you must perform a clean installation of Windows 8.

Upgrading Windows 8.1 Editions

In Windows 8.1, the Anytime Upgrade feature from Windows 7 and Windows Vista is replaced by an Add Features to Windows 8.1 control panel, which enables retail users to purchase and install upgrades.

The fairly complicated Anytime Upgrade matrix from Windows 7 and Vista is now reduced to a few basic options. If you are running the core Windows 8.1 product, you can purchase an upgrade to Windows 8.1 Pro and, if desired, add Windows Media Center as well. Users already running the Pro edition can add Windows Media Center for a fee.

In all of these cases, the existing operating system installation remains in place, and all applications, settings, and data files are unchanged. The Add Features to Windows 8.1 control panel enables you to purchase upgrades online and download them immediately, or if you already have a product key for an upgraded version, you can apply the upgrade immediately.

Windows 8.1 Enterprise is excluded from this feature, as it is only available to volume licensing customers.

Upgrading from Windows 8

All licensed users of Windows 8 are entitled to a free update to Windows 8.1. However, unlike upgrades from Windows 7, this update is available through the Windows Store. Updates of this type preserve all of the user profiles, applications, settings, and data files, but it might be necessary to install some updated drivers after the completion of the process is complete.

Windows 8.1 supports upgrades from any Windows 8 edition that is the same or lower than the 8.1 edition you are installing. Table 1-4 lists the upgrade paths from Windows 8 editions to Windows 8.1 editions.

Table 1-4

In-place Upgrade Paths from Windows 8 to Windows 8.1

	TO WINDOWS 8.1	TO WINDOWS 8.1 PRO	TO WINDOWS 8.1 ENTERPRISE
From Windows 8	Yes	Yes	Yes
From Windows 8 Pro	No	Yes	Yes
From Windows 8 Enterprise	No	No	Yes
From Windows 8.1 Pro	No	No	Yes

Upgrading from Windows 7

Windows 7 is the only down-level operating system from which you can perform an in-place upgrade to Windows 8.1. However, there are limits to this upgrade process.

To perform an in-place upgrade from Windows 7 to Windows 8.1, you run the Windows 8.1 Setup.exe program from within Windows 7 and select the Upgrade option. Users can purchase a Windows 8.1 upgrade disk or download the operating system after purchasing it at an upgrade price.

Generally speaking, you can upgrade any Windows 7 edition to Windows 8.1. The distinction between home and business versions in Windows 7 is essentially gone in Windows 8.1, so you can now upgrade Windows 7 Home Basic or Home Premium to Windows 8.1 Pro, something you could not do when upgrading Windows Vista to Windows 7.

However, when upgrading in place from Windows 7 to Windows 8.1, you can choose to keep your personal files, but you cannot keep your user profiles, Windows configuration settings, and applications. This is a departure from the Windows 7 to Windows 8 upgrade, which did enable you to keep these things. In fact, some administrators find it preferable to perform upgrades in two stages: from Windows 7 to Windows 8, retaining all of the profiles and settings, and then from Windows 8 to Windows 8.1, which also retains the profiles and settings.

For administrators in an enterprise environment, in-place upgrades take much more time to complete and are often unreliable or inconsistent in their results. Generally speaking, a migration of settings to a clean Windows 8.1 installation is a much better solution.

TAKE NOTE*

Windows 8.1 does not support in-place upgrades of 32-bit to 64-bit operating systems under any circumstances, or vice versa.

Upgrading from Earlier Windows Versions

Windows 8.1 does not support in-place upgrades from any Windows versions prior to Windows 7. However, there are techniques available that can preserve some of your existing data.

Users running Windows Vista and Windows XP cannot perform any sort of in-place upgrade to Windows 8.1. The setup program will not allow you to select the upgrade option when it is running on one of those operating systems. For Windows Vista and Windows XP users, there is not choice but to perform a clean installation of Windows 8.1. It is possible, however, to perform a migration of user profiles and configuration settings, although the process is unwieldy.

In an operating system migration, you copy the system configuration settings and personal files from the old operating system to the new one, using a program such as the User State Migration Tool. This process preserves many–but not all–of the existing user settings from the old system. Migration does not preserve third-party applications, so you must re-install and configure them after the Windows 8.1 installation is completed.

Migrations do not preserve as much of the existing system configuration as in-place upgrades, but they do result in a more uniform, and usually more stable, Windows 8.1 computer.

X REF

For more information on migrating older operating systems to Windows 8.1, see Lesson 3, "Migrating and Configuring User Data".

SKILL SUMMARY

IN THIS LESSON, YOU LEARNED:

- Windows 8 was a major release that represented a fundamental departure in Windows operating system design. Windows 8.1 is an incremental upgrade that refines the innovations in Windows 8 and provides some additional capabilities.

- The first new element in Windows 8.1 faced by users and support staff alike is the Start screen, which replaces the familiar Start menu from previous versions of Windows.

- Apps are programs that launch from the Start screen and run exclusively in the WinRT environment. Most of the tiles that appear on the default Windows 8.1 Start screen launch apps, and many others are available for purchase (or for free) through the Windows Store.

- There are no less than six editions of Windows 7, but Microsoft has reduced that number down to four for Windows 8.1, one of which is a specialized version for tablets and other portable devices.

- In some cases, the most convenient way to deploy Windows 8.1 on existing computers is to perform an upgrade from another operating system. However, there are many Windows versions, and not all of them support upgrades to Windows 8.1.

Knowledge Assessment

Multiple Choice

Select one or more correct answers for each of the following questions.

1. The general public in the United States will be able to purchase all of the Windows 8.1 editions in retail stores except which of the following?
   a. Windows 8.1
   b. Windows 8.1 Pro
   c. Windows 8.1 Enterprise
   d. Windows 8.1 RT

2. Which of the following operating system editions can you not upgrade in place to the core Windows 8.1 edition?
   a. Windows 7 Starter
   b. Windows 7 Home Basic
   c. Windows 7 Home Premium
   d. Windows 7 Professional

3. What is the maximum amount of system memory supported by the 32-bit versions of Windows 8.1?
   a. 2 GB
   b. 4 GB
   c. 16 GB
   d. 128 GB

4. The Add Features to Windows 8 control panel replaces which of the following Windows 7 features?
   a. Programs and features
   b. Windows Update
   c. Anytime Upgrade
   d. Upgrade Assistant

5. Which of the following Windows 8 editions are not capable of joining an Active Directory Domain Services domain?
   a. Windows 8.1
   b. Windows 8.1 RT
   c. Windows 8.1 Pro
   d. Windows 8.1 Enterprise

6. You have 20 tablet computers to deploy to traveling salesmen. The computers will have to run Microsoft Office, as well as several apps from the Windows Store. Which of the following Windows 8.1 editions is most suitable for these tablets?
   a. Windows 8.1
   b. Windows 8.1 RT
   c. Windows 8.1 Pro
   d. Windows 8.1 Enterprise

7. Which of the following terms best describes the fly-out panel that appears on the right side of the Windows 8.1 Start screen contains buttons?
   a. Icons
   b. Buttons
   c. Tokens
   d. Charms

8. Which of the following operating systems can you upgrade in place to Windows 8.1?
   a. Windows 8
   b. Windows 7
   c. Windows Vista
   d. Windows XP

9. Which of the following elements can be retained when you upgrade a computer running Windows 7 to Windows 8.1?
   a. Operating system configuration settings
   b. Applications installed on the Vista computer
   c. The user's personal data files
   d. Application configuration settings

10. Which of the following Windows operating system versions required Microsoft to develop and maintain separate SKUs for each language?
    a. Windows 8.1
    b. Windows 7
    c. Windows Vista
    d. Windows XP

Best Answer

Choose the letter that corresponds to the best answer. More than one answer choice may achieve the goal. Select the BEST answer.

1. Which product or combination of products would provide the closest experience to the Windows 7 Ultimate Edition product?
   a. Windows 8.1
   b. Windows 8.1 RT
   c. Windows 8.1 Pro
   d. Windows 8.1 Enterprise
   e. Windows Media Server

2. Which of the following represents the best way to deploy a bilingual French-English version of Windows 8.1?
   a. Purchase separate French and English versions of Windows 8.1 and install them one after the other on the same computer.
   b. Purchase separate French and English versions of Windows 8.1, install the English version, and then change the installed product key to the one from the French version.
   c. Purchase Windows 8.1, select one of the desired languages during the operating system installation, and then download and install the language pack for the other language.
   d. Install Windows 8.1 with one of the desired languages, and then change to the other language in Control Panel, as needed.

3. Which of the following is the best way to display the All Apps icon on a Windows 8.1 computer with a touch screen?
   a. Swipe a finger up from the bottom edge of the screen.
   b. Press the WIN key.
   c. Swipe a finger from the right side to the center of the screen.
   d. Right-click the background of the Start screen.

4. Which of the following is the best way to determine whether you can upgrade your computer to Windows 8.1?
   a. Boot the system from a Windows 8.1 installation disk.
   b. Start the Windows 8.1 Setup program from an installation disk while the old operating system is running.
   c. Run the Microsoft Upgrade Assistant application.
   d. Run Windows Update to determine whether the new operating system is available for download.

5. For which of the following operating systems is there no upgrade pricing to Windows 8.1?
   a. Windows 8
   b. Windows 7
   c. Windows Vista
   d. Windows XP
   e. Windows 2000

Matching and Identification

Match the following terms with their corresponding definitions.

_____ **a)** Windows 8.1 RT
_____ **b)** Upgrade Assistant
_____ **c)** In-place upgrade
_____ **d)** Windows 8.1 Enterprise
_____ **e)** Windows 8.1 Pro
_____ **f)** Windows 8.1 32-bit
_____ **g)** Multilingual user interface
_____ **h)** Edge UI
_____ **i)** Charms
_____ **j)** Live tiles

1. Supports no more than 4 GB of memory
2. Available as a retail product
3. Runs on an ARM processor
4. Icons that display information supplied by the applications they run
5. Supported fully only from Windows 8
6. Integrated into the language neutral Windows 8 operating system
7. Appears when you swipe a finger from the side of a touch screen to the center
8. Specifies possibility of performing an in-place upgrade
9. Available only through volume licensing programs
10. Icons on fly-out screens

Build a List

1. Place the following charms in the order in which they appear in the Windows 8.1 edge UI, from top to bottom.
   _____ Share
   _____ Devices
   _____ Search
   _____ Settings
   _____ Start

2. Arrange the following Windows 8.1 operating systems in order from most capable to least capable.
   _____ Windows 8.1 RT
   _____ Windows 8.1 Enterprise
   _____ Windows 8.1
   _____ Windows 8.1 Pro

3. Specify the correct order of steps for running the Windows 8.1 Upgrade Assistant.
   _____ Save data
   _____ Download Upgrade Assistant
   _____ View the *Windows 8 For You* page
   _____ Examine results
   _____ Browse to the *Buy Windows 8* page
   _____ Open Internet Explorer
   _____ Run Upgrade Assistant

■ Business Case Scenarios

Scenario 1-1: Selecting a Windows 8.1 Edition

You are a private computer consultant, and a new client has approached you about upgrading his small business network. The network currently consists of eight Windows XP workstations and a single server running Windows Server 2008 R2. The server is functioning as a domain controller and the eight workstations are members of an Active Directory Domain Services domain. The workstations each have 1 GB of memory and a 1.8-GHz processor. The video cards support DirectX 9 and have WDDM drivers available from the manufacturer. Three of the workstations are located in a warehouse across town, while the other five in the main office run Microsoft Office applications almost exclusively. The server is also located in the main office. There have been problems with sluggish performance on the warehouse computers when they attempt to access server files. Which edition of Windows 8.1 would you select for the workstations to provide the features and performance they require? Explain your answer.

Scenario 1-2: Building a Network

A business owner called Ortiz approaches you about the possibility of designing a network for deployment at his new branch office in Bolivia. He has already purchased twenty computers and shipped them to the site. Each computer has 1 GB of memory, a 1 GHz processor, and an 80 GB hard drive. He wants to connect the computers into an ActiveDirectory Domain Services network that will be used primarily for accessing Web-based applications. Because he will be operating the network in a South American country, Mr. Ortiz wants to use the core Windows 8.1 product for his workstations, as this is the most economical solution he can find. Will this be an adequate solution for his needs? Explain why or why not.

2 LESSON

Installing Windows 8.1

70-687 EXAM OBJECTIVE

Objective 1.2 – Install Windows 8.1. This objective may include but is not limited to: install as Windows to Go; migrate from previous versions of Windows to Windows 8.1; upgrade from Windows 7 or Windows 8 to Windows 8.1; install to a VHD; install additional Windows features; configure Windows for additional languages.

LESSON HEADING	EXAM OBJECTIVE
Understanding the Windows 8.1 Boot Environment	
Introducing Windows PE	
What's New in Windows PE	
Understanding Windows PE Limitations	
Using Windows PE	
Performing a Clean Installation	
Installing Third-Party Device Drivers	
Working with Installation Partitions	
Installing to a VHD	Install to a VHD
Installing Language Support	Configure Windows for additional languages
Installing Additional Features	Install additional Windows features
Upgrading to Windows 8.1	
Preparing to Upgrade	
Upgrading from Windows 7 to Windows 8.1	Upgrade from Windows 7 or Windows 8 to Windows 8.1
Upgrading from Windows 8 to Windows 8.1	
Upgrading Windows 8.1 Editions	
Migrating from previous Windows Versions	Migrate from previous versions of Windows to Windows 8.1
Installing Windows to Go	Install as Windows to Go

KEY TERMS

Application Compatibility Toolkit
    (ACT)
clean installation
system recovery disk
Upgrade Assistant program
User State Migration Tool (USMT)

virtual hard disk (VHD)
Volume Activation
    Management Tool (VAMT)
Windows 8.1 Assessment and
    Deployment Kit (ADK)
Windows Easy Transfer

Windows PE 5.0
Windows Recovery Environment
Windows To Go

Understanding the Windows 8.1 Boot Environment

THE BOTTOM LINE Windows 8 eliminates DOS from the installation process and provides a new boot environment.

Those who have performed clean installations of standalone Windows XP systems should recall that the very beginning of the process, immediately after the system boots from the installation disk, consists of several character-based (that is, non-graphical) screens. On these screens, you opt to perform the installation, agree to the terms of the End User License Agreement (EULA), select the drive partition on which you want to install Windows XP, and then watch as the program copies the installation files from the CD-ROM to a temporary folder on the hard disk.

These screens are character-based because all of the Windows operating systems up to and including Windows XP required an MS-DOS boot at the beginning of the installation process. The MS-DOS boot was necessary because the computer required an operating system to run the installation program and to gain access to the disk drives.

This need for an MS-DOS boot became increasingly problematic over the years for several reasons, including the limited disk and networking support in MS-DOS. Microsoft needed a new solution.

Introducing Windows PE

All of the Windows versions since Windows Vista, and including Windows 8.1 eliminate the need for MS-DOS as an underlying operating system for the installation process. To replace the MS-DOS boot, Windows 8.1 includes Windows Preinstallation Environment 5.0 (Windows PE).

Windows PE 5.0 is a stripped-down operating system, based on the Windows 8.1 kernel, which enables system administrators to boot a computer that has no operating system installed and initiate the operating system setup process. When compared to MS-DOS, Windows PE has a number of distinct advantages, including the following:

- **Native 32-bit or 64-bit support** – Windows PE is a native 32-bit or 64-bit operating system that enables the computer to address memory just as the full Windows 8.1 operating system does. MS-DOS is a 16-bit OS and is relatively limited in its memory addressing capabilities.

- **Native 32-bit or 64-bit driver support** – Because Windows PE is a 32-bit or 64-bit OS, it can use the same drivers as a full Windows 8.1 installation. System administrators therefore do not have to search for antiquated 16-bit real mode network drivers as they did with MS-DOS.

- **Internal networking support** – Windows PE includes its own internal TCP/IP networking stack and is capable of functioning as a Windows file sharing client. This means that after booting Windows PE, an administrator only has to supply a driver for the network adapter and the networking stack is complete.

- **Internal NTFS support** – Windows PE includes internal support for the NTFS file system used by Windows 8.1, as well as the FAT file systems that MS-DOS supports. This means that when you boot a system using Windows PE, you can read from and write to existing NTFS drives in the computer, as well as create and format new NTFS partitions. It is even possible to create and manage dynamic volumes using Windows PE.

- **Scripting language support** – Windows PE includes internal support for a subset of the Win32 application programming interface (API), meaning that it is possible to run some Windows programs in the preinstallation environment. Windows PE also includes support for .NET Framework (WinPE_NetFx), Windows PowerShell (WinPE_PowerShell), Windows Management Instrumentation (WMI) and Windows Script Host, which makes it possible for administrators to create scripts that are far more powerful than MS-DOS batch files.

- **Flexible boot options** – Windows PE can boot from a variety of media, including CD-ROMs, DVD-ROMs, USB devices, such as flash disks and floppy drives, or a Windows Deployment Services (WDS) server. The computer can then run the Windows PE operating system from a variety of media, including the DVD, a temporary folder on a hard disk, a USB flash drive, a RAM disk, or a network share.

+ MORE INFORMATION

Windows PE 5.0 is available in both 32-bit and 64-bit versions. You must use the 32-bit version of Windows PE to install the 32-bit version of Windows 8.1 and the 64-bit version of Windows PE to install the 64-bit version of Windows 8.1.

What's New in Windows PE

The latest version of Windows PE, versions 5.0, is packaged with a variety of tools you can use to customize the Windows PE environment.

The most important development in the latest versions of Windows PE (3.0, 4.0, and 5.0) is that anyone can obtain them. Prior to Windows 7, Microsoft made Windows PE available only to customers with service agreements. Now, it's available for free in a standalone version as part of the ***Windows 8.1 Assessment and Deployment Kit (Windows ADK)***.

The Windows 8.1 ADK includes the following components:

- ***Application Compatibility Toolkit (ACT)*** – Enables administrators to test, detect, and prioritize application compatibility issues

- **Deployment Tools** – Includes tools that enable administrators to capture, manage, and deploy system images

- ***User State Migration Tool (USMT)*** – Scriptable command line tools that enable administrators to migrate user profile information to newly installed Windows 8.1 workstations

TAKE NOTE*

Windows 8.1 ADK, including Windows PE 5.0, is available free of charge from the Microsoft Download Center.

- *Volume Activation Management Tool (VAMT)* – Enables administrators to manage the activation of product keys for Microsoft products, obtained through retail and volume channels
- **Windows Performance Toolkit (WPT)** – Provides a graphical interface that administrators can use to analyze system performance data
- **Windows Assessment Toolkit** – Includes tools that enable administrators to simulate user activity and examine its effect on the computer
- **Windows Assessment Services** – Includes tools that enable administrators to remotely manage computers in a laboratory environment
- **Windows Preinstallation Environment (Windows PE)** – Provides a minimized version of the Windows operating system for installation and maintenance purposes

Understanding Windows PE Limitations

Microsoft intends Windows PE to be a reduced subset of the Windows 8.1 operating system, only providing sufficient capability to perform certain installation, diagnostic, and recovery functions while running from a minimized hardware environment, such as a RAM drive.

Because there was never any intention for Windows PE to function as a full-time operating system, and to facilitate its rapid deployment and execution, there are certain inherent limitations in the product, such as the following:

- Windows PE does not support the entire collection of Win32 APIs as a full installation of Windows 8.1 does. Microsoft limits the APIs in Windows PE primarily to those providing disk and network input/output functions, as well as certain APIs that make it possible to run basic programs. Reducing the API support enables Windows PE to run in a smaller memory space than Windows 8.1.

TAKE NOTE*

Because Windows PE requires a relatively small memory space, the entire operating system can run from a RAM disk. A RAM disk is a driver that allocates a section of active memory for use as a virtual disk drive, complete with drive letter. Because the RAM disk is based in memory it is much faster than a hard disk drive, but it is also volatile; all of its contents are lost when the computer restarts. Running the Windows 8.1 Setup program from a RAM disk enables all of the operating system file handles to remain open throughout the installation process, allowing you to remove the boot device, if necessary. By contrast, running the Setup program directly from a DVD makes it impossible to remove the disk (to load third-party drivers, for example) without interrupting the installation procedure. In the same way, running the Setup program from a temporary folder on a hard disk interferes with partition creation and management functions that might be needed during the installation.

- Windows PE automatically stops and reboots the computer after 72 hours of continuous operation. This deliberate limitation prevents individuals from using the product as a permanent operating environment.
- Windows PE will not fit on a floppy disk, but it is possible to create bootable Windows PE CD-ROMs, DVD-ROMs, and USB flash drives.
- You must use the 32-bit version of Windows PE to install the 32-bit version of Windows 8.1, and the 64-bit version of Windows PE to install the 64-bit Windows 8.1.

- While it is possible to modify the Windows PE registry when the operating system is running, all registry keys are reset to their default values each time the operating system restarts. It is possible to make permanent changes to the registry, but to do so you must make the changes offline by manually editing the registry while Windows PE is not running.

- While you can create drive letter assignments in a Windows PE session, these assignments are not persistent between sessions.

- Windows PE does not have file server or Remote Desktop capabilities, nor does it support the Microsoft .NET framework or the Common Language Runtime (CLR), Windows on Windows 32 (WOW32), Windows on Windows 64 (WOW64), Virtual DOS Machine (VDM), OS/2, or POSIX subsystems.

- Windows PE does not support the installation of Windows Installer package (.msi) files.

- Windows PE can access Distributed File System (DFS) folders, but only those in stand-alone DFS roots.

Using Windows PE

In addition to functioning as a platform for individual installations of Windows 8.1, Windows PE is useful for other scenarios that require a basic operating system with minimal resource usage.

Some of the other scenarios that can make use of Windows PE are as follows:

- **Custom deployments** – Windows 8.1 uses Windows PE during the default installation procedure, but it is possible for administrators to build their own unattended installation routines using Windows PE as a platform to run scripts and deploy customized disk images on fleets of workstations. You can even use Windows PE to deploy operating systems other than Windows 8.1.

- **System troubleshooting** – If a Windows 8.1 computer fails to start, or if it crashes repeatedly, a technician can launch the *Windows Recovery Environment* (Windows RE), which is simply another name given to Windows PE on a computer with Windows 8.1 already installed. In the Windows RE environment, the technician can use Windows' built-in troubleshooting utilities or run third-party or custom diagnostic tools.

- **System recovery** – OEMs who build their own computers typically supply their customers with a *system recovery disk* rather than an operating system installation disk. A system recovery disk contains image files that can restore the computer to its original state, just as it was when it left the factory. OEMs can use Windows PE to build recovery solutions that automate the process of setting up Windows 8.1, installing specific drivers, installing applications, and configuring the entire system to create a standardized environment.

■ Performing a Clean Installation

THE BOTTOM LINE

A *clean installation* is the simplest way to deploy Windows 8.1 on a new computer or a computer with a partition that you are willing to reformat (losing all of the data on the partition in the process).

If a computer is brand new and has no operating system installed on it, then it cannot start until you supply a boot disk, such as the Windows 8.1 installation disk. During the installation you will select the disk partition on which you want to install Windows, and the Setup program will copy the operating system files there.

If the computer has an operating system installed on it, and you have already backed up all of the data that you want to preserve, then you are ready to boot the computer from the Windows 8.1 installation disk. During the setup process you can erase a partition on the disk in preparation for installing Windows there.

TAKE NOTE ✳   The following procedure is for an installation of Windows 8.1 Pro. Although the installation procedure for the other editions is nearly identical, you might see minor differences in the procedure.

 PERFORM A CLEAN INSTALLATION

GET READY. Prepare the computer for the Windows 8.1 installation by making sure that all of its external peripheral devices are connected and powered on.

1. Turn on the computer and insert the Windows 8.1 installation disk into the DVD drive.

2. Press any key to boot from the DVD (if necessary).

   A progress indicator screen appears as Windows is loading files.

TAKE NOTE ✳   The device that a PC uses to boot is specified in its system (or BIOS) settings. In some cases, you might have to modify these settings to enable the computer to boot from the Windows 8.1 DVD. If you are not familiar with the operation of a particular computer, watch the screen carefully as the system starts and look for an instruction specifying what key to press to access the system settings.

3. The computer loads the Windows graphical interface and the Windows Setup screen appears, as shown in Figure 2-1.

Figure 2-1

The *Windows Setup* page

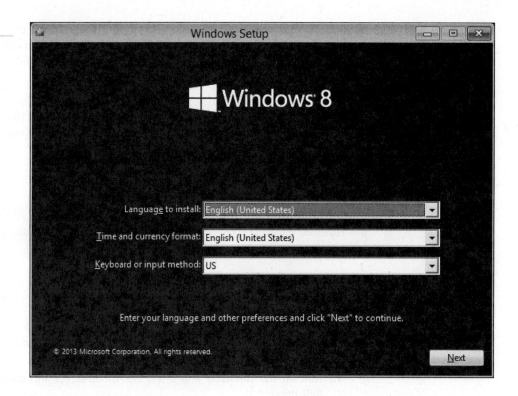

4. Using the drop-down lists provided, select the appropriate Language to install, Time and currency format, and Keyboard or input method and then click Next.

The *Windows 8.1 Install now* page appears.

5. Click the Install now button.

The *License terms* page appears.

TAKE NOTE* Depending on the Windows 8 edition you are installing and the type of license, you might be required to type in a product key at this time.

6. Select the I accept the license terms checkbox and then click Next. The *Which type of installation do you want?* page appears, as shown in Figure 2-2.

Figure 2-2

The *Which type of installation do you want?* page

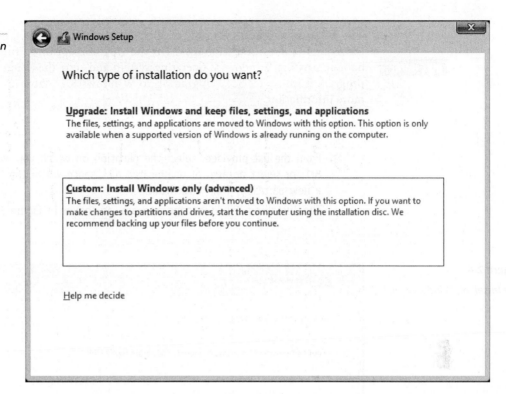

7. Click the **Custom: Install Windows only (advanced)** option.

The *Where do you want to install Windows?* page appears, as shown in Figure 2-3.

Figure 2-3

The *Where do you want to install Windows?* page

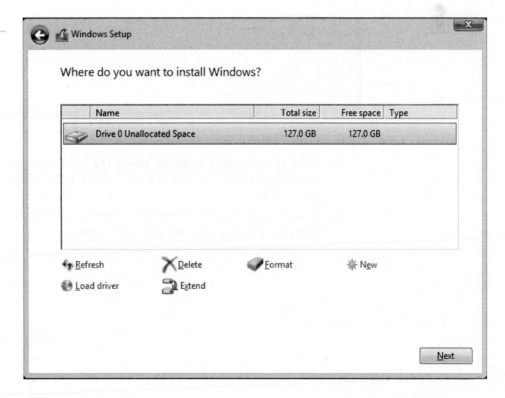

TAKE NOTE *

The Upgrade option is currently disabled because you booted the computer using the Windows 8.1 installation disk. For the Upgrade option to function, you must boot an existing Windows 7 operating system and start the Windows 8.1 installation program from there. See "Upgrading to Windows 8.1" later in this lesson for more information.

8. From the list provided, select the partition on which you want to install Windows 8.1, or select an area of unallocated disk space where the Setup program can create a new partition. Then click Next.

The Installing Windows page appears, as shown in Figure 2-4.

Figure 2-4

The *Installing Windows* page

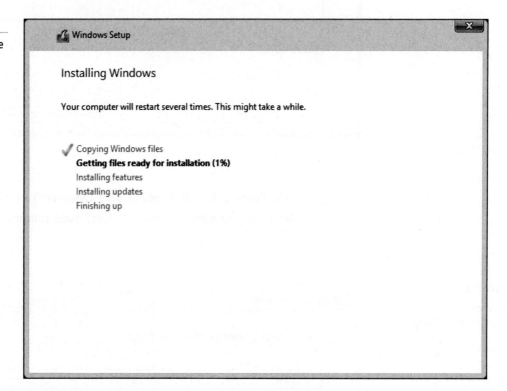

9. After several minutes, during which the Setup program installs Windows 8.1, the computer reboots and the Personalize page appears, as shown in Figure 2-5.

10. Select a color for your screen background and in the PC name text box, type a name for the computer, and then click Next.

Figure 2-5

The *Personalize* page

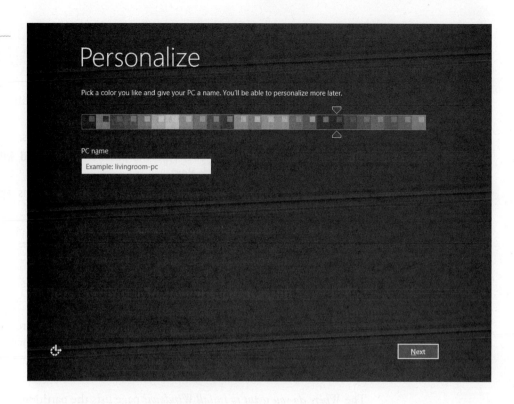

The Settings page appears.

 If the computer is connected to a Windows network, then the name you specify for the computer must be unique on that network.

11. Click **Use Express Settings**. The *Sign in to your Microsoft account* page appears, as shown in Figure 2-6.

Figure 2-6

The *Sign in to your Microsoft account* page

TAKE NOTE* If you do not have a Microsoft account, you can click the *Create a new account* link to obtain one or create a traditional local Windows account without an email address.

12. In the *Email address* text box, type the address associated with a Microsoft account and then click Next.

   The *Enter your Microsoft account password* page appears.

13. In the Password text box, type the password associated with your Microsoft account and then click **Next**.

   A series of screens introducing Windows 8.1 functions appear, followed by the Windows 8.1 Start screen.

At this point, you can remove the installation disk from the drive.

Installing Third-Party Device Drivers

During the Windows 8.1 installation procedure, the Setup program enables you to select a disk partition or an area of unallocated disk space where you want to install the operating system.

The *Where do you want to install Windows?* page lists the partitions on all of the hard disks that the Setup program can detect with its default drivers. In most cases, all of the computer's hard disks will appear in the list; If they do not, it is probably because Windows PE does not include a driver for the computer's drive controller.

If the hard disk drives in the computer are connected to a third-party controller, rather than the one integrated into the motherboard, the list of partitions might appear empty, and you will have to supply a driver before the Setup program can see the disks. Check the controller manufacturer's website for a driver supporting Windows 8.1. If none is available, use the most recent Windows 7 driver.

➕ MORE INFORMATION

There are several reasons why a computer might employ a third-party disk controller, rather than the one integrated into the motherboard. The computer might have a relatively old motherboard and more modern drives whose capabilities are not supported by the older controller. The computer might also be using SCSI (Small Computer Systems Interface) or SAS (Serial Attached SCSI) rather than SATA (Serial ATA) or IDE (Integrated Drive Electronics) hard drives, and a SCSI or SAS host adapter that is not supported by Windows PE. Finally, the computer might be using a specialized controller that provides advanced disk management technologies, such as RAID (Redundant Array of Independent Disks).

To install a third-party disk driver, use the following procedure:

 INSTALL A THIRD-PARTY DISK DRIVER

GET READY. If, during a Windows 8.1 installation, no disk partitions or unallocated space appear on the *Where do you want to install Windows?* page, you must install the appropriate driver for your disk controller using the following procedure before the installation can continue.

1. On the *Where do you want to install Windows?* page, click the **Load Driver** button.

   A *Load Driver* message box appears, as shown in Figure 2-7.

Figure 2-7

The *Load Driver* message box

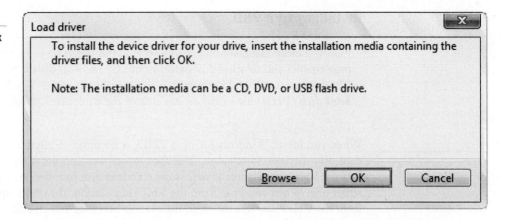

2. Insert the storage medium containing the driver into the computer. You can supply drivers on a CD, DVD, USB flash drive, or floppy disk.

3. Click **OK** if the driver is in the root directory of the storage medium or click **Browse** if it is necessary to locate the driver in the directory structure of the disk. When the driver loads, the partitions and unallocated space on the associated disks appear in the list on the *Where do you want to install Windows?* page.

4. Select the partition or area of unallocated space where you want to install Windows 8.1 and then continue with the rest of the installation procedure, as covered earlier in this lesson.

Because the Windows setup program is running from a RAM drive, it is possible to remove the Windows 8.1 installation disk from the DVD drive and insert another disk containing drivers. You will later have to re-insert the Windows 8.1 disk to complete the installation.

Working with Installation Partitions

In addition to installing disk drivers, the *Where do you want to install Windows?* page enables you to create, manage, and delete the partitions on your disks.

In addition to *Refresh* and *Load driver* there are four additional buttons on the page. These buttons have the following functions:

- **Delete** – Removes an existing partition from a disk, permanently erasing all of its data. You might want to delete partitions to consolidate unallocated disk space, enabling you to create a new, larger partition.

- **Extend** – Enables you to make an existing partition larger, as long as there is unallocated space available immediately following the selected partition on the disk.

- **Format** – Enables you to format an existing partition on a disk, thereby erasing all of its data. There is no need to format any new partitions you create for the install, but you might want to format an existing partition to eliminate unwanted files prior to installing Windows 8.1 on it.

- **New** – Creates a new partition of a user-specified size in the selected area of unallocated space.

Installing to a VHD

During a clean installation of Windows 8.1, the *Where do you want to install Windows?* page enables you to select any partition on any physical disk as the destination for the Windows system files. However, it is also possible to install Windows 8.1 on a *virtual hard disk (VHD)* file stored on any one of the computer's physical disks.

When you install Windows 8.1 on a VHD, it becomes an alternative boot device to the standard disk partition installation. The boot loader that appears when you start the computer lists the VHD installation as well as the standard disk installation, enabling you to select either one. When you boot from the VHD installation, the entire operating systems loads from the VHD file, and the main installation becomes inaccessible.

This ability makes it possible to maintain any number of independent Windows 8.1 installations on a single computer and boot into any one as needed.

To install Windows 8.1 to a VHD file, use the following procedure.

CERTIFICATION READY
Install to a VHD
Objective 1.2

 INSTALL WINDOWS 8.1 TO A VHD

GET READY. Prepare the computer for the Windows 8.1 installation by making sure that all of its external peripheral devices are connected and powered on.

1. Turn on the computer and then insert the Windows 8.1 installation disk into the DVD drive.
2. Press any key to boot from the DVD (if necessary).
   A progress indicator screen appears as Windows is loading files.
3. The computer switches to the Windows graphical interface and the Windows Setup screen appears.
4. Using the drop-down lists provided, select the appropriate Language to install, Time and currency format, and Keyboard or input method and then click **Next**.
   The *Windows 8.1 Install now* page appears.
5. Press Shift+F10. A Command Prompt window appears.
6. At the command prompt, type **diskpart** and then press **Enter**.
   A Diskpart prompt appears.
7. At the Diskpart prompt, type the following command and then press **Enter**.
   create vdisk file=C:\filename.vhd maximum=*disksize* **type=fixed|expandable**
   size specifies the size of the disk in megabytes, *fixed* specifies a fixed size virtual disk file, and *expandable* specifies a virtual disk file that resizes to accommodate the allocated data. The default is **fixed**.
8. Type **select vdisk file=C:\filename.vhd** and then press **Enter**.
9. Type **attach vdisk** and then press **Enter**.
10. Type **exit** and then press **Enter** to close the Diskpart prompt.
11. Type **exit** and then press **Enter** to close the Command Prompt window.
12. Click the *Install now* button.
    The *License terms* page appears.
13. Select the **I accept the license terms** checkbox and then click **Next**.
    The *Which type of installation do you want?* page appears.
14. Click the **Custom: Install Windows only (advanced)** option.
    The *Where do you want to install Windows?* page appears, with the new VHD you created appearing as one of the disks available for selection.

15. From the list provided, select the partition representing the VHD you just created, and then click **Next**.

The *Installing Windows* page appears.

16. Proceed with the rest of the installation in the normal manner.

Once you have completed the installation, you can select the VHD installation from the boot loader each time you start the computer.

Installing Language Support

As described in Lesson 1, "Evaluating Hardware Readiness and Capability," Windows 8.1 simplifies the process of installing support for different languages by making the operating system itself language neutral and packaging all localized information in the form of language packs.

CERTIFICATION READY
Configure Windows for additional languages
Objective 1.2

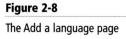

Once you install Windows 8.1 using one particular language, you can add others using the Language control panel applet. To install an additional language pack, use the following procedure.

 INSTALL A LANGUAGE PACK

GET READY. Log on to Windows 8.1 using an account with administrative privileges.

1. From the desktop, right-click the Start button and, on the context menu, select Control Panel. The Control Panel window appears.

2. Click Add a language. The Language applet appears.

3. Click Add a language. The Add a language page appears, as shown in Figure 2-8.

Figure 2-8

The Add a language page

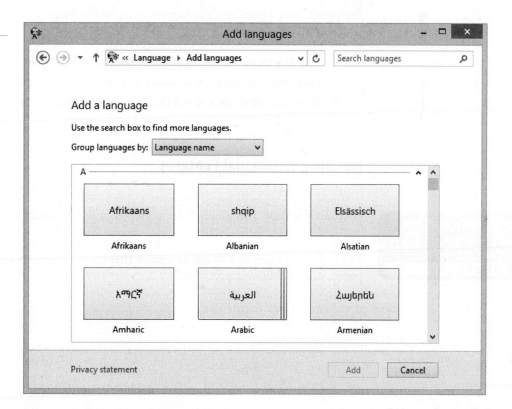

4. Scroll down the list, select the language you want to install, and click Add. If there are multiple variants of the language available, click Open, select the vatiant you want to install, and click Add. The new language appears in the list of installed languages.

5. Click the Options link for the new language you just added. A Language options page appears, as shown in Figure 2-9.

Figure 2-9

The Language options page

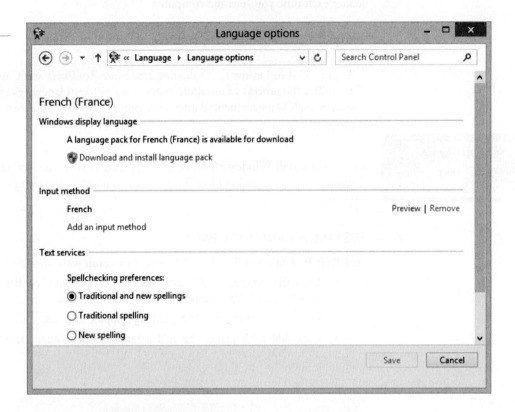

6. Click Download and install language pack. A User Account Control message box appears.

7. Click Yes. The system downloads and installs the selected language pack.

8. When the installation is completed, click Restart Now. The system restarts.

Installing Additional Features

Windows 8.1 includes many programs and features that the setup program does not install by default. This prevents the Windows from consuming resources unnecessarily.

CERTIFICATION READY
Install additional
Windows features
Objective 1.2

To add these features to a Windows system after the operating system installation is completed, use the following procedure.

INSTALL WINDOWS FEATURES

GET READY. Log on to Windows 8.1 using an account with administrative privileges.

1. From the desktop, right-click the Start button and, on the context menu, select Control Panel. The Control Panel window appears.

2. Click Programs > Turn Windows features on or off. The Turn Windows features on or off window appears, as shown in Figure 2-10.

Figure 2-10

The Turn Windows features on or off window

3. Select the checkboxes for the features you want to install and click OK. The system installs the selected features.

4. Click Close.

■ Upgrading to Windows 8.1

THE BOTTOM LINE

To the workstation user, performing an in-place upgrade to Windows 8 is a relatively simple procedure, but the activities the Setup program performs behind the scenes are highly complex.

During the upgrade process, the Setup program creates a new Windows folder and installs the Windows 8.1 operating system files into it.

While in-place upgrades often proceed smoothly, the complexity of the upgrade process and the large number of variables involved means that there are many things that can potentially go wrong. To minimize the risks involved, it is important for an administrator to take the upgrade process seriously, prepare the system beforehand, and have the ability to troubleshoot any problems that might arise. The following sections discuss these subjects in greater detail.

Preparing to Upgrade

Before you begin an in-place upgrade to Windows 8.1, you should perform a number of preliminary procedures to ensure that the process goes smoothly and that the user data is protected.

Consider the following before you perform any upgrade to Windows 8:

- **Run Upgrade Assistant** – To be sure that the computer is capable of running the Windows 8.1 edition you plan on installing, run Upgrade Assistant and take note of its advisories regarding the computer's hardware and software. If it is necessary to perform hardware upgrades, do so before installing Windows 8.1, making sure that the new hardware is operational before proceeding.

For more information on Windows 8.1's hardware requirements, and on running the Upgrade Assistant program, see Lesson 1, "Evaluating Hardware Readiness and Capability."

- **Check hardware compatibility** – The *Upgrade Assistant program* can point out hardware inadequacies in the computer, especially in regard to the Windows 8.1 system requirements. If it is necessary to upgrade hardware, make certain that the products you purchase are certified for use with Windows 8.1. The Upgrade Assistant program can also identify devices that might not function under Windows 8. However, it is sometimes possible to make such devices run properly with a driver or firmware upgrade. It is a good idea to perform an inventory of the computer's primary components before you perform the upgrade, and consider the age and capabilities of each one. It is always best to locate potential hardware incompatibilities before you perform the upgrade procedure.

- **Search for updated drivers** – As part of your hardware inventory, be sure to consider the age of the device drivers installed on the computer. Check hardware manufacturers' websites for driver updates, especially those that are specifically intended to provide support for Windows 8.1. In some cases it might be preferable to install the new drivers while the old operating system is still running, but if the manufacturer provides separate Windows 7, Windows 8, and Windows 8.1 drivers, wait until you have installed Windows 8. Even if no updates are available, it is a good idea to gather all of the drivers for the computer's hardware together and copy them to a removable storage medium, such as a writable CD or flash drive. This way, if the Setup program requires a driver during the upgrade process, you have it available.

- **Check application compatibility** – Upgrade Assistant can point out possible application compatibility problems, but you can sometimes solve these problems by updating or upgrading the application. Create an inventory of the software products installed on the computer and check the manufacturers' websites for updates, availability of upgrades, and announcements regarding support for Windows 8.1. For example, if the computer is running Microsoft Office, use the Office Online website to download the latest updates. Check the applications' system requirements as well. Install any free updates that are available and consider the need for paid upgrades. In an enterprise environment, you should test all applications for Windows 8.1 compatibility, no matter what the manufacturer says, before you perform any operating system upgrades. However, for standalone clients, testing usually isn't practical. The best you can do is to inform the user that there might be problems with specific applications and warn them that there might be additional costs involved for new versions or different products.

- **Check disk space** – Make sure that there is at least 20 gigabytes of disk space free on the partition where the old operating system is installed. During the upgrade procedure, sufficient disk space is needed to hold both operating systems simultaneously. After the upgrade is complete, you can remove the old Windows files, freeing up some additional space.

- **Ensure computer functionality** – Make sure that the old operating system is running properly on the computer before you begin the upgrade process. You must start an in-place upgrade from within an earlier Windows version so you cannot count on Windows 8.1 to correct any problems that prevent the computer from starting or running the Setup program.

- **Perform a full backup** – Before you perform any upgrade procedure you should back up the entire system, or at the very least the essential user files. You can use Windows Easy Transfer if no other tool is available. Removable hard drives make this a simple process, even if the client does not have a suitable backup device in the computer.

- **Purchase Windows 8** – Be sure to purchase the appropriate Windows 8 edition for the upgrade, and have the installation disk and product key handy. For more information on the allowed upgrade paths to Windows 8, see Lesson 1.

Upgrading from Windows 7 to Windows 8.1

Once you complete the steps in the previous section, you are ready to perform an in-place upgrade from Windows 7 to Windows 8.1.

CERTIFICATION READY
Upgrading from
Windows 7 to Windows 8.1
Objective 1.2

To upgrade a computer running Windows 7 to Windows 8 while preserving all files and settings, use the following procedure:

 UPGRADE WINDOWS 7 TO WINDOWS 8.1

GET READY. Turn on the computer running Windows 7 and make sure you have the Windows 8.1 installation disk and product key ready.

1. Insert the Windows 8.1 installation disk into the DVD drive.

   An Autoplay dialog box appears.

2. Click **Run setup.exe**.

   The *Get important* updates page appears.

3. Select No, thanks and click Next.

   The License terms page appears.

4. Select the *I accept the license terms* checkbox and click Accept.

   The *Choose what to keep* page appears.

5. Click Next.

   The *Ready to install* page appears.

6. Click Install.

   The *Installing Windows 8.1* page appears, displaying a progress indicator. The system restarts several times, and eventually the Region and Language page appears.

TAKE NOTE

If you do not have a Microsoft account, you can click the *Create a new account* link to obtain one or create a traditional local Windows account without an email address.

7. Configure the Country or region, App language, Keyboard layout, and Time zone settings as needed and click Next. The Personalize page appears.
8. In the PC name text box, enter a name for your computer and click Next. The Settings page appears.
9. Click Use express settings. The Sign in to your Microsoft account page appears.
10. Type the address associated with a Microsoft account and then click Next. The *Enter your Microsoft account password* page appears.
11. In the Password text box, type the password associated with your Microsoft account and then click **Next**. A series of screens introducing Windows 8.1 functions appear, followed by the Windows 8.1 Start screen.

As noted in Lesson 1, when upgrading from Windows 7 to Windows 8.1, you can copy your personal files from the old operating system to the new one, but you cannot copy user profiles, applications, or operating system configuration settings.

Upgrading from Windows 8 to Windows 8.1

As mentioned in Lesson 1, Windows 8.1 is a free upgrade to all licensed Windows 8 users.

The Windows Store app in Windows 8 displays products that are suited to the computer running it. If you are currently running Windows 8, the store will present you with the opportunity to download and install Windows 8.1 free of charge.

TAKE NOTE

Windows 8 and Windows 8 Pro are upgradable through the Windows Store, but Windows 8 Enterprise is not.

This upgrade is actually more of an update, because it does not completely replace the operating system, as an in-place upgrade from Windows 7 to Windows 8.1 does. The Windows 8 to Windows 8.1 update replaces certain files in the operating system and adds some new ones, but it does not have to migrate user profile information and other data from one copy of the operating system to another. In an enterprise environment, this is an upgrade that can easily be performed by the end user, without the need for a service call.

Upgrading Windows 8.1 Editions

One of the main advantages of the new architecture that Microsoft devised for Windows 8 is that it makes upgrades to other editions incredibly simple.

There are basically two scenarios in which an end user might be in a position to upgrade Windows 8.1 from one edition to another. If you are running the core Windows 8.1 product, you might want to upgrade to Windows 8.1 Pro. Among other things, this provides the ability to join the computer to an Active Directory Domain Services domain. This is likely to be a frequently encountered situation, as many computers sold by original equipment manufacturers (OEMs) have the core version of Windows 8.1 already installed on them.

The other possibility is that of a Windows 8.1 Pro user who wants to add the Windows 8.1 Media Center Pack. Both the Windows 8.1 Pro upgrade and the Windows 8.1 Media Center

Pack are available directly through the operating system, using the Add features to Windows 8.1 control panel applet.

To upgrade a Windows 8 installation to another edition, use the following procedure.

 USE THE ADD FEATURES TO WINDOWS 8.1 CONTROL PANEL

GET READY. Start the Windows 8.1 computer and log on using an account with administrative privileges.

1. On the Windows 8.1 computer, open the charms bar and then click **Search**.
   The Search bar appears.
2. With the Settings option selected, type **add features** in the text box.
   The *Add features to Windows 8.1* application appears in the results display.
3. Click **Add features to Windows 8.1**.
   A User Account Control message box appears.
4. Click **Yes**.
   The *Add features to Windows 8.1* control panel appears, displaying the *How do you want to get started?* page, which specifies the currently installed Windows 8.1 version.
5. Click **I want to buy a product key online**.
   A *Here's what we found* page appears, displaying the product options available for the computer.
6. Click the **Choose** button for the upgrade that you want to purchase.
   A Microsoft Store Wizard appears to step you through the process of purchasing the upgrade.
7. Follow the instructions to purchase and then install the upgrade.

Migrating from Previous Windows Versions

> There is no direct upgrade path from Windows Vista or Windows XP to Windows 8.1. The only way to retain any of your system information from these earlier operating systems while installing Windows 8.1 is to perform a migration, either side-by-side or wipe-and-load, as described in Lesson 3, "Migrating and Configuring User Data."

CERTIFICATION READY
Migrating from previous versions of Windows to Windows 8.1
Objective 1.2

A migration is when you perform a clean installation of Windows 8.1 and then transfer selected data from an existing installation of a previous Windows version. For example, if you are running Windows 7 and don't want to perform an in-place upgrade to Windows 8.1, you can install a clean copy of Windows 8.1 and migrate your essential data from Windows 7.

Windows 8.1, Windows 8, Windows RT, and Windows 7 all include a tool called ***Windows Easy Transfer*** that enables you to copy the valuable data from a source operating system to a destination operating system. In the Windows versions prior to 8.1, you can use Windows Easy Transfer to migrate user profiles, Windows settings, and personal files, and you can transfer the data using a variety of media, including external storage devices, network drives, and a special Easy Transfer cable. There were also compatible versions of the tool available for Windows Vista and Windows XP.

In Windows 8.1, however, Microsoft has taken the first steps towards deprecating the Windows Easy Transfer tool. The Windows 8.1 version can only transfer files (not settings or profiles), and only from Windows 7, Windows RT, and Windows 8. You can't even transfer data from one Windows 8.1 system to another.

There is another tool that can migrate data into Windows 8.1, called the User State Migration Tool (USMT), This is a command line tool designed primarily for use by administrators.

■ Installing Windows To Go

THE BOTTOM LINE

Windows To Go is a new feature in Windows 8.1 that enables administrators to deploy system images on removable USB drives.

When a user plugs a Windows To Go drive into a remote computer, the system loads the complete Windows 8.1 environment from the removable medium, including applications and any other data incorporated into the image file. The user can therefore access a familiar environment on any computer with hardware sufficient to run Windows 8.1.

Once Windows 8.1 is loaded from the Windows To Go drive, the storage subsystem on the host computer is disabled, so that no remnants of the Windows To Go environment are left on that computer. Users can therefore load Windows To Go on any computer, without worrying about leaving any confidential information behind, and enterprise administrators can permit temporary visitors to use their own computers.

For security purposes, Windows To Go supports the use of BitLocker, bypassing the Trusted Platform Module (TPM) because the feature is designed for use on different computers.

To create a Windows To Go drive, use the following procedure.

CERTIFICATION READY
Install as Windows to Go
Objective 1.2

 CREATE A WINDOWS TO GO DRIVE

GET READY. Start the Windows 8.1 computer and log on using an account with administrative privileges.

1. Plug the USB drive into an available port.
2. Insert a Windows 8.1 Enterprise installation disk into a drive.
3. On the Windows 8.1 computer, open the charms bar and then click **Search**.
   The Search bar appears.
4. With the Settings option selected, type **windows to go** in the text box.
   The *Windows To Go* application appears in the results display.
5. Click **Windows To Go**.
   The *Create a Windows To Go Workspace Wizard* appears, displaying the *Choose the drive you want to use* page, as shown in Figure 2-11.

Figure 2-11

The *Choose the drive you want to use* page

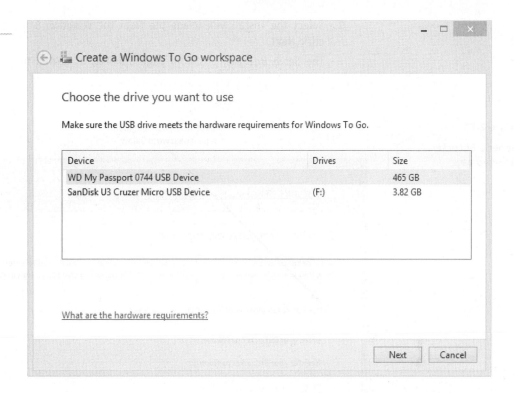

6. Select the USB device you want to convert to a Windows To Go drive from the device list and then click **Next**.

   The *Choose a Windows 8.1 Image* page appears, as shown in Figure 2-12.

Figure 2-12

The *Choose a Windows 8.1 image* page

Create a Windows To Go workspace

Choose a Windows 8 image

Pick an Enterprise image below or add a location to search for one. The image contains the operating system and app files.

Name	Location
Windows 8 Enterprise	F:\sources\install.wim

Add search location

Where can I find an image file?

Next   Cancel

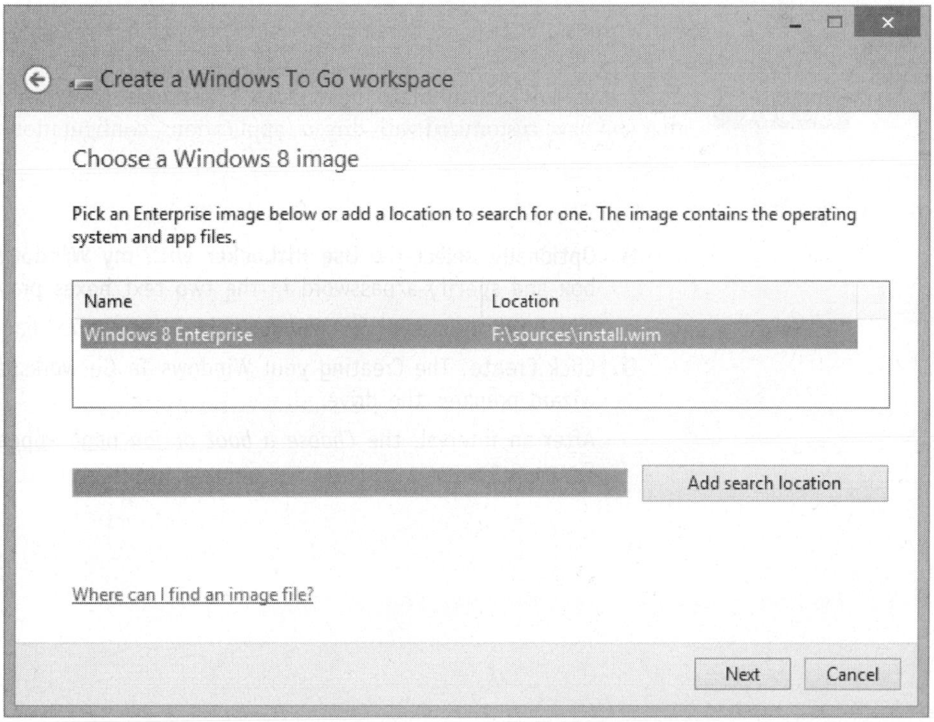

7. Select the Install.wim image file from the Windows 8 installation disk and then click **Next**.

The *Set a BitLocker password* page appears, as shown in Figure 2-13.

Figure 2-13

The *Set a BitLocker password* page

Select this option and then type a password below

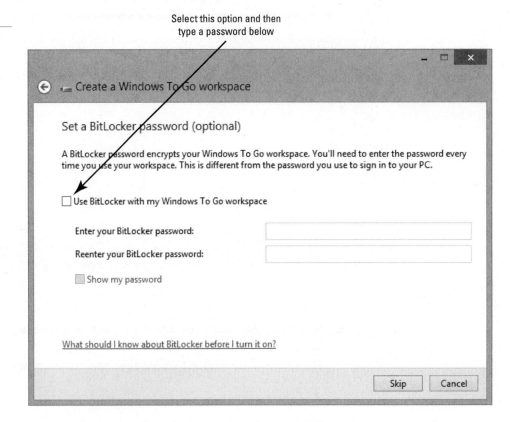

You can use any system image file to create a Windows To Go workspace, including an image that you have customized with drivers, applications, configuration settings, and data files.

8. Optionally, select the **Use BitLocker with my Windows To Go workspace** check-box and specify a password in the two text boxes provided. Then click **Next**.

The *Ready to create your Windows To Go workspace* page appears.

9. Click **Create**. The Creating your Windows To Go workspace page appears as the wizard prepares the drive.

After an interval, the *Choose a boot option* page appears, as shown in Figure 2-14.

Figure 2-14

The *Choose a boot option* page

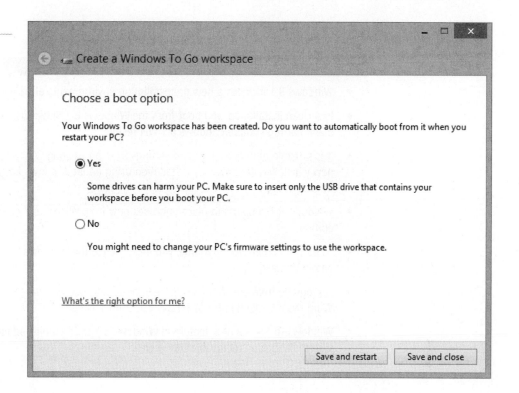

The process of creating a Windows To Go workspace can be a lengthy one, as long as 30 minutes or more, depending on the size of the image file you select.

TAKE NOTE*

10. Select **Yes** and then click **Save and close**.
11. Remove the USB device from computer.

You can now use the USB device to a boot any computer with hardware sufficient to run Windows 8.1 into the Windows To Go workspace.

TAKE NOTE*

Converting a USB drive to a Windows To Go workspace modifies its volume attributes. To decommission the device so that it becomes usable as a standard USB storage drive again, you must use the Diskpart utility to run the clean command on the drive, which removes all data, formatting, and initialization information.

SKILL SUMMARY

IN THIS LESSON, YOU LEARNED:

- Windows 8.1 includes a new preinstallation environment called Windows PE.

- In a clean installation, you boot from the Windows 8.1 Setup disk and create or select a blank partition where Windows 8.1 will reside.

- It is possible to migrate files and settings from an existing Windows installation to a newly installed Windows 8.1 installation using either Windows Easy Transfer or User State Migration Tool.

- Windows 8.1 supports in-place upgrades only from Windows 7 or another Windows 8.1 edition.

- To perform an in-place upgrade, you must launch the Windows 8.1 Setup program from within Windows 7.

- To upgrade from one Windows 8.1 edition to another, you can use the Add features to Windows 8.1 found in the Windows 8.1 Control Panel.

- Windows To Go is a new feature in Windows 8.1 that enables administrators to deploy system images on removable USB drives.

Knowledge Assessment

Multiple Choice

Select the correct answer for each of the following questions.

1. Which of the following are migration types supported by Windows Easy Transfer?
   a. Clean installation
   b. Side-by-side
   c. Wipe–and-load
   d. Single sideload

2. A computer running Windows PE will automatically reboot after how long?
   a. 24 hours
   b. 48 hours
   c. 72 hours
   d. 96 hours

3. When a serious problem occurs with Windows 8.1, you might be able to repair it by starting the Windows PE operating system and running diagnostic tools. In this scenario, Windows PE is called by which of the following names?
   a. Windows RT
   b. Windows RE
   c. Windows ARM
   d. Windows Repair

4. It is possible to remove the Windows 8.1 installation disk to supply the Setup program with drivers because Windows PE runs on which of the following?
   a. USB disk
   b. Ramdisk
   c. Scratch disk
   d. DVD

5. Which of the following upgrades can you purchase through the *Add features to Windows 8.1* control panel?
   a. Windows 7 Professional to Windows 8.1 Pro
   b. Windows 8.1 to Windows 8.1 Pro
   c. Windows 8.1 to Windows 8.1 Enterprise
   d. Windows 8.1 Pro to Windows 8.1 Enterprise

6. Which of the following mechanisms provides security in Windows To Go?
   a. IPsec
   b. Trusted Platform Module (TPM)
   c. BitLocker
   d. Kerberos

7. Which of the following tools must you use while installing Windows 8.1 to a virtual hard disk (VHD) file?
   a. Scanstate.exe
   b. Loadstate.exe
   c. Vdisk.exe
   d. Diskpart.exe

8. As a preinstallation environment, Windows PE is a vast improvement over MS-DOS because it includes internal support for which of the following?
   a. Networking
   b. .NET Framework
   c. NTFS
   d. 64-bit drivers

9. Which of the following is not included in the Windows Assessment and Deployment Kit?
   a. Activation Management Tool (VAMT)
   b. User State Migration Tool (USMT)
   c. Application Compatibility Toolkit (ACT)
   d. Windows Easy Transfer
   e. Windows Assessment Services

Best Answer

Choose the letter that corresponds to the best answer. More than one answer choice may achieve the goal. Select the BEST answer.

1. Which of the following tools is the best choice when you are performing a scripted migration in an enterprise environment?
   a. Windows Easy Transfer
   b. User State Migration Tool
   c. Update Assistant
   d. AppLocker

2. Which of the following operating systems provides the easiest migration to Windows 8.1?
   a. Windows 8
   b. Windows 7
   c. Windows Vista
   d. Windows XP

3. Which of the following are the two best reasons why Windows PE is a better installation environment for Windows 8.1 than MS-DOS?
   a. Windows PE boots faster than MS-DOS
   b. Windows PE includes internal networking support
   c. Windows PE supports the NTFS file system
   d. Windows PE boots from floppy drives

Matching and Identification

1. Match the following terms with their corresponding definitions.
   _____ a) wipe-and-load migration
   _____ b) Windows PE
   _____ c) Upgrade Assistant
   _____ d) side-by-side migration
   _____ e) Windows To Go
   _____ f) Windows Easy Transfer
   _____ g) Windows 8.1 Assessment and Deployment Kit
   _____ h) Virtual hard disk
   _____ i) system recovery disk
   _____ j) Windows RE
       1. Environment similar to Windows PE, used for troubleshooting
       2. Image of an entire hard disk stored as a single file
       3. Transfers user profiles data using two computers
       4. Replaces MS-DOS as system boot medium
       5. Determines whether an in-place upgrade is possible
       6. Contains an image of a computer in its newly installed state
       7. Transfers user profile data using one computer
       8. Installs a system image to a removable drive
       9. Wizard-based data migration utility
       10. Includes Windows PE and the User State Migration Tool

Build a List

1. Place the following steps for installing Windows 8.1 with a third party disk driver in the correct order.
   _____ a) Click Custom: Install Windows Only.
   _____ b) Accept the license terms for the installation.
   _____ c) Boot the computer from a Windows 8.1 installation disk.
   _____ d) Select the partition where you want to install Windows.
   _____ e) Click Install now.
   _____ f) Personalize the installation.
   _____ g) Click the Load Driver button.
   _____ h) Insert the disk containing the third party driver.
   _____ i) Select appropriate language, time and currency, and keyboard settings.

2. Place the following steps for installing Windows To Go in the correct order.
   _____ a) Launch the Windows To Go application.
   _____ b) Plug a removable drive into the computer's USB port.
   _____ c) Specify a password for BitLocker security.
   _____ d) Launch the Create a Windows To Go Workspace Wizard.
   _____ e) Insert a Windows 8.1 installation DVD into the disk drive.
   _____ f) Close the Create a Windows To Go Workspace Wizard.
   _____ g) Click Create.
   _____ h) Select the removable drive as the target for the Windows To Go image.
   _____ i) Choose Yes for the automatic boot option.
   _____ j) Select the Install.wim image from the installation disk as the source image.

Business Case Scenarios

Scenario 2-1: Upgrading Windows 8.1 Editions

You are working as a desktop support technician at a computer store, and a customer approaches you with a laptop computer he purchased three years ago. The computer came with Windows XP Home Basic installed on it, and the customer has already purchased a copy of Windows 8.1 core edition. He now wants to upgrade the computer to Windows 8.1 without affecting his files and also use the computer to log on to the Active Directory Domain Services domain at his office. Explain in detail the procedure you would have to use to fulfill the customer's request.

Scenario 2-2: Understanding the Difference Between a Side-by-Side Migration and a Wipe-and-Load Migration

You have been assigned the task of migrating 50 workstations running Windows 8 to Windows 8.1. However, your supervisor does not understand the difference between a side-by-side migration and a wipe-and-load migration. Explain the difference between the two migration types.

3 LESSON

Migrating and Configuring User Data

70-687 EXAM OBJECTIVE

Objective 1.3 – Migrate and configure user data. This objective may include but is not limited to: migrate user profiles; configure folder location; configure profiles, including profile version, local, roaming, and mandatory.

LESSON HEADING	EXAM OBJECTIVE
Configuring User Profiles	Configure profiles, including profile version, local, roaming, and mandatory
Using Roaming Profiles	
Using Mandatory User Profiles	
Managing Profile Compatibility	
Migrating User Profiles	Migrate user profiles
Using Windows 8.1 Easy Transfer	
Using the User State Migration Tool	
Configuring Folder Location	Configure folder location

KEY TERMS

folder redirection

Group Policy Management Editor console

Group Policy object (GPO)

local user profile

mandatory user profile

roaming user profile

side-by-side migration

task sequence

user profile

User State Migration Tool (USMT)

Windows Easy Transfer

wipe-and-load migration

Configuring User Profiles

↓
THE BOTTOM LINE

As discussed in Lesson 2, "Installing Windows 8.1," a *user profile* is a series of folders, associated with a specific user account, that contain personal documents, user-specific registry settings, Internet favorites, and other personalized information—everything that provides a user's familiar working environment. On a Windows 8.1 computer, user profiles are stored in the Users folder, in subfolders named for the user accounts.

CERTIFICATION READY
Configure profiles, including profile version, local, roaming, and mandatory
Objective 1.3

On computers running Windows 8.1, user profiles automatically create and maintain the desktop settings for each user's work environment on the local computer in a folder beneath C:\Users. The system creates a new user profile for each user logging on at the computer for the first time.

Each of these user folders contains a separate user profile for that person. A typical user profile consists of the following folders, some of which are hidden, plus a hidden registry file.

- AppData
- Contacts
- Desktop
- Documents
- Downloads
- Favorites
- Links
- Music
- Pictures
- Saved Games
- Searches
- Videos

When a user logs on at the workstation using a local or domain account, the system loads that individual's profile and uses it throughout the session until the user logs off. During the session, the Documents folder in the user's profile becomes the operative Documents folder for the system, as do all the other folders in the profile.

There are three main types of user profiles, as follows:

- *Local user profile* – A profile that Windows 8.1 automatically creates when each user logs on at the computer for the first time. The local user profile is stored on the computer's local hard disk.
- *Roaming user profile* – A copy of a local user profile that is stored on a shared folder on the network, making it accessible from anywhere on the network. A roaming user profile merges any changes with the local user profile to the server during the log off process.
- *Mandatory user profile* – A roaming profile that users cannot change. Administrators use mandatory user profiles to enforce particular desktop settings for individuals or for a group of users. A fourth variation, called a super-mandatory profile, requires the user to access the server-based profile or the logon fails.

Using Roaming Profiles

To support users who work at multiple computers on the same network, administrators can create roaming user profiles.

A *roaming user profile* is simply a copy of a local user profile that is stored on a network share (to which the user has appropriate permissions), so that the user can access it from any computer on the network. No matter which computer a user logs on from, he or she always receives the files and desktop settings from the profile stored on the server.

To enable a user to access a roaming user profile, rather than a local profile, you must open the user's *Properties* sheet to the Profile tab, as shown in Figure 3-1, and specify the location of the roaming profile in the Profile Path field.

Figure 3-1

The *Profile* tab of a domain user's *Properties* sheet

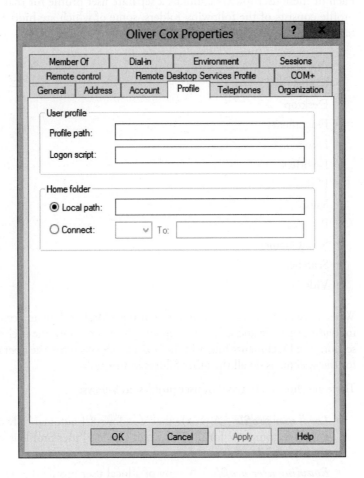

For a local user account, you use the Local Users and Groups snap-in – available through the Computer Management console – to access the user's Properties sheet. For Active Directory Domain Services (AD DS) domain users, you use the Active Directory Users and Computers console to access a user's Properties sheet.

The path to the roaming profile folder that you specify on the Profile tab should use Universal Naming Convention (UNC) notation, in the form *server\share\folder*.

To use a single server folder to store profiles for multiple users, you can create subfolders named for the users and add the *%username%* environment variable to the profile path. For example, you can specify the same profile path, such as *\\Fileserver1\Profiles\Users\%username%,* for all of your users, and each one will receive a roaming profile in a separate subfolder, named using his or her account, in the Users folder, in the Profiles share, on a server called Fileserver1.

Then, the next time the user logs on, Windows 8.1 accesses the roaming user profile in the following manner:

1. During the user's first logon, the computer copies the entire contents of the roaming profile to the appropriate subfolder in the Users folder on the local drive. Having the roaming user profile contents stored on the local drive enables the user access to the profile during later logons, even if the server containing the roaming profile is unavailable.

2. The computer applies the roaming user profile settings to the computer, making it the active profile.

3. As the user works, the system saves any changes he or she makes to the user profile to the copy on the local drive.

4. When the user logs off, the computer replicates any changes made to the local copy of the user profile back to the server where the roaming profile is stored.

5. The next time the user logs on at the same computer, the system compares the contents of the locally stored profile with the roaming profile stored on the server. The computer copies only the roaming profile components that have changed to the copy on the local drive, which makes the logon process shorter and more efficient.

You should create roaming user profiles on a file server that you back up frequently, so that you always have copies of your users' most recent profiles. To improve logon performance for a busy network, place the users' roaming profiles folder on a member server (in the same site) instead of a domain controller.

Using Mandatory User Profiles

A *mandatory user profile* is simply a read-only roaming user profile.

When accessing a mandatory profile, users receive files and desktop settings from a server-based profile, just as they would with any roaming profile, and they can modify their desktop environments while they are logged on. However, because the profile is read-only, the system cannot save any profile changes back to the server when the users log off. The next time the user logs on, the server-based profile will be the same as during the previous logon.

Windows 8.1 downloads the mandatory profile settings to the local computer each time the user logs on. You can assign one mandatory profile to multiple users who require the same desktop settings, such as a group of users who all do the same job. Because the profile never changes, you do not have to worry about one user making changes that affect all of the other users. Also, a mandatory profile makes it possible to modify the desktop environment for multiple users by changing only one profile.

To create a mandatory user profile, you rename the Ntuser.dat file in the folder containing the roaming profile to Ntuser.man. The Ntuser.dat file consists of the Windows 8.1 system registry settings that apply to the individual user account and contains the user environment settings, such as those controlling the appearance of the desktop. Renaming this file with a .man extension makes it read-only, preventing the client computers from saving changes to the profile when a user logs off.

Managing Profile Compatibility

User profiles created with Windows 8 and Windows 8.1 are compatible with each other, but they are not compatible with profiles created in Windows 7 or earlier versions. If you use a computer running Windows 8 or Windows 8.1 to access a roaming profile created with Windows 7, the newer operating system automatically upgrades the profile to its new format, rendering it unusable with Windows 7.

In an environment where users might log on to workstations running different versions of Windows, you must create and maintain separate profiles for each version. To control which profile a workstation uses based on the operating system version, you can use a Group Policy setting called *Set roaming profile path for all users logging onto this computer.*

Located in the Computer Configuration\Policies\Administrative Templates\System\User Profiles folder of a **Group Policy object (GPO)**, this policy, shown in Figure 3-2, overrides any profile specified in a user's account properties.

Figure 3-2

The *Set roaming profile path for all users logging onto this computer* dialog box

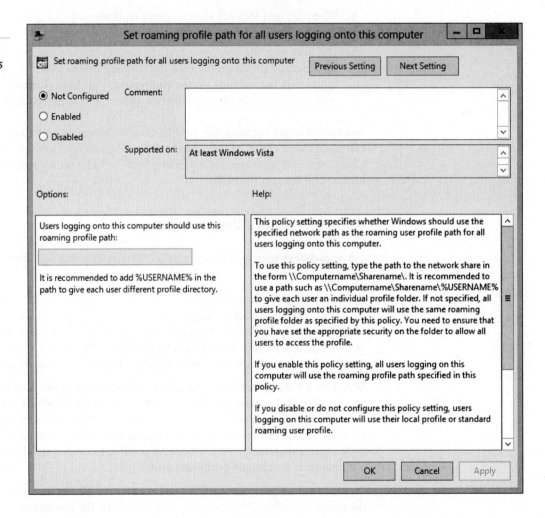

When you specify a path for the roaming profiles the computer will use, you must add the %USERNAME% variable to the Universal Naming Convention path, as in the following example: \\Server\share\%USERNAME%. This appends a folder named for each user to the path, so every user still maintains a unique profile.

To support profiles for multiple Windows versions, you must create a separate GPO for each version and configure each GPO to be applied only to the computers running that version. For example, in an AD DS environment, you can create separate OUs called Win7Clients and Win8Clients and move the computer objects running each operating system into the appropriate OU. Then you create a separate GPO for each operating system, containing the *Set roaming profile path for all users logging on to this computer* policy, and link it to the correct OU. The policy setting for each GPO should point to a subfolder intended only for computers running that specific operating system version.

■ Migrating User Profiles

↓
THE BOTTOM LINE

Performing a clean installation of Windows 8.1 on a user's workstation does not necessarily mean that the user has to lose his or her personal files and folders, operating system and application settings, and Internet favorites. Using tools supplied with Windows 8.1 or the Windows Assessment and Deployment Kit (ADK), you can sometimes migrate these elements from one operating system to another.

CERTIFICATION READY
Migrate user profiles
Objective 1.3

In some cases, performing a clean installation of Windows 8.1 is a perfectly adequate solution. You might be working with a brand new computer, or the user might not have any important data to carry over from the previous operating system. However, most experienced computer users have settings and data they want to keep, data that is typically stored in a Windows user profile.

A user profile is a series of folders, associated with a specific user account, that contain personal documents, user-specific registry settings, Internet favorites, and other personalized information—everything that provides a user's familiar working environment. On a standalone Windows XP workstation, user profiles are stored in the Documents and Settings folder, in subfolders named for the user accounts. Starting in Windows Vista and continuing through Windows 8.1 workstations, the subfolders are found in the Users folder. On a workstation that is joined to an Active Directory Domain Services (AD DS) domain, the user profiles are also stored on a network server.

➕ **MORE INFORMATION**

User profiles consist of files, such as a user's personal documents and Internet favorites, stored in appropriate profile folders, and settings stored in a registry file. The registry settings include basic display parameters, such as the colors, themes, and images you have designated for your Windows desktop, as well as configuration parameters for specific applications. Windows loads the profile information into memory each time that particular user logs on to Windows, and saves any changes the user has made to the profile when logging off. User profiles make it possible for different users to maintain their own individual settings on one Windows computer.

In Windows versions up to Windows 8, there are two basic methods for deploying a new operating system to a client while retaining the user profile settings: upgrade and migration. In an upgrade, you install a newer version of the operating system on a computer running an earlier version, retaining all of the user profile files and settings. In a migration, you copy the user profile information from the old operating system to some temporary medium and transfer it to a new, clean Windows installation.

Upgrading to Windows 8.1 from Windows 8 or Windows 7, however, does not preserve the user profiles from the older operating system, and migrating user profile data to Windows 8.1 is also more difficult than it was in Windows 8.

Microsoft has created two different tools for migrating data to new Windows installations which are as follows:

- **Windows Easy Transfer** – Designed for the migration of a single computer, Easy Transfer is a wizard-based utility that makes it possible to migrate user profile information for multiple users from one computer to another.
- **User State Migration Tool** – Designed for large-scale enterprise deployments, User State Migration Tool is a command line utility that can migrate profile information for multiple users on multiple computers.

In the following sections, you learn the procedure for using Windows Easy Transfer to migrate user profile settings from an existing Windows 7 workstation to a new Windows 8 workstation. You also learn some basic facts about using the User State Migration Tool.

Using Windows 8.1 Easy Transfer

Windows Easy Transfer is a tool that can migrate user profile information from an existing Windows computer to a new computer with a clean installation of Windows.

To use the tool, you must run the wizard on both computers, either simultaneously or sequentially. On the source computer, the wizard scans for user profiles and other data and enables you to select what you want to transfer. You then select the medium for the transfer, in the form of a direct connection or a temporary storage device, such as a removable disk.

In Windows 8.1, Microsoft has begun to deprecate the Windows Easy Transfer tool by limiting its capabilities. Unlike earlier versions, which could transfer data from Windows Vista and Windows XP, the version in Windows 8.1 can only work with Windows 8 and Windows 7. In addition, the Windows 8.1 version can only transfer files from these operating systems; it cannot transfer user profiles and Windows configuration settings.

This deprecation is largely due to the increased use of the Microsoft account in Windows 8.1. When you log on to Windows 8.1 using a Microsoft account, you have the ability to store Windows configuration settings in the cloud and access them from other computers. This enables users to create a consistent working environment on multiple machines, downloading settings as needed from the cloud.

TAKE NOTE

For administrators and users accustomed to using Windows Easy Transfer, and for situations where migration of user profiles from Windows 7 or earlier is imperative, there is a viable workaround. Instead of performing a clean installation of Windows 8.1, you can install Windows 8 and use its version of Windows Easy Transfer to migrate the user profiles and other data from the earlier operating system. Then you can upgrade from Windows 8 to Windows 8.1, retaining the user profile information you migrated.

The following sections detail the differences when using Windows Easy Transfer with Windows 8 and Windows 8.1 as the destination.

TRANSFERRING DATA TO WINDOWS 8

When transferring data to Windows 8, *Windows Easy Transfer* migrates user profile data from one computer to another in a variety of scenarios. As long as you are working with the user accounts from one single computer, Windows Easy Transfer can function in virtually any hardware configuration. Some of the options you can select are as follows:

- **Number of computers** – Windows Easy Transfer supports both side-by-side and wipe-and-load migrations. In a ***side-by-side migration***, you have two computers running simultaneously; one is the source computer containing the user profile information you want to transfer, and the other is the destination computer running Windows 8 to which you want to transfer the profile information. In a ***wipe-and-load migration***, you have only one computer, which initially contains the user profile settings you want to transfer. After saving the profile information to a removable storage medium, you perform a clean Windows 8 installation, wiping out all data on the computer's hard disk, and then transfer the profile data from the removable medium back to the computer.
- **Direct or indirect** – When you are performing a side-by-side migration, you can use Windows Easy Transfer with the computers connected together directly, using a cable or a network, or connected indirectly, using a removable storage medium.
- **Storage medium** – Windows Easy Transfer can use virtually any storage medium to transfer profile data between computers, as long as it provides sufficient storage space and is accessible by both machines. You can use a writable CD or DVD, a USB flash drive, an external hard drive, or a network share. Floppy disks are not supported because they have insufficient capacity.

The procedure for migrating files consists of two basic elements: saving the user profile information on the existing computer and transferring the information to the new computer. Using the capabilities of Windows Easy Transfer, you should be able to satisfy the requirements of virtually any standalone user that wants to move to Windows 8 without performing an upgrade. The most common scenarios are likely to be the following:

- A user purchases a new computer on which he wants to run Windows 8, but he also wants to retain the files and settings from his existing Windows computer.
- A user wants to install Windows 8 on her existing Windows computer and retain all of her files and settings, but she wants to avoid performing an upgrade to maximize her Windows 8 performance.

Once you have selected the data you want to transfer on the source computer, you run the Windows Easy Transfer Wizard on the destination computer, which enables you to select the data you want to transfer, as shown in Figure 3-3.

TRANSFERRING DATA TO WINDOWS 8.1

The version of Windows Easy Transfer included with Windows 8.1 is compatible with the Windows 8 and Windows 7 versions as sources. It is not compatible with earlier Windows versions of the tool, even the ones available from the Microsoft Download Center that are designed for Windows 8 compatibility.

No matter what data you choose to save when running Windows Easy Transfer on a Windows 7 or Windows 8 source system, the version included with Windows 8.1 can only transfer files; it cannot import Windows settings. In addition, the Windows 8.1 version functions only as a transfer destination; it cannot save data for transfer to other systems.

The Windows 8.1 version of Windows Easy Transfer only supports migrations using a removable storage device, such as an external hard drive or a USB flash drive. There are no options to use a network connection or an Easy Transfer cable. When you use the tool to open a transfer file created with an earlier version that contains user profiles, an error message appears stating that the settings in the file cannot be transferred; Windows Easy Transfer can only transfer files. The wizard then enables you to select files for transfer from the source you selected, as shown in Figure 3-3.

Windows 8.1

Figure 3-3

The *What do you want to use to transfer items to your new PC?* page

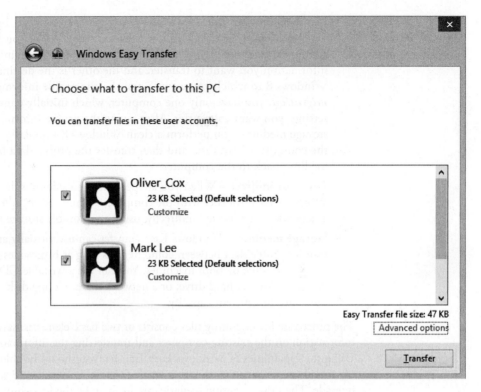

Using the User State Migration Tool

The *User State Migration Tool (USMT)* has the same basic capabilities as previous versions of Windows Easy Transfer. The primary difference between the two is that USMT is a command line program that lacks a graphical interface.

USMT's command line interface is not a disadvantage, although individuals that prefer graphical utilities might perceive it as such. The command line interface enables administrators to incorporate USMT tasks into scripts, making it more suitable for large-scale deployments than Windows Easy Transfer.

For administrators, USMT is the more capable tool for migrating user profiles to Windows 8.1. Unlike the Windows 8.1 version of Windows Easy Transfer, USMT can migrate user profile data from computers running Windows 7, Windows 8, and Windows 8.1.

USMT is not supplied with Windows 8.1 itself. You must obtain it by downloading the Windows Assessment and Deployment Kit for Windows 8.1 from the Microsoft Download Center. USMT consists primarily of three command line executables, as follows:

- Scanstate.exe – Captures user profile data from a Windows 7, Windows 8, or Windows 8.1 computer and stores it on a removable drive or network share.
- Loadstate.exe – Imports user profile data previously captured by the Loadstate tool into a computer running Windows.
- Usmtutils.exe – Performs ancillary functions related to the user profile migration process, such as extraction from compressed stores and verification of store integrity.

Each of these programs supports a variety of command line parameters that enable you to specify a storage location and control what data the programs save and restore.

USMT is designed primarily to be integrated into an automated Windows deployment procedure. Windows ADK includes a variety of tools that make it possible to automate large scale deployments by creating scripts that perform all of the steps required to roll **out Windows to a large fleet of workstations**.

For example, Windows ADK enables administrators to incorporate migration tasks into an installation script called a ***task sequence***. A properly configured task sequence can save the user profile data on a workstation to a network share, perform a clean Windows 8.1 installation on the workstation, and then load the saved user profile data, all with little or no user interaction required.

The USMT version provided in Windows ADK for Windows 8.1 is version 6.3. This version of the tool can migrate user profile data from source computers running Windows 7, Windows 8, and Windows 8.1 only. The tool also supports migrations from 32-bit Windows versions to 64-bit versions (but not from 64-bit to 32-bit).

USMT version 6.3 does not support migrations from Windows Vista or Windows XP. However, the tool remains compatible with migration stores created using earlier versions of USMT. If you need to migrate user profiles from Windows Vista or Windows XP to Windows 8.1, you can do so by using the Scanstate.exe program from USMT version 5 to capture data from the source operating systems, and then use the Loadstate.exe program from version 6.3 to import the data into Windows 8.1.

In addition to the command line interface, the other big advantage to using USMT for large scale deployments is the ability to customize the migration process. USMT uses XML (Extensible Markup Language) files to control the migration process. The default XML files supplied with the program—called MigApp.xml, MigDocs.xml, and MigUser.xml—enable it to migrate the most common user data sources, but it is also possible to modify these or create your own XML files to migrate specific application settings and data.

■ Configuring Folder Location

THE BOTTOM LINE

It is preferable to store user data on a network share rather than the local workstation for several reasons, including the following:

- **Backups** – Backing up one or two servers is much faster, easier, and often cheaper than backing up multiple workstations.
- **Mobility** – With all data files stored on a network shared folder, users can work from any computer and move to another location as needed.
- **Replacement** – Deploying new client computers in the place of older ones is a simple matter of replacing the hardware; no migration of data files is necessary.

To change folder locations, you use a feature called ***folder redirection***, which is simply a means of storing a copy of certain user profile folders on another computer, usually a file server. The process is completely invisible to the workstation user. Once the folders are redirected to the server, that user can log on at any workstation and the system copies the redirected folders to the user's local profile on that computer.

CERTIFICATION READY
Configure folder
location
Objective 1.3

To implement folder redirection on Windows 8.1, you must join the workstation to an Active Directory Domain Services domain and create a Group Policy Object (GPO) that specifies which folders to redirect and where to store them.

The Group Policy settings for folder redirection are located in the following path: User Configuration\Policies\Windows Settings\Folder Redirection, as shown in Figure 3-4.

Figure 3-4

The Folder Redirection policies in a GPO

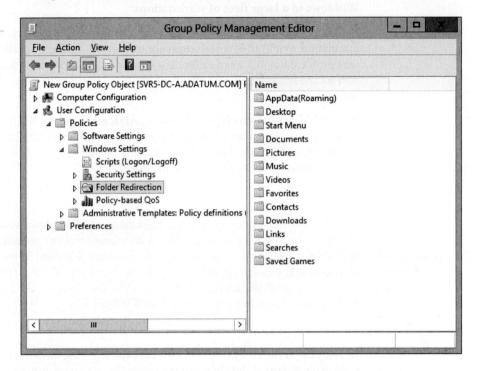

You can use the **Group Policy Management Editor console** to modify the Folder Redirection settings in a GPO by right-clicking one of the folders under the Folder Redirection node and opening its *Properties* sheet, as shown in Figure 3-5.

Figure 3-5

The *Properties* sheet for a Folder Redirection policy

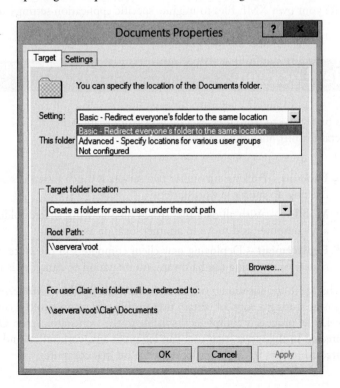

Table 3-1 lists the settings for the Folder Redirection folders and explains their functions.

Table 3-1

Folder Redirection Group
Policy Settings

SETTING	FUNCTION
Setting	• Basic – Redirect Everyone's Folder To The Same Location – Causes workstations to redirect the folder for all users to the same server share • Advanced – Specify locations for various user groups – Causes workstations to redirect the folders to different locations based on group memberships • Follow the Documents folder – Allows the Pictures, Music, and Videos folders to be redirected as subfolders of the Documents folder
Target Folder Location	• Create A Folder For Each User Under The Root Path – Causes workstations to create a separate folder for each user on the server share • Redirect to the following location – Causes workstations to redirect the folder to a single location for all users • Redirect to the local userprofile location – Causes work-stations to redirect the folder to the user's local userprofile location
Root Path	Specifies the server share where you want to store the redirected folders, in UNC format (\\server\share\folder).
Grant The User Exclusive Rights To [the folder]	Prevents anyone except the user from receiving permission to access the redirected folder.
Move The Contents Of [the folder] To The New Location	Causes the workstation to copy the contents of the redirected folders on its local drive to the target folder on the server share.
Also Apply Redirection Policy To Windows 2000, Windows 2000 Server, Windows XP, And Windows Server 2003 Operating Systems	Provides compatibility with earlier operating systems that use different folder names in their user profiles, such as My Documents.
Policy Removal	• Leave the folder in the new location when policy is removed – Causes the workstation to direct the folders back to the local drives without copying their contents from the server, thus rendering those contents inaccessible • Redirect The Folder Back To The Local Userprofile Location When Policy Is Removed – Causes the workstation to copy the contents of the redirected folders back to the local drive in the event that an administrator disables the Folder Redirection Group Policy settings

SKILL SUMMARY

IN THIS LESSON, YOU LEARNED:

- A user profile is a series of folders, associated with a specific user account, that contain personal documents, user-specific registry settings, Internet favorites, and other personalized information—everything that provides a user's familiar working environment.

- A roaming user profile is simply a copy of a local user profile that is stored on a network share (to which the user has appropriate permissions), so that the user can access it from any computer on the network.

- A mandatory user profile is simply a read-only roaming user profile.

- Windows Easy Transfer is a tool that migrates data from an existing Windows computer to a new computer with a clean installation of Windows 8.1.

- The User State Migration Tool (USMT) has the same basic capabilities as Windows Easy Transfer. The primary difference between the two is that USMT is a command line program that lacks a graphical interface.

- Folder redirection is a Windows 8.1 feature that is simply a means of storing a copy of certain user profile folders on another computer, usually a file server.

■ Knowledge Assessment

Multiple Choice

Select one or more correct answers for each of the following questions.

1. What is the term used to describe a read-only copy of a user profile stored on a network share?
   a. mandatory profile
   b. super-mandatory profile
   c. roaming profile
   d. search profile

2. Which of the following are the two types of migration supported by Windows Easy Transfer?
   a. wipe-and-load
   b. side-by-side
   c. preview-and-wipe
   d. copy-and-redirect

3. Which of the following are command line programs? (Choose two.)
   a. Windows Easy Transfer
   b. Scanstate
   c. Folder Redirection
   d. Loadstate

4. Which of the following tools do you use to configure folder redirection?
   a. File Explorer
   b. Computer Management
   c. Active Directory Users and Computers
   d. Group Policy Management Editor

5. Which of the following storage media can you NOT use for a migration in any version of Windows Easy Transfer?
   a. RAM disk
   b. Network share
   c. USB flash drive
   d. CD-ROM

6. Which of the following Setting values in Folder Redirection creates a folder for each user beneath a single parent folder?
   a. Redirect
   b. Basic
   c. Advanced
   d. Not configured

7. How many computers are required for a wipe-and-load migration?
   a. 1
   b. 2
   c. 3
   d. 4

8. Which of the following user profile types can only be stored on server drives?
   a. Local
   b. Mandatory
   c. Roaming
   d. Super-mandatory

9. On a computer running Windows 8.1, local user profiles are located in which of the following folders?
   a. C:\Windows
   b. C:\Users
   c. C:\Documents and Settings
   d. C:\Profiles

Best Answer

1. Which of the following are valid reasons why redirecting users' folders to server drives is a good idea?
   a. Because backing up servers is faster and easier than backing up workstations.
   b. Replacing workstations is easier when they do not hold any user data.
   c. Users can log on from any workstation and access their data.
   d. Files take up less storage space on server drives.

2. Which is the best type of profile to use if you want to prevent users from logging on if the profile is not available?
   a. Local
   b. Roaming
   c. Mandatory
   d. Super-mandatory

3. Which of the following is the best explanation for why it is necessary to include %USERNAME% in the path for roaming profiles?
   a. Because Windows servers automatically create a folder called %USERNAME%, where it stores profiles.
   b. Because %USERNAME% is a variable replaced by the system with the user's account name.
   c. Because the inclusion of %USERNAME% causes the profile to roam.
   d. Because including %USERNAME% enables the system to create a separate profile for each user.

Matching and Identification

1. Match the following terms with their corresponding definitions.
    _____ **a)** Folder redirection
    _____ **b)** User State Migration Tool
    _____ **c)** Windows Easy Transfer
    _____ **d)** Mandatory user profile
    _____ **e)** Wipe-and-load migration
    _____ **f)** Roaming profile
    _____ **g)** Side-by-side migration
    _____ **h)** Super-mandatory profile
    _____ **i)** Task sequence
    _____ **j)** Group Policy object
    1. Wizard-based utility
    2. Enables Windows 8.1 to store profile folders on server drives
    3. Command line utility
    4. Transfers profile data to a newly installed computer
    5. Denied logon if profile is not available
    6. Saves profile data to an external storage device
    7. Server-based user profile
    8. Container for Folder Redirection and other settings
    9. Read-only profile
    10. Script containing Scanstate and Loadstate commands

Build a List

1. Place the steps of the following process by which Windows 8.1 accesses and updates roaming profiles in the correct order.
    _____ The workstation applies the roaming profile settings.
    _____ The workstation copies the roaming profile to the local drive.
    _____ As the user works, the workstation makes changes to the profile on the local drive.
    _____ The workstation copies the changes from the local profile to the roaming profile.
    _____ The user logs on.
    _____ The user logs off.

2. Place the steps of the following procedure for configuring Folder Redirection in the correct order.
    _____ Close the Group Policy Object Editor console.
    _____ Log on to a domain controller.
    _____ Open the GPO in the Group Policy Object Editor console.
    _____ Close the Group Policy Management console.
    _____ Create a new Group Policy object.
    _____ Log off of the domain controller.
    _____ Configure the Folder Redirection policies.
    _____ Browse to the Folder Redirection folder in User Configuration node.
    _____ Open the Group Policy Management Console.

■ Business Case Scenario

Scenario 3-1: Deploying Windows 8.1

Alice has been assigned the task of deploying Windows 8.1 on her department's existing workstations. To facilitate future support efforts, she wants to perform clean Windows 8.1 installations on all of the computers now running Windows XP. When presenting her action plan to her superiors, Alice states that there is no need to perform any type of upgrade or data migration from the existing computers before wiping their drives and installing Windows 8.1.

Which of the following could combine to explain why this is so?

a. The computers already have all of their data folders redirected to server drives.
b. Folder redirection is configured using Group Policy objects stored in Active Directory.
c. The users all have roaming profiles stored on network servers.
d. Windows 8.1 automatically creates a new profile for each user.

4 LESSON

Working with Disks and Devices

70-687 EXAM OBJECTIVE

Objective 2.1 – Configure devices and device drivers. This objective may include but is not limited to: install, update, disable, and roll back drivers; resolve driver issues; configure driver settings, including signed and unsigned drivers; manage driver packages.

LESSON HEADING	EXAM OBJECTIVE
Working with Devices and Drivers	
Understanding Device Drivers	
Working with Devices	Install, update, disable, and roll back drivers Manage driver packages
Using Device Manager	Install, update, disable, and roll back drivers Configure driver settings, including signed and unsigned drivers Resolve driver issues

KEY TERMS

device driver	**digital signature**	**public key cryptography**
Device Manager	**protected checksum**	

■ Working with Devices and Drivers

THE BOTTOM LINE

A computer is a collection of hardware devices, each of which requires a software component called a device driver to function. Windows 8.1 includes a large library of device drivers, but it is still sometimes necessary to obtain them yourself.

As most people know, a PC is a collection of hardware devices, all of which are connected together and installed inside or connected to a single case. Disk drives, keyboards, mice, cameras, and printers are all types of devices. To communicate with the operating system running on the computer, each device also requires a software element called a *device driver*. The device driver provides the operating system with information about a specific device.

70

For example, when you use a word processing application to save a file to a hard disk, the application issues a generic WriteFile function call to the operating system. The application knows nothing specific about the disk drive hardware; it just issues an instruction to store a particular file there. When the operating system processes the function call, it accesses the device driver for the hard disk drive, which provides detailed information about how to communicate with the drive. If the user selects a different target location for the file, the operating system accesses the device driver for that location, whether it's a hard drive or USB flash drive.

In most cases the information the device driver provides is integrated into the Windows interface. For example, the Properties sheet for a printer includes generic system information, such as which port the printer is connected to and who is permitted to use it. Other tabs, and particularly the Device Settings tab, as shown in Figure 4-1, are based on hardware-specific information provided by the device driver.

Figure 4-1

The *Device Settings* tab of a printer's *Properties* sheet

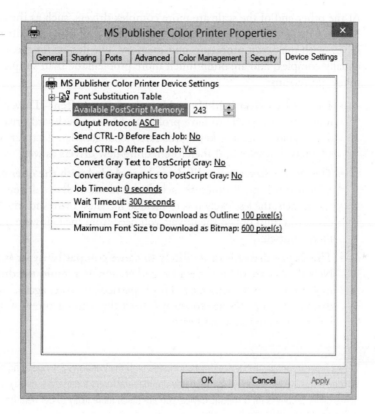

In addition to providing information about a device, drivers also permit the operating system to modify the hardware configuration settings of the device. For example, when you configure a printer to print a document in landscape mode instead of portrait mode, the printer device driver generates the appropriate command and sends it to the hardware.

Understanding Device Drivers

The process of installing a hardware device consists primarily of identifying the device and installing a device driver for it. This process can occur during the operating system installation or at a later time, but the steps are fundamentally the same.

A major part of the Windows 8.1 installation process consists of identifying the devices in the computer and installing the appropriate drivers for them. The Windows 8.1 installation package includes hundreds of driver packages for many different devices, which is why many installations finish without any user intervention. Sometimes, however, you might have to supply device drivers yourself.

UNDERSTANDING DRIVER COMPLEXITY

Virtually every component in a PC requires a device driver, but they can vary greatly in complexity. Many of the standard computer devices are so standardized that their drivers operate virtually invisibly. When was the last time you had a problem with a keyboard driver, for example? Nearly every computer has a keyboard and the generic keyboard driver included with Windows 8.1 functions properly in almost every case. If you have a keyboard with special features, you might need a special driver to access them, but the basic keyboard functions will still work, even without it.

At the other end of the scale are more complex drivers, such as those for graphics adapters. Many of the graphics adapters on the market are really self-contained computers in themselves, with their own processors and memory. The drivers for these complex devices are equally complex, and are often much more problematic than simple keyboard drivers, for the following reasons:

- **The device driver is likely to be revised more often** – Drivers that are required to do more are more likely to have problems. Generic keyboard drivers can go for years without upgrades, because keyboards rarely change. Manufacturers often release new graphics adapters, however, and therefore require new drivers as well.
- **The device driver is less likely to be included with the operating system** – The Windows 8.1 installation disk includes hundreds of device drivers, but the older the operating system gets, the less likely it is to include the latest drivers for the newest devices. In these cases, you must obtain the drivers you need from the hardware manufacturer and install them yourself.
- **The device driver is more likely to cause compatibility or functionality problems** – New devices are often rushed to market, and as a result, the drivers that ship with them might not be fully debugged. This is particularly true, again, with graphic adapter drivers. It is a good idea to always check the manufacturer's web site for the latest drivers before installing new hardware.

+ MORE INFORMATION

With a few exceptions, the device drivers included with the Windows 8.1 operating system, as well as all other Windows versions, are supplied by the hardware manufacturers themselves, not by Microsoft. Therefore, if you experience driver problems for a specific device, you are much more likely to get help from the hardware manufacturer than from Microsoft.

CREATING A DRIVER UPDATE POLICY

As an IT Professional, you are likely to be working with many different computers, each containing many devices. Keeping up with the drivers for all of these devices can be difficult, and you also must consider whether installing each driver update is necessary and, above all, safe.

There are two basic schools of thought when it comes to updating drivers. The "latest is the greatest" school advocates downloading and installing every new driver that is released, while the "if it ain't broken, don't fix it" school prefers to leave things as they are until it experiences a problem. Both of these philosophies have their advantages and disadvantages, and unfortunately, this is not likely to be a question that is best answered with a hard and fast rule or a company policy.

Other than supporting new hardware, there are three main reasons why hardware manufacturers release new driver updates:

- To address problems with the previous driver release(s)
- To implement new features
- To enhance performance of the device

The question of whether to update a Windows 8.1 driver is most easily answered for the first of these reasons. If you are experiencing the problem that the update is designed to address, then you should install it. Otherwise, you probably should not. As to the other two reasons, new features and enhanced performance are certainly desirable, but you should be sure that the driver update does not introduce new problems at the same time.

As a general rule, it is a good idea to test all driver updates before deploying them, especially in an enterprise environment. A comprehensive testing program will apply a new update to all of the workstation environments currently in use on production networks and run them through a realistic program of everyday tasks under typical operating conditions.

Another good safety measure is to avoid installing driver updates as soon as they are released. Waiting at least a week or so gives the manufacturer time to address any major issues that arise.

Above all, the question of whether to install driver updates should depend on the hardware devices involved and the policies and reputation of the hardware manufacturer. Some manufacturers release driver updates frequently and haphazardly, while others are more careful. Examining the manufacturer's support web site is a good way to ascertain how they deal with hardware problems and how often they release driver updates.

UNDERSTANDING DRIVER SIGNING

As with any other software component, device drivers have the potential to damage a computer configuration. Unscrupulous programmers can conceivably alter device drivers by adding their own malware, and the average user, downloading the driver from the Internet, would never know the difference. For that reason, Microsoft has instituted the practice of digitally signing the device drivers they have tested and approved.

A signed driver is a device driver that includes a ***digital signature***. The signer uses a cryptographic algorithm to compute the digital signature value and then appends that value to the device driver. A signer is an organization, or publisher, that uses a private key to create the digital signature for the device driver. This process ensures that the device driver does come from the authentic publisher and that someone has not maliciously altered it.

> **+ MORE INFORMATION**
>
> ***Public key cryptography*** is an encryption method based on a pair of keys, called the public key and the private key. As the names imply, the public key is freely available to anyone and the private key is kept secret by its owner. Any code that is digitally encrypted using the public key can only be decrypted by the holder of the private key. In the same way, any code that is encrypted using the private key, can only be decrypted by the public key. It is the latter example that publishers use for driver signing. The signer encrypts the device driver using its private key. The fact that the user can decrypt the driver using that signer's public key confirms that owner of the private key has signed it, and that the software has not been modified.

Generally, the process the publisher uses to create the digital signature starts by running the device driver files through a hash algorithm and then using the publisher's private key to transform the hash result cryptographically. The resulting value is the digital signature of the device driver.

The digital signature value is a ***protected checksum***. A protected checksum is the value of an algorithmic function that is dependent on the contents of the data object and that is stored together with the data object. Its purpose is to protect the data object against active attacks that attempt to change the checksum to match changes that a malicious individual has made to the data object. Thus, the properties of a cryptographic hash ensure that when a malicious individual attempts to change the data object, the digital signature no longer matches the object.

If Windows 8.1 perceives a problem with a digital signature of a device driver, it alerts you with one of the following messages during the installation attempt:

- **Windows can't verify the publisher of this driver** – Either a certification authority has not verified the digital signature or the driver does not contain a digital signature. Only install this driver if you obtained it from the original manufacturer's disk.
- **This driver has been altered** – Someone has altered this driver after the verified publisher has digitally signed it, possibly with malicious intent. The driver package may now include malware that could harm your system or steal information. Only install this driver if you obtained it from the original manufacturer's disk.
- **Windows cannot install this driver** – x64-based versions of Windows 8.1 cannot install a device driver that someone has altered after the verified publisher has digitally signed it or one that that lack a valid digital signature altogether.

As with earlier 64-bit versions of Windows, Windows 8.1 requires device drivers to be digitally signed, or it will not install them. Also, Windows 8.1 checks to see if a driver has been modified. If it has, Windows 8.1 will again refuse to install it.

BYPASSING DIGITAL SIGNATURE REQUIREMENTS

Also different in Windows 8 and Windows 8.1 is the procedure to bypass the digital signature requirements. In Windows 7 and earlier versions, you can interrupt the boot process by pressing the F8 key, which displays an advanced boot options menu. One of the options in this menu is Disable Driver Signing, which enables the system to load drivers regardless of their signatures.

However, one of the design imperatives in Windows 8.1 is faster booting, and the designers were successful to the point at which, depending on the system hardware, the interval during which a user can press the F8 key can be as small as 200 ms. Windows 8.1 therefore has a different method for modifying the boot options, as described in the following procedure.

 ACCESS ADVANCED BOOT OPTIONS

GET READY. Log on to Windows 8.1 using an account with Administrator privileges.

1. Mouse over the lower-right corner of the screen, and when the fly-out menu appears, click the Settings charm.

   The Settings menu appears.

2. Select **Change PC Settings**.

   The *PC Settings* menu appears.

3. Select **Update and Recovery**.

   The *Update and Recovery* menu appears.

4. Click **Recovery**. The Recovery screen appears, as shown in Figure 4-2.

Figure 4-2

The *Recovery screen*

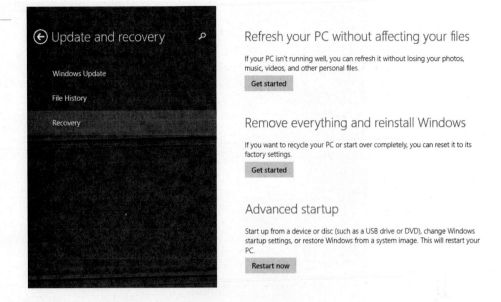

5. Under Advanced Startup, select **Restart Now**.

   The system restarts and the *Choose an Option* screen appears, as shown in Figure 4-3.

Figure 4-3

The *Choose an option* menu

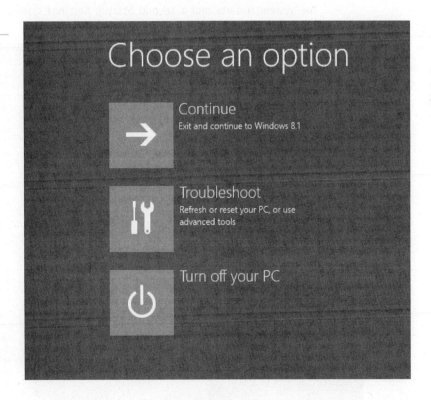

6. Select **Troubleshoot**.

   The *Troubleshoot* screen appears.

7. Select **Advanced Options**.

The *Advanced Options* screen appears, as shown in Figure 4-4.

Figure 4-4

The *Advanced options* screen

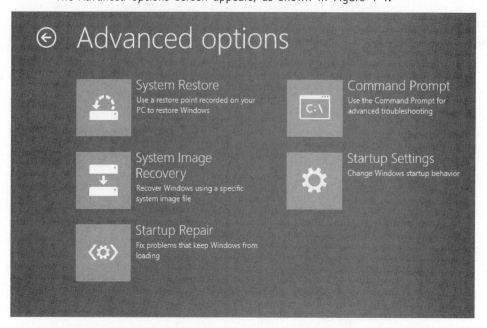

8. Select **Startup Settings**.

The *Startup Settings* page appears.

9. Click **Restart**.

The system restarts and a second Startup Settings screen appears, as shown in Figure 4-5.

Figure 4-5

The *Startup Settings* menu

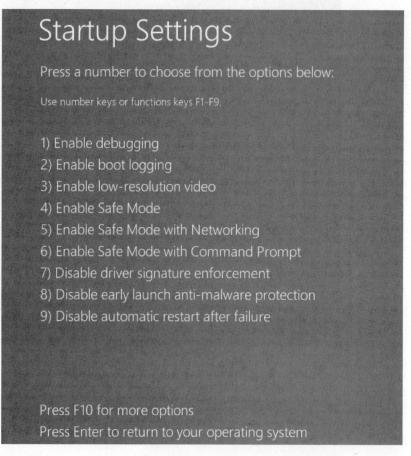

10. Press **7** to disable driver signature enforcement.

The system starts, loading all drivers, whether signed or not, or altered or not.

11. Log on to Windows 8.1 in the normal manner.

Working with Devices

> Windows 8.1 is, in most cases, able to detect the devices connected to a computer when you install the operating system, as well as any new devices you attach later.

Most PCs use USB (Universal Serial Bus) connections for peripheral devices, and Plug and Play is an integral part of the USB standard. When you connect a printer, a camera, a scanner, or another type of device to a computer running Windows 8.1 using a USB port, the system usually detects it, adds it to the *Devices and Printers* control panel, as shown in Figure 4-6, and installs the appropriate device driver for it.

Figure 4-6

The *Devices and Printers* control panel

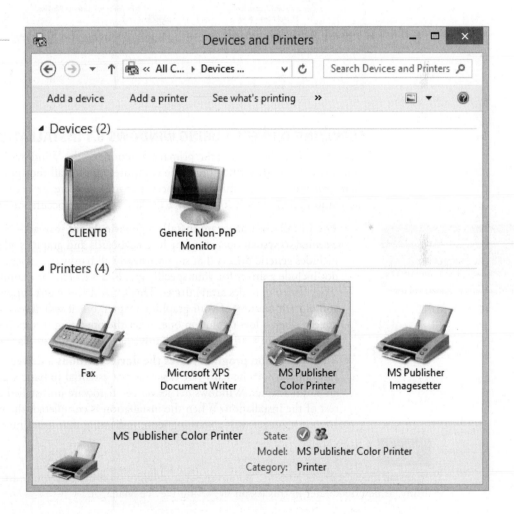

CERTIFICATION READY
Install, update, disable, and roll back drivers
Objective 2.1

You can also manually install a device by selecting *Add a device*, to display the *Choose a device or a printer to add to this PC* page, as shown in Figure 4-7.

Figure 4-7

The *Choose a device or a printer to add to this PC* page

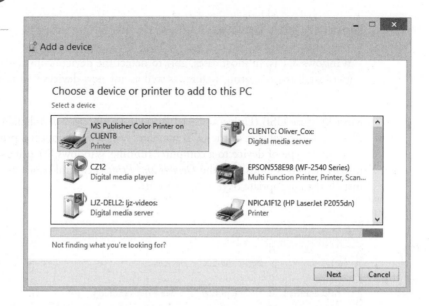

SUPPLYING DRIVERS DURING WINDOWS 8.1 INSTALLATION

As mentioned earlier, one of the primary functions of the Windows 8.1 installation program is to identify the hardware devices in the computer and install the appropriate device drivers for them. For most devices, this process occurs invisibly. There are occasions, however, when the installation program fails to identify a device. When this occurs, one of three things happens:

CERTIFICATION READY
Install, update, disable, and roll back drivers
Objective 2.1

- **The installation program installs a generic driver instead** – For devices that are essential to system operation, such as keyboards and graphics adapters. Windows 8.1 includes generic drivers that support nearly all hardware devices. If Windows 8.1 does not include a driver for your specific graphics adapter, for example, it installs a generic VGA (video graphics array) driver. This VGA driver won't support the high resolutions and esoteric features of your graphics adapter, but it will at least display an image on your screen, albeit a low-resolution one. After the operating system installation is completed, you can obtain a driver for your hardware and install it in place of the generic driver.

- **The installation program leaves the device without a driver and completes the installation** – If the hardware device is not essential to basic system operation, such as an audio adapter, Windows 8.1 leaves the hardware uninstalled and proceeds with the rest of the installation. When the installation is completed, the hardware appears in Device Manager with a warning icon, indicating that it has no driver.

X REF

To install a device driver after the Windows 8.1 installation is complete, you must use the Device Manager utility, as described later in this lesson in "Using Device Manager."

- **The installation program permits you to supply an alternate driver or, failing that, halts** – The sole exception to the preceding condition is when the installation program cannot access a disk drive with sufficient free space to install Windows 8.1. When this happens, the setup program halts, unless you are able to supply the device driver for an unrecognized mass storage hardware device. For example, if your hard drives are connected to an interface adapter that Windows 8.1 does not recognize, you can click Load Driver on the installation program's *Where do you want to install windows?* page, and specify the location of a driver for the adapter.

UPDATING DRIVERS WITH WINDOWS UPDATE

The Windows Update web site was originally designed to provide users with operating system updates, but it now includes a large library of device driver updates as well. The driver packages distributed through Windows Update have all undergone Windows Hardware Quality Labs (WHQL) testing and have received the Windows logo.

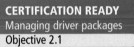

CERTIFICATION READY
Install, update, disable, and roll back drivers
Objective 2.1

When you access the Windows Update web site manually, Windows 8.1 transmits a list of installed hardware and device version numbers to the site. If there are any updated drivers available for your hardware, the web site makes them available, usually as an optional download.

If Windows 8.1 is configured to use automatic updating, the system will download drivers only for hardware devices that do not have a driver installed. If you use Device Manager to search for updated drivers, Windows 8.1 examines the drivers that are available and only downloads a new driver if it is a better match for the device than the one that is currently installed.

MANAGING DRIVER PACKAGES

Depending on the nature and complexity of the device, drivers can consist of one or two files, or they can be large installations consisting of many programs and files. The collection of all the software components needed for a device to be supported in Windows 8.1 is called a *driver package*. Apart from the driver files themselves, a driver package can include an installation program, such as a setup information (INF) file or a driver catalog (CAT) file. The package might also include property pages, install wizard pages, icons, utilities, and so on.

CERTIFICATION READY
Managing driver packages
Objective 2.1

During the life of a Windows 8.1 installation, the system typically downloads and installs multiple versions of device driver packages over time. These multiple versions can occupy a lot of disk space needlessly. To locate and eliminate the outdated driver packages, you can run the Disk Cleanup application, as shown in Figure 4-8.

Figure 4-8

The Disk Cleanup application

When you run Disk Cleanup, it scans the computer's hard disk for deletable files, including device driver packages. Selecting the Device driver packages option causes the program to delete packages that have been superseded by newer versions; the latest versions remain on the drive.

> **TAKE NOTE** * Obviously, deleting the previous versions of a driver package prevents the Roll Back Driver button in Device Manager from functioning.

In addition, during a Windows 8.1 installation, the Setup program copies the files for all included driver packages and operating system components from the installation medium to a directory called WinSxS, the side-by-side component store. This enables you to add devices later and install their drivers without having to supply an installation medium.

The drawback of this arrangement is that the WinSxS directory also occupies a significant amount of disk space, much of which is, in many cases, devoted to data that will never be used. You cannot just delete this directory to reclaim the space, however. This is because many of the files in the WinSxS folder are hardlinks mapped to locations in system folders, such as System32 and Program Files.

Fortunately, Windows 8.1 includes a new /AnalyzeComponentStore parameter for the Deployment Image Servicing and Management tool (DISM.exe) that enables you to analyze the Windows Component Store for driver packages and other files that can be deleted. To use this parameter, you run the following command from an elevated command prompt:

```
DISM /Online /Cleanup-Image /AnalyzeComponentStore
```

Typical results of this command are shown in Figure 4-9. If DISM.exe finds deletable files, you can initiate a cleanup using the Disk Cleanup tool or the following command:

Figure 4-9

The Disk Cleanup application

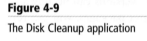

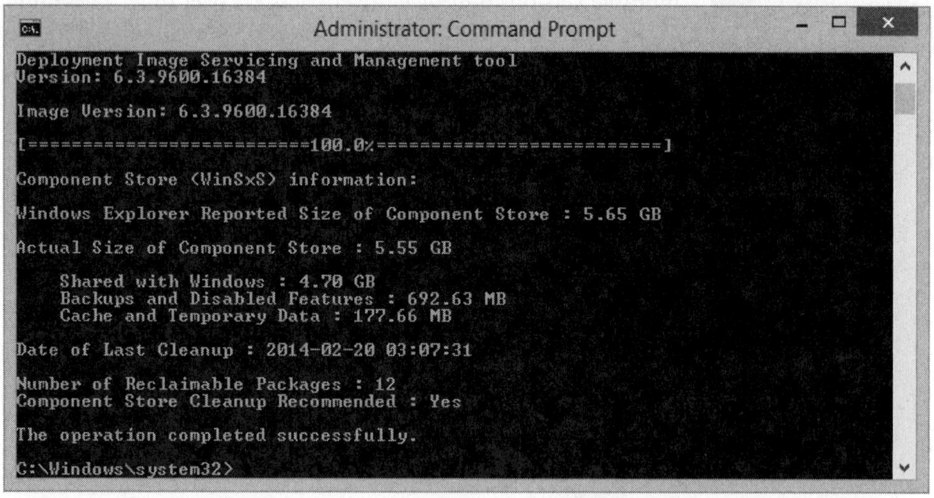

```
Deployment Image Servicing and Management tool
Version: 6.3.9600.16384

Image Version: 6.3.9600.16384

[===========================100.0%===========================]

Component Store (WinSxS) information:

Windows Explorer Reported Size of Component Store : 5.65 GB

Actual Size of Component Store : 5.55 GB

    Shared with Windows : 4.70 GB
    Backups and Disabled Features : 692.63 MB
    Cache and Temporary Data : 177.66 MB

Date of Last Cleanup : 2014-02-20 03:07:31

Number of Reclaimable Packages : 12
Component Store Cleanup Recommended : Yes

The operation completed successfully.

C:\Windows\system32>
```

```
DISM /Online /Cleanup-Image /StartComponentCleanup /ResetBase
```

Using Device Manager

> The primary Windows 8.1 tool for managing devices and their drivers is called **Device Manager**. You can use Device Manager to get information about the devices installed in the computer, as well as install, update, and troubleshoot device drivers.

Although it is not immediately apparent, Device Manager is a snap-in for the Microsoft Management Console (MMC). This means that there are many ways that you can access Device Manager, including the following:

- On the Windows 8.1 desktop, right-click the Start button and, from the context menu that appears, select Device Manager.
- Open the Windows 8.1 Control Panel and select Hardware and Sound and, under Devices and Printers, click Device Manager.
- Open the Computer Management console from the Administrative Tools program group in the System and Security control panel and click Device Manager in the left pane.
- Run the Microsoft Management Console shell application (Mmc.exe), select File, Add/ Remove Snap-in, and select Device Manager from the list of snap-ins provided.
- Open the Run dialog box and type the file name of the Device Manager snap-in (Devmgmt.msc) in the Open text box, and then click OK.

Each of these procedures launches the Device Manager and displays a window with an interface like that shown in Figure 4-10.

Figure 4-10

The *Windows 8.1 Device Manager* display

When you launch Device Manager while logged on with a standard user account, a message box appears, warning you that you can only view the settings in the console. To modify settings in Device Manager, you must log on with an account that has Administrative privileges.

VIEWING DEVICE PROPERTIES

Device Manager is capable of displaying information in the following four modes:

- **Devices by type** – Displays a list of device categories, which you can expand to show the devices in each category. This is the default Device Manager view.
- **Devices by connection** – Displays a list of the interfaces that hardware devices use to communicate with the computer. Expanding a connection shows the devices using that connection.
- **Resources by type** – Displays a list of resource types, including Direct Memory Access (DMA), Input/Output (I/O), Interrupt Request (IRQ), and Memory, which you can expand to show the resources of each type and the devices that are using them.

- **Resources by connection** – Displays a list of resource types, including Direct Memory Access (DMA), Input/Output (I/O), Interrupt Request (IRQ), and Memory, which you can expand to show the connection associated with each individual resource and the device using each connection.

To examine the properties of a device, locate it in the tree display and double-click it to open its *Properties* sheet, as shown in Figure 4-11.

Figure 4-11

A Device Manager *Properties* sheet

The tabs on the Properties sheet vary depending on the nature of the device you select, but virtually all devices have the following tabs:

- **General** – Displays the name of the device, its type, manufacturer, and location in the system. The Device Status box indicates whether the device is functioning and, if not, provides troubleshooting help.
- **Driver** – Displays the device driver's provider, date, version, and digital signer. The tab also provides buttons you can use to display driver details, update, roll back, or uninstall the driver, and enable or disable the device.
- **Details** – Displays extensive information about the driver and its properties.
- **Events** – Displays events associated with the driver.
- **Resources** – Displays the hardware resources being used by the device and indicates whether there are any conflicts with other devices in the computer.

CERTIFICATION READY
Configure driver settings, including signed and unsigned drivers
Objective 2.1

ENABLING AND DISABLING DEVICES

With Device Manager, you can disable any device in the computer, using any of the following procedures:

- Select the device and then choose Disable from the Action menu
- Right-click the device and then choose Disable from the context menu
- Open the device's Properties sheet and then click the Disable button on the Driver tab

CERTIFICATION READY
Install, update, disable,
and roll back drivers
Objective 2.1

Disabling a device does not affect the hardware in any way or uninstall the device driver, it simply renders the device inoperative until you enable it again. Obviously, you cannot disable devices that are necessary for the system to function, such as the processor, and some devices that are currently in use require you to restart the system before they can be disabled.

TAKE NOTE*

Disabling a device releases the hardware resources it was using back to the operating system. If you restart the computer with the device disabled, Windows might reassign those hardware resources to other devices. If you then re-enable the device, the computer might allocate different hardware resources to it than it had originally.

CERTIFICATION READY
Install, update, disable,
and roll back drivers
Objective 2.1

UPDATING DRIVERS

When you update a driver using Device Manager, you can point to a location on your computer where you have already saved the new driver, or you can run a search of your computer and the Internet. To update a device driver, use the following procedure.

UPDATE A DEVICE DRIVER

GET READY. Log on to Windows 8.1 using an account with Administrator privileges.

1. Open Device Manager and locate the device that you want to update.
2. Double-click the device you want to update, so that its Properties sheet appears.
3. Click the *Driver* tab and then click the **Update Driver** button.

    The *How do you want to search for driver software?* page appears, as shown in Figure 4-12.

Figure 4-12

The *How do you want to search for driver software?* page

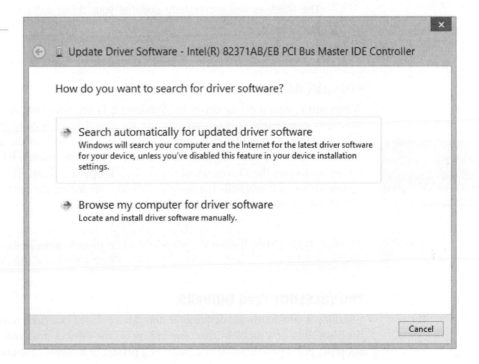

4. Click *Browse my computer for driver software* to specify a location for the driver or to select from a list of installed drivers, as shown in Figure 4-13, or click *Search automatically for updated driver software* to initiate a search for a driver.

Figure 4-13

The *Browse for driver software on your computer* page

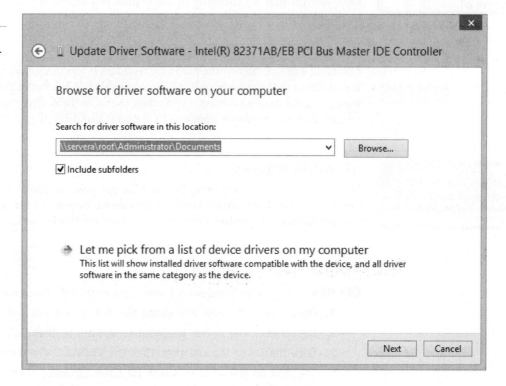

5. Locate the driver you want to install and then click **Next**.

The *Windows has successfully updated your driver software* page appears.

6. Click **Close**.

7. Close the *Device Manager* console.

ROLLING BACK DRIVERS

When you update a device driver in Windows 8.1, the operating system does not discard the old driver completely. It is not uncommon for new drivers to cause more problems than they solve, and many users find that they would prefer to go back to the old version. Windows 8.1 makes this possible with the Roll Back feature, which you initiate by clicking the Roll Back Driver button on the Driver tab of the device's Properties sheet. This procedure uninstalls the current driver and reinstalls the previous version, returning the device to the state before you performed the most recent driver update.

CERTIFICATION READY
Install, update, disable, and roll back drivers
Objective 2.1

 The Roll Back Driver button is active only when there is a previous version of the current driver available on the system. Otherwise, the button is grayed out.

TROUBLESHOOTING DRIVERS

Installing a new hardware device or a new device driver is a risky undertaking. There is always the possibility of a problem that, depending on the devices involved, could be trivial or catastrophic. For a peripheral device, such as a printer, a hardware misconfiguration or faulty driver would probably just cause the new device to malfunction. However, if the device involved is a graphics adapter, a bad driver could prevent the system from functioning.

To troubleshoot hardware or driver problems, consider some of the following techniques:

CERTIFICATION READY
Resolve driver issues
Objective 2.1

- Open the Properties sheet for the device and check the Device Status box on the General tab. If the device is malfunctioning, this tab informs you of its status and enables you to launch a troubleshooter.

- Open the Device Manager and delete the device entirely. Then restart the system and allow Windows 8.1 to detect and install the device over again. This process will cause Windows to re-allocate hardware resources to the device, which could resolve the problem if it was caused by a hardware resource conflict.

- If the device or driver malfunction prevents the system from running properly, as in the case of a bad graphics driver that prevents an image from appearing on the screen, you can start the computer in Safe Mode by using the Advanced Boot Options procedure described earlier in this lesson. Safe Mode loads the operating system with a minimal set of generic devices drivers, bypassing the troublesome ones, so you can uninstall or troubleshoot them.

SKILL SUMMARY

IN THIS LESSON, YOU LEARNED:

- Device drivers are software components that enable applications and operating systems to communicate with specific hardware devices. Every hardware device you install in a computer must have a corresponding driver.

- Plug and Play is a standard that enables computers to detect and identify hardware devices, and then install and configure drivers for those devices. PnP dynamically assigns hardware resources to each device, and can reconfigure devices at will to accommodate each component's special needs.

- The drivers included with Windows 8.1 have all been digitally signed to ensure that they have not been modified since they were published.

- Device Manager is an MMC snap-in that lists all hardware devices in the computer and indicates problems with hardware identification or driver configuration. Using Device Manager, you can enable and disable devices, update and roll back drivers, and manage device and device driver properties.

Knowledge Assessment

Multiple Choice

Select one or more correct answers for each of the following questions.

1. Which of the following are the three main reasons why manufacturers release driver updates?
   a. To address problems with previous driver versions
   b. To enhance device performance
   c. To add new driver features
   d. To fulfill Microsoft testing requirements

2. Under which of the following conditions will Windows 8.1 fail to load an unsigned device driver?
   a. When you modify the Windows startup settings by disabling driver signature enforcement
   b. When you are running the 32-bit version of Windows 8.1
   c. When you are running the 64-bit version of Windows 8.1
   d. When you are running the Windows 8.1 Enterprise edition

3. All digitally signed device drivers included with Windows 8.1 have undergone testing by which of the following bodies?
   a. The manufacturer
   b. Windows Hardware Quality Lab
   c. American National Standards Institute (ANSI)
   d. Internet Engineering Task Force (IETF)

4. What does the Windows 8.1 installation program do when it does not have a device driver for the specific model of graphics adapter installed in the computer?
   a. The installation program prompts the user to supply an appropriate driver for the adapter.
   b. The installation program searches the Internet for an appropriate driver for the adapter.
   c. The installation program installs a generic driver for the adapter.
   d. The installation program halts, because it is unable to supply an appropriate driver.

5. Which of the following tasks are you unable to perform using the Windows 8.1 Device Manager application?
   a. Install a new hardware device
   b. Update an existing device driver
   c. Roll back an installed device driver to a previous version
   d. Disable a device driver

6. Which of the following is not a tab found on Properties sheets in Device Manager?
   a. General
   b. Driver
   c. Details
   d. Events
   e. Advanced

7. Which of the following statements about public key cryptography are true?
   a. Data encrypted with a user's public key can only be decrypted with that same public key.
   b. Data encrypted with a user's private key can only be decrypted with that same private key.
   c. Data encrypted with a user's public key can only be decrypted with that same user's private key.
   d. Data encrypted with a user's private key can only be decrypted with that same user's public key.

8. What typically happens after you delete a device using Device Manager?
   a. Device Manager immediately reinstalls the device
   b. The system reinstalls the device during the next restart
   c. You must reinstall the device manually
   d. The device is permanently removed from the system

9. Which of the following is the default view of the Device Manager?
   a. Resources by connection
   b. Resources by type
   c. Devices by connection
   d. Devices by type

Best Answer

1. Which of the following is the best reason for rolling back a driver?
   a. Because a newly installed device fails to function
   b. Because a newly released driver update is buggy
   c. Because the installed driver is not digitally signed
   d. Because there is no Windows 8.1 driver available for the device

2. Which of the following devices is most likely to have drivers that cause problems with Windows 8.1?
   a. A new ergonomic keyboard
   b. A five year old serial mouse
   c. The latest high performance graphics adapter
   d. The network adapter integrated into your motherboard

Build a List

1. Place the following steps of the procedure for disabling driver signature enforcement in the proper order.
   _____ Select General.
   _____ Open the fly-out menu and click the Settings charm.
   _____ Click Advanced Options.
   _____ Press 7 to disable driver signature enforcement
   _____ Log on to Windows 8.1 with Administrator privileges.
   _____ Click Troubleshooting
   _____ Click Restart
   _____ Click Change PC Settings.
   _____ Scroll down and under Advanced Startup, click Restart Now
   _____ Click Startup Settings

Business Case Scenario

Scenario 4-1: Troubleshooting Graphics Drivers

A user asks you to troubleshoot his Windows 8.1 workstation, which is behaving erratically. He has recently purchased and installed a new graphics adapter, and ever since then, he sees occasional wavy lines in the display. You run Device Manager on the system and note the manufacturer, model, and version number of the device driver for the graphics adapter. Then, you check the adapter manufacturer's web site and discover that there is a new driver available for the adapter. After downloading and installing the driver update, you restart the system. The system appears to start normally, except that the graphical interface has been replaced by incomprehensible noise. Because you can't see the display, you can't work with the system. What should you do return the computer to an operational state?

5 LESSON

Installing and Configuring Desktop Apps and Windows Store Apps

70-687 EXAM OBJECTIVE

Objective 2.2 – Install and configure desktop apps and Windows Store apps. This objective may include but is not limited to: install and repair applications by using Windows Installer; configure default program settings; modify file associations; manage access to Windows Store.

LESSON HEADING	EXAM OBJECTIVE
Configuring Program Defaults	
Setting Default Programs	Configure default program settings
Modifying File Associations	Modify file associations
Modifying Autoplay Settings	
Setting Program Access Defaults	
Using Windows Installer	Install and repair applications by using Windows Installer
Configuring Application Compatibility	
Troubleshooting Program Compatibility	
Setting Compatibility Modes	
Configuring Application Compatibility Policies	
Installing and Configuring Windows Store Apps	Manage access to Windows Store
Installing, Reinstalling and Updating Windows Store Apps	
Disabling the Windows Store	

KEY TERMS

compatibility mode

Group Policy Management console (gpmc.msc)

Local Group Policy editor (gpedit.msc)

Program Compatibility Assistant (PCA)

Program Compatibility Troubleshooter

■ Configuring Program Defaults

↓ THE BOTTOM LINE	Windows 8.1 is, above all, a platform for running applications, and the operating system includes many controls that facilitate that function.

Administrators must often work with applications that are technically outdated, and Windows 8.1 provides compatibility settings that help those applications to run efficiently. Administrators might also need to control which applications are associated with specific file types and specific user activities, such as sending an email message or inserting a DVD. The Default Programs control panel in Windows 8.1, as shown in Figure 5-1, contains controls for all of these functions.

Figure 5-1

The *Default Programs* control panel

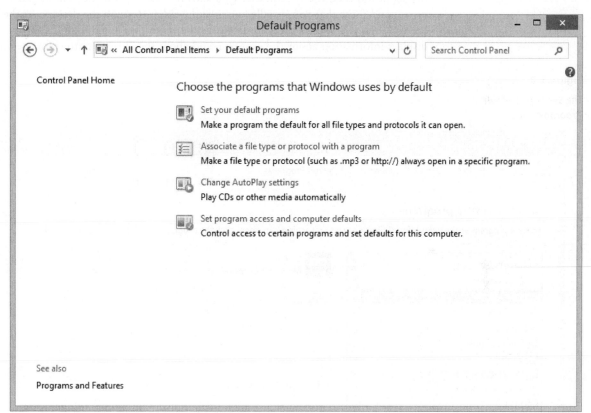

Setting Default Programs

The Set Default Programs interface enables you to specify which file types are associated with an application. With these associations in place, a user can simply double-click a file, and the application will launch itself and load that file.

Many applications have their own file types, and those types are associated with the application when you install it. For example, Microsoft Word is associated with the Microsoft Word Document (.docx) file type, and there is rarely any reason for an administrator or user to change it.

CERTIFICATION READY
Configure default
program settings
Objective 2.2

Other file types, however, can be opened by multiple applications, and administrators and users can use program defaults to select their favorite applications for particular file types. For example, you might want to change the default program for MP3 music files to your favorite music player application. For image files, such as Windows Bitmaps, you might want to select either an image viewer or an image editor.

Many applications reset the system defaults, to take control over certain file types. This can occur when you install the application, or in some cases, every time you launch the application. In some instances, you might have two or more applications competing for the same file types, each of which resets the program defaults in its favor each time you run it. Most well-behaved programs let you control this behavior, but in the event that one does not, you can use the control panel to change the program defaults.

When you click the *Set your default programs* link in the Default Programs control panel, the *Set your default programs* page appears. On this page, the Programs box contains a list of all the applications on the system, those installed by default with the Windows 8.1 operating system and those that you installed afterwards, either through the desktop or the Windows Store. When you select a program from the list, as shown in Figure 5-2, the rest of the page displays information about the program, and about the current status of its default file types.

Figure 5-2

The *Set Your Default Programs* page

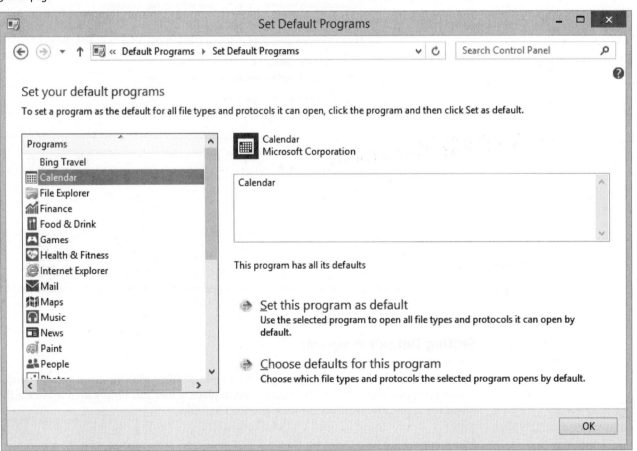

In addition, there are two links at the bottom of the page, as follows:

- **Set this program as default** – If the program is not currently associated with all of its default file types, this link resets those defaults.
- **Choose defaults for this program** – Opens the *Set program associations* page, as shown in Figure 5-3, in which you can select the file types that you want to associate with the program.

Figure 5-3

The *Set Program Associations* page

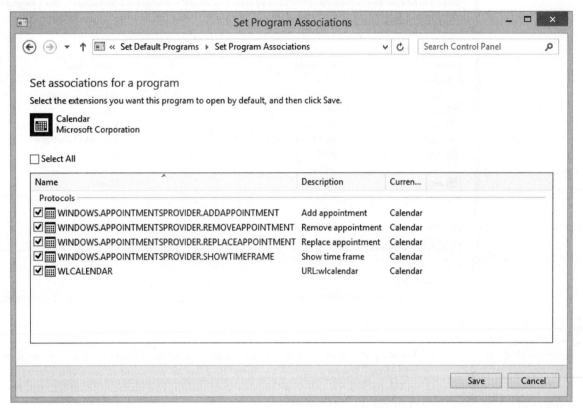

Modifying File Associations

The Default Programs control panel enables you to select a program and choose the file types that are associated with it. However, you can also approach the problem from the other direction, by selecting a file type and then choosing the program to be associated with it.

CERTIFICATION READY
Modify file associations
Objective 2.2

When you click the *Associate a file type or protocol with a program* link in the Default Programs control panel, the *Set Associations* page appears, as shown in Figure 5-4.

Figure 5-4

The *Set Associations* page

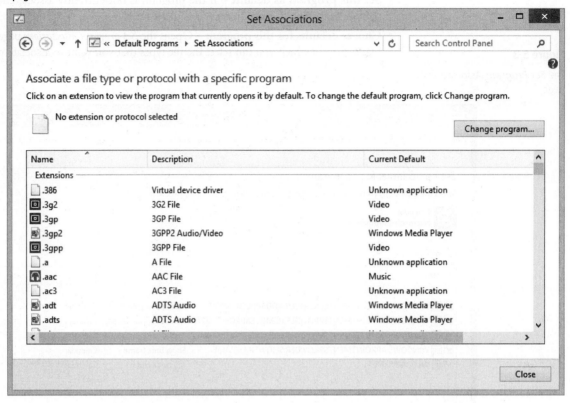

Scrolling down in the list, you can select any of the file extensions registered on the system and click Change Program to open the *How do you want to open this type of file* box, as shown in Figure 5-5. By selecting another application, you change the association between the file type and the application.

Figure 5-5

The *How do you want to open this type of file* box

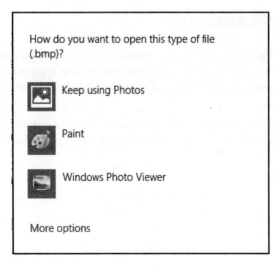

Modifying Autoplay Settings

Autoplay defines the actions that Windows takes when you insert a new removable medium, such as a CD, DVD, or USB flash drive, in to the computer.

When you click *Change Autoplay settings* in the Default Programs control panel, the *AutoPlay* dialog box appears, as shown in Figure 5-6. This dialog box enables you to select from a variety of actions for different media types and different types of content.

Figure 5-6

The *AutoPlay* dialog box

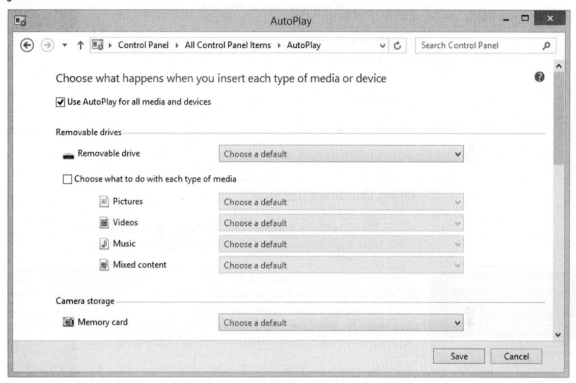

Setting Program Access Defaults

The Default Programs control panel also enables you to create a program configuration that specifies which applications Windows 8.1 should use to perform specific tasks, such as browse the Web, send email, and play media files.

When you click *Set program access and computer defaults*, the dialog box shown in Figure 5-7 appears.

The three options on this page enable you to select an all-Microsoft solution, stick with the applications your system is currently using, or select a combination of the two.

Figure 5-7

The *Set Program Access* and *Computer Defaults* dialog box

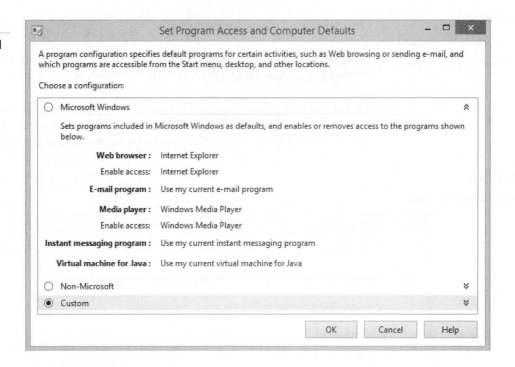

Using Windows Installer

> Windows Installer is a software installation, repair, and removal engine that can simplify the process of deploying applications on Windows computers.

CERTIFICATION READY
Install and repair applications by using Windows Installer
Objective 2.2

Windows Installer is based on a file format that includes the application files and instructions for their installation in a single package, with an .msi extension. Many Windows updates and other operating system components are provided as Windows Installer packages. Third-party developers are also encouraged to use the Windows Installer format, and there are utilities available that enable administrators to create their own packages.

Windows operating systems, including Windows 8.1, have a program called Msiexec.exe, which you can use to install Windows Installer packages, or, depending on the command line options you use, repair or uninstall an existing installation. To view the command line parameters options supported by Msiexec.exe, run the program from a command prompt with administrative privileges, as shown in Figure 5-8.

Figure 5-8

Command line parameters for qsiexec.exe

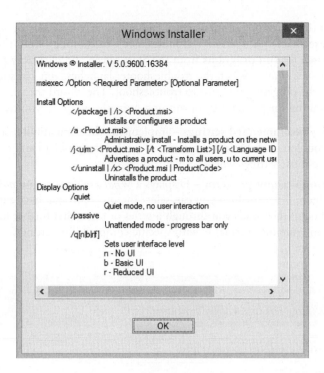

Configuring Application Compatibility

THE BOTTOM LINE

Windows 8.1 includes a number of security features that can alter the ability of certain applications to run. Administrators must therefore take measures to ensure the compatibility of their legacy applications.

One example of these features, data execution prevention (DEP), prevents applications from executing code in certain areas of memory. Another, mandatory integrity control (MIC), defines four integrity levels that Windows assigns to running processes, which specify the amount of access that the processes receive to system resources.

As a result of features like these, some programs that run perfectly well in older versions of Windows, particularly Windows XP and earlier, cannot run on Windows 8.1. For enterprise network administrators, deploying Windows 8.1 can be a massive undertaking in itself. The prospect of upgrading all of their applications as well can be reason enough to delay or even cancel the project.

Fortunately, Windows 8.1 includes a number of compatibility tools and features that can provide administrators with several ways to run their applications successfully. These tools and features are discussed in the following sections.

Troubleshooting Program Compatibility

The simplest method of coping with an application compatibility issue in Windows 8.1 is to run the Program Compatibility Troubleshooter.

The *Program Compatibility Troubleshooter* is a wizard-based solution that users or administrators can use to automatically configure an executable file to use an appropriate Windows 8.1 compatibility mechanism. Thus, the troubleshooter is not a compatibility mechanism in itself; it is just a method for applying other mechanisms.

To run the Program Compatibility Troubleshooter, right-click an executable file or a shortcut to an executable file and select Troubleshoot Compatibility from the context menu. You can also search for **run programs** from the Start screen and click *Run programs made for previous versions of Windows*. When the troubleshooter launches, you can specify the name and location of the program you want to troubleshoot. The wizard then it attempts to determine what is preventing the program from running properly and gives you two options, as follows:

- **Try recommended settings** – implements the compatibility settings that the troubleshooter has determined will resolve the problem and configures the executable to use those settings whenever you run it.

- **Troubleshoot program** – Displays a *What problems do you notice?* page, shown in Figure 5-9, on which you can select the problems you have experienced. The troubleshooter then leads you through a series of pages that further identify the problem and configure the executable with specific compatibility settings.

Figure 5-9

The *What problems do you notice?* page in the Program Compatibility Troubleshooter

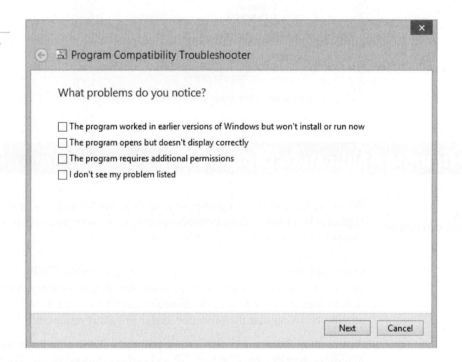

Setting Compatibility Modes

The Program Compatibility Troubleshooter is essentially a wizard that simplifies the process of selecting compatibility mode settings for an executable. However, you can also configure those same compatibility mode settings manually.

To configure the *compatibility mode* settings for an application, you must open the Properties sheet for the application's executable file (or a shortcut pointing to that executable file) and select the Compatibility tab, as shown in Figure 5-10.

Selecting the *Run the program in compatibility mode for* checkbox, you can select a previous version of Windows from the drop-down list, under which you were able to run the program successfully.

Figure 5-10

The *Compatibility* tab of an executable's Properties sheet

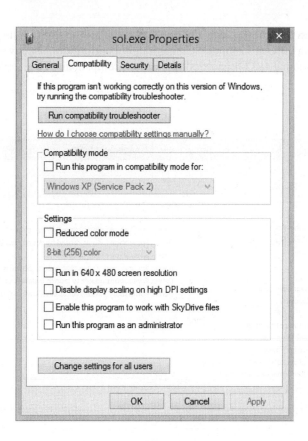

This setting does not emulate the earlier operating system versions in every way, so the successful execution of the program is not guaranteed, but in many cases, applications that do not run properly in Windows 8.1 can run with this setting enabled.

In addition to the version emulations, you can also select any or all of the following compatibility mode settings:

- **Reduced color modes** – Causes the program to run with an 8-bit or 16-bit color depth
- **Run in 640 x 480 screen resolution** – Causes the program to run at a limited screen resolution
- **Disable display scaling on high DPI images** – Disables application resizing due to large font sizes
- **Enable this program to work with OneDrive files** – Gives the program the ability to open and save files to a OneDrive folder
- **Run this program as an administrator** – Executes the program with elevated privileges

By default, the executable or shortcut you select retains the compatibility mode settings for the user currently logged on. You can also click *Change settings for all users* to apply the same settings to all of the computers users.

Configuring Application Compatibility Policies

The Program Compatibility Troubleshooter, and to some extent the compatibility mode settings themselves, are designed to be easily accessible and understandable to the end user. However, in some enterprise network environments, administrators manage compatibility issues themselves, and would prefer that users not see Windows 8.1 compatibility warnings.

To suppress application compatibility warnings, administrators can use the Group Policy settings located in a GPO at Computer Configuration\Policies\Administrative Templates\System\ Troubleshooting and Diagnostics\Application Compatibility Diagnostics, as shown in Figure 5-11.

Figure 5-11

The *Application Compatibility Diagnostics* Group Policy settings

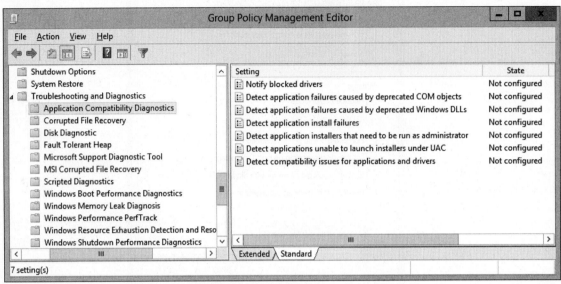

The Application Compatibility Diagnostics settings are as follows:

- **Notify blocked drivers** – Specifies whether the ***Program Compatibility Assistant (PCA)*** should notify users when drivers are blocked for compatibility reasons

- **Detect application failures caused by deprecated COM objects** – Specifies whether the PCA should attempt to detect the creation of COM objects that no longer exist in Windows 8.1

- **Detect application failures caused by deprecated windows DLLs** – Specifies whether the PCA should detect attempts to load DLLs that no longer exist in Windows 8.1

- **Detect application install failures** – Specifies whether the PCA should attempt to detect application installation failures and prompt to restart the installation in compatibility mode

- **Detect application installers that need to be run as administrator** – Specifies whether the PCA should detect application installations that fail due to a lack of administrative privileges and prompt to restart the installation as an administrator

- **Detect applications unable to launch installers under UAC** – Specifies whether the PCA should detect the failure of child installer processes to launch due to the lack of elevated privileges

- **Detect compatibility issues for applications and drivers** – Specifies whether the PCA should detect failures during application installation and runtime, and drivers blocked due to compatibility issues

Administrators can also limit users' access to compatibility mode controls using Group Policy. These settings are located in Computer Configuration\Administrative Templates\Windows Components\Application Compatibility, as follows:

- **Prevent access to 16-bit applications** – Disables the MS-DOS subsystem on the computer, preventing 16-bit applications from running.

- **Remove Program Compatibility Property Page** – Removes the Compatibility tab from the Properties sheets of executables and shortcuts.
- **Turn off Application Telemetry** – Disables the application telemetry engine, which tracks anonymous usage of Windows system components by applications.
- **Turn off Application Compatibility Engine** – Prevents the computer from looking up applications in the compatibility database, boosting system performance but possible affecting the execution of legacy applications.
- **Turn off Program Compatibility Assistant** – Disables the PCA, preventing the system from displaying compatibility warnings during application installations and start-ups.
- **Turn off Inventory Collector** – Prevents the system from inventorying applications, files, devices, and drivers on the system and sending the resulting information to Microsoft.
- **Turn off Switchback Compatibility Engine** – Prevents the computer from providing generic compatibility mitigations to older applications, thus boosting performance.
- **Turn off Steps Recorder** – Prevents the computer from capturing the steps taken by the user.

Installing and Configuring Windows Store Apps

THE BOTTOM LINE

The Windows Store is a central location for purchasing and downloading thousands of new apps for Windows 8.1 devices. Understanding the process for installing, updating, and configuring apps as well as managing access to the Windows Store is critical when it comes to not only supporting your users but aligning their needs with your company's policies.

CERTIFICATION READY
Manage access to
Windows Store
Objective 2.3

The **Windows Store** provides access to both traditional apps as well as Windows apps (for example, packaged apps). **Windows apps** use the new Windows user interface (UI) designed to display and work across Windows 8.1 devices with different form factors and display sizes.

There are currently thousands of Windows 8.1 apps available within the store, and the number is continuing to grow on a daily basis. Each of these apps must meet a certain benchmark for quality and functionality to be placed in the store.

With so many apps to choose from, why not just open them up to everyone? If you're using a Windows 8.1 device for personal use, there might be no reason to restrict access to the Store or the apps. On the other hand, if you use a Windows 8.1 device in your work environment, your company most likely has a policy that defines the standards, restrictions, and procedures for end users who have authorized access to sensitive company data.

As an administrator, it is your responsibility to configure and manage access to the Windows Store to align with these policies.

Installing, Reinstalling, and Updating Windows Store Apps

To install, reinstall, and update Windows Store apps, you need a Microsoft account and an Internet connection. Using a Microsoft account enables you to not only access Windows Store apps but synchronize key files and settings in the cloud and across multiple Windows 8.1 devices, providing a consistent interface and access to the same content on all your devices.

A **Microsoft account** (formerly called **Windows Live ID**) includes an email address and a password that enables you to sign in to all Microsoft sites and services. If you don't have one, you can create a new Microsoft account, by using an existing email address or by requesting a new one.

INSTALLING AND UNINSTALLING WINDOWS STORE APPS

You can visit the Windows Store page by clicking the Store tile on the Windows 8.1 Start screen.

Once on the Store page, shown in Figure 5-12, you find free and paid apps grouped into categories such as Spotlight, Games, Social, Photo, Books & Reference, Productivity Tools, Business, and News & Weather. These categories are visible across the top of the screen with each category featuring selected apps of interest. Each group is further divided into the sub-categories: paid, free, and new releases.

Figure 5-12

The Windows Store page

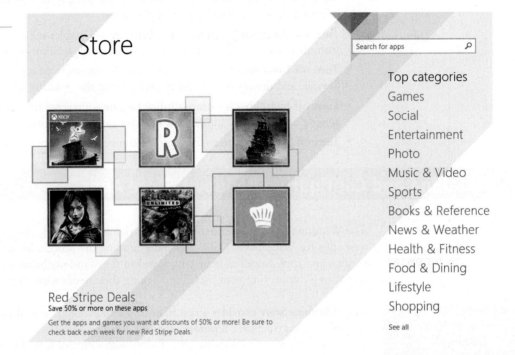

If you're not looking for a specific app, you can simply browse through the categories to find a program that interests you. If you know the type of app you want or the name of the app, start typing the word while inside the Store to perform a search, as shown in Figure 5-13.

Figure 5-13

Searching the Windows Store

Each app is represented by a tile that once selected, takes you to a ***purchase page*** (also called an ***app listing page***). From there you can gather information such as the app's download size, its publisher, and a detailed description of its features.

After reviewing the details on the app listing page, you are ready to start the installation. For free apps, you just click *Install*. For paid apps, you select either the *Try* link or the *Buy* link. Selecting Buy asks that you confirm the purchase by entering your Microsoft account password and specifying a payment method.

Once the installation completes, you receive a notification message. If you click the message, you can use the app immediately; otherwise, you will find a tile for the app on your Windows 8.1 Start screen.

If you decide after using the app that you no longer need it, you can right-click the app's tile and choose Uninstall from the menu that appears along the bottom of the Windows Start screen.

REINSTALLING WINDOWS STORE APPS

Each time you install a Windows app on a device, it's saved to your Microsoft account and the device is added to the list of devices allowed to run it. This provides you with two capabilities. First, you can install the app on up to five Windows 8.1 devices using the same account. Second, if you uninstall a Windows App, you can reinstall it quickly. The steps you use to install an app on additional Windows 8.1 devices and reinstall the app you removed on your existing device are the same.

 INSTALL OR REINSTALL AN APP

GET READY. To install or reinstall an app, perform the following steps:

1. Click the **Store** tile to open the Windows Store page.
2. Right-click and choose **Your Apps.**
3. Click **Apps not installed on this PC.**
4. Select the app(s) you want to install.
5. Click **Install.**

If you reach the maximum number of devices, you will need to remove one of them to add the app to a new device. You can do this by performing the steps in the next exercise.

UPDATING WINDOWS STORE APPS

On a daily basis, Microsoft checks to see whether there are any updates for the apps you've previously downloaded from the Windows Store. If any are found, a number indicator appears on the Store tile.

To see the actual apps requiring updates, click the *Store* tile and select the *Updates* link.

By default, all updates are selected automatically and clicking *Install* starts the update process, as shown in Figure 5-14. If for some reason you don't want to update all your apps at one time, you can click or touch each app to exclude it.

Figure 5-14

Managing update options

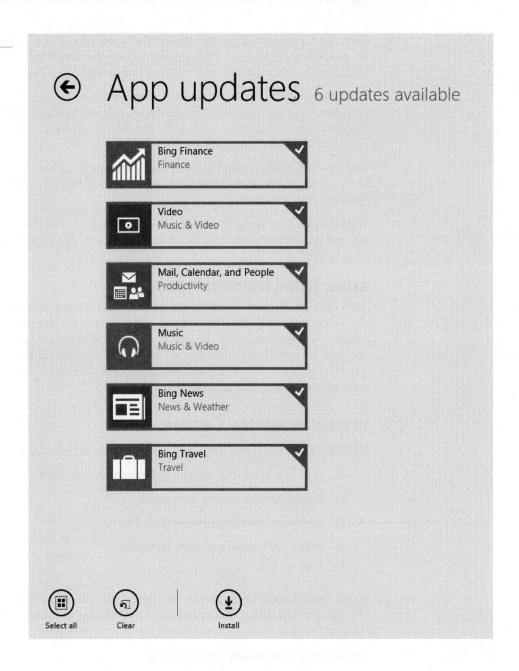

By default, Windows 8.1 is configured to download Windows app updates (but not install them) automatically in the background when your device is idle. If you don't want this to occur, you need to either change the appropriate setting on the Windows 8.1 device or use Group Policy to control the setting.

On a Windows 8.1 device, you can turn off the automatic download updates for apps by performing the steps in the following exercise.

DISABLE AUTOMATIC UPDATE DOWNLOADS

GET READY. To disable the automatic download updates for apps, perform the following steps:

1. Click the **Store** tile to open the Windows Store page.

2. Move your mouse to the upper-right corner and then click **Settings**.

3. Click **App Updates**.

4. Move the slider to the left to set it to **No**, as shown in Figure 5-15.

Figure 5-15

Turning off app updates on
Windows 8.1

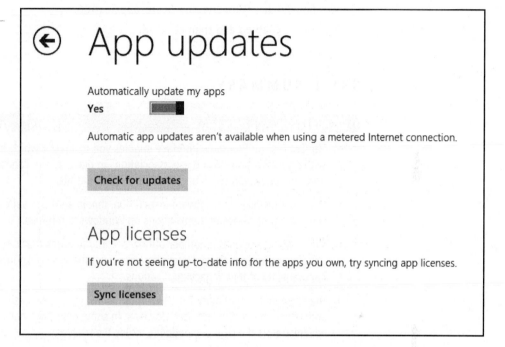

To change the setting through Group Policy, you can use either the *Local Group Policy editor (gpedit.msc)* or the *Group Policy Management console (gpmc.msc)*. Browse to the Computer Configuration\Policies\Administrative Templates\Windows Components\Store node and enable the *Turn off automatic download of updates* policy.

■ Disabling the Windows Store

THE BOTTOM LINE

To maintain control over the apps installed on Windows 8.1 computers, you can disable access to the Windows Store completely. This is common in corporate environments where you want to maintain consistency between computers in the domain and reduce the time and complexity of having to troubleshoot multiple configurations.

If your company policy dictates that access to the Windows Store should be disabled, you can easily configure it through the Local Group Policy editor (gpedit.msc) for a single computer or use GPMC if you are working in a domain-based environment.

DISABLE STORE ACCESS

GET READY. To disable access to the Store for all users working on a specific Windows 8.1 client computer, perform the following steps using the Local Group Policy editor:

1. From the Windows desktop, right-click the Start button and, from the context menu, select Run.

2. In the *Run* dialog box, type **gpedit.msc**.

3. Browse to the Computer Configuration\Administrative Templates\Windows Components\Store node.

4. Double-click **Turn off the Store application**.

5. Select **Enabled** and then click **OK**.

SKILL SUMMARY

IN THIS LESSON, YOU LEARNED:

- The Set Default Programs interface enables you to specify which file types are associated with an application. With these associations in place, a user can simply double-click a file, and the application will launch itself and load that file.

- Windows Installer is a software installation, repair, and removal engine that can simplify the process of deploying applications on Windows computers.

- Windows 8.1 includes a number of new security features that can alter the ability of certain applications to run. Administrators must therefore take measures to ensure the compatibility of their legacy applications.

- The Program Compatibility Troubleshooter is designed to be easily accessible and understandable to the end user. However, in some enterprise network environments, administrators manage compatibility issues themselves.

- The Windows Store is Microsoft's central location for distributing and purchasing Windows apps (also called *Packaged apps*).

- Each Windows app is represented by a tile in the Windows Store. Selecting the tile takes you to a purchase page where you can find additional information and install the app. Once installed, the app appears on your Windows 8.1 Start screen as a tile.

- You can install Windows apps on up to five Windows 8.1 devices. Because the apps are saved to your Microsoft account, you can access them from any device using the Your Apps menu.

- When updates are ready for Windows Apps, a number indicator appears on the Store tile. By default, updates are only downloaded; the user must initiate the actual update process.

- You can turn off automatic updates through App Updates and by using Group Policy, which can be configured using the Local Group Policy editor or the Group Policy Management console.

- Disabling access to the Windows Store can be accomplished via the Local Group Policy editor or the Group Policy Management console.

Knowledge Assessment

Multiple Choice

Select one or more correct answers for each of the following questions.

1. Which of the following is not an emulation mode supported by Windows 8.1?
   a. Windows 2000
   b. Windows 95
   c. Windows 98
   d. Windows XP SP2
   e. Windows Vista

2. Which of the following is the file name extension associated with Windows Installer packages?
   a. exe
   b. com
   c. msi
   d. win

3. Which of the following controls are intended for use by the Windows 8.1 end user? (Choose all that apply.)
   a. Program Compatibility Troubleshooter
   b. Application Compatibility Policies
   c. Application Virtualization Sequencer
   d. Compatibility mode

4. Which of the following is not one of the links in the Default Programs control panel?
   a. Set your default programs
   b. Associate a file type or protocol with a program
   c. Change Autoplay settings
   d. Set program access and computer defaults
   e. Change Windows Installer Properties

5. Which of the following tasks is Windows Installer not capable of performing? (Choose all that apply.)
   a. Installing an application on the local system
   b. Deploying an application on multiple remote systems
   c. Repairing an application the local system
   d. Uninstalling an application on a remote system

6. Which of the following are Windows 8.1 mechanisms that can prevent older applications from running properly? (Choose all that apply.)
   a. Data execution prevention
   b. Security zones
   c. Mandatory integrity control
   d. Microsoft Application Virtualization

7. What is the maximum number of Windows 8.1 devices on which you can install a Windows app?
   a. 1
   b. 3
   c. 5
   d. 10

8. Which of the following can be used to turn off automatic download of updates from the Windows store on a Windows 8.1 computer? (Select all that apply.)
   a. Windows Store > Settings > App Updates > Move slider to No
   b. gpedit.msc
   c. gpmc.msc
   d. AppLocker

9. Which represents the correct path for disabling the *Turn off the Store application* using the Local Group Policy editor?
   a. Computer Configuration > Windows Components > Store
   b. Computer Configuration > Administrative Templates > Windows Store
   c. Computer Configuration > Administrative Templates > Windows Components > Store
   d. Computer Configuration > Administrator Templates > Windows Components > Windows Store

10. Which of the following are true regarding updating Windows apps from the Windows Store?
    a. Only the user can update the apps, but they can be downloaded automatically in the background.
    b. A number indicator appears on the Store icon that will inform you of the number of updates available.
    c. Free Windows apps cannot be updated.
    d. The updates are downloaded and installed in the background.

Matching and Identification

Complete the following exercise by matching the terms with their corresponding definitions.

_____ a) Compatibility mode
_____ b) File association
_____ c) Autoplay default
_____ d) Program access default
_____ e) Windows Installer
_____ f) Application Compatibility Policies
_____ g) Program Compatibility Troubleshooter

1. Packages applications and installation instructions
2. Launches applications based on file name extensions
3. Can prevent users from seeing compatibility warnings
4. Associates an application with a specific task
5. Supports applications designed for older operating systems
6. Controls what happens when you insert a removable medium
7. Wizard-based solution for outdated applications

Best Answer

1. Which of the following is the most likely situation in which an administrator might want to modify the file associations on Windows 8.1 workstations?
   a. When he has just deployed an application with a unique file name extension
   b. When the workstations have two or more applications installed that can open the same file type
   c. When there are two applications with different file types that use the same file name extension
   d. When an application can open multiple file types

2. Which of the following is the most logical reason for changing the default Autoplay settings?
   a. To prevent a media sharing system from automatically playing movie DVDs when you insert them
   b. To prevent burner software from writing to a DVD using a CD format
   c. To enforce DVD-ROM burning standards.
   d. To use Windows Installer to install the application on the removable medium.

3. Which of the following is the best command to use to deploy a Windows Installer package and restart the workstation without any interaction from the user?
   a. Msiexec.exe app.msi /n
   b. Msiexec.exe app.msi /passive /n
   c. Msiexec.exe app.msi /quiet /restart
   d. Msiexec.exe app.msi /quiet /n /forcerestart

4. Which of the following Program Compatibility Troubleshooter problems could most likely be resolved by changing the application's compatibility mode?
   a. The program worked in earlier versions of Windows but won't install or run now.
   b. The program opens but doesn't display correctly
   c. The program requires additional permissions
   d. I don't see my problem listed

5. You have 25 Windows 8.1 computers in a Windows Active Directory domain named *contoso.com*. Which of the following tools should be used to disable the automatic download of updates from the Windows Store on all of them with the least amount of administrative effort?
   a. Local Group Policy editor
   b. Group Policy Management console
   c. Turn off via App Updates in the Windows Store
   d. Delete the automatic updates registry key

6. To uninstall a Windows app that you recently purchased on one of your Windows 8.1 devices last week but now would like to reinstall, which of the following options best describes the process to reinstall it?
   a. Visit the Windows Store, browse through the categories to find the app, and reinstall it at no charge.
   b. Visit the Windows Store, browse through the categories to find the app, and pay for the app to reinstall it.

    c. Visit the Windows Store, access Your Apps, and click Apps not installed on this PC. Select and install.

    d. Remove the app from one of your other Windows 8.1 devices, access Your Apps, and click Apps not installed on this PC. Select and install.

7. As the administrator for a network that has 50 Windows 8.1 client computers, which of the following approaches can be used to initiate Windows app updates on the users' machines?

    a. Configure a Group Policy.

    b. Configure a Local Policy.

    c. Turn on automatic download/install of Windows Apps.

    d. Ask users to perform updates when they see the indicator on their Store tile.

Build a List

1. After deleting a Windows App that is installed on four other Windows 8.1 devices, specify the correct order of steps required to reinstall the Windows app.

    _____ **a)** Click **Apps not installed on this PC.**

    _____ **b)** Select the Windows logo key to open the Windows Start menu and select the Store tile.

    _____ **c)** Select the app you want to install.

    _____ **d)** Right-click and select **Your Apps.**

    _____ **e)** Click **Install.**

2. In order of first to last, specify the tasks that must be completed to disable access to the Windows Store using the Local Group Policy editor.

    _____ **a)** Click **Computer Configuration > Administrative Templates > Windows Components > Store.**

    _____ **b)** Click **Enabled** and then click **OK.**

    _____ **c)** Press the **Windows logo key + r.**

    _____ **d)** Double-click **Turn off the Store application.**

    _____ **e)** In the Run dialog box, type gpedit.msc.

■ Business Case Scenario

Scenario 5-1: Application Errors

Alice is the help desk supervisor at Wingtip Toys, Ltd. and she has noticed an increasing number of similar help calls from users in the company's main office. The users are all running Windows 8.1 on their workstations, and many of the complaints involve errors writing data to specific memory addresses, the type of errors not often seen in Windows 8. After examining the errors in Event Viewer and looking a one of the computers involved, Alice determines that a group of users in the main office are running old games that were designed on MS-DOS and Windows 95. All of the authorized applications on the workstations are designed to run on Windows 8.1.

How can Alice prevent all of the main office users from running this downlevel software without having to create rules excluding each game individually?

Controlling Access to Local Hardware and Applications

LESSON **6**

70-687 EXAM OBJECTIVE

Objective 2.3 – Control access to local hardware and applications. This objective may include but is not limited to: configure application restrictions, including Software Restriction Policies and AppLocker; manage installation of and access to removable devices; configure Assigned Access.

LESSON HEADING	EXAM OBJECTIVE
Configuring Hardware Restrictions	
Controlling Device Installation	
Controlling Removable Storage Access	Manage installation of and access to removable devices
Configuring Application Restrictions	Configure application restrictions, including Software Restriction Policies and AppLocker
Using Software Restriction Policies	
Using AppLocker	
Configuring Assigned Access	Configure Assigned Access

KEY TERMS

application control policies

AppLocker

certificate rules

default rule

executable rules

hash rules

network zone rules

packaged app rules

path rules

script rules

software restriction policies

Windows Installer rules

■ Configuring Hardware Restrictions

THE BOTTOM LINE

Data storage technology has advanced to the point at which anyone can carry enormous amounts of information in a device no larger than a postage stamp. The storage capacities of flash memory cards, USB flash drives, and portable hard drives are increasing at an exponential rate, and for many administrators, this represents a critical threat.

109

High-capacity removable disks and drives are dangerous to enterprise networks in that they can allow data in, as well as carry it out. Users can easily introduce unauthorized software into the environment, and they can also copy corporate data and carry it out. One way to minimize these threats is to limit the ability to use these devices on enterprise workstations.

Windows Server 2012 R2 and Windows 8.1 both support Group Policy settings that enable administrators to limit user access to specific types of removable storage devices. As with most Group Policy settings, administrators can deploy them on Windows 8.1 computers individually by modifying the Local Security Policy settings, but in an enterprise environment, it is usually more practical to create a Group Policy Object (GPO) with the appropriate settings and link it to an Active Directory Domain Services (AD DS) object.

Controlling Device Installation

> The Device Installation Restrictions folder in a GPO contains policy settings that enable you to prevent Windows computers from installing and updating device drivers under specific conditions.

The policies in the Computer Configuration/Policies/Administrative Templates/System/Device Installation/Device Installation Restrictions folder, shown in Figure 6-1, enable you to specify if or when the computers on your network can install drivers for hardware devices.

Figure 6-1

The Device Installation Restrictions policies

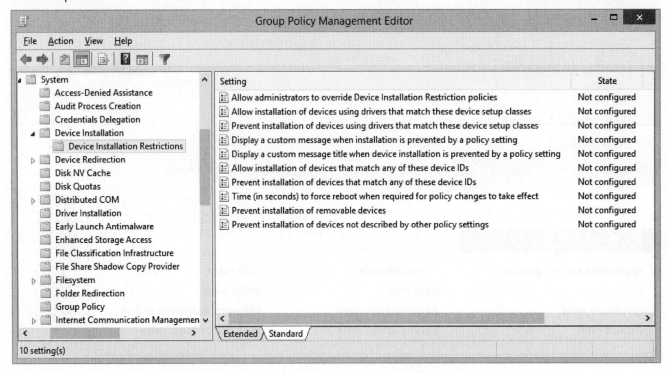

For example, the *Prevent installation of removable devices* setting enables you to prevent computers from installing any devices which the drivers identify as removable. This would therefore prevent users from inserting USB flash drives or portable hard drives for the first time.

The policy also prevents any drivers for removable devices already installed on the system from being updated. However, the policy does nothing to inhibit the functionality of drivers that are already installed.

For more granular control over device installation, you can use any of the following additional policies:

- **Allow/Prevent installation of devices that match any of these device IDs** – Enables you to allow or prevent installation or update of device drivers based on their Plug and Play hardware IDs. Use this *Allow* setting only when the *Prevent installation of devices not described by other policy settings* is also enabled.

- **Allow/Prevent installation of devices using drivers that match these device setup classes** – Enables you to allow or prevent installation or update of device drivers based on the globally unique identifiers (GUIDs) of their setup classes. Use this *Allow* setting only when the *Prevent installation of devices not described by other policy settings* is also enabled.

- **Prevent installation of devices not described by other policy settings** – Provides a prohibition against the installation or update of all devices not named in the *Allow installation of devices that match any of these device IDs* and/or *Allow installation of devices using drivers that match these To device setup classes* policies.

- **Allow administrators to override Device Installation Restriction policies** – Provides members of the Administrators group with the ability to install and update device drivers regardless of all other policy settings.

Controlling Removable Storage Access

CERTIFICATION READY
Manage installation of and access to removable devices
Objective 2.3

> In many enterprise situations, administrators might want to prevent people from using some or all removable storage devices, both to protect company data and prevent the introduction of malware.

To implement policies controlling removable storage access, use the following procedure.

⊙ CONFIGURE REMOVABLE STORAGE ACCESS POLICIES

GET READY. Log on to Windows 8.1 using an account with Administrator privileges.

1. Open the Windows Control Panel and select System and Security > Administrative Tools.

> **TAKE NOTE★**   To run the Group Policy Management console on a computer running Windows 8.1, you must first download and install Remote Server Administration Tools for Windows 8.1, available from the Microsoft Download Center.

2. Double-click Group Policy Management. The Group Policy Management console appears.
3. Browse to the Group Policy Objects folder.
4. Right-click the folder and, from the context menu, select New Group Policy object. The New GPO dialog box appears.
5. Type a name for the Group Policy object in the Name text box and click OK.
6. Right-click the GPO you created and, in the context menu, select Edit. The Group Policy Management Editor appears.
7. Browse to the Computer Configuration/Policies/Administrative Templates/System/ Removable Storage Access folder, as shown in Figure 6-2.

Figure 6-2

The Removable Storage
Access policies

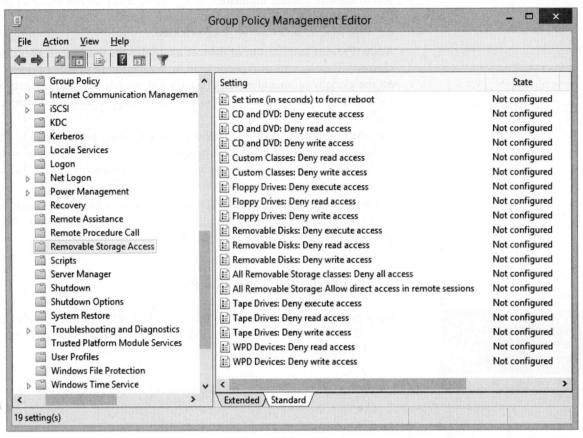

8. For control over access to specific types of removable storage, configure any of the following policy settings:

- **All Removable Storage classes: Deny all access** – Enables you to block access to all classes of removable storage device. This policy takes precedence over all of the policy settings for individual classes.

- **All Removable Storage: Allow direct access in remote sessions** – Enables users to access removable storage devices directly during remote sessions.

- **CD and DVD: Deny read/write/execute access** – Enables you to deny users read, write, and/or execute access to all of the CD or DVD drives in the computer.

- **Custom Classes: Deny read/write access** – Enables you to deny users read and/or write access to custom device classes identified by their GUIDs.

- **Floppy Drives: Deny read/write/execute access** – Enables you to deny users read, write, and/or execute access to all of the floppy drives in the computer, including USB floppy drives.

- **Removable Disks: Deny read/write/execute access** – Enables you to deny users read, write, and/or execute access to all of the removable disks in the computer.

- **Tape Drives: Deny read/write/execute access** – Enables you to deny users read, write, and/or execute access to all of the tape drives in the computer.

TAKE NOTE*

For control at the user level, the same policies appear in the User Configuration/Policies/Administrative Templates/System/Removable Storage Access folder.

- **WPD Devices: Deny read/write access** – Enables you to deny users read and/or write access to all of the Windows Portable Devices in the computer, including smartphones, MP3 players, and cameras.

9. Close the Group Policy Management Editor console.

10. Close the Group Policy Management console.

Configuring Application Restrictions

THE BOTTOM LINE In an enterprise environment, administrators often prefer to limit the applications their users are permitted to run. In Windows 8.1, there are two ways of doing this.

Restricting the applications that users can run on their computers is one step towards creating a consistent workstation environment. Workstations that are identically configured are easier to support and limit the possibility of malware infiltration.

Windows 8.1 supports two mechanisms for restricting application, both of which you can deploy using Group Policy settings: software restriction policies and AppLocker. These mechanisms are discussed in the following sections.

CERTIFICATION READY
Configure application restrictions, including Software Restriction Policies and AppLocker
Objective 2.3

Using Software Restriction Policies

Software restriction policies are rules that specify which applications users can run.

Software restriction policies are Group Policy settings that enable administrators to specify the programs that are allowed to run on workstations by creating rules of various types. Software restriction policies have been around for years, and their main advantage is that you can create one set of policies that apply to Windows XP, Windows Vista, and Windows 7 workstations, as well as Windows 8 and Windows 8.1. The disadvantage of software restriction policies is that, unlike the newer AppLocker feature, you can only create rules manually and individually.

CREATING RULES

The software restriction policy rules that you can create include the following:

- *Certificate rules* – Identify applications based on the inclusion of a certificate signed by the software publisher. An application can continue to match this type of rule, even if the executable file is updated, as long as the certificate remains valid.
- *Hash rules* – Identify applications based on a digital fingerprint that remains valid even when the name or location of the executable file changes.
- *Network zone rules* – Identify Windows Installer (.msi) packages downloaded with Internet Explorer based on the security zone of the site from which they are downloaded.
- *Path rules* – Identify applications by specifying a file or folder name or a registry key. The potential vulnerability of this type of rule is that any file can match the rule, as long as it is the correct name or location.

To create rules, use the following procedure.

CREATE SOFTWARE RESTRICTION POLICY RULES

GET READY. Log on to Windows 8.1 using an account with Administrator privileges.

1. Open the Windows Control Panel and select System and Security > Administrative Tools.

2. Double-click Group Policy Management. The Group Policy Management console appears.

3. Browse to the Group Policy Objects folder.

4. Right-click the folder and, from the context menu, select New Group Policy object. The New GPO dialog box appears.

5. Type a name for the Group Policy object in the Name text box and click OK.

6. Right-click the GPO you created and, in the context menu, select Edit. The Group Policy Management Editor appears.

7. Browse to the Computer Configuration\Policies\Windows Settings\Security Settings\Software Restriction Policies folder.

8. Right-click the Software Restriction Polices object and, from the context menu, select New Software Restriction Policies. The policies appear, as shown in Figure 6-3.

Figure 6-3

Software Restriction Policies

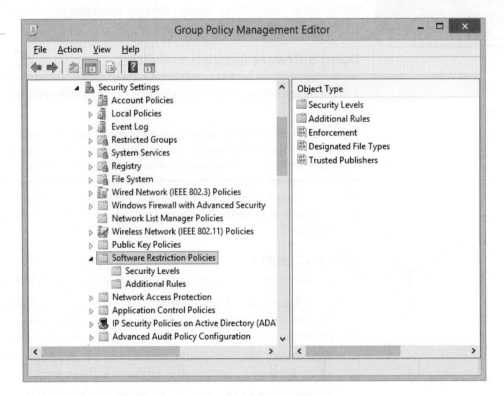

9. Right-click the Additional Rules folder and, from the context menu, select New Path Rule. The *New Path Rule* dialog box appears, as shown in Figure 6-4.

Figure 6-4

The *New Path Rule* dialog box

10. In the *Path* text box, type the path to the file you want to restrict.
11. In the *Security level* drop-down list, select an appropriate value and click OK.
12. Close the Group Policy Management Editor console.
13. Close the Group Policy Management console.

There is also a fifth type of rule – the ***default rule*** – that applies when an application does not match any of the other rules you have created. To configure the default rule, you select one of the policies in the Security Levels folder and click *Set As Default* on its *Properties* sheet.

TAKE NOTE*

The most common way to implement software restriction policies is through Group Policy objects linked to Active Directory Domain Services containers, so that administrators can apply their policy settings to large numbers of computers simultaneously. However, it is also possible to configure software restriction policies on individual computers using Local Security Policy.

CONFIGURING RULE SETTINGS

Software restriction policies can work in three ways, based on the settings you choose for each of the rules. The three possible settings are as follows:

- **Disallowed** – Prevents an application matching a rule from running.
- **Basic user** – Allows all applications not requiring administrative privileges to run. Allows applications that do require administrative privileges to run only if they match a rule.
- **Unrestricted** – Allows an application matching a rule to run

The most restrictive – and the most secure – way to use the settings is to set the default rule to Disallowed and then create additional Unrestricted rules for the applications you want your users to be able to run. This prevents them from launching any applications other than the ones you specify. The reverse of this method is to set the default rule to Unrestricted and use additional Disallowed rules to specify applications that you want to prevent users from running.

Although the most obvious way of using these settings is to creates rules for individual applications, there are other alternatives also. You can, for example, create rules that prevent users from running applications from anywhere other than the Program Files folder, and then use NTFS permissions to prevent them from installing new application to Program Files.

RESOLVING CONFLICTS

It is possible to create rules in such a way that conflicts occur because more than one rule applies to a single application. When this is the case, the more specific rule takes precedence over the less specific. Thus, the order of precedence is as follows:

1. Hash rules
2. Certificate rules
3. Path rules
4. Zone rules
5. Default rule

Using AppLocker

AppLocker is a feature first introduced in Windows 7 that enables administrators to create application restriction rules much more easily than software restriction policies.

Software restriction policies can be a powerful tool, but they can also require a great deal of administrative overhead. If you elect to disallow all applications except those matching the rules you create, there are a great many programs in Windows 8.1 itself that need rules, in addition to the applications you want to install. Administrators must also create the rules manually, which can be an onerous chore.

AppLocker, also known as *application control policies*, is essentially an updated version of the concept implemented in software restriction policies. AppLocker also uses rules, which administrators must manage, but the process of creating the rules is much easier, thanks to a wizard-based interface.

AppLocker is also more flexible than software restriction policies. You can apply AppLocker rules to specific users and groups and also create rules that support all future versions of an application. The primary disadvantage of AppLocker is that you can only apply the policies to computers running Windows 7, Windows 8, Windows 8.1, Windows Server 2008 R2, Windows Server 2012 and Windows Server 2012 R2.

UNDERSTANDING RULE TYPES

The AppLocker settings are located in Group Policy objects in the Computer Configuration\
Policies\Windows Settings\Security Settings\Application Control Policies\AppLocker container, as shown in Figure 6-5.

Figure 6-5

AppLocker settings

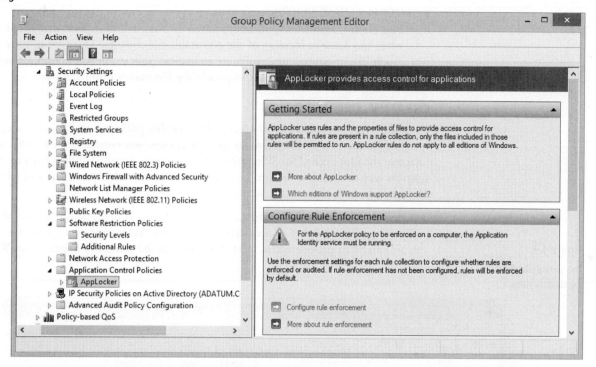

The AppLocker container in a GPOIn the AppLocker container, there are four nodes that contain the basic rule types, as follows:

- *Executable Rules* – Contains rules that apply to files with .exe and .com extensions.
- *Windows Installer Rules* – Contains rules that apply to Windows Installer packages with .msi and .msp extensions.
- *Script Rules* – Contains rules that apply to script files with .ps1, .bat, .cmd, .vbs, and .js extensions.
- *Packaged app Rules* – Contains rules that apply to applications purchased through the Windows Store.

TAKE NOTE✱

You can also configure AppLocker to use DLL rules, which require administrators to create rules that provide users with access to all of the dynamic link libraries (DLLs) in an application, as well as the executables. This option, while more secure, can incur a significant performance penalty, because AppLocker must confirm access to each of an application's DLLs before it can load. To configure this option, open the *Properties* sheet for the AppLocker container, click the *Advanced* tab, and select the *Enable the DLL rule collection* checkbox.

Each of the rules you create in each of these containers can allow or block access to specific resources, based on one of the following criteria:

- **Publisher** – Identifies code-signed applications by means of a digital signature extracted from an application file. You can also create publisher rules that apply to all future versions of an application.

- **Path** – Identifies applications by specifying a file or folder name. The potential vulnerability of this type of rule is that any file can match the rule, as long as it is the correct name or location.
- **File Hash** – Identifies applications based on a digital fingerprint that remains valid even when the name or location of the executable file changes. This type of rules functions much like its equivalent in software restriction policies; in AppLocker, however, the process of creating the rules and generating file hashes is much easier.

CREATING DEFAULT RULES

By default, AppLocker blocks all executables, installer packages, and scripts, except for those specified in *Allow* rules. Therefore, to use AppLocker, you must create rules that enable users to access the files needed for Windows and the system's installed applications to run. The simplest way to do this is to right-click each of the three rules containers and select *Create Default Rules* from the context menu.

The default rules for each container, as shown in Figure 6-6, are standard rules that you can replicate, modify, or delete as necessary. You can also create your own rules instead, as long as you are careful to provide access to all the resources the computer needs to run Windows.

Figure 6-6

The default AppLocker executable rules

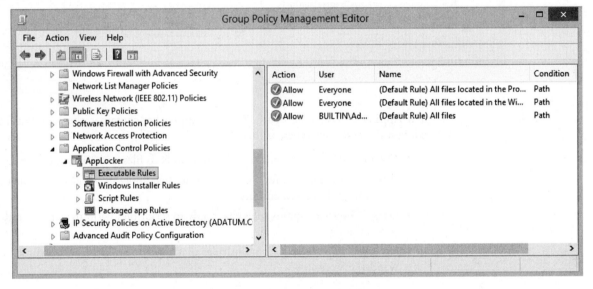

> **TAKE NOTE**
>
> To use AppLocker, Windows 8.1 requires the Application Identity service to be running. By default, this service uses the manual startup type, so you must start it yourself in the Services console before Windows 8.1 can apply the AppLocker policies. This behavior is deliberate. With AppLocker, it is relatively easy to inadvertently create a set of rules that omits access to executables or other files that Windows needs to run, thus disabling the operating system. If this should occur, simply restarting the computer will cause the operating system to load without the Application Identity service, preventing AppLocker from loading. Only when you are certain that you have configured your rules properly should you change the startup type for the Application Identity service to automatic.

CREATING RULES AUTOMATICALLY

The greatest advantage of AppLocker over software restriction policies is the ability to create rules automatically. When you right-click one of the three rules containers and select *Create Rules Automatically* from the context menu, an *Automatically Generate Rules* wizard appears, as shown in Figure 6-7.

Figure 6-7

The *Automatically Generate Executable Rules* wizard

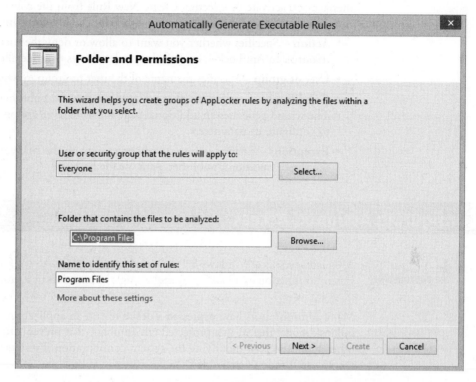

After specifying the folder to be analyzed and the users or groups to which the rules should apply, a *Rule Preferences* page appears, as shown in Figure 6-8.

Figure 6-8

The *Rule Preferences* page of the *Automatically Generate Executable Rules* wizard

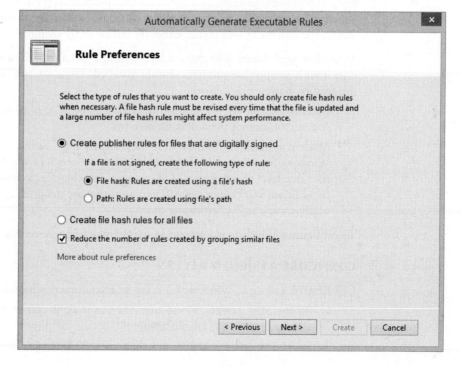

The wizard then displays a summary of its results in the *Review Rules* page and adds the rules to the container.

CREATING RULES MANUALLY

In addition to creating rules automatically, you can also do it manually, using a wizard-based interface you activate by selecting Create New Rule from the context menu for one of the three rule containers. The wizard prompts you for the following information:

- **Action** – Specifies whether you want to allow or deny the user or group access to the resource. In AppLocker, explicit deny rules always override allow rules.

- **User or group** – Specifies the name of the user or group to which the policy should apply.

- **Conditions** – Specifies whether you want to create a publisher, path, or file hash rule. The wizard generates an additional page for whichever option you select, enabling you to configure its parameters.

- **Exceptions** – Enables you to specify exceptions to the rule you are creating, using any of the three conditions: publisher, path, or file hash.

■ Configuring Assigned Access

 THE BOTTOM LINE
Assigned access is a Windows 8.1 feature that enables you to configure a Windows 8.1 system to function as a kiosk, running a single application in a protected environment.

Many administrators have expressed a desire to run an application on a Windows computer in kiosk mode, that is, in a protected environment that prevents the user from running any other applications or modifying the system configuration. Previously, the only way to do this was to use Windows embedded.

It is now possible, in Windows 8.1, to associate a local user account with a single Windows app, so that the app launches when the user logs on to the system. Once in that app, the user cannot launch another app. The system also suppresses all notifications, and disables all of the key combinations, gestures, and shortcuts that provide access to the underlying system components. For example, the user cannot press the Windows key to display the Start screen, or display the charms fly-out menu, either by mouse or by swiping.

To use Assigned Access, you create a local account specifically for that purpose, and you associate it with an app that you have already installed. There are two important limitations to this feature, however, as follows:

- Local accounts only – You must use a local account, created solely for use with Assigned Access. You cannot use a domain account.

- Modern apps only – You can only use Modern apps – either purchased from the Windows Store or sideloaded – with Assigned Access. Desktop applications do not have the same level of security as Modern apps, and therefore cannot function in kiosk mode. In addition, you cannot use Modern apps that are designed to modify the system configuration, such as PC Settings or Store.

To configure a Windows 8.1 system to use Assigned Access, use the following procedure.

 CONFIGURE ASSIGNED ACCESS

GET READY. Log on to Windows 8.1 using an account with administrative privileges.

1. On the Start screen, mouse over the lower right corner or swipe in from the right side to display the charms menu.

2. Select the Settings charm and then click PC Settings. The *PC Settings* page appears.

3. Click Accounts. The *Accounts* page appears.

4. Click Other accounts. The *Manage other accounts* page appears, as shown in Figure 6-9.

Figure 6-9

The *Manage other accounts* page

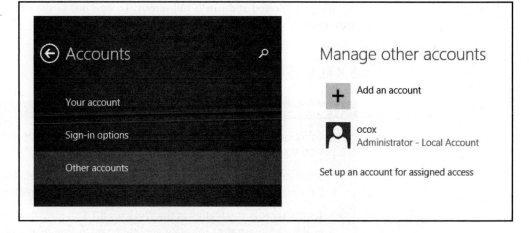

5. Click Add an account. The *How will this person sign in?* page appears.

6. Click sign in without a Microsoft account. The *Add a user* page appears.

7. Click Local account. A second *Add a user* page appears.

8. In the User name text box, type a name for the Assigned Access account, and in the Password and Reenter password textboxes, type the password you want to use for the account. Then type a password hint in the remaining textbox and click Next.

9. Once the account is created, click Finish. The new account appears on the *Manage other accounts* page.

10. Restart the computer, log on using the new account, and install the desired app.

11. Click Set up an account for assigned access. The *Set up an account for assigned access* page appears, as shown in Figure 6-10.

12. Click Choose an account and select the account you just created.

Figure 6-10

The Set up an account for assigned access page

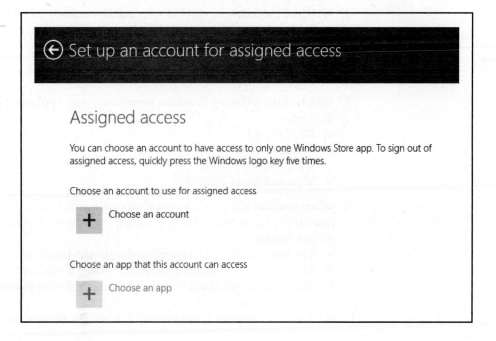

13. Click Choose an app and select the app you want the account to run.

14. Click the back arrow to return to the *Manage other accounts* page.

The next time anyone logs on using the account you have configured, the system with load the app you selected and run it full screen. To sign out at the end of the session, the user must tap the Windows key five times in succesion.

SKILL SUMMARY

IN THIS LESSON, YOU LEARNED:

- Using Group Policy, you can restrict user access to removable storage devices on their workstations.

- Software restriction policies are Group Policy settings that enable administrators to specify the programs that are allowed to run on workstations by creating rules of various types.

- AppLocker is a new feature in the Windows 8.1 Enterprise and Ultimate editions that enables administrators to create application restriction rules much more easily.

■ Knowledge Assessment

Multiple Choice

Select one or more correct answers for each of the following questions.

1. Which of the following software restriction policy rule types takes the highest precedence?
   a. Certificate rules
   b. Hash rules
   c. Default rules
   d. Zone rules

2. Which of the following types of rules can be manually created in AppLocker?
   a. Publisher rules
   b. Certificate rules
   c. Path rules
   d. File hash rules

3. Which of the following Windows versions support AppLocker policies? (Choose all that apply.)
   a. Windows 8.1
   b. Windows Vista
   c. Windows Server 2003
   d. Windows Server 2008 SP2

4. When you enable the Prevent installation of removable devices policy in a GPO and link that GPO to a domain, what is the effect on the devices already installed on computers in that domain?
   a. The policy has no effect on removable devices that have already been installed.
   b. The policy causes already-installed removable devices to be uninstalled.
   c. The policy allows already-installed removable devices to function, but prevents their drivers from being updated.
   d. The policy disables already-installed removable devices, but does not uninstall them.

5. Which of the following rule types can *not* be used to create software restriction policies?
   a. Hash rules
   b. Certificate rules
   c. Path rules
   d. Code rules

6. When creating an AppLocker rules manually, which of the following is *not* information the wizard prompts you to supply?
   a. Conditions
   b. User or group
   c. Function
   d. Action

7. Which of the following is *not* a setting for software restriction policies?
   a. Basic user
   b. Disallowed
   c. Advanced user
   d. Unrestricted

Best Answer

1. Which of the following statements is the primary reason why AppLocker is an improvement over software restriction policies?
   a. AppLocker has more rule types than software restriction policies.
   b. AppLocker can generate its own rules automatically.
   c. AppLocker can be deployed in Group Policy objects in Active Directory.
   d. AppLocker requires the Application Identity service to be running.

2. Which of the following statements is the primary reason why you must start the Application Identity service manually before using AppLocker?
   a. Because AppLocker needs the Application Identity service to be running in order to function.
   b. Because the Application Identity service will hang the system if it starts with Windows.
   c. Because requiring the manual start prevents improperly configured AppLocker rules from permanently hanging the system.
   d. Because Windows 8.1 does not support starting the Application Identity service automatically.

Matching and Identification

Complete the following exercise by matching the terms with their corresponding definitions.

_____ a) Path rules
_____ b) Windows Installer Rules
_____ c) Certificate rules
_____ d) Executable Rules
_____ e) Hash rules
_____ f) Packaged app Rules
_____ g) Default rule
_____ h) Network zone rules
_____ i) Script Rules
_____ j) DLL rules

   1. Applies to files with .exe and .com extensions
   2. Applies to packages with .msi and .msp extensions
   3. Applies to files with .ps1, .bat, .cmd, .vbs, and .js extensions

4. Applies to Windows Store purchases
5. Applies to digitally signed applications
6. Applies to applications with a digital fingerprint
7. Applies to packages downloaded with Internet Explorer
8. Applies to applications with a specific file or folder name
9. Applies to libraries, as well as executables
10. Applies to applications that do not match any other rule type

■ Business Case Scenario

Scenario 6-1: Using AppLocker

Sophie is planning on using AppLocker to control access to applications on a new network she has constructed for the Research and Development department at a major aerospace firm. The software developers in the department have recently deployed a new application called Virtual Wind Tunnel, which is based on government project research and is therefore classified. All of the full-time personnel have sufficient clearance to use the application, but the interns in the department do not. Sophie has placed the user accounts for everyone in the department into a security group called ResDev. The interns are also members of a group called RDint.

How can Sophie use AppLocker to provide everyone in the department with access to the Virtual Wind Tunnel application without changing the group memberships and without having to apply policies to individual users?

Configuring Internet Explorer 11 and Internet Explorer for the Desktop

70-687 EXAM OBJECTIVE

Objective 2.4 – Configure Internet Explorer 11 and Internet Explorer for the Desktop. This objective may include but is not limited to: configure compatibility view; configure Internet Explorer 11 settings, including add-ons, downloads, security, and privacy.

LESSON HEADING	EXAM OBJECTIVE
Administering Internet Explorer	
Configuring Internet Explorer	Configure compatibility view Configure Internet Explorer 11 settings, including add-ons, downloads, security, and privacy
Securing Internet Explorer	Configure Internet Explorer 11 settings, including add-ons, downloads, security, and privacy
Understanding Protected Mode	
Configuring Security Zones	
Configuring the SmartScreen Filter	
Using InPrivate Mode	
Browsing with Certificates	

KEY TERMS

accelerators

add-ons

certification authority (CA)

compatibility logging

Compatibility View

InPrivate Filtering

InPrivate Mode

Mandatory Integrity Control (MIC)

phishing

protected mode

public key infrastructure (PKI)

Secure Sockets Layer (SSL)

security zones

SmartScreen Filter

social engineering

Trusted Sites zone

■ Administering Internet Explorer

THE BOTTOM LINE   Administrators must be familiar with the administrative controls in Internet Explorer (IE) to protect users from Internet predators.

Windows 8.1 includes the latest version of the Internet Explorer web browser, Version 11, which enhances the features introduced in earlier versions. For administrators, these changes are likely to result in an increasing number of "user error" calls as users become accustomed to the new tools and the changes to the interface. Internet Explorer 11 also includes security tools that you must know how to configure for maximum effectiveness.

The chief innovation in IE10 and 11 is that the browser now has two distinct interfaces. When you launch IE from the desktop, you see the same familiar screen arrangement as in previous versions, with a menu bar and tabs across the top. When you launch IE by clicking the tile on the Start screen, however, you initially see a screen with a dark-colored address bar along the bottom, as shown in Figure 7-1, but that soon disappears, leaving the entire screen filled with the webpage content.

Figure 7-1

The IE Start screen interface

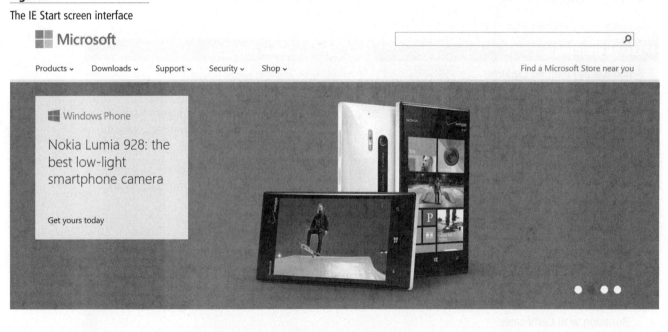

TAKE NOTE *

The controls described in the following sections pertain to the desktop version of IE. The *Start* screen version does not include all of the features and controls found in the desktop version.

This *Start* screen version of IE is equipped with an interface designed specifically for touch screens and is based on the full-screen paradigm found in other *Start* screen applications. Browser controls appear when you right-click the mouse or swipe in from an edge of the screen, but for the most part, the entire screen is occupied by content.

Although the look of this *Start* screen version of IE is different from the desktop version, they are in fact the same application. As with many other apps, the basic controls for the *Start* screen IE appear in an *Internet Explorer Settings* fly-out panel, as shown in Figure 7-2. The desktop version of IE retains the Internet Options tabbed dialog box familiar from previous *versions*.

Figure 7-2

The *Internet Explorer Settings* panel

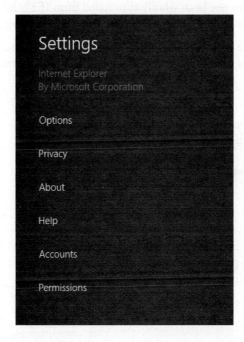

Configuring Internet Explorer

IE includes new features that administrators must be able to use and *configure*.

As with earlier versions, IE satisfies most users' needs with no adjustment. However, some of the new features in IE require configuration. The following sections examine the configuration procedures that desktop technicians might have to perform for their clients.

CONFIGURING COMPATIBILITY VIEW

The standards that developers use when creating websites, like most standards, are in a continual state of development. Browsers like IE, therefore, must be designed to properly display pages that conform to the latest version standards. IE11 operates in a default standards mode that enables it to display pages created using Cascading Style Sheets 3, Hypertext Markup Language version 5 (HTML5), Web Sockets, and other standards.

CERTIFICATION READY
Configure compatibility view
Objective 2.4

The problem with this regular development was that many of the pages on the Internet still conformed to older versions of the standards. In previous versions of IE, the browser could not display them properly, and to accommodate these older pages, IE included a feature called *Compatibility View*, which enabled the browser to display older pages properly, as if they were loaded in a previous version of IE.

In these earlier IE versions, the most easily visible indication of Compatibility View was the broken window Compatibility View button that appeared at the right end of the IE address box. When a website designed to earlier standards did not display properly, clicking this button switched IE into Compatibility View mode, which could sometimes improve the appearance of the site by displaying it using IE version 7 standards.

IE 11 eliminates the Compatibility View button, however, because its standards mode is natively more compatible than previous versions, and because forcing IE7 compatibility is likely to break more pages than it can fix on today's web. Many of the web servers in use today add meta tags to the pages they serve, enabling the browser to automatically compensate for standards version discrepancies.

Compatibility View has not been wholly eliminated from IE11, however. You can still enable Compatibility View by selecting Tools/Compatibility View Settings from the Tools menu.

When you do this, the *Compatibility View Settings* dialog box appears, as shown in Figure 7-3. In this dialog box, you can maintain a list of websites for which you want to use *Compatibility View* all of the time.

Figure 7-3

The IE *Compatibility View Settings* dialog box

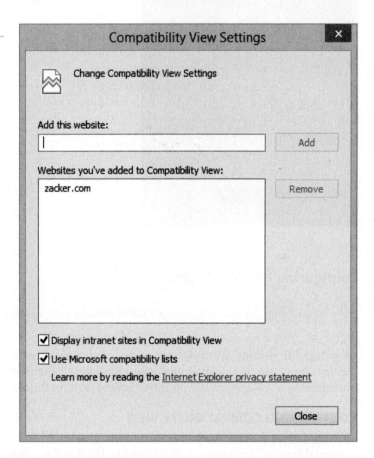

In addition to maintaining individual lists on each computer, Microsoft also maintains its own list of sites that can benefit from Compatibility View. When you select the *Use Microsoft compatibility lists* checkbox on the Compatibility View Settings dialog box, IE includes the Microsoft-supplied sites in the computer's list.

TAKE NOTE*

Any META tags in a webpage's code specifying a rendering standard override the presence of the site in the computer's Compatibility View list.

For website developers, it is possible to include tags in HTML files that cause IE to view the page in Compatibility View mode. For example, to render a page using the IE Version 7 standards, you can include the following code in the page's HEAD section:

```
<meta http-equiv="X-UA-Compatible" content="IE=7" />
```

For workstations on an Active Directory Domain Services (AD DS) network, administrators can configure Compatibility View settings using Group Policy. The settings are located in the Computer Configuration\Policies\Administrative Templates\Windows Components\Internet Explorer\Compatibility View container of every GPO.

The policy settings for Compatibility View are as follows:

- **Turn on Internet Explorer 7 Standards Mode** – Causes IE versions 8 to 10 to render all webpages in the Standards Mode from the previous version of the browser. This improves compatibility with older websites, but can negatively affect the appearance of sites designed to the current standard.
- **Turn off Compatibility View** – Disables the Compatibility View feature in IE, preventing users from configuring the Compatibility View settings.
- **Turn on Internet Explorer Standards Mode for local intranet** – Causes IE to display all intranet content using the current Standards Mode, and prevents users from modifying this behavior.
- **Turn off Compatibility View button** – Prevents the broken page icon from appearing on the address box in IE versions 8 to 10.
- **Include updated website lists from Microsoft** – Forces IE to use the Microsoft site compatibility lists when displaying webpages.
- **Use Policy List of Internet Explorer 7 sites** – Enables administrators to create a common list of sites that IE should display using Compatibility View mode.
- **Use policy List of Quirks Mode sites** – Enables IE to identify itself to servers with an IE7 user agent string and operate in quirks mode, which supports incomplete standards, as opposed to standard mode.

MANAGING ADD-ONS

CERTIFICATION READY
Configure Internet Explorer 11 settings, including add-ons, downloads, security, and privacy
Objective 2.4

IE is designed to be a versatile platform that can interact with a variety of other resources on the computer, on the network, and on the Internet. One of the ways that IE does this is through the use of add-ons. *Add-ons* are separate software components, created by Microsoft or by third parties, that interact with the basic functions of the web browser. Add-ons can provide an interface between the browser and another software product or between the browser and a specific site on the Internet.

The four basic types of add-ons supported by IE are as follows:

- **Toolbars and Extensions** – Enable the browser to open and manipulate websites or file types that IE does not support natively. Some applications add their own toolbars to IE, enabling you to work with their documents within an IE session.
- **Search Providers** – Enable the user to perform searches directly from the IE interface using search engines on the Internet or the local network.
- **Accelerators** – Enable users to send text or other media they select in an IE browser window to another application, such as an email client, or an Internet resource, such as a blog.
- **Tracking Protection** – Enables users to install or maintain a list of sites that the IE should prevent from sharing your browsing habits with other sites.

⚠ **WARNING** As with any Internet download, be sure that you install add-ons provided only by sources that you trust. Add-ons can easily contain various types of malware that can damage your system.

Microsoft provides a few add-ons with IE in Windows 8.1, and also maintains gallery sites, from which you can download add-ons created by third parties. Some applications come with their own add-ons, which they install along with the application itself. Some websites also make add-ons available directly from their own pages.

To work with the IE add-ons on a particular Windows 8.1 computer, you open the *Manage Add-ons* dialog box, as shown in Figure 7-4, by clicking Tools\Manage Add-ons from either the menu bar or the Tools toolbar button.

Figure 7-4

The *Manage Add-ons* dialog box

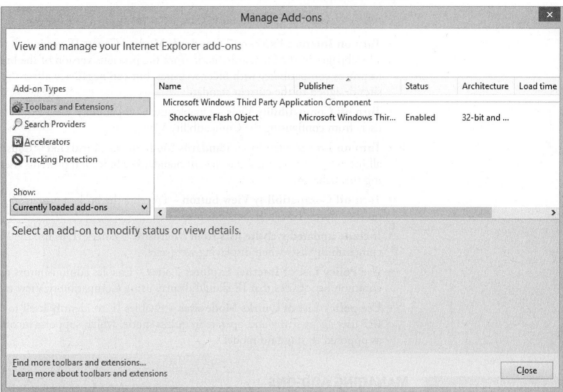

When you select one of the categories in the *Add-on Types* list, you see a list of the computer's currently-installed add-ons. With the controls that appear on the bottom pane of the dialog box, you can temporarily disable an add-on, remove it permanently, or select it as the default add-on of that type.

TAKE NOTE*

Only the desktop version of IE11 supports the use of add-ons. The *Start* screen version does not.

CONFIGURING SEARCH OPTIONS

Search providers are one of the most useful types of IE add-on. By default, the *Instant Search* box found in IE enables users to perform searches using Microsoft's Bing engine. To use other search engines, you must first install them to the list of search providers. Search providers are add-ons specifically designed to support the syntax required by other search engines.

IE supports virtually any type of search provider, not just the well-known web search engines such as Google. You can also add search providers for specific topics or sites, such as *Wikipedia* and *The New York Times*. Finally, you can add internal search engines of your own design, so that users can search your corporate intranet.

Adding Search Providers

To add search providers to the *Instant Search* list, use the following procedure:

ADD A SEARCH PROVIDER

GET READY. Log on to Windows 8.1 and then perform the following steps:

1. On the **Start** screen, click the **Desktop** tile.

   The Windows desktop appears.

2. In the taskbar, click the **Internet Explorer icon**.

   The IE window appears.

3. Click the down arrow on the right side of the search icon and then, from the context menu, select **Add**.

   The *Add-ons* page of the IE gallery appears, as shown in Figure 7-5.

Figure 7-5

The *Add-ons* page of the IE gallery

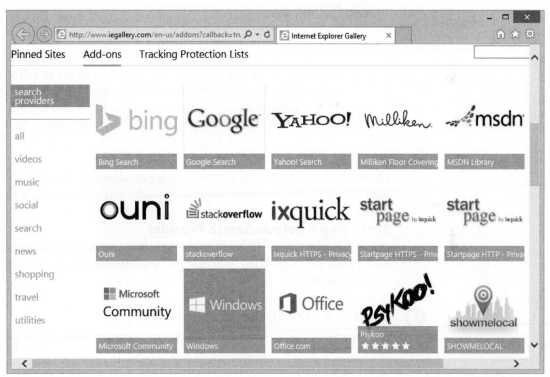

4. Click the tile for one of the web search or topic search providers.

   A page dedicated to that provider appears.

5. Click **Add to Internet Explorer**.

   An *Add Search Provider* dialog box appears, as shown in Figure 7-6.

Figure 7-6

The *Add Search Provider*
dialog box

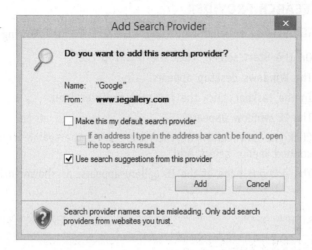

6. If you want the selected provider to replace Bing as the IE default, select the *Make this my default search provider* checkbox. If you want the provider to provide suggestions as you type searches, select the *Use search suggestions from this provider* checkbox. Then, click **Add** to add the selected provider to the *Instant Search* list.

Once you configure IE with multiple search providers, you can click the down arrow on the right side of the *Search* icon to select the provider you want to use for a particular search.

Specifying a Default Search Provider

When you first open an IE window, the default search providers *Bing*. Once you have added other search providers, you can specify a different default provider, using the following procedure:

 SPECIFY A DEFAULT SEARCH PROVIDER

GET READY. Log on to Windows 8.1 and then perform the following steps:

1. On the **Start** screen, click the **Desktop tile**.

   The Windows desktop appears.

2. In the taskbar, click the **Internet Explorer icon**.

   The IE window appears.

3. Click the **Tools** icon, and then from the context menu that appears, select **Manage Add-ons**.

   The *Manage Add-ons* dialog box appears.

4. Select **Search providers in the Add-on types** list, as shown in Figure 7-7.

Figure 7-7

The Search Providers list in the
Manage Add-ons dialog box

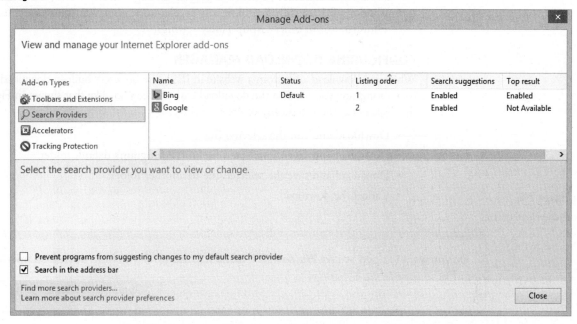

5. Select one of the search providers you installed earlier and click **Set as default**. The *Status* indicator changes to show the selected provider as the default.
6. Click **Close**.

CONFIGURING ACCELERATORS

Like search providers, *accelerators* enable users to send content to other resources, in the form of applications running on the computer or other sites on the Internet. However, instead of the user typing content into a search box, accelerators enable you to highlight content in a browser window and select the accelerator for the resource you want to receive that content.

By default, IE includes accelerators that enable users to email content, find it on a map, or translate it to another language. By clicking the *Find more accelerators* link on the *Manage Add-ons* dialog box, you can install new accelerators from the Microsoft Add-ons Gallery, using them to replace or augment the default ones.

Administrators can control the use of accelerators on Windows 8.1 computers using Group Policy. The settings are located in the Computer Configuration\Policies\Administrative Templates\Windows Components\Internet Explorer\Accelerators container.

The Accelerators Group Policy settings are as follows:

- **Add non-default Accelerators** – Enables administrators to specify additional accelerators to be installed on Windows 8.1 computers. Users can also add their own non-default accelerators at will, but they cannot modify or remove the accelerators specified by the administrator.
- **Add default Accelerators** – Causes Windows 8.1 computers to deploy the accelerators included with IE by default. Default. Users can also add their own accelerators at will, but they cannot modify or remove the default accelerators.

- **Turn off Accelerators** – Prevents Windows 8.1 computers from running any IE accelerators.
- **Restrict Accelerators to those deployed through Group Policy** – Prevents Windows 8.1 users from adding any accelerators other than those specified by the administrator in other Group Policy settings.

CONFIGURING DOWNLOAD MANAGER

When you download a file from a website in IE11, the browser's built-in download manager takes over, prompting you confirm the download with a dialog box like that shown in Figure 7-8. From this dialog box, you can do any of the following:

- Download and run the selected file.
- Download and save the selected file to the program's default folder.
- Download and save the selected file to another folder.
- Cancel the download.

Figure 7-8

IE download options

Do you want to open or save **Windows8.1-KB269....msu** (67.5 MB) from **download.microsoft.com**?   ✕

Open   Save ▼   Cancel

When you choose an option to proceed with the download, the process begins and control is immediately returned to the browser, so you can continue working as the download proceeds.

When the download finishes, the dialog box shown in Figure 7-9 appears, providing you with the following options:

- Run the selected file.
- Open the folder containing the file in File Explorer.
- Open the Download Manager window.

Figure 7-9

IE downloaded file options

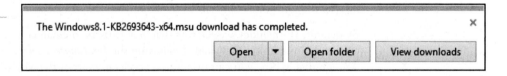

The Windows8.1-KB2693643-x64.msu download has completed.   ✕

Open ▼   Open folder   View downloads

The *View Downloads* window, shown in Figure 7-10, provides you with access to all of your previous downloads. You can also click Options to change the default download folder and select whether the manager should notify you when downloads are complete.

Figure 7-10

The IE View Downloads window

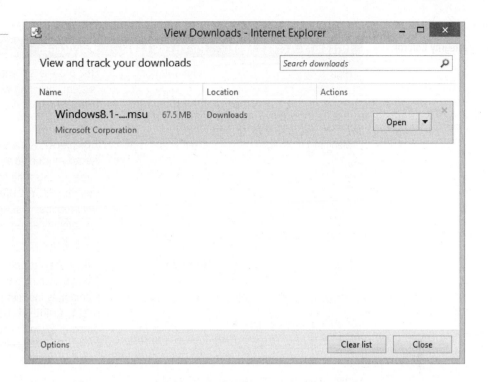

▪ Securing Internet Explorer

THE BOTTOM LINE

Apart from its performance features, IE includes a number of important security enhancements that help to protect users from malware incursions and other Internet dangers.

CERTIFICATION READY
Configure Internet Explorer 11 settings, including add-ons, downloads, security, and privacy
Objective 2.4

The web browser is the primary application that most people use to access the Internet, and as a result it is also a major point of weakness from a security perspective. The security improvements included in the Windows 8.1 release of IE provide users with the highest degree of protection possible without compromising their Internet experiences.

Understanding Protected Mode

One of the most important security features in IE is that, by default, the browser operates in what Microsoft refers to as *protected mode*. Protected mode is an operational state designed to prevent attackers that do penetrate the computer's defenses from accessing vital system components.

Protected mode is essentially a way to run IE with highly reduced privileges. Windows 8.1 includes a security feature called *Mandatory Integrity Control (MIC)*, which assigns various integrity access levels to processes running on the computer. These integrity access levels control what system resources the process is allowed to access. Table 7-1 shows the integrity levels assigned by MIC.

Table 7-1

Mandatory Integrity Control

INTEGRITY ACCESS LEVEL	PRIVILEGE LEVEL	PRIVILEGES
High	Administrator	The process is granted full access to the system, including write access to the Program Files folder and the HKEY_LOCAL_MACHINE registry key.
Medium	User	The process is granted limited access to the system, including write access to user-specific areas, such as the user's Documents folder and the HKEY_CURRENT_USER registry key. All processes that are not explicitly assigned an integrity access level receive this level of access.
Low	Untrusted	The process is granted minimal access to the system, including write access only to the Temporary Internet Files\Low folder and the HKEY_CURRENT_USER\Software\Microsoft\Internet Explorer/LowRegistry registry key

In Windows 8.1, IE protected mode means that it runs as a low-integrity procedure. The browser application can therefore write to only low-integrity disk locations, such as the Temporary Internet Files folder and the standard IE storage areas, including the History, Cookies, and Favorites folders.

What this means is that even if attackers manage to gain access to the computer through a web browser connection, there is little they can do to damage the system because they do not have access to vital system areas. For example, even if an attacker manages to upload a destructive application to the system, he or she cannot force it to load each time the system starts by adding it to the Startup group.

Protected mode is not a complete defense against malware in itself. IE10 and Windows 8.1 have many other security mechanisms that work in combination. Protected mode is designed to limit the damage that attackers can do if they manage to penetrate the other security measures.

DETECTING PROTECTED MODE INCOMPATIBILITIES

Because IE on Windows 8.1 runs in protected mode by default, it is possible that web-based applications designed to run on earlier versions might not run properly. These applications might be designed to write to a disk area that is inaccessible while in protected mode, or they might not know how to handle the new prompts in IE.

However, you might find that applications that did not run under IE version 7 now do run in IE11, using the default settings. This is because in IE7, websites in the local intranet zone ran in protected mode by default. In IE8 and later, Microsoft changed the defaults, and disabled protected mode for local intranet sites, as shown in Figure 7-11.

Figure 7-11

Protected Mode disabled

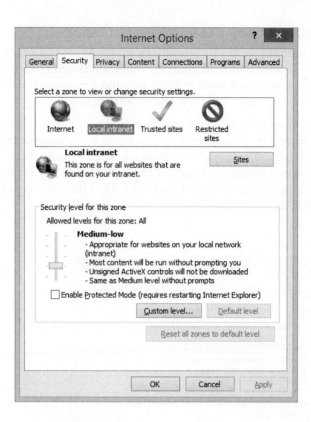

Comprehensive testing of all web-based applications should be an essential part of every Windows 8.1 or IE deployment. To gather information about application incompatibilities, enable *Turn on* **compatibility logging** setting in the Local Group Policy, located in the Computer Configuration\Administrative Templates\Windows Components\Internet Explorer folder or the User Configuration\Administrative Templates\Windows Components\Internet Explorer folder.

Once you enable the *Turn on compatibility logging* policy, Windows 8.1 begins logging all information blocked by the IE security settings. The logged data appears in the *Event Viewer* console in the IE application log.

RESOLVING PROTECTED MODE INCOMPATIBILITIES

Once you have determined the exact source of your application's incompatibility, you can use the following techniques to try to resolve the problem.

- **Move the site to the Trusted Sites zone** – IE maintains different security zones that provide applications with different levels of privileges. Sites in the Internet zone run in protected mode, with minimal privileges, but if you move them to the *Trusted Sites zone*, they do not run in protected mode, and receive elevated privileges.

- **Disable protected mode in IE** – Although Microsoft does not recommend this practice, you can disable protected mode by selecting a zone and clearing the Enable Protected Mode checkbox. Disabling protected mode causes IE to apply the medium integrity access level to the zone.

- **Modify the application** – Probably the most difficult and time-consuming option, you can also modify the application itself so that it can run properly using the minimal privileges provided by protected mode.

INTRODUCING ENHANCED PROTECTED MODE

In addition to the protection provided by protected mode, IE11 includes an extension of that feature, called Enhanced Protected Mode. Enhanced Protected Mode uses the same basic philosophy as protected mode to block unauthorized access to addition system resources, such as personal information and corporate network resources.

Enhanced Protected Mode runs by default in the *Start* screen version of IE11, but it is disabled by default in the desktop version because it is incompatible with some of the more popular plug-ins. The *Start* screen version does not support plug-ins, so this is not a problem, but when you check *Enable Enhanced Protected Mode* in the *Advanced* tab of the *Internet Options* dialog box, as shown in Figure 7-12, IE11 disables any installed add-ins that are not compatible.

Figure 7-12

Enabling *Enhanced Protected Mode*

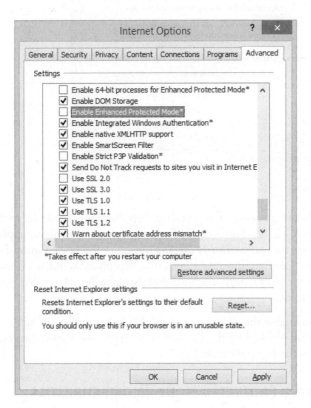

Configuring Security Zones

> With the appropriate development tools and programming expertise, web-based applications can do virtually anything that traditional software applications do, which can be either a good or a bad thing.

For companies developing their own in-house software, web browsers provide a stable, proven technological base. However, a web-based intranet application is likely to require extensive access to system resources. An intranet application might have to install software on the computer, for example, or change system configuration settings.

Granting this type of access is acceptable for an internal application, but you could not grant the same privileges to an Internet website. Imagine what it would be like to surf the Internet if every site you accessed had the ability to install any software it wanted on your computer, or modify any of your system configuration settings. Your computer would likely be rendered inoperative within a matter of hours.

To provide different levels of access to specific applications, IE divides the addresses accessible with the web browser into several different *security zones*, each of which has a different set of privileges. The four zones are as follows:

- **Internet** – All website that are not listed in the other three zones fall into this zone. Sites in the Internet zone run in protected mode and have minimal access to the computer's drives and configuration settings.
- **Local intranet** – IE automatically detects sites that originate from the local intranet and places them in this zone. Sites in this zone do not run in protected mode and have significant access to the system, including the ability to run certain scripts, ActiveX controls, and plug-ins.
- **Trusted sites** – This zone provides the most elevated set of privileges and is intended for sites that you can trust not to damage the computer. By default, there are no sites in this zone; you must add them manually.
- **Restricted sites** – This zone has the most reduced set of privileges and runs in protected mode. It is intended for websites that are known to be malicious, but which users still must access for some reason. As with the Trusted sites zone, this zone is empty by default.

There are two ways to modify the default zone settings in IE. You can assign websites to specific zones, or you can modify the security settings of the zones themselves. These two procedures are described in the following sections.

ADDING SITES TO A SECURITY ZONE

The easiest way to modify the security settings that IE imposes on a specific website is to manually add the site to a different security zone. The typical procedure is to add a site to the Trusted sites zone, to increase its privileges, or add it to the Restricted sites zone, to reduce its privileges. To do this, use the following procedure.

 ADD A SITE TO A SECURITY ZONE

GET READY. Log on to Windows 8.1 and then perform the following steps:

1. On the **Start** screen, click the **Desktop tile**.
   The Windows desktop appears.
2. In the taskbar, click the **Internet Explorer icon**.
   The IE window appears.
3. Click the **Tools** icon and select **Internet Options**.
   The *Internet Options* dialog box appears.
4. Click the **Security** tab, as shown in Figure 7-13.

Figure 7-13

The *Security* tab of the
Internet Options
dialog box

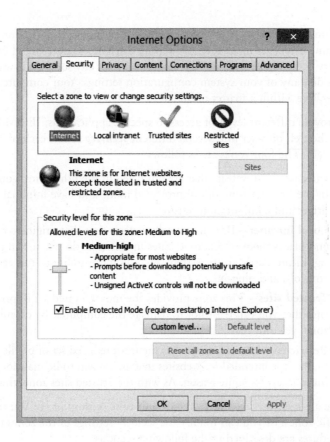

5. Select the zone, either **Trusted sites** or **Restricted sites**, to which you want to add a **site**.

6. Click **Sites**.

   The *Trusted sites* or *Restricted sites* dialog box appears.

7. Type the URL of the website you want to add to the zone into the *Add this website to the zone* text box, and then click **Add**.

   The URL appears in the *Websites* list.

8. Click **Close** to close the *Trusted sites* or *Restricted sites* dialog box.

9. Click **OK** to close the *Internet Properties* sheet.

CONFIGURING ZONE SECURITY

In addition to placing sites into zones, it is also possible to modify the properties of the zones themselves. Before you do this, however, you should consider that changing a zone's security properties will affect all of the sites in that zone. Decreasing the privileges allocated to a zone could prevent some sites in that zone from functioning properly. Increasing the privileges of a zone could open up security holes that attackers might be able to exploit.

To modify the security properties of a zone, use the following procedure:

 MODIFY SECURITY ZONE SETTINGS

GET READY. Log on to Windows 8.1 and then perform the following steps:

1. On the **Start** screen, click the **Desktop tile**.

   The Windows desktop appears.

2. In the taskbar, click the **Internet Explorer icon**.

   The IE window appears.

3. Click the **Tools** icon and select **Internet Options**.

   The *Internet Options* dialog box appears.

4. Click the **Security** tab.

5. Select the zone for which you want to modify the security settings.

6. In the *Security level for this zone* box, adjust the slider to increase or decrease the security level for the zone. Moving the slider up increases the protection for the zone and moving the slider down decreases it.

7. Select or clear the **Enable protected mode** checkbox, if desired.

8. To exercise more precise control over the zone's security settings, click **Custom level**.

   The *Security Settings* dialog box for the zone appears, as shown in Figure 7-14.

Figure 7-14

The *Security Settings* dialog box for the *Local Intranet Zone*

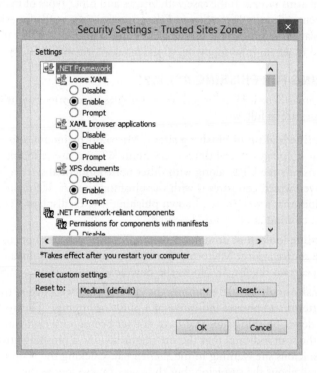

9. Select radio buttons for the individual settings in each of the security categories. The radio buttons typically make it possible to enable a setting, disable it, or prompt the user before enabling it.

10. Click **OK** to close the *Security Settings* dialog box.

11. Click **OK** to close the *Internet Options* dialog box.

Configuring the SmartScreen Filter

Social engineering is a term that describes any attempt to penetrate the security of a system by convincing people to disclose secret information.

Many would-be attackers have realized that discovering a user's password with an elaborate software procedure is a lot more difficult than simply calling the user on the telephone and asking for it. When asked for information by an authoritative-sounding person saying that they work for the IT department, most people are eager to help and are all too willing to give out information that should be kept confidential.

Phishing is a technique that takes social engineering to a mass scale. Instead of convincing-sounding telephone callers, phishing uses convincing-looking websites that urge users to supply personal information, such as passwords and account numbers.

For example, an attacker might send out thousands of email messages directed at customers of a particular bank, urging them to update their account information or risk having their accounts closed. Unsuspecting users click the hyperlink in the email and are taken to a webpage that looks very much like that of the actual bank site, but it isn't. The page is part of a bogus site set up by the attacker and probably copied from the bank site. This false site proceeds to ask the user for information such as bank account numbers, PINs, and passwords, which the attacker can then use to access the account.

Defending against phishing is more a matter of educating users than competing in a technological arms race, as is the case with viruses and other types of malware. IE11 includes a component called the *SmartScreen Filter* that examines traffic for evidence of phishing activity and displays a warning to the user if it finds any. It is up to the user to recognize the warning signs and to refrain from supplying confidential information to unknown parties.

FILTERING FOR PHISHING ATTACKS

The IE SmartScreen Filter uses three techniques to identify potential phishing websites. These techniques are as follows.

- **Online lookup of phishing sites** – Microsoft maintains a list of known phishing sites that it updates several times every hour. When a user attempts to access a websites, IE transmits the URL, along with other nonconfidential system information, to a Microsoft server, which compares it with the phishing site list. If the online lookup process determines that a website is a known phishing site, IE displays a warning. However, the user can continue to the site, if desired.

- **Online lookup of download sites** – When a user attempts to download a file, IE checks the source against Microsoft's list of known malicious software sites. If the source site appears on the list, IE blocks the download and displays a warning.

- **Onsite analysis** – IE examines the code of each webpage as the system downloads it for patterns and phrases indicative of a phishing attempt. This technique provides a means to detect phishing sites that have not yet been positively identified and reported as such. If the scan indicates that the site might include a phishing attempt, IE displays a yellow suspicious site warning in the *Address* bar. Clicking the warning button displays more detail about the suspicion, but the user can also ignore the warning and proceed.

DISABLING SMARTSCREEN FILTER

When you run IE11 for the first time, you can elect to set up the browser by using express settings, or by configuring settings individually.

The express settings option enables the SmartScreen Filter, but you can disable it at any time by clicking the Tools icon and selecting Safety> Turn off SmartScreen Filter, to display the Microsoft SmartScreen Filter dialog box.

Phishing sites present no danger other than the temptation to reply to requests for confidential information. It is possible to turn the SmartScreen Filter off and remain safe from phishing attempts, as long as you follow one simple rule: Don't trust hyperlinks. Never supply a password or any other confidential information to a website unless you type the URL yourself and you are sure that it is correct.

Most successful phishing attempts occur when a user clicks a hyperlink in an email or another website. It is a simple matter to create a hyperlink that looks like http://www.woodgrovebank.com, but which actually points to a server run by an evil attacker in another domain. However, as long as you yourself type www.woodgrovebank.com in the browser's *Address* bar, you are assured of accessing the true website of Woodgrove Bank.

Using InPrivate Mode

> IE has always maintained a record of each user's activities, in the form of temporary files, cookies, and a browsing history.

The user could delete these elements individually after the fact, but there was no easy way to prevent IE from gathering them all in the first place. *InPrivate Mode* is a feature in IE11 that enables you to surf the Internet without leaving any record of your activities.

InPrivate Mode consists of the following two technologies:

- **InPrivate Browsing** – Prevents IE from maintaining a permanent record of the user's activities during browsing session.
- *InPrivate Filtering* – Prevents third-party websites from compiling information about an IE user's browsing practices.

USING INPRIVATE BROWSING

To use InPrivate Browsing, you click the Safety button on the toolbar and select InPrivate Browsing. A new IE window appears, as shown in Figure 7-15. The InPrivate Browsing policies apply during the entire browsing session, including any additional tabs you create in that IE window.

Figure 7-15

InPrivate Browsing in IE

During the browsing session, IE stores some information temporarily, such as that found in cookies and temporary files, and deletes it when you terminate the session by closing the browser window. However, there is some information that IE does not store at all, including the browsing history, any data you supply in forms, and *Address* bar and AutoComplete data.

USING INPRIVATE FILTERING

Many Internet websites incorporate content from third-party providers, such as advertisements, maps, and videos. As a user browses to various sites that use these same providers, they can build up a profile of the user's browsing habits, and use that information to target them for specific types of ads. InPrivate Filtering enables you to block specific providers – or all providers – from gathering that information.

You can open a browser window that uses InPrivate Filtering by clicking the Tools button in the toolbar and selecting InPrivate Filtering.

CONFIGURING INPRIVATE MODE USING GROUP POLICY

AD DS administrators can configure InPrivate Mode settings for Windows 8.1 users all over the network using Group Policy. The policy settings are located in the Computer Configuration\Policies\Administrative Templates\Windows Components\Internet Explorer\ Privacy container.

The policy settings for InPrivate Mode are as follows:

- **Establish InPrivate Filtering threshold** – Specifies the number of sites in which a third-party content provider must be found before the site is blocked. The range of allowable values is 3 to 30.

- **Establish Tracking Protection threshold** – Specifies the number of first-party sites that a third-party item can be referenced from before it is blocked. The range of allowable values is 3 to 30.

- **Prevent the computer from loading toolbars and Browser Helper Objects when InPrivate Browsing starts** – Disables all toolbars and browser helper objects (BHOs) during InPrivate Browsing sessions.

- **Turn off collection of InPrivate Filtering data** – Specifies whether Windows 8.1 computers should collect InPrivate filtering data.

- **Turn off InPrivate Browsing** – Disables InPrivate Browsing for all browsing sessions. When you disable the setting, InPrivate Browsing is available for use

- **Turn off InPrivate Filtering** – Disables InPrivate Filtering for all browsing sessions. When you disable the setting, InPrivate Filtering is available for use.

- **Turn off Tracking Protection** – Disables Tracking Protection for all browsing sessions. When you disable the setting, Tracking Protection is available for use.

Browsing with Certificates

> *Secure Sockets Layer (SSL)* is the protocol that most websites use when establishing secure connections with clients over the Internet.

SSL communication is based on the exchange of digital certificates. A digital certificate is a credential, issued by a trusted party, that confirms the identity of the web server and enables the client and the server to exchange encrypted traffic.

SSL communications are based on a *public key infrastructure (PKI)*, which requires two encryptions keys, a public one and a private one. Data encrypted using the public key can only be decrypted with the private key, and in the same way, data encrypted with the private key can only be encrypted using the public key. A web server participating in a PKI receives a digital certificate from a *certification authority (CA)*, which contains its public key. The server also generates a private key, which it stores locally.

When a web server on the Internet establishes an SSL connection with a client, it transmits its certificate. Then, when the server sends data encrypted with its private key to a client, the fact that the client can successfully decrypt the data using the public key from the certificate confirms the identity of the server. When the client transmits data encrypted using the public key, only the possessor of the private key – the server – can decrypt it.

When a Windows 8.1 IE user connects to a site that is secured using SSL, a lock appears in the address bar, along with the name of the organization to which the CA issued the certificate, as shown in Figure 7-16.

Figure 7-16

A secure connection in IE11

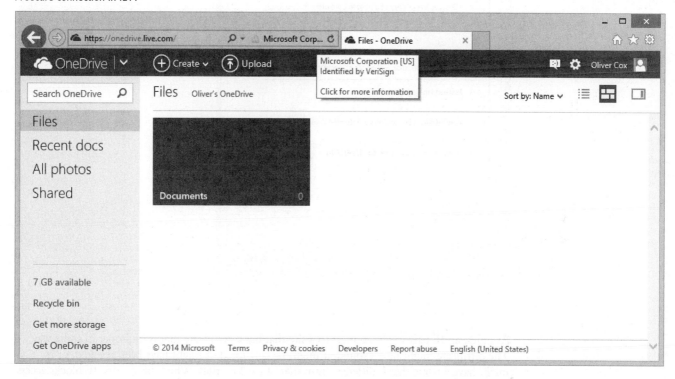

Clicking the lock icon displays more information about the site, including the identity of the CA that issued the certificate.

For even more information, you can click the *View certificates* link to open the *Certificate* dialog box, as shown in Figure 7-17. In most cases, the CA is a commercial entity, such as VeriSign or Thawte, which is in the business of issuing certificates to clients. If you trust the CA that issued the certificate, then you should trust the website that possesses it.

Figure 7-17

The *Certificate* dialog box

At times, an IE user might connect to a site that has a certificate that is improper in some way. The certificate might have expired, it might be corrupted, it might have been revoked, or it might have a name that is different from that of the site itself. When this occurs, IE blocks access to the site and displays a warning screen stating that there is a problem with the certificate. The user can then opt to close the browser window or ignore the warning and continue on to the site.

SKILL SUMMARY

IN THIS LESSON, YOU LEARNED:

- Many of the pages on the Internet still conform to old standards, and IE11 might not display them properly. To accommodate these pages, IE11 includes a feature called Compatibility View, which enables the browser to display older pages properly.

- One of the ways that IE interacts with other resources is through the use of add-ons. Add-ons are separate software components, created by Microsoft or by third parties, that interact with the basic functions of the web browser.

- Accelerators enable users to send content to other resources, in the form of applications running on the computer or other sites on the Internet. Accelerators enable you to highlight content in a browser window and select the accelerator for the resource you want to receive that content.

- Protected mode is a way to run IE with highly reduced privileges. Enhanced protected mode provides more protection, at the cost of compatibility with some add-ons.

(continued)

- Phishing is a technique that uses convincing-looking websites that urge users to supply personal information, such as passwords and account numbers. IE8 includes a SmartScreen Filter that examines traffic for evidence of phishing activity and displays a warning to the user if it finds any.

- To provide different levels of access to specific applications, IE divides the addresses accessible with the web browser into several different security zones, each of which has a different set of privileges.

■ Knowledge Assessment

Multiple Choice

Select one or more correct answers for each of the following questions.

1. What are the names of the two security zones in IE that have no sites in them by default? (Choose all that apply.)
   a. Internet
   b. Local intranet
   c. Trusted sites
   d. Restricted sites

2. Which of the following is NOT one of the add-on types supported by IE?
   a. Toolbars and Extensions
   b. Search Providers
   c. Accelerators
   d. SmartScreen Filtering

3. What does a broken window icon in the IE address bar indicate?
   a. A failure to successfully download a certificate from the website
   b. A webpage that is incompatible with IE
   c. A failure to update a subscribed RSS feed
   d. A failure to print a document from IE

4. Which of the following can be used to highlight content in a browser window instead of typing content directly into the browser's search box?
   a. Accelerator
   b. Search Provider
   c. RSS Feed
   d. Toolbars and Extensions

5. When you subscribe to an RSS Feed in IE, the content is updated how frequently by default?
   a. Weekly
   b. Daily
   c. Hourly
   d. Monthly

6. When downloading a file from a website in IE11, the browser's built-in download manager manages the process. Which of the following are valid options from within the download manager? (Choose all that apply.)
   a. Download and run the selected file.
   b. Download and save the selected file into the program's default folder.
   c. Download and save the selected file to another folder.
   d. Cancel the download.

7. Which of the following are true regarding IE in Windows 8.1 and the use of mandatory integrity control? (Choose all that apply.)
   a. IE runs as a low integrity access level.
   b. IE runs at a medium integrity access level.
   c. IE can write to the History, Cookies, and Favorites folders.
   d. IE runs at a high integrity access level.

8. By default, there are no sites included in which of these IE security zones; you must add them manually. (Choose all that apply.)
   a. Trusted sites
   b. Restricted sites
   c. Local intranet
   d. Internet

9. Which of the following represent techniques used by IE to identify potential phishing websites? (Choose all that apply.)
   a. Online lookup of phishing sites
   b. Onsite analysis
   c. Online lookup of download sites
   d. Offline lookup of download sites

Best Answer

Choose the letter that corresponds to the best answer. More than one answer choice may achieve the goal. Select the BEST answer.

1. The company is designing a new web-based application that is likely to require extensive access to system resources. Users will connect to it over their local network segment. To make sure the application works as planned, in which security zone should the website be placed to allow it to function at its full capability?
   a. Trusted sites zone
   b. Internet zone
   c. Local intranet zone
   d. Restricted sites zone

2. A new company has just installed Windows 8.1 on their computers. They want to be able to protect themselves against phishing attacks. Which combinations below will ensure they are using the best approach to defend against these types of attacks?
   a. Prevent browsing to any sites that are not included in the Trusted sites zone
   b. Educate users on how to recognize phishing attacks and use SmartScreen Filter to display warnings if the site is suspicious.
   c. Prevent browsing to any sites that are not included in the Local intranet zone.
   d. Place a list of known phishing sites into each user's Restricted sites zone

3. Several users on the network do sensitive research for the company using IE on 50 Windows 8.1 computers. They do not want IE to maintain a permanent record of their activities during their browser sessions? What is the best approach to use to address their need?
   a. Configure InPrivate Browsing on each of the computers.
   b. Configure InPrivate Browsing on a subset of the computers and direct the users to only browse when working at those computers.
   c. Configure InPrivate Browsing using Group Policy and apply it to the users' computers.
   d. Configure InPrivate Browsing using Group Policy and apply it to a subset of the computers; ask users to work on those computers only.

4. In Windows 8.1, IE runs in protected mode. Which of the following best describes the capabilities of IE when running in this mode?
   a. IE can write to the Temporary Internet files folder.
   b. IE can write to the Temporary Internet files and the History folders.
   c. IE can write to the Temporary Internet files, History, and Cookies folders.
   d. IE can write to the Temporary Internet files, History, Cookies, and Favorites folder.

5. The company is considering upgrading to Windows 8.1 but is concerned that some of their web-based applications may not be compatible. What is the best way to test for incompatibilities?
   a. Upgrade a few computers to Windows 8.1 and ask users to report any problems they have to the help desk.
   b. Upgrade all computers to Windows 8.1 and ask users to report any problems they have to the help desk.
   c. Upgrade a subset of computers that use all of the web-based applications and turn on compatibility logging via the Local Group policy.
   d. Upgrade a subset of computers that use all of the web-based applications. Ask users to report any problems. If problems are found, clear the Enable Protected Mode checkbox in the Local Intranet zone.

Matching and Identification

Complete the following exercise by matching the terms with their corresponding definitions.

    _____ a) Add-ons
    _____ b) Social engineering
    _____ c) Security zones
    _____ d) Accelerators
    _____ e) SmartScreen Filter
    _____ f) Protected mode
    _____ g) InPrivate Mode
    _____ h) Compatibility View

1. Describes any attempt to penetrate the security of a system by convincing people to disclose secret information.
2. Enables browser to display older pages properly.
3. Enables surfing the Internet without leaving any record of your activities.
4. Enable users to highlight content in a browser window instead of using the search box.
5. Examines traffic for evidence of phishing activity.
6. Used by IE to divide websites and assign different sets of privileges to each.
7. Provides a way to run IE with highly reduced privileges.
8. Software components that interact with the basic functions of the web browser.

Build a List

1. In order of first to last, specify the correct order of steps to configure a default Search Provider.
       _____ On the Start screen, click the **Desktop tile**.
       _____ Click the **Tools** icon, and from the context menu that appears, select **Manage Add-ons**.
       _____ Select one of the search providers you installed earlier and click **Set as default**.
       _____ Select **Search providers in the Add-on types** list,
       _____ Click **Close**.
       _____ In the taskbar, click the **Internet Explorer icon**.

2. Specify the correct order of steps to add a site to a Security Zone.

_____ Click the **Tools** icon and select **Internet Options**.

_____ In the taskbar, click the **Internet Explorer icon**.

_____ Type the URL of the website you want to add to the zone into the *Add this website to the zone* text box, and then click **Add**.

_____ Click **Sites**.

_____ On the Start screen, click the **Desktop tile**.

_____ Click **Close** to close the *Trusted sites* or *Restricted sites* dialog box.

_____ Select the zone, either **Trusted sites** or **Restricted sites**, to which you want to add a site.

_____ Click **OK** to close the Internet Properties sheet.

_____ Click the **Security** tab.

■ Business Case Scenarios

Scenario 7-1: Using the SmartScreen Filter

Several employees at the company you work for have recently been victims of identity theft. These incidents were the result of emails received by the victims requesting that they supply personal bank account information to a website or risk having their accounts closed. The website was, of course, not legitimate, and attackers used the information collected there to transfer funds from the victims' accounts. The company has recently upgraded all of the company workstations to Windows 8.1, and you are examining the capabilities of the SmartScreen Filter in the IE. Your superiors have told you that you can use any of the new IE security features for the company workstations, as long as they do not consume any additional Internet bandwidth.

Explain to your supervisor the various methods IE uses to protect against phishing attacks, and specify which ones you intend to use for the company workstations.

Scenario 7-2: Resolving Application Compatibility Issues

A web-based site is needed by all users on the company's network in order to perform research on the company's competitors. After installing Windows 8.1, calls start coming into the help desk indicating there are compatibility problems with the site. What are some techniques that can be tried to address the problem?

Configuring Hyper-V

70-687 EXAM OBJECTIVE

Objective 2.5 – Configure Hyper-V. This objective may include but is not limited to: create and configure virtual machines, including integration services; create and manage checkpoints; create and configure virtual switches; create and configure virtual disks, move a virtual machine's storage.

LESSON HEADING	EXAM OBJECTIVE
Creating Virtual Machines with Hyper-V	
Installing Hyper-V	
Using Hyper-V Manager	
Creating a Virtual Machine Using Hyper-V Manager	Create and configure virtual machines, including integration services
Configuring Virtual Machine Settings	
Configuring Guest Integration Services	
Managing Checkpoints	Create and manage checkpoints
Managing Virtual Switches	
Understanding Virtual Switches	Create and configure virtual switches
Creating Virtual Hard Disks	
Understanding Virtual Hard Disk Formats	Create and configure virtual disks
Managing and Configuring Virtual Hard Disks	
Moving Virtual Machine Storage	Move a virtual machine's storage

KEY TERMS

Dynamic Memory	**Hyper-V Manager**	**virtual hard disks (VHDs)**
Hyper-V	**checkpoint**	**virtualization**
hypervisor	**VHDX**	

■ Creating Virtual Machines with Hyper-V

THE BOTTOM LINE

Hyper-V virtualization technology has been providing virtualized server environments since Windows Server 2008. Windows 8.1 is the first Windows client version to include Hyper-V. Hyper-V supports a large range of virtualization features, many of which are included in Windows 8.1. This lesson introduces the client Hyper-V functionality in Windows 8.1, explains how it differs from Windows Server 2012 R2 Hyper-V, and explains how to effectively configure and manage the Hyper-V features and functions in Windows 8.1.

Hyper-V provides the capability to share a computer's hardware with one or more operating systems that run inside the same computer. The technology that enables this to happen is called a *hypervisor*. The hypervisor keeps the host or parent operating system separate from all the virtual machines installed. This allows for the installation and running of multiple guest operating systems as separate and secure virtual machines, all within one physical host computer. *Virtualization* is the technology that provides dramatic reductions in power consumption while increasing the utilization of data centers and individual servers, thereby saving money and resources. Microsoft has provided Hyper-V as a free component in 64-bit Windows 8.1 Pro and Enterprise editions only. Hyper-V also has additional machine hardware requirements, as follows:

- Windows 8.1 Pro or Enterprise edition (64-bit)
- Second Level Address Translation (SLAT) processor
- 4GB RAM

> **+ MORE INFORMATION**
>
> SLAT is a required feature for Hyper-V. SLAT leverages AMD-V Rapid Virtualization Indexing (RVI) and Intel VT Extended Page Tables (NPT) technology to allow users to run virtual instances of operating systems on their PC as if they were standard desktop applications. SLAT ensures that the end-user experience for all applications is optimized.

Installing Hyper-V

Client Hyper-V is available to install in Windows 8.1 Pro and Enterprise 64-bit editions only.

The hypervisor requires the 64-bit operating system to be able to act as a host for other 64-bit operating systems such as Windows Server 2012 R2. In the following exercise, you install Hyper-V.

 INSTALL CLIENT HYPER-V

GET READY. Log on to the Windows 8.1 computer with administrative privileges. To install the Hyper-V feature, perform the following steps:

1. On the Windows desktop, right-click the Start button and, from the context menu, select **Control Panel**.

   The *Control Panel* window appears.

2. Click **Programs**, and then in the *Programs* window, click **Turn Windows Features on or off**.

3. In the *Windows Features* window, expand the **Hyper-V** and **Hyper-V Management Tools nodes,** as shown in Figure 8-1.

Figure 8-1

Installing Hyper-V

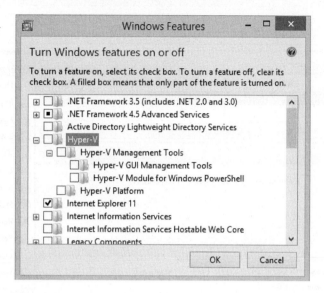

4. Select the Hyper-V Management Tools and Hyper-V Platform check boxes and click OK. Windows installs the Hyper-V feature.

5. Close the Programs window.

With the Client Hyper-V feature and management tools installed, the Hyper-V Manager and Hyper-V Virtual Machine Connection applications are available from the Windows 8.1 Start screen and the desktop.

The two new tiles you see after logging in with an administrative account are:

- **Hyper-V Manager** – The management console for creating and managing your virtual machines and setting up your test network.

- **Hyper-V Virtual Machine Connection** – Enables you to connect to a virtual machine that you have already created, much like the Remote Desktop Connection utility.

USING WINDOWS POWERSHELL

You can also enable Client Hyper-V using Windows PowerShell from a command line:

```
Enable-WindowsOptionalFeature -online -FeatureName
Microsoft-Hyper-V-all
```

Using Hyper-V Manager

Hyper-V Manager is a Microsoft Management Console (MMC) 3.0 snap-in application that enables you to manage the hypervisor on a local or remote computer.

When you start Hyper-V Manager from the desktop, the Microsoft Management Console window appears with the Hyper-V snap-in loaded (as shown in Figure 8-2).

Figure 8-2

Hyper-V Manager

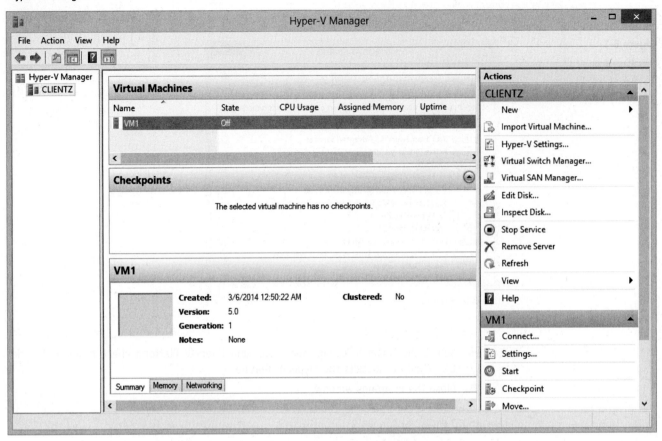

The Hyper V Manager snap-in consists of five panes. Their names and functions are listed as follows:

- Hyper-V Hosts – Provides local and remote connections to any number of Hyper-V host computers. The authenticated user and the computer account must have permissions to connect to the remote hosts.
- Virtual Machines – Lists all of the virtual machines contained in the currently selected Hyper-V host.
- Actions – The top section relates to the Hyper-V host computer, and the bottom relates to the currently selected virtual machine. All host networking and settings are configured in this pane.
- Checkpoints – Contains all saved checkpoints of the currently selected virtual machine.
- VM tabs – Provides a view of the currently selected virtual machine, with each tab showing a different area of functionality. The Replication tab appears only if the Hyper-V host and the virtual machine are enabled for replication using Hyper-V replica. Summary, Memory, and Networking tabs are always available. Double clicking on the Virtual Machine image connects the user to the VM.

Creating a Virtual Machine Using Hyper-V Manager

Hyper-V Manager is the only graphical tool available for creating a virtual machine. There are also Windows PowerShell cmdlets available for virtual machine creation.

CERTIFICATION READY
Create and configure virtual machines, including integration services.
Objective 2.5

A virtual machine consists of a virtual hard disk, some XML configuration files, and any checkpoints created in the environment when in use. You can create and manage all of these using Hyper-V Manager.

CREATE A VIRTUAL MACHINE USING HYPER-V MANAGER

GET READY. Log on to the Windows 8.1 computer with administrative privileges and run Hyper-V Manager. To create a virtual machine, perform the following steps:

1. Select a server and in the *Action* pane, click **New** > **Virtual Machine**.
   The *New Virtual Machine Wizard* starts. Click **Next**.
2. On the *Specify Name and Location* page, shown in Figure 8-3, type the name of the virtual machine and click **Next**.

Figure 8-3

The New Virtual Machine Wizard

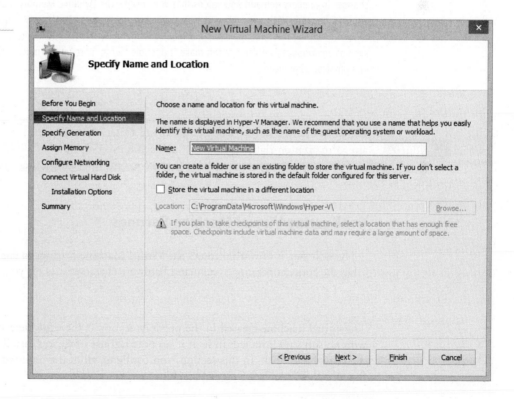

3. On the *Specify Generation* page, select the generation of the virtual machine you want to create, and click **Next**.
4. On the *Assign Memory* page, type the amount of startup memory required and choose whether to use dynamic memory for this virtual machine, and then click **Next**.
5. On the *Configure Networking* page, in the *Connection* drop-down box, select the desired network. This box is populated from the Virtual Networks created earlier in the Virtual Switch Manager. Click **Next**.

6. On the *Connect Virtual Hard Disk* page, select **Create a virtual hard disk**, choose the location, and then click **Next**.

7. On the *Installation Options* page, select **Install an operating system later**, and then click **Next**.

8. On the *Completing the New Virtual Machine Wizard* page, check the settings for the new VM and click **Finish**. Once completed, the new virtual machine appears in the Virtual Machines list of the Hyper-V Manager.

If you click *Start* in the Actions pane for the virtual machine (or right-click on the virtual machine and click *Start*), the machine starts. If you click *Connect*, a window opens (similar to a remote connection to the virtual machine) and you can see that the virtual machine has indeed started. However, because there is no operating system installed on the hard disk, a Boot failure error message displays. The next step in creating a viable virtual machine is to configure the necessary settings and install an operating system.

> **+ MORE INFORMATION**
>
> **Dynamic Memory** is a Hyper-V feature that helps you use physical memory more efficiently. With Dynamic Memory, Hyper-V treats memory as a shared resource that can be reallocated automatically among running virtual machines. Dynamic Memory adjusts the amount of memory available to a virtual machine, based on changes in memory demand and values that you specify. The Dynamic Memory feature enables memory to be adjusted between VM's even when they are switched on. As a result, Hyper-V can distribute memory more efficiently among the running virtual machines configured with Dynamic Memory. Depending on factors such as workload, this efficiency can make it possible to run more virtual machines at the same time on one physical computer.

> **TAKE NOTE*** Unlike Windows Server 2012 Standard and Datacenter, Windows 8.1 does not come with any virtualization rights. Every virtual machine you create in a Windows 8.1 Hyper-V environment needs a valid end user license for the operating system you install on it.

Configuring Virtual Machine Settings

> The next step is to work through the Virtual Machine Settings to ensure the virtual machine has the correct operating system and hardware characteristics for your desired purpose.

The virtual machine created in the previous section is the equivalent of a bare metal computer with no software installed on it. It is no practical use until you install an operating system on the virtual hard disk. In this section, you configure all of the required settings to create a fully functional Windows 8.1 virtual machine.

 CONFIGURE VIRTUAL MACHINE SETTINGS

GET READY. Log on to the Windows 8.1 computer with administrative privileges and run Hyper-V Manager. To configure a virtual machine, perform the following steps:

1. In the *Virtual Machines* pane click the newly created virtual machine, and then in the *Actions* pane for the virtual machine, click **Settings**.

   The *Settings* dialog box for that virtual machine appears, as shown in Figure 8-4.

Figure 8-4

The Settings dialog box for a
virtual machine

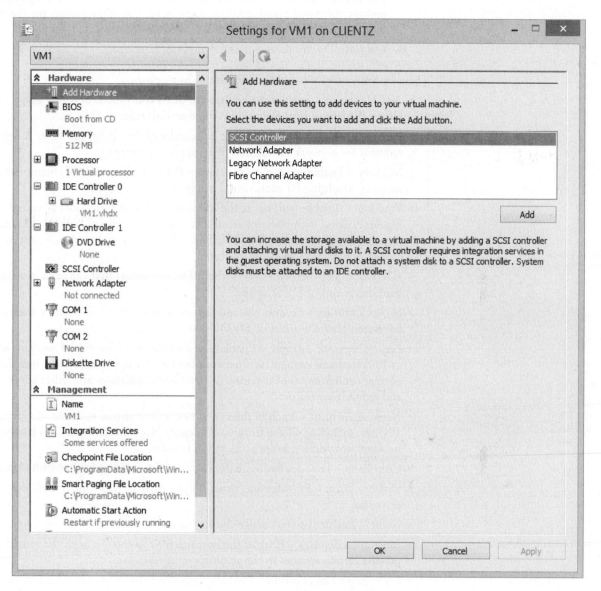

2. For a Generation 1 VM, in the *Hardware* section, under the *IDE Controller 1*
   section, click **DVD Drive**. For a Generation 2 VM, you must create a new DVD drive
   in the SCSI Controller section.

   This screen provides the options to connect the VM directly to the host computer's
   DVD drive, or to use an image file (*.iso, for example), or to have no media at
   all. In this instance, insert your Windows 8.1 DVD disc into the host machine DVD
   drive and click **Physical CD/DVD drive**. (The drop-down box enables you to choose
   which drive letter to use if the host has more than one optical drive.)

3. Click **OK**.

   By placing a DVD into the host DVD drive, the virtual machine also has access to
   the inserted DVD.

4. In the *Virtual Machines* pane of Hyper-V Manager, right-click the virtual machine and click **Start**. Then right-click the VM and click **Connect**.

The virtual machine starts, and the remote connection window opens. The boot process commences and because there is no operating system on the virtual hard disk, the VM boots from the DVD drive or DVD image.

5. Complete the Windows 8.1 setup process as normal.

There are many more Virtual Machine settings, as follows:

- Add Hardware – Enables the addition of SCSI controllers, network adaptors, and Fibre Channel adaptors to the virtual machine architecture.
- BIOS – Enables you to change the boot order of the virtual machine. A legacy NIC is required for network installation of an operating system.
- Memory – Enables you to set the startup RAM, Dynamic RAM, memory buffer, and memory weighting for each virtual machine.
- Processor – Enables you to set the number of Virtual Processors allocated to the virtual machine, along with resource control settings to balance virtual machine usage of physical resources across the whole host. There are as many virtual processors available as there are cores in the host machine.
- IDE Controller – Provides two virtual IDE controllers that can each have two devices, hard drives and/or DVD drives.
- SCSI Controller – Enables the addition of multiple SCSI controllers, each of which can have multiple hard drives or DVD drives.
- Legacy Network Adaptor – Enables the connection of the virtual machine to a network at 100Mbps and enables PXE network booting for operating system installation. Also enables configuration of dynamic or static MAC addresses and other advanced security and redundancy features.
- Network Adaptor – Enables the connection of the virtual machine to a network at 10Gbps, including all the features of a legacy NIC, but also provides bandwidth management and hardware acceleration features.
- Com Ports – Provides two virtual serial ports for communication with legacy devices.
- Diskette Drive – Provides one virtual floppy drive to allow the use of .vfd virtual floppy drive files.
- Name – Enables you to change the virtual machine name.
- Integration Services – Enables the host machine to interact with the virtual machine and provide certain services to the guest operating systems.
- Checkpoint File Location – Enables you to store the VM checkpoint in a location other than the default. Once you have created a checkpoint, this cannot be changed.
- Smart Paging File Location – Enables you to store the smart-paging file in a specific location, for speed or redundancy. This provides a reliable way to keep virtual machines running when there is not enough physical memory available. If a virtual machine is configured with a lower minimum memory than its startup memory and Hyper-V needs additional memory to restart it, Hyper-V smart paging is used to bridge the gap between minimum and startup memory.
- Automatic Start Action – Enables the automatic start of a virtual machine when the host starts (or to start only if it was running when the host shut down).
- Automatic Stop Action – Enables the virtual machine state to be saved when the host shuts down, or the virtual machine is to be turned off, or the guest operating system is to be shut down.

> **USING WINDOWS POWERSHELL**
>
> Windows PowerShell 4.0 Cmdlets enable you to configure Hyper-V virtual machines settings such as `Get-VMMemory` and `Set-VMMemory,` which enable you to access and configure the memory settings on a particular virtual machine. The following example enables dynamic memory on virtual machine VM1, sets its minimum, startup, and maximum memory, its memory priority, and sets its buffer:
>
> ```
> Set-VMMemory VM1 -DynamicMemoryEnabled $true -MinimumBytes 64MB
> -StartupBytes 256MB -MaximumBytes 2GB -Priority 80 -Buffer 25
> ```

Configuring Guest Integration Services

> In some cases, certain Hyper-V guest operating system features do not function properly using the OS's own device drivers. Hyper-V, therefore, includes a software package called *guest integration services*, which Hyper-V installs on your virtual machines for compatibility purposes.

Some of the functions provided by the guest integration services package are as follows:

- *Operating system shutdown* enables the Hyper-V Manager console to remotely shut down a guest operating system in a controlled manner, eliminating the need for you to log on and manually shut the system down.
- *Time synchronization* enables Hyper-V to synchronize the operating system clocks in parent and child partitions.
- *Data Exchange* enables the operating systems on parent and child partitions to exchange information, such as OS version information and fully qualified domain names.
- *Heartbeat* implements a service in which the parent partition sends regular heartbeat signals to the child partitions, which are expected to respond in kind. A failure of a child partition to respond indicates that the guest OS has frozen or malfunctioned.
- *Backup* allows backup of Windows virtual machines using Volume Shadow Copy Services.
- *Guest services* enables you to copy files to running VMs that are not accessible through standard virtual network connections. Guest services, which is disabled by default, uses the VMBus, a high-speed conduit between the host computer and the guest computers.

The Windows 8.1, Windows 8, Windows Server 2012 R2, and Windows Server 2012 operating systems have the latest guest integration services software built in, so you do not need to install the package on VMs running those operating systems as guests. Earlier versions of Windows, however, have previous versions of the guest integration services package that need to be upgraded, and some Windows versions do not include the package at all.

> **TAKE NOTE***   For Linux guest operating systems, you must download and install Linux Integration Services Version 3.5 for Hyper-V from the Microsoft Download Center.

To upgrade the guest integration services on a Windows guest OS, use the following procedure.

 INSTALL GUEST INTEGRATION SERVICES

GET READY. Log on to the server running Windows 8.1 using an account with administrative privileges and run Hyper-V Manager.

1. In the **Actions** pane, start the virtual machine on which you want to install the guest integration services and click **Connect.** A Virtual Machine Connection window appears.

2. From the **Actions** menu of the Virtual Machine Connection window, choose *Insert Integration Services Setup Disk*. Hyper-V mounts an image of the guest integration services disk to a virtual disk drive and displays an Autoplay window.

3. Click *Install Hyper-V Integration Services*. A message box appears, asking you to upgrade the existing installation.

4. Click **OK**. The system installs the package and prompts you to restart the computer.

5. Click **Yes** to restart the computer.

After you install or upgrade the guest integration services, you can enable or disable each individual function by opening the *Settings* dialog box for the virtual machine and selecting the *Integration Services* page, as shown in Figure 8-5.

Figure 8-5

Integration Services settings for a virtual machine

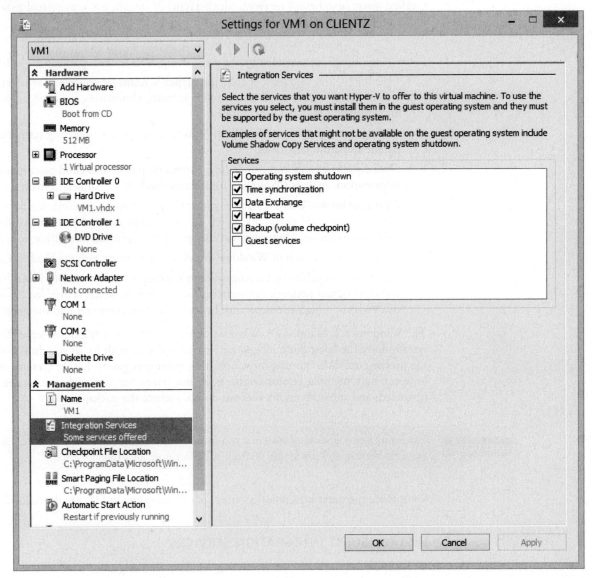

Now, you are ready to configure and manage the virtual machine as though you were working on a physical server. You can modify the network configuration, enable remote desktop, and install applications.

Managing Checkpoints

↓
THE BOTTOM LINE

Hyper-V provides a feature that enables a user to take a point-in-time image of the current settings and configuration and even the system state of a virtual machine. This image is called a *checkpoint* and is useful in testing changes to a setup or installation of software. If the changes fail, there is no need to uninstall or redo the actions; the ability to apply any checkpoint at any time enables quick and easy testing and reverting.

Hyper-V is a perfect tool for testing software development platforms and deployment of changes to production environments. It is normal for these changes to lead to errors and systems failures. The use of checkpoint data to recover from these errors andm to reset the VM to a previous point in time can save a considerable amount of time and effort when testing systems.

CERTIFICATION READY
Create and manage
checkpoints
Objective 2.5

Checkpoint data files are stored as .avhd files. Taking multiple checkpoints can quickly consume storage space. Checkpoint data files usually are located in the same folder as the virtual hard disk by default. Checkpoints are not recommended for use in production environments.

+ MORE INFORMATION

If the virtual machine is imported with checkpoints, they are stored in their own folder. If the virtual machine has no checkpoints and you modify the virtual machine checkpoint setting, all checkpoints you take afterwards will be stored in the folder you specify.

 CONFIGURE SNAPSHOTS

GET READY. Log on to the Windows 8.1 computer with administrative privileges and run Hyper-V Manager. To configure a Virtual Machine checkpoint, perform the following steps:

1. In the *Virtual Machines* pane, select virtual machine, and in the *Action* pane for the virtual machine, click **Start**.
2. Right-click the virtual machine and click **Checkpoint**.

    A checkpoint is created and appears in the Checkpoint pane for the virtual machine. The default checkpoint name is the name of the virtual machine with the date and time of the checkpoint in parentheses.
3. Right-click the checkpoint and select **Rename**, then type **Post Install**, and press **Enter**.
4. In the Actions pane, click **Connect**.
5. In the virtual machine on the *Windows 8.1 Start* screen, type **Notepad** and press **Enter**. Type some words in the Notepad window and save the document as after-checkpoint.txt in the default documents library.
6. In Hyper-V Manager, right-click the virtual machine and select **Revert**.

The virtual machine shuts down and the previous version saved in the checkpoint starts up. The document you just created in Notepad is not in the library, because you created the checkpoint before you created the file. Because you did not take another checkpoint after creating the document and before you reverted, the document is lost.

There are several other functions that you can perform on a checkpoint. You do this by right-clicking an individual checkpoint. The options are as follows:

- Settings – Opens the Virtual Machine Settings dialog for the particular checkpoint. A checkpoint file saves the hardware settings for a virtual machine and maintains them separately from the other checkpoints.
- Apply – Applies the chosen checkpoint and loads the virtual machine in the state that was present when it was created. If the virtual machine was saved or off when the checkpoint was taken, that is how the virtual machine will appear once applied. Likewise, if the virtual machine was running when the checkpoint was taken, it will reappear as a running virtual machine.
- Rename – Enables you to give the chosen checkpoint a meaningful and relevant name.
- Delete Checkpoint – Deletes all the checkpoint files.
- Delete Checkpoint Subtree – Removes the whole checkpoint subtree.
- Help – Provides basic Hyper-V help screens.

Managing Virtual Switches

 THE BOTTOM LINE   Hyper-V provides a software-based Layer 2 network switch. This switch enables virtual machines to connect to external networks and virtual networks on Hyper-V hosts.

The virtual switch sits between the host's physical network adapter, and the virtual machine's virtual network adapter to provide a layer of abstraction as well as additional security for the host and virtual machines.

Understanding Virtual Switches

A Hyper-V virtual switch is a software-based layer-2 network switch that is available in Hyper-V Manager when you install the Hyper-V server role. The switch includes the capability to connect virtual machines to both virtual networks and the physical network. In addition, a Hyper-V virtual switch provides policy enforcement for security, isolation, and service levels.

The Hyper-V virtual switch introduces several features and enhanced capabilities for virtual machines and multiple-tenant isolation, traffic shaping, protection against malicious virtual machines, and simplified troubleshooting.

The Hyper-V virtual switch enables independent software vendors (ISVs) to create extensible plug-ins (known as Virtual Switch Extensions) that can provide enhanced networking and security capabilities. Virtual Switch Extensions that you add to the Hyper-V virtual switch are listed in the Virtual Switch Manager feature of Hyper-V Manager.

The most important features of Hyper-V virtual switch are as follows:

- **ARP/ND Poisoning (spoofing) protection** – Provides protection against a malicious virtual machine using Address Resolution Protocol (ARP) spoofing to steal IP addresses from other virtual machines. Provides protection against attacks that can be launched for IPv6 using Neighbor Discovery (ND) spoofing.
- **DHCP Guard protection** – Protects against a malicious virtual machine representing itself as a Dynamic Host Configuration Protocol (DHCP) server for man-in-the-middle attacks.
- **Port Access Control Lists (ACLs)** – Provides traffic filtering based on Media Access Control (MAC) or Internet Protocol (IP) addresses/ranges, which enables you to set up virtual network isolation.

- **Trunk mode to a Virtual Machine** – Enables administrators to set up a specific VM as a virtual appliance, and then direct traffic from various VLANs to that virtual machine.
- **Network traffic monitoring** – Enables administrators to review traffic that is traversing the network switch.
- **Isolated (private) VLAN** – Enables administrators to segregate traffic on multiple VLANs to more easily establish isolated tenant communities.

There are three different types of virtual switches:

- **External:** Connects directly to a physical NIC, enabling the virtual machines to communicate with the external network as well as the host computer. Note that a physical NIC can be part of only one external network.
- **Internal:** Enables the virtual machines to communicate together and with the host computer.
- **Private:** Enables the virtual machines to communicate with each other, but not with the host computer.

CREATE AND CONFIGURE A VIRTUAL SWITCH

CERTIFICATION READY
Create and configure
virtual switches
Objective 2.5

GET READY. Log on to the Windows 8.1 computer with administrative privileges and run Hyper-V Manager. To create and configure a virtual switch, perform the following steps:

1. In the *Action* pane, click **Virtual Switch Manager**.

   The *Virtual Switch Manager* dialog box appears, as shown in Figure 8-6.

Figure 8-6

Virtual Switch Manager

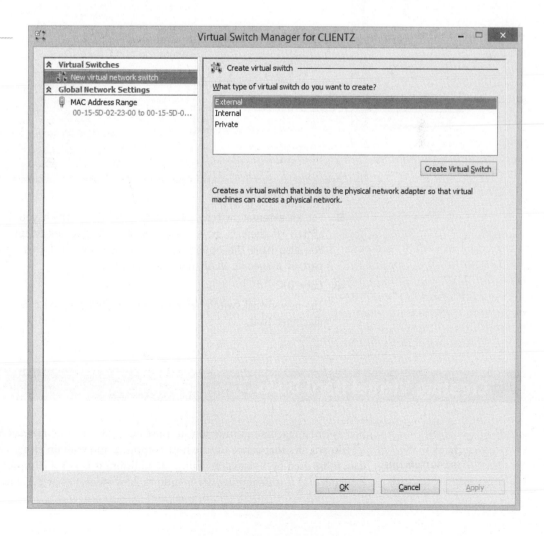

2. Select which type of virtual switch you would like to create; in this instance, and click **Create Virtual Switch**.

The *Virtual Switch Properties* page appears, as shown in Figure 8-7.

Figure 8-7

Virtual Switch Properties

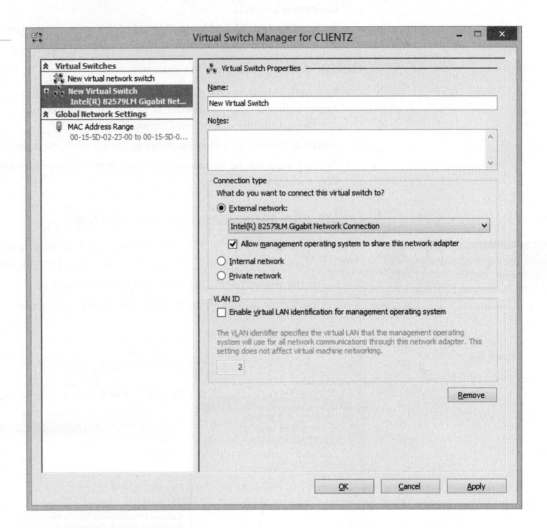

3. For an external switch, select the network to which you want to connect the switch (if there is more than one physical network adapter in the host computer). You also have the opportunity to set a VLAN ID if this network switch is to be part of a specific VLAN number. Click **OK**.

4. Click **OK**.

The new virtual switch has now been created and you can connect any of your virtual machines to it.

■ Creating Virtual Hard Disks

THE BOTTOM LINE

For a virtual machine to function, it must have one or more *virtual hard disks (VHDs)*. VHDs are files that reside on the host computer and contain either an operating system or data to be used by a virtual machine. In addition, it is possible to boot a physical machine from a VHD if it is running the Windows 7, Windows 8, or 8.1 operating system.

Understanding Virtual Hard Disk Formats

Virtual hard disks can be one of two different formats:

- **VHD**—A VHD file can be as large as 2040 GB (just under 2TB) in size and was the original format used in the predecessor to Hyper-V (Virtual PC).
- **VHDX**—A newer more efficient VHD format that can be as large as 64TB.

VHDX disks may have many advanced features, including the following:

- Support for virtual hard disk storage capacity of up to 64 TB.
- Protection against data corruption during power failures by logging updates to the VHDX metadata structures.
- Improved alignment of the virtual hard disk format to work well on large sector disks.
- Larger block sizes for dynamic and differencing disks, which enables these disks to attune to the needs of the workload.
- A 4-KB logical sector virtual disk that provides for increased performance when used by applications and workloads that are designed for 4-KB sectors.
- The ability to store custom metadata about the file that the user might want to record, such as operating system version or patches applied.
- Efficiency in representing data (also known as "trim"), which results in smaller file size and enables the underlying physical storage device to reclaim unused space. (Trim requires physical disks directly attached to a virtual machine or SCSI disks, and trim-compatible hardware.)

TAKE NOTE * The VHDX format is not compatible with versions of Hyper-V or operating systems below Windows Server 2012 and Windows 8. If you are creating a VM that is likely to be moved to a Hyper-V host running on Windows Server 2008R2 or Windows Server 2008, then it is necessary to use the VHD format.

 CREATE VIRTUAL HARD DISKS

GET READY. Log on to the Windows 8.1 computer with administrative privileges and run Hyper-V Manager. To create a virtual hard disk, perform the following steps:

CERTIFICATION READY
Create and configure
virtual disks
Objective 2.5

1. In the *Action* pane, click **New** > **Hard Disk**.

   The *New Virtual Hard Disk Wizard* appears.

2. Click **Next**. The Choose Disk Format page appears, as shown in Figure 8-8.

Figure 8-8

The *Choose Disk Format* page

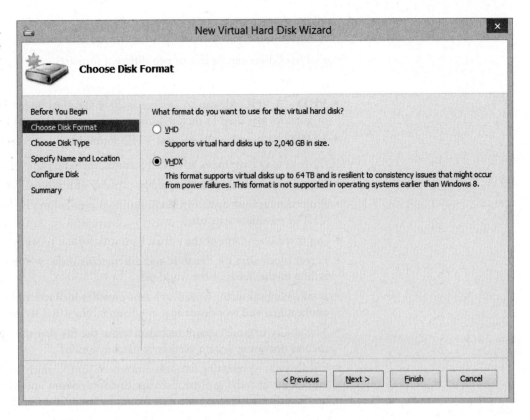

3. Choose the VHD or VHDX format for the disk you want to create, and click **Next**. The *Choose Disk Type* page appears.

4. Select one of the following disk types and click **Next**.

- **Fixed** – Provides better performance, especially on servers with high disk activity. The VHD file is the same size as the disk and does not change.

- **Dynamically expanding** – Makes better use of disk space but does not perform as quickly as a fixed disk type. The VHD file created is initially small but grows as data is added to the disk.

- **Differencing** – Linked to a parent disk. The parent disk is a read only disk, normally with a prepared and generalized version of an operating system installed. The differencing disk holds all subsequent changes made to the disk. This enables one installation of an operating system or parent disk to be used by many differencing disks without making any changes to the parent. This type of disk is not recommended in a production environment. The use of a single parent does introduce a single point of failure to all virtual machines using differencing disks based on that parent.

5. The *Specify Name and Location* page appears.

6. Type a name for the disk and click **Next**. The *Configure Disk* page appears.

7. Specify the size for a new blank disk or choose to copy the contents of a specified physical or virtual disk. Then click **Next**. The *Completing the New Virtual Hard Disk Wizard* page appears.

8. Click **Finish**.

➕ MORE INFORMATION
It is also possible to create a VHD from the Add Hard Disk page of the VM settings dialog box. You can also use this interface to attach a previously created VHD to a VM.

Managing and Configuring Virtual Hard Disks

Having created a new virtual hard disk, the next step is to attach the hard disk to a virtual machine. You do this in a VM's Settings dialog box. You can attach a hard disk to an IDE controller or a SCSI controller, the latter without. The latter maybe attached without switching the VM off, which is a useful facility. It is also possible to attach many hard disks to a SCSI controller than to an IDE one.

It is possible that a VHD may require some changes after it has been in use for some time. Using the *Edit Disk Wizard* in Hyper-V Manager, it is possible to convert the format and type of the original disk. The software actually does this by copying the contents to a new disk of a different type or format. In addition, you can compact or expand the disk's size.

There is one other useful utility available. Inspect a disk. This enables a user to see the size, location, format, type and file size of the disk, as shown in Figure 8-9.

Figure 8-9

Inspecting a virtual hard disk

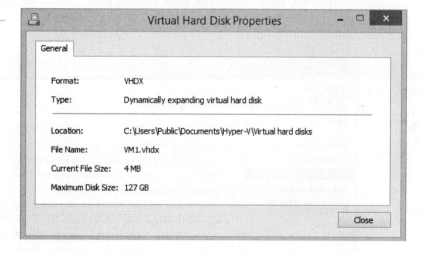

Inspect a disk is available in the Actions pane of Hyper-V Manager, or from the Add disk page of the virtual machine's Settings dialog box.

Moving Virtual Machine Storage

If you find that a virtual machine you created previously is running short on disk space at its present location, Hyper-V enables you to move it to another location using a feature called Live Migration.

Live Migration is a Hyper-V feature that enables you to move a vitual hard disk file to another location without shutting down the virtual machine. When you move a virtual machine, Hyper-V creates a mirror image of the VHD and, optionally, the VM configuration files as well, and then switches from using the original copy to the mirror images. You can leave the original image in place, for use as a backup, or you can remove it to reclaim the disk space. To use Live Migration to move a virtual machine's storage, use the following procedure.

CERTIFICATION READY
Move a virtual machine's storage
Objective 2.5

MOVE VIRTUAL MACHINE STORAGE

GET READY. Log on to the Windows 8.1 computer with administrative privileges and run Hyper-V Manager.

1. In the Virtual Machines pane, select a VM and in the Actions pane, click Move. The Move Wizard for the selected VM appears.

2. Click Next. The Choose Move Type page appears.

+ MORE INFORMATION

On the Windows Server 2012 R2 Hyper-V implementation, Live Migration can not only move a VM to another disk or to shared storage, it can also move an entire VM to another Hyper-V host server on the network without shutting it down, enabling administrators to redistribute their server loads without interrupting service. To option to do this appears on the Choose Move Type page.

---

3. Click Next. The Choose Move Options page appears, as shown in Figure 8-10.

Figure 8-10

The Choose Move Options page

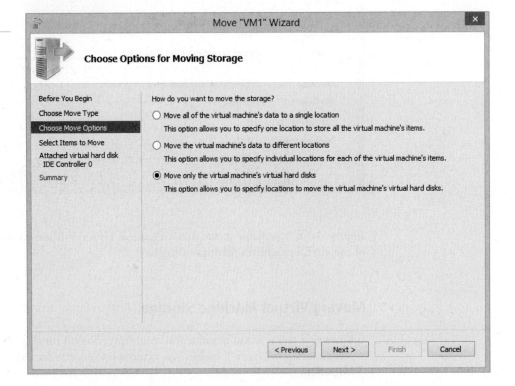

4. Specify whether you want to move all of the VM's data to a single location, all of the data to multiple locations, or just the VHDs to another location, and click Next. The Select Items to Move page appears.

5. Select the VHDs and/or other elements you want to migrate and click Next. The Choose a new location for attached virtual hard disk page appears.

6. Specify the location where you want to move the VHD file and click Next. The Completing Move Wizard page appears.

   If you opted to move the entire VM to separate locations, additional pages appear enabling you to specify locations for the VM's configuration files, checkpoints, and Smart Paging data.

7. Click Finish. The wizard copies the selected items to the locations you specified and switches the VM to those migrated images.

SKILL SUMMARY

IN THIS LESSON YOU LEARNED:

- Hyper-V virtualization technology has been providing virtualized server environments since Windows Server 2008. Hyper-V supports a large range of virtualization features, many of which are included in Windows 8.1 in a feature called Hyper-V.

- Hyper-V provides the capability to share a computer's hardware with one or more operating systems that run inside the same computer. The technology that enables this to happen is called a hypervisor. The hypervisor requires the 64-bit operating system to be able to act as a host for other 64-bit operating systems such as Windows Server 2012 R2.

- Hyper-V Manager is a Microsoft Management Console (MMC) snap-in application that enables management of the hypervisor on a local or remote machine.

- A virtual machine consists of a virtual hard disk, some XML configuration files, and any checkpoints created in the environment when in use. All of these can be created and managed using Hyper-V Manager.

- Dynamic Memory is a Hyper-V feature that treats memory as a shared resource that can be reallocated automatically among running virtual machines based on changes in memory demand and values that you specify.

- Hyper-V checkpoints enable a user to take a point-in-time image of the current settings and configuration and even the system state of a virtual machine.

- Hyper-V provides a software-based Layer 2 network switch. This switch enables virtual machines to connect to external networks and virtual networks on Hyper-V hosts.

- For a virtual machine to function, it must have one or more Virtual Hard Disks (VHDs). VHDs are files that reside on the host computer and contain either an operating system or data to be used by a virtual machine.

- Virtual hard disks can be one of two different formats: VHD—A VHD file can be as large as 2040 GB (just under 2TB) in size and was the original format used in the predecessor to Hyper-V (Virtual PC). VHDX—A new more efficient VHD format that can be as large as 64TB. VHDX disks have many advanced features.

■ Knowledge Assessment

Multiple Choice

1. Which of the following virtual hard disk types can be used to reduce physical hard disk storage in a production environment?
   a. Dynamically expanding
   b. Parent
   c. Fixed
   d. Differencing

2. Which of the following allows a virtual hard disk size of up to 64TB?
   a. VHDX
   b. VHD
   c. VFD
   d. VMDK

3. How many IDE controllers can a virtual machine have?
   a. 7
   b. 4
   c. 1
   d. 2

4. Which Hyper-V client utility is used to convert a VHD into a VHDX format?
   a. Create Disk
   b. Inspect Disk
   c. Edit Disk
   d. Add Disk

5. Which of the following is a requirement for using the VHDX format? (Choose all that apply.)
   a. Windows 8.1
   b. Windows Server 2012 R2
   c. Hard Disk of 4TB in size
   d. Virtual SCSI disk controller

6. Which VHD type is not recommended for use in a production environment? (Choose all that apply.)
   a. Differencing
   b. Fixed
   c. Dynamically expanding
   d. Encrypted

7. What is a requirement for booting a virtual machine from a network to install an operating system?
   a. Legacy network adaptor
   b. Network adaptor
   c. virtual switch extension
   d. Bandwidth management

8. Which of the following statements about the Virtual Switch Manager in Hyper-V client is not true?
   a. MAC address ranges can be specified.
   b. An external network may allow the host computer to share the network adaptor.
   c. The Private virtual switch is the default type when creating a new switch.
   d. VLAN IDs are not enabled by default

9. Which of the following is not a valid integration service in Hyper-V client?
    a. Operating system shutdown
    b. Heartbeat
    c. application integration
    d. volume checkpoint backups

10. Which of the following is not a virtual network adaptor advanced feature?
    a. DCHP guard
    b. Router guard
    c. NIC teaming
    d. Virtual machine queue

Best Answer

Choose the letter that corresponds to the best answer. More than one answer choice may achieve the goal. Select the BEST answer.

1. Which virtual format provides the capability to create a disk of 1.5TB in a Hyper-V client?
    a. VHD
    b. VHDX
    c. VFD
    d. VMDK

2. Which virtual hard disk type increases performance in a production environment?
    a. Dynamically expanding
    b. Parent
    c. Fixed
    d. Differencing

3. Which type of virtual switch enables communication between a virtual machine and the host computer?
    a. Private
    b. Internal
    c. External
    d. Virtual

4. To provide a host computer with the capability to share a network adaptor, which of the following should be enabled?
    a. An external network
    b. Virtual machine queue
    c. Private network
    d. IPSec task offloading

5. To allow a network adaptor to use a specific MAC address, which of the following should be used?
    a. Virtual Switch Manager
    b. Virtual Machine Settings
    c. Host Network adaptor settings
    d. MAC address spoofing

Matching and Identification

1. Identify which of the following are Hyper-V virtual hard disk format resource records.
    _____ a) VFD
    _____ b) VMDK

_____ c) VHD
_____ d) WIM
_____ e) VHDX
_____ f) UDIF
_____ g) VDI

Build a list

1. Identify the correct order in which a virtual hard disk is created? Not all steps will be used.

   _____ a) Choose the operating system.
   _____ b) Choose a disk format.
   _____ c) Enable BitLocker Drive Encryption.
   _____ d) Configure the disk.
   _____ e) Choose disk type.
   _____ f) Copy disk data.
   _____ g) Specify a name and location.

■ Business Case Scenarios

Scenario 8-1: Choosing a Suitable VHD Format

When creating multiple virtual machines using Windows 8.1 Professional, to minimize the host computers use of hard disk space, in a development environment, which implementation of a virtual hard disk format and type for all the virtual hard disks involved is best?

Scenario 8-2: Choosing a Virtual Network Switch

How do you create a small test network using Hyper-V client for which the test network must not be able to communicate with the Internet or with the host computer?

Scenario 8-3: Managing VM disks

A number of test networks run on a Windows 8.1 Hyper-V client system. One virtual machine runs out of space on its main VHD. The virtual machine can be powered down to achieve results. Which solution should be implemented to fix the problem?

Configuring IP Settings

70-687 EXAM OBJECTIVE

Objective 3.1 – Configure IP settings. This objective may include but is not limited to: configure name resolution; connect to a network; configure network locations.

LESSON HEADING	EXAM OBJECTIVE
Networking Basics	
The Physical Layer	
The Data-Link Layer	
The Network Layer	Configure name resolution
The Transport Layer	
The Upper Layers	
Connecting to a Network	Connect to a network
Installing Network Support	
Using the Network and Sharing Center	Configure network locations
Managing Network Connections	
Using TCP/IP Tools	
Using Ipconfig.exe	
Using Ping.exe	
Using Tracert.exe	
Using Nslookup.exe	

KEY TERMS

8P8C connectors

Automatic Private IP Addressing (APIPA)

classless inter-domain routing (CIDR)

connectionless protocol

connection-oriented protocol

data encapsulation

datagram

frame

Internet Protocol (IP)

media access control (MAC) addresses

network address translation (NAT)

Open Systems Interconnection (OSI) reference model

packet-switching networks

ports

protocols

router

socket

stateless address autoconfiguration

subnet mask

unshielded twisted pair (UTP)

■ Networking Basics

↓
THE BOTTOM LINE

The networking modifications introduced in Windows Vista were the most significant changes to the Windows networking engine since it was first incorporated into the operating system in Windows 95. Windows 8.1 networking now includes a revamped TCP/IP stack and a variety of new tools that simplify the networking process, for both users and administrators.

Networking is one of the primary functions of Windows 8.1. Most Windows computers are connected to either a private local area network (LAN) or to the Internet, and many are connected to both. These connections provide users with access to remotely-stored data, shared resources, network-attached hardware, and the virtually unlimited information and services available on the Internet.

To promote interoperability between hardware manufacturers' products, computer networks are, for the most part, based on independent standards. The networking capabilities built into Windows 8.1 are implementations of those standards. Before you work directly with the Windows 8.1 networking tools, it is helpful to have a firm grasp of the underlying principles on which they were designed.

Computer networking is a highly complex process, but most of the technology operates invisibly, both to the user and the administrator. Computers on a network communicate using *protocols*, which are nothing more than languages that all of the computers understand. These protocols operate on different levels, forming what is commonly known as a networking stack or protocol stack. The most common method for illustrating the operations of the networking stack is the ***Open Systems Interconnection (OSI) reference model***, which consists of seven layers, as shown in Figure 9-1.

Figure 9-1

The OSI reference model

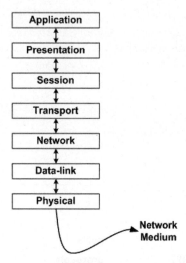

The following sections examine the functions provided by each of the seven model layers and the protocols that implement them.

The Physical Layer

> At the bottom of the OSI model is the physical layer, which represents the hardware that forms the network.

The physical layer of the OSI model consists of the cable or the radio signals that carry data from one system to another and the network interface adapters, which are the hardware components in the computers that provide the connection to the physical network.

Most cabled networks use a type of cable called *unshielded twisted pair (UTP)*, which is similar to the cable used for telephone wiring. UTP cable consists of four pairs of wires, with each pair twisted individually. At either end of each cable run are modular *8P8C connectors* (often incorrectly referred to as RJ45 connectors), which are similar to the RJ11 connectors used for telephones.

A network interface adapter is the component that provides the connection to the network. Most of the computers manufactured today have Ethernet network or wireless interface adapters integrated into their motherboards, but the adapter can also take the form of an expansion card that you install into the computer or an external device that connects to a Universal Serial Bus (USB) port. For wireless networking, the cables and cable connectors are replaced by radio transceivers that transmit the same data using a different kind of signal.

XREF

For more information on wireless networking, see Lesson 10, "Configuring Network Settings."

The Data-Link Layer

> As you move up beyond the physical layer, the subsequent layers of the OSI model are realized in software, as protocols that provide different types of communications.

Most Windows networks use a protocol called Ethernet at the data-link layer. Local area networks are sometimes described as *packet-switching networks*, which means that the messages generated by each computer are divided up into small pieces called packets, which the computer transmits individually over the network. A single file might be divided into hundreds or thousands of packets, each of which is transmitted separately. The packets might take different routes to the destination, and might even arrive there in a different order. The data-link layer protocol at the receiving computer is responsible for putting the pieces back together to reassemble the file.

➕ **MORE INFORMATION**

The cable on a packet-switching network, at any given moment, can be carrying packets generated by dozens of different computers. The alternative to a packet-switching network is called a circuit-switching network, in which two systems establish a dedicated connection that they use exclusively until their transaction is completed. The most common example of a circuit-switching network is the public switched telephone network (PSTN), the standard land-based telephone system.

TAKE NOTE *

There are other data-link layer protocols, but the vast majority of LANs today use Ethernet. Two computers must both be running the same data-link layer protocol to communicate.

For the packets to reach their destination, they have to know where they are going. Therefore, they require an address. Just like letters mailed in the post office, each packet needs an address identifying the computer that will be its destination. Ethernet is the protocol responsible for addressing the packets at the data-link layer, which it does by surrounding the data it receives from the network layer just above it with a header and footer, as shown in Figure 9-2. This header and footer and the data they contain are collectively called a *frame* and the process of applying the frame is called *data encapsulation*. The header and footer perform the same functions as the envelope does to a letter, protecting the contents and displaying the address of the recipient.

Figure 9-2

Data-link layer data
encapsulation

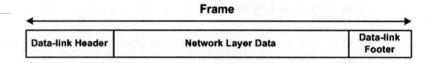

The addresses computers use at the data-link layer are six-byte hexadecimal sequences, usually hard-coded into each network interface adapter by the manufacturer. These sequences are called hardware addresses or *media access control (MAC) addresses*. The first three bytes of a hardware address identify the manufacturer of the network interface adapter, and the last three bytes identify the adapter itself.

In addition to addresses, the Ethernet header contains other information that helps to direct and protect the data in the packet. Each Ethernet frame contains a code that identifies the network-layer protocol that generated the data in the packet, and a checksum that the receiving system will use to confirm that the packet has not been altered in transit.

The Network Layer

The protocols that Windows uses by default at the network and transport layers are collectively called TCP/IP. TCP is the Transmission Control Protocol and IP is the *Internet Protocol*.

IP is the network layer protocol that performs many important networking functions. These functions are described in the following sections.

IP ROUTING

The term internet (with a lowercase "i") literally means a network of networks. The Internet as we know it (with a capital "I") is a huge conglomeration of networks, all connected together by devices called routers. A *router* is simply a device that connects one network to another. When you install a LAN in a home or office, and connect it to the Internet, you are actually installing a router that connects your network to another network belonging to an Internet service provider (ISP).

+ MORE INFORMATION

Windows 8.1 itself can function as a router. When a Windows 8.1 computer is connected to two networks, such as a LAN and an ISP's network, you can activate the Internet Connection Sharing (ICS) feature, which enables Windows 8.1 to route packets between the networks. In most cases, however, routers are not general-purpose computers, but rather specialized devices that are dedicated to routing functions.

IP is the primary end-to-end protocol used on most data networks. Data-link layer protocols like Ethernet are actually LAN protocols; they are designed to send packets from one system to another system on the same local network. An *end-to-end protocol* like IP is responsible for the complete transmission of a packet from its source to its final destination on another network.

To get to that final destination, packets must be passed from router to router, through many different networks. A single packet might pass through dozens of routers before it reaches its destination network. The IP protocol is responsible for this routing process. Every TCP/IP system maintains a routing table that functions as the road map to other networks. By examining the destination address on each packet, and comparing it with the information in the routing table, IP decides which router to send the packet to next. The next router to receive the packet does the same thing, and step by step, the packet makes its way to the destination. Actually, each router the packet passes through is called a *hop*, so it is really a hop-by-hop process.

IPv4 ADDRESSING

IP has its own addressing system, which it uses to identify all of the devices on a network. Every network interface in a computer, and every device that is directly connected to a TCP/IP network, must have an IP address. IP addresses are independent of the hardware addresses assigned to network interface adapters. A Windows 8.1 computer that is connected to a LAN has both a hardware address and an IP address.

As mentioned earlier, data-link layer protocols like Ethernet are LAN protocols; their addresses are only used to transmit packets to other systems on the same local network. The IP address in a given packet, on the other hand, always identifies the packet's final destination, even if it is on another network. This is why IP is called an end-to-end protocol. When you use your web browser to connect to a site on the Internet, the packets your computer generates contain the IP address of the destination site, but at the data-link layer, they carry the hardware address of a router on the local network that they can use to access the Internet. Thus, the data-link layer and the network layer both have their own addressing systems, and the two addresses do not have to point to the same destination.

The current standard for IP is version 4 (IPv4), which defines a 32-bit address space. Each address is split into two parts:

- **Network identifier** – As the name implies, specifies the network on which a particular system is located.
- **Host identifier** – Specifies a particular network interface (also called a *host*) on the network.

Unlike hardware addresses, however, which always use three bytes for the network and three bytes for the interface, IP addresses can have variable numbers of network bits and host bits. To locate the division between the network identifier and the host identifier, TCP/IP systems use a mechanism called a ***subnet mask***.

Subnet Masking

IPv4 addresses are expressed in dotted decimal notation, that is, four eight-bit numbers, separated by dots (or periods), such as 192.168.3.64. An eight-bit binary number, when expressed in decimal form, can have any value from 0 to 255. A subnet mask is also a 32-bit number, expressed in dotted decimal notation, such as 255.255.255.0. The difference between a subnet mask and an IPv4 address is that a subnet mask consists, in binary form, of a series of consecutive ones followed by a series of consecutive zeroes. When you compare the binary values of the subnet mask to those of the IPv4 address, the one bits in the mask represent the network identifier, while the 0 bits represent the host identifier.

For example, a Windows 8.1 computer might be configured with the following IPv4 address and subnet mask:

- **IP address:** 192.168.3.64
- **Subnet mask:** 255.255.255.0

The whole concept of the subnet mask is easier to understand if you convert both values from decimal to binary, as follows:

- **IP address:** 11000000 10101000 00000011 100000000
- **Subnet mask:** 11111111 11111111 11111111 00000000

In binary form, you can see that the first 24 bits of the subnet mask are ones. Therefore, the first 24 bits of the IPv4 address form the network identifier. The last eight bits of the mask are zeroes, so the last eight bits of the address are the host identifier. As a result, in decimal form, the network identifier is 192.168.3 and the host identifier is 64.

The original IP standard defines three classes of IP addresses, based on the byte divisions of their subnet masks. These classes, and their characteristics, are shown in Table 9-1.

Table 9-1

IPv4 Address Classes

	CLASS A	CLASS B	CLASS C
Subnet mask	255.0.0.0	255.255.0.0	255.255.255.0
First bit values (binary)	0	10	110
First byte value (decimal)	0–127	128–191	192–223
Number of network identifier bits	8	16	24
Number of host identifier bits	24	16	8
Number of possible networks	126	16,384	2,097,152
Number of possible hosts	16,777,214	65,534	254

Classless Inter-Domain Routing (CIDR)

In practical use, the IP address classes proved to be wasteful, and when the Internet first experienced a massive period of growth in the 1990s, it was feared that there might at some time be a shortage of addresses. To avoid assigning entire addresses of a particular class to networks that didn't have that many hosts, the IETF eventually published a new standard for assigning IP addresses called *classless inter-domain routing (CIDR)*.

CIDR differs from traditional addressing (now called *classful addressing*) by allowing the division between the network identifier and the host identifier to fall anywhere in an IPv4 address; it does not have to fall on one of the eight-bit boundaries. For example, a subnet mask of 255.255.240.0 translates into a binary value of 11111111 11111111 11110000 00000000, meaning that the network identifier is 20 bits long and the host identifier is 12 bits. This falls between a Class B and a Class C address, and enables ISPs to assign clients only the number of addresses they need, which conserves the IP address space.

CIDR also introduced a new syntax for IP network address references. In classful notation, an address like 172.23.0.0 was assumed to be a Class B address and use the standard 255.255.0.0 Class B subnet mask. In CIDR notation, the network address is followed by a slash and the number of bits in the network identifier. Therefore, 172.23.0.0/16 would be the CIDR equivalent of a Class B address. An address that used the 255.255.240.0 subnet mask described earlier would therefore look something like 172.23.0.0/20.

Private IP Addressing

Computers that are connected directly to the Internet must use IPv4 addresses that are registered with the Internet Assigned Numbers Authority (IANA). This is to prevent the duplication of IP addresses on the Internet. The IANA assigns blocks of network identifiers to ISPs, who assign them in turn to their customers. Once an organization is assigned a network identifier, it is up to the network administrators to assign a unique host identifier to each computer on the network.

Private LANs do not need registered addresses, so they can use network identifiers from three special ranges of private addresses that are reserved for that purpose. The three private address ranges are shown in Table 9-2.

Table 9-2

IPv4 Private Addresses

ADDRESS CLASS	IPV4 PRIVATE ADDRESS RANGE	SUBNET MASK
Class A	10.0.0.0 through 10.255.255.255	255.0.0.0
Class B	172.16.0.0 through 172.31.255.255	255.255.0.0
Class C	192.168.0.0 through 192.168.255.255	255.255.255.0

Internet routers do not forward these private addresses, so computers that use them are theoretically not accessible from the Internet. However, most networks today that use private IP addresses provide their computers with Internet access using a technology such as ***network address translation (NAT)***.

NAT is a feature built into many routers that takes the packets destined for the Internet that are generated by the computers on a private network, substitutes a registered address for the computer's private address, and then forwards the packets to the Internet destinations. When the Internet servers send replies, the NAT router does the same thing in reverse. As a result, an entire private network can share a single registered address.

Assigning IP Addresses

Windows 8.1 computers can acquire IP addresses in the following three ways:

- **Manual configuration** – It is possible for administrators to manually assign IP addresses to hosts and configure each computer to use the address assigned to it. However, this method requires much more time and effort than the other alternatives, and is prone to error.

- **Dynamic Host Configuration Protocol (DHCP)** – DHCP is a client/server application and protocol that enables clients to obtain IP addresses from a pool provided by a server, and then return the addresses to the pool when the clients no longer need them. Windows 8.1 includes a DHCP client, which it uses by default. The Windows server products all include a full-featured DHCP server, which you can configure to assign any range of addresses in a variety of ways.

- *Automatic Private IP Addressing (APIPA)* – When a Windows 8.1 computer with no IP address starts, and it fails to locate a DHCP server on the network, the TCP/IP client automatically configures itself using an address in the 169.254.0.0/16 network. This enables computers on a small network with no DHCP server to communicate without the need for manual configuration.

CERTIFICATION READY
Configure name
resolution
Objective 3.1

DNS NAME RESOLUTION

All TCP/IP communication is based on IP addresses, and in TCP/IP parlance, each network interface in a computer is called a host. In addition to IP addresses, hosts can also have names, and the host names are grouped together in units called domains. When users access a website on the Internet, they do so by specifying or selecting a DNS name, which consists of a host name and two or more domain names (such as www.adatum.com), not an IP address. This is because names are far easier to remember and use than IP addresses.

For TCP/IP systems to use these friendly host names, they must have some means of discovering the IP address associated with a specific name. This discovery process is called name resolution, and the application that resolves names into IP addresses is the Domain Name System (DNS).

DNS is a client/server application that is essentially a distributed database. Information about the names and addresses of Internet computers is distributed among thousands of DNS servers, all over the world. Virtually all operating systems have a DNS client, called a resolver, that enables it to send a host name to a DNS server and receive the IP address associated with that name in return.

In its most basic form, the DNS name resolution process consists of a resolver submitting a name resolution request to the DNS server specified in its TCP/IP configuration settings. When the server does not possess information about the requested name, it forwards the request to another DNS server on the network, a process called recursion. The second server generates a response containing the IP address of the requested name and returns it to the first server, which relays the information in turn to the resolver. In actual practice, the DNS name resolution process can be considerably more complex, but the basic message exchanges are essentially the same.

IPv6 ADDRESSING

When the IP protocol was first developed, in the late 1970s, the Internet was an experimental network used only by a few hundred engineers and scientists. At that time, the 32-bit address space defined in the IPv4 standard seemed enormous. No one could have foreseen the explosive growth of the Internet that began in the 1990s, and which soon threatened to deplete the existing supply of IP addresses.

To address this situation, work began in the 1990s on a new revision of the IP protocol, known as Internet Protocol Version 6, or IPv6. IPv6 expands the address space from 32 to 128 bits, which is large enough to provide more than 6.7×10^{23} addresses for each square meter of the Earth's surface.

Because this address space is so huge, IPv6 supports multiple subnet levels, and not just one, as in IPv4. Individual hosts can also have multiple IPv6 addresses for various purposes, with little chance of the address space being depleted in the foreseeable future. IPv6 supports automatic assignment of addresses, in both stateful and stateless configurations.

IPv6 also simplifies the packet header format by moving some of the IPv4 header information to optional fields. This reduces the size of routing tables and decreases the processing burden on routers throughout the IPv6 universe.

IPv6 Address Format

Unlike IPv4 addresses, which use decimal notation, IPv6 addresses use hexadecimal notation, in the form of eight two-byte values, separated by colons, as follows:

XX:XX:XX:XX:XX:XX:XX:XX

Each X is a hexadecimal value for one byte, resulting in a total of 16 bytes, or 128 bits. An example of an IPv6 address would be as follows:

FDC0:0000:0000:02BD:00FF:BECB:FEF4:961D

To simplify the address somewhat, you can remove the leading zeroes, leaving you with the following:

FDC0:0:0:02BD:FF:BECB:FEF4:961D

TAKE NOTE*

In hexadecimal (or base 16) notation, each digit can have a value from 0 to 9 or A to F, for a total of 16 possible values. Remember, an eight-bit (one-byte) number can have 256 possible values. If each hexadecimal digit can have 16 values, two digits are required to express the 256 possible values for each byte of the address ($16^2 = 256$). This is why some of the two-byte values in the sample IPv6 address require four digits.

To simplify the notation further, you can eliminate the zero blocks from an address and replace them with a double colon, as follows:

```
FDC0::02BD:FF:BECB:FEF4:961D
```

Subnetting IPv6

To identify the network bits of an address, IPv6 uses the same type of notation as CIDR, in which the address is followed by a slash and a decimal value specifying the size of the network prefix, as in the following example:

```
FDC0::02BD/64
```

This notation is the only way to identify subnets in IPv6; there are no subnet masks.

Understanding IPv6 Address Types

Much as IPv4 supports unicast, broadcast, and multicast addresses, IPv6 has three address types, as follows:

- **Unicast** – Identifies a single network interface in a computer or other device. Packets addressed to a unicast address are delivered to one node only.
- **Anycast** – Identifies a set of network interfaces. Packets addressed to an anycast address are delivered only to the interface closest to the source (by number of hops).
- **Multicast** – Identifies a group of multiple network interfaces. Packets addressed to a multicast address are delivered to all of the interfaces designated as members of the group. One standard multicast address, known as the "all nodes" multicast group, performs the role of the IPv4 broadcast address, so there is no need for an explicit broadcast address type in IPv6.

IPv6 addresses each have a scope, which defines the area within which the address is unique. The scopes defined in the IPv6 standards are as follows:

- **Node local unicast** – Limited to an individual interface. This is the equivalent to the loopback address in IPv4.
- **Link local unicast** – Limited to systems on the directly-attached network.
- **Unique local unicast** – Routable within an organization. The IPv6 equivalent of the 10.0.0.0/8, 172.16.0.0/16, and 192.168.0.0/24 private network addresses in IPv4.
- **Site local unicast** – Limited to interfaces at a single site. Once intended to be the equivalent of private IPv4 addresses, this scope is now deprecated.
- **Organization local** – Designed to span multiple sites belonging to an individual organization.
- **Global** – Unique throughout the IPv6 universe.

IPv6 Name Resolution

Name resolution for computers with global IPv6 addresses is provided by the Domain Name System (DNS), just as it is in IPv4. For computers with link-local addresses, which might not have access to a DNS server, the system uses the *Link Local Multicast Name Resolution (LLMNR)* protocol.

To use LLMNR, systems transmit name query request messages as multicasts to the local network. The request contains the name the computer is trying to resolve. The other computers on the local network, on receiving the messages, compare the requested name with their own names. The computer with the requested name then replies with a message containing its IP address, which it transmits as a unicast to the original requestor.

IPv6 Address Autoconfiguration

At the time IPv4 was conceived, there were some data-link layer implementations that required network administrators to manually assign addresses to the network interface hardware for media access control purposes. The designers of IPv4 therefore decided to design an addressing system that was completely independent from the underlying protocol at the data-link layer.

Today, all network interface adapters have factory-assigned hardware addresses, so IPv6 derives its host identifiers from those hardware addresses. There is therefore no need for APIPA or NAT or DHCP host address assignments.

IPv6 address assignment is much more of an automatic process than in IPv4. A technique called ***stateless address autoconfiguration*** enables computers to configure their own addresses after transmitting router solicitation multicasts to the routers on the network and receiving router advertisement messages in return. For situations where stateless autoconfiguration is not appropriate, Windows 8.1 workstations can use DHCP for stateful network address autoconfiguration instead.

IPv6 Transition

More than ten years after the initial publication of the IPv6 standard, and despite its almost universal operating system and router support, the vast majority of the systems on the Internet still rely on IPv4. However, the inclusion of IPv6 support in Windows 8.1 and Windows Server 2012 R2 makes the operating systems ready for the transition when it occurs. Windows 8.1, by default, installs support for both IPv4 and IPv6 addressing when it detects a network interface adapter in the computer, as shown in Figure 9-3. Microsoft refers to this as Windows 8.1's *dual IP stack*.

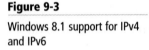

Figure 9-3

Windows 8.1 support for IPv4 and IPv6

In addition, the DHCP Server application in Windows Server 2012 R2 supports both addressing standards, so when a Windows 8.1 computer requests IP addresses, the DHCP server can supply both IPv4 and IPv6 information. Windows 8.1 applications that are capable of using IPv6 do so by default; otherwise, applications revert to IPv4.

As the transition from IPv4 to IPv6 proceeds, there are times when it is necessary for computers running IPv6-only applications to exchange messages over an IPv4-only network. For example, computers at different locations cannot communicate over the Internet using IPv6, because as of this writing, the Internet still uses IPv4. However, Windows 8.1 (and Windows Server 2012 R2) support a number of transition mechanisms that make this communication possible, including the following:

- **IPv4-compatible addresses** – A hybrid IPv6/IPv4 address that enables an IPv6 system to communicate using an IPv4 infrastructure. The address format consists of 96 bits of zeroes, followed by an IPv4 address in its standard dotted decimal notation, as in the following example:
  `::192.168.1.99`.

- **IPv4-mapped addresses** – A hybrid IPv6/IPv4 address that enables an IPv6 system to recognize an IPv4-only system. The address format consists of 80 bits of zeroes, followed by 16 bits of ones, followed by an IPv4 address in its standard dotted decimal notation, as in the following example:
  `::ffff:192.168.1.99`.

- **6to4** – A tunneling technology that enables computers to transmit IPv6 packets over an IPv4 network. The 6to4 address that an IPv6 system uses when connecting to the IPv6 Internet through an intermediate IPv4 network takes the following format: 2002:<first 16 bits of the IPv4 address>:<second 16 bits of the IPv4 address>::/16. For example, the IPv4 address 192.168.1.99 would appear as follows:
  `2002:C0A8:0163::/16`.

- **Teredo** – A tunneling protocol that enables computers to transmit IPv6 packets through NAT routers that do not support IPv6. A Teredo address consists of a 32-bit prefix: 2001:0000, followed by the IPv4 address of the Teredo server, 16 flag bits, and the UDP port number and public IPv4 address of the NAT router. These last 48 bits are obfuscated by having their bit values reversed.

> **TAKE NOTE**
>
> Tunneling is a networking technique that enables systems to encapsulate packets within other packets, for security or compatibility purposes. In the case of 6to4, for example, a computer encapsulates IPv6 packets within IPv4 packets using UDP, so that the system can transmit them over an IPv4 network.

NETWORK LAYER DATA ENCAPSULATION

Earlier in this lesson, you learned how data-link layer protocols encapsulate data for transmission, much as an envelope encapsulates a letter for mailing. IP encapsulates data as well, so that it can provide the address of the system that is the packet's final destination. In fact, IP performs its encapsulation first, by adding a header to the data it receives from the transport layer protocol. This header includes the packet's source and destination IP addresses, as well as other information that facilitates the transmission of the packet.

After IP adds its header, it sends the packet down to the data-link layer, where Ethernet adds its own header and footer to the packet. Thus, the data-link layer packet that gets transmitted over the network consists of transport layer data, encapsulated within an IP packet, which is called a *datagram*, which is in turn encapsulated within an Ethernet frame, as shown in Figure 9-4.

Figure 9-4

IP data encapsulation

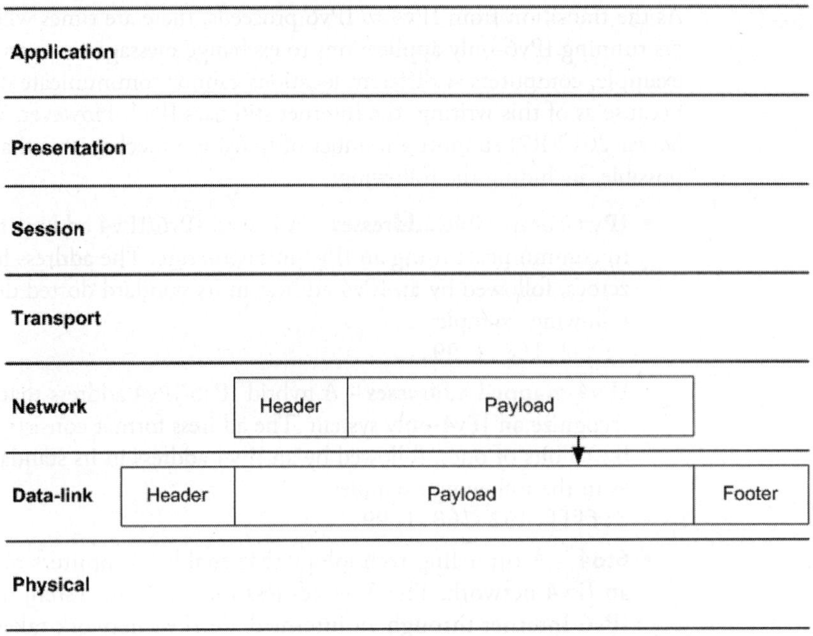

Application

Presentation

Session

Transport

Network		Header	Payload	

Data-link	Header	Payload		Footer

Physical

As with Ethernet, one of the functions of the IP header is to identify the protocol that generated the data in the datagram. The Protocol field in the IP header uses codes standardized by the IANA to specify the transport layer protocol that created the packet.

The Transport Layer

The OSI reference model calls for the network and transport layers to provide a flexible quality of service, so that applications can operate at peak efficiency.

There are two types of protocols that operate at the network and transport layers:

- **Connection-oriented** – A *connection-oriented protocol* is one in which two communicating systems establish a connection before they transmit any data. Once the connection is established, the computers exchange packets with complex headers designed to provide error detection and correction. A connection-oriented protocol ensures bit-perfect data transmissions, but at the price of greatly increased overhead.

- **Connectionless** – A *connectionless protocol* does not require the establishment of a connection, nor does it perform error detection or correction. Systems simply transmit their packets to the destination, without knowing if the destination system is ready to accept data, or if it even exists. Connectionless protocols do not guarantee delivery of their data, but they operate with a very low overhead that conserves network bandwidth.

IP, at the network layer, is a connectionless protocol, and there is no connection-oriented alternative at that layer. At the transport layer, TCP is the connection-oriented protocol, and the connectionless alternative is the User Datagram Protocol (UDP).

CONNECTION-ORIENTED PROTOCOLS

Applications that use TCP require every bit of data they transmit to be received properly at the destination. For example, if you download a service pack from the Microsoft website, a single garbled bit could render the package useless. Using the combination of TCP and IP guarantees that every message eventually arrives intact. If a packet is damaged or lost, the systems retransmit it. However, to use TCP, the systems must exchange extra packets to establish a connection and append a 20-byte header to each packet. This adds up to a lot of extra data that have to be transmitted over the network.

CONNECTIONLESS PROTOCOLS

Applications that use UDP are not terribly concerned if a packet goes astray. There are two reasons why this can be so. Either the messages are so small that the systems can easily retransmit them if they do not receive a response, or the data transmitted by the application is of a type that can tolerate the loss of an occasional packet.

An example of the former reason is the Domain Name System (DNS) communications that are a part of every Internet transaction. When you type a URL into your web browser, the first thing the system does is send a UDP message to a DNS server requesting the IP address corresponding to the domain name in the URL. This is a tiny message that fits in a single packet, so it's not worth transmitting several additional packets to establish a TCP connection. It's more economical just to retransmit the DNS request if no response if forthcoming.

A good example of the latter reason is streaming video. A video stream consists of large amounts of data, but unlike a file transfer, a few missing bits will not cause a catastrophic failure. A few packets lost from a video stream due to damaged UDP packets might mean a few lost frames, but that would hardly be noticeable to the viewer. The alternative, using TCP to transmit all of the packets, would provide a perfect viewing experience for the user, but at the cost of vastly increased bandwidth.

PORTS AND SOCKETS

Just like the network and data-link layers, transport layer protocols encapsulate the data they receive from the layer above by appending a header to each packet, as shown in Figure 9-5. Unlike the lower layers, however, transport layer protocols are not concerned with addressing packets to the correct system. This addressing is performed by IP and Ethernet, so there is no need for it here. However, transport layer protocols are concerned with identifying the applications that created the packet and to which the packet will ultimately be delivered.

Figure 9-5

Transport layer data encapsulation

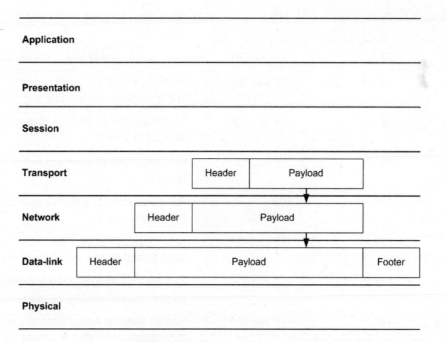

As with the protocol codes included in IP headers, the TCP and UDP headers both contain codes that identify specific applications running on the system. The codes are called *ports*, and the combination of an IP address and a port number is called a *socket*. For example, the standard port number for the Hypertext Transfer Protocol (HTTP), the application layer protocol used for web communications, is 80. If your web browser is sending an HTTP request to a web server with the IP address 192.168.87.33, the web server application on that computer can be identified by the socket 192.168.87.33:80.

There are two basic types of port numbers: *well-known port numbers*, which are numbers permanently assigned to specific applications, and *ephemeral port numbers*, which are random values created automatically by client applications. In the previous example, the web browser is using the well-known HTTP port 80 as the destination for its packets, but the source port would be an ephemeral port number created by the system running the browser.

This system works because the client is initiating contact with the server. The client has to know the port number to use in its messages to the server, so it uses a well-known port. There is no need for the client to have a well-known port number because the server will be able to discover the client's ephemeral port number from its incoming messages.

Table 9-3

Well-Known Port Numbers Used by TCP and UDP

Some of the most common well-known port numbers are listed in Table 9-3.

SERVICE NAME	PORT NUMBER	PROTOCOL	FUNCTION
ftp-data	20	TCP	FTP data channel; used for transmitting files between systems
ftp	21	TCP	FTP control channel; used by FTP-connected systems for exchanging commands and responses
Ssh	22	TCP and UDP	SSH (Secure Shell) Remote Login Protocol; used to security log on to a computer from another computer on the same network and execute commands.
telnet	23	TCP	Telnet; used to execute commands on network-connected systems
Smtp	25	TCP	Simple Mail Transport Protocol (SMTP); used to send email messages
Domain	53	TCP and UDP	DNS; used to receive host name resolution requests from clients
Bootps	67	TCP and UDP	Bootstrap Protocol (BOOTP) and DHCP servers; used to receive TCP/IP configuration requests from clients
Bootpc	68	TCP and UDP	BOOTP and DHCP clients; used to send TCP/IP configuration requests to servers
http	80	TCP	HTTP; used by Web servers to receive requests from client browsers
pop3	110	TCP	Post Office Protocol 3 (POP3); used to retrieve email requests from clients
nntp	119	TCP and UDP	Network News Transfer Protocol; used to post and distribute messages to, and retrieve them from, Usenet servers on the Internet.
ntp	123	TCP and UDP	Network Time Protocol; used to exchange time signals for the purpose of synchronizing the clocks in network computers.
imap	143	TCP and UDP	Internet Message Access Protocol version 4; used by email client programs to retrieve messages from a mail server
snmp	161	TCP and UDP	Simple Network Management Protocol (SNMP); used by SNMP agents to transmit status information to a network management console
https	443	TCP and UDP	Hypertext Transfer Protocol Over TLS/SSL;

TRANSPORT LAYER DATA ENCAPSULATION

The headers that the TCP and UDP protocols add to the data they receive from the application layer are vastly different in size and complexity. The headers for both protocols contain source and destination port numbers. The UDP header includes little else, except for a checksum used to check for errors in the header. The TCP header, on the other hand, includes a multitude of fields that implement additional services, including the following:

- **Packet acknowledgment** – Informs the sender which packets have been delivered successfully.
- **Error correction** – Informs the sender which packets must be retransmitted.
- **Flow control** – Regulates the rate at which the sending system transmits its data.

The Upper Layers

> The application layer is the top of the networking stack, and as such, it provides the entrance point for programs running on a computer.

Windows applications themselves have no networking capabilities. They simply make function calls to application layer protocols, which in turn initiate the entire network communications process.

TAKE NOTE* In TCP/IP, the session and presentation layers do not have individual protocols dedicated to them. In most cases, application layer protocols include functions attributed to all of the top three layers.

For example, a mail client is a program that enables you to send messages to users on other computers, but the mail program knows nothing about the nature of your network. When you send an email message to someone, the client takes the message and the address of the intended recipient and packages it using an application layer protocol called Simple Mail Transfer Protocol (SMTP). SMTP creates a properly formatted email message and passes it down to the proper protocol at the next lower layer in the networking stack, the transport layer, which for this application is TCP.

TCP then adds its header, passes the packet down to IP at the network layer, which encapsulates it and passes it down to Ethernet at the data-link layer, which adds its frame and transmits it over the network. Thus, by the time the email message reaches the network, it has been encapsulated four times, by SMTP, TCP, IP, and Ethernet, as shown in Figure 9-6.

Figure 9-6

Application layer data encapsulation

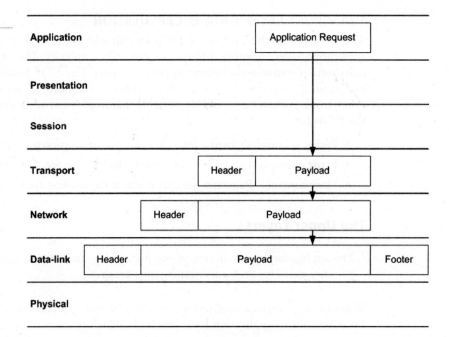

When the packet arrives at its final destination, the networking stack on the receiving computer performs the same steps in reverse. The system passes the incoming packets up through the layers, with each one removing its header and using the header information to pass the contents to the correct protocol at the next higher layer. Finally, the packet arrives at its final terminus, which is an application running on the destination computer, in this case, an email server.

■ Connecting to a Network

THE BOTTOM LINE

The networking capabilities in Windows 8.1 have been designed to minimize the threat of intrusion from outsiders while providing users with a simple and reliable networking experience. The following sections examine some of the networking tools and concepts in Windows 8.1.

CERTIFICATION READY
Connect to a network
Objective 3.1

Networking provides Windows 8.1 with an open door to a virtually unlimited array of resources, but an open door can let things in as easily as it lets things out. This makes security a primary concern for Windows 8.1 administrators. Windows 8.1 includes a variety of tools and features that enable users and administrators to manage the operating system's networking capabilities and help to protect it against unauthorized access. Many of these features operate invisibly to both users and administrators.

Some of the tools that desktop technicians must use regularly, and the concepts they support, are discussed in the following sections:

Installing Network Support

Windows 8.1 usually is able to detect a network interface adapter in a computer and automatically install and configure the networking client.

The installation of Windows 8.1's networking support is usually automatic. When Windows 8.1 detects a network interface adapter in the computer, either during the operating system installation or afterwards, it installs a device driver for the adapter, as well as the components of the default networking stack, which are as follows:

- **Client for Microsoft Networks** – Provides application layer services that enable programs to access shared files and printers on the network.
- **File and Printer Sharing for Microsoft Networks** – Enables the computer to share its files and printers with other users on the network.
- **QoS Packet Scheduler** – Enables the network client to prioritize network traffic based on bandwidth availability and changing network conditions.
- **Microsoft Network Adapter Multiplexor Protocol** – Provides support for network adapter load balancing and failover.
- **Microsoft LLDP Protocol Driver** – Provides Link Layer Discovery Protocol support for Microsoft Data Center Networking (DCN).
- **Link Layer Topology Discovery Mapper I/O Driver and Link Layer Topology Discovery Responder** – Implement the protocol that enables Windows 7 Windows 8.1 to compile a map of the computers on the network.
- **Internet Protocol Version 6 (TCP/IPv6)** – Provides support for the IPv6 network layer protocol, including 128-bit IP addresses.
- **Internet Protocol Version 4 (TCP/IPv4)** – Provides support for the IPv4 network layer protocol, including 32-bit IP addresses.

The first time that the computer connects to a network, Windows 8.1 presents the user with the option to turn on network discovery and find PCs, devices, and content on the network, as shown in Figure 9-7.

Figure 9-7

Windows 8.1 Networks controls

Do you want to find PCs, devices, and content on this network, and automatically connect to devices like printers and TVs?

We recommend that you do this on your home and work networks.

Yes   No

Depending on your selection, the system configures the computer to use one of three network location designations. These selections are actually combinations of network discovery and file sharing settings, which determine how much access the workstation user will have to the network and how much access network users will have to the workstation.

These three network location options are as follows:

- **Private** – Indicates that the computer is connected to a private workgroup or HomeGroup network and not directly connected to the Internet. This means that it is safe for the computer to share its files and discover other computers.
- **Public** – Indicates that the computer is connected to a network in a public place, such as an airport or coffee shop "hot spot" for wireless computers, or is connected directly to the

Internet without an intervening router. This means that the computer and its shares cannot be seen or accessed from the network, nor can the system create or join a HomeGroup network. In addition, some applications might not be able to access the network.

- **Domain** – Indicates that the computer is connected to an Active Directory Domain Services (AD DS) domain. This option is set automatically when you join the computer to the domain.

These Network controls are accessible through the Network and Sharing Center in the Control Panel. Clicking Change advanced sharing settings opens the windows, as shown in Figure 9-8.

Figure 9-8

Windows 8.1 Network sharing controls

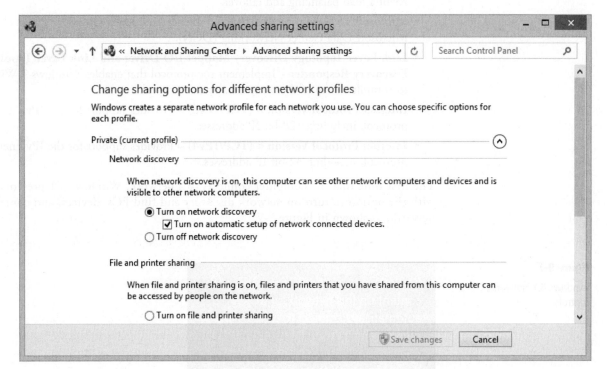

Using the Network and Sharing Center

The Network and Sharing Center is a centralized console that provides technical specialists and system administrators with access to most of the major networking tools included with Windows 8.1.

The Windows 8.1 Network and Sharing Center provides a central access point for all of the network connections on the computer. Many of the common network configuration and administration tasks that technicians perform on Windows 8.1 computers start by opening the Network and Sharing Center. As with many Windows tools, there are several ways to open the Network and Sharing Center, two of which are as follows:

- Click the Search charm, select Settings, and search for "Network and Sharing Center."
- From the Desktop, right-click the Start button and click Control Panel. Then click Network and Internet > Network and Sharing Center.

When the Network and Sharing Center appears, you see a window like the one shown in Figure 9-9.

Figure 9-9

The Network and Sharing
Center

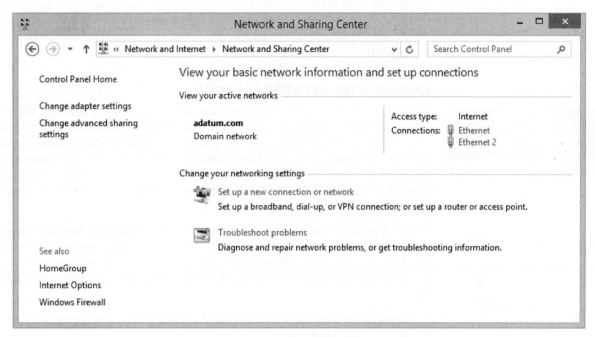

The Network and Sharing Center main window consists of the following elements:

- **Task list (left pane)** – Contains links that enable you to manager network adapter settings and configure sharing parameters.
- **View your active networks (top right)** – Displays the name of the network and other information, such as the network location (private, domain, or public), whether the workstation is connected to a local network, the Internet, or both, and the name of the network connection(s) in the system. There are also links the enable you to view the current status of the network connection(s).
- **Change your networking settings (bottom right)** – Contains links that enable you to create new network connections or troubleshoot existing ones.

UNDERSTANDING NETWORK DISCOVERY

Network Discovery is an important security concept first introduced in Windows Vista. It enables users to control critical network firewall controls with a single switch. Windows Firewall is a feature that was first introduced in the Windows XP Service Pack 2 release, and is now included in Windows 8.1 as well.

Network Discovery is a Windows 8.1 feature that simplifies the task of firewall configuration by enabling you to block or allow the protocols and ports needed for the computer to browse and access the network.

When you modify the Network Discovery settings in the Network and Sharing Center, by clicking *Change advanced sharing settings*, you control whether the computer can see and be seen by the other systems on the network. It is critical to understand that this setting works in both directions.

When a Windows 8.1 computer has Network Discovery turned off, it cannot browse the other computers on the network. At the same time, the other computers on the network cannot browse to the Windows 8.1 computer. However, it is still possible for the Windows 8.1

computer to access network resources. The difference is that the user must know the names and locations of those resources; it is not possible to browse to them.

The default state of the Network Discovery setting is dependent on the network location, as set manually by the user or automatically by the computer. Computers configured with the Private and Domain location have Network Discovery turned on, and Public computers have it turned off.

CHANGING THE NETWORK LOCATION

CERTIFICATION READY
Configure network
locations
Objective 3.1

After you select the initial network location during the network interface adapter installation, Windows 8.1 attempts to detect the type of location whenever you connect to a different network. If, for example, your laptop computer used the Private location when you installed Windows 8.1 on your home network, and you later take the computer to a coffee shop with a wireless network, Windows 8.1 will most likely detect the change and alter the network location to Public. This turns the Network Discovery and file sharing options off, for greater security.

Unlike Windows 7, in which you can easily change the network location using the Network and Sharing Center controls, changing the network location is more difficult in Windows 8.1. In most cases, when Windows 8.1 is unable to detect the network type for any reason, it errs on the side of caution and sets the network location to Public, which is the most secure option.

One method for detecting the problem and changing the Public setting to Private is to use the HomeGroup Troubleshooter, as in the following procedure.

CHANGE THE NETWORK LOCATION USING HOMEGROUP TROUBLESHOOTER

GET READY. Log on to Windows 8.1 using an account with administrative capabilities and then perform the following steps:

1. Open the **Network and Sharing Center**.

   The *Network and Sharing Center* window appears.

2. Click the **HomeGroup** or **Available to join** link.

   The *Share with other home computers* page appears.

3. Click **Start the HomeGroup troubleshooter**.

   The *Troubleshoot and help prevent computer problems* page appears, as shown in Figure 9-10.

Figure 9-10

The *Troubleshoot and help prevent computer problems* page

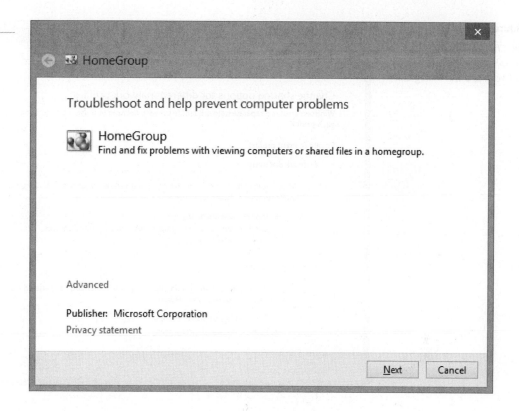

4. Click **Next**. The *Troubleshoot network problems* page appears.
5. Click **Troubleshoot network problems**.

   The troubleshooter should detect the problem and offer to change the network location to Private.
6. Click **Apply this fix**. After the fix is applied, you can select whether you want to join the computer to a homegroup or not.

When you select the option to join a homegroup network, the system searches for existing homegroups on the network. If it fails to find one, the system creates a new homegroup network and supplies a password for it. For more information on homeroup networking, see Lesson 13, "Configuring Shared Resources."

CONFIGURING ADVANCED SHARING SETTINGS

With some limitations, you can manually change the Network Discovery and other sharing settings, whichever network location the system is using, by using the following procedure:

 CONFIGURE ADVANCED SHARING

GET READY. Log on to Windows 8.1 using an account with administrative capabilities and then perform the following steps:

1. Open the **Network and Sharing Center**.

   The *Network and Sharing Center* window appears.
2. In the left pane, click **Change advanced sharing settings**.

   The *Change sharing options for different network profiles* dialog box appears.
3. Click the down arrow for the network location whose settings you want to modify, to produce the display shown in Figure 9-11.

Figure 9-11

The *Change sharing options for different network profiles* dialog box

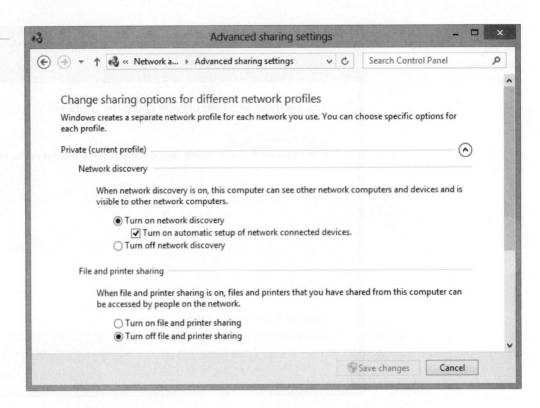

4. Configure the following settings by selecting from the options provided:
   - **Network Discovery** – Enables the computer to see other devices on the network and renders it visible from the network
   - **Turn on automatic setup of network connected devices** – Enables the system to automatically configure itself to access printers and other network devices.
   - **File and printer sharing** – Enables network users to access the files and printers shared on the computer
   - **Public folder sharing** – Enables network users to access the Public folders on the computer
   - **Media streaming** – Enables network users to access media files on the computer, and enables the computer to locate media files on the network
   - **File sharing connections** – Specifies whether clients accessing the computer's shares must use 128-bit encryption
   - **Password protected sharing** – Specifies whether network users accessing the computer's shares must have local user accounts with passwords
   - **HomeGroup connections** – Specifies whether Windows 8.1 should manage HomeGroup connections automatically
5. Click **Save Changes**.
   The *Network and Sharing Center* window reappears.

Managing Network Connections

Windows 8.1 creates and configures local area connections automatically, but you can also manage and modify the properties of the connections manually.

When Windows 8.1 detects a network interface adapter, it creates a network connection automatically, installs the TCP/IP networking components, and configures it to use DHCP to obtain IP addresses and other network configuration settings. To view and modify the Properties of a local area connection, use the procedures in the following sections.

VIEWING A CONNECTION'S STATUS

Each local area connection on a Windows 8.1 system has a status dialog box that displays real time information about the connection. To view the status of a connection, use the following procedure.

 VIEW CONNECTION STATUS

GET READY. Log on to Windows 8.1 using an account with administrative capabilities and then perform the following steps:

1. Open the **Network and Sharing Center**.

    The *Network and Sharing Center* window appears.

2. In the *View your active networks* section, click **Ethernet** or the name of the connection whose status you want to view.

    The Ethernet Status dialog box appears, as shown in Figure 9-12.

Figure 9-12

The *Ethernet Status* dialog box

3. Click **Details**. The Network Connection Details dialog box appears, as shown in Figure 9-13.

Figure 9-13

The *Network Connection Details* dialog box

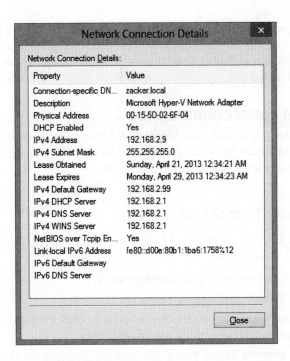

4. Click **Close** to close the *Network Connection Details* dialog box.

5. Click **Close** to close the *Local Area Connection Status* dialog box.

The *Ethernet Status* dialog box displays basic information about the connection, such as its speed, which version(s) of IP it is using, and how long the computer has been connected. In the Activity area, you can see the number of bytes that the computer has sent and received in a real-time display, so you can tell if the network connection is currently functional.

The *Network Connection Details* page displays the configuration settings for the network connection, including the TCP/IP settings obtained using DHCP.

CONFIGURING IPv4 SETTINGS

Most networks today use DHCP to configure the TCP/IP configuration settings of their workstations. DHCP automates the configuration process and prevents the duplication of IP addresses. However, there are still some situations in which it is desirable or necessary to configure the Windows 8.1 TCP/IP client manually. To do this, use the following procedure:

 CONFIGURE IPv4 SETTINGS

GET READY. Log on to Windows 8.1 using an account with administrative capabilities and then perform the following steps:

1. Open the **Network and Sharing Center**.

   The *Network and Sharing Center* window appears.

2. Click **Change adapter settings**.

   The Network Connections window appears.

3. Right-click the connection you want to manage and, from the context menu, select **Properties**.

   The connection's *Properties* sheet appears.

4. Select **Internet Protocol Version 4 (TCP/IPv4)** and then click **Properties**.

   The Internet Protocol Version 4 (TCP/IPv4) Properties sheet appears, as shown in Figure 9-14.

Figure 9-14

The *Internet Protocol Version 4 (TCP/IPv4) Properties* sheet

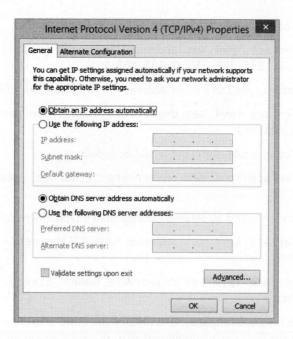

5. Select the **Use the following IP address** option and then enter appropriate values for the following parameters:
   - **IP address** – A 32-bit IPv4 address, in dotted decimal notation.
   - **Subnet Mask** – An appropriate mask indicating which part of the IP address is the network identifier and which part the host identifier.
   - **Default Gateway** – The IP address of the router on the local network that the computer should use to access other networks and/or the Internet.

6. Select the **Use The Following DNS Server Addresses** option and then enter appropriate values for the following parameters:
   - **Preferred DNS Server** – The IP address of the DNS server the computer should use to resolve host and domain names into IP addresses
   - **Alternate DNS Server** – The IP address of a DNS server that the computer should use if the preferred DNS server is unavailable

➕ **MORE INFORMATION**

Clicking the Advanced button opens the Advanced TCP/IP Settings dialog box, in which you can configure multiple IP addresses, subnet masks, default gateways, DNS servers, and WINS servers for client computers with special requirements.

7. Click **OK** to close the *Internet Protocol Version 4 (TCP/IPv4) Properties* sheet.
8. Click **OK** to close the connection's *Properties* sheet.

The command line alternative to this graphical interface is a program called Netsh.exe. Netsh. exe is a powerful tool that you can use interactively or with command line parameters to configure virtually any Windows 8.1 networking setting. To configure the basic IPv4 parameters for a network connection, you use the following syntax:

```
netsh interface ipv4 set address connection_name
static ip_address subnet_mask default_gateway
```

An example of an actual command would be as follows:

```
netsh interface ipv4 set address "Ethernet" static
192.168.1.23 255.255.255.0 192.168.1.1
```

Then, to configure the DNS server address, you would use the following command syntax:

```
netsh interface ipv4 set dnsservers connection_name
static ip_address
```

An example of an actual command would be as follows:

```
netsh interface ipv4 set dnsservers "Ethernet" static
192.168.1.99
```

To configure a connection to obtain its settings from a DHCP server, use the following commands:

```
netsh interface ipv4 set address name="Ethernet"
source=dhcp
```

```
netsh interface ipv4 set dnsservers name="Ethernet"
source=dhcp
```

Prior to Windows 8, configuring IP addresses and other network interface settings with Windows PowerShell was a complicated affair involving scripts and Windows Management Instrumentation (WMI) classes. Windows PowerShell 3.0 and 4.0, however, have a NetTCPIP module that includes cmdlets that simplify these tasks.

To configure the basic settings for a network interface, including the IP address, the subnet mask, and the default gateway address, you use the New-NetIPAddress cmdlet with the following syntax:

```
New-NetIPAddress –InterfaceIndex <number>
-Ipaddress <address> -PrefixLength <number>
-DefaultGateway <address>
```

To determine the index number of the network interface you want to configure, you run the Get-NetIPInterface cmdlet. Once you have the index number, you can configure the interface, as in the following example:

```
New-NetIPAddress –InterfaceIndex 12 -IPaddress
192.168.4.55 -PrefixLength 24 -DefaultGateway
192.168.4.1
```

The one essential parameter that the New-NetIPAddress cmdlet cannot configure is the DNS server address the system will use. To configure this, you must use the Set-DNSClientServerAddress cmdlet, with the followng syntax:

```
Set-DNSClientServerAddress –InterfaceIndex <number> -
ServerAddresses ("10.0.0.1","10.0.0.7"]
```

CONFIGURING IPv6 SETTINGS

Because most computers use IPv6 autoconfiguration or DHCP, manual configuration of the Windows 8.1 IPv6 implementation is rarely necessary, but it is possible.

The procedure for configuring IPv6 using the graphical interface is the same as that for IPv4, except that, in the *Local Area Connection Properties* sheet, you select Internet Protocol Version 6 (TCP/IPv6) and click Properties. The Internet Protocol Version 6 (TCP/IPv6) Properties sheet appears, as shown in Figure 9-15.

Figure 9-15

The *Internet Protocol Version 6 (TCP/IPv6) Properties* sheet

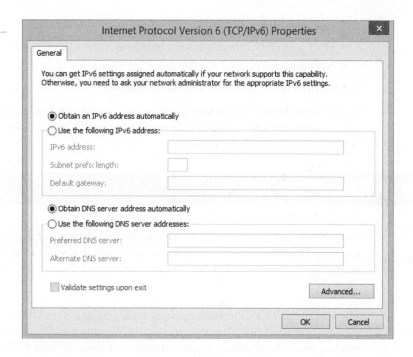

To configure IPv6 from the command prompt, you use Netsh.exe in the same way you would for IPv4, substituting the ipv6 parameter for ipv4 and an IPv6 address for the IPv4 address and subnet mask, as in the following example:

```
netsh interface ipv6 set address "Ethernet" static
FE80::7166:22E6:1D18:BDAA
```

To configure DNS server addresses, use a command like the following:

```
netsh interface ipv6 set dnsservers "Ethernet" static
FE80::7166:22E6:1D18:BD01
```

RUNNING NETWORK DIAGNOSTICS

The Network and Sharing Center shows the devices on the network and their status. Improperly configured devices have yellow warning signs on their icons and non-functioning connections have red X's on them.

When a networking problem exists, clicking a warning icon launches Windows Network Diagnostics. This utility attempts to automatically discover the cause of the problem and displays possible solutions.

➕ **MORE INFORMATION**

You can also launch Windows Network Diagnostics by opening the Network Connections window, right-clicking one of the network connections, and selecting Diagnose from the context menu.

Unlike previous troubleshooting tools, Network Diagnostics does not just display error messages, it tells you in clear language what might be wrong and what you have to do to repair the problem. The Network Diagnostics Framework (NDF) includes troubleshooting routines for wireless as well as wired networks. Problems that the system can diagnose include the following:

- Broken or detached cable connections
- IP address and subnet mask problems

- Default gateway problems
- DNS and DHCP configuration problems
- Networking hardware configuration problems
- Internet server addresses and service settings

If, after identifying a networking problem, the system can repair it automatically, it provides a link that you can select to have it do so. Otherwise, it displays a list of manual fixes that you can perform to address the problem.

■ Using TCP/IP Tools

↓
THE BOTTOM LINE

Virtually all network operating systems today include support for the TCP/IP protocols, and TCP/IP traditionally includes some basic tools that you can use to troubleshoot network connectivity problems yourself.

The traditional TCP/IP troubleshooting tools originated on UNIX systems, and as a result, they are command line tools that you run in Windows 8.1 by opening a Command Prompt window first. The Windows implementations of these utilities generally use the same syntax as they did on UNIX.

This section examines some of the most common TCP/IP utilities and their purposes.

Using Ipconfig.exe

All Windows operating systems, including Windows 8.1, have a graphical interface for configuring network connections, but the configuration display capabilities of the UNIX ifconfig program have been retained in a command line tool called Ipconfig.exe.

When you run Ipconfig.exe with the/all parameter at the Windows 8.1 command prompt, you see a display like the one shown in Figure 9-16.

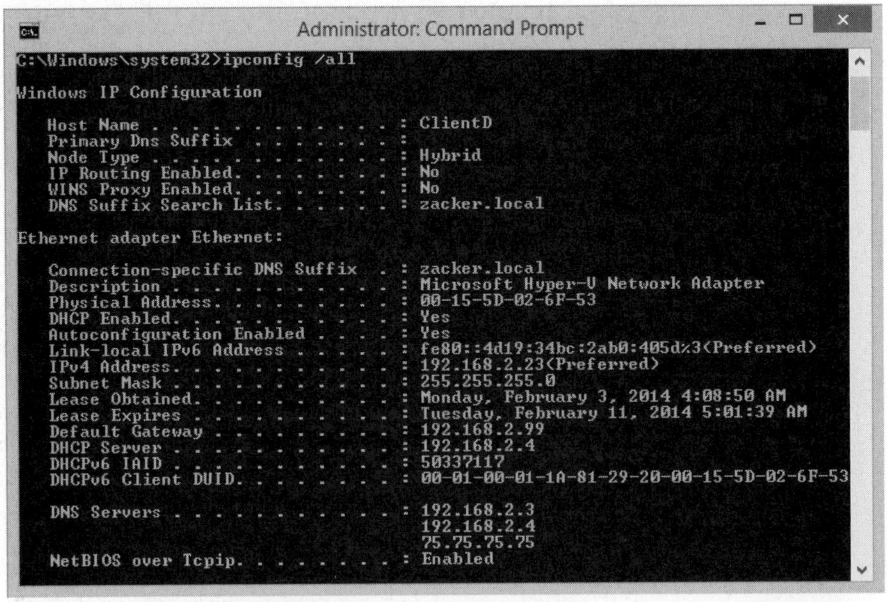

Figure 9-16

The Ipconfig.exe display

The value of Ipconfig.exe is particularly apparent when a Windows 8.1 computer auto-configures its TCP/IP client or uses DHCP to obtain its IP address and other TCP/IP configuration parameters. A DHCP-configured computer does not display any configuration information in the Ethernet Properties sheet; it just shows that the DHCP client is activated. One of the few ways to see what settings the DHCP server has assigned to the computer (without examining the DHCP server itself) is to use Ipconfig.exe.

In addition to displaying the DHCP-obtained configuration settings, Ipconfig.exe also enables you to manually release the IP address the system obtained from the DHCP server and renew existing address leases. By running Ipconfig.exe with the /release and /renew command-line parameters, you can release or renew the IP address assignment of one of the network interfaces in the computer or for all of the interfaces at once.

Using Ping.exe

Ping is the most basic of TCP/IP utilities, and is included in some form with every TCP/IP implementation. On Windows 8.1 systems, the program is called Ping.exe.

Ping.exe can tell you if the TCP/IP stack of another system on the network is functioning normally. The Ping.exe program generates a series of Echo Request messages using the Internet Control Message Protocol (ICMP) and transmits them to the computer whose name or IP address you specify on the command line. The basic syntax of the Ping program is as follows:

```
ping target
```

The *target* variable contains the IPv4 or IPv6 address or name of any computer on the network. Because Ping.exe is a TCP/IP utility, the target computer can be running any operating system, not just Windows. You can use DNS host and domain names or Windows NetBIOS names in Ping commands. Ping resolves the name into an IP address before sending the Echo Request messages, and it then displays the address in its output.

TCP/IP computers respond to any *Echo Request* messages they receive that are addressed to them by generating Echo Reply messages and transmitting them back to the sender. When the pinging computer receives the Echo Reply messages, it produces a display like the one shown in Figure 9-17.

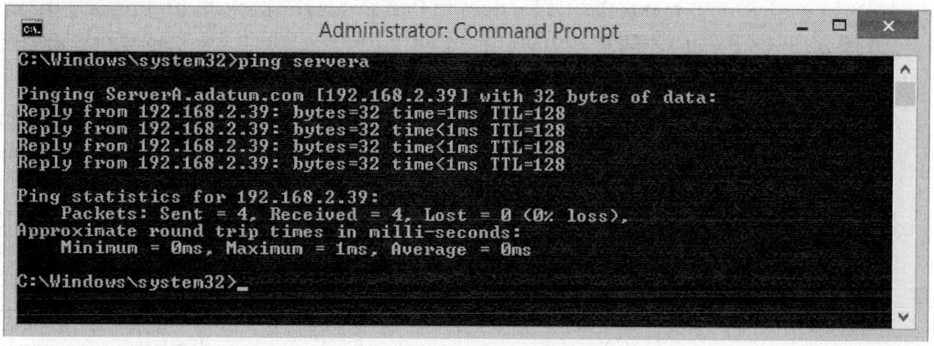

Figure 9-17

The Ping.exe display

In Windows 8.1's Ping.exe implementation, the display shows the IP address of the computer receiving the Echo Requests, the number of bytes of data included with each request, the elapsed time between the transmission of each request and the receipt of each reply, and the value of the Time To Live (TTL) field in the IP header.

In this example, the target computer was on the same local area network (LAN), so the time measurement is very short—less than 1 millisecond. When pinging a computer on the

Internet, the interval is likely to be longer. A successful Ping result like this one indicates that the target computer's networking hardware is functioning properly, as are its TCP/IP protocols, at least as high as the network layer of the OSI model. If a Ping test fails, there might be a firewall blocking the ICMP traffic between the two systems. If there is no firewall, then the Ping test failure indicates that there is a problem in one or both of the computers or in the network medium connecting them.

Ping.exe also has a series of command-line switches that you can use to modify the operational parameters of the program, such as the number of Echo Request messages it generates and the amount of data in each message. To display the syntax of the program, type `ping /?` at the command prompt.

Using Tracert.exe

Traceroute is another UNIX program that was designed to display the path that TCP/IP packets take to their final destination. Called traceroute in UNIX, in Windows 8.1 it is implemented as Tracert.exe. Because of the nature of IP routing, the path from a packet's source to its destination on another network can change from minute to minute, especially on the Internet. Tracert.exe displays a list of the routers that are currently forwarding packets to a particular destination.

Tracert.exe is a variation on Ping.exe. The program uses ICMP Echo Request and Echo Reply messages just like Ping, but it modifies the messages by changing the value of the TTL field in the IP header. The values in the TTL field prevent packets from getting caught in router loops that keep them circulating endlessly around the internetwork. On a Windows 8.1 computer, the default value for the TTL field is relatively high, 128. Each time a packet passes from one network to another, the router connecting the networks reduces the TTL value by one. If the TTL value ever reaches zero, the router processing the packet discards it and transmits an ICMP error message back to the original sender.

Tracert.exe works by modifying the TTL values in the successive Ping.exe packets that it transmits to a target computer. When you run Tracert.exe from the command prompt with a *target* parameter, the program generates its first set of Echo Request messages with TTL values of 1. When the messages arrive at the first router on their path to the destination, the router decrements the TTL values to 0, discards the packets, and reports the errors to the sender. The error messages contain the router's address, which Tracert.exe displays as the first hop in the path to the destination.

Tracert.exe's second set of Echo Request messages use a TTL value of 2, causing the second router on the path to discard the packets and generate error messages. The Echo Request messages in the third set have a TTL value of 3, and so on. Each set of packets travels one hop farther than the previous set before causing a router to return error messages to the source. The list of routers displayed by the program as the path to the destination is the result of these error messages.

The following is an example of a Tracert.exe display:

```
Tracing route to www.fineartschool.co.uk [173.146.1.1] over a maximum
of 30 hops:

  1    <10 ms     1   ms   <10  ms    192.168.2.99
  2    105 ms    92   ms    98  ms    qrv1-67terminal01.cpandl.com
  3    101 ms   110   ms    98  ms    qrv1.cpandl.com
```

4	123	ms	109	ms	118	ms	svcr03-7b.cpandl.com
5	123	ms	112	ms	114	ms	clsm02-2.cpandl.com
6	136	ms	130	ms	133	ms	sl-gw19-pen-6-1-0-T3.fabrikam.com
7	143	ms	126	ms	138	ms	sl-bb9-pen-4-3.fabrikam.com
8	146	ms	129	ms	133	ms	sl-bb20-pen-12-0.fabrikam.com
9	131	ms	128	ms	139	ms	sl-bb20-nyc-13-0.fabrikam.com
10	130	ms	134	ms	134	ms	sl-gw9-nyc-8-0.fabrikam.com
11	147	ms	149	ms	152	ms	sl-demon-1-0.fabrikam.com
12	154	ms	146	ms	145	ms	ny2-backbone-ge021.fabrikam.com
13	230	ms	225	ms	226	ms	tele-backbone-ge023.adatum.co.uk
14	233	ms	220	ms	226	ms	tele-core-3-fxp1.adatum.co.uk
15	223	ms	224	ms	224	ms	tele-access-1-14.adatum.co.uk
16	236	ms	221	ms	226	ms	tele-service-2-165.adatum.co.uk
17	220	ms	224	ms	210	ms	www.fineartschool.co.uk

```
Trace complete.
```

In this example, Tracert.exe displays the path between a computer in Pennsylvania and one in the United Kingdom. Each of the hops contains the elapsed times between the transmission and reception of three sets of Echo Request and Echo Reply packets. In this trace, you can clearly see the point at which the packets begin traveling across the Atlantic Ocean. At hop 13, the elapsed times increase from approximately 150 to 230 milliseconds (ms) and stay in that range for the subsequent hops. This additional delay of only 80 ms is the time it takes the packets to travel the thousands of miles across the Atlantic Ocean.

Ping.exe simply tells you whether two TCP/IP systems are having trouble communicating. It can't pinpoint the location of the problem. A failure to contact a remote computer could be due to a problem in your workstation, in the remote computer, or in any of the routers in between. Tracert.exe can tell you how far your packets are going before they run into the problem.

Using Nslookup.exe

The *Nslookup.exe* command-line utility enables you to generate DNS request messages and transmit them to specific DNS servers on the network. The advantage of Nslookup. exe is that you can test the functionality and the quality of the information on a specific DNS server by specifying it on the command line.

The basic command-line syntax of Nslookup.exe is as follows:

```
nslookup DNSname DNSserver
```

- **DNSname** specifies the DNS name that you want to resolve
- **DNSserver** specifies the DNS name or IP address of the DNS server that you want to query for the name specified in the *DNSname* variable

There are also many additional parameters that you can include on the command line to control the server query process. The output generated by Nslookup.exe in Windows 8.1 looks like the one shown in Figure 9-18.

Figure 9-18

The Nslookup.exe display

The Nslookup.exe utility has two operational modes: command-line and interactive. When you run Nslookup.exe with no command-line parameters, the program displays its own prompt from which you can issue commands to specify the default DNS server to query, resolve multiple names, and configure many other aspects of the program's functionality.

SKILL SUMMARY

IN THIS LESSON, YOU LEARNED:

- The networking stack used on Windows 8.1 computers corresponds roughly to the seven-layer OSI reference model.

- The OSI (Open Systems Interconnection) reference model consists of seven layers: physical, data-link, network, transport, session, presentation, and application.

- Ethernet, the data-link layer protocol used on most LANs, consists of physical layer specifications, a frame format, and a MAC mechanism.

- The network and transport layer protocols work together to provide an end-to-end communication service that achieves the quality of service required by the application requesting network services.

- The functions of the session, presentation, and application layers are often combined into a single application layer protocol.

- Windows 8.1 includes support for both the IPv4 and IPv6 protocols. IPv6 increases the IP address space from 32 to 128 bits, simplifies the routing process, and improves address autoconfiguration.

- Network Discovery is a Windows 8.1 feature that simplifies the task of firewall configuration by enabling you to block or allow the protocols and ports need for the computer to browse and access the network.

- Most networks use DHCP to configure their TCP/IP clients, but it is still possible to configure them manually, using a graphical interface or the Netsh.exe command line utility.

- Windows 8.1 includes a variety of command line TCP/IP tools, including Ipconfig.exe, Ping.exe, Tracert.exe, and Nslookup.exe.

Knowledge Assessment

Multiple Choice

Select one or more correct answers for each of the following questions.

1. Which of the following is the primary method for transmitting IPv6 traffic over an IPv4 network?
   a. Subnetting
   b. Tunneling
   c. Supernetting
   d. Contracting

2. Which of the following is the IPv6 equivalent to a private IPv4 address?
   a. Link-local unicast address
   b. Global unique unicast address
   c. Unique local unicast address
   d. Anycast address

3. Which of the following is an automatic tunneling protocol used by Windows operating systems that are located behind NAT routers?
   a. Teredo
   b. 6to4
   c. ISATAP
   d. APIPA

4. What kind of IP address must a system have to be visible from the Internet?
   a. Registered
   b. Binary
   c. Class B
   d. Subnetted

5. What subnet mask would you use when configuring a TCP/IP client with an IPv4 address on the 172.16.32.0/19 network?
   a. 255.224.0.0
   b. 255.240.0.0
   c. 255.255.224.0
   d. 255.255.240.0
   e. 255.255.255.240

6. This protocol is responsible for addressing packets at the data link layer?
   a. Internet Protocol
   b. Transmission Control Protocol
   c. Ethernet
   d. CIDR

7. Windows 8.1 computers can acquire IP addresses in which of the following ways? Select all that apply.
   a. APIPA
   b. Manual configuration
   c. DHCP
   d. TCP/IP

8. Which of the following are true statements regarding IPv4 and IPv6 addressing? Select all that apply.
   a. IPv4 addresses are 32 bits in length
   b. IPv4 addresses are 128 bits in length
   c. IPv6 addresses are 128 bits in length
   d. IPv4 and IPv6 support stateful and stateless configuration

9. Computers with link-local addresses, that do not have access to a DNS server, use this protocol?
    a. Link Local Name Resolution
    b. Link Local Multicast Name Resolution
    c. Link Local Unicast Name Resolution
    d. Link Local Anycast Name Resolution

10. In which layer of the OSI model would packet acknowledgment, error correction and flow control services typically be handled.?
    a. Network layer
    b. Physical layer
    c. Transport layer
    d. Data Link layer

Best Answer

Choose the letter that corresponds to the best answer. More than one answer choice may achieve the goal. Select the BEST answer.

1. A computer is currently experiencing connectivity problems. The network administrator is unsure whether the source of the problem is the local computer, the remote computer or one of the routers between the two. Which tool would most likely provide the information needed to answer these questions and pinpoint the location of the problem?
    a. nslookup
    b. ping
    c. netstat
    d. tracert

2. Two computers are configured to communicate on a local network segment 192.168.2.0/24? Computer A is currently assigned 192.168.2.17 and Computer B is assigned 192.168.2.22. A new administrator adds a third computer (Computer C) to the network and forgets to configure its IP address. If the DHCP server were *temporarily* unavailable, which of the following would most likely be the result?
    a. Computer C would be assigned an address automatically
    b. Computer C would be assigned an APIPA address
    c. Computer C would be assigned an APIPA address and not be able to communicate with the other two computers
    d. Computer C would be assigned an APIPA address and not be able to communicate with the other two computers. Once the DHCP server came back online, all computers will be able to communicate.

3. The network administrator is currently having problems connecting and gathering information from a Windows 8.1 computer using telnet. He wants to use telnet on a very limited basis. Which of the following would represent the best approach to solve this problem?
    a. Turn the Windows Firewall off on the target computer.
    b. Disable the Windows Firewall on the target computer temporarily.
    c. Configure the target computer's Windows Firewall to allow traffic directed to port 23, 20, and 21.
    d. Configure the target computer's Windows Firewall to allow traffic directed to port 23; complete the work and then block the port until he needs to connect at a late date/time.

4. When troubleshooting computers and networks, it's wise to use the OSI model as a guide. If a user is experiencing problems with resolving host names to IP addresses, which layer of the OSI model would you focus on to quickly resolve the problem?
   a. Data Link
   b. Physical Layer
   c. Network Layer
   d. Application Layer

5. A network administrator is trying to locate where packets are being delayed in transit. She uses the tracert command and receives the following information. Which of these hops would be the source of the delay?
   a. <100 ms   103 ms   <130 ms
   b. <210 ms   200 ms   <205 ms
   c. <250 ms   210 ms   <240 ms
   d. <375 ms   300 ms   <360 ms

Matching and Identification

Complete the following exercise by matching the terms with their corresponding definitions.

_____ a) ipconfig
_____ b) IPv6
_____ c) media access control address
_____ d) network address translation
_____ e) connectionless protocol
_____ f) connection-oriented protocol
_____ g) Transmission Control Protocol
_____ h) Internet Protocol
_____ i) packet switching network
_____ j) Automatic Private IP Addressing (APIPA)

1. Used to view the settings assigned to a DHCP-enabled client
2. Allows computers on network without DHCP to communicate with each other when not assigned manual IP addresses
3. A protocol that does not perform error detection or correction.
4. Uses 128-bit addresses
5. Protocol in which two system establish a connection before they transmit any data.
6. A hardware address used at the data link layer
7. Also referred to as a local area network.
8. Feature built into routers; substitutes a registered address for the computer's private address and then forwards to destination
9. A connectionless protocol found at the Network Layer
10. A connection-oriented protocol found at the Transport Layer.

Build a List

1. In order of first to last, specify the correct order of steps to view connection status.
   _____ Open the **Network and Sharing Center**.
   _____ Click **Close** to close the *Network Connection Details* dialog box.
   _____ Click **Close** to close the *Local Area Connection Status* dialog box
   _____ Click **Details**. The *Network Connection Details* dialog box appears.
   _____ In the *View your active networks* section, click **Ethernet** or the name of the connection whose status you want to view.

2. Specify the correct order of steps to configure IPv4 settings.

_____ Click **Change adapter settings**.

_____ Select **Internet Protocol Version 4 (TCP/IPv4)** and then click **Properties**.

_____ Select the **Use The Following DNS Server Addresses** option and then enter appropriate values for the following parameters (preferred DNS Server, alternate DNS server.

_____ Right-click the connection you want to manage and, from the context menu, select **Properties**.

_____ Open the **Network and Sharing Center**.

_____ Click **OK** to close the *Internet Protocol Version 4 (TCP/IPv4) Properties* sheet.

_____ Select the **Use The Following IP Address** option and then enter appropriate values for IP address, subnet mask, and default gateway).

_____ Click **OK** to close the connection's *Properties* sheet.

3. Specify the correct order of steps to configure Advanced Sharing settings.

_____ Open the **Network and Sharing Center**.

_____ Configure the following settings by selecting from the options provided (Network Discovery, Turn on automatic setup of network connected device, file/printer sharing, public folder sharing, media streaming, file sharing connections, password protected sharing, and HomeGroup connections)

_____ Click **Save Changes**.

_____ Click the down arrow for the network location whose settings you want to modify.

_____ In the left pane, click **Change advanced sharing settings**. The *Change sharing options for different network profiles* dialog box appears.

Business Case Scenarios

Scenario 9-1: Using Port Numbers

While you are installing an Internet web server on your company network, the owner of the company tells you that he also wants to build a web server for internal use by the company's employees. This intranet web server will not contain confidential information, but it should not be accessible from the company's Internet website. To do this, you create a second site on the web server. The Internet site uses the well-known port number for web servers, which is 80. For the intranet site, you select the port number 283. Assuming that the web server's IP address on the internal network is 10.54.3.145, what should the users on the company network do to access the intranet website with Microsoft Internet Explorer?

Scenario 9-2: Configuring TCP/IP Clients

Mark is setting up a small Ethernet network in his home by installing network adapters in three computers running Windows 8.1 and connecting them to a switch. Mark only uses one of the computers to access the Internet with a dial-up modem, but he wants to be able to access files and his printer from any one of the three systems. After he installs the network interface adapters, he notes that the default networking components have been installed on all three systems, and he sets about configuring their TCP/IP configuration parameters manually. Of the settings on the Internet Protocol Version 4 (TCP/IPv4) Properties sheet, which must Mark configure to provide the network connectivity he desires, and which can he leave blank?

Configuring Network Settings

70-687 EXAM OBJECTIVE

Objective 3.2 – Configure networking settings. This objective may include but is not limited to: connect to a wireless network; manage preferred wireless networks; configure network adapters; configure location-aware printing.

LESSON HEADING	EXAM OBJECTIVE
Configuring Network Settings	
Understanding Wireless Security	
Evaluating Wireless Networking Hardware	
Using Wired Equivalent Privacy	
Selecting an Authentication Method	
Using Wi-Fi Protected Access	
Connecting to Wireless Networks	Connect to a wireless network
Managing Preferred Wireless Networks	Manage preferred wireless networks
Prioritizing Networks in Windows 8.1	
Removing Wireless Networks/Profiles	
Configuring Network Adapters	Configure network adapters
Configuring Location-Aware Printing	Configure location-aware printing

KEY TERMS

ad hoc mode

Advanced Encryption System (AES)

data tampering

denial of service

eavesdropping

infrastructure mode

Institute of Electrical and Electronic Engineers (IEEE)

location-aware printing

masquerading

mobile broadband networks

Network and Sharing Center

network adapter

Network List Service

Network Location Awareness service

open system

passphrases

service set identifier (SSID)

Temporal Key Integrity Protocol (TKIP)

shared secret

WiFi Protected Access

Wired Equivalent Privacy (WEP)

wireless profile

Wireless Profile Manager

WPA2 Enterprise

WPA2 Personal

■ Configuring Network Settings

THE BOTTOM LINE

Configuring, connecting and troubleshooting a computer's network settings is a key skill set that every administrator must have in order to ensure their users can access the resources they need. Administrators must be able to understand how Windows 8.1 functions in both wired and wireless networks, how it selects a wireless network to connect to, and how it can be configured to locate default printers when users work across multiple networks.

In this lesson, you learn the basics for connecting to wireless networks and the compatibility and security issues you face when configuring your Windows 8.1 computer. The wireless trend continues to grow and companies need to have someone who can ensure their users are staying connected while still maintaining a secure operating environment.

As employees move between home, work, the local coffee shop, and other public hotspots, Windows 8.1 must be able to differentiate between the locations while still providing a streamlined approach to connecting and using those networks. As the administrator, you must know how Windows 8.1 functions in these environments and how to remove connections that are no longer valid.

The setup of your network adapters (wired, wireless) can be accomplished with minimal effort in Windows 8.1 but you must know how to perform basic configuration of the adapters when you need to troubleshoot connectivity problems or address wireless performance issues.

Finally, with so many users taking advantage of mobile devices, they are looking for you to help them configure their Windows 8.1 computers so they can easily locate, connect and print to printers located on multiple networks.

Understanding Wireless Security

Wireless networks are subject to many of the same security threats as cabled networks, but the medium they use makes it easier for attackers to penetrate them.

Establishing a wireless connection is not difficult, but establishing a secure one can be. Wired networks typically rely on physical security to protect the privacy of their communications. A potential intruder must have physical access to the network cable to connect to the network. This is not the case with wireless networks. If a wireless network is not properly secured, an intruder in a car parked outside can use a laptop to gain full access to the network's communications.

Connecting to a wireless network can grant an attacker access to resources on an organization's internal network, or it might enable the attacker to access the Internet while hiding his or her identity. Some of the specific types of attacks to which an unsecured wireless network is subject are as follows:

- *Eavesdropping* – Attackers can capture traffic as a wireless computer communicates with a wireless access point (WAP). Depending on the type of antennae the devices use and their transmitting power, an attacker might be able to eavesdrop from hundreds of feet away.
- *Masquerading* – Attackers might be able to gain access to restricted network resources by impersonating authorized wireless users. This enables the attacker to engage in illegal activities or attack hosts on remote networks while disguised with another identity.

- *Attacks against wireless clients* – Attackers can launch a network-based attack on a wireless computer that is connected to an ad hoc or untrusted wireless network.
- *Denial of service* – Attackers can jam the wireless frequencies by using a transmitter, preventing legitimate users from successfully communicating with a WAP.
- *Data tampering* – Attackers can delete, replay, or modify wireless communications with a man-in-the-middle attack. A man-in-the-middle attack is when an intruder intercepts network communications and modifies the contents of the packets before sending them on to their destination.

The concerns over the abuse of wireless networks are far from theoretical. Intruders have a wide variety of tools available for detecting, connecting to, and abusing wireless networks. As with most aspects of security, technology can be used to limit the wireless network vulnerabilities. Specifically, you must configure the network computers so that all wireless communications are authenticated and encrypted. This provides protection similar to that offered by the physical security of wired networks.

Evaluating Wireless Networking Hardware

Selecting the right wireless hardware requires that you have a good understanding of the wireless standards. The standards supported by your hardware dictate the range, data rates, and overall compatibility with other devices.

The 802.11 standards published by the *Institute of Electrical and Electronic Engineers (IEEE)* dictate the frequencies, transmission speeds, and ranges of wireless networking products.

Table 10-1

IEEE Wireless Networking Standards

Table 10-1 lists the IEEE 802.11 standards and their capabilities.

IEEE STANDARD	RELEASE DATE	STATUS	DATA RATE	INDOOR RANGE	OUTDOOR RANGE
802.11a	1999	Ratified	54 Mb/sec	~30 meters	~100 meters
802.11b	1999	Ratified	11 Mb/sec	~35 meters	~110 meters
802.11g	2003	Ratified	54 Mb/sec	~35 meters	~110 meters
802.11n	2009	Ratified	600 Mb/sec (4x4 MIMO)	~70 meters	~250 meters
802.11ac	2014	Ratified	1.73 Gb/sec (8x8 MIMO)	Up to 30% over 802.11n	Up to 30% over 802.11n

+ MORE INFORMATION

IEEE 802.11n equipment increases wireless networking speeds by using multiple transmitter and receiver antennae on each device in a process called multiple-input multiple-output (MIMO). For example, a device using a 2x2 MIMO format has two transmitters and two receivers, operating at different frequencies. The sending system splits its data into two signals for transmission, and the receiving device reassembles the signals into a single data stream. This process is called spatial multiplexing. The only potential drawback to this arrangement is the depletion of the available frequency bandwidth by having too many devices in proximity to each other.

Most of the wireless networking hardware now available supports the 802.11b and 802.11g standards. There are also many 802.11n products on the market, some of which are based on the draft standard, while others are certified as conforming to the ratified standard published in late 2009.

As a general rule, devices supporting the newer, faster standards are capable of falling back to slower speeds when necessary. For example, an 802.11g WAP almost always support computers with 802.11b hardware as well. If you're involved in hardware evaluation or selection, compatibility problems among the basic 802.11 standards are relatively rare. The possibility of purchasing incompatible hardware is likely only if you adopt a proprietary technology.

There is, however, another compatibility factor to consider apart from the IEEE 802.11 standards, and that is the security protocols the wireless devices support. Two main security protocols are used in the wireless LAN devices on the market today: *Wired Equivalent Privacy (WEP)* and *WiFi Protected Access* (WPA and WPA2). WEP has been around for some time, and is supported by virtually all wireless LAN products. WPA and WPA2 are comparatively recent, and some older devices do not support them.

Unfortunately, wireless devices cannot fall back from one security protocol to another. You must use WEP or WPA on your network, and all of your devices must support the one you choose. WPA and WPA2 are inherently more secure than WEP, so they are usually preferable. If the network has any devices that do not support WPA, you must either replace them or settle for WEP.

Using Wired Equivalent Privacy

Although WEP is inherently weak when it comes to wireless security, there are still networks and hardware that use this protocol and its authentication methods. Understanding its limitations will help you to secure it as best as possible while still justifying the need to management to move to a more secure protocol.

WEP is a wireless security protocol that helps protect transmitted information by using a security setting, called a shared secret or a shared key, to encrypt network traffic before sending it. To use WEP, administrators must configure all of the devices on the wireless network with the same shared secret key. The devices use that key to encrypt all of their transmissions. Any outside party, who gains possession of that key can, at the very least, read the contents of the transmitted packets, and at worst, participate on the network.

Unfortunately, the cryptography used by WEP is relatively weak, and programs that can analyze captured traffic and derive the key from it are readily available. These factors have resulted in WEP becoming one of the most frequently cracked network encryption protocols today.

In addition to its weak cryptography, another factor contributing to WEP's vulnerability is that the protocol standard doesn't provide any mechanism for automatically changing the shared secret. On wireless networks with hundreds of hosts, manually changing the shared secret on a regular basis is a practical impossibility. Therefore, on most WEP networks, the same shared secret tends to stay in place indefinitely. As with any cryptographic function, the longer a system uses the same code, the more time an attacker has to penetrate that code. A static WEP installation that uses the same permanent key gives attackers sufficient opportunity to crack the shared secret and all the time they need to gain access to the network.

If administrators could change the shared secret on a regular basis, however, they would be able to prevent an attacker from gathering enough data to crack the WEP key, and this would significantly improve WEP's privacy. There are techniques for dynamically and automatically changing the shared secret to dramatically reduce WEP's weaknesses, such as the 802.1X authentication protocol.

Selecting an Authentication Method

> Selecting the right type of authentication for a WEP network will provide an additional level of protection when the WEP client connects to the wireless access point.

The initial WEP standards provided for two types of computer authentication:

- *Open system* enables any client to connect without providing a password
- *Shared secret* requires wireless clients to authenticate by using a secret key

Fortunately, choosing between open system and shared secret authentication is easy: always use open system authentication. On the surface this might seem illogical, because open system authentication does not require any proof of identity while shared key authentication requires knowledge of a secret key. However, shared secret authentication actually weakens security because most WEP client implementations use the same secret key for both authentication and WEP encryption. If a malicious user captures the authentication key and manages to penetrate its code, then the WEP encryption key is compromised as well.

Therefore, although shared secret authentication is stronger than open system for authentication, it weakens the WEP encryption. If you use open system authentication, any computer can easily join your network. However, without the WEP encryption key the unauthorized clients cannot send or receive wireless communications, and abuse the wireless network.

Using Wi-Fi Protected Access

> Wi-Fi Protected Access improves upon the authentication and encryption features of WEP by providing stronger encryption and built-in authentication support.

To address the weaknesses of WEP, the Wi-Fi Alliance, a consortium of the leading wireless network equipment vendors, developed Wi-Fi Protected Access (WPA). WPA can use the same authentication mechanisms and encryption algorithms as WEP, which enables manufacturers to add support for WPA to existing products with a simple software or firmware upgrade.

There are two encryption options for WPA, as follows:

- *Temporal Key Integrity Protocol (TKIP)* – Implemented in the original WPA standard, TKIP encrypts data using the RC4 algorithm with a 128-bit key. This is the same algorithm as WEP, but TKIP virtually eliminates WEP's most exploited vulnerability by using a unique encryption key for each packet.
- *Advanced Encryption System (AES)* – Implemented in the WPA2 standard, AES uses a different and more secure encryption algorithm, called Counter Cipher Mode with Block Chaining Message Authentication Code Protocol (CCMP). However, while it is possible to upgrade some legacy WEP equipment to support WPA-TKIP, most equipment cannot be upgraded to support AES. As a result, a wireless network will probably not be able to use AES encryption unless the organization chooses equipment that specifically supports it.

In its current form, WPA has two operational modes, as follows:

- *WPA2-Personal* – Also known as WPA-PSK or pre-shared key mode, an administrator selects a passphrase that is automatically associated with the dynamically generated security settings. A passphrase is a combination of words and characters used to authenticate the wireless connection. This passphrase is stored with the network settings in the WAP and on each of the networked computers. Only wireless devices with the WPA passphrase can join the network and decrypt network transmissions.

- **WPA2-Enterprise** – Also known as WPA-802.1X or WPA-RADIUS, requires an authentication server using Remote Authentication Dial-In User Service (RADIUS) and the 802.1X authentication protocol, as implemented in the Network Policy and Access Services role in Windows Server 2008 R2. Although more difficult to implement and configure, the use of RADIUS and 802.1X is more secure. This combination provides centralized administration, auditing, and logging, and eliminates the need for a shared passphrase, which is a potential vulnerability.

■ Connecting to Wireless Networks

THE BOTTOM LINE

When connecting Windows 8.1 to a wireless network, the process can differ depending upon whether or not the wireless network is broadcasting its network name.

The process for connecting a Windows 8.1 computer to a wireless network is very simple when the network is broadcasting its *service set identifier (SSID)*. The SSID is the name for the wireless network. Any wireless network that is broadcasting its name appears in the list of available networks in Windows 8.1. If you hold your mouse over the network name without clicking, you can see the security type (e.g., WEP, WPA2) used and the wireless protocol required (e.g., 802.11g, 802.11n).

CERTIFICATION READY
Connect to a wireless network
Objective 3.2

If you click the network, Windows 8.1 scans for the security settings and then prompts you to type the correct security key. Once you type the correct key, you have the option of enabling sharing on the network. If you are working on a private network (home,work), sharing is recommended. If you are on a public network, make sure you do not turn on sharing. After you are connected, the network icon in the task tray shows a small bar graph indicating the strength of the wireless signal. To disconnect, you simply click the network on the list and choose Disconnect.

 CONNECT TO A WIRELESS NETWORK BROADCASTING ITS SSID

GET READY. In order to complete this exercise, you need to have a wireless network in range and know its assigned security key. To connect to a wireless network that is broadcasting its SSID, perform the following steps:

1. From the *Start* menu, press the **Windows logo key** + c to open the *Charms* bar.
2. On the *Charms* bar click **Settings**.
3. In the *Settings* menu, click the **wireless network icon** (see Figure 10-1).

   The word *Available*, shown under the icon, indicates you are currently within range of one or more wireless networks. If you were already connected to a wireless network, you would see its name under the wireless network icon.

Figure 10-1

Selecting the wireless network icon

4. On the *Networks* menu, you see a list of wireless networks that are within range. Click the network to which you want to connect.

   If this were a network that you wanted to connect to one time only, you would uncheck the option *Connect automatically*. The default setting causes Windows 8.1 to always connect to the network automatically when it is within range.

5. Click **Connect**.

6. In the *Enter the network security key* field, type the security key for the network and then click **Next**.

Your computer is now connected to the network you selected. The network will now show its status as *Connected* in the *Networks* menu.

If you need to connect to a wireless network that is not broadcasting its SSID, the process is a little more involved. Because the network is not broadcasting, it does not appear in the list of available networks. This means you have to enter information such as the network's SSID (network name), security type, encryption type and security key to connect to it.

Because the network does not appear on your network list, you must connect to it by using the ***Network and Sharing Center***. The Network and Sharing Center provides a central location for network configuration controls (changing settings, managing wireless networks, network sharing settings).

 CONNECT TO A HIDDEN WIRELESS NETWORK

GET READY. To connect to a hidden wireless network that is not broadcasting its SSID, perform the following steps:

1. From the *Start* menu, press the **Windows logo key** + **c** to open the Charms bar.
2. On the *Charms* bar click **Settings**.
3. From the *Settings* menu, click **Control Panel**.
4. In the *Control Panel*, click **Network and Internet** > **Network and Sharing Center**.
5. From the *Network and Sharing Center*, click **Set up a new connection or network**.
6. Under *Choose a connection option*, choose **Manually connect to a wireless network** and then click **Next**. The *Manually connect to a wireless network* page appears, as shown in Figure 10-2.

Figure 10-2

The *Manually connect to a wireless network* page

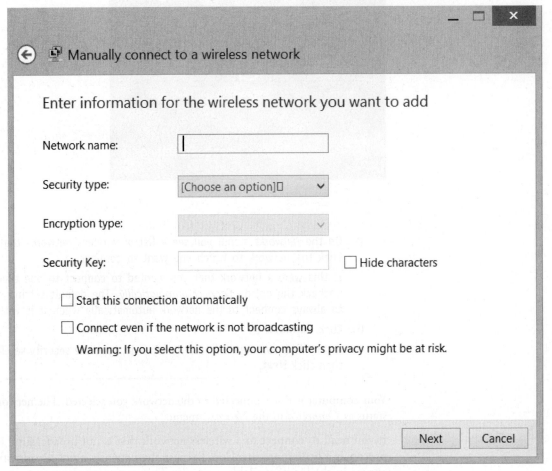

7. Type the *Network name*, choose the *Security type* and *Encryption type* and then type the *Security Key* for the wireless network.

8. Click **Next** to continue.

9. When the success message appears, click **Close**.

10. If the network is within range, you see its signal strength (series of full bars) by checking the network icon in the task tray.

■ Managing Preferred Wireless Networks

↓
THE BOTTOM LINE

When multiple wireless networks are within range of your Windows 8.1 computer, it needs to make a decision on which one to connect to. Windows 8.1 has automated this process for you (meaning that you do not have to manage preferred networks yourself) but having a good understanding of how this works helps you manage both your wireless and mobile broadband connections more effectively.

Once your Windows 8.1 computer has been configured to use a wireless network adapter, it connects to the wireless network you specified after entering the appropriate security key. But, what if there are multiple wireless networks in the same range?

CERTIFICATION READY
Manage preferred
wireless networks
Objective 3.2

In Windows 7, you could view a list (via *Network and Sharing Center, Manage wireless networks*) of wireless networks that you had connected to and then rename, remove, or move these networks up and down in the priority list. Windows 7 would then attempt to connect to the networks in the order you specified. The process for prioritizing networks is very different in Windows 8.1.

Prioritizing Networks in Windows 8.1

Windows 8.1 determines the connection priority automatically based on the type of network to which you are connected. The highest priority network is always an Ethernet (wired) connection with Wi-Fi and then *mobile broadband networks* preferred when Ethernet is not available.

Mobile broadband networks provide high-speed Internet access through portable devices and require a data plan with a mobile broadband provider.

When you connect to a new Wi-Fi network from a Windows 8.1 computer, Windows adds the new network to the list of wireless networks on your computer. If you connect to another wireless network, while in range of the first one, the second network is now preferred over the first. To see the list of networks, click the wireless network icon in your task tray.

If you connect to a mobile broadband network while a Wi-Fi network is within range, the mobile broadband network is the preferred network for that specific session only. The next time you attempt to connect and both the mobile broadband and the Wi-Fi network are within range, the Wi-Fi network is preferred.

Windows 8.1 is designed to learn your preferences and adjust the list of networks for you. If you want to move a network up in the priority list, you simply have to connect automatically when the network is in range.

For example, in Figure 10-3, a computer running Windows 8.1 is connected to a wireless network called Contoso1 and also has a second wireless network, called Contoso2, within range.

Figure 10-3

Connecting to a preferred network

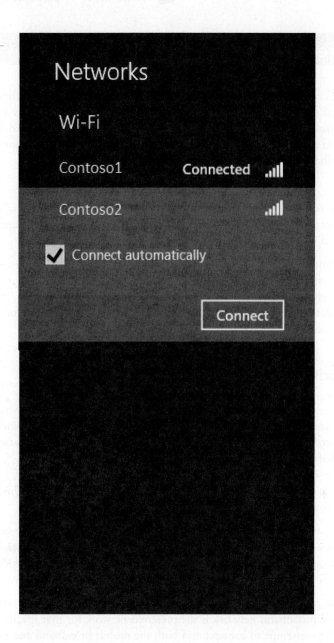

Because Windows 8.1 is currently connected to Contoso1, it is treating it as the preferred network. This means anytime the computer is within range, it automatically connects to Contoso1. If you connect to Contoso2 manually, selecting the Connect automatically checkbox, Windows 8.1 makes a note of this and use Contoso2 as the preferred network the next time you are within range of the two networks.

Removing Wireless Networks/Profiles

Wireless profiles contain information that allows you to connect to wireless networks automatically. Understanding how to delete them will help you to maintain an updated list of only valid networks.

Another key difference between Windows 7 and Windows 8.1 is the absence of a Wireless Profile Manager in Windows 8.1. In Windows 7, the ***Wireless Profile Manager*** was used to create, delete, and modify wireless profiles. A ***wireless profile*** is a file in Windows 8.1 that stores information about a wireless network that you use on a repeated basis. The profile includes the wireless network name, the security type, encryption type and any security keys or ***passphrases*** used to connect to the wireless network. The main benefit of the profile is that is allows you to connect to the wireless network automatically when you are within range.

Over time, the list of wireless networks and profiles can become large and you may want to remove them from the list. This is very common when you connect using public Wi-Fi spots (library, coffee shops, fast food restaurants, etc.). Although Windows 8.1 no longer provides the Wireless Profile Manager, you can use the following commands to first show the wireless profiles on your computer and then delete the profile if the wireless network is no longer in range.

To view all wireless profiles currently stored on your computer, from a command prompt, type the following and then press Enter:

```
netsh wlan show profiles
```

To delete a wireless profile that is no longer within range, from a command prompt, type the following and press Enter. Be sure to replace *<profile name>* with the actual name of the profile you want to remove:

```
netsh wlan delete profile name="<profile name>"
```

Configuring Network Adapters

THE BOTTOM LINE

In order for Windows 8.1 to communicate on a network using a wireless or wired network adapter, you must understand the options available for configuring these types of interfaces. These configuration settings can allow you to troubleshoot problems with the adapter.

A ***network adapter*** (network interface card [NIC], ethernet adapter, wireless adapter, Wi-Fi card) is the hardware component used to connect your Windows 8.1 computer to a wired or wireless network.

The easiest way to access the configuration settings for a network adapter is to use the Network and Sharing Center. To configure the network adapter click the *Change adapter settings* link, which takes you to the Network Connections dialog box shown in Figure 10-4.

Figure 10-4

The Network Connections
window

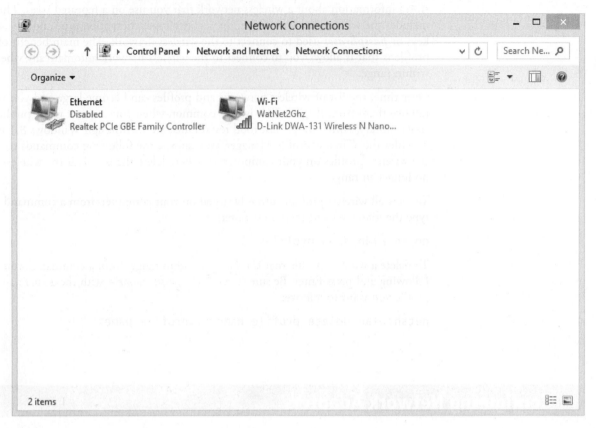

CERTIFICATION READY
Configure network
adapters
Objective 3.2

After accessing the Network Connections dialog box, you see any wired and wireless network adapters installed on the computer. To disable a network connection without affecting its configuration, you can right-click the adapter and then choose Disable from the context menu. To re-enable a disabled connection, you choose Enable from the context menu.

Disabling and enabling a network adapter can sometimes help you to solve connection problems. It can also prevent wireless interference with other devices and improve battery life when a wireless connection is no longer needed.

In addition to enabling and disabling adapters, you can also perform additional configuration tasks by right-clicking the adapter, choosing Properties, and then clicking Configure. This opens the network adapter's Properties sheet. The configuration options available differ depending on the network adapter manufacturer as well as the adapter type (wired or wireless).

In Figure 10-5, you can see this wireless network adapter has two property settings that you can configure: Beacon Interval and Wireless Mode.

Figure 10-5

Advanced configuration
options for a wireless network
adapter

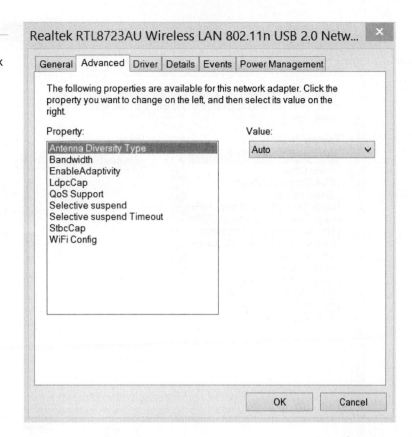

Depending upon the capabilities of the wireless adapter, you can configure additional settings in the advanced properties including whether the wireless network adapter supports ad hoc networks and how the adapter determines when to switch to another access point based on signal strength. When working in ***ad hoc mode***, you are configuring the wireless network adapter to connect to other computers who are also using wireless network adapters. You can also configure the wireless network adapter to work in ***infrastructure mode***. In infrastructure mode, the wireless network adapter is configured to connect to other computers through a wireless access point.

In the case of a wired adapter, you access the advanced configuration options in exactly the same way, but the adapter has a completely different set of options, as shown in Figure 10-6.

Figure 10-6

Advanced configuration options for a wired network adapter

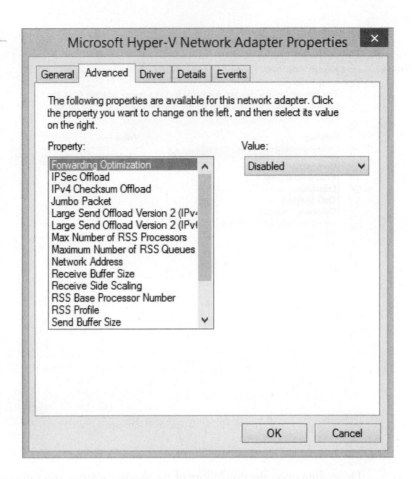

Just as with wireless network adapters, wired network adapter settings can vary according to the manufacturer. The settings enable you to troubleshoot and/or enable additional performance improvements.

Configuring Location-Aware Printing

THE BOTTOM LINE

As users become more mobile, they need to be able to easily locate, connect and print to printers located on multiple networks. These printers might be located on a home, office, airport or coffee shop's network.

Users who work from laptop computers often find themselves connecting to different printers depending upon where they are working from at any given point in time. For example, they may have a specific printer they like to use while at work while needing to switch to a different printer when connected to their home network. In either case, when the user connects from work or from home, they often have to set and reset the default printer to ensure their documents go to the right device. Windows 8.1 has a feature called *location-aware printing* that can make the process of moving between networks and connecting to printers much simpler.

➕ MORE INFORMATION
Location-aware printing is only available for computers that run on batteries (e.g., laptops).

Configure location-aware
printing
Objective 3.2

Location-aware printing, works by telling Windows 8.1 Pro to update and select the default printer based on the currently connected network. By configuring the default network for each printer, documents are automatically sent to the right printer whether the user is working from home or at work.

Location-aware printing depends upon the ***Network Location Awareness service*** and the ***Network List Service*** to determine network information. The Network Location Awareness service collects and stores configuration information for the networks and notifies programs when the information is changed. The Network List Service identifies the networks to which the computer is connected. If either of these services are not running or malfunctioning, Windows 8.1 is not able to detect changes in networks and cannot adjust the default printer accordingly. You can confirm these services are functioning properly by pressing the Windows logo key + r, typing services.msc in the Run dialog box and then reviewing their status in the Services console.

To configure location-aware printing, you must be running a portable computer with Windows 8.1 Pro or Windows 8.1 Enterprise and need to connect to printers on at least two different networks.

 CONFIGURE LOCATION-AWARE PRINTING

GET READY. Configure location-aware printing on a Windows 8.1 laptop by logging in with administrative privileges and performing the following steps:

> **TAKE NOTE** ✱   In this lesson, it is assumed that you have two printers available that are located on different networks (home and office)

1. From the *Start* menu, press the **Windows logo key + w**, type **devices**, and then choose **Devices and Printers** from *Results*.
2. Select the printer you want to configure and then in the menu bar, click **Manage default printers**.
3. In the *Manage Default Printers* dialog box (see Figure 10-7), select the **Change my default printer when I change networks** option.

Figure 10-7

The Manage Default Printers
dialog box

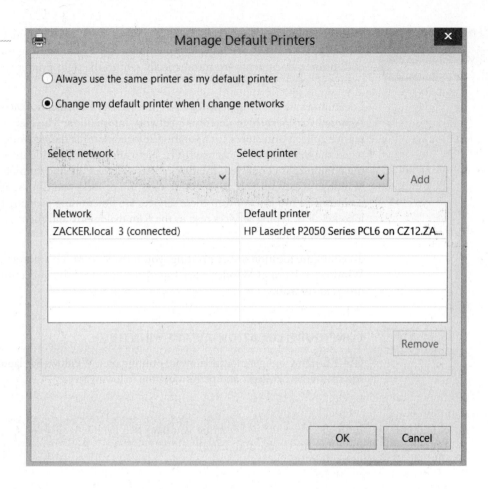

4. In the *Select network* drop-down list, choose a network, and then, in the *Select printer* drop-down list, choose the printer that will be the default printer for that network.

5. Click **Add**.

6. To close the *Manage Default Printers* dialog box, click **OK**.

7. Close the *Device and Printers* dialog box.

SKILL SUMMARY

- The Institute of Electrical and Electronic Engineers dictate the frequencies, transmission speeds, and ranges of wireless network products.

- The Wired Equivalent Privacy (WEP) and WiFi Protected Access (WPA/WPA2) are the two main security protocols used in wireless LAN devices.

- WiFi Protected Access was designed to address the weaknesses of WEP and uses two encryption options: Temporal Key Integrity Protocol (TKIP) and Advanced Encryption System (AES).

- If a wireless network is broadcasting its SSID (network name) and it is within range of your Windows 8.1 computer, it appears in the list of available networks. You can simply click the network and enter the appropriate security key to connect.

- If a wireless network is not broadcasting its SSID, you have to enter information such as the network's SSID, security type, encrypting type and security key manually by going through the Network and Sharing Center.

- Windows 8.1 automates the process of managing the preferred network when it is within range. Unlike Windows 7 which allowed you to set the priority of one network over another, Windows 8.1 determines the priority based on the type of network you are connected to and the order in which you connect to the network.

- A wireless profile is a file that contains the wireless SSID, security type and encryption type and security keys. The main benefit of the profile is that is allows you to connect to the wireless network automatically when you are within range. The netsh tool can be used to view and delete these profiles.

- If you do not want Windows 8.1 to automatically connect to a network, you can use the *Forget this network* option if you are currently in range or the netsh wlan delete profile name="<profile name>" command if the network is no longer within range of your computer.

- Ad hoc mode is used when you configure a wireless network adapter to bypass a WAP and connect directly to other wireless computers. Infrastructure mode is used when you want the wireless adapter to connect to a WAP.

- Location-aware printing, available on Windows 8.1 computers that have batteries only (e.g., laptops) allows you to configure a default printer for each network you connect to. This ensures a user's print jobs are directed to the appropriate printer when they are working from home or the office.

- The Network Location Awareness services and the Network List Service are required in order for location-aware print to work. If either of these two services is not functioning, Windows 8.1 is not able to detect changes in networks and cannot adjust the default printer accordingly.

Knowledge Assessment

Multiple Choice

Select one or more correct answers for each of the following questions.

1. What type of attack is used to gain access to restricted network resources by impersonating authorized wireless users?
   a. eavesdropping
   b. data tampering
   c. denial of service
   d. masquerading

2. When a wireless network broadcasts this information to potential wireless clients, it appears in the list of available networks in Windows 8.1.
   a. WPA
   b. WEP
   c. SSID
   d. Beacon

3. Which of the following are included in a wireless profile? Select all that apply.
   a. SSID
   b. Security type
   c. Encryption type
   d. Security keys

4. In which mode would you configure a wireless client to connect through a wireless access point (WAP)?
   a. Ad hoc mode
   b. Infrastructure mode
   c. WAP mode
   d. Implementation mode

5. Which Windows 8.1 feature would you use to configure a default printer for each network the computer connects to?
   a. WAP
   b. Location-aware processing
   c. Location-aware printing
   d. Beacons

6. You are connected to a wireless network at a local coffee shop and want to make sure the next time you are in range of the network that Windows 8.1 does not automatically connect to it. What should you do before moving out of range of the network?
   a. Right-click the network and then choose *Forget this network*.
   b. Run the `netsh wlan delete profile "<profile name>"` command.
   c. Run the `netsh delete profile name="<profile name>"` command.
   d. Run the `netsh wlan delete name="<profile name>"` command.

7. Which of the following represents the correct order that Windows 8.1 uses to prioritize networks?
   a. Ethernet, Wi-Fi and then mobile broadband networks.
   b. Mobile, Wi-Fi and then Ethernet.
   c. Ethernet, mobile broadband and then Wi-Fi.
   d. Windows 8.1 allows you to set the priority via the *Manage wireless networks* option.

8. Which command would you use to view all wireless profiles currently stored on your Windows 8.1 computer?
   a. `netsh wlan show wireless profiles`
   b. `netsh wlan show profiles`
   c. `netsh wlan show profiles = all`
   d. `netsh wlan show profiles` *<all profiles>*

9. You are currently connected to a mobile broadband network while a Wi-Fi network is within range. Which of the following statements are true on how Windows 8.1 manages these connections in regard to priority? Select all that apply.
   a. The mobile broadband network is preferred for this session only.
   b. The mobile broadband network is always the preferred network.
   c. The Wi-Fi network is preferred the next time you are within range of both networks.
   d. The Wi-Fi network forces the mobile broadband network to disconnect and replace it with the Wi-Fi network that is in range.

Best Answer

Choose the letter that corresponds to the best answer. More than one answer choice may achieve the goal. Select the BEST answer.

1. You are thinking about purchasing new wireless hardware for your company. Your wireless clients need to connect to a WAP. These clients are sometimes as far away as 50 meters from the WAP but most of the time are within 35 meters. What IEEE Wireless networking standard would you recommend?
   a. IEEE 802.11a
   b. IEEE 802.11b
   c. IEEE 802.11n
   d. IEEE 802.11g

2. You would like to setup location-aware printing on your Windows 8.1 computer. After opening *Devices and Printers*, you cannot find the option *Manage Default Printers* on the menu bar. What is the most likely reason?
   a. You do not have administrative privileges.
   b. You are logged in to a Windows 8.1 Pro desktop computer.
   c. You are logged in to a Windows 8.1 Enterprise desktop computer.
   d. You are not logged in to a Windows 8.1 Pro/Enterprise laptop.

3. You would like to prevent wireless interference with other devices and improve battery life on your laptop. What is the best way to disable your wireless connection when it is not in use?
   a. Delete the wireless adapters from the *Network Connections* dialog box.
   b. Right-click the wireless network and choose *Forget this network*.
   c. Right-click the wireless network adapter and choose Disable.
   d. Turn off your laptop when not connecting to the wireless network.

4. Your network consists of both Windows 7 and Windows 8.1 desktops and laptops. All of the computers are configured to connect to a WAP using AES. There is no pre-shared key is being used. If you needed to add another Windows 8.1 laptop, what security setting would you recommend to use on the computer?
   a. WPA2-Personal
   b. WPA-Personal AES
   c. WPA-Enterprise AES
   d. WPA2-Enterprise

5. You are running a Windows 8.1 computer that has a wireless adapter installed. What is the easiest way to determine the security type and wireless protocol being used by the network that is currently in range and broadcasting its SSID?
   a. Contact the administrator of the WAP.
   b. Use a third-party tool to scan the network for wireless configurations.
   c. Under the *Networks* menu, move your mouse over the visible network.
   d. Review the properties of the wireless network adapter after you connect.

Matching and Identification

Complete the following exercise by matching the terms with their corresponding definitions.

_____ a) Passphrase
_____ b) Location-aware printing
_____ c) Mobile broadband network
_____ d) Ad hoc mode
_____ e) Infrastructure mode

1. Configures wireless adapter to connect through a WAP.
2. Words and characters used to authenticate a wireless connection.
3. Feature that allows you to set default printer for each network you connect to.
4. Configures wireless adapter to connect to other wireless computers bypassing the WAP.
5. Provide high-speed access through portable devices; requires data plan.

Build a List

1. In order of first to last, specify the order of steps you would use to connect to a wireless network broadcasting its SSID.
   _____ In the *Settings* menu, click the **Network icon**.
   _____ From the Windows 8.1 *Start* menu, press the **Windows logo key + c**, to open the *Charms* bar.
   _____ Click **Connect**.
   _____ When prompted, Do *you want to turn on sharing between PCs and connect to devices on this network?* Click **Yes, turn on sharing and connect to devices**.
   _____ In the *Networks* menu, choose the network you want to connect to
   _____ On the *Charms* bar click **Settings**.
   _____ In the *Enter the network security key* field, type the security key for the network and then click **Next**.

2. Specify the correct order of steps required to keep Windows 8.1 from automatically connecting to a wireless network that used for a one time task while you are still within range of the network.

_____ From the Windows 8.1 task tray, click your wireless connection icon.

_____ Make sure your computer is currently within range of the network you want to remove.

_____ From the *Networks* menu, locate the network you want to remove.

_____ Right-click the network and choose **Forget this network**.

3. In order of first to last, specify the steps needed to configure location-aware printing on a Windows 8.1 laptop.

_____ Under *Select network* click the down arrow and choose a network and then under *Select printer* choose the printer that will be used as the default printer for that network.

_____ To close the *Manage Default Printers* dialog box, click **OK**.

_____ Click the printer you want to configure and then in the menu bar, choose **Manage default printers**.

_____ Click **Add**.

_____ Close the *Device and Printers* dialog box.

_____ In the *Manage Default Printers* dialog box, click **Change my default printer when I change networks**.

_____ From the Windows 8.1 Start menu, press the **Windows logo key + w**, type **devices** and then choose **Devices and Printers** from *Results*.

Business Case Scenarios

Scenario 10-1: Troubleshooting Location-Aware Printing

You currently have two users in your company that work from home on Wednesday's. After setting up their Windows 8.1 laptops to use location-aware printing, you discover the computers are not defaulting to the appropriate printer when they connect to a network. How would you troubleshoot this problem?

Scenario 10-2: Deleting Wireless Networks No Longer in Range

A few of your Windows 8.1 laptop users recently returned from a convention where they used the local wireless network extensively. They have no intention of every going back to that convention and want to know how to delete the wireless profile from their machines. What would you tell them?

Configuring and Maintaining Network Security

70-687 EXAM OBJECTIVE

Objective 3.3 – Configure and maintain network security. This objective may include but is not limited to: configure Windows Firewall; configure Windows Firewall with Advanced Security; configure connection security rules (IPsec); configure authenticated exceptions; configure network discovery.

LESSON HEADING	EXAM OBJECTIVE
Defending Against Malware	
Using Windows 8.1 Action Center	
Using Windows Firewall	Configure Windows Firewall Configure Windows Firewall with Advanced Security Configure network discovery Configure authenticated exceptions Configure connection security rules (IPsec)

KEY TERMS

authenticated exception	IP Security (IPsec)	tunneling
filter	malware	
firewall	rules	

■ Defending Against Malware

↓
THE BOTTOM LINE

Malware is one of the primary threats to Windows 8.1 security, and the operating system includes a variety of tools that you can use to combat it. The following sections examine these tools and how to implement and configure them.

Windows 8.1 holds security as one its primary goals. Beginning with the Windows XP Service Pack 2 release, Windows has monitored the state of the security mechanisms included with the operating system and warns the user if any components are misconfigured, outdated, or not functioning.

Chief among the threats to Windows 8.1 computers is malicious software created specifically for the purpose of infiltrating or damaging a computer system without the user's knowledge or consent. This type of software includes a variety of technologies, including viruses, Trojan horses, worms, spyware, and adware. The term most commonly used to collectively refer to these malicious software technologies is *malware*.

The types of malware to which Windows 8.1 is susceptible range from the relatively innocuous to the extremely destructive. The effects they can have on a Windows 8.1 computer include the following:

- Collect usage information about the computer user and transmit to an Internet server.
- Display advertisements on the user's system.
- Use the system's email address book to send spam.
- Attach code to document files that spreads to other files on any system opening the document.
- Install and run a program that enables a remote user to take control of the system.
- Damage or destroy the files stored on the computer.
- Infiltrate the computer's boot sector and spread to other systems.

Malware is, in most cases, introduced onto a computer by a deliberate action on the part of a user. Someone opens an email attachment, installs an infected program, or accesses a dangerous website, and the malicious code is introduced to the system. Windows 8.1 includes a variety of tools that try to prevent users from inadvertently infecting their computers and also attempt to block the activities of malicious software programs once they are present.

Security is a pervasive concern throughout the Windows 8.1 operating system, and as a result there are some Windows 8.1 security mechanisms that are discussed elsewhere in this text:

- In Lesson 7, "Configuring Internet Explorer 11 and Internet Explorer for the Desktop," you learn about the security features included in Internet Explorer.
- In Lesson 14, "Configuring File and Folder Access," you learn about the permissions Windows uses to control access to files and other system resources.

Using Windows 8.1 Action Center

The Windows 8.1 Action Center ensures that your system is protected from malware intrusion by notifying you if any of the Windows 8.1 security mechanisms are not running properly.

Like the Network and Sharing Center, the ***Action Center*** is a centralized console that enables users and administrators to access, monitor, and configure the various Windows 8.1 security mechanisms. The primary function of the Action Center is to provide an automatic notification system that alerts users when the system is vulnerable.

Action Center is a service that starts automatically and runs continuously on Windows 8.1 computers, by default. The service constantly monitors the different security mechanisms running on the computer. If Action Center detects a mechanism that is not functioning properly for any of several reasons, it displays an icon in the notification area (formerly known as the taskbar tray) to inform the user of the condition, as shown in Figure 11-1.

Figure 11-1

The *Action Center* menu in the notification area

The Windows 8.1 Action Center is not limited to monitoring Microsoft security solutions. The service can also monitor third-party programs for their currency and operational status.

TAKE NOTE *

ACCESSING ACTION CENTER

When a user clicks the notification area icon to open the Action Center window (or opens it from the Control Panel), the system displays information about the problems it has discovered, and links to possible solutions.

For example, the Action Center window shown in Figure 11-2 contains Spyware and unwanted software protection and Virus protection warnings. Clicking *Find an app online to help protect my PC* opens a webpage on Microsoft's site linking to various providers of virus protection software.

Figure 11-2

The *Action Center* window

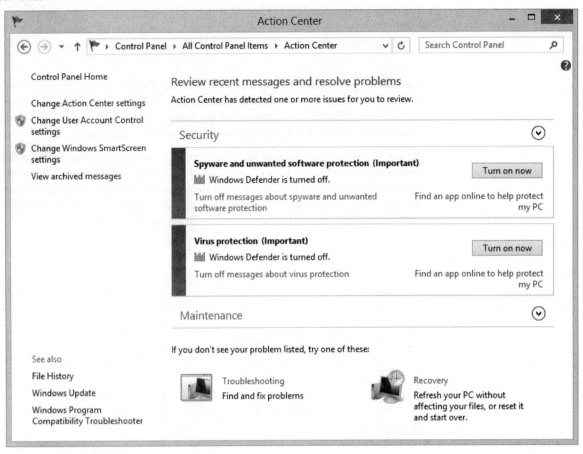

The Action Center window is divided into two main sections: Security and Maintenance. The Security section, in addition to monitoring the computer's security status, provides users with a single point of access to information about Windows 8.1 security, in the form of the following indicators:

- Network firewall
- Windows Update
- Virus Protection
- Spyware and unwanted software protection
- Internet security settings
- User Account Control
- Windows SmartScreen
- Network Access Protection
- Windows activation

The Maintenance section contains these indicators:

- Check for solutions to problem reports
- Automatic maintenance
- HomeGroup

- File History
- Drive status
- Device software

Each of these indicators displays the current status of the security or maintenance feature and, if appropriate, supplies a link to the controls for that feature.

Links to other related features appear on the left side of the window, including a link to the *Change Action Center Settings* window. From this window, you can control which messages appear in the *Action Center* interface.

Using Windows Firewall

> Windows Firewall protects Windows 8.1 computers by blocking dangerous traffic, both incoming and outgoing. A *firewall* is a software program or hardware device that protects a computer by allowing certain types of network traffic in and out of the system while blocking others.

Firewalls are essentially packet filters that examine the contents of packets and the traffic patterns to and from the network to determine which packets should be allowed passage through the filter.

Network connections are all but ubiquitous in the computing world these days. All business computers are networked, and virtually all home computers have an Internet connection. Many homes have local area networks as well. Network connections provide Windows 8.1 users with access to virtually unlimited resources, but any door that allows data out can also allow data in. Some of the hazards that firewalls protect against are as follows:

- Trojan horse applications that users inadvertently download and run can open a connection to a computer on the Internet, enabling an attacker on the outside to run programs or store data on the system.
- A mobile computer can be compromised while connected to a public network and then brought onto a private network, compromising the resources there in turn.
- Network scanner applications can probe systems for unguarded ports, which are essentially unlocked doors that attackers can use to gain access to the system.
- Attackers that obtain passwords by illicit means, such as social engineering, can use remote access technologies to log on to a computer from another location and compromise its data and programming.

UNDERSTANDING FIREWALLS

Firewalls typically base their filtering on the TCP/IP characteristics at the network, transport, and application layers of the Open Systems Interconnection (OSI) reference model, as follows:

- **IP addresses** – Represent specific computers on the network.
- **Protocol numbers** – Identify the transport layer protocol being used by the packets.
- **Port numbers** – Identify specific applications running on the computer.

To filter traffic, firewalls use *rules*, which specify which packets are allowed to pass through the firewall and which are blocked. Firewalls can work in two ways, as follows:

- Admit all traffic, except that which conforms to the applied rules.
- Block all traffic, except that which conforms to the applied rules.

Generally speaking, blocking all traffic by default is the more secure arrangement. From the firewall administrator's standpoint, you start with a completely blocked system, and then start testing your applications. When an application fails to function properly because network access is blocked, you create a rule that opens up the ports the application needs to communicate.

This is the method that the Windows Firewall service in Windows 8.1 uses by default for incoming network traffic. The default rules preconfigured into the firewall are designed to admit the traffic used by standard Windows networking functions, such as file and printer sharing. For outgoing network traffic, Windows Firewall uses the other method, allowing all traffic to pass except that which conforms to a rule.

MONITORING WINDOWS FIREWALL

Windows Firewall is one of the programs monitored by the Action Center service. The main *Action Center* window indicates whether Windows Firewall is running, and also whether any third-party firewall products are running.

When you open the Windows Control Panel and click System and Security > Windows Firewall, a *Windows Firewall* window appears, displaying the firewall's status in greater detail, as shown in Figure 11-3.

Figure 11-3

The *Windows Firewall* window

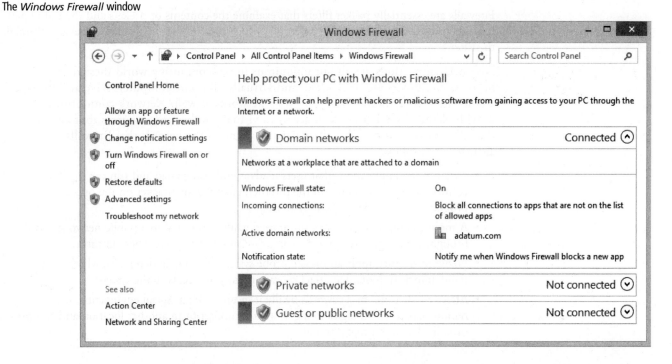

The Windows Firewall window contains expandable headings for the computer's network locations: public, guest or private, and domain (if the computer is joined to an Active Directory Domain Services domain). Each of the headings contains information on

- whether the computer is connected to a domain, private, or public network,
- whether the Windows Firewall service is currently turned on or off,
- whether inbound and outbound connections are blocked, or
- whether users are notified when a program is blocked.

Windows Firewall maintains a separate profile for each of the network locations, so you can have a different firewall configuration for each one. Whenever you are working with Windows Firewall settings, you must be conscious of the profile to which the settings apply.

USING THE WINDOWS FIREWALL CONTROL PANEL

On the left side of the Windows Firewall window is a series of links that enable you to configure Windows Firewall to allow a specific app or feature through its barrier, change the firewall notification settings, turn Windows Firewall on and off, restore the default firewall settings, and configure advanced firewall settings.

Clicking *Change notification settings* or *Turn Windows firewall on or off* displays the *Customize settings for each type of network* dialog box, as shown in Figure 11-4. As in the *Windows Firewall* window, controls for the domain profile only appear when the computer is joined to an AD DS domain.

CERTIFICATION READY
Configure Windows Firewall
Objective 3.3

Figure 11-4

The *Customize settings for each type of network* dialog box

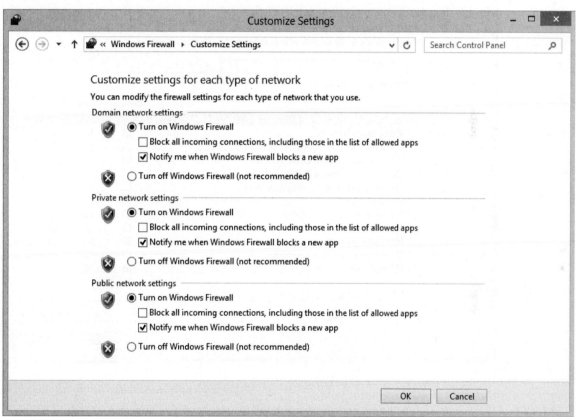

Using this interface, you can turn Windows Firewall completely on or off for each of the network locations and configure each location to block all incoming traffic and notify the user when the firewall blocks a program.

BLOCKING INCOMING CONNECTIONS

Selecting the *Block all incoming connections, including those in the list of allowed apps* checkbox enables you to increase the security of your system by blocking all unsolicited attempts to connect to your computer. Note, however, that this does not prevent you from performing common networking tasks, such as accessing websites and sending or receiving emails. These activities are not unsolicited connection attempts; they begin with the client contacting the server first. When the firewall detects the outgoing traffic from your web browser to a web server on the Internet, for example, it knows that it should admit the incoming response from the server.

ALLOWING PROGRAMS THROUGH THE FIREWALL

Users might want to modify the firewall settings in other ways also, typically because a specific application requires access to a port not anticipated by the firewall's preconfigured rules. Clicking *Allow an app or feature through Windows Firewall* opens the *Allow apps to communicate through Windows Firewall* dialog box, as shown in Figure 11-5. In this dialog box, you can open up a port through the firewall for specific programs and features installed on the computer, simply by selecting the appropriate checkboxes.

Figure 11-5

The *Allow apps to communicate through Windows Firewall* dialog box

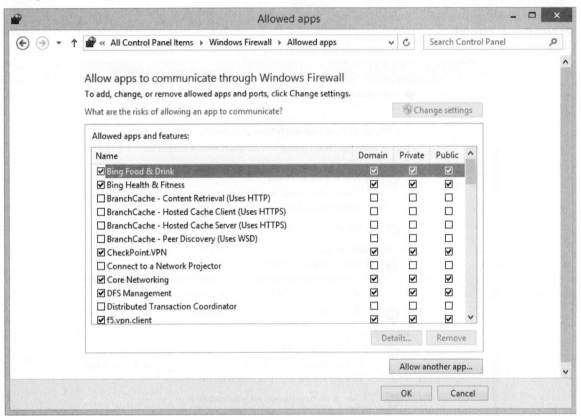

Opening a port in your firewall is an inherently dangerous activity. The more holes you make in a wall, the greater the likelihood that intruders will get in. For this reason, the Windows Firewall controls in the Windows 8.1 Control Panel are quite limited. In Windows 8.1, you cannot open up specific port numbers using Control Panel; you can only select from a list of installed applications and features. For full access to Windows Firewall, you must use the Windows Firewall with Advanced Security console, as discussed in the next section.

USING THE WINDOWS FIREWALL WITH ADVANCED SECURITY CONSOLE

The Windows Firewall with Advanced Security snap-in for Microsoft Management Console (MMC) provides direct access to the rules that control the behavior of Windows Firewall. To access the console, you can run a search for the program from the Start screen, or, from the Windows Control Panel, click System and Security > Administrative Tools > Windows Firewall with Advanced Security. The Windows Firewall with Advanced Security console appears, as shown in Figure 11-6.

Figure 11-6

The *Windows Firewall with Advanced Security* snap-in

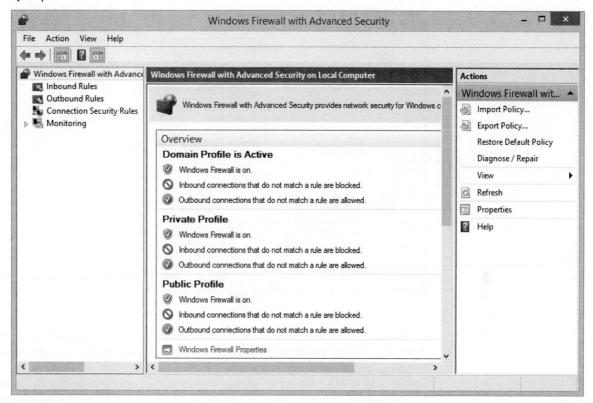

Configuring Profile Settings

CERTIFICATION READY
Configure Windows Firewall
with Advanced Security
Objective 3.3

At the top of the center pane, in the Overview section, are status displays for the computer's three possible network locations. Windows Firewall maintains separate profiles for each of the three possible network locations: domain, private, and public. If you connect the computer to a different network, as in the case of a laptop computer that you bring to an Internet "hot spot" in a coffee shop, Windows Firewall loads a different configuration for that profile and a different set of rules.

Unlike the Windows Firewall control panel, the Windows Firewall with Advanced Security console always displays all three network location profiles, even if the computer is not joined to a domain. This enables you to work with the rules in any of the profiles, whether that profile is active or not. As you can tell from the Overview display, the default Windows Firewall settings call for the same basic configuration for all three profiles: the firewall is turned on, incoming traffic is blocked unless it matches a rule, and outgoing traffic is allowed unless it matches a rule. You can change this default behavior by clicking the Windows Firewall Properties link, which displays the *Windows Firewall with Advanced Security on Local Computer Properties* sheet, as shown in Figure 11-7.

Figure 11-7

The *Windows Firewall with Advanced Security on Local Computer Properties* sheet

On this properties sheet, each of the three location profiles has a tab with identical controls that enables you to modify the default profile settings. You can, for example, configure the firewall to shut down completely when it is connected to a domain network, and turn the firewall on with its most protective settings when you connect the computer to a public network. You can also configure the firewall's notification option, which specifies whether the firewall should display a message to the user when it blocks a program, and its logging behavior.

The most important settings in this properties sheet are those that establish the default behavior for each profile, because these settings determine the nature of the rules that Windows Firewall will use. In the default settings, *Inbound connections* is set to *Block*, so the rules you create must allow certain types of traffic to pass through the firewall. If you change the default to allow inbound connections, then you must create rules that block certain types of traffic. The setting for *Outbound connections* are the opposite, by default.

Creating Rules

Selecting apps and features in the Windows Firewall control panel is a relatively friendly method for working with firewall rules. In the *Windows Firewall with Advanced Security* console, you can work with the rules in their raw form. Selecting either Inbound Rules or Outbound Rules in the left pane displays a list of all the rules operating in that direction, as shown in Figure 11-8. The rules that are currently operational have a checkmark in a green circle, while the rules not in force are grayed out.

Figure 11-8

The *Inbound Rules* list in the
*Windows Firewall with
Advanced Security* console

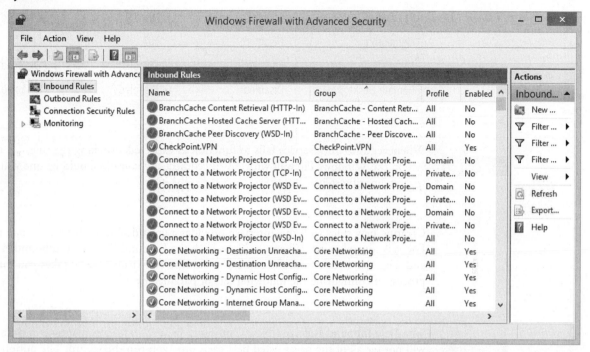

> **TAKE NOTE*** It is important to remember that in the Windows Firewall with Advanced Security console, you are always working with a complete list of rules for all of the profiles, while in the *Windows Firewall Settings* dialog box, you are working only with the rules that apply to the currently active profile.

CERTIFICATION READY
Configure network
discovery
Objective 3.3

The default rules for three profiles differ, with the public profile providing the most secure environment and the private profile the least. Table 11-1 lists some of the primary networking services in Windows 8.1 and their default firewall settings for each profile. This is a highly simplified list, as most of these services use a variety of protocols that each require their own rules for incoming and outgoing traffic. When you modify the default networking behavior in Windows 8.1 – such as when you enable Network Discovery in the Advanced Sharing Settings control panel – the controls change the default settings for the Windows Firewall rules.

> **TAKE NOTE*** For more information on Network Discovery and its relationship to Windows Firewall, see "Understanding Network Discovery" in Lesson 9, "Configuring IP Settings."

Table 11-1

Default Windows Firewall
Rules Settings

	PRIVATE	PUBLIC	DOMAIN
Core Networking	Enabled	Enabled	Enabled
File and Printer Sharing	Enabled	Disabled	Disabled
Homegroup	Disabled	N/A	N/A
Network Discovery	Enabled	Disabled	Disabled
Remote Desktop	Disabled	Disabled	Disabled

TAKE NOTE ✱

Whenever a network service fails to function as expected, checking the rules for that service in the Windows Firewall with Advanced Security console should be one your first troubleshooting steps.

Creating new rules with this interface provides a great deal more flexibility than the Windows Firewall control panel. When you right-click the Inbound Rules or Outbound Rules node and select New Rule from the context menu, the New Rule Wizard takes you through the process of configuring the following sets of parameters:

TAKE NOTE ✱

The New Inbound Rule and New Outbound Rule Wizards are adaptive, meaning that you will not see all of the pages listed here each time you run the wizard. The option you select on the Rule Type page determines what additional pages appear next.

- **Rule Type** – Specifies whether you want to create a program rule, a port rule, a variant on one of the predefined rules, or a custom rule. This selection determines which of the following pages the wizard displays.
- **Program** – Specifies whether the rule applies to all programs, to one specific program, or to a specific service.
- **Protocol and Ports** – Specifies the protocol and the local and remote ports to which the rule applies. This enables you to specify the exact types of traffic that the rule should block or allow.
- **Scope** – Specifies the IP addresses of the local and remote systems to which the rule applies. This enables you to block or allow traffic between specific computers.
- **Action** – Specifies the action the firewall should take when a packet matches the rule. You configure the rule to allow traffic if it is blocked by default, or block traffic if it is allowed by default. You can also configure the rule to allow traffic only when the connection between the communicating computers is secured using IPsec. This is called an *authenticated exception*.
- **Profile** – Specifies the profile(s) to which the rule should apply: domain, private, and/or public.
- **Name** – Specifies a name and (optionally) a description for the rule.

CERTIFICATION READY
Configure authenticated exceptions
Objective 3.3

The rules you can create using the New Rule Wizards range from simple program rules to highly complex and specific rules that block or allow only specific types of traffic between specific computers. The more complicated the rules become, however, the more you have to know about TCP/IP communications in general and the specific behavior of your applications. Modifying the default firewall settings to accommodate some special applications is relatively simple, but creating an entirely new firewall configuration is a formidable task.

Importing and Exporting Rules

The process of creating and modifying rules in the Windows Firewall with Advanced Security console can be time-consuming, and repeating the process on multiple computers even more so. Therefore, the console makes it possible for you to save the rules and settings you have created by exporting them to a policy file.

A *policy file* is a file with a .wfw extension that contains all of the property settings in a Windows Firewall installation, as well as all of its rules, including the preconfigured rules and the ones you have created or modified yourself. To create a policy file, you select Export Policy from the Action menu in the Windows Firewall with Advanced Security console, and specify a name and location for the file.

You can then duplicate the rules and settings on another computer by copying the file and using the Import Policy function to read in the contents.

> **TAKE NOTE** * When you import policies from a file, the console warns you that all existing rules and settings will be overwritten. You must therefore be careful not to create custom rules on a computer, and then expect to import other rules using a policy file.

Using Filters

Although what a firewall does is sometimes referred to as packet filtering, in the Windows Firewall with Advanced Security console, the term *filter* is used to refer to a feature that enables you to display rules according to the profile they apply to, their current state, or the group to which they belong.

For example, to display only the rules that apply to the public profile, click Action > Filter By Profile > Filter By Public Profile. The display changes to show only the rules that apply to the public profile. In the same way, you can apply a filter that causes the console to display only the rules that are currently turned on, or the rules that belong to a particular group. Click Action > Clear All Filters to return to the default display showing all of the rules.

Configuring Connection Security Rules

Windows 8.1 includes a feature in Windows Firewall that incorporates IPsec data protection into the Windows Firewall. The *IP Security (IPsec)* standards are a collection of documents that define a method for securing data while it is in transit over a TCP/IP network. IPsec includes a connection establishment routine, during which computers authenticate each other before transmitting data, and a technique called *tunneling*, in which data packets are encapsulated within other packets for their protection.

> **➕ MORE INFORMATION**
>
> Data protection technologies such as the Windows 8.1 Encrypting File System (EFS) and BitLocker protect data while it is stored on a drive. However, they do nothing to protect data while it is being transmitted over the network, because they both decrypt the data before sending it. IPsec, by contrast, protects data while it is in transit.

In addition to inbound and outbound rules, the Windows Firewall with Advanced Security console enables you to create connection security rules, using the New Connection Security Rule Wizard. Connection security rules defines the type of protection you want to apply to the communications that conform to Windows Firewall rules.

CERTIFICATION READY
Configure connection
security rules (IPsec)
Objective 3.3

When you right-click the Connection Security Rules node and select New Rule from the context menu, the New Connection Security Rule Wizard takes you through the process of configuring the following sets of parameters:

- **Rule Type** – Specifies the basic function of the rule, such as to isolate computers based on authentication criteria, to exempt certain computers (such as infrastructure servers) from authentication, to authenticate two specific computers or groups of computers, or to tunnel communications between two computers. You can also create custom rules combining these functions.

- **Endpoints** – Specifies the IP addresses of the computer that will establish a secured connection before transmitting any data.

- **Requirements** – Specifies whether authentication between two computers should be requested or required in each direction.

- **Authentication Method** – Specifies the type of authentication the computers should use when establishing a connection.

- **Profile** – Specifies the profile(s) to which the rule should apply: domain, private, and/or public.

- **Name** – Specifies a name and (optionally) a description for the rule.

CONFIGURING WINDOWS FIREWALL WITH GROUP POLICY

As with many other Windows 8.1 features, configuring Windows Firewall on individual computers is not practical in an enterprise network environment. However, it is possible to configure firewall settings on Windows workstations using Group Policy.

When you browse to the Computer Configuration\Policies\Windows Settings\Security Settings\ Windows Firewall with Advanced Security node in a GPO, you see the interface shown in Figure 11-9, which is similar to that of the Windows Firewall with Advanced Security console.

Figure 11-9

The *Windows Firewall with Advanced Security* node in a GPO

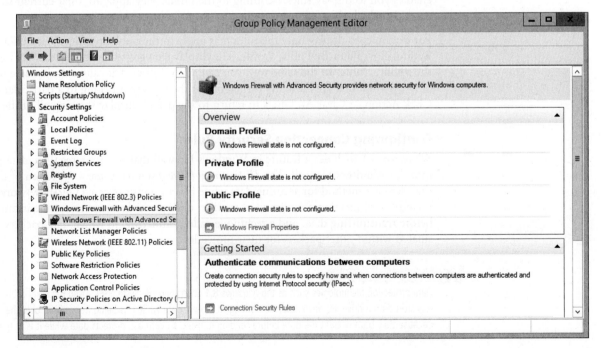

Clicking Windows Firewall Properties opens a dialog box with the same controls as the Windows Firewall with Advanced Security on Local Computer Properties sheet and clicking Inbound Rules and Outbound Rules launches the same wizards as the console.

SKILL SUMMARY

IN THIS LESSON, YOU LEARNED:

- Malware is malicious software created specifically for the purpose of infiltrating or damaging a computer system without the user's knowledge or consent. This type of software includes a variety of technologies, including viruses, Trojan horses, worms, spyware, and adware.

- Action Center is a centralized console that enables users and administrators to access, monitor, and configure the various Windows 8.1 security mechanisms.

- Windows Firewall is a software program that protects a computer by allowing certain types of network traffic in and out of the system while blocking others.

- You configure Windows Firewall by creating rules that specify what types of traffic to block and/or allow.

■ Knowledge Assessment

Multiple Choice

Select one or more correct answers for each of the following questions.

1. Which of the following mechanisms is used most often used in firewall rules to allow traffic onto the network?
   a. Protocol numbers
   b. IP addresses
   c. Port numbers
   d. Hardware addresses

2. Which of the following actions can you not perform from the Windows Firewall control panel? (Choose all that apply.)
   a. Turn Windows firewall off for all three profiles
   b. Manage firewall exceptions for the domain profile
   c. Allow a program through the firewall in all three profiles
   d. Create firewall exceptions based on port numbers

3. Connection security rules require that network traffic allowed through the firewall use which of the following security mechanisms?
   a. IPsec
   b. EFS
   c. UAC
   d. PIV

4. Windows Firewall uses three profiles to represent the type of network to which the server is connected. What are the three profiles?
   a. Private, Temporary, and Authenticated
   b. Public, DMZ, and Private

    c. Internet, Secure, and Private

    d. Domain, Private, and Public

5. When a user attempts to visit an Internet-based web server, what is the default action of the Windows Firewall?

    a. The firewall will not permit the user to visit a non-corporate website.

    b. The firewall by default will not block client-initiated network traffic.

    c. The firewall will block the web request unless the user is already authenticated.

    d. The firewall will block all outbound traffic.

6. In the Windows Firewall With Advanced Security console, while creating a new rule, the Program page specifies whether the _____.

    a. rule applies to all programs, to one specific program

    b. rule applies to all users, to one specific user

    c. rule applies to all systems, to one specific system

    d. rule applies to all programs, to one specific program, or to a specific service

7. By exporting the Windows Firewall policy, you have a file with a .wfw extension that contains _____.

    a. all the rules you have created or modified

    b. preconfigured rules to be applied to another firewall

    c. all its rules, including the preconfigured rules and the ones you have created or modified

    d. firewall settings as specified by the Group Policy settings

Best Answer

Choose the letter that corresponds to the best answer. More than one answer choice may achieve the goal. Select the BEST answer.

1. What is the primary objective of a firewall?

    a. To permit traffic in and out for legitimate users, and to block the rest

    b. To authenticate and authorize users past the network perimeter

    c. To compare traffic information against a list of known valid traffic

    d. To protect a network by allowing certain types of network traffic in and out of the system

2. Windows Firewall Customize Settings contains three profiles (Public, Private and Domain). What differentiates these profiles from each other?

    a. Public is for servers accessible to temporary users. Private is for servers on an internal network. Domain is for servers in which users are all authenticated.

    b. Public is for servers accessible to unauthenticated users. Private is for inaccessible servers. Domain is for servers accessible only to authenticated users.

    c. Public is for servers accessible to temporary users. Private is for servers on an internal network. Domain is for servers across multiple sites.

    d. Public is for servers accessible to unauthenticated users. Private is for servers on a private network. Domain is for servers spanning different domain groups.

3. Windows Firewall allows you to create inbound, outbound, and connection security rules for individual servers or systems. How can you do this for multiple systems?

    a. You can delegate to administrators the task of performing the same configuration to their local servers.

    b. You can create a new Group Policy object (GPO) and create matching rules to match the desired configuration. Then deploy the GPO to other systems on the network.

    c. You can visit individual systems and configure them as you have the initial system.

    d. You can create a new GPO and you can import settings from a policy file created earlier. Then deploy the GPO to other systems on the network.

4. What is the primary benefit of configuring Windows Firewall through the Windows Firewall With Advanced Security snap-in for the Microsoft Management Console?

    a. The Microsoft Management Console offers a more familiar interface than the Windows Firewall control panel.

    b. The Microsoft Management Console snap-in applies the rules faster than the Windows Firewall control panel.

    c. Compared to the Windows Firewall control panel, the Microsoft Management Console can be brought up in fewer clicks.

    d. The Microsoft Management Console snap-in offers full access compared to the Windows Firewall control panel.

5. When creating a firewall exception, what is the difference between opening a port and allowing an application?

    a. Opening a port is permanent, and thus is less risky than allowing an application.

    b. Allowing an application opens the specified port only while the program is running, and thus is less risky.

    c. Both options are available in the Windows Firewall with Advanced Security console.

    d. There is no functional difference between opening a port and allowing an application.

Build a List

1. Specify the order of steps for processing an application in Windows Firewall.

    _____ Click Allow an app or feature through Windows Firewall. The Allowed Apps dialog box appears.

    _____ Scroll down in the Allowed apps and features list and select the check box for the application you want to allow through the firewall.

    _____ Log on to Windows 8, using an account with administrator privileges.

    _____ Click OK to close the Allowed Apps dialog box.

    _____ Open the Control Panel and click System and Security > Windows Firewall. The Windows Firewall window appears.

2. In order of first to last, specify the order of steps for creating Windows Firewall rules.

    _____ From the Action menu, select Export Policy. The Save As combo box appears.

    _____ Log on to Windows 8, using an account with administrator privileges.

    _____ Modify the inbound or outbound firewall rules or create new rules as needed.

    _____ Open the Control Panel and select System & Security > Administrative Tools > Windows Firewall With Advanced Security. The Windows Firewall with Advanced Security console appears.

    _____ In the left pane, select the Windows Firewall with Advanced Security on Local Computer node.

    _____ In the File Name text box, type a name for the policy file and click Save.

■ Business Case Scenarios

Scenario 11-1: Configuring Windows Firewall

You are a desktop technician in the IT department of a small corporation. Today is the day of the company picnic and, as the junior member of the department, you have been left in charge of the entire corporate network while everyone else is out of the office. Shortly after 2:00 PM, an email arrives from the company's biggest customer, complaining that they can't access the web server they use to place their orders. After checking the web server logs, it seems clear that the server is undergoing a denial-of-service attack, because there are suddenly hundreds of Internet computers repeatedly trying to access it. What temporary modifications could you make to Windows Firewall on the Windows 8 computer that stands between the web server and the Internet that would allow customers to access the web server while blocking the attackers?

Configuring Remote Management

70-687 EXAM OBJECTIVE

Objective 3.4 – Configure remote management. This objective may include but is not limited to: choose the appropriate remote management tools; configure remote management settings; modify settings remotely by using MMCs or Windows PowerShell; configure Remote Assistance, including Easy Connect.

LESSON HEADING	EXAM OBJECTIVE
Using Remote Access Technologies	Choose the appropriate remote management tools
Using Microsoft Management Console	Modify settings remotely by using MMCs or Windows PowerShell
Using Remote Assistance	Configure Remote Assistance, including Easy Connect
Using Remote Desktop	
Using Windows Remote Management	Configure remote management settings

KEY TERMS

Microsoft Management Console (MMC)

Remote Assistance

Remote Desktop

Remote Desktop Protocol (RDP)

Windows PowerShell

Windows Remote Management

WinRS.exe

■ Using Remote Access Technologies

THE BOTTOM LINE

Remote access technologies enable a user on one computer to effectively take control of another computer on the network. For desktop administrators, this capability can save many hours of travel time.

A main objective for desktop administrators working on large corporate networks is to minimize the amount of travel from site to site to work on individual computers. Some of the troubleshooting tools included with Windows 8 are capable of managing services on remote

CERTIFICATION READY
Choose the appropriate remote management tools
Objective 3.4

computers as well as on the local system. For example, most MMC snap-ins have this capability, enabling technicians to work on systems throughout the enterprise without traveling. However, most snap-ins are specialized tools used only for certain administration tasks. For comprehensive access to a remote computer, Windows 8 includes two tools that are extremely useful to the desktop technician: Remote Assistance and Remote Desktop.

Using Microsoft Management Console

The shortcuts to various Microsoft Management Console (MMC) tools that appear in Windows 8.1 are all configured to manage resources on the local system.

CERTIFICATION READY
Modify settings remotely by using MMCs or Windows PowerShell
Objective 3.4

However, many of the snap-ins supplied with Windows 8.1 enable you to manage other Windows computers on the network as well. There are two ways to access a remote computer using an *Microsoft Management Console (MMC)* snap-in.

- Redirect an existing snap-in to another system.
- Create a custom console with snap-ins directed to other systems.

To connect to and manage another system using an MMC snap-in, you must launch the console with an account that has administrative credentials on the remote computer. The exact permissions required depend on the functions performed by the snap-in. If your credentials do not provide the proper permissions on the target computer, you will be able to load the snap-in, but you will not be able to read information from or modify settings on the target computer.

REDIRECTING A SNAP-IN

A snap-in that is directed at a specific system typically has a Connect To Another Computer command in its Action menu. Selecting this command opens a *Select Computer* dialog box, as shown in Figure 12-1, in which you can specify or browse to another computer on the network. Once you select the name of the computer you want to manage and click OK, the snap-in element in the scope pane changes to reflect the name of the computer you selected.

Figure 12-1

The *Select Computer* dialog box in an MMC console

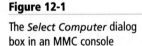

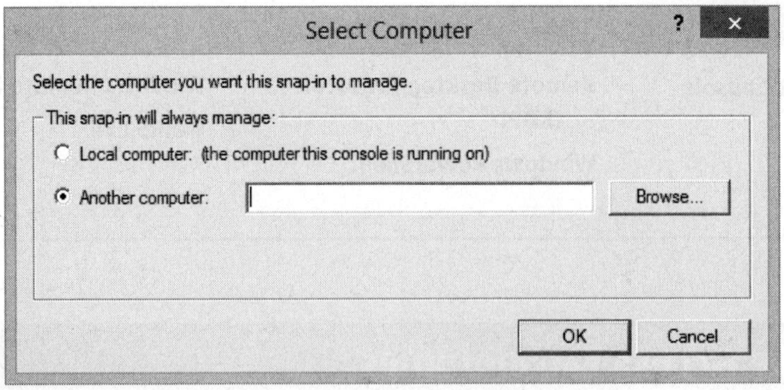

Not every snap-in has the ability to connect to a remote computer, because some do not need it. For example, the Active Directory Domain Services consoles automatically locate a domain controller for the current domain and access the directory service from there. There is no need to specify a computer name. However, you will find Change Domain and Change Domain Controller commands in the Action menu in these consoles, which enable you to manage a different domain or select a specific domain controller in the present domain.

The other factor that can affect the ability of an MMC snap-in to connect to a remote computer is the existence of Windows Firewall rules that block the necessary network traffic between the computers. The traffic that an individual snap-in requires and whether the default Windows Firewall rules restrict it depends on the functions that the snap-in performs.

TAKE NOTE *

For more information on Windows Firewall and how to manipulate its rules, see Lesson 11, "Configuring and Maintaining Network Security."

CREATING A REMOTE CONSOLE

Connecting to a remote computer by redirecting an existing console is convenient for impromptu management tasks, but it is limited by the fact that you can access only one computer at a time. You also have to open the console and redirect it every time you want to access the remote system. A more permanent solution is to create a custom console with snap-ins that are already directed at other computers.

When you add a snap-in to a custom console, you select the computer you want to manage with that snap-in. You can also add multiple copies of the same snap-in to a custom console, with each one pointed at a different computer. This adds a whole new dimension to MMC's functionality. Not only can you create custom consoles containing a variety of tools, you can also create consoles containing tools for a variety of computers. For example, you can create a single console containing multiple instances of the Event Viewer snap-in, with each one pointing to a different computer. This enables you to monitor the event logs for computers all over the network from a single console.

Using Remote Assistance

> *Remote Assistance* is a Windows 8.1 feature that enables an administrator, trainer, or technical specialist at one location to connect to a distant user's computer, chat with the user, and either view all of the user's activities or take complete control of the system.

Remote Assistance eliminates the need for administrative personnel to travel to a user's location for any of the following reasons:

- **Technical support** – A desktop administrator can use Remote Assistance to connect to a remote computer to modify configuration parameters, install new software, or troubleshoot user problems.

- **Troubleshooting** – By connecting in read-only mode, an expert can observe a remote user's activities and determine whether improper procedures are the source of problems the user is experiencing. The expert can also connect in interactive mode to try to recreate the problem or to modify system settings to resolve it. This is far more efficient than trying to give instructions to inexperienced users over the telephone.

- **Training** – Trainers and help desk personnel can demonstrate procedures to users right on their systems, without having to travel to their locations.

TAKE NOTE *

In Microsoft interfaces and documentation, the person connecting to a client using Remote Assistance is referred to as an expert or a helper.

To receive remote assistance, the computer running Windows 8.1 must be configured to use the Remote Assistance feature in one of the following ways:

- **Using Control Panel** – Open Control Panel and click System and Security > System > Remote settings. In the System Properties sheet, on the Remote tab, select the *Allow Remote Assistance connections to this computer* checkbox, as shown in Figure 12-2. By clicking the Advanced button, the user can specify whether the expert can take control of the computer or simply view activities on the computer. The user can also specify the amount of time that the invitation for remote assistance remains valid.

Figure 12-2

The Remote tab of the System Properties sheet

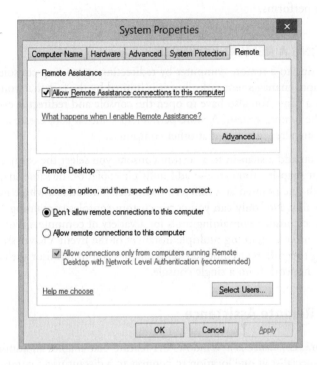

- **Using Group Policy** – Use the Group Policy Object Editor snap-in for MMC to access the computer's Local Computer Policy settings. Browse to the Computer Configuration > Administrative Templates > System > Remote Assistance container and enable the Configure Solicited Remote Assistance policy, as shown in Figure 12-3. The Solicited Remote Assistance policy also enables you to specify the degree of control the expert receives over the client computer, the duration of the invitation, and the method for sending email invitations. The Configure Offer Remote Assistance policy enables you to specify the names of users or groups that can function as experts, and whether those experts can perform tasks or just observe. You can also configure these same settings in Group Policy object (GPO) linked to an Active Directory Domain Services (AD DS) domain, site, or organizational unit object.

Figure 12-3

The Solicited Remote
Assistance policy in the Group
Policy Object Editor console

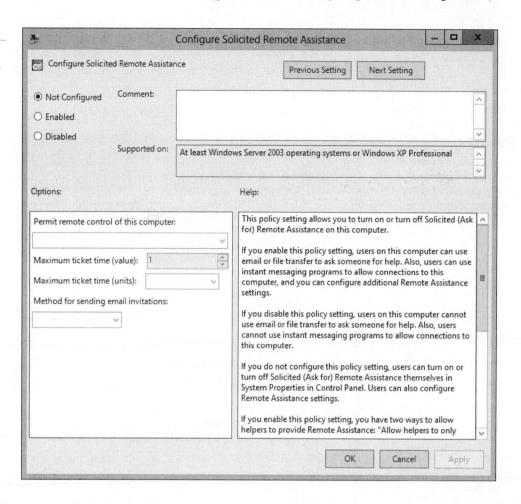

CERTIFICATION READY
Configure Remote
Assistance, including
Easy Connect
Objective 3.4

CREATING AN INVITATION

To request a Remote Assistance session, a client must issue an invitation and send it to a particular expert. The client can send the invitation using email, or save it as a file to be sent to the expert in some other manner. To create an invitation, use the following procedure:

 TAKE NOTE*

It is also possible for an expert to initiate a Remote Assistance connection to the client by specifying the client's computer name or IP address. However, Windows 8.1 cannot establish the session unless the client approves the connection.

CREATE AN INVITATION

GET READY. Log on to Windows 8.1 and then perform the following steps:

1. Open the *Windows Control Panel* and click **System and Security > Action Center > Troubleshooting > Get help from a friend**.

   The *Use Remote Assistance to contact someone you trust for help* page appears.

2. Click **Invite someone to help you.**

   The Windows Remote Assistance Wizard appears, displaying the *How do you want to invite your trusted helper?* page, as shown in Figure 12-4.

Figure 12-4

The *How do you want to invite your trusted helper?* page in the Windows Remote Assistance wizard

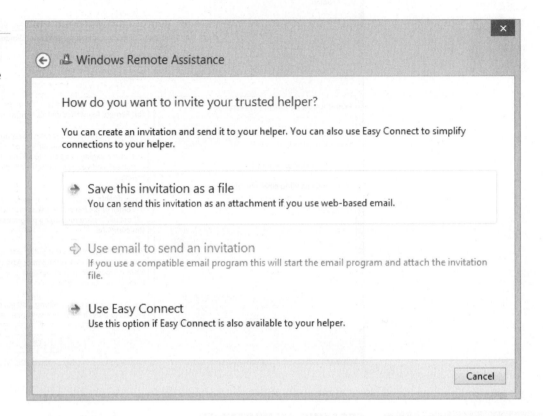

3. Click **Save this invitation as a file.**

   A *Save As combo* box appears.

4. Specify a name for the invitation file and the location of the folder in which the wizard should create the invitation and then click **Save.**

5. The Windows Remote Assistance window appears, as shown in Figure 12-5, displaying the password you must supply to the helper or expert.

TAKE NOTE *

You can also opt to send an invitation to the helper via email or by using Easy Connect.

Figure 12-5

The *Give your helper the invitation file and password* page of the Windows Remote Assistance wizard

Once the expert receives the invitation, invoking it launches the Remote Assistance application, which enables the expert to connect to the remote computer. If you select the Easy Connect option, you receive only a password, which you must supply to the expert. As long as the expert is running Windows 7 or newer, the password alone provides Remote Assistance access to the remote computer.

Using the Remote Assistance interface, the user and the expert can talk or type messages to each other and, by default, the expert can see everything that the user is doing on the computer. If the client computer is configured to allow remote control, the expert can also click the Take Control button and operate the client computer interactively.

SECURING REMOTE ASSISTANCE

Because an expert offering remote assistance to another user can perform virtually any activity on the remote computer that the local user can, this feature can be a significant security hazard. An unauthorized user who takes control of a computer using Remote Assistance can cause almost unlimited damage. However, Remote Assistance is designed to minimize the dangers. Some of the protective features of Remote Assistance are as follows:

- **Invitations** – No person can connect to another computer using Remote Assistance unless that person has received an invitation from the client. Clients can configure the effective lifespan of their invitations in minutes, hours, or days to prevent experts from attempting to connect to the computer later.

- **Interactive connectivity** – When an expert accepts an invitation from a client and attempts to connect to the computer, a user must be present at the client console to grant the expert access. You cannot use Remote Assistance to connect to an unattended computer.

- *Client-side control* – The client always has ultimate control over a Remote Assistance connection. The client can terminate the connection at any time, by pressing the Esc key or clicking Stop Control (ESC) in the client-side Remote Assistance page.

- **Remote control configuration** – Using the System Properties sheet or the Remote Assistance Group Policy settings, users and administrators can specify whether experts are permitted to take control of client computers. An expert who has read-only access cannot modify the computer's configuration in any way using Remote Assistance. The group policies also enable administrators to grant specific users expert status, so that no one else can use Remote Assistance to connect to a client computer, even with the client's permission.

- **Firewalls** – Remote Assistance uses Transmission Control Protocol (TCP) port number 3389 for all its network communications. For networks that use Remote Assistance internally and are also connected to the Internet, it is recommended that network administrators block this port in their firewalls to prevent users outside the network from taking control of computers that request remote assistance. However, it is also possible to provide remote assistance to clients over the Internet, which would require leaving port 3389 open.

Using Remote Desktop

While Remote Assistance is intended to enable users to obtain interactive help from other users, *Remote Desktop* is an administrative feature that enables users to access computers from remote locations, with no interaction required at the remote site.

Remote Desktop is essentially a remote control program for Windows computers; there are no invitations and no read-only capabilities. When you connect to a computer using Remote Desktop, you can operate the remote computer as though you were sitting at the console and perform most configuration and application tasks.

➕ **MORE INFORMATION**

One of the most useful application of Remote Desktop is to connect to servers, such as those in a locked closet or data center, that are not otherwise easily accessible. In fact, some administrators run their servers without monitors or input devices once the initial installation and configuration of the computer is complete, relying solely on Remote Desktop access for everyday monitoring and maintenance.

Remote Desktop is essentially an implementation of the Remote Desktop Services (formerly known as Terminal Services) technology built into the Windows server operating systems. When you use Remote Desktop Services on a server to host a large number of clients, you must purchase licenses for them. However, Windows 8.1 allows a single Remote Desktop connection for administrative purposes, without the need for a separate license.

The Remote Desktop Connection client communicates with a host computer using the *Remote Desktop Protocol (RDP)*. This protocol essentially transmits screen information, keystrokes, and mouse movements between the two computers. Any applications you launch in the client are still running on the remote computer, using its processor, memory, and storage resources.

When you connect to a computer using Remote Desktop, you must log on, just as you would if you were sitting at the console, meaning that you must have a user account and the appropriate privileges to access the host system. After you log on, the system displays the desktop configuration associated with your user account, and you can then proceed to work as you normally would.

ACTIVATING REMOTE DESKTOP

By default, the Remote Desktop Services service that powers the server side of Remote Desktop is not started on computers running Windows 8.1. Before you can connect to a distant computer using Remote Desktop, you must start it using the controls on the Remote tab of the System Properties sheet, which you access from the Control Panel. Select the *Allow remote connections to this computer* option and, depending on your security needs, you can select the checkbox requiring Network Level Authentication.

TAKE NOTE* Because Remote Desktop requires the remote user to perform a standard logon, it is inherently more secure than Remote Assistance, and needs no special security measures such as invitations and session passwords. However, you can also click Select Users in the Remote tab to display a Remote Desktop Users dialog box, in which you can specify the names of the users or groups that are permitted to access the computer using Remote Desktop. All users with Administrator privileges are granted access by default.

USING THE REMOTE DESKTOP CONNECTION CLIENT

In addition to the Remote Desktop Services service, Windows 8 includes the Remote Desktop Connection client program needed to connect to a host computer. To connect to a remote computer with the client, use the following procedure.

 RUN THE REMOTE DESKTOP CLIENT

GET READY. Log on to Windows 8.1 and then perform the following steps:

1. On the Windows 8.1 computer, on the Start screen, type **remote** to initiate a search and in the results display, click **Remote Desktop Connection**. The *Remote Desktop Connection* dialog box appears.

2. Click **Show options**.

   The dialog box expands to show additional controls, as shown in Figure 12-6.

Figure 12-6

The General tab in the expanded *Remote Desktop Connection* dialog box

3. On the *General* tab, type the name of the host computer you want to access in the *Computer* text box. Then click the **Display** tab, as shown in Figure 12-7.

Figure 12-7

The Display tab in the *Remote Desktop Connection* dialog box

4. In the *Display configuration* box, use the slider to select the desired size for the image of the host computer's desktop that will appear on the client system.

5. In the *Colors* box, select the desired color depth using the dropdown list.

6. Click the **Local Resources** tab, as shown in Figure 12-8.

Figure 12-8

The Local Resources tab in the *Remote Desktop Connection* dialog box

7. Using the controls provided, specify which of the resources on the remote computer you want to bring to your local computer, including sound, printers, clipboard, smart cards, ports, drives, and other Plug and Play devices.

8. In the *Keyboard* box, specify how you want the client to handle the Windows key combinations you press on your local computer.

9. Click the **Experience** tab, as shown in Figure 12-9.

Figure 12-9

The Experience tab in the *Remote Desktop Connection* dialog box

On the *Experience* tab, you can enhance the performance of the Remote Desktop Connection client by eliminating nonessential visual effects from the display information transmitted over the network.

10. Select one of the network connection speeds from the dropdown list or choose the items you want to suppress by clearing their checkboxes.

11. Click **Connect** to initiate the connection process.

A *Windows Security* dialog box appears.

12. Supply *User Name* and *Password* values to log on to the remote computer, and then click **OK**.

A *Remote Desktop* window appears containing an image of the remote computer's desktop.

Using Windows Remote Management

Using Windows Remote Management, administrators can execute programs from the command line on remote computers without having to open a Remote Desktop session.

CERTIFICATION READY
Configure remote
management settings
Objective 3.4

Windows Remote Management is a Windows 8.1 service that enables administrators to execute commands on remote computers, using Windows PowerShell or the Windows Remote Shell (WinRS.exe) command line program. However, Windows 8.1 does not start the service by default or configure the computer to allow remote management communications. To do this, you must complete the following procedure.

 CONFIGURE REMOTE MANAGEMENT

GET READY. Log on to Windows 8.1 using an account with administrative privileges and then perform the following steps:

1. Open a Command Prompt with Administrator privileges.

TAKE NOTE＊ If you are working on a computer that is a member of a workgroup, a User Account Control message box appears, in which you must click Yes to continue.

2. Execute the following command:

`winrm quickconfig`

The command prompts you to start the WinRM service.

3. Type **y** and then press **Enter** to continue.

The command prompts you to create a listener for incoming remote management requests and configure the required firewall exception.

4. Type **y** and then press **Enter** to continue, as shown in Figure 12-10.

Figure 12-10

Configuring a listener and firewall exception

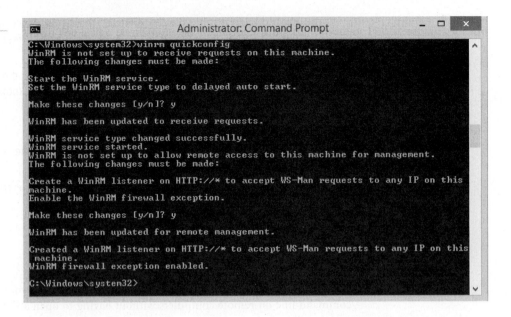

5. **Close** the *Administrator: Command Prompt* window.

The WinRM.exe program will fail to configure the required firewall exception if the computer's network location is set to Public. The computer must use either the Private or Domain location settings for the remote management configuration process to succeed.

In addition to this manual method, you can also configure Windows Remote Management using the Group Policy settings found in the Computer Configuration\Policies\Administrative Templates\Windows Components\Windows Remote Management (WinRM)\WinRM Service container of every Group Policy object (GPO).

USING WINRS.EXE

Once you have configured the Remote Management service, you can execute commands on other computers that have been similarly configured. To execute a command from the Windows 8.1 command prompt, you must use the **WinRS.exe** program.

To use WinRS.exe, you frame the command you want to execute on the remote computer as follows:

`winrs –r:computer [-u:user] [-p:password] command`

- **–r:computer** – Specifies the name of the computer on which you want to execute the command, using a NetBIOS name or a fully qualified domain name (FQDN).
- **-u:user** – Specifies the account on the remote computer that you want to use to execute the command.
- **-p:password** – Specifies the password associated with the account specified in the –u parameter. If you do not specify a password on the command line, WinRS.exe prompts you for one before executing the command.
- **command** – Specifies the command (with arguments) that you want to execute on the remote computer.

You can configure the behavior of WinRS.exe using the Group Policy settings found in the Computer Configuration\Policies\Administrative Templates\Windows Components\Windows Remote Shell container of every Group Policy object (GPO).

CERTIFICATION READY
Modify settings remotely
by using MMCs or
Windows PowerShell
Objective 3.4

USING WINDOWS POWERSHELL REMOTE COMMANDS

It is also possible to execute commands on remote computers using *Windows PowerShell* version 3, the version included with Windows 8.1. Like WinRS.exe, Windows PowerShell requires the Windows Remote Management service to be configured and running on both computers. The configuration parameters are exactly the same.

To execute a Windows PowerShell command on a remote computer, you must open an elevated Windows PowerShell session and use the following syntax:

```
icm computer {command}
```

- **computer** – Specifies the name of the computer on which you want to execute the command.
- **{command}** – Specifies the Windows PowerShell command you want to execute of the remote computer. The command must be enclosed in curly brackets.

> **➕ MORE INFORMATION**
>
> The icm command is an alias for the Invoke-Command cmdlet, which you can use in its place, if desired. For information on the other parameters supported by the Invoke-Command cmdlet, see the help screens for the cmdlet.

SKILL SUMMARY

IN THIS LESSON, YOU LEARNED:

- The shortcuts to various Microsoft Management Console (MMC) tools that appear in Windows 8.1 are all configured to manage resources on the local system. However, many of the snap-ins supplied with Windows 8.1 enable you to manage other Windows computers on the network as well.

- Remote Assistance is a Windows 8.1 feature that enables an administrator, trainer, or desktop technician at one location to connect to a distant user's computer, chat with the user, and either view all the user's activities or take complete control of the system.

- Remote Desktop is an administrative feature that enables users to access computers from remote locations, with no interaction required at the remote site.

- Windows Remote Management is a Windows 8.1 service that enables administrators to execute commands on remote computers, using Windows PowerShell or the Windows Remote Shell (WinRS.exe).

■ Knowledge Assessment

Multiple Choice

Select one or more correct answers for each of the following questions.

1. Which of the following remote access solutions requires a user to be present at the remote site and allow the connection to be established?
   a. Remote Desktop
   b. Remote Assistance
   c. WinRM
   d. WinRS.exe

2. Which of the following are true statements regarding the capabilities of Remote Desktop connections? Select all that apply.
   a. Allows you to operate the remote computer as if you were sitting at its console.
   b. Requires a separate license for each connection.
   c. Communicates with the host computer over RDP.
   d. Requires that you have an account on the remote computer to access the system.

3. Which of the following use Windows Remote Management to execute commands on remote computers? Select all that apply.
   a. RDP
   b. WinRS.exe
   c. Windows PowerShell
   d. Remote Assistance

4. To receive remote help, the computer running Windows 8.1 can be configured to use remote assistance. Where can this setting be configured? Select all that apply.
   a. Control Panel > System and Security > System > Remote settings > Remote tab
   b. Using the Group Policy Object Editor snap-in
   c. Control Panel > System > Remote settings > Remote tab
   d. Control Panel > System and Security > Remote settings > Remote tab

5. Which of the following can be used to initiate a Remote Assistance session? Select all that apply.
   a. Create and send invitation via email.
   b. Create and send invitation via file.
   c. Accept an approve a remote assistance connection on the client computer.
   d. Through a chat session.

6. Which of the following are true statements regarding the use of snap-ins? Select all that apply.
   a. Not all snap-ins have the ability to connect to a remote computer.
   b. The Windows Firewall can block a snap-in's functionality.
   c. A single console can only manage one instance of each snap-in.
   d. A single console can be created that contains multiple instances of the same snap-in (e.g., Event Viewer).

7. Remote Assistance can provide which of the following benefits to administrative personnel?
   a. Installing of software.
   b. Observing a remote user's activities.
   c. Assisting a remote user who has lost connectivity to the Internet.
   d. Training end users on their local system.

8. Which of the following names are used to describe the person connecting to a client using Remote Assistance? Select all that apply.
   a. Remote Expert
   b. Expert
   c. Assistant
   d. Helper

9. Remote Assistance provides which of the following protective features? Select all that apply.
   a. Invitations
   b. Interactive connectivity
   c. Client-side control
   d. A valid user account on the client computer

10. Which command is used to start the Windows Remote Management service from a command prompt?
- **a.** `winrm quickconfig`
- **b.** `winrm startconfig`
- **c.** `win quickconfig`
- **d.** `winrm quickconfig/start`

Best Answer

Choose the letter that corresponds to the best answer. More than one answer choice may achieve the goal. Select the BEST answer.

1. Which tool would work best when it comes to passively observing and assisting a remote user as they attempt to learn a new program while still providing interactive assistance when necessary?
   - **a.** Remote Desktop
   - **b.** Remote Assistance
   - **c.** Windows PowerShell
   - **d.** WinRS.exe

2. An administrator has setup a remote computer for one of the company's employees. She knows the IP address and the computer's name. Which option would allow her to remotely assist the employee with the least amount of effort assuming the employee is currently sitting in front of their computer?
   - **a.** Have the remote employee send an invitation via email.
   - **b.** Have the remote employee send an invitation via chat.
   - **c.** Have the remote employee call the administrator and then walk them through the setup of a Remote Assistance connection.
   - **d.** Initiate a Remote Assistance connection to the remote employee's computer by specifying its name and IP address. Ask the remote employee to accept the connection.

3. A junior administrator would like the ability to take full control of a remote computer to perform a service pack upgrade. The computer is currently stored in a locked room in which she does not currently have the key. Which of the following options would ensure she can access the computer with the least amount of effort?
   - **a.** Find someone who has a key to the room and ask them to let her in.
   - **b.** Use Remote Desktop to connect to the server and perform the service pack upgrade.
   - **c.** Configure the computer for Remote Assistance and then send an invitation to her email address.
   - **d.** Contact the help desk and submit a ticket to upgrade the computer at a later date and time.

4. There are 25 Windows 8.1 computers on the Windows domain. You want to configure them for Remote Management. What is the most efficient way to accomplish this task?
   - **a.** Visit each computer and run the `winrm quickconfig` command.
   - **b.** Visit each computer and configure the Local Group Policy to start the Windows Remote Management service automatically.
   - **c.** Use Remote Desktop to connect to each computer and run the `winrm quickconfig` command.
   - **d.** Configure Windows Remote Management using Group Policy and apply it to the selected computers in the domain.

5. Which of the following best describes what happens if you attempt to connect to another computer using an MMC snap-in without the appropriate level of permissions on the target computer?
   a. The snap-in will not load
   b. The snap-in will load but you will not be able to read information from or modify settings on the target computer.
   c. The snap-in will load but you will have to provide the appropriate credentials to be able to read information from the target computer.
   d. The snap-in will load with read permission only but you will not be able to make any modifications to the target computer.

Matching and Identification

Complete the following exercise by matching the terms with their corresponding definitions.

_____ a) Remote Assistance
_____ b) WinRS.exe
_____ c) Remote Desktop
_____ d) Remote Desktop Protocol (RDP)
_____ e) Windows Remote Management
_____ f) Windows PowerShell
_____ g) Microsoft Management Console
_____ h) Invitation
_____ i) Invoke-Command
_____ j) TCP port number 3389

1. Administrative feature that enables users to access computers from remote locations, with no interaction required at the remote computer.
2. A service that enables administrators to execute commands on remote computers using Windows PowerShell or WinRS.exe.
3. Used to execute a command from the Windows 8.1 command prompt.
4. Used by Remote Assistance for all its network communications.
5. Provides an interface for system administrators to configure and monitor the local and remote systems.
6. Allows an expert/helper to chat and take control of a remote computer.
7. Transmits screen information, keystrokes and mouse movements between two computers.
8. A command line shell and scripting language.
9. The *icm* command is an alias for this cmdlet.
10. Sent by email, file, or chat to an Expert/Helper to get help.

Build a List

1. In order of first to last, specify the correct order of steps to create a Remote Assistance invitation.
   _____ a) Open the *Windows Control Panel* and click **System and Security > Action Center > Troubleshooting > Get help from a friend.**
   _____ b) Click **Save this invitation as a file.**
   _____ c) The Windows Remote Assistance window appears displaying the password you must supply to the helper or expert.
   _____ d) Click **Invite someone to help you.**
   _____ e) Specify a name for the invitation file and the location of the folder in which the wizard should create the invitation and then click **Save.**

2. Specify the correct order of steps to run the Remote Desktop Client.

_____ **a)** On the Windows 8.1 computer, open the charms bar and then click **Search**.

_____ **b)** Click the **Experience** tab.

_____ **c)** Select one of the network connection speeds from the dropdown list or choose the items you want to suppress by clearing their checkboxes.

_____ **d)** In the _Keyboard_ box, specify how you want the client to handle the Windows key combinations you press on your local computer.

_____ **e)** Using the controls provided, specify which of the resources on the remote computer you want to bring to your local computer.

_____ **f)** With the Apps option selected, type **remote** and, in the results display, click **Remote Desktop Connection**.

_____ **g)** Click **Connect** to initiate the connection process.

_____ **h)** On the _General_ tab, type the name of the host computer you want to access in the Computer text box. Then click the **Display** tab.

_____ **i)** Supply _User Name_ and _Password_ values to log on to the remote computer, and then click **OK**. A Remote Desktop window appears containing an image of the remote computer's desktop.

_____ **j)** Click the **Local Resources** tab.

_____ **k)** In the _Display configuration_ box, use the slider to select the desired size for the image of the host computer's desktop that will appear on the client system.

_____ **l)** In the Colors box, select the desired color depth using the dropdown list.

_____ **m)** Click **Show options**.

3. Specify the correct order of steps to configure Remote Management.

_____ **a)** Open a Command Prompt with Administrator privileges.

_____ **b)** Type **y** and then press **Enter** to continue.

_____ **c)** Type **y** and then press **Enter** to continue.
The command prompts you to create a listener for incoming remote management requests and configure the required firewall **exception**.

_____ **d)** Execute the following command: winrm quickconfig
The command prompts you to start the WinRM service.

_____ **e)** **Close** the _Administrator: Command Prompt_ window.

■ Business Case Scenario

Scenario 12-1: Troubleshooting Remote Assistance

Joe is a new IT Director who is tasked with making sure his Windows 8.1 computer users can be assisted remotely. On his first day at the company, Joe was told that the Remote Assistance feature was not working for users after a new firewall was installed. What might be causing the problem and how should it be addressed?

13 LESSON

Configuring Shared Resources

70-687 EXAM OBJECTIVE

Objective 4.1 – Configure shared resources. This objective may include but is not limited to: configure shared folder permissions; configure HomeGroup settings; configure libraries; configure shared printers; set up and configure OneDrive.

LESSON HEADING	EXAM OBJECTIVE
Sharing Files and Folders	
Understanding Folder Sharing in Windows 8.1	
Sharing with Homegroups	Configure HomeGroup settings
Using Libraries	Configure libraries
Creating a Homegroup	
Joining a Homegroup	
Working with Homegroups	
Sharing the Public Folder	
Sharing a Folder	
Managing Share Permissions	Configure shared folder permissions
Combining Share and NTFS Permissions	
Using OneDrive	Set up and configure OneDrive
Working with Printers	
Understanding the Windows Print Architecture	
Sharing a Printer	Configure shared printers
Configuring Printer Security	
Accessing a Shared Printer	

KEY TERMS

homegroups	print device	printer control language (PCL)
homegroup networking	print server	printer driver
local printer	printer	OneDrive

Sharing Files and Folders

THE BOTTOM LINE

Windows 8.1 is capable of functioning as both a client and a server on a network, meaning that users can access files on other computers, as well as share files and folders on their own computers with other network users.

For network users to be able to access your files, you must first create a network share out of a specific drive or folder. Once you have created a share, users on the network can browse to it in Windows Explorer and access the files there, just as if they were on a local drive.

Understanding Folder Sharing in Windows 8.1

When compared with versions prior to Windows Vista, Windows 8.1 provides additional methods for sharing files and folders, as well as additional security mechanisms to protect the computer from intrusion.

Windows 8.1 provides three basic methods for sharing the files and folders on the computer: any folder sharing, public folder sharing, and homegroup sharing. Table 13-1 lists the capabilities of each sharing method.

The type of sharing method you elect to use depends on the size and formality of the network to which the computer is connected. For home users, homegroup networking is simple to set up and use. For small business networkers, Public folder sharing is often the easiest method, one that users can easily maintain for themselves on a day-to-day basis. For larger networks, Windows domain networks, or any network with more elaborate security requirements, any folder sharing is preferable.

Table 13-1

Windows 8.1 sharing features

Any Folder Sharing	Public Folder Sharing	Homegroup Sharing
Shares files from any location	Places all shared files in a single location	Shares files from their default library locations
Enables you to set different sharing permissions for individual network users	Uses the same sharing permissions for all network users	Enables you to set the same sharing permissions for all network users or set different sharing permissions for individual users
Access can be limited to network users with a user account and password on your computer	Access can be limited to network users with a user account and password on your computer	Access can be limited to network users with a user account and password on your computer
Individual users can be granted read-only or read/write access to the share	Can be configured as a read-only share or a read/write share	Individual users can be granted read-only or read/write access to the share
Shares files from their original locations	Requires you to copy or move files to be shared to the Public folder	Shares files from their original locations

Sharing with Homegroups

Homegroup networking is a Windows 8.1 feature that enables computers configured to use the Private network location to share the contents of their respective libraries among themselves.

Using *homegroups*, Windows 8.1 users can share their documents, printers, pictures, music, and videos with other Windows 8.1 users connected to the same home network. A home network has a single read-only homegroup by default, with the individual users selecting what they want to share.

Homegroups are relatively limited, when compared to any folder sharing, because you can only share the contents of the libraries in the user's profile. However, compared to Public folder sharing, homegroups don't require users to copy or move files to a Public folder.

CERTIFICATION READY
Configure HomeGroup Settings
Objective 4.1

In the default homegroup networking configuration, all of the users that join the homegroup have read-only access to all of the libraries the other users have elected to share. However, it is possible for each user to configure the system to provide read/write access, and to share libraries only with specific users.

Using Libraries

The redesigned File Explorer interface in Windows 8.1 retains much from its Windows Explorer predecessors in Windows 7 and Windows Vista,

When you open a File Explorer window in Windows 8.1 (as shown in Figure 13-1), left pane retains the Favorites and Network folder from earlier versions, as well as the This PC folder, which was formerly called Computer in previous Windows versions. Missing, however, in Windows 8.1 is the Libraries folder. The libraries still exist in Windows 8.1; they just don't appear in the File Explorer interface by default.

Figure 13-1

A File Explorer window

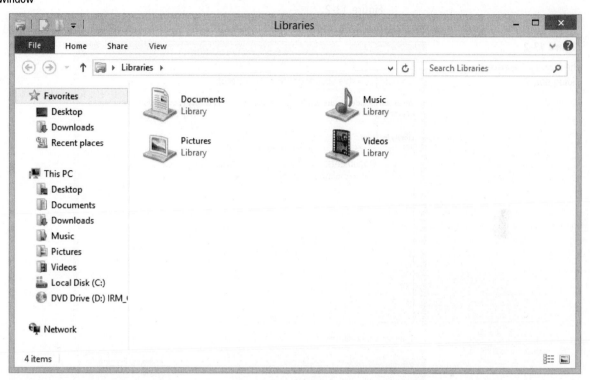

 CERTIFICATION READY
Configure file libraries
Objective 4.1

Libraries enable users to aggregate files in multiple locations – and even on multiple computers – into a single folder that makes them appear as though they are all on a local drive. By default, File Explorer has four libraries, called Documents, Music, Pictures, and Videos. Users can also create as many additional libraries as they need.

Each library consists of one or more locations, and each location is a folder on the local or a network computer. For example, the Documents library has two locations: the user's My Documents folder and the Public Documents folder. When you look at the Documents library, you see the files in both locations.

If you add more locations to the library, the files in those locations appear in the library as well. In every library, one of the locations is designated as the save location; this is where files go that the user saves to the library.

To restore the Libraries folder to File Explorer, all you have to do is click the View tab and, in the *Navigation pane* drop-down list, select *Show libraries*.

To add your own locations to a library, use the following procedure.

⊙ **ADD LIBRARY LOCATIONS**

GET READY. Log on to Windows 8.1 using an account with Administrator privileges. If you plan to add network folders to the library, make sure that Network Discovery and File and Printer Sharing all turned on. Then perform the following steps:

1. Open **File Explorer** and select the **Libraries** folder.
2. Select one of the four library icons in the right pane.

   A *Manage* menu appears with a *Library Tools* header.
3. Click the Manage tab, and in the ribbon that appears, click the **Manage Library** button.

   The Library Locations dialog box appears for the library you selected, as shown in Figure 13-2.

Figure 13-2

The *Library Locations* dialog box

4. Click **Add**.

   An Include Folder combo box appears for the library you selected.
5. Browse to the folder you want to add, select it, and then click **Include Folder**.

   The folder appears in the list of library locations.
6. Click **OK**.

   The contents of the folder you added appear in the library.
7. **Close** the *File Explorer* window.

TAKE NOTE*

Any folder you add to a library in Windows 8.1 must be indexed. If you attempt to added a folder that cannot be indexed, an error message appears.

In addition to File Explorer windows, libraries also appear in Open and Save As combo boxes.

Creating a Homegroup

When a Windows 8.1 computer uses the Private network location, the computer attempts to detect an existing homegroup on the network.

Unlike Windows 7, Windows 8.1 does not enable you to explicitly select a network location when you install the operating system. If your system is configured to use the public location, you can change it by opening the Local Security Policy console, browsing to the

Security Settings\Network List Manager Policies folder, opening the *Properties* sheet for the appropriate network type (such as Unidentified Network) and selecting the Private Location Type option, as shown in Figure 13-3.

Figure 13-3

The *Unidentified Network Properties* sheet

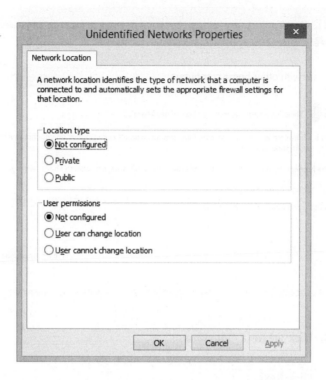

If the system does not detect a homegroup, the Network and Sharing Center control panel contains a link providing access to the Create a Homegroup Wizard.

To create a homegroup, use the following procedure.

 CREATE A HOMEGROUP

GET READY. Log on to Windows 8.1 using an account with Administrator privileges. Make sure that the system is configured to use the Private network location and then perform the following steps:

1. Open the *Control Panel* and then click **Network and Internet > Network and Sharing Center**.

   The *Network and Sharing Center* control panel appears.

2. Click the **Ready to create** link.

   The HomeGroup control panel appears, as shown in Figure 13-4.

Figure 13-4

The *HomeGroup* control panel, with no HomeGroup installed

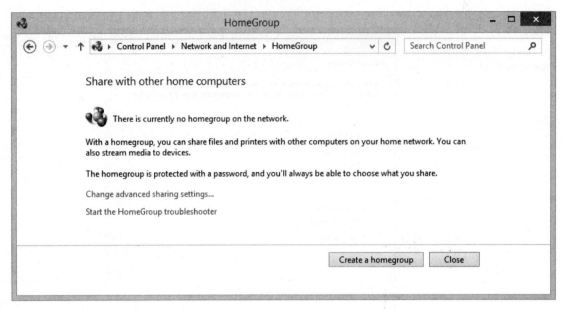

3. Click Create a **HomeGroup**.

   The *Create a HomeGroup* wizard appears.

4. Click **Next**.

   The *Share with other homegroup members* page appears, as shown in Figure 13-5.

Figure 13-5

The *Share with other home-group members* page

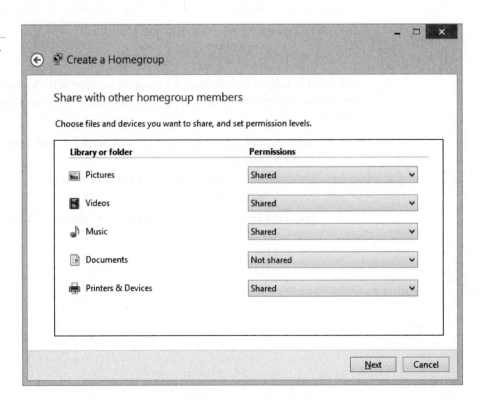

5. Select the libraries that you want to share and then click **Next**.

The wizard creates the homegroup and assigns it a password. The *Use this password to add other computers to your homegroup* page appears, as shown in Figure 13-6.

Figure 13-6

The *Use this password to add other computers to your homegroup* page

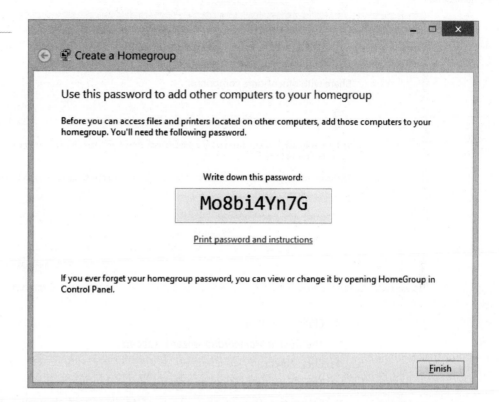

Create a Homegroup

Use this password to add other computers to your homegroup

Before you can access files and printers located on other computers, add those computers to your homegroup. You'll need the following password.

Write down this password:

Mo8bi4Yn7G

Print password and instructions

If you ever forget your homegroup password, you can view or change it by opening HomeGroup in Control Panel.

Finish

6. Click **Finish**.

The wizard closes and the HomeGroup control panel changes to reflect its current status.

Joining a Homegroup

When a Windows 8.1 computer using the Private network location does detect a homegroup on the network, the Network and Sharing Center control panel appears with an Available to Join link.

To join an existing homegroup, use the following procedure.

 JOIN A HOMEGROUP

GET READY. Log on to Windows 8.1 using an account with Administrator privileges. Make sure that the system is configured to use the Private network location and then perform the following steps:

1. Open the *Control Panel* and click **Network and Internet** > **Network and Sharing Center**.

The *Network and Sharing Center* control panel appears.

2. Click the **Available to join** link.

The HomeGroup control panel appears, as shown in Figure 13-7.

Figure 13-7

The *HomeGroup* control
panel, showing the homegroup
found on the network

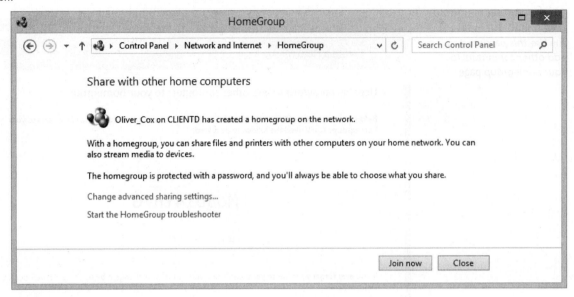

3. Click **Join Now**.

   The *Join a HomeGroup* wizard appears.

4. Click **Next**.

   The *Share with other homegroup members* page appears.

5. Select the libraries that you want to share and then click **Next**.

   The *Type the homegroup password* page appears, as shown in Figure 13-8.

Figure 13-8

The *Type the homegroup
password* page

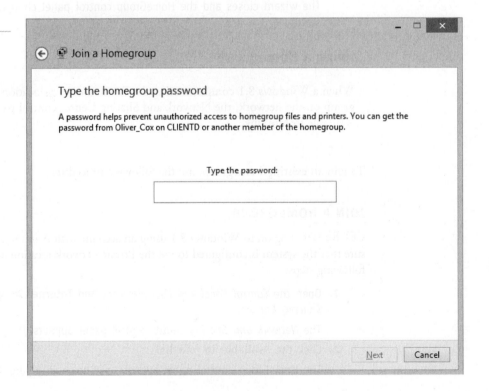

6. In the *Type the password* text box, type the password supplied by the *Create a HomeGroup* wizard and then click **Next**.

7. The *You have joined the homegroup* page appears.

8. Click **Finish**.

   The wizard closes and the HomeGroup control panel changes to reflect its current status.

Working with Homegroups

Once you have joined a computer to a homegroup, the shared libraries of the other computers on the network appear in File Explorer in the Homegroup container, as shown in Figure 13-9.

Figure 13-9

Homegroup shares in File Explorer

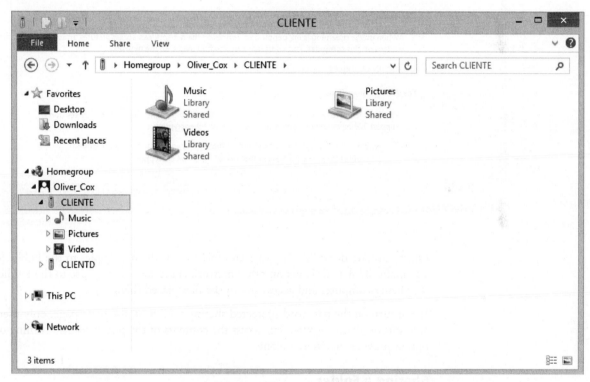

To modify the default homegroup sharing configuration, you can select one of your shared libraries in File Explorer and click Share in the toolbar. Using the controls that appear in the ribbon, you can change other homegroup users' access to the library from Read to Read/Write. You can also limit access to specific homegroup users, or prevent anyone on the network from accessing that library.

Sharing the Public Folder

Sharing files and folders using the Public folder is the simplest way to give your clients file sharing capability.

All you have to do to activate Public folder sharing in Windows 8.1 is enable Network Discovery and select the *Turn on sharing so anyone with network access can read and write files in the Public folders* option on the *Advanced sharing settings* control panel, as shown in Figure 13-10.

Figure 13-10

Sharing the Public folder

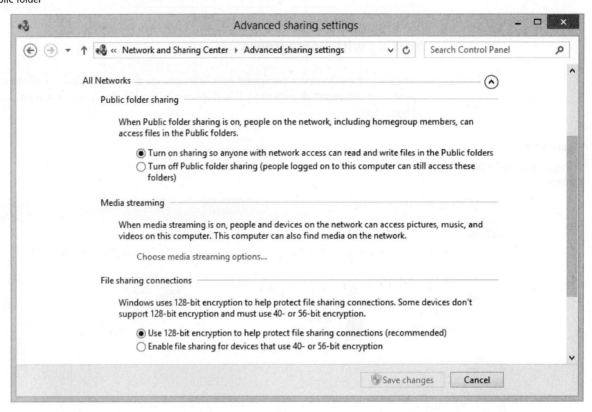

Once you have done this, any files and folders that the user copies to the Public folder are automatically shared. Users on other network computers can browse to the Public share on the client's computer and access any of the files placed there.

If you turn on the password protected sharing option on the same page, only users with accounts on that computer can access the contents of the public folder. Turning off that option provides access to anyone.

Sharing a Folder

The real power and flexibility of Windows 8.1 file sharing is found in the any folder sharing capability.

With any folder sharing, you have full control over what material on the computer is shared, which users are permitted to access the shared material, and what degree of access each user is granted.

To share a folder on a Windows 8.1 computer, use the following procedure.

SHARE A FOLDER

GET READY. Log on to Windows 8.1 using an account with Administrator privileges. Make sure that Network Discovery, File and Printer Sharing, and Password Protected Sharing are all turned on. Then perform the following steps:

1. Open **File Explorer** and expand the **Computer** node and the **Local Disk (C:)** drive.
2. Right-click a folder on the C: drive and, from the context menu, select **Properties**. The folder's *Properties* sheet appears.
3. Click the **Sharing** tab to display the interface shown in Figure 13-11.

Figure 13-11

The Sharing tab of a folder's *Users Properties* sheet

4. Click **Advanced Sharing**.

The *Advanced Sharing* dialog box appears, as shown in Figure 13-12.

Figure 13-12

The *Advanced Sharing* dialog box

➕ **MORE INFORMATION**

If you click Share on the Sharing tab, or if you right-click a folder and select Share from the context menu, Windows 8.1 takes you to the File Sharing Wizard, which is a simplified method for creating a share. The wizard is designed for end users and provides a limited set of features, as well as a means for informing network users that a new share is available. Administrators will usually want to use the Advanced Sharing interface. It is possible to disable the wizard entirely by clearing the Use Sharing Wizard checkbox on the View tab of the Folder Options control panel.

5. Select the **Share this folder** checkbox.

   By default, the name of the folder you are sharing appears as the name of the share, but you can change the name, if desired, without affecting the name of the original folder.

6. The number of users permitted to access the share simultaneously is 20 by default. To conserve system resources and network bandwidth, you can reduce this number by adjusting the value in the *Limit the number of simultaneous users to* spin box.

➕ **MORE INFORMATION**

It is possible to create a share that is invisible to users browsing the network simply by appending a dollar symbol ($) to the share name. For example, each drive in the computer has an administrative share that the setup program creates during the operating system installation, called C$, D$, and so on. These shares do not appear in File Explorer, but you can still access them by specifying the share name in a command line. Any additional hidden shares that you create are also accessible, though invisible.

7. Click **OK** to create the share and close the *Advanced Sharing* dialog box.
8. **Close** the *Users Properties* sheet.

If you return to File Explorer and browse to the computer in the Network container, you can now see the shared folder there.

Managing Share Permissions

> Windows 8.1 shares have their own permission system, which is completely independent from the other Windows permission systems.

CERTIFICATION READY
Configure shared folder permissions
Objective 4.1

For network users to access shares on a Windows 8.1 computer with Password protected sharing enabled, they must have user accounts on the sharing computer (or in a domain to which both computers are joined) and you must grant them the appropriate permissions.

To set share permissions, use the following procedure:

 SET SHARE PERMISSIONS

GET READY. Log on to Windows 8.1 using an account with Administrator privileges. Make sure that Network Discovery, File Sharing, and Password Protected Sharing are all turned on and then perform the following steps:

1. Open **File Explorer** and browse to the folder you shared earlier.
2. Right-click the shared folder and, from the context menu, select **Properties**. The folder's *Properties* sheet appears.
3. Click the **Sharing** tab and then click **Advanced Sharing**.

   The *Advanced Sharing* dialog box appears.
4. Click **Permissions**.

The *Permissions* dialog box for the folder appears, as shown in Figure 13-13. As with all of the Windows permission systems, the top half of the dialog box lists the security principals that have been granted permissions, and the bottom half displays the permissions granted to the selected principal.

Figure 13-13

The *Permissions for Documents* dialog box for a shared folder

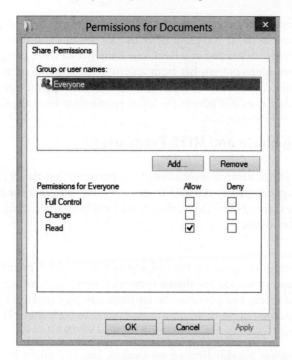

5. Click **Add**. The *Select Users or Groups* dialog box appears.
6. In the *Enter the object names to select* text box, type the name of the security principal you want to add and click **OK**.

   The user or group is added to the *Group or user names* list.
7. In the Permissions list for the user or group, select or clear the checkboxes to **Allow** or **Deny** the user any of the permissions shown in Table 13-2.

Table 13-2

Share Permissions and Their Functions

SHARE PERMISSION	ALLOWS OR DENIES SECURITY PRINCIPALS THE ABILITY TO:
Read	• Display folder names, file names, file data, and attributes • Execute program files • Access other folders within the shared folder
Change	• Create folders • Add files to folders • Change data in files • Append data to files • Change file attributes • Delete folders and files • Perform all actions permitted by the Read permission
Full Control	• Change file permissions • Take ownership of files • Perform all tasks allowed by the Change permission

8. Click **OK** to close the *Permissions* dialog box.

9. Click **OK** to close the *Advanced Sharing* dialog box.

10. Click **Close** to close the folder's *Users Properties* sheet.

When assigning share permissions, be aware that they do not combine in the same way that NTFS permissions do. If you grant Alice the Allow Read and Allow Change permissions to the C:\Test Folder share, and at a later time deny her all three permissions to the C:\ share, the Deny permissions prevent her from accessing the any files on the C:\ share, but she can still access the C:\Test Folder share because of the Allow permissions. In other words, the C:\ Test Folder share does not inherit the Deny permissions from the C:\ share.

Combining Share and NTFS Permissions

It is crucial for desktop technicians to understand that the NTFS and share permission systems are completely separate from each other, and that for network users to access files on a shared NTFS drive, they must have both the correct NTFS and the correct share permissions.

The share permission system is the simplest of the Windows permission systems, and provides only basic protection for shared network resources. Share permissions provide only three levels of access, compared to the far more complex system of NTFS permissions. Generally speaking, network administrators prefer to use either NTFS or share permissions, but not both.

TAKE NOTE*

The *Effective Access* display in the Advanced Security Settings dialog box shows only the effective NTFS permissions, not the share permissions that might also constrain the user's access.

Share permissions provide limited protection, but this might be sufficient on some small networks. Share permissions are also the only alternative on a computer with FAT32 drives, because the FAT file system does not have its own permission system as NTFS does.

On networks already possessing a well-planned system of NTFS permissions, share permissions are not really necessary. In this case, you can safely grant the Full Control share permission to Everyone, and allow the NTFS permissions to provide security. Adding share permissions to the mix only complicates the administration process, without providing any additional security.

■ Using OneDrive

THE BOTTOM LINE

OneDrive is Microsoft's personal, cloud-based storage service. Every user who applies for a Microsoft account receives free cloud storage. You can use this storage to back up local files, to share files with your other devices, or to share files with other users. OneDrive is also where Windows 8.1 stores the personalization settings that you choose to sync using your Microsoft account.

CERTIFICATION READY
Set up and configure OneDrive
Objective 4.1

After logging on using a Microsoft account, users can access their OneDrive storage space is several ways, including the following:

- **Through the web** – By browsing to http://onedrive.com and logging on with your Microsoft account, you can access your storage space directly, as shown in Figure 13-14. Using this interface, you can manage your files, perform uploads and downloads, and even open your files in web-based versions of Microsoft Office applications.

Figure 13-14

The Microsoft OneDrive
website

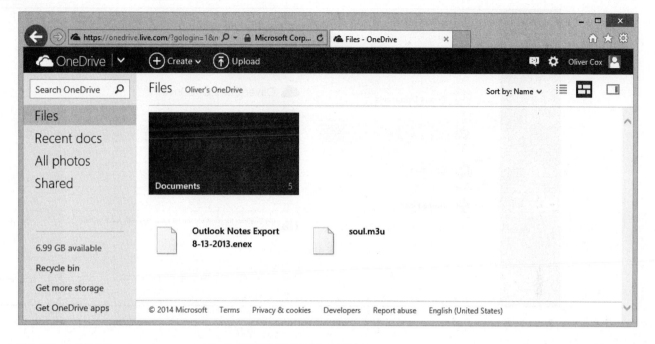

- **Through the OneDrive app** – Windows 8.1 creates a folder in your user profile on the local drive, and synchronizes the contents of that folder with your OneDrive space in the cloud. You simply drop files into your OneDrive folder and the app automatically uploads them to your storage space. You can access the files on multiple computers, so that they all maintain the latest versions. To manage your OneDrive settings, click OneDrive on the PC Settings screen to display the interface.

- **Through a desktop application** – Many software developers are incorporating OneDrive into the storage options for their applications. For example, Microsoft Office 2013 enables you to access files directly from your OneDrive space, as shown in Figure 13-15, and save revised versions there. When an application is designed to access OneDrive directly, the synchronization app is not needed.

Figure 13-15

OneDrive access in Microsoft Office 2013

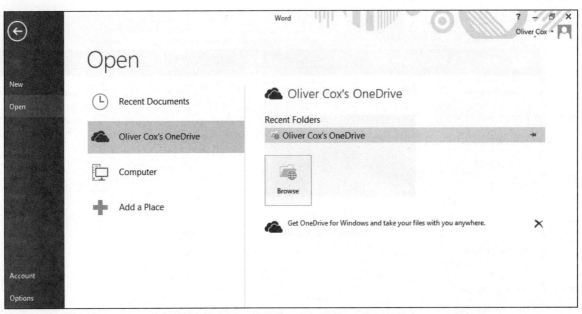

■ Working with Printers

THE BOTTOM LINE

The printer is one of the most common external devices you find connected to a PC. To manage printers in Windows 8.1, you work with the Devices and Printers control panel or the Print Management snap-in for Microsoft Management Console (MMC).

Windows 8.1, like the other Windows versions, provides a great deal of flexibility in its handling and management of printers. As a client, a Windows 8.1 computer can have a print device directly attached to one of its ports, or it can access a device located elsewhere on the network. Windows 8.1 can also function as a print server, enabling other users on the network to send print jobs to the computer, which feeds them to a printer. The following sections examine the various printer functions possible with Windows 8.1.

Understanding the Windows Print Architecture

Printing in the Windows environment involves a number of different roles and components, and the names used to refer to these roles and components can sometimes be confusing. You can avoid confusion by making sure that you understand the terms used for the print components and how they work together.

Printing in Microsoft Windows typically involves the following four components:

- **Print device** – A *print device* is the actual hardware that produces hard copy documents on paper or other print media. Windows 8.1 supports both *local print devices*, which are directly attached to the computer's parallel, serial, Universal Serial Bus (USB), or IEEE 1394 (FireWire) ports, or *network interface print devices*, which are connected to the network, either directly or through another computer.

- **Printer** – In Windows parlance, a *printer* is the software interface through which a computer communicates with a print device. Windows 8.1 supports numerous interfaces, including parallel (LPT), serial (COM), USB, IEEE 1394, Infrared Data Access (IrDA), and Bluetooth ports, and network printing services such as lpr, Internet Printing Protocol (IPP), and standard TCP/IP ports.

> **TAKE NOTE***
>
> The most common misuse of the Windows printing vocabulary is the confusion of the terms printer and print device. Many sources use the term printer to refer to the printing hardware, but in Windows, the two are not equivalent. For example, you can add a printer to a Windows 8.1 computer without a physical print device being present. The computer can then host the printer, print server, and printer driver. These three components enable the computer to process the print jobs and store them in a print queue until the print device is actually available.

- **Print server** – A *print server* is a computer (or standalone device) that receives print jobs from clients and sends them to print devices that are either locally attached or connected to the network.

- **Printer driver** – A *printer driver* is a device driver that converts the print jobs generated by applications into an appropriate string of commands for a specific print device. Printer drivers are designed for a specific print device and provide applications with access to all of the print device's features.

UNDERSTANDING WINDOWS PRINTING

The four printing components work together to process the print jobs produced by Windows applications and turn them into hard copy documents, as shown in Figure 13-16.

Figure 13-16

The Windows print architecture

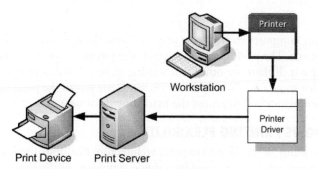

Before you can print documents in Windows, you must install at least one printer. To install a printer in Windows, you must do the following:

- Select a specific manufacturer and model of print device.
- Specify the port (or other interface) the computer will use to access the print device.
- Supply a printer driver specifically created for that print device.

When you print a document in an application, you select the printer that will be the destination for the print job.

The printer is associated with a printer driver that takes the commands generated by the application and converts them into a language understood by the printer, which is called a *printer control language (PCL)*. PCLs can be standardized, as in the case of the PostScript language, or they can be proprietary languages developed by the print device manager.

The printer driver enables you to configure the print job to use the various capabilities of the print device. These capabilities are typically incorporated into the printer's Properties dialog box, like the one shown in Figure 13-17.

Figure 13-17

A Windows printer's Properties dialog box

Once the computer converts the print job into the appropriate PCL, it stores the job in a print queue. The print queue then sends the job to the print device when the device is ready to receive it. If there are other jobs waiting to be printed, a new job might wait in the print queue for some time. When the server sends the job to the print device, the device reads the PCL commands and produces the hard copy document.

WINDOWS PRINTING FLEXIBILITY

The flexibility of the Windows print architecture manifests itself in how the roles of these components can be performed by a single computer, or distributed around a network.

When you connect a print device to a standalone Windows 8.1 computer, for example, the computer supplies the printer, printer driver, and print server functions. However, you can also connect the computer to a local area network (LAN) and share the printer with other users. In this arrangement, the computer with the print device attached to it functions as a print server. The other computers on the network are the print clients.

In this network printing arrangement, each client supplies its own printer and printer driver. As before, the application sends the print jobs to the printer and the printer driver converts the application commands to PCL commands. The client computer then sends the PCL print jobs over the network to the print server on the computer with the attached print device. Finally, the print server sends the jobs to the print device.

This is only the most basic of network printing arrangements. A multitude of possible variations exist to enable you to create a network printing architecture that supports your organization's printing needs. Some of the more advanced possibilities are as follows:

- Print devices do not necessarily have to be connected to computers. Many print devices have integrated network interfaces that enable them to connect directly to the LAN and function as their own print servers. You can also purchase standalone print server devices that connect a print device to a network. In these cases, print devices have their own IP addresses, which clients use to communicate with the devices.

- You can connect a single print server to multiple print devices. This is called a printer pool. On a busy network with many print clients, the print server can distribute large numbers of incoming jobs among several identical print devices to provide timely service. Alternatively, you can connect print devices that support different forms and paper sizes to a single print server, which will distribute jobs with different requirements to the appropriate print devices.

- You can connect multiple print servers to a single print device. By creating multiple print servers, you can configure different priorities, security settings, auditing, and monitoring parameters for different users. For example, you can create a high-priority print server for company executives, while junior users send their jobs to a lower priority server. This ensures that the executives' jobs get printed first, even if the servers are both connected to the same print device.

ADDING A LOCAL PRINTER

The most common configuration for home, small business, or workgroup users is to connect a print device directly to a computer running Windows 8.1 or another version of Windows, and then add a printer and printer driver. This enables local users to print their own jobs, and it also makes it possible to share the printer with other network users.

To add a local printer to a Windows 8.1 computer, use the following procedure:

TAKE NOTE* This procedure is necessary only if the print device is connected (or will be connected) to the computer by a parallel (LPT) port or serial (COM) port interface. This is because these interfaces are not capable of automatically detecting connected devices. If your print device connects to the computer using USB, IEEE 1394, IrDA, Bluetooth, or any other auto-detecting technology, simply connecting the print device will cause the computer to detect it and install it automatically.

 ADD A LOCAL PRINTER

GET READY. Log on to Windows 8.1 using an account with Administrator privileges and then perform the following steps:

1. Open the **Control Panel** and click **Hardware and Sound > Devices and Printers**. The Devices and Printers control panel appears, as shown in Figure 13-18.

Figure 13-18

The *Devices and Printers* control panel

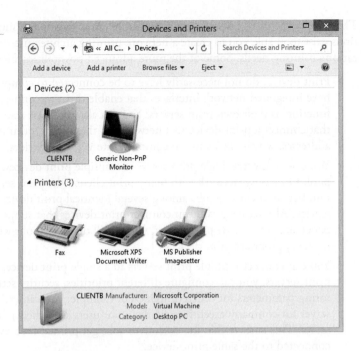

2. Click **Add a printer**.

   The *Add Printer* wizard appears, and begins searching for printers, while displaying the *Searching for available printers* page.

3. When the *No printers were found* page appears, click **Next**, and when the *Find a printer by other options* page appears, click **Next** again (see Figure 13-19).

Figure 13-19

The *Find a printer by other options* page

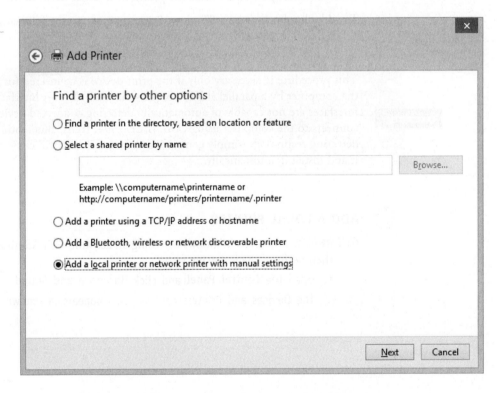

4. Select the *Add a local printer or network printer with manual settings* option and click **Next**.

   The *Choose a printer port* page appears, as shown in Figure 13-20.

Figure 13-20

The *Choose a printer port* page

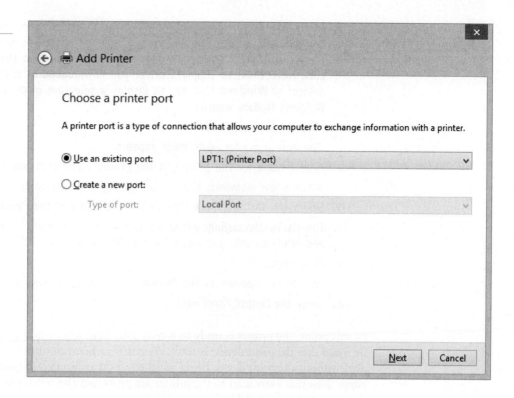

5. Select the **Use an existing port** option and then select the LPT or COM port to which the print device is connected.

6. Click **Next** to continue.

The *Install the printer driver* page appears, as shown in Figure 13-21.

Figure 13-21

The *Install the printer driver* page

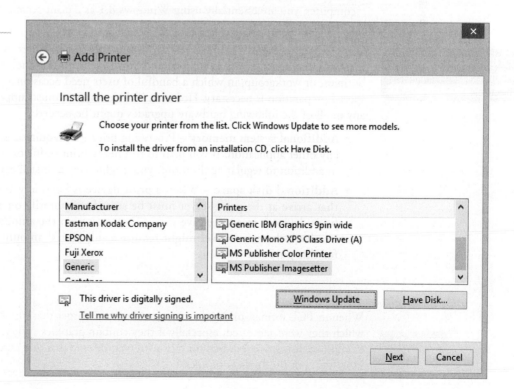

7. In the Manufacturer column, scroll down and select the manufacturer of your print device. Then, in the Printers column, select the specific model of print device you want to install. If your print device does not appear in the list, you must either click **Have Disk**, to supply a driver you downloaded or that came with the print device; or **Windows Update**, to display a selection of drivers available from the Windows Update website.

8. Click **Next** to continue.

   The *Type a printer name* page appears.

9. Type a name for the printer in the *Printer name* text box and then click **Next**.

   After a few moments, the *Printer sharing* page appears.

10. Select the **Do not share this printer option** and then click **Next**.

11. The *You've successfully added the printer* page appears. If the printer is connected and ready to use, you can click the *Print a test page* button.

12. Click **Finish**.

    The printer appears in the Devices and Printers control panel.

13. **Close** the *Control Panel* window.

At this point, the printer is ready to receive jobs from applications, but this does not necessarily mean that the print device is ready. As stated earlier, you can complete this entire procedure without the print device being attached to the computer, or turned on, or loaded with paper. Jobs that users send to the printer are processed and remain in the print queue until the print device is available for use.

Sharing a Printer

A *local printer* is, of course, available for use by anyone working at the computer to which it is attached. However, you can also share the printer with other users in a homegroup, workgroup, or domain. When you share a printer connected to a Windows 8.1 computer, you are essentially using Windows 8.1 as a print server.

CERTIFICATION READY
Configure shared printers
Objective 4.1

Using Windows 8.1 as a print server can be a simple or a complex matter, depending on how many clients the server has to support and how much printing they do. For a home, small business, or workgroup, in which a handful of users need occasional access to the printer, no special preparation is necessary. However, if the computer must support heavy printer use, any or all of the following hardware upgrades might be needed:

- **Additional system memory** – Processing print jobs requires system memory, just like any other application. If you plan to run heavy print traffic on a Windows 8.1 computer, in addition to regular applications, you might want to install extra system memory.

- **Additional disk space** – When a print device is busy, any additional print jobs that arrive at the print server must be stored temporarily on a hard drive until the print device is free to receive them. Depending on the amount of print traffic involved, the print server might require a substantial amount of temporary storage for this purpose.

TAKE NOTE*

When in PCL format, print jobs can often be much larger than the document files from which they were generated, especially if they contain graphics. When estimating the amount of disk space required for a print server, be sure that you consider the size of the PCL files, not the application files.

- **Make the computer a dedicated print server** – In addition to memory and disk space, using Windows 8.1 as a print server requires processor clock cycles, just like any other application. On a computer handling heavy print traffic, standard user applications might experience a substantial performance degradation. If you need a print server to handle heavy traffic, you might want to consider using the computer for print server tasks exclusively and move the user(s) elsewhere.

TAKE NOTE*

If you plan on using a Windows computer as a dedicated print server, Windows 8.1 might not be your best choice as an operating system. As with all of the workstation versions of Windows, Windows 8.1 is limited to ten simultaneous network connections, so no more than ten clients can print at any one time. If you need a print server that can handle more than ten connections, you must use a server operating system, such as Windows Server 2012 R2.

To share a printer on a Windows 8.1 computer, you must enable the appropriate settings in the Network and Sharing Center, just as you have to do to share files and folders. To share printers, the following Sharing and Discovery settings must be turned on:

- Network Discovery
- File and Printer Sharing

In addition, if the Password Protected Sharing setting is turned on, users must be logged on and have appropriate permissions to use the printer.

To share a printer that is already installed on a Windows 8.1 computer, use the following procedure:

➔ SHARE A PRINTER

GET READY. Log on to Windows 8.1 using an account with Administrator privileges and then perform the following steps:

1. Open the **Control Panel** and then click **Hardware and Sound** > **Devices and Printers**.

   The *Devices and Printers* control panel appears.

2. Right-click one of the printer icons in the window and then, from the context menu, select **Printer Properties**.

   The printer's *Properties* sheet appears

3. Click the **Sharing** tab, as shown in Figure 13-22.

Figure 13-22

The Sharing tab of a printer's *Properties* sheet

4. Select the **Share this printer** checkbox.

   The printer name appears in the Share name text box. You can accept the default name or supply one of your own. Select the *Render print jobs on client computers* checkbox if you want to use the printer drivers on the individual client computers. Leaving this box unchecked will force the print server on the computer hosting the printer to process all of the jobs.

> **TAKE NOTE***
>
> If the computer is a member of an Active Directory domain, an additional *List printer in the directory* checkbox appears in this dialog box. Selecting this checkbox creates a new printer object in the Active Directory Domain Services database, which enables domain users to locate the printer by searching the directory.

5. Click **OK** to close the *Properties* sheet for the printer.
6. The printer icon in the Printers control panel now includes a symbol indicating that it has been shared.

Configuring Printer Security

> Just like NTFS files and folders, Windows printers have their own permissions, which enable you to control who has access to the printer and to what degree.

When Password Protected Sharing is turned on in the Windows 8.1 Network and Sharing Center, users must log on to the computer with a user account that requires a password before they can access a shared printer. In addition, the user account must have the appropriate permissions to use the printer.

Printer permissions are much simpler than NTFS permissions; they basically dictate whether users are allowed to merely use the printer, manage documents submitted to the printer, or manage the properties of the printer itself. To assign permissions for a printer, use the following procedure:

 ASSIGN PRINTER PERMISSIONS

GET READY. Log on to Windows 8.1 using an account with Administrator privileges and then perform the following steps:

1. Open the **Control Panel** and then click **Hardware and Sound** > **Devices and Printers.** The *Devices and Printers* control panel appears.

2. Right-click one of the printer icons in the window and then, from the context menu, select **Printer Properties.**

    The printer's *Properties* sheet appears

3. Click the **Security** tab, as shown in Figure 13-23.

    The top half of the display lists all of the security principals currently possessing permissions to the selected printer. The bottom half lists the permissions held by the selected security principal.

Figure 13-23

The Security tab of a printer's *Properties* sheet

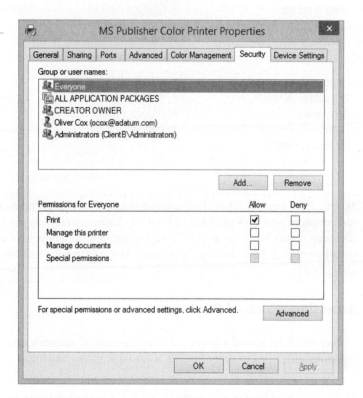

4. Click **Add.**

    The *Select Users or Groups* dialog box appears.

TAKE NOTE*

When you assign permissions on a standalone computer, you select local user and group accounts to be the security principals that receive the permissions. However, if the computer is a member of an Active Directory Domain Services domain, you assign permissions to domain users, groups, and other objects by default.

5. In the *Enter the object names to select* text box, type a user or group name, and then click **OK**.

The user or group appears in the *Group or user names* list.

6. Select the user or group you added, and select or clear the checkboxes in the bottom half of the display to Allow or Deny the user any of the standard permissions shown in Table 13-3.

7. Click **OK** to close the *Properties* sheet.

Table 13-3

Basic Printer Permissions

PERMISSION	CAPABILITIES	SPECIAL PERMISSIONS	DEFAULT ASSIGNMENTS
Print	• Connect to a printer • Print documents • Pause, resume, restart, and cancel the user's own documents	• Print • Read Permissions	Assigned to the Everyone special identity
Manage This Printer	• Cancel all documents • Share a printer • Change printer properties • Delete a printer • Change printer permissions	• Print • Manage Printers • Read Permissions • Change Permissions • Take Ownership	Assigned to the Administrators group
Manage Documents	• Pause, resume, restart, and cancel all users' documents • Control job settings for all documents	• Manage Documents • Read Permissions • Change Permissions • Take Ownership	Assigned to the Creator Owner special identity

TAKE NOTE* As with NTFS permissions, there are two types of printer permissions: basic permissions and advanced permissions. Each of the three basic permissions consists of a combination of advanced permissions. As with NTFS, you can work directly with the advanced permissions by clicking Advanced on the Security tab, to display the Advanced Security Settings dialog box.

Accessing a Shared Printer

Once you have shared a printer, it is available to all network users with the appropriate permissions, just as a shared folder is available to the network.

To access a shared printer from Windows 8.1, use the following procedure.

 ACCESS A SHARED PRINTER

GET READY. Log on to Windows 8.1 using any user account and then perform the following steps:

1. Open the **Control Panel** and then click **Hardware and Sound** > **Devices and Printers**.

The *Devices and Printers* control panel appears.

2. Click Add a printer.

   The *Add Printer Wizard* appears and begins searching the network for shared printers.

3. If the printer you want appears, select it and then click Next to install it. If it does not appear, click *The printer that I want isn't listed* to display the *Find a printer by other options* page.

4. Select the proper option to browse for a network printer, enter a printer's IP address or hostname, or add a Bluetooth or wireless printer\UNC name or URL for a printer, or. Then click Next.

   When you have selected a printer, the *You've successfully added the printer* page appears.

5. Click Finish. The printer appears in the *Devices and Printers* control panel.

6. Close the *Control Panel* window.

In addition to using the Add Printer wizard, there are several other ways to access shared network printers. If the computer is a member of a homegroup, then all of the printers shared by other members of the same homegroup automatically appear in the Devices and Printers control panel.

When browsing the network in File Explorer, you can see the shared printers for each computer on the network, as shown in Figure 13-24. By right-clicking a printer in any File Explorer window and selecting Connect from the context menu, you can access any printer for which you have the appropriate permissions. Any other Windows 8 mechanism that can display the shared printers on the network provides access to them in the same way.

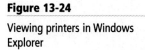

Figure 13-24

Viewing printers in Windows Explorer

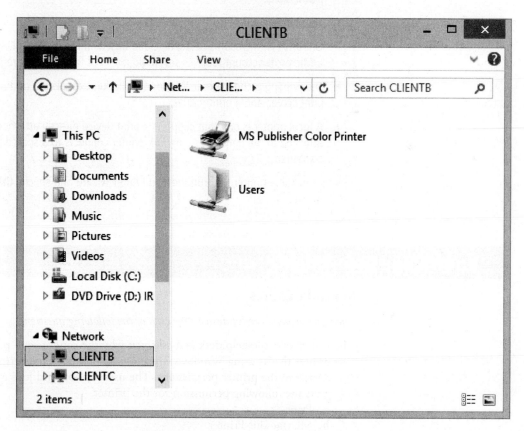

When the computer hosting the printer is a member of an Active Directory Domain Services domain, the ability to locate shared printers is enhanced even further. Opting to list the printer in the Active Directory database creates an object for the printer, and in this object you can specify a lot of information about the print device, including its location and its capabilities.

Recording this information in the printer object makes it possible for users to locate printers by searching the directory for specific characteristics. For example, if a user on a large corporate network needs to find a color duplex printer on the third floor, running a directory search with the appropriate keywords will enable the user to locate the required printer.

SKILL SUMMARY

IN THIS LESSON, YOU LEARNED:

- Windows 8.1 provides three basic methods for sharing the files and folders on the computer: any folder sharing, public folder sharing, and homegroup sharing.

- Homegroup networking is a Windows 8.1 feature that enables computers configured to use the Home network location to share the contents of their respective libraries among themselves.

- Libraries enable users to aggregate files in multiple locations – and even on multiple computers – into a single folder that makes them appear as though they are all on a local drive.

- Sharing files and folders using the Public folder is the simplest way to give your clients file sharing capability.

- Windows 8.1 has several sets of permissions, which operate independently of each other, including NTFS permissions, share permissions, registry permissions, and Active Directory permissions.

- Share permissions provide rudimentary access control for all of the files on a network share.

- OneDrive is Microsoft's personal, cloud-based storage service. Every user who applies for a Microsoft account receives seven gigabytes of free cloud storage.

- The printing architecture in Windows is modular, consisting of the print device, a printer, a print server, and a printer driver.

- A local printer is one that supports a print device directly attached to the computer or attached to the network. A network printer connects to a shared printer hosted by another computer.

- To install a printer, you run the Add Printer wizard and specify the printer driver and port to use.

■ Knowledge Assessment

Multiple Choice

Select one or more correct answers for each of the following questions.

1. A user calls the help desk and asks you why she cannot send print jobs to a shared printer that is using Windows 8.1 as a print server. You determine that the problem is related to the printer permissions. The user cannot send jobs to the printer because she lacks the following permission for the printer.
   a. Print
   b. Manage this Printer
   c. Manage all Printers
   d. Manage Documents

2. To share a folder with network users on a public network, you must first open the Network and Sharing Center and do which of the following? (Choose all that apply.)
   a. Enable DHCP
   b. Turn on Network Discovery
   c. Enable File and Printer Sharing
   d. Create a homegroup

3. In the Windows printing architecture, which of the following are the hardware components. (Choose all that apply.)
   a. Printer
   b. Print driver
   c. Print device
   d. Print server

4. The primary function of a printer driver is to take printer commands generated by applications and convert them into what format?
   a. Printer control language
   b. Print server
   c. Analog
   d. Binary

5. What must you do to create a shared folder called DOCS and hide it from network users?
   a. Append an percent sign to the name (DOCS%)
   b. Append a dollar sign to the name (DOCS$)
   c. Type the name in all lowercase letters (docs)
   d. Append an exclamation point to the name (DOCS!)

6. Share level permissions provide which of the following levels of access? (Choose all that apply.)
   a. Read
   b. Full Control
   c. Change
   d. Modify

7. If a user is granted the share permission Allow READ to a folder named Sales and also has the share permission Allow CHANGE to the same folder as part of her membership in the Finance Group. What is her effective permission to the Sales folder? (Choose all that apply.)
   a. She can create folders, files, and change data in the files in the Sales folder.
   b. She can change file permissions for files in the Sales folder.
   c. She can delete files and folders in the Sales folder.
   d. She can execute any program files located in the Sales folder.

8. Which basic Printer permission is needed to allow a user to cancel all of their documents currently queued on a print device?
   a. Print
   b. Manage this printer
   c. Manage documents
   d. Manage all documents

9. Which of the following methods can be used to access OneDrive storage space? (Choose all that apply.)
   a. Through the web (http://onedrive.com)
   b. By using the OneDrive Desktop app
   c. Through an Office 2013 application
   d. By using an FTP client

10. Which type of permissions apply when you are connecting to a resource locally or across the network?
    a. NTFS file permissions only
    b. Share folder permissions
    c. NTFS and Share permissions
    d. NTFS file and folder permissions

Best Answer

Choose the letter that corresponds to the best answer. More than one answer choice may achieve the goal. Select the BEST answer.

1. You are the administrator of a network with several print devices, all of which are hosted by Windows 8.1 computers. These print devices are shared with all users on the network. One of the print devices is malfunctioning and must be sent out for repair. Which of the following is the most practical way to prevent users from sending jobs to the printer while the print device is unavailable?
   a. Delete the printer on the computer functioning as the print server.
   b. Revoke the Print permission from all of the users.
   c. Modify the printer.
   d. Stop sharing the printer.

2. A folder named Marketing contains each month's sales forecasts. This folder needs to be accessible over the local network so that a subset of the Marketing team (Interns) can have read only access to view the data. Of the following, which would provide the most efficient approach for providing the access needed for those in the Interns group?
   a. Share permission: Full Control (Interns group), NTFS permission: Read (assigned to each Intern's individual user account)
   b. Share permissions: Read (Interns group), NTFS permission: Modify (assigned to each Intern's individual user account)
   c. Share permission: Read (Everyone group), NTFS permission: Read (assigned to the Interns group)
   d. Share permission: Full Control (Interns group), NTFS permission: Read (assigned to the Interns group)

3. There are currently five users on a Windows 8.1 network. One of the Windows 8.1 computers is currently configured as a print server. If the number of users is expected to double every 6 months for the next year, what is the best approach to use for to ensure you are able to handle the future growth?
   a. Add additional memory on the Windows 8.1 print server.
   b. Add additional hard drive space on the Windows 8.1 print server.
   c. Make the computer a dedicated print server.
   d. Replace the Windows 8.1 computer with a Windows Server 2012 R2 print server.

4. A new printer has been added to the company network. What is the least amount of privileges you can provide for a junior administrator to allow them to print documents while also being able to pause, resume, restart, and cancel all of their own documents?
   a. Print
   b. Manage This Printer
   c. Manage Documents
   d. Print and Manage Documents

5. Due to tight deadlines, the Executives' print jobs need to have a higher priority than other print jobs on the network. What is the best approach to use to ensure Executives print jobs are always a higher priority than other users while keeping costs down?
   a. Create multiple printers, associate them with different print devices and then assign the Execs Group a priority of 77 and everyone else a priority of 1.
   b. Create multiple printers, associate them with different print devices and then assign the Execs Group a priority of 77 and everyone else a priority of 72.
   c. Purchase a new print device, share it on the network so that only the members of the Execs Group can print to it.
   d. Purchase new print devices for each member of the Execs Group and connect it directly to their computers.

Matching and Identification

Complete the following exercise by matching the terms with their corresponding definitions.

_____ a) Homegroups
_____ b) OneDrive
_____ c) Local printer
_____ d) Libraries
_____ e) Printer pool
_____ f) Manage this Printer
_____ g) Printer control language
_____ h) Share permissions
_____ i) Printer driver
_____ j) Print server

1. A basic printer permission; allows you to cancel all documents and change printer properties.
2. Enable users to aggregate files in multiple locations.
3. Can be standardized (PSL) or can be proprietary languages developed by the print device manager.
4. Microsoft's personal, cloud-based storage service.
5. Receives print jobs from clients and sends them to print devices.
6. Provide rudimentary access control for all of the files on a network share.
7. Converts print jobs into commands for a specific print device.
8. Supports a print device directly attached to the computer.
9. Designed to share only libraries.
10. A single print server connected to multiple print devices.

Build a List

1. In order of first to last, specify the correct order of steps to assign printer permissions.
   _____ Click the **Security** tab.
   _____ Click **Add**. The *Select Users or Groups* dialog box appears.
   _____ In the *Enter the object names to select* text box, type a user or group name, and then click **OK**.
   _____ Click **OK** to close the *Properties* sheet.
   _____ Right-click one of the printer icons in the window and then, from the context menu, select **Printer Properties**.
   _____ Select the user or group you added, and select or clear the checkboxes in the bottom half of the display to Allow or Deny the user any of the standard permissions.
   _____ Open the **Control Panel** and then click **Hardware and Sound** > **Devices and Printers**.

2. Specify the correct order of steps to set a printer's priority.

_____ Right-click one of the printer icons in the window and then, from the context menu, select **Printer Properties**.

_____ Set the *Priority* spin box to a number representing the highest priority you want to set for the printer. Higher numbers represent higher priorities. The highest possible priority is 99.

_____ Open the **Control Panel** and then click **Hardware and Sound > Devices and Printers**.

_____ Click the **Security** tab.

_____ Click the **Advanced** tab.

_____ Add the users or groups that you want to provide with high-priority access to the printer and assign them the *Allow Print* permission.

_____ Create an identical printer using the same printer driver and pointing to the same print device. Leave the *Priority* setting to its default value of *1* and then leave the default permissions in place.

_____ Rename the printers, specifying the priority assigned to each one.

_____ Revoke the *Allow Print* permission from the *Everyone* special identity.

_____ Inform the privileged users that they should send their jobs to the high-priority printer.

_____ Click **OK** to close the *Properties* sheet.

3. Specify the correct order of steps to add a library location.

_____ Click the **Manage Library** button in the ribbon.

_____ Select one of the four library icons in the right pane.

_____ **Close** the *File Explorer* window.

_____ Click **OK**. The contents of the folder you added appear in the library.

_____ Open **File Explorer** and select the **Libraries** folder.

_____ Browse to the folder you want to add, select it, and then click **Include Folder**.

_____ Click **OK** to close the *Internet Properties* sheet.

_____ Click **Add**. An *Include Folder* combo box appears for the library you selected.

■ Business Case Scenarios

Scenario 13-1: Enhancing Print Performance

You are a desktop support technician for a law firm with a group of ten legal secretaries who provide administrative support to the attorneys. All of the secretaries use a single, shared, high-speed laser printer that is connected to a dedicated Windows 7 print server. The secretaries print multiple copies of large documents on a regular basis, and although the laser printer is fast, it is kept running almost constantly. Sometimes the secretaries have to wait 20 minutes or more after submitting a print job for their documents to reach the top of the queue. The office manager has offered to purchase additional printers for the department. However, the secretaries are accustomed to simply clicking the Print button, and don't like the idea of having to examine multiple print queues to determine which one has the fewest jobs before submitting a document. What can you do to provide the department with a printing solution that will enable the secretaries to utilize additional printers most efficiently?

Scenario 13-2: Understanding Printing Priorities

Jack has the Allow Print, Allow Manage Documents, and Allow Manage Printers permissions to a printer with a priority of 1. Jill has the Allow Print permission to a printer with a priority of 10, connected to the same print device. If Jack and Jill both submit a print job at exactly the same time, whose print job will be processed first?

Configuring File and Folder Access

70-687 EXAM OBJECTIVE

Objective 4.2 – Configure file and folder access. This objective may include but is not limited to: encrypt files and folders by using Encrypting File System (EFS); configure NTFS permissions; configure disk quotas; configure file access auditing.

LESSON HEADING	EXAM OBJECTIVE
Managing Permissions	
Understanding the Windows Permission Architecture	
Managing NTFS Permissions	Configure NTFS permissions
Using the Encrypting File System	
Encrypting a Folder with EFS	Encrypt files and folders by using Encrypting File System (EFS)
Determining Whether a File or Folder is Encrypted	
Configuring Disk Quotas	Configure disk quotas
Configuring File Access Auditing	Configure file access auditing

KEY TERMS

access control list (ACL)

access control entries (ACEs)

advanced permissions

Active Directory permissions

auditing

basic permissions

effective access

Encrypting File System (EFS)

NTFS

NTFS permissions

NTFS quotas

permissions

Registry permissions

security principal

Share permissions

■ Managing Permissions

THE BOTTOM LINE

In Lesson 20, "Managing Local Storage," you learn how to prepare hard disk drives so that users can store files on them. To control access to the disks and other resources, Windows 8.1 uses permissions.

Permissions are privileges granted to specific system entities, such as users, groups, or computers, enabling them to perform a task or access a resource. For example, you can grant a specific user permission to read a file, while denying that same user the permissions needed to modify or delete the file.

Windows 8.1 has several sets of permissions, which operate independently of each other. As an administrator, you should be familiar with the operation of the following four permission systems:

- *NTFS permissions* – Control access to the files and folders stored on disk volumes formatted with the NTFS file system. To access a file, whether on the local system or over a network, a user must have the appropriate NTFS permissions.

- *Share permissions* – Control access to files and folders shared over a network. To access a file over a network, a user must have appropriate share permissions and appropriate NTFS permissions.

- *Registry permissions* – Control access to specific parts of the Windows registry. An application that modifies registry settings or a user attempting to manually modify the registry must have the appropriate registry permissions.

- *Active Directory permissions* – Control access to specific parts of an Active Directory hierarchy. Although Windows 8.1 cannot host an Active Directory Domain Services domain, desktop technicians might require these permissions when servicing computers that are members of a domain.

All of these permission systems operate independently of each other and can conceivably combine to provide increased protection to a specific resource. For example, Alice might grant Ralph the NTFS permissions needed to access the budget spreadsheet stored on her computer. If Ralph sits down at Alice's computer and logs on as himself, he will be able to access that spreadsheet. However, if Ralph is working at his own computer, he will not be able to access the spreadsheet until Alice creates a share containing the file and until she grants Ralph the proper share permissions.

TAKE NOTE *

Although all of these permissions systems are operating all the time, administrators do not necessarily have to work with them all on a regular basis. In fact, you might not ever have to manually alter a Registry or Active Directory permission. However, many technicians have to work with NTFS and share permissions on a daily basis.

Understanding the Windows Permission Architecture

Permissions protect files, folders, shares, registry keys, and Active Directory objects.

To store permissions, each of these elements has an *access control list (ACL)*. An ACL is a collection of individual permissions, in the form of *access control entries (ACEs)*. Each ACE consists of a *security principal* (that is, the name of the user, group, or computer being granted the permissions) and the specific permissions assigned to that security principal. When you manage permissions in any of the Windows 8.1 permission systems, you are actually creating and modifying the ACEs in an ACL.

It is crucial to understand that, in all of the Windows operating systems, permissions are stored as part of the element being protected, not the security principal being granted access. For example, when you grant a user the NTFS permissions needed to access a file, the ACE you create is stored in the file's ACL; it is not part of the user account. You can move the file to a different location, and in most cases, its permissions go with it.

To manage permissions in Windows 8.1, you use the controls in the Security tab of the element's Properties dialog box, like the one shown in Figure 14-1, with the security principals listed at the top and the permissions associated with them at the bottom. All of the Windows permission systems use the same interface, although the permissions themselves differ.

Figure 14-1

The Security tab of a *Documents Properties* dialog box

UNDERSTANDING BASIC AND ADVANCED PERMISSIONS

The permissions protecting a particular system element are not like the keys to a lock, which provide either full access or no access at all. Permissions are designed to be granular, enabling you to grant specific degrees of access to security principals.

You can use NTFS permissions to control not only who has access to Alice's spreadsheet, but also the degree to which each user has access. You might grant Ralph permission to read the spreadsheet and also modify it, while Ed can only read it, and Trixie cannot see it at all.

To provide this granularity, each of the Windows permission systems has an assortment of permissions that you can assign to a security principal in any combination. Depending on the permission system you are using, you might have literally dozens of different permissions available for a single system element.

If this is all starting to sound extremely complex, don't worry. Windows provides preconfigured permission combinations that are suitable for most common access control chores. When you open the Properties dialog box for a system element and look at its Security

TAKE NOTE*

Prior to Windows 8 and Windows Server 2012, basic and advanced permissions were known as standard and special permissions, respectively.

tab, the permissions you are seeing are called ***basic permissions***. Basic permissions are actually combinations of ***advanced permissions***, which provide the most granular control over the element.

For example, the NTFS permission system has 14 advanced permissions that you can assign to a folder or file. However, there are also six basic permissions, which are various combinations of the 14 advanced permissions. In most cases, you will only have to work with the basic permissions. Many administrators rarely, if ever, work directly with the advanced permissions.

If you do find it necessary to work with advanced permissions directly, Windows makes it possible. When you click the Advanced button on the Security tab of any Properties dialog box, an Advanced Security Settings dialog box appears, as shown in Figure 14-2, which enables you to access the ACEs for the selected system element directly.

Figure 14-2

The *Advanced Security Settings for Documents* dialog box

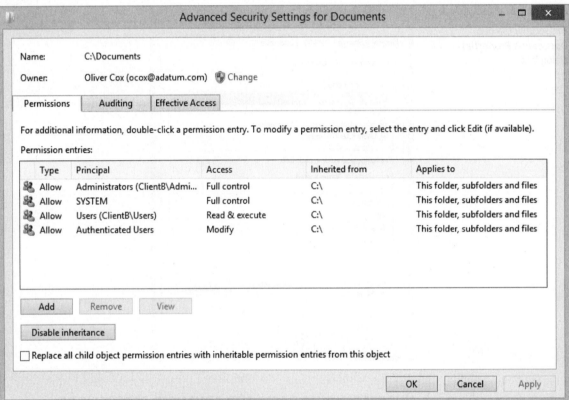

ALLOWING AND DENYING PERMISSIONS

When you assign permissions to a system element, you are, in effect, creating a new ACE in the element's ACL. There are two basic types of ACEs: *Allow* and *Deny*. This makes it possible to approach permission management tasks from two directions:

- **Additive** – Start with no permissions and then grant Allow permissions to individual security principals to provide them with the access they need.

- **Subtractive** – Start by granting all possible Allow permissions to individual security principals, providing them with full control over the system element, and then grant them Deny permissions for the access you don't want them to have.

Most administrators prefer the additive approach, because Windows, by default, attempts to limit access to important system elements. In a properly designed permission hierarchy, the use of Deny permissions is often not needed at all. Many administrators frown on their use, because combining Allow and Deny permissions in the same hierarchy can make it difficult to determine the effective permissions for a specific system element.

INHERITING PERMISSIONS

The most important principle in permission management is that permissions tend to run downwards through a hierarchy. The tendency of permissions to flow downwards through a file system or other hierarchy is called permission inheritance. Permission inheritance means that parent elements pass their permissions down to their subordinate elements.

For example, when you grant Alice Allow permissions to the root of the D: drive, all of the files and subfolders on the D: drive inherit those permissions, and Alice can access them. The principle of inheritance simplifies the permission assignment process enormously. Without it, you would have to grant security principals individual Allow permissions for every file, folder, share, object, and key they need to access. With inheritance, you can grant access to an entire file system by creating one set of Allow permissions.

In most cases, whether they do it consciously or not, system administrators take inheritance into account when they design their file systems and Active Directory trees. The location of a system element in a hierarchy is often based on how the administrators plan to assign permissions. For example, the section of a directory tree shown in Figure 14-3 is intended to be a place where network users can temporarily store files that they want other users to access.

Figure 14-3

A sample xfer directory structure

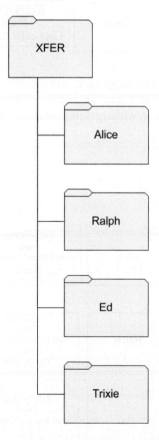

Because the administrator has assigned all users the Allow Read and Allow List Folder Contents basic permissions to the xfer folder, as shown in Figure 14-4, everyone is able to read the files in the xfer directory. Because the assigned permissions run downwards, all of the subfolders beneath xfer inherit those permissions, so all of the users can read the files in all of the subfolders as well.

Figure 14-4

Granting *Allow* permissions to the xfer folder

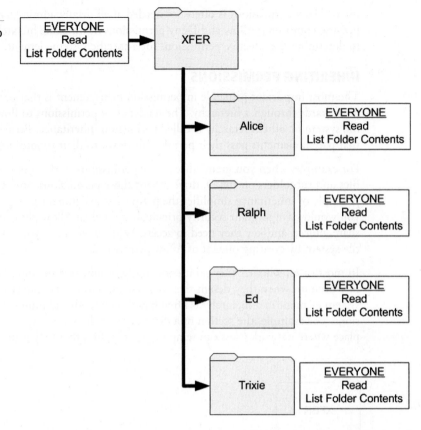

The next step is for the administrator to assign each user the Allow Full Control permission to his or her own subfolder, as shown in Figure 14-5. This enables each user to create, modify, and delete files in his or her own folder, without compromising the security of the other users'

Figure 14-5

Granting *Full Control* to individual user folders

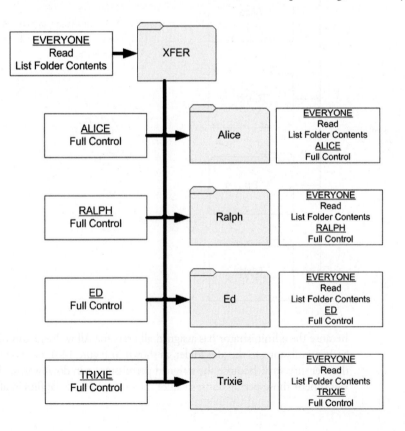

folders. Because the user folders are at the bottom of the hierarchy, there are no subfolders to inherit the Full Control permissions.

There are some situations in which an administrator might want to prevent subordinate elements from inheriting permissions from their parents. There are two ways to do this:

- **Turn off inheritance** – When you assign advanced permissions, you can configure an ACE not to pass its permissions down to its subordinate elements. This effectively blocks the inheritance process.

- **Deny permissions** – When you assign a Deny permission to a system element, it overrides any Allow permissions that the element might have inherited from its parent objects.

UNDERSTANDING EFFECTIVE ACCESS

A security principal can receive permissions in many different ways, and it is important for an administrator to understand how these permissions interact. *Effective access* is the combination of Allow permissions and Deny permissions that a security principal receives for a given system element, whether explicitly assigned, inherited, or received through a group membership. Because a security principal can receive permissions from so many sources, it is not unusual for those permissions to conflict, so there are rules defining how the permissions combine to form the effective permissions. These rules are as follows:

- **Allow permissions are cumulative** – When a security principal receives Allow permissions from more than one source, the permissions are combined to form the effective permissions. For example, if Alice receives the Allow Read and Allow List Folder Contents permissions for a particular folder by inheriting them from its parent folder, and receives the Allow Write and Allow Modify permissions to the same folder from a group membership, Alice's effective permissions for the folder is the combination of all four permissions. If you then explicitly grant Alice's user account the Allow Full Control permission, this fifth permission is combined with the other four.

- **Deny permissions override Allow permissions** – When a security principal receives Allow permissions, whether explicitly, by inheritance, or from a group, you can override those permissions by granting the principal Deny permissions of the same type. For example, if Alice receives the Allow Read and Allow List Folder Contents permissions for a particular folder by inheritance, and receives the Allow Write and Allow Modify permissions to the same folder from a group membership, explicitly granting her the Deny permissions to that folder prevents her from accessing it in any way.

- **Explicit permissions take precedence over inherited permissions** – When a security principal receives permissions by inheriting them from a parent or from group memberships, you can override those permissions by explicitly assigning contradicting permissions to the security principal itself. For example, if Alice inherits the Deny Full Access permission for a folder, explicitly assigning her user account the Allow Full Access permission to that folder overrides the denial.

Of course, instead of examining and evaluating all of the possible permission sources, you can just open the Advanced Security Settings dialog box, click the Effective Access tab, and select a security principal to display its current effective permissions for the selected file or folder, as shown in Figure 14-6.

Figure 14-6

The Effective Access tab of the *Advanced Security Settings for Documents* dialog box

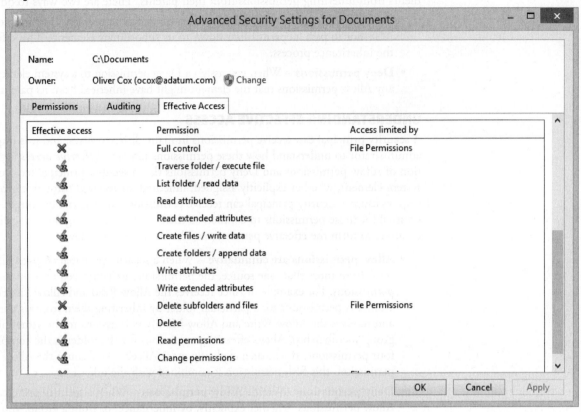

Managing NTFS Permissions

> Windows 8.1 supports two primary file systems, NTFS and FAT, but the majority of Windows installations today use NTFS.

NTFS, the primary Windows file system, is required to implement various security and administrative features in Windows. NTFS is a journaling file system that can recover from disk errors more readily than the earlier FAT32 file system. It also supports the Unicode character set and long file names (up to 255 characters).

NTFS permissions are available to drives formatted with NTFS. The advantage of NTFS permissions is that they affect local users as well as network users and they are based on the account employed by each individual user at the Windows logon, regardless of where the user is connecting.

Along with the additional functionality that NTFS provides comes the potential for complex configurations that can lead to administration headaches. If you don't have a thorough understanding of various permissions and their relationships, it can be difficult to sort out a permission problem when it occurs.

CERTIFICATION READY
Configure NTFS
permissions
Objective 4.2

In the NTFS permission system, the security principals involved are typically users and groups, which Windows refers to as security identifiers (SIDs). When a user attempts to access an NTFS file or folder, the system reads the user's security access token, which contains the SIDs for the user's account and all of the groups to which the user belongs. The system then compares these SIDs to those stored in the file or folder's ACEs to determine what access the user should have. This process is called authorization.

ASSIGNING BASIC NTFS PERMISSIONS

Most Windows system administrators work with basic NTFS permissions almost exclusively. This is because there is no need to work directly with advanced permissions for most common access control tasks. To assign basic NTFS permissions, use the following procedure:

 ASSIGN BASIC NTFS PERMISSIONS

GET READY. Log on to Windows 8.1 using an account with Administrator privileges, and then perform the following steps:

1. Open the desktop and click the **File Explorer** icon on the taskbar. A *File Explorer* window appears.

2. In the Computer container, right-click the **Local Disk (C:)** drive and then, on the context menu, point to **New** and select **Folder**. Give the folder the name **Test Folder**.

3. Right-click the **Test Folder** folder you created and then, from the context menu, select **Properties**. The *Test Folder Properties* sheet appears.

4. Click the **Security** tab. The top half of the resulting display lists all of the security principals currently possessing permissions to the Test Folder folder. The bottom half lists the permissions held by the selected security principal.

5. Click **Edit**. The *Permissions for Test Folder* dialog box appears, as shown in Figure 14-7. The interface is the same as that of the Security tab on the Properties sheet, except that the permissions are now represented by checkboxes, indicating that you can modify their states.

Figure 14-7

The *Permissions for Test Folder* dialog box

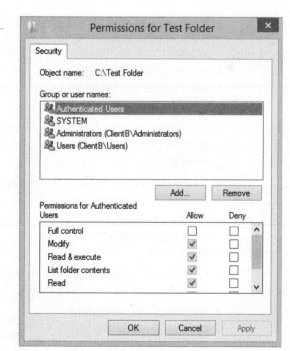

6. Click **Add**. The Select Users or Groups dialog box appears.

TAKE NOTE * When you assign permissions on a computer using the Private or Public network location, you select local user and group accounts to be the security principals that receive the permissions. However, if the computer is a member of an Active Directory Domain Services domain, the default is to assign permissions to domain users, groups, and other objects.

7. In the Enter the object names to select text box, type **Guest** and then click **OK**. The Guest user account appears on the *Permissions for Test Folder* dialog box in the Group or user names list.

8. Select the **Guest** user and then, in the *Permissions for Guest* box, select or clear the **Allow** checkbox or **Deny** checkbox to allow or deny the user any of the basic permissions shown in Table 14-1.

Table 14-1

NTFS Basic Permissions

BASIC PERMISSION	WHEN APPLIED TO A FOLDER, ENABLES A SECURITY PRINCIPAL TO:	WHEN APPLIED TO A FILE, ENABLES A SECURITY PRINCIPAL TO:
Full Control	• Modify the folder permissions. • Take ownership of the folder. • Delete subfolders and files contained in the folder. • Perform all actions associated with all of the other NTFS folder permissions.	• Modify the file permissions. • Take ownership of the file. • Perform all actions associated with all of the other NTFS file permissions.
Modify	• Delete the folder. • Perform all actions associated with the Write and the Read & Execute permissions.	• Modify the file. • Delete the file. • Perform all actions associated with the Write and the Read & execute permissions.
Read & Execute	• Navigate through restricted folders to reach other files and folders. • Perform all actions associated with the Read and List Folder Contents permissions.	• Perform all actions associated with the Read permission. • Run applications.
List Folder Contents	• View the names of the files and subfolders contained in the folder.	• Not applicable
Read	• See the files and subfolders contained in the folder. • View the ownership, permissions, and attributes of the folder.	• Read the contents of the file. • View the ownership, permissions, and attributes of the file.
Write	• Create new files and subfolders inside the folder. • Modify the folder attributes. • View the ownership and permissions of the folder.	• Overwrite the file. • Modify the file attributes. • View the ownership and permissions of the file.

9. Click **OK** to close the *Permissions for Test Folder* dialog box.

10. Click **OK** to close the Test folder Properties sheet.

> **TAKE NOTE** *
>
> Assigning permissions to the single folder you created takes only a moment, but for a folder with a large number of subordinate files and subfolders the process can take a long time because the system must modify the ACL of each folder and file.

ASSIGNING ADVANCED NTFS PERMISSIONS

If you ever have the need to work with advanced NTFS permissions directly, Windows 8.1 provides the tools to do so. To view and manage the advanced NTFS permissions for a file or folder, use the following procedure.

 ASSIGN ADVANCED NTFS PERMISSIONS

GET READY. Log on to Windows 8 using an account with Administrator privileges, and then perform the following steps:

1. Open **File Explorer** and expand the **Local Disk** (C:) drive.

2. Right-click the **Test Folder** folder you created earlier and then, from the context menu, select Properties. The *Test Folder Properties* sheet appears.

3. Click the Security tab, and then click **Advanced**. The *Advanced Security Settings for Test Folder* dialog box appears. This dialog box is as close as the Windows graphical interface can come to displaying the contents of an ACL. Each of the lines in the Permission entries list is essentially an ACE, and includes the following information:

   • **Type** – Specifies whether the entry allows or denies the permission.

   • **Name** – Specifies the name of the security principal receiving the permission.

   • **Permission** – Specifies the name of the basic permission being assigned to the security principal. If the entry is used to assign advanced permissions, the word *Advanced* appears in this field.

   • **Inherited From** – Specifies whether the permission is inherited and if so, where it is inherited from.

   • **Apply To** – Specifies whether the permission is inherited by subordinate objects and if so, by which ones.

   This dialog box also contains the following two controls:

   • **Disable inheritance** – A button that enables you to specify whether the file or folder should inherit permissions from parent objects. Clicking it causes a Block Inheritance message box to appear, enabling you to choose whether to convert inherited permissions for the selected object into explicit permissions or remove all of the inherited permissions from the object. If you choose the former, the effective access stays the same, but the file or folder is no longer dependent on the parent for permission inheritance. If you change the permissions on the parent objects, the file or folder remains unaffected.

   • **Replace all child object permissions with inheritable permission entries from this object** – Causes subordinate objects to inherit permissions from this file or folder, to the exclusion of all permissions explicitly assigned to the subordinate objects.

4. Click **Add**. A *Permission Entry for Test Folder* dialog box appears.

5. Click **Select a principal**. The *Select Users or Groups* dialog box appears.

6. In the *Enter the object names to select text* box, type **Guest,** and then click **OK**. The Guest user appears in the *Permission Entry for Test Folder* dialog box appears, as shown in Figure 14-8.

Figure 14-8

The *Permission Entry for Test Folder* dialog box

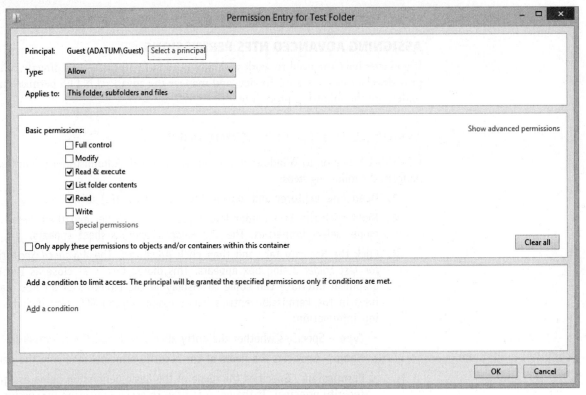

7. In the *Type* drop-down list, specify whether you want to allow or deny the permissions you assign using this dialog box.

8. In the *Applies to* dropdown list, select which subordinate elements should receive the permissions you assign using this dialog box.

9. Click the **Show advanced permissions** link.

10. In the *Advanced permissions* list, select or clear the checkboxes to assign the user any of the advanced permissions shown in Table 14-2.

Table 14-2

NTFS Advanced Permissions

ADVANCED PERMISSION	FUNCTIONS
Traverse Folder/Execute File	• The Traverse Folder permission allows or denies security principals the ability to move through folders that they do not have permission to access, so as to reach files or folders that they do have permission to access. This permission applies to folders only. • The Execute File permission allows or denies security principals the ability to run program files. This permission applies to files only.
List Folder/Read Data	• The List Folder permission allows or denies security principals the ability to view the file and subfolder names within a folder. This permission applies to folders only. • The Read Data permission allows or denies security principals the ability to view the contents of a file. This permission applies to files only.
Read Attributes	Allows or denies security principals the ability to view the NTFS attributes of a file or folder.
Read Extended Attributes	Allows or denies security principals the ability to view the extended attributes of a file or folder.
Create Files/Write Data	• The Create Files permission allows or denies security principals the ability to create files within the folder. This permission applies to folders only. • The Write Data permission allows or denies security principals the ability to modify the file and overwrite existing content. This permission applies to files only.
Create Folders/Append Data	• The Create Folders permission allows or denies security principals to create subfolders within a folder. This permission applies to folders only. • The Append Data permission allows or denies security principals the ability to add data to the end of the file but not to modify, delete, or overwrite existing data in the file. This permission applies to files only.
Write Attributes	Allows or denies security principals the ability to modify the NTFS attributes of a file or folder.
Write Extended Attributes	Allows or denies security principals the ability to modify the extended attributes of a file or folder.
Delete Subfolders and Files	Allows or denies security principals the ability to delete subfolders and files, even if the Delete permission has not been granted on the subfolder or file.
Delete	Allows or denies security principals the ability to delete the file or folder.
Read Permissions	Allows or denies security principals the ability to read the permissions for the file or folder.
Change Permissions	Allows or denies security principals the ability to modify the permissions for the file or folder.
Take Ownership	Allows or denies security principals the ability to take ownership of the file or folder.
Synchronize	Allows or denies different threads of multithreaded, multiprocessor programs to wait on the handle for the file or folder and synchronize with another thread that might signal it.

11. Click **OK** to close the *Permission Entry for Test Folder* dialog box.

12. Click **OK** to close the second *Advanced Security Settings for Test Folder* dialog box.

13. Click **OK** to close the first *Advanced Security Settings for Test Folder* dialog box.

14. Click **OK** to close the *Test Folder Properties* sheet.

USING ICACLS.EXE

In addition to configuring NTFS permissions graphically, you can also use the Icacls.exe command line utility. Using Icacls.exe, you can grant or revoke basic or advanced permissions by allowing or denying them to specific security principals. The syntax for granting permissions is as follows:

```
icacls.exe filespec /grant[:r] security_id:(permissions)
[/T][/C][/L][/Q]
```

- *filespec* – Specifies the file or folder whose ACL you want to modify.
- **:r** – Causes the assigned permissions to replace any previously assigned ones. Without the :r switch, the program adds the permissions to the existing ones.
- *security_id* – Specifies the name or security ID of the user or group to whom you want to assign permissions.
- *permissions* – Specifies the permissions you want to assign to the security principal, using the following abbreviations:
    - ° F (Full Control)
    - ° M (Modify)
    - ° RX (Read and Execute)
    - ° R (Read)
    - ° W (Write)
- **/T** – Executes the command on all of the files and subfolders contained in the filespec.
- **/C** – Proceeds with the operation despite the occurrence of errors.
- **/L** – Performs the operation on a symbolic link rather than the actual destination.
- **/Q** – Prevents the program from displaying success messages.

> **+ MORE INFORMATION**
> You can also use Icacls.exe to manage advanced permissions. For more information on using Icacls.exe, see Microsoft's TechNet website.

In addition to granting permissions, you can also use the /*deny* parameter to assign Deny permissions and the /remove parameter to erase permissions from an ACL.

UNDERSTANDING RESOURCE OWNERSHIP

As you study the NTFS permission system, it might occur to you that it seems possible to lock out a file or folder—that is, assign a combination of permissions that permits access to no one at all, leaving the file or folder inaccessible. In fact, this is true.

A user with administrative privileges can revoke his or her own permissions, as well as everyone else's, preventing them from accessing a resource. However, the NTFS permissions system includes a "back door" that prevents these orphaned files and folders from remaining permanently inaccessible.

Every file and folder on an NTFS drive has an owner, and the owner always has the ability to modify the permissions for the file or folder, even if the owner has no permissions him- or herself. By default, the owner of a file or folder is the user account that created it. However, any account possessing the Take Ownership advanced permission (or the Full Control basic permission) can take ownership of the file or folder.

The other purpose for file and folder ownership is to calculate disk quotas. When you set quotas specifying the maximum amount of disk space particular users can consume, Windows calculates a user's current disk consumption by adding up the sizes of all the files and folders that the user owns.

■ Using the Encrypting File System

THE BOTTOM LINE

The Encrypting File System (EFS) protects users' data by encrypting and decrypting it on the fly as the user works.

The *Encrypting File System (EFS)* is a feature of NTFS that encodes the files on a computer so that even if an intruder can obtain a file, he or she will be unable to read it. The entire system is keyed to a specific user account, using the public and private keys that are the basis of the Windows public key infrastructure (PKI). The user who creates a file is the only person who can read it.

As the user works, EFS encrypts the files he or she creates using a key generated from the user's public key. Data encrypted with this key can be decrypted only by the user's personal encryption certificate, which is generated using his or her private key.

TAKE NOTE*

Only Windows 8.1 Pro and Windows 8.1 Enterprise support EFS.

When the user logs on to the computer, the system gains access to the keys that are necessary to encrypt and decrypt the EFS-protected data. To that user, the encryption process is completely invisible, and usually does not have a major impact on system performance. The user creates, accesses, and saves files in the normal manner, unaware that the cryptographic processes are taking place.

If another user logs on to the computer, he or she has no access to the other user's private key, and therefore cannot decrypt the encrypted files. An attacker can conceivably sit down at the computer and try to copy the files off to a flash drive, but he or she will receive an "Access Denied" error message, just as if he or she lacked the appropriate NTFS permissions for the files.

There are two main restrictions when implementing EFS:

- EFS is a feature of the NTFS file system, so you cannot use EFS on FAT drives.
- You cannot use EFS to encrypt files that have already been compressed using NTFS compression.

CERTIFICATION READY
Encrypt files and folders by using Encrypting File System (EFS)
Objective 4.2

Encrypting a Folder with EFS

In Windows 8.1, you can use File Explorer to encrypt or disable EFS on any individual files or folders, as long as they are on an NTFS drive.

To encrypt a file or folder, use the following procedure.

 ENCRYPT A FOLDER

GET READY. Log on to Windows 8.1, and then to encrypt a folder, perform the following steps:

1. Open **File Explorer**. The File Explorer window appears.
2. Right-click a file or folder and then, from the context menu, select Properties. The **Properties** sheet for the file or folder appears.
3. On the General tab, click **Advanced**. The *Advanced Attributes* dialog box appears, as shown in Figure 14-9.

Figure 14-9

The *Advanced Attributes* dialog box

4. Select the **Encrypt contents to secure data** checkbox, and then click **OK**.

5. Click **OK** to close the Properties sheet. If you selected a folder that contains files or subfolders, a *Confirm Attribute Changes* dialog box appears, asking you to choose whether to apply changes to the folder only, or to the folder and all of its subfolders and files.

 TAKE NOTE* If you elect to apply changes to the selected folder only, EFS does not encrypt any of the files that are currently in the folder. However, any files that you create, copy, or move to the folder after you enable EFS will be encrypted.

6. Select a confirmation option and click **OK**. Depending on how many files and folders there are to be encrypted, the process could take several minutes.

Determining Whether a File or Folder is Encrypted

Administrators commonly receive calls from users who are unable to access their files because they have been encrypted using EFS and the user is unaware of this fact. To resolve the problem, you must first determine whether their files are encrypted or not, and whether the user has the proper NTFS permissions.

File Explorer displays the names of encrypted files in green, by default, but this setting is easily changed in the Folder Options dialog box. To verify that a folder or file is encrypted, use the following procedure:

VIEW THE ENCRYPTION ATTRIBUTE

GET READY. To view the encryption attribute, log on to Windows 8.1, and then perform the following steps:

1. Open File Explorer. The **File Explorer** window appears.

2. Right-click a file or folder and then, from the context menu, select **Properties**. The Properties sheet for the file or folder appears.

   3. On the General tab, click **Advanced**. The *Advanced Attributes* dialog box appears. If the Encrypt contents to secure data checkbox is selected, the file or folder is encrypted.

   4. Click **OK** to close the *Advanced Attributes* dialog box.

   5. Click **OK** to close the *Properties* sheet.

Configuring Disk Quotas

THE BOTTOM LINE

Managing disk space is a constant concern for server administrators, and one way to prevent users from monopolizing large amount of storage is to implement quotas. Windows 8.1 supports storage quotas through the NTFS file system. Windows Server also supports a more elaborate quota system as part of File Server Resource Manager. This section discusses only the NTFS implementation.

NTFS quotas enable administrators to set a storage limit for users of a particular volume. Depending on how you configure the quota, users exceeding the limit can be denied disk space, or just receive a warning. The space consumed by individuals users is measured by the size of the files they own or create.

CERTIFICATION READY
Configure disk quotas
Objective 4.2

NTFS quotas are relatively limited in that you can set only a single limit for all of the users of a volume. The feature is also limited in the actions it can take in response to a user exceeding the limit. The quotas in File Server Resource Manager, by contrast, are much more flexible in the nature of the limits you can set and the responses of the program, which can send email notifications, execute commands, and generate reports, as well as log events.

To configure NTFS disk quotas for a volume, use the following procedure.

 CONFIGURE DISK QUOTAS

GET READY. To configure disk quotas, log on to Windows 8.1 using an account with administrative privileges, and then perform the following steps:

   1. Click the **File Explorer** icon in the taskbar. The File Explorer window appears.

   2. In the Folders list, expand the **This PC** container, right-click a volume and, from the context menu, select **Properties**. The *Properties* sheet for the volume appears.

   3. Click the **Quota** tab to display the interface shown in Figure 14-10.

Figure 14-10

The Quota tab of a volume's *Properties* sheet

4. Select the **Enable quota management** checkbox to activate the rest of the controls.

5. If you want to prevent users from consuming more than their quota of disk space, select the **Deny disk space to users exceeding quota limit** checkbox.

6. Select the **Limit disk space to** radio button and specify amounts for the quota limit and the warning level.

7. Select the **Log event** checkboxes to control whether users exceeding the specified limits should trigger log entries.

8. Click **OK** to create the quota and close the *Properties* sheet.

9. **Close** Windows Explorer.

■ Configuring File Access Auditing

THE BOTTOM LINE

Local Policies enable administrators to set user privileges on the local computer that govern what users can do on the computer and determine if the system should track them in an event log. Tracking events, a process referred to as *auditing*, is an important part of monitoring and managing activities on a computer running Windows 8.1.

The Audit Policy section of a Group Policy Object (GPO) enables administrators to log successful and failed security events, such as logons and logoffs, account access, and file or object access. You can use auditing to track both user activities and system activities. Planning to audit requires that you determine the computers to be audited and the types of events you wish to track. Object access auditing enables you to select specific shares, files, and folders for monitoring, as well as any other type of object in the operating system.

When you consider what events to audit, you must decide whether you wish to audit successes or failures, or both. Tracking successful events enables you to determine how often

CERTIFICATION READY
Configure file access auditing
Objective 4.2

users access network resources. This information can be valuable when planning your resource usage and budgeting for new resources. Tracking failed events can help you determine when security breaches occur or are attempted. The policy settings available for auditing are shown in Figure 14-11.

Figure 14-11

Audit Policies in the Windows 8.1 Local Computer Policy

When an audited event occurs, Windows 8.1 writes an event to the security log on the computer where the event took place. You can then review the audited events in the Event Viewer console.

You must decide which computers, resources, and events you want to audit. It is important to balance the need for auditing against the potential information overload that would be created if you audited every possible type of event. The following guidelines can help you to plan your audit policy:

- **Audit only pertinent items**. Determine the events you want to audit and consider whether it is more important to track successes or failures of these events. You should only plan to audit events that will help you gather network information. When auditing object access, be specific about the type of access you want to track. For example, if you want to audit read access to a file or folder, make sure you audit the read events, not Full Control. Auditing of Full Control would trigger writes to the log for every action on the file or folder. Auditing uses system resources to process and store events. Therefore, auditing unnecessary events will create overhead on your server and make it more difficult to monitor the logs.

- **Archive security logs to provide a documented history**. Keeping a history of event occurrences can provide you with supporting documentation. You can use this documentation to support the need for additional resources based on the usage of a particular resource. In addition, it provides a history of events that might indicate past security breach attempts. If intruders have administrative privileges, they can clear the log, leaving you without a history of events that document the breach.

- **Configure the size of your security logs carefully**. You need to plan the size of your security logs based on the number of events that you anticipate logging. Event Log Policy settings can be configured under the Computer Configuration\Windows Settings\ Security Settings\Event Log node of a GPO.

You can view the security logs using the Event Viewer console and configure it to monitor any number of event categories, including the following:

- **System events** – Events that trigger a log entry in this category include system startups and shutdowns; system time changes; system event resources exhaustion, such as when an event log is filled and can no longer append entries; security log cleaning; or any event that affects system security or the security log.
- **Policy change events** – Policy change audit log entries are triggered by events such as user rights assignment changes, establishment or removal of trust relationships, IPsec policy agent changes, and grants or removals of system access privileges.
- **Account management events** – This setting triggers an event that is written based on changes to account properties and group properties. Log entries written due to this policy setting reflect events related to user or group account creation, deletion, renaming, enabling, or disabling.
- **Logon events** – This setting logs events related to successful user logons on a computer. The events are logged to the Security Log on the computer that processes the request.

Implementation of your plan requires awareness of several factors that can affect the success of your audit policy. You must be aware of the administrative requirements to create and administer a policy plan. Two main requirements are necessary to set up and administer an Audit Policy. First, you must have the Manage Auditing and Security Log user right for the computer on which you want to configure a policy or review a log. This right is granted by default to the Administrators group. However, if you wish to delegate this task to someone else, such as a container administrator, that person must possess the specific right. Second, any files or folders to be audited must be located on NTFS volumes.

Implementation of your plan requires that you specify the categories to be audited and, if necessary, configure files or other objects for auditing. To configure an audit policy, use the following procedure.

 CONFIGURE AN AUDIT POLICY

GET READY. To configure an audit policy, log on to Windows 8.1, using an account with Administrator privileges, and then perform the following steps:

1. Open a Command Prompt window with Administrative Privileges and type **gpedit. msc**. A Local Group Policy Editor console appears.

2. Browse to the Computer Configuration\\Windows Settings\Security Settings\Local Policies node and select **Audit Policy**. The audit policy settings appear in the right pane.

3. Double-click the **Audit object access** setting. The *Properties* sheet for the policy appears, as shown in Figure 14-12.

Figure 14-12

The *Properties* sheet for a policy setting

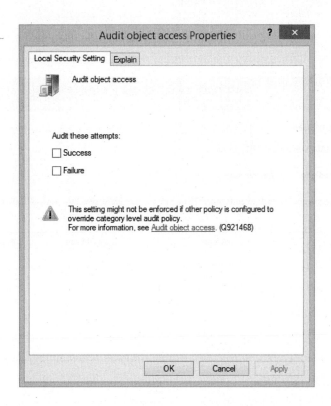

4. Select the appropriate checkbox(es) to audit Success, Failure, or both.

5. Click **OK** to close the setting's Properties sheet.

6. **Close** the *Local Group Policy Editor* console.

You have now configured an audit policy that will enable you to track object accesses. However, configuring files or other objects for auditing is necessary when you have configured the Audit object access policy. This requires additional setup steps, which are described in the following procedure.

 CONFIGURE FILES AND FOLDERS FOR AUDITING

GET READY. Log on to a Windows 8.1 computer, on which you have configured the Audit object access policy, using an account with Administrator privileges. To configure files and folders for auditing, perform the following steps:

1. Open File Explorer, right-click the file or folder you want to audit and, from the context menu, select **Properties.**

   The *Properties* sheet for the file or folder appears.

2. Click the **Security** tab. Then click **Advanced.**

   The *Advanced Security Settings* dialog box appears.

3. Click the **Auditing** tab, as shown in Figure 14-13.

Figure 14-13

The Auditing tab in a folder's
Properties sheet

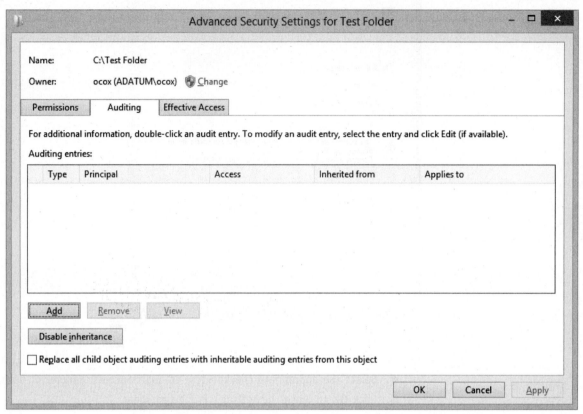

4. Click **Add**.

   The *Auditing Entry* page appears.

5. Click **Select a Principal**.

   The *Select User, Computer, Service Account, or Group* dialog box appears.

6. Select the users or groups to be audited and then click **OK**.

   The users or groups appear in the *Auditing Entry* dialog box for the object.

7. From the *Type* drop-down list, specify whether you want to audit failures, successes, or both.

8. From the *Applies to* drop-down list, specify which descendent objects should be audited.

9. Select the basic permissions you want to audit for this object and click **OK**. The new Auditing entry appears in the *Advanced Security Settings* dialog box.

10. Create additional auditing entries, if desired, and then click **OK**.

11. Click **OK** to close the object's *Advanced Security Settings* dialog box.

12. Click **OK** to close the object's Properties sheet.

13. Close the *File Explorer* window.

You have now configured auditing for files and folders within the Windows 8.1 operating system. Events corresponding to the settings you have selected will now be recorded in the security log.

SKILL SUMMARY

IN THIS LESSON, YOU LEARNED:

- Windows 8.1 has several sets of permissions, which operate independently of each other, including NTFS permissions, share permissions, registry permissions, and Active Directory permissions.

- NTFS permissions enable you to control access to files and folders by specifying just what tasks individual users can perform on them.

- The Encrypting File System (EFS) is a feature of NTFS that encodes the files on a computer so that even if an intruder can obtain a file, he or she will be unable to read it.

- NTFS quotas enable administrators to set a storage limit for users of a particular volume. Depending on how you configure the quota, users exceeding the limit can be denied disk space, or just receive a warning.

Knowledge Assessment

Multiple Choice

Select one or more correct answers for each of the following questions.

1. Which of the following NTFS features is incompatible with EFS encryption?
   a. Compression
   b. IPsec
   c. Permissions
   d. Parental controls

2. Which of the following is the best description of a security principal?
   a. The person granting permissions to network users
   b. The network resource receiving permissions
   c. A collection of individual special permissions
   d. An object that assigns permissions

3. Which of the following statements about effective access is not true?
   a. Inherited permissions take precedence over explicit permissions.
   b. Deny permissions always override Allow permissions.
   c. When a security principal receives Allow permissions from multiple groups, the permissions are combined to form the effective access permissions.
   d. Effective access includes both permissions inherited from parents and permissions derived from group memberships.

4. Which of the following statements is not true in reference to resource ownership?
   a. One of the purposes for file and folder ownership is to calculate disk quotas.
   b. Every file and folder on an NTFS driver has an owner.
   c. It is possible for any user possessing the Take Ownership special permission to assume the ownership of a file or folder.
   d. It is possible to lock out a file or folder by assigning a combination of permissions that permits access to no one at all, including the owner of the file or folder.

5. Which of the following statements about permissions are true?
   a. ACLs are composed of ACEs.
   b. Basic permissions are composed of advanced permissions.
   c. All permissions are stored as part of the protected resource.
   d. All of the above.

6. In the NTFS permission system, combinations of advanced permissions are also known as _____ permissions.
    a. special
    b. basic
    c. share
    d. standard

7. Which of the following computers would restrict you from implementing EFS? Select all that apply.
    a. A computer with a hard drive formatted with FAT32 only.
    b. A computer with an NTFS volume that has been compressed.
    c. A computer with an NTFS volume.
    d. A computer with a hard drive formatted with FAT only.

8. When an audited event occurs, Windows 8.1 writes the event to which log?
    a. Security Log
    b. Application Log
    c. System Log
    d. Setup Log

9. After setting quota limits on an NTFS volume, you want to be able to monitor how much disk space users are consuming while still allowing them to go over the default quota limit you set for them. Which option must *not* be selected for this to work?
    a. Deny disk space to users exceeding quota limit
    b. Enable quota management
    c. Limit disk space to
    d. Log event when a user exceeds their quota limit

Best Answer

Choose the letter that corresponds to the best answer. More than one answer choice may achieve the goal. Select the BEST answer.

1. Which of the following is key reason for assigning permissions when configuring file and share access?
    a. Creates redundancy for file storage, providing a fault-tolerant file archive.
    b. Enables configuring offline files, improving performance.
    c. Improves data security, granting file and share access only to the users who need it.
    d. Assigns ownership to specific users, instilling responsibility and personal accountability.

2. Alice needs NTFS permission system support. She doesn't presently need encryption or compression, but might at a later date. Which file system is the best choice for Alice?
    a. The traditional NTFS file system
    b. The new ReFS file system introduced in Windows Server 2012
    c. The FAT file system
    d. The NFS file system

3. Which of the following sets of permissions is responsible for controlling access to files and folders stored on a local disk volume?
    a. Share permissions
    b. NTFS permissions
    c. Registry permissions
    d. Active Directory permissions

4. Knowing how permissions can be cumulative or override each other is an important factor in understanding what?
   a. Permission inheritance
   b. Explicitly assigned permissions
   c. Permission precedence
   d. Effective access

5. A user wants to be able to provide access to a folder named MyDocs. The MyDocs folder should be accessible over the network but still prevent unauthorized users from accessing the folder and its contents while logged on to the computer locally. The files are not sensitive but only the authorized users should be able to make changes. Which of the following combinations will best meet this need?
   a. Share permissions only
   b. NTFS permissions only
   c. Combined Share and NTFS permissions
   d. Share and NTFS permissions combined with EFS

6. A user has Allow Read and Allow List Folder Contents permissions for a subfolder named Forecasts. The permissions are inherited from the Sales folder. The user also has Allow Write and Allow Modify permission to the Forecasts folder as part of their membership in the SalesTeam group. Which of the following best describes her effective permissions to the Forecasts folder?
   a. Allow Write
   b. Allow Write and Allow Modify
   c. Allow Write, Allow Modify, Allow Read, Allow List Folder Contents
   d. Allow Read and Allow Write

7. There are several sensitive files on your Windows 8.1 computer stored in a folder named Sales. Inside the Sales folder are several files that provide confidential forecast information. What is the best way to protect those files that you need to access over the network while still protecting them from someone sitting at your computer and attempting to copy the files to a flash drive.
   a. Encrypt the folder using EFS.
   b. Encrypt the folder using EFS and secure the files with NTFS permissions.
   c. Share the folder and secure the files with NTFS permissions.
   d. Share the folder, secure the files with NTFS and use EFS to encrypt the folder and its contents.

Matching and Identification

Complete the following exercise by matching the terms with their corresponding definitions.

_____ a) NTFS quotas
_____ b) Effective access
_____ c) Auditing
_____ d) Access control entry (ACE)
_____ e) Security principal
_____ f) Permissions
_____ g) Share permissions
_____ h) NTFS permissions
_____ i) Permission inheritance
_____ j) Security identifier
   1. Tracking events that take place on the local computer.
   2. The name of a user, group, or computer being granted permission.
   3. The combination of Allow permissions and Deny permissions that a security principal receives for a given system element.

4. Enables administrators to set a storage limit for users of a particular volume.
5. Control access to files and folders shared over a network.
6. Used to protect files, folders, shares, registry keys, and Active Directory objects.
7. Consists of the security principal and the specific permission assigned to that security principal.
8. The tendency of permissions to flow downwards through a file system or other hierarchy.
9. Control access to the files and folders stored on disk volumes formatted with the NTFS file system.
10. These are included in the security access token for each user's account and all the groups to which the user belongs.

Build a List

1. In order of first to last, specify the correct order of steps to encrypt a folder.
   _____ Right-click a file or folder and then, from the context menu, select **Properties**.
   _____ Select the **Encrypt contents to secure data** checkbox, and then click **OK**.
   _____ Open **File Explorer**.
   _____ Click **OK** to close the *Properties* sheet. If you selected a folder that contains files or subfolders, a *Confirm Attribute Changes* dialog box appears.
   _____ On the General tab, click **Advanced**.
   _____ Select a confirmation option and click **OK**.

2. In order of first to last, specify the correct order of steps to view the encryption attribute.
   _____ Click **OK** to close the *Properties* sheet.
   _____ On the General tab, click **Advanced**. The *Advanced Attributes* dialog box appears. If the Encrypt contents to secure data checkbox is selected, the file or folder is encrypted.
   _____ Right-click a file or folder and then, from the context menu, select **Properties**.
   _____ Click **OK** to close the *Advanced Attributes* dialog box.
   _____ Open **File Explorer**.

3. In order of first to last, specify the correct order of steps to configure a disk quota.
   _____ Click the File Explorer icon in the taskbar.
   _____ Select the **Limit disk space to** radio button and specify amounts for the quota limit and the warning level.
   _____ Click the Quota tab.
   _____ In the Folders list, expand the **Computer** container, right-click a volume and, from the context menu, select Properties.
   _____ If you want to prevent users from consuming more than their quota of disk space, select the **Deny disk space to users exceeding quota limit** checkbox.
   _____ Select the **Enable quota management** checkbox to activate the rest of the controls.
   _____ Select the Log event checkboxes to control whether users exceeding the specified limits should trigger log entries.
   _____ Click **OK** to create the quota and close the *Properties* sheet.

■ Business Case Scenarios

Scenario 14-1: Rescuing Orphaned Files

Heidi, a junior desktop technician, approaches her supervisor ashen-faced. A few minutes earlier, the president of the company called the help desk and asked Heidi to give his new assistant the permissions needed to access his personal budget spreadsheet. As she was attempting to assign the permissions, she accidentally deleted the BUDGET_USERS group from the spreadsheet's access control list. Heidi is now terrified because that group was the only entry in the file's ACL. Now no one can access the spreadsheet file, not even the president or the Administrator account. Is there any way to gain access to the file, and if so, how?

Scenario 14-2: Assigning Permissions

Tom works for the help desk for a corporate network and receives a call from a user named Leo, who is requesting access to the files for a new classified project called Trinity. The Trinity files are stored in a shared folder on a file server, which is locked in a secured underground data storage facility in New Mexico. After verifying that the user has the appropriate security clearance for the project, Tom creates a new group on the file server called TRINITY_USERS and adds Leo's user account to that group. Then, he adds the TRINITY_USER group to the access control list for the Trinity folder on the file server, and he assigns the group the following NTFS permissions:

- Allow Modify
- Allow Read & Execute
- Allow List Folder Contents
- Allow Read
- Allow Write

Some time later, Leo calls Tom back to tell him that while he is able to access the Trinity folder and read the files stored there, he has been unable to save changes back to the server. What is the most likely cause of the problem?

Configuring Authentication and Authorization

70-687 EXAM OBJECTIVE

Objective 4.3 – Configure authentication and authorization. This objective may include but is not limited to: configure user rights; manage credentials; manage certificates; configure biometrics; configure picture password; configure PIN; set up and configure Microsoft account; configure virtual smart cards; configure authentication in workgroups or domains; configure User Account Control (UAC) behavior.

LESSON HEADING	EXAM OBJECTIVE
Working with Users and Groups	
Understanding Local and Domain Users	Configure authentication in workgroups or domains
Understanding Local and Domain Groups	
Creating and Managing Local Users and Groups	
Using the User Accounts Control Panel	Set up and configure Microsoft Account
Using the Local Users and Groups Snap-in	
Working with Domain Users and Groups	
Authenticating and Authorizing Users	
Working with Passwords	Manage credentials
Using PIN and Picture Passwords	Configure PIN Configure picture password
Using Smart Cards	
Using Virtual Smart Cards	Configure virtual smart cards
Managing Certificates	Manage certificates
Using Biometrics	Configure biometrics
Configuring User Account Control	Configure User Account Control (UAC) behavior
Understanding Recommended UAC Practices	
Using Secure Desktop	
Configuring User Account Control	
Elevating Privileges	
Troubleshooting Authentication Issues	
Authorizing Users	Configure user rights

KEY TERMS

Active Directory

authentication

authorization

brute force

directory service

domain

domain controller

group

homegroup

multifactor authentication

pass-through
    authentication

Personal Identity Verification
    (PIV)

user rights

virtual smart card

Windows Biometric Framework

workgroup

Working with Users and Groups

THE BOTTOM LINE

The user account is the fundamental unit of identity in the Windows operating systems. In computer terminology, the term *user* has two meanings; it can refer to the human being that is operating the computer, or it can be an operating system element that represents a single human user.

From a programming perspective, a user account is a relatively simple construct, no more than a collection of properties that apply to the human being or other entity that the user account represents. These properties can include information about the user, such as names and contact information, and identifying characteristics, such as passwords.

+ MORE INFORMATION

Most user accounts represent humans, but Windows also employs user accounts to provide system processes and applications with access to secured resources. These accounts are no different from standard user accounts structurally; the only difference is that they are created and managed automatically by the operating system or an application.

As an operating system element, the user account and its properties are vital components in two of the most important Windows functions:

- *Authentication* – The process of verifying that the identity of the person operating the computer is the same as the user account the person is employing to gain access. Typically, to be authenticated, the human user must supply some piece of information associated with the user account, such as a password, demonstrate some personal characteristic, such as a fingerprint; or prove access to an identifying possession, such as a smart card.

- *Authorization* – The process of granting an authenticated user a specific degree of access to specific computer or data resource. In Windows, a user account is associated with permissions that grant the human user access to files and folders, printers, and other resources.

The first thing a human user does with a Windows system is authenticate him- or herself, a process typically referred to as logging on. The human user specifies the name of a user account and supplies a password or other identifying token. Once the authentication is successful, the person is known by that user name throughout the Windows session, and the operating system grants access to specific resources using that name.

As the authenticated user begins working with the operating system, the authorization process occurs whenever the user attempts to access certain resources or perform specific tasks. All of the Windows permission systems, including NTFS, share, registry, and *Active Directory* permissions, are user-based. The access control list (ACL) for each permission-protected resource contains a list of users and the degree of access each user is granted to the resource.

Another user-based Windows element, completely separate from the permission systems, is called *user rights*. User rights are specific operating system tasks, such as Shut Down the System or Allow Log On Through Remote Desktop Services, which can only be performed by certain users designated by a system administrator.

A *group* is another type of entity that Windows uses to represent a collection of users. System administrators can create groups for any reason and with any name, and then use them just as they would a user account. Any permissions or user rights that an administrator assigns to a group are automatically inherited by all members of the group.

➕ MORE INFORMATION

The concept of group inheritance is one of the fundamental principles of network administration. On all but the smallest networks, administrators typically assign permissions to groups, rather than individual users, and then control access by adjusting group memberships. For example, if a person performing a particular job needs access to a variety of different network resources, it might take an administrator some time to assign all of the rights and permissions that person needs to an individual user account. Later, if that job should be taken over by another person, the administrator has to go through the entire process again twice, once to remove the rights and permissions from the old user's account and once to grant the same rights and permissions to the new user. By creating a group to represent the job, the administrator only has to grant the rights and permissions to the group once. When someone new takes over the job, the administrator only has to remove the departed user from the group and add the new user.

Understanding Local and Domain Users

The concept of users and groups is complicated in Windows because there are two completely separate user account systems: local users and domain users. Which user account system a Windows computer uses depends on whether it is a member of a workgroup or an Active Directory Domain Services domain.

CERTIFICATION READY
Configure authentication in workgroups or domains
Objective 4.3

Windows 8.1 supports three types of networks: homegroups, workgroups, and domains, as described in the following sections.

INTRODUCING THE HOMEGROUP

New in Windows 7, a *homegroup* is a simplified networking paradigm that enables users connected to a home network to share the contents of their libraries without the need for creating user accounts and permissions. For more information on creating and using homegroups, see in Lesson 13, "Configuring Shared Resources."

INTRODUCING THE WORKGROUP

A *workgroup* is a collection of computers that are all peers. A peer network is one in which every computer can function as both a server, by sharing its resources with other computers; and a client, by accessing the shared resources on other computers.

On a workgroup network, each computer has its own set of users and groups that it uses to control access to its own resources. For example, if you want to use one computer to access resources on all four of the other computers on a five-node workgroup network, you must have a user account on each of those four computers. As you connect to each computer, you are authenticated and authorized by each one. If effect, you are logging on to each computer individually.

TAKE NOTE*

Although it is technically a separate authentication process every time a workgroup computer accesses another computer, this does not necessarily mean that users have to supply account names and passwords each time they connect to another computer. If a user has accounts with the same name and password on multiple workgroup computers, then the authentications occur automatically, with no user intervention. This is called *pass-through authentication*. If the passwords for the accounts are different, however, a manual authentication is necessary for each one.

INTRODUCING THE DOMAIN

A **domain** is a collection of computers that all utilize a central directory service for authentication and authorization. A **directory service** is a collection of logical objects that represent various types of network resources, such as computers, applications, users, and groups. Each object consists of attributes that contain information about the object.

> **TAKE NOTE ***
>
> Do not confuse an Active Directory Domain Services (AD DS) domain with a Domain Name System (DNS) domain. An AD DS domain is a collection of Windows computers and other related objects that are all joined to the Windows directory service. A DNS domain is a collection of Internet host names used by computers that can be running any operating system.

To create a domain, you must have at least one Windows server with the Active Directory Domain Services (AD DS) role installed. This server is called a **domain controller**. Each of the computers then joins the domain, and is represented by a computer object. In the same way, administrators create user objects that represent human users. In Windows networking, the main difference between a domain and a workgroup is that users log on to the domain once, rather than each computer individually. When users attempt to access network resources, the individual computers hosting the resources send authorization requests to the domain controller, rather than handling the authorizations themselves.

DIFFERENTIATING LOCAL AND DOMAIN USERS

The primary advantage of a domain over a workgroup is that administrators only have to create one user account for each person, while workgroups can require many different user accounts for one person. If, on a workgroup network, a user's password is lost or compromised, someone must change that password on every computer where that user has an account. On a domain, there is only one user account for each person, so only one password change is needed.

Windows 8.1 computers always have a need for local user accounts, for administrative access to the system, if no other reason. For networking purposes, though, it is typical to use local user accounts or domain user accounts, but not both. Workgroup networks are typically small and informal, with users administering their own computers. Domain networks are usually larger, and have dedicated network administrators responsible for managing user accounts and controlling access to network resources.

Local and domain users are different in several important ways. You use different tools to create and manage the two types of users, and the user accounts themselves are different in composition. As mentioned earlier, a user account consists of attributes, which contain information about the user. Domain users have many more attributes than local users.

As a demonstration of this, Figures 15-1 and 15-2 contain the *Properties* sheets of a Windows 8.1 local user account and an AD DS domain user account. Notice that the Properties sheet for the local user has only 3 tabs, while the domain user's sheet has 13. This means that the domain user account can store a great deal more information about the user, and can access many more different kinds of network resources.

Figure 15-1

The *Properties* sheet for a local user

Figure 15-2

The *Properties* sheet for a domain user

Table 15-1 lists some of the other differences between local and domain users.

Table 15-1

Frequently Asked Questions
About Local and Domain Users

QUESTION	LOCAL USERS	DOMAIN USERS
What tools do you use to manage the user accounts?	The User Accounts control panel applet or the Local Users and Groups snap-in for Microsoft Management Console (MMC)	The Active Directory Users and Computers MMC snap-in
Where are the user accounts stored?	In the Security Accounts Manager (SAM) on the local computer	On the Active Directory Domain Services domain controllers
What can you access with the user account?	Local computer resources only	All domain and network resources
What restrictions are there on the user name?	Each user name must be unique on the computer	Each user name must be unique in the directory

As an administrator, the type of user accounts you work with depends/. on the nature of your networks you manage and their security requirements. Small businesses are more likely to use workgroup networking, in which case you will be working with local user accounts. Depending on the capabilities of the users, you might have to set up all of the user accounts for all of the computers on the network, or you might be able to show the users how to create accounts on their own computers. Local users are relatively simple to create and manage, and a workgroup network often is a casual affair.

If your client is a medium or large business, it is more likely to be running an AD DS domain, in which case you will be working primarily with domain user accounts. The question of whether to host a Windows domain is a major decision that an organization usually makes when they are designing and installing the network. Hosting a Windows domain is a costly undertaking, both in terms of the additional hardware and software required, and in terms of the time and effort needed for planning and deployment.

INTRODUCING BUILT-IN LOCAL USERS

As mentioned earlier, Windows 8.1 (like the other Windows workstation operating systems) always has a need for local user accounts. When you perform a standard interactive installation of Windows 8.1, you are required to create one user account. In addition, the Setup program automatically creates a number of other user accounts.

The following user accounts are built-in on Windows 8.1:

- **Administrator** – During a typical Windows 8.1 installation, the Setup program creates an Administrator account and makes it a member of the Administrators group, giving it complete access to all areas of the operating system. However, the Setup program leaves the account in a disabled state and does not assign it a password.

- **New User Account** – During the operating system installation process, the installer must specify the name for a new user account, which the Setup program creates and adds to the Administrators group. This grants the new account full access to the operating system. The installer specifies the password for this account. Windows 8.1 uses this account for its initial logons.

- **Guest** – This account is designed for users that require only temporary access to the computer, and who do not need high levels of access. The Guest account is disabled, by default, and is a member only of the Guests group, which provides it with only the most rudimentary access to the system.

In addition to these accounts, Windows 8.1 also creates a number of system and service accounts, none of which you have to manipulate directly.

 TAKE NOTE *

After the Windows 8.1 installation is completed, you might want to consider enabling the Administrator account and assigning it a strong password. This will provide you with administrative access to the system, even if your main user account becomes compromised.

Understanding Local and Domain Groups

Just as there are local and domain users, there are local and domain groups as well. Whether local or domain, a group is essentially just a collection of users and, in some cases, other groups. As mentioned earlier, by assigning rights and permissions to a group, you assign those rights and permissions to all of its members.

USING LOCAL GROUPS

When compared to domain groups, local groups are quite simple, and are defined more by what they cannot do than what they can do. Local groups are subject to the following restrictions:

- You can only use local groups on the computer where you create them.
- Only local users from the same computer can be members of local groups.
- When the computer is a member of an AD DS domain, local groups can have domain users and domain global groups as members.
- Local groups cannot have other local groups as members. However, they can have domain groups as members.
- You can only assign permissions to local groups when you are controlling access to resources on the local computer.
- You cannot create local groups on a Windows server computer that is functioning as a domain controller.

INTRODUCING BUILT-IN LOCAL GROUPS

Windows 8.1 includes a number of built-in local groups that are already equipped with the permissions and rights needed to perform certain tasks. You can enable users to perform these tasks simply by adding them to the appropriate group. Table 15-2 lists the Windows 8.1 built-in local groups and the capabilities they provide to their members.

TAKE NOTE *

Some of the built-in local groups in Windows 8.1, such as Administrators, Backup Operators, and Remote Desktop Users, are created for the convenience of system administrators so that they can easily grant certain privileges to users. Other groups, such as IIS_USRS and Replicator, are designed to support automated functions that create their own system user accounts. There is no need to manually add users to these groups.

Table 15-2

Windows 8.1 Built-in Local Groups and Their Capabilities

BUILT-IN LOCAL GROUP	GROUP FUNCTION
Access Control Assistance Operators	Members can remotely query authorization permissions for resources on this computer.
Administrators	Members have full administrative access to the entire operating system. By default, the Administrator user and the user account created during the operating system installation are both members of this group.
Backup Operators	Members have user rights enabling them to override permissions for the sole purpose of backing up and restoring files, folders, and other operating system elements.
Cryptographic Operators	Members are capable of performing cryptographic operations.
Distributed COM Users	Members are capable of launching, activating, and using distributed COM objects.
Event Log Readers	Members can read the computer's event logs.
Guests	Members have no default user rights. By default, the Guest user account is a member of this group.
Hyper-V Administrators	Members have full control of all Hyper-V features.
IIS_IUSRS	Group used to provide privileges to dedicated Internet Information Services users.
Network Configuration Operators	Members have privileges that enable them to modify the computer's network configuration settings.
Performance Log Users	Members have privileges that enable them to schedule the logging of performance counters, enable trace providers, and collect event traces on this computer, both locally and from remote locations.
Performance Monitor Users	Members have privileges that enable them to monitor performance counter data on the computer, both locally and from remote locations.
Power Users	Members possess no additional capabilities in Windows 8.1, In previous Windows versions, the Power Users group provided privileges for a limited number of administrative functions, but in Windows 8.1, the group is included solely for reasons of backwards compatibility.
Remote Desktop Users	Members can log on to the computer from remote locations, using Terminal Services or Remote Desktop.
Remote Management Users	Members can access Windows Management Instrumentation (WMI) resources using management protocols.
Replicator	When the computer is joined to a domain, this group provides the access needed for file replication functions. The only member should be a user account dedicated solely to the replication process.
Users	Members can perform most common tasks, such as running applications, using local and network printers, and locking the server. However, members are prevented from making many system-wide configuration changes, whether they do so accidentally or deliberately.
WinRM RemoteWMIUsers_	Members can access Windows Management Instrumentation (WMI) resources using management protocols.

The built-in local groups in Windows 8.1, although created by the operating system, are groups like any other. You can modify their properties, change their names, and assign new rights and permissions to them. However, it's a better idea to create your own groups and assign whatever additional rights and permissions you need to them. You can make a single user a member of multiple groups, and the permissions from all of the groups will be combined.

INTRODUCING SPECIAL IDENTITIES

Another type of element in Windows 8.1 (and all other Windows operating systems) is a special identity, which functions much like a group. A *special identity* is essentially a placeholder for a collection of users with a similar characteristic. For example, the Authenticated Users special identity represents all of the users that are logged on to the computer at a given instant. You can assign rights and permissions to a special identity just as you would to a group.

When the access control list (ACL) for a system resource contains a special identity in one of its access control entries (ACEs), the system substitutes the users that conform to the special identity at the moment the ACL is processed.

TAKE NOTE*

It's important to understand that the set of computers represented by a special identity can change from minute to minute. The Authenticated Users special identity changes every time a user logs on or off, for example. When you assign rights and permissions to a special identity, the users who receive those rights and permissions are not those who conform to the special identity at the time you make the assignment, but rather those who conform to the special identity at the time the special identity is read from the ACL.

Table 15-3 lists the special identities included in Windows 8.

Table 15-3

Windows 8.1 Special Identities and Their Constituents

SPECIAL IDENTITY	FUNCTION
All Application Packages	Includes all Windows Store apps
Anonymous Logon	Includes all users who have connected to the computer without authenticating
Authenticated Users	Includes all users with a valid local user account whose identities have been authenticated. The Guest user is not included in the Authenticated Users special identity, even if it has a password.
Batch	Includes all users who are currently logged on through a batch facility such as a task scheduler job
Console Logon	Includes all users that are logged on to the computer's physical console
Creator Group	Includes the primary group of the user who created or most recently took ownership of the resource
Creator Owner	Includes only the user who created or most recently took ownership of a resource
Dialup	Includes all users who are currently logged on through a dial-up connection
Everyone	Includes all members of the Authenticated Users special identity plus the Guest user account

(continued)

Table 15-3

(continued)

SPECIAL IDENTITY	FUNCTION
Interactive	Includes all users who are currently logged on locally or through a Remote Desktop connection
IUSR	Account used to provide anonymous access to webpages through Internet Information Services (IIS)
Local Service	Provides all services configured to run as a local service with the same privileges as the Users group
Network	Includes all users who are currently logged on through a network connection
Network Service	Provides all services configured to run as a network service with the same privileges as the Users group
Owner Rights	Represents the current owner of an object
Remote Interactive Logon	Includes all users who are currently logged on through a Remote Desktop connection
Service	Includes all security principals who have logged on as a service
System	Provides the operating system with all of the privileges it needs to function
Terminal Server User	Includes all users who are currently logged on to a Terminal Services server that is in Terminal Services version 4.0 application compatibility mode
This Organization Certificate	Account used by the default IIS user

Creating and Managing Local Users and Groups

THE BOTTOM LINE

Windows 8.1 provides two separate interfaces for creating and managing local user accounts: the User Accounts control panel applet and the Local Users and Groups snap-in for the Microsoft Management Console (MMC). Both of these interfaces provide access to the same Security Account Manager (SAM) where the user and group information is stored, so any changes you make using one interface will appear in the other.

Microsoft designed the User accounts control panel applet and the Local Users and Groups snap-in for computer users with different levels of expertise, and they provide different degrees of access to the Security Account Manager, as follows:

- **User Accounts** – Microsoft designed the User accounts control panel applet for relatively inexperienced end users; it provides a simplified interface with extremely limited access to user accounts. With this interface, it is possible to create local user accounts and modify their basic attributes, but you cannot create groups or manage group memberships (except for the Administrators group).
- **Local Users and Groups** – Microsoft includes this MMC snap-in as part of the Computer Management console; it provides full access to local users and groups, as well as all of their attributes. Designed more for the technical specialist or system administrator, this interface is not difficult to use, but it does provide access to controls that beginning users generally do not need.

TAKE NOTE* Both the User accounts control panel applet and the Local Users and Groups snap-in are capable of working with local users and local groups only. You cannot create and manage domain users and groups using these tools. To work with domain users and groups, you must use a domain tool, such as Active Directory Users and Computers, which is supplied with the server operating system that is hosting the Active Directory Domain Services domain.

Using the User Accounts Control Panel

As described earlier, the first local user account on a Windows 8.1 computer is the one created during the operating system installation process. The Setup program prompts the installer for an account name, and creates a new user account with administrative privileges. The program also creates the Administrator and Guest accounts, both of which are disabled by default.

CERTIFICATION READY
Set up and configure
Microsoft Account
Objective 4.3

When the Windows 8.1 installation process is completed, the system restarts. Because only one user account is available, the computer automatically logs on using that account. This account has administrative privileges, so at this point you can create additional user accounts or modify the existing ones.

CREATING A NEW USER ACCOUNT

In Windows 8.1, you can create a local user account based on an existing Microsoft account. A Microsoft account provides access to an Internet-based authentication service with which users can access all of their personal data stored in the Microsoft cloud. This includes OneDrive (formerly known as SkyDrive), a personal storage space in the cloud where users can store their data files and their Windows operating system configuration settings.

When you create a local user account using a Microsoft account, you specify your email address and your password. Windows 8.1 uses the information from your Microsoft account to create a local user, and configures Windows 8.1 to synchronize its configuration elements with the service on the Internet. This way, if you log on to another Windows 8.1 computer using that same account, you can download your desktop configuration, favorites, and other settings from the cloud and reproduce your home configuration on the other machine.

The User accounts control panel applet provides access to existing local accounts, but when creating new accounts, the system transfers you to the *Accounts* page of the *PC Settings* app. Adding a user through this interface takes you through the same procedure as the new user creation process in the Windows 8.1 installation.

To create a new user account with the User accounts control panel applet, use the following procedure:

CREATE A NEW USER ACCOUNT

TAKE NOTE*
This procedure is valid only on Windows 8.1 computers that are part of a workgroup. When you join a computer to an AD DS domain, you can only create new local user accounts with the Local Users and Groups snap-in.

GET READY. Log on to Windows 8.1 using an account with Administrator privileges and then perform the following steps:

1. On the Start screen, click the **Desktop tile**.

   The Windows Desktop appears.

2. Right-click the **Start** button and, from the context menu, select **Control Panel**.

   The *Control Panel* window appears.

3. Click **User Accounts and Family Safety**.

   The *User Accounts and Family Safety* window appears.

4. Click **User Accounts**.

Figure 15-3

The *User Accounts* control panel applet

The *User Accounts* control panel applet appears, as shown in Figure 15-3.

5. Click **Manage another account**.

The *Choose the user you would like to change* page appears.

6. Click **Add a new user in PC settings**.

The *PC Settings* screen appears, displaying the *Accounts* page, as shown in Figure 15-4.

Figure 15-4

The *Accounts* page in the *PC Settings* screen

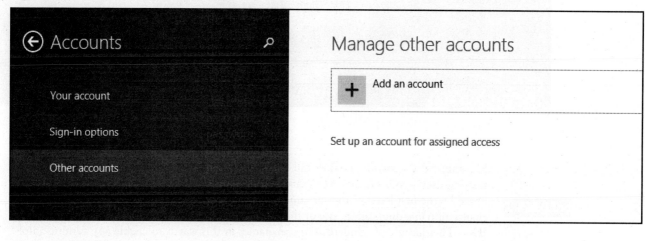

7. Click **Add an account.**

   The *How will this person sign in?* screen appears.

8. Click **Sign in without a Microsoft account.**

   An *Add a user* screen appears, describing the differences between a Microsoft account and a local account.

9. Click **Local account.**

   An *Add a user* form appears, as shown in Figure 15-5.

Figure 15-5

The *Add a user* form

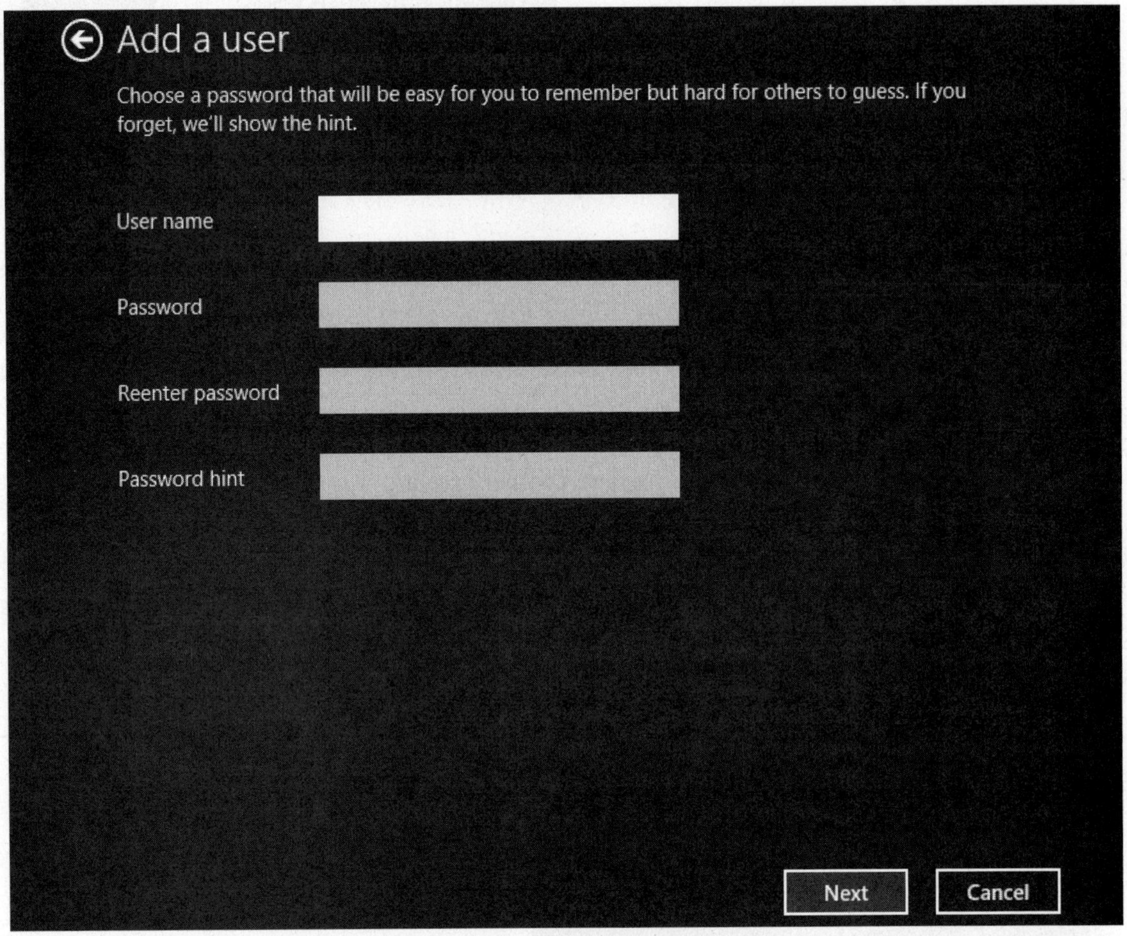

TAKE NOTE*

Recommended network practices call for administrators to use a standardized system for creating user account names. For example, smaller networks often use the first name followed by the first letter of the surname, such as JohnD. For larger networks with a greater chance of name duplication, use of the first initial plus the surname is common, such as JDoe. The purpose of standardizing user names in this way is to enable any administrator to determine the account name for any user.

10. In the *User name* text box, type the new user's account name.

11. In the *Password* and *Reenter password* text boxes, type the password for the new account.

12. In the *Password hint* text box, type a phrase related to the password and click Next.

    A page appears displaying the new account, with a checkbox enabling you to turn on Family Safety.

13. Click **Finish**.

The new account appears on the *Users* page of the *PC Settings* screen.

This procedure provides only the most rudimentary access to the user account attributes. Apart from supplying a name for the account, all you can do is specify a password. Local accounts created in this way are Standard users, not Administrators. To modify the account type, you must return to the User accounts control panel applet.

What the User accounts control panel applet refers to as an account type is actually a group membership. Selecting the Standard user option adds the user account to the local Users group, while selecting the Administrator option adds the account to the Administrators group.

MANAGING A USER ACCOUNT

To see the modifications you can make to an existing local user account with the User accounts control panel applet, use the following procedure:

 MANAGE USER ACCOUNTS

GET READY. Log on to Windows 8.1 using an account with Administrator privileges and then perform the following steps:

1. On the Start screen, click the **Desktop tile**.

   The Windows Desktop appears.

2. Right-click the **Start** button and, from the context menu, select **Control Panel**.

   The Control Panel window appears.

3. Click **User Accounts and Family Safety**.

   The *User Accounts and Family Safety* window appears.

4. Click **User Accounts**.

   The *User accounts* control panel applet appears.

5. Click **Manage another account**.

   The *Choose the account you would like to change* page appears.

6. Click one of the existing accounts.

   The *Make changes to [user's] account* page appears, as shown in Figure 15-6.

Figure 15-6

The *Make changes to [user's] account* page

7. Click **Change the account name**.

The *Type a new account name for [user] account* page appears.

8. Type a new name for the account in the *New account name* text box, and then click **Change Name**.

The *Make changes to [user's] account* page reappears.

9. Click **Change the account type**.

The *Choose a new account type for [user]* page appears.

10. Select the **Standard** or **Administrator** radio button, and then click **Change Account Type**.

The *Make changes to [user's] account* page reappears.

11. Click **Delete the account**.

The *Do you want to keep [user's] files?* page appears.

12. Click **Delete Files** to delete the user profile, or click **Keep Files** to save it to the desktop.

The *Are you sure you want to delete [user's] account?* page appears.

13. Click **Delete Account**.

The *Choose the account you would like to change* page reappears.

14. Close the User accounts control panel applet window.

CREATING A WINDOWS 8.1 ACCOUNT FROM A MICROSOFT ACCOUNT

If, during the Windows 8.1 installation, you opt to create your first account by specifying a Microsoft account – formerly called a ***Windows Live ID*** – the procedure is the same as when you supply an email address during the *Add a user* process described earlier.

For several years, Windows Live has been Microsoft's attempt to consolidate all of its online services under a single sign-on. If you have ever used Microsoft's Live Messenger application or stored files on OneDrive, or used any one of Microsoft's other online services, then you probably already have a Microsoft account registered using your email address.

When you specify your email address on the *How will this person sign in?* screen, the system searches for a Microsoft account that uses that address, and either prompts you for the account password or, if it fails to find one, displays a *Create a Microsoft Account* form with which you can create a new account, as shown in Figure 15-7. The system then uses the Microsoft account information to create a new local account on the Windows 8.1 system.

Figure 15-7

The *Create a Microsoft Account* page

The sole difference between the local account created during the Windows 8.1 installation and one that you create later is that the one created during the installation uses the Administrator account type. This is because it is the only functional account on the system and must have full access. Accounts that you create later through the User accounts control panel are standard user accounts.

TAKE NOTE*

With a Microsoft account, you can purchase apps from the Windows Store and synchronize your system settings with other computers by storing them in the cloud. However, this synchronization cannot begin until you verify the use of your Microsoft account for that purpose. Microsoft sends an email message to the address you supplied, confirming that you want to use the account with your specific computer. Once you respond to that email, the connection between your Windows 8.1 computer and your Microsoft account is fully activated.

Using the Local Users and Groups Snap-in

The User accounts control panel applet provides only partial access to local user accounts, and no access to groups other than the Users and Administrators groups. The Local Users and Groups snap-in, on the other hand, provides full access to all of the local user and group accounts on the computer.

By default, the Local Users and Groups snap-in is part of the Computer Management console. However, you can also load the snap-in by itself, or create your own MMC console with any combination of snap-ins you wish.

OPENING THE LOCAL USERS AND GROUPS SNAP-IN

You can open the Local Users and Groups snap-in in one of three ways, as follows:

- Open the Control Panel and select **System and Security** > **Administrative Tools** > **Computer Management**
- Launch Microsoft Management Console (Mmc.exe), choose **File** > **Add/Remove Snap-In**, and then select the **Local Users and Groups** snap-in.
- Open the **Run** dialog box and type **Lusrmgr.msc** in the *Open* text box.

Each of these three methods provides access to the same snap-in and the same controls for creating, managing, and deleting local users and groups.

CREATING A LOCAL USER

To create a local user account with the Local Users and Groups snap-in, use the following procedure:

 CREATE A NEW USER

GET READY. Log on to Windows 8.1 using an account with Administrator privileges and then perform the following steps:

1. Open the *Computer Management* console.
2. In the left pane of the console, expand the *Local Users and Groups* node and click **Users**.

   A list of the current local users appears in the middle pane, as shown in Figure 15-8.

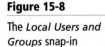

Figure 15-8

The *Local Users and Groups* snap-in

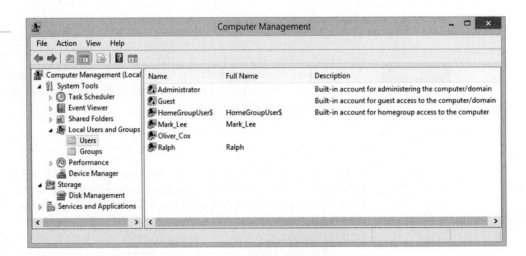

3. Right-click the **Users** folder and, from the context menu, select **New User**. The New User dialog box appears, as shown in Figure 15-9.

Figure 15-9

The *New User* dialog box

4. In the *User name* text box, type the name you want to assign to the user account.

5. Specify a *Full name* and a *Description* for the account, if desired.

6. In the *Password* and *Confirm password* text boxes, type a password for the account.

7. Select or clear the four checkboxes to control the following functions:

   • **User must change password at next logon** – Forces the new user to change the password after logging on for the first time. Select this option if you want to assign an initial password and have users control their own passwords after the first logon. You cannot select this option if you have selected the *Password never expires* checkbox. Selecting this option automatically clears the *User cannot change password* checkbox.

   • **User cannot change password** – Prevents the user from changing the account password. Select this option if you want to retain control over the account password, such as when multiple users are logging on with the same user account. This option is also commonly used to manage service account passwords. You cannot select this option if you have selected the *User must change password at next logon* checkbox.

   • **Password never expires** – Prevents the existing password from ever expiring. This option automatically clears the *User must change password at next logon* checkbox. This option is also commonly used to manage service account passwords.

   • **Account is disabled** – Disables the user account, preventing anyone from using it to log on.

8. Click **Create**.

   The new account is added to the detail pane and the console clears the dialog box, leaving it ready for the creation of another user account.

9. Click **Close**.

10. Close the *Computer Management* console.

MANAGING LOCAL USERS

Local user accounts on a Windows 8.1 computer are not nearly as complex as domain users, but the Local Users and Groups snap-in provides full access to all of the attributes they do possess. To modify a user's attributes, use the following procedure:

 MANAGE A USER

GET READY. Log on to Windows 8.1 using an account with Administrator privileges and then perform the following steps:

1. Open the *Computer Management* console.
2. In the console's left pane, expand the *Local Users and Groups* subheading, and then click **Users**.

   A list of the current local users appears in the middle pane.
3. Double-click one of the existing user accounts.

   The *Properties* sheet for the user account appears.
4. If desired, modify the settings on the General tab, as described in the *Create a new user* procedure, earlier in this lesson.
5. Click the **Member Of** tab.
6. To add the user to a group, click the **Add** button.

   The *Select Groups* dialog box appears, as shown in Figure 15-10.

Figure 15-10

The *Select Groups* dialog box

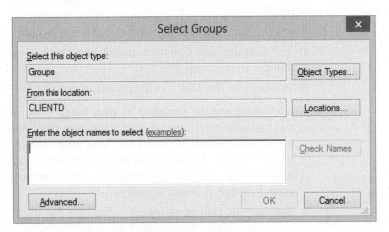

7. Type the name of the local group to which you want to add the user in the text box, and then click **OK**.

   The group is added to the *Member of* list. You can also type part of the group name and click **Check Names** to complete the name or click **Advanced** to search for groups.
8. Click the **Profile** tab.

   The interface shown in Figure 15-11 appears.

Figure 15-11

The *Profile* tab of a user's *Properties* sheet

9. Type a path or file name into any of the following four text boxes as needed:

   - **Profile path** – To assign a roaming or mandatory user profile to the account, type the path to the profile stored on a network share using Universal Naming Convention (UNC) notation, as in the example \\server\share\folder.

   - **Logon script** – Type the name of a script that you want to execute whenever the user logs on.

   - **Local path** – To create a home folder for the user on a local drive, specify the path in this text box.

   - **Connect** – To create a home folder for the user on a network drive, select an unused drive letter and type the path to a folder on a network share using UNC notation.

10. Click **OK** to save your changes and close the *Properties* sheet.

11. Close the *Computer Management* console.

For more information on roaming and mandatory user profiles, see "Understanding User Profiles" in Lesson 3, "Migrating and Configuring User Data".

CREATING A LOCAL GROUP

To create a local group with the Local Users and Groups snap-in, use the following procedure:

 CREATE A LOCAL GROUP

GET READY. Log on to Windows 8.1 using an account with Administrator privileges and then perform the following steps:

1. Open the Computer Management console.

2. In the console's scope pane, expand the *Local Users and Groups* node and click **Groups**.

   A list of the current local groups appears in the details pane.

3. Right-click the **Groups** folder and then, from the context menu, select **New Group**.

   The *New Group* dialog box appears, as shown in Figure 15-12.

Figure 15-12

The *New Group* dialog box

4. In the *Group name* text box, type the name you want to assign to the group. This is the only required field in the dialog box.

5. If desired, specify a *Description* for the group.

6. Click the **Add** button.

   The *Select Users* dialog box appears.

7. Type the names of the users that you want to add to the group, separated by semicolons, in the text box, and then click **OK**.

   The users are added to the Members list. You can also type part of a user name and click **Check Names** to complete the name or click **Advanced** to search for users.

8. Click **Create** to create the group and populate it with the user(s) you specified. The console then clears the dialog box, leaving it ready for the creation of another group.

9. Click **Close**.

10. Close the Computer Management console.

Local groups have no user-configurable attributes other than a members list, so the only modifications you can make when you open an existing group are to add or remove members. As noted earlier in this lesson, local groups cannot have other local groups as members, but if the computer is a member of a Windows domain, a local group can have domain users and domain groups as members.

TAKE NOTE *

To add domain objects to a local group, you click the Add button on the group's Properties sheet and, when the Select Users dialog box appears, change the Object Types and Location settings to those of the domain. Then, you can select domain users and groups just as you did local users in the previous procedure.

Working with Domain Users and Groups

> To create and manage AD DS domain users and groups on a Windows 8.1 workstation, you must install the Remote Server Administration Tools for Windows 8.1 package, turn on the Active Directory Users and Computer snap-in under Turn Windows features on or off, and have the appropriate Active Directory permissions.

Creating and managing AD DS domain users and groups is beyond the scope of the 70-687 exam, but suffice it to say that you cannot use any of the tools discussed so far in this lesson to work with domain objects. To create domain users and groups, you must use the Active Directory Users and Computers console, which is included with the Windows Server operating systems.

To manage domain objects on a Windows 8.1 workstation, you must download and install Remote Server Administration Tools for Windows 8.1, which is available from the Microsoft Download Center. Once you have installed the appropriate package for your processor platform, the Remote Server Administration Tools are available for activation in the Windows Features dialog box, which is accessible from the Programs and Features control panel.

▪ Authenticating and Authorizing Users

THE BOTTOM LINE

> As mentioned earlier in this lesson, authentication and authorization are two of the most important functions of Windows 8.1. Authentication confirms the identification of a user accessing computer or network resources, and authorization specifies which resources the user is permitted to access.

Network resources require varying levels of security, and administrators are often responsible for seeing to it that users have access only to the information they need to do their jobs, and no more. Authentication is crucial to this process, because before you can provide access to protected resources, you must confirm the identity of those to whom you are providing access.

The user authentication process is typically based on one or more of the following:

- **Something the user knows** – A secret shared between the user and the management – usually in the form of a password – is the simplest and most common form of authentication. However, users can forget, share, or otherwise compromise passwords, often without knowing it.

- **Something the user has** – A token of some kind, carried by the user, such as a smart card, can serve as proof of identity. While tokens can easily be lost or stolen, users are typically aware of the loss, and the time during which the system is compromised is brief.

- **Something the user is** – Biometric identification is the use of physical characteristics to confirm a user's identity. Fingerprints are the most commonly-used biometric identifier, but there are also technologies that are based on ocular scans, facial recognition, and other characteristics.

Because each of these identification methods has inherent weaknesses, networks requiring high security often use more than one. For example, a network that issues smart cards to users nearly always requires some sort of password as well. This technique is known as *multifactor authentication*.

Authentication is nearly always a balance between security and convenience, and nowhere is this more true than in user authentication. As an administrator responsible for network security, you could conceivably demand that your users log on each day by typing 72-character passwords, scanning security bracelets permanently fastened to their wrists, and having their identities confirmed with a blood sample. There are, however, likely to be objections to this treatment from users.

Working with Passwords

Passwords are the most common user identifier on Windows networks, primarily because they do not require any additional hardware or software. Passwords can provide excellent security as well, as long as they are used properly.

When left to their own devices, users tend to employ password policies that can compromise their effectiveness as a security mechanism. Potential intruders can obtain passwords in two possible ways: by cracking them or by discovering them.

Cracking is the process of repeatedly guessing passwords until you find the right one. Cracking is a mathematical process, in which a software program tries all of the possible passwords until it finds the right one. This is sometimes known as a *brute force* process.

Password discovery is a process in which the intruder tries to guess a password based on the user's personal information, or tries to dupe the user into supplying the password. This is also known as social engineering.

These methods are possible only when users compromise their passwords in some way. Some of the ways in which users can weaken the security of their passwords are as follows:

- **Short passwords** – Shorter passwords are mathematically easier to guess. A three-character alphabetical password has 26^3, or 17,576, possible values. Increasing the password to seven characters increases the number of possible values to 26^7, or over eight billion, password combinations.

- **Simple passwords** – Passwords that use only lowercase characters are also mathematically easier to guess than those that use mixed lowercase and uppercase characters. A seven-character password using upper and lowercase characters would have 52^7, or over one trillion, possible values. Passwords that use numerical characters and symbols as well increase their strength even further.

- **Unchanging passwords** – A brute force attack takes time to try every possible password combination, so changing passwords forces an attacker to start all over again. The fewer the possible password combinations an attacker has to try, the more frequently you should change the password.

- **Predictable passwords** – Users often select passwords based on predicable values, such as birthdays, or names of children and pets. Attackers that have access to this type of information can make more educated password guesses.

Windows 8.1 includes features that can provide users with a more convenient password experience, and also compel them to obey network password selection and maintenance policies that minimize these potential weaknesses. Some of these features are discussed in the following sections.

CONFIGURING PASSWORD POLICIES

Windows 8.1 supports a number of Group Policy settings that administrators can use to enforce password security practices on individual computers or on Active Directory Domain Services (AD DS) networks. By enforcing these password practices, you can ensure that your systems remain secure, even though the end users are responsible for their own passwords.

To configure password policies on a workgroup system, you must use the Local Security Policy console. The password policies you can use are listed in Table 15-4.

Table 15-4

Windows Password
Policy Settings

PASSWORD POLICY SETTINGS	VALUES AND FUNCTION
Enforce Password History	Specifies the number of unique passwords that users have to supply before Windows 8.1 permits them to reuse an old password. Possible values range from 0 to 24. The default value is 0.
Maximum Password Age	Specifies how long a single password can be used before Windows 8.1 forces the user to change it. Possible values range from 0 to 999. A value of 0 causes the password never to expire. The default value is 42 days.
Minimum Password Age	Specifies how long a single password must be used before Windows 8.1 permits the user to change it. Possible values range from 0 to 998. The default value is 0 days, which enables the user to change the password immediately.
Minimum Password Length	Specifies the minimum number of characters Windows 8.1 permits in user-supplied passwords. Possible values range from 0 to 14. The default value is 0, which means that no password is required.
Password Must Meet Complexity Requirements	When enabled, indicates that passwords supplied by users must be at least six characters long, with no duplication of any part of the user's account name; and must include characters from at least three of the following four categories: uppercase letters, lowercase letters, numbers, and symbols. By default, this policy is disabled.
Store Passwords Using Reversible Encryption	When enabled, causes Windows 8.1 to store user account passwords using a less effective encryption algorithm. This policy is designed to support authentication protocols that require access to the user's password, such as the Challenge Handshake Authentication Protocol (CHAP). From a security perspective, this policy is functionally equivalent to using plaintext passwords. The default value is disabled.

In an enterprise network environment, administrators generally prefer to configure these settings using AD DS Group Policy, so they can distribute them to large numbers of workstations simultaneously. To configure password policies on an AD DS network, you must run the Group Policy Management Console and create a Group Policy Object (GPO), which you then link to a domain, site, or organizational unit object in your AD DS tree. The password policies in a GPO are located in the Computer Configuration\Policies\Windows Settings\Security Settings\Account Policies\Password Policies node. The policy settings themselves are exactly the same.

TAKE NOTE * The Group Policy Management Console is supplied with the Windows Server operating systems and installed automatically on AD DS domain controllers. To manage AD DS Group Policy settings on a Windows 8.1 workstation, you must download and install the Remote Server Administration Tools for Windows 8.1 package.

CONFIGURING ACCOUNT LOCKOUT POLICIES

It is possible to penetrate any password-protected resource, given enough time and an unlimited number of access attempts. The brute force approach to password penetration is supported by programs designed to try thousands of different character combinations in an attempt to find the one that matches the password.

Windows 8.1 can protect against brute force password penetration techniques by limiting the number of unsuccessful logon attempts allowed by each user account. When a potential infiltrator exceeds the number of allowed attempts, the system locks the account for a set period of time. To impose these limits, you can use Local Security Policy for stand-alone computers, or Group Policy for AD DS networks, to configure the policy settings listed in Table 15-5.

Table 15-5

Windows Account Lockout Policy Settings

ACCOUNT LOCKOUT POLICY SETTING	VALUES AND FUNCTION
Account Lockout Duration	Determines the period of time that must pass after a lockout before Windows 8.1 automatically unlocks a user's account. The policy is not set by default, as it is viable only in conjunction with the Account Lockout Threshold policy. Possible values range from 0 to 99999 minutes (about 10 weeks). A low setting (5 to 15 minutes) is usually sufficient to reduce attacks significantly without unreasonably affecting legitimate users who are mistakenly locked out. A value of 0 requires an administrator to unlock the account manually. When the Account Lockout Threshold policy is activated, this policy is activated as well and set to a default value of 30 minutes.
Account Lockout Threshold	Specifies the number of invalid logon attempts that will trigger an account lockout. Possible values range from 0 to 999. A value that is too low (as few as three, for example) may cause lockouts due to normal user error during logon. A value of 0 prevents accounts from ever being locked out. The default value is 0.
Reset Account Lockout Counter After	Specifies the period of time that must pass after an invalid logon attempt before the lockout counter resets to zero. Possible values range from 1 to 99999 minutes, and must be less than or equal to the account lockout duration. When the Account Lockout Threshold policy is activated, this policy is activated as well and set to a default value of 30.

USING CREDENTIAL MANAGER

Users and administrators alike often become frustrated when forced to re-enter passwords whenever they have to access a protected resource. This is one reason why Microsoft modified the default behavior of User Account Control beginning in Windows 7 to eliminate elevation prompts for administrative operating system tasks.

CERTIFICATION READY
Manage credentials
Objective 4.4

Credential Manager is a Windows 8.1 tool that stores the user names and passwords people supply to servers and web sites in a protected area called the Windows Vault. When a user selects the *Remember my credentials* checkbox while authenticating in Windows Explorer, Internet Explorer, or Remote Desktop Connection, the system adds the credentials to the Windows Vault.

From the Credential Manager window in Control Panel, you can see the resources for which the Windows Vault contains credentials, as shown in Figure 15-13, although you cannot view the passwords themselves.

Figure 15-13

The *Credential Manager* window

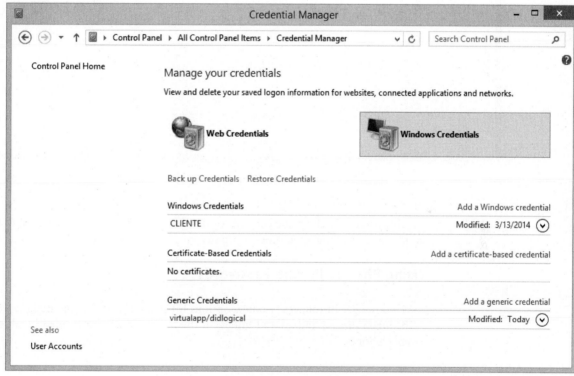

It is also possible to add credentials directly to the vault using Credential Manager, by clicking *Add a Windows credential,* or one of the similar links. The interface shown in Figure 15-14 then appears, in which you can specify the address of a resource and the credentials that go with it. In the same way, you can specify a resource and select a certificate from the computer's store.

Figure 15-14

The *Add a Windows Credential* window

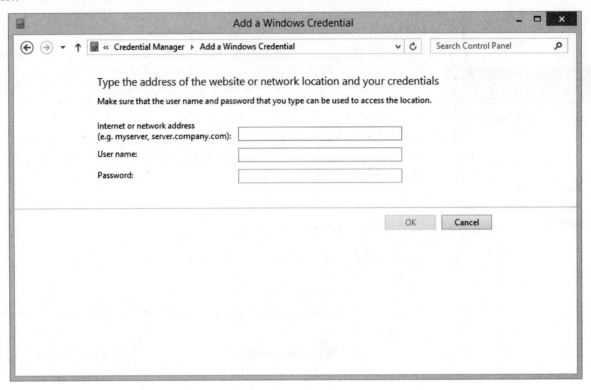

Finally, you can back up the contents of the Windows Vault from Credential Manager and restore it to the same or another computer, to protect the credentials or migrate them.

Using PIN and Picture Passwords

Windows 8.1 introduces two new options for password processing, designed to simplify the logon process and take advantage of the touch interfaces provided in tablets and smartphones.

On the *Accounts* page of the *PC Settings* screen, shown in Figure 15-15, you can change the password of your local user account, and you can also replace the password entirely, with either a numerical PIN or a picture and a sequence of gestures.

Figure 15-15

The *Users* page of the *PC Settings* screen

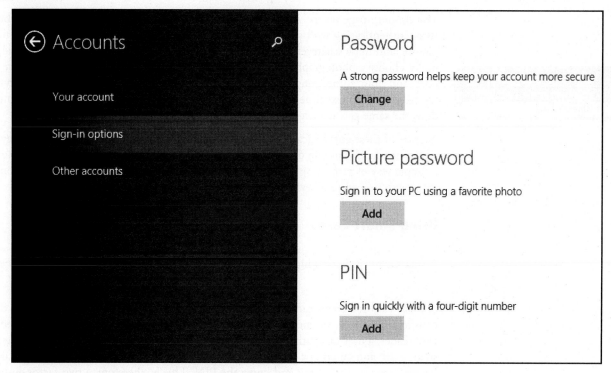

CERTIFICATION READY
Configure PIN
Objective 4.4

A PIN password is a four-digit number that a user can employ to log on in place of a password. PIN passwords are designed for use on portable devices with small screens, on which it is easier to display and use a numerical keypad than a full virtual keyboard.

When you click the Create a PIN button, you must first re-authenticate with your account password, and then the system displays a Create a PIN screen, as shown in Figure 15-16, on which you enter and verify the four-digit PIN you want to use. The next time you log on, the system prompts you for your PIN instead of your password.

Figure 15-16

The *Create a PIN* screen

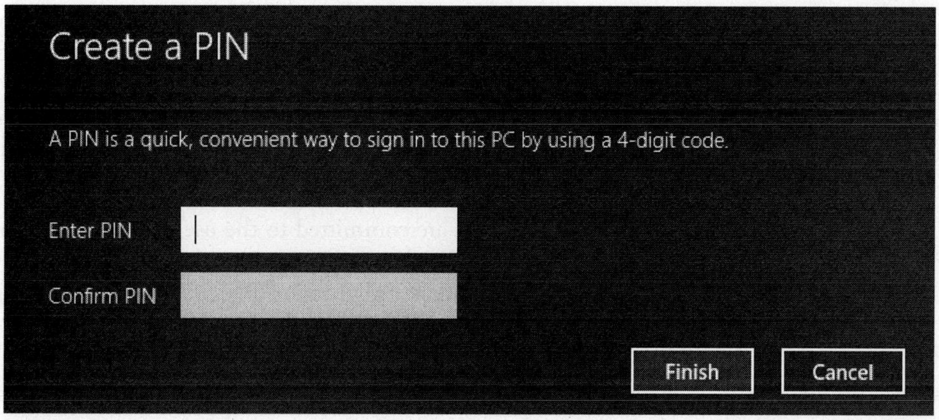

Create a PIN

A PIN is a quick, convenient way to sign in to this PC by using a 4-digit code.

Enter PIN

Confirm PIN

[Finish]   [Cancel]

Picture passwords are designed to take advantage of touch interfaces by replacing the standard alphanumeric password with a picture. Instead of typing in a password, the user must duplicate a sequence of three gestures – taps, circles, or lines – on the picture, using the touch screen.

The *Accounts* page on the *PC Settings* screen also has a Create a Picture Password button. After authenticating with your standard password, you are given the opportunity to select a picture, and draw whatever sequence of three gestures you want on it. For example, you might choose a photograph of a person's face, and for your gestures tap the left eye, circle the nose, and draw a line along the mouth. After performing the gestures twice, the system saves the pattern. The next time you logon, the system displays your selected picture, and you must draw the same gestures on it to complete the authentication.

CERTIFICATION READY
Configure picture password
Objective 4.4

Neither of these authentication methods is as secure as a strong password, and they are not recommended for use on devices that contain sensitive data. However, for casual use, they are a simple way of protecting a portable device, without forcing the user to type a complex password on a tiny, virtual keyboard.

Using Smart Cards

Smart cards provide a high-security alternative to passwords for user authentication.

A smart card is a credit card-like device that contains a chip, on which is stored a digital certificate that serves as an identifier for a particular user. On a computer equipped with a card reader, a user can authenticate him- or herself by specifying a user name, inserting the smart card, and entering a PIN associated with the card. To log on successfully, a user must have possession of the card and know the PIN. This is, therefore, a two-factor authentication.

Smart cards are more secure than passwords, because there is no practical way to duplicate the information they contain by guessing or brute force attack. It is possible for users to have their smart cards lost or stolen, but without the PIN, the card is useless. In addition, users in most cases, know when this occurs and can report it. An administrator can then revoke the certificate on the card, rendering it invalid.

Smart cards provide additional security in three ways, as follows:

- The private keys and other information stored on the smart card cannot be exported to another medium and reused.
- Smart cards can perform encryption and decryption right on the chip, so it is not possible for malware running on the computer to penetrate these functions.
- To prevent the use of a lost or stolen smart card, the number of PIN entry attempts is limited. Too many attempts locks the card until an administrator intervenes.

Windows has supported smart card authentication for some time, but until Windows 7, you had to install a third-party device driver along with the card reader hardware. By including support for the **Personal Identity Verification (PIV)** standard, published by the National Institute of Standards and Technology (NIST), Windows 8.1 can now obtain drivers for PIV smart cards from Windows Update, or use a PIV minidriver included with the operating system.

For organizations that are committed to the use of smart cards for authentication, there are two smart card-related Group Policy settings that Windows 8.1 supports. These settings, located in the Computer Configuration\Policies\Windows Settings\Security Settings\Local Policies\Security Options node, are as follows:

- **Interactive Logon: Require Smart Card** – Configures Windows 8 to allow only smart card user authentications.

- **Interactive Logon: Smart Card Removal Behavior** – Specifies how Windows 8.1 should behave when a user removes the smart card from the reader while logged on to the computer. The possible values are as follows:
  - **No action** – Enables the user to remove the smart card without affecting the session. This is the default setting.
  - **Lock Workstation** – Disables the workstation while leaving the session open until the user reinserts the smart card. This enables the user to leave the workstation temporarily without leaving the smart card and without having to log off.
  - **Force Logoff** – Causes the workstation to log the user off as soon as the smart card is removed.
  - **Disconnect if a Remote Desktop Services session** – Disconnects the computer from the Remote Desktop Services server without logging the user off from the session. The user can then resume the session by reinserting the smart card at the same or another computer.

Using Virtual Smart Cards

Virtual smart cards provide the security of a smart card without the additional expense.

CERTIFICATION READY
Configure virtual smart cards
Objective 4.3

The greatest impediment to the use of smart cards for authentication is the additional expense required to purchase and deploy the cards themselves and equip computers with card readers. To address this problem, Windows 8.1 introduces the ability to create and use virtual smart cards.

A *virtual smart card* is a solution that utilizes the hardware already built into the computer to duplicate the capabilities of an external, physical smart card. In Windows 8.1, virtual smart cards use the Trusted Platform Module (TPM) found in many of today's computers to encrypt the user's certificate and other information before storing it on the hard disk.

A TPM is a dedicated cryptographic processor chip that is similar to that found on a smart card. All cryptographic functions associated with the authentication process are performed by the TPM and isolated from software running on the computer. With a virtual smart card encrypted by the TPM, the user only has to supply the correct PIN to authenticate and gain access to the system. This also provides a two-factor authentication, because the user must have possession of the computer and the PIN.

Because many computers already come equipped with a TPM, a virtual smart card deployment incurs no additional hardware costs for cards and readers, and yet it provides the same three protections as conventional smart cards, listed in the previous section. The information encrypted by the TPM, even though it is stored on the hard disk, can only be decrypted by that TPM. Therefore, the information cannot be experted and used on another computer. TPM chips also have the same cryptographic capabilities and similar anti-brute force capabilities as physical smart cards.

To create and deploy virtual smart cards in an AD DS domain environment, you must install the Active Directory Certificate Services role on a Windows server to create a Certification Authority. Then, you create a certificate template containing the settings that the server will use when issuing new certificates.

Once the server infrastructure is in place, you can use the Tpmvscmgr.exe command line program in Windows 8.1 to create the virtual smart card and secure it with a PIN. Then, you use the Certificates snap-in to request a certificate from the certification authority and store it on the virtual smart card, which appears in the snap-in as *Identity Device (Microsoft Profile)*. Once the system has retrieved the certifiuate, the virtual smart card appears as an icon on the Windows Logon screen. Click the icon and supply the PIN you specified when creating the virtual smart card, and the authentication is completed.

Managing Certificates

Windows 8.1 uses digital certificates for a variety of authentication tasks, internally, on the local network, and on the Internet. Every user account has a certificate store containing a variety of certificates obtained by various means.

Windows 8.1 creates some certificates itself, such as the self-signed certificate it uses for the Encrypting File System. Others it downloads from other computers, such as servers on the Internet. In most cases, activities involving certificates are invisible to the user. Windows 8.1 obtains most of the certificates it needs automatically and stores them for future use.

CERTIFICATION READY
Manage certificates
Objective 4.4

However, it is possible for users to manage their certificate stores directly, including creating backups of certificates for disaster recovery or migration purposes. Windows 8.1 includes a Certificates snap-in for MMC that provides access to the certificate store, but the snap-in is not accessible from the Start menu or the Control Panel.

To access the Certificates snap-in, type **cert** on the Start screen and, in the Results list, click **Manage user certificates** to load the snap-in and point it at the current user account, as shown in Figure 15-17.

Figure 15-17

The *Certificates* snap-in

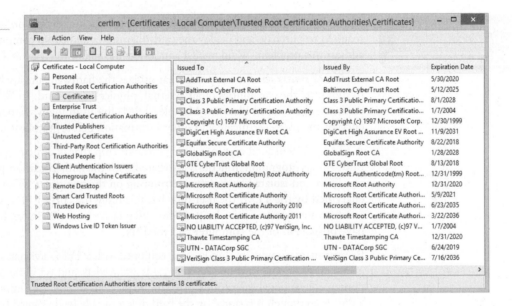

Double-clicking one of the certificates in the store displays a Certificate dialog box like the one shown in Figure 15-18. This dialog box contains information about the certificate and the data stored in it.

Figure 15-18

A *Certificate* dialog box

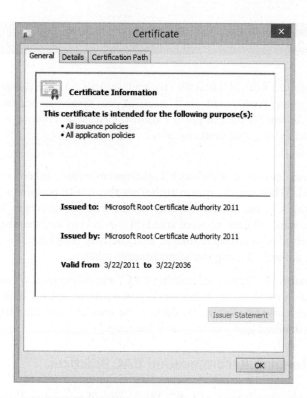

To back up a certificate to a file, right-click it in the snap-in and, in the context menu, select All Tasks > Export, to launch the Certificate Export Wizard. This wizard prompts you to select a format for the file, and the location where you want to save it.

Using Biometrics

> Biometric authentication uses a scan of a physical characteristic to confirm the identity of a user.

Biometric authentication is theoretically more secure than a token-based or secret-based authentication method, because the identifying characteristic is difficult or impossible to duplicate. Even the grisly stories of severed body parts being used to fool biometric scanners are (hopefully) fictitious, as the technology exists to confirm that a finger or other appendage is still connected to a living body.

CERTIFICATION READY
Configure biometrics
Objective 4.4

There are a great many third-party biometric authentication solutions available, many of which take the form of finger print scanners. Prior to Windows 7, the operating system included no support for biometric devices at all, and required the third-party vendor to supply a complete software solution along with the hardware. However, Windows 8.1 includes a component called the ***Windows Biometric Framework***, which provides a core biometric functionality and a Biometric Device control panel.

Even with the Windows Biometric Framework, however, the reliability of these technologies and the security they provide can vary widely. Most biometric solutions include a secondary authentication method, such as a password or a smart card, for when the biometric scan fails. Others are multifactor solutions, requiring both a biometric scan and another form of authentication.

■ Configuring User Account Control (UAC)

THE BOTTOM LINE

Preventing users from accidentally changing settings on your computer and stopping malware from gaining system-wide access to your system are vulnerabilities that *User Account Control (UAC)* can protect against. UAC is a Windows 8.1 feature that prevents unauthorized changes to your computer.

CERTIFICATION READY
Configure User Account Control (UAC) behavior
Objective 4.3

When a user logs on to Windows 8.1, the system issues a token, which indicates the user's access level. Whenever the system authorizes the user to perform a particular activity, it consults the token to see whether the user has the required privileges. In previous versions of Windows, standard users received standard user tokens and members of the Administrators group received administrative tokens. Every activity performed by an administrative user was, therefore, authorized using the administrative token.

On a Windows 8.1 computer running UAC, a standard user still receives a standard user token, but an administrative user receives two tokens: one for standard user access and one for administrative user access. By default, the standard and administrative users both run using the standard user token most of the time.

Understanding Recommended UAC Practices

Despite the introduction of UAC, Microsoft still recommends that all Windows users log on with a standard user account, except when they are logging on for administrative purposes only.

As compared to earlier Windows versions, Windows 8 and Windows 8.1 and UAC simplify the process by which standard users can gain administrative access, making the use of standard user accounts less frustrating, even for system administrators.

PERFORMING ADMINISTRATIVE TASKS WITH A STANDARD USER ACCOUNT

When a standard user attempts to perform a task that requires administrative privileges (for example, changing the system time or date), the system displays a *credential prompt,* as shown in Figure 15-19, requesting that the user supply the name and password for an account with administrative privileges.

Figure 15-19

Receiving a credential prompt

PERFORMING ADMINISTRATIVE TASKS WITH AN ADMINISTRATIVE ACCOUNT

When an administrator attempts to perform a task that requires administrative access, the system switches the account from the standard user token to the administrative token. This is known as *Admin Approval Mode*.

Before the system permits the user to employ the administrative token, it might require the human user to confirm that he or she is actually trying to perform an administrative task (for example, installing an application). To do this, the system generates an elevation prompt. An *elevation prompt* is the message box shown in Figure 15-20. This confirmation prevents unauthorized processes, such as those initiated by malware, from accessing the system using administrative privileges.

Figure 15-20

Receiving an elevation prompt

In Windows 8 and Windows 8.1, administrators are faced with elevation prompts far less frequently than in previous versions. In response to complaints from users, Microsoft has modified the default UAC behavior so that elevation prompts appear only when an application attempts to perform an administrative task.

TAKE NOTE* The system component that is responsible for recognizing the need for elevated privileges and generating elevation prompts is called the Application Information Service (AIS). AIS is a Windows 8.1 service that has to be running for UAC to function properly. Disabling this service prevents applications that require administrative access from launching, resulting in Access Denied errors.

WARNING It is still possible for a malware program to imitate the secure desktop and create its own artificial elevation or credential prompt, but an artificial prompt cannot provide the program with genuine access to administrative functions. The only possible danger is that a malware program could use an artificial credential prompt to harvest administrative account names and passwords from unsuspecting users.

Using Secure Desktop

By default, whenever Windows 8.1 displays an elevation prompt or a credential prompt, it does so using the secure desktop.

The *secure desktop* is an alternative to the interactive user desktop that Windows normally displays. When Windows 8.1 generates an elevation or credential prompt, it switches to the secure desktop, suppressing the operation of all other desktop controls and permitting only Windows processes to interact with the prompt. The object of this is to prevent malware from automating a response to the elevation or credential prompt and bypassing the human reply.

Configuring User Account Control

Windows 8.1 enables User Account Control by default, but it is possible to configure several of its properties.

In Windows 8.1, there are UAC settings available through the Control Panel. To configure UAC through the Control Panel, use the following procedure.

 REVIEW UAC SETTINGS

GET READY. Log on to Windows 8.1 using an account with Administrator privileges.

1. On the Windows 8.1 Start menu, type **uac**, and then from *Results*, choose **Change User Account Control settings**.

2. The *User Account Control Settings* box appears as shown in Figure 15-21.

Figure 15-21

Reviewing UAC setting options

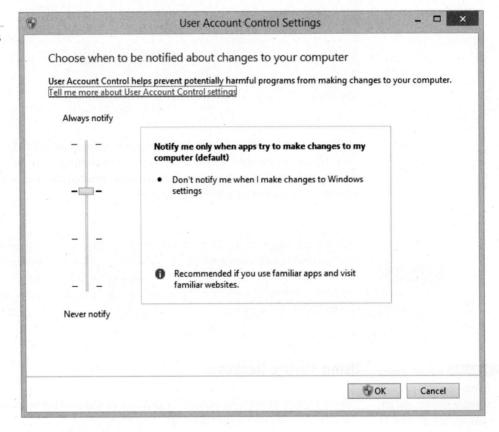

3. Read the current setting and then drag the slider up and down to each setting to review its description.
   - Always notify me
   - Notify me only when apps try to make changes to my computer (default)
   - Notify me only when apps try to make changes to my computer (do not dim my desktop)
   - Never notify me

4. In the *User Account Control Settings* box, click **Cancel**.

In Windows 7, you can fully disable UAC in the Control Panel, but with the Windows 8.1 Control Panel, you cannot. Even if you move the slider to *Never notify me*, you are not turning off UAC but just receiving less notifications and running all processes at a medium integrity level. Although it is possible to turn it off via a registry edit on a Windows 8.1 computer, doing so increases your vulnerability to malware attacks and is not recommended.

Although the UAC controls in Windows 8.1 are improved, the most granular control over UAC properties is still through Local Security Policy, or on an Active Directory-based network using Group Policy. The available policy settings are listed in Table 15-6.

Table 15-6

UAC Local Security Policy Settings

POLICY SETTING	VALUES AND FUNCTIONS
User Account Control: Admin Approval Mode for the Built-in Administrator account	• When enabled, the built-in Administrator account uses Admin Approval Mode. By default, any operation that requires elevation of privilege prompts the user to approve the operation. • When disabled (default), the built-in Administrator account runs with full administrative privilege.
User Account Control: Allow UIAccess applications wto prompt for elevation without using the secure desktop	• When enabled, causes User Interface Accessibility programs to disable the secure desktop when displaying elevation prompts used by a standard user. • When disabled, elevation prompts use the secure desktop, unless the *User Account Control: Switch to the secure desktop when prompting for elevation* policy is enabled.
User Account Control: Behavior of the elevation prompt for administrators in Admin Approval Mode	• When set to *Elevate without prompting*, administrative users are elevated to the administrative token with no consent or credentials from the human user. • When set to *Prompt for credentials on the secure desktop*, administrative users are elevated to the administrative token only after the presentation of a credential prompt on the secure desktop, to which the user must supply a valid administrative account name and password, even if he or she is already logged on using such an account. If valid credentials are entered, the operation continues with the user's highest available privilege. • When set to *Prompt for consent on the secure desktop*, administrative users are elevated to the administrative token only after the presentation of an elevation prompt on the secure desktop and the consent of the human user. The user is prompted to select Permit or Deny. If they select Permit, the operation continues with the user's highest available privilege. • When set to *Prompt for credentials*, administrative users are elevated to the administrative token only after the presentation of a credential prompt to which the user must supply valid administrative account name and password. If valid credentials are entered, the operation continues with the applicable privilege. • When set to *Prompt for consent*, administrative users are elevated to the administrative token only after the presentation of an elevation prompt on the secure desktop

(continued)

Table 15-6

(continued)

POLICY SETTING	VALUES AND FUNCTIONS
	and the consent of the human user. The user is prompted to select Permit or Deny. If they select Permit, the operation continues with the user's highest available privilege. • When set to *Prompt for consent for non-Windows binaries (Default)*, When an operation for a non-Microsoft application requires elevation of privilege, administrative users are prompted to select either Permit or Deny. If they select Permit, the operation continues with the highest available privilege.
User Account Control: Behavior of the elevation prompt for standard users	• When set to *Prompt for credentials (default)*, standard users attempting to perform an administrative function receive a credential prompt, to which the user must supply a valid administrative account name and password. • When set to *Automatically deny elevation requests*, suppresses the credential prompt and prevents standard users from being elevated to an administrative token. When an operation requires elevation of privilege, a configurable access denied error message is displayed. • When set to *Prompt for credentials on the secure desktop*, standard users attempting to perform an administrative function receive a credential prompt on the secure desktop, to which the user must supply a valid administrative account name and password.
User Account Control: Detect application installations and prompt for elevation	• When enabled, an attempt to install an application causes standard users to receive credential prompt and administrative users to receive an elevation prompt. The user must supply authentication credentials or consent before the installation can proceed. This is the default setting. • When disabled, elevation and credential prompts are suppressed during application installations, and the installation fails. This setting is for use on enterprise desktops that use an automated installation technology, such as Microsoft System Center Configuration Manager.
User Account Control: Only Elevate executables that are signed and validated	• When enabled, requires successful public key infrastructure (PKI) signature verifications on all interactive applications that request administrative access. Unsigned applications will not run. • When disabled, both signed and unsigned applications run. This is the default setting.
User Account Control: Only elevate UIAccess applications that are installed in secure locations	• When enabled, Windows 8.1 provides access to the protected system user interface only if the executable is located in the \Program Files, \Windows\system32, and \ Program Files (x86) folders on the system drive. If the executable is not located in one of these folders, access is denied, despite a positive response to the elevation prompt. This is the default setting.

(continued)

Table 15-6

(continued)

POLICY SETTING	VALUES AND FUNCTIONS
User Account Control: Run all administrators in Admin Approval Mode	• When disabled, the folder location checks are omitted, so any application can be granted access to the protected system user interface upon successful completion of the elevation prompt. • When enabled, the built-in Administrator account and all other users who are members of the Administrators group can run in Admin Approval Mode. A change in the value of this policy does not take effect until the system is restarted. This is the default setting. • When disabled, the AIS service is disabled and does not automatically start. When the system starts, the Windows Security Center warns the user that operating system security is reduced and provides the ability to activate UAC.
User Account Control: Switch to the secure desktop when prompting for elevation	• When enabled, causes Windows 8.1 to display all elevation prompts on the secure desktop, which can receive messages only from Windows processes. This is the default setting. • When disabled, causes Windows 8.1 to display all elevation prompts on the interactive user desktop.
User Account Control: Virtualize file and registry write Failures to per-user locations	• When enabled, allows non-UAC-compliant applications to run by redirecting write requests to protected locations, such as the Program Files and Windows folders or the HKLM\Software registry key, to alternative locations in the registry and file system. This process is called *virtualization*. This is the default setting. • When disabled, virtualization is disabled, and non-UAC-compliant applications attempting to write to protected locations fail to run. This setting is recommended only when the system is running UAC-compliant applications exclusively.

Elevating Privileges

Ever since the Windows Vista release, Microsoft has made a concerted effort to persuade users not to log on to Windows for their everyday tasks using an administrative account. This practice not only makes accidental configuration changes more possible, it also increases the likelihood of intrusion by malevolent attackers.

The preferred mechanism for performing tasks that require administrative privileges is to use the Run As feature to execute a program using another account. Shortcuts in the Start menu have a *Run as administrator* option in their context menus, which causes standard users to receive a credential prompt and administrators to receive an elevation prompt, according to the system's normal User Account Control (UAC) practices.

It is also possible to use the Runas.exe command line program to execute an application using any other account. The syntax for the Runas.exe program is as follows:

```
runas [/user:domain\user] [/profile] [/noprofile] [/savecred]
[/smartcard] [/env] [/netonly] [/trustlevel] [/showtrustlevels]
"program.exe /parameter"
```

- **/user:domain\user** – Specifies the account that Runas.exe should use to execute the program. The account can be specified in the form *domain\user* or *user@domain*. The *domain* variable can also be the name of a standalone workstation and *user* a local *user* account.
- **/profile** – Causes the Runas.exe program to load the profile of the account specified by the /user parameter. This is the default value.
- **/noprofile** – Prevents the Runas.exe program from loading the profile of the account specified by the /user parameter. Without the profile, the program cannot access the EFS-encrypted files belonging to the account specified by the /user parameter.
- **/savecred** – Causes the Runas.exe program to save the credentials for the account specified by the /user parameter in the Windows Vault or, in the case of a previously-saved account, to use the credentials saved in the vault.
- **/smartcard** – Specifies that the credentials for the account specified by the \user parameter will be supplied using a smart card.
- **/env** – Causes the Runas.exe program to use the current environment, rather than the one of the account specified by the /user parameter.
- **/netonly** – Specifies that the credentials of the account specified by the /user variable are for remote access only.
- **"program.exe/parameter"** – Specifies the name of the application that Runas.exe should run with elevated privileges, along with any of the application's necessary command line parameters.

A typical example of a Runas command line would appear as follows:

```
runas /user:example\administrator "notepad.exe \script.vbs"
```

When you run the command, the program prompts for the password to the Administrator account, loads the user profile for the account, executes Notepad.exe, and then loads the Script.vbs file.

Troubleshooting Authentication Issues

The most common problem related to authentication experienced by Windows 8.1 users is password loss. There is no way for a user or an administrator to read a password from a user account on a Windows system, whether it is stored in the Security Account Manager (SAM), the Windows Vault, or an AD DS domain controller.

When a user loses a Windows 8.1 account password, there is no way to reclaim it; the only solution is to reset (that is, change) the password. There are two ways of doing this: either the user resets his or her own password or an administrator resets it.

To reset your own password, you must supply the old one first. If you cannot do this, because you have lost or forgotten the old password, the only solution is to use a password reset disk. The password reset disk supplies the old password for you, enabling you to reset the password to a new value.

The problem with this solution is that you must have created a password reset disk before losing your password. In the User accounts control panel applet, the *Make changes to your user account* page for each user has a link that enables the user to run the Forgotten Password Wizard and create a password reset disk, using a floppy disk or a USB flash drive.

When a user loses his or her password, and does not have a password reset disk, the only alternative is for an administrator to reset the password, using either the Local Users and Groups snap-in or the Manage Accounts page of the User accounts control panel applet. Administrators can reset passwords without having to supply the old password first.

The problem, however, is that an administrative reset causes the user to lose access to all EFS-encrypted files, all certificates in the user's personal certificate store, and all passwords stored in the Windows Vault. These passwords might be recoverable from a backup of the Windows Vault or the EFS key, but it would be a lot easier if the user had created a password reset disk in the first place.

Authorizing Users

> Authentication confirms a user's identity. Authorization grants the user access to certain resources.

A successful authentication confirms that a user is who he or she purports to be, but logging on successfully does not guarantee access to system resources. Some authenticated users have full access to the system, while others might have nearly none. The difference between the two is the resources that they are authorized to access.

USING PERMISSIONS

The most commonly-used mechanisms for authorizing users in Windows 8.1 are the NTFS, share, and registry permission systems. By adjusting permissions in the protected resources, administrators can specify who should have access to them and what degree of access users should receive.

For more information on managing permissions, see Lesson 13, "Configuring Shared Resources" and Lesson 15, "Configuring File and Folder Access."

CONFIGURING USER RIGHTS

Some people confuse the concept of user permissions with that of user rights; in Windows 8.1, these are two different concepts. In Windows 8.1, *user rights* are policies that define specific operating system functions. For example, in order to sit down at a Windows 8.1 computer and log on, users must not only have accounts, they also must possess the *Allow log on locally* user right.

Administrators can assign user rights to individual users, but as with permissions, this practice is rare. The more practical alternative is to assign user rights to groups and then add individual users to the groups as needed.

In fact, Windows 8.1 does this for you, by default. The built-in local groups on a computer running Windows 8.1 receive their special capabilities through default user rights assignments. For example, the Remote Desktop Users group has been assigned the *Allow log on through Remote Desktop Services* user right.

To assign user rights to users or groups, you can open the Local Security Policy snap-in on a Windows 8.1 workstation and browse to Security Settings\Local Policies\User Rights Assignment, as shown in Figure 15-22. In an AD DS environment, you open a GPO and browse to the Computer Configuration\Policies\Windows Settings\Security Settings\Local Policies\User Rights Assignment node. In both interfaces, there are 44 user rights assignments that you can grant to local or domain users and groups.

CERTIFICATION READY
Configure user rights
Objective 4.4

Figure 15-22

The *User Rights Assignment* node in the *Local Security Policy* snap-in

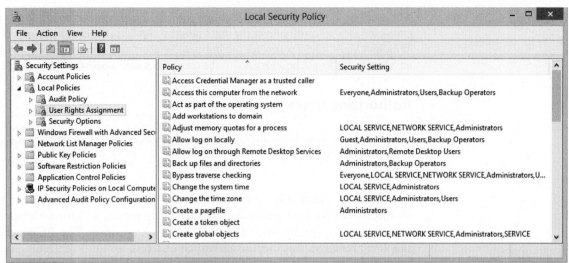

SKILL SUMMARY

IN THIS LESSON, YOU LEARNED:

- The user account is the fundamental unit of identity in the Windows operating systems.

- A group is an identifying token that Windows uses to represent a collection of users.

- A workgroup is a collection of computers that are all peers. A peer network is one in which every computer can function as both a server, by sharing its resources with other computers, and a client, by accessing the shared resources on other computers.

- A domain is a collection of computers that all utilize a central directory service for authentication and authorization.

- Windows 8.1 provides two separate interfaces for creating and managing local user accounts: the User Accounts (or user Accounts and Family Safety) control panel and the Local Users and Group snap-in for the Microsoft Management Console (MMC).

- Windows 8.1 supports a number of Group Policy settings that administrators can use to enforce password security practices on individual computers or on Active Directory Domain Services (AD DS) networks.

- Credential Manager is a Windows 8 tool that stores the user names and passwords people supply to servers and web sites in a protected area called the Windows Vault.

- The User Account Control (UAC) feature is designed to protect your computer from settings being changed accidentally and stop malware from gaining system-wide access to your system. In Windows 8.1, you cannot fully disable UAC without resorting to a registry edit, which is not recommended.

- The UAC feature displays two types of prompts. The credential prompt requests a user name and password when a standard user attempts to perform a task that requires administrative privilege. The elevation prompt prevents unauthorized processes, such as those initiated by malware, from accessing the system using administrative privileges.

■ Knowledge Assessment

Multiple Choice

Select one or more correct answers for each of the following questions.

1. Which of the following account lockout policy modifications could you make to ensure that user passwords cannot be intercepted by analyzing captured packets?
   a. Increase the Enforce Password History value.
   b. Enable the Password Must Meet Complexity Requirements setting.
   c. Decrease the Account Lockout Threshold value.
   d. Disable the Store Passwords Using Reversible Encryption policy.

2. Which of the following policy modifications would make it harder for intruders to penetrate user passwords by a brute force attack? (Choose all that apply.)
   a. Increase the value of the Reset Account Logon Counter After policy.
   b. Enable the Password Must Meet Complexity Requirements policy.
   c. Increase the Account Lockout Threshold value.
   d. Reduce the value of the Minimum Password Age policy.

3. The built-in local groups on a Windows 8.1 workstation receive their special capabilities through which of the following mechanisms?
   a. Security options
   b. Windows firewall rules
   c. NTFS permissions
   d. User rights

4. When you log on to a newly-installed Windows 8.1 computer for the first time, why can you not use the Administrator account?
   a. Local Security Policy prevents its use.
   b. The Administrator account has no password.
   c. There is no Administrator account.
   d. The Administrator account is disabled.

5. Which of the following statements is true?
   a. The User accounts control panel applet can create local users and local groups only.
   b. The User accounts control panel applet can create local and domain users.
   c. The User accounts control panel applet can create local users only.
   d. The User accounts control panel applet can create local users, local groups, domain users, and domain groups.

6. This Windows element contains a list of users for each permission-protected resource and the degree of access each user has to the resource.
   a. Access control list (ACL)
   b. Authorization control list (ACL)
   c. Authentication control list (ACL)
   d. Access control entry (ACE)

7. Your Windows 8.1 computer is currently a member of a workgroup that includes four other Windows 8.1 computers. If you want to access resources on all four of these computers, you must have a user account on how many of them?
   a. 1
   b. 5
   c. 4
   d. 2

8. Which of the following statements are true regarding domain and local user accounts? (Choose all that apply.)
   a. Local user accounts are stored in the Security Account Manager (SAM) database.
   b. Domain accounts can access local computer resources only.
   c. Local user accounts are created using the Active Directory Users and Computers MMC snap-in.
   d. Domain user accounts must be unique within the directory.

9. You have set the Account Lockout Duration policy setting to 15 and the Account Lockout Threshold to 3. What would be the result? (Choose all that apply.)
   a. A user will have to wait 15 minutes before Windows 8 automatically unlocks their account.
   b. The Administrator will have to unlock the user's account manually.
   c. A user will be allowed 3 invalid logon attempts before they are locked out.
   d. The user may get locked out due to normal user error during logon.

10. Which of the following provides you with the strongest level of password protection on a computer that contains sensitive data?
    a. PIN
    b. Picture Password
    c. A password created using 7 alphabetical characters.
    d. A password created using 7 characters including upper case, lower case, numerical characters and symbols.

11. Which of the following is the default configuration for User Account Control (UAC) in Windows 8.1?
    a. Always notify me
    b. Notify me only when apps try to make changes to my computer
    c. Notify me only when apps try to make changes to my computer (do not dim my desktop)
    d. Never notify me

12. Which of the following is the effect of setting the UAC configuration to *Never notify me* in Windows 8.1?
    a. It fully disables UAC
    b. It results in less notifications but does not fully disable UAC
    c. It allows the processes to run at a medium integrity level
    d. No notifications will be displayed

Best Answer

Choose the letter that corresponds to the best answer. More than one answer choice may achieve the goal. Select the BEST answer.

1. You would like to implement an identification method that would provide the best security when it comes to protecting sensitive information on your network. Which of the following would you recommend?
   a. PIN + Smart Card.
   b. Use 7 character passwords that are a combination of numbers, characters, and symbols.
   c. Use 8 character passwords that use alphanumeric characters.
   d. Use picture passwords.

2. You have a resource that you want to make available to only selected users on your domain-based network. Which of the following would provide the most efficient method of assigning and managing access to the resource as users join and leave the company?
   a. Assign permissions for the resource to each individual user's account.
   b. Assign permissions for the resource to a group that contains the selected users' accounts.
   c. Assign permission for the resource to the Authenticated Users group
   d. Assign permission for the resource to the Everyone group.

3. You would like to configure an Account Lockout Threshold policy that will protect your system from brute force attacks while still preventing lockouts from normal user error. Which value would you recommend for the Account Lockout Threshold setting?
   a. 1
   b. 2
   c. 3
   d. 5

4. A user lost their password and requested that an administrator reset it for them. Of the options listed below for resetting the password, which would have the least impact on the user assuming they have EFS-encrypted files on their computer?
   a. Using a password reset disk.
   b. Restoring from a backup of the Windows Vault.
   c. Using a backup of the user's EFS key.
   d. Resetting the user's password via the Local Users and Groups snap-in.

5. You want to configure an account lockout policy that will provide the best protection for your system against failed password attempts while still allowing you to know when someone has attempted to access your system. Which setting will allow you to accomplish this?
   a. Set the Account lockout threshold to lock out after 5 failed password attempts and the Account lockout duration to 0.
   b. Set the Account lockout threshold to lock out after 10 failed password attempts and the Account lockout duration to 1.
   c. Set the Account lockout threshold to lock out after 20 failed password attempts and the Account lockout duration to 10.
   d. Set the Account lockout threshold to lock out after 100 failed password attempts and the Account lockout duration to 100.

6. To have more granular control over UAC property settings on a Windows 8.1 computer that is joined to a workgroup, which of the following tools would you recommend?
   a. Group Policy
   b. Local Security Policy
   c. User Account Control Settings via Control Panel
   d. Edit the registry directly

Matching and Identification

Complete the following exercise by matching the terms with their corresponding definitions.

_____ **a)** Authentication
_____ **b)** Account Lockout Threshold
_____ **c)** Windows Biometric Framework
_____ **d)** User rights
_____ **e)** Authorization
_____ **f)** Group
_____ **g)** Workgroup
_____ **h)** Directory service
_____ **i)** Multifactor authentication
_____ **j)** Personal Identity Verification (PIV)

1. Allows Windows 8.1 to obtain drivers for smart cards from Windows Update or use a mini driver included with the operating system.
2. Specifies the number of invalid logon attempts that will trigger an account lockout.
3. The process of granting an authenticated user a specific degree of access to specific data resources.
4. The process of verifying that the identity of the person operating the computer is the same as the user account the person is employing to gain access.
5. Provides a core biometric functionality and a Biometric Device control panel.
6. Collection of computers that are all peers.
7. Policies that define specific operating system functions (e.g., allow log on locally).
8. Involves using more than one identification method.
9. Collection of logical objects that represent various types of network resources.
10. Used to represent a collection of users.

Build a List

1. In order of first to last, specify the correct order of steps create a Local Group.
   _____ Open the Computer Management console.
   _____ Right-click the **Groups** folder and then, from the context menu, select **New Group**.
   _____ Specify a Description for the group.
   _____ Type the names of the users that you want to add to the group, separated by semi colons, in the text box, and then click **OK**.
   _____ Click **Create** to create the group and populate it with the user(s) you specified.
   _____ Close the Computer Management console.
   _____ In the Group name text box, type the name you want to assign to the group.
   _____ Click the **Add** button.
   _____ In the console's scope pane, expand the Local Users and Groups node and click **Groups**.
   _____ Click **Close**.

2. Specify the correct order of steps to back up an existing Windows 8.1 certificate.
   _____ Right-click the certificate you want to backup and choose **All Tasks > Export** certificate.
   _____ Click the **Search** charm, choose **Settings** and then type **cert** in the search box.
   _____ Select the *file format* you want to use.
   _____ In the *Results* list, click **Manage user certificates** to load the snap-in.
   _____ Type a *name* for the file, browse to the location where you want to store the file and then click **Finish**.

3. You want to configure an Account Lockout Policy. Specify the correct order of steps to accomplish the task.
   _____ Open Control Panel and then click **System and Security > Administrative Tools**.
   _____ Double-click the policy you want to configure to open its' Properties sheet.
   _____ Expand the Account Policies header, and then click **Account Lockout Policy**.
   _____ Double-click **Local Security Policy**.
   _____ Configure the policy by setting a value using the spin box, radio button, or other control and then click **OK**.
   _____ Close the Local Security Policy console and the Administrative Tools window.

4. Someone accidentally changed the default setting for UAC to Never notify me. To return the Windows 8.1 computer to the recommended default setting, specify the correct order of steps to accomplish this task.

_____ In the *User Account Control Settings box, move the slider to Notify me only when apps try to make changes to my computer.*

_____ Log on to the Windows 8.1 computer with Administrator privileges.

_____ Click **OK**.

_____ From the Windows 8.1 Start menu, press the **Windows logo key + w**, type **uac**, and then from Results, choose **Change User Account Control** settings.

Business Case Scenarios

Scenario 15-1: Using Password and Account Lockout Policies

You are working on a corporate network owned by a company with several government contracts to develop classified technology. You have been assigned the task to create a set of password and account policy settings that meet the following criteria:

- Users must change passwords every four weeks and cannot reuse the same passwords for one year.

- User passwords must be at least 12 characters long, case sensitive, and consist of letters numbers and symbols.

- Users are allowed no more than three unsuccessful logon attempts before the account is permanently locked down until released by an administrator.

In the following table, enter the values for the policies that will meet these requirements.

POLICY SETTING	VALUE
Enforce Password History	
Maximum Password Age	
Minimum Password Age	
Minimum Password Length	
Password Must Meet Complexity Requirements	
Store Passwords Using Reversible Encryption	
Account Lockout Threshold	
Account Lockout Duration	
Reset Account Lockout Counter After	

Scenario 15-2: Recovering a Lost Password

A junior administrator has just informed you that a user on your network has lost their password. She would like to reset the password for the user. What advice would you provide her?

Scenario 15-3: Troubleshooting Access Denied Errors

One of your users was recently issued a new Windows 8.1 computer that was configured by a new administrator in your department. The user reports she received an access denied message while trying to view her disk properties using the Disk Management tool. The message was as follows: *You do not have access rights to Logical Disk Manager on Win8Pro.*

You remember the new administrator talking about local security policies and that he had been testing them a few days earlier. You suspect this could be the source of the problem. How would you troubleshoot this?

Configuring Remote Connections

70-687 EXAM OBJECTIVE

Objective 5.1 – Configure remote connections. This objective may include but is not limited to: configure remote authentication; configure Remote Desktop settings; configure virtual private network (VPN) connections and authentication; enable VPN reconnect; configure broadband tethering.

LESSON HEADING	EXAM OBJECTIVE
Using BranchCache	
Understanding Network Infrastructure Requirements	
Understanding BranchCache Communications	
Configuring BranchCache Settings	
Using Remote Network Connections	
Understanding Virtual Private Networking	
Authenticating Remote Users	Configure remote authentication Configure virtual private network (VPN) connections and authentication
Creating a VPN Connection	Configure virtual private network (VPN) connections and authentication Enable VPN reconnect
Creating a Broadband Connection	
Using Broadband Tethering	Configure broadband tethering
Using Remote Desktop	Configure Remote Desktop settings
Using DirectAccess	

KEY TERMS

BranchCache

DirectAccess

Extensible Authentication
   Protocol (EAP)

Internet Key Exchange, Version 2
   (IKEv2)

Layer 2 Tunneling Protocol
   (L2TP)

Microsoft Challenge Handshake
   Authentication Protocol

Point-to-Point Protocol (PPP)

Point-to-Point Tunneling
   Protocol (PPTP)

Protected Extensible
   Authentication Protocol
   (PEAP)

Secure Password
   (EAP-MSCHAPv2),

Secure Socket Tunneling
   Protocol (SSTP)

tunneling

virtual private network
   (VPN)

VPN Reconnect

■ Using BranchCache

THE BOTTOM LINE

BranchCache is a feature in Windows 8.1 and Windows Server 2012 R2 that enables networks with computers at remote locations to conserve bandwidth by storing frequently-accessed files on local drives.

Caching is a process in which computers copy frequently-used data to an intermediate storage medium so they can satisfy subsequent requests for the same data more quickly or less expensively. For example, virtually all computers have an area of high-speed memory between the system processor and the main system memory that functions as a cache. Repeated requests for the same data can be satisfied more quickly from the cache memory than the slower main memory. BranchCache works in much the same way, except that it is a disk storage cache that reduces the traffic between branch office computers and a server at another site.

Wide area network (WAN) connections between offices are slower and more expensive than the local area network (LAN) connections within an office. When a computer in a branch office requires a file stored on a server at the main office, the server must transmit the file over a WAN connection. If twenty computers at the branch office require that same file, the server must transmit it twenty times, using twenty times the WAN bandwidth.

BranchCache is a feature that can store a copy of the file on a computer (or computers) at the branch office site, so that the server only has to transmit the files over the WAN connection once. All of the subsequent requests access the file from the cache on the local network.

Understanding Network Infrastructure Requirements

To use BranchCache, you must have a server running Windows Server 2008 R2, Windows Server 2012, or Windows Server 2012 R2 at the main office and computers running Windows Server 2008 R2, Windows Server 2012, Windows Server 2012 R2, Windows 7, Windows 8, or Windows 8.1 at the branch office.

BranchCache is a client/server application that supports two operational modes, as follows:

- *Distributed cache mode* – Each Windows workstation on the branch office network caches data from the content server on its local drive and shares that cached data with other local workstations.

- *Hosted cache mode* – Windows workstations on the branch office network cache data from the content server on a branch office server, enabling other workstations to access the cached data from there.

Obviously, the major difference between the two modes is the need for a second, branch-office server in hosted cache mode, which makes the caching process more efficient, but which adds to the expense of the implementation. In distributed cache mode, each workstation is responsible for maintaining its own cache and processing cache requests from the other workstations on the local network.

Understanding BranchCache Communications

BranchCache clients and servers exchange relatively small messages among themselves, to coordinate their caching activities.

TAKE NOTE*

Only Windows 8.1 Enterprise includes BranchCache support for the SMB, HTTP, and BITS protocols. The BranchCache implementation in Windows 8.1 Pro supports only BITS traffic.

BranchCache supports file requests using Server Message Blocks (SMB), the standard Windows file sharing protocol, Hypertext Transfer Protocol (HTTP), the standard protocol for web communications, and the Background Intelligent Transfer Service (BITS). The traffic transmitted over the WAN consists primarily of small messages containing client requests and metadata replies, as well as one single copy of every requested file.

It is critical to understand that BranchCache is a read-only caching application. The metadata messages described here occurs only when branch office clients are requesting files from the content server, not when they are writing modified files back to the server. BranchCache does not support write caching, which is a far more complicated process, because the systems must account for the possibility of conflicts between multiple versions of the same file.

Configuring BranchCache Settings

To implement BranchCache on your network, you must install the appropriate modules on your server(s) and configure Group Policy settings on both servers and clients.

BranchCache requires a minimum of one content server and one or more branch office workstations. You can install additional content servers at any location that serves files to branch offices.

At the branch office, a typical BranchCache installation in distributed cache mode can support up to 50 workstations. To use hosted cache mode, you must have a branch office server at each location where there are branch office workstations.

CONFIGURING A CONTENT SERVER

To use BranchCache on your network, your files must be stored on a content server running Windows Server 2008 R2, Windows Server 2012, or Windows Server 2012 R2. To support SMB requests, the server must have the BranchCache for Network Files role service installed in the File and Storage Services role. To support HTTP and BITS requests, you must install the BranchCache feature.

Once you have installed the required BranchCache modules, you must configure a Group Policy setting called Hash Publication for BranchCache. This setting is located in the Computer Configuration\Policies\Administrative Templates\Network\Lanman Server node of a Group Policy object (GPO) or in Local Computer Policy.

The Hash Publication for BranchCache setting, shown in Figure 16-1, enables the server to respond to file requests from BranchCache clients with metadata instead of the files themselves. In this setting, you can stipulate that the server publish hash metadata for all of its shared files or for only the shares you select.

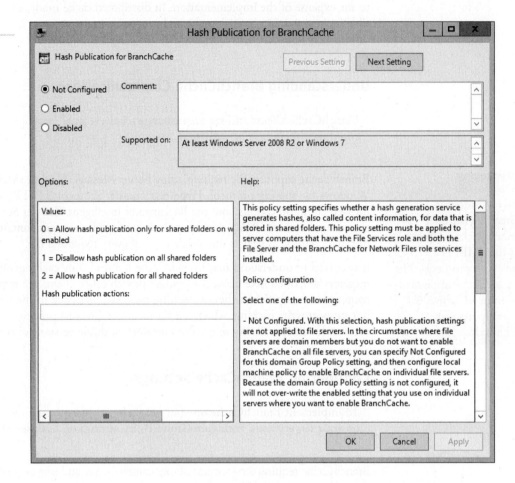

If you select the *Allow hash publication only for shared folders on which BranchCache is enabled* option, you must configure each share for which you want to enable BranchCache by opening the share's Properties sheet in the Windows Server 2012 or Windows Server 2012 R2 Server Manager console, as shown in Figure 16-2, or the Windows Server 2008 R2 Share and Storage Management console, and selecting an appropriate option.

Figure 16-2

A share's *Properties* sheet in Windows Server 2012 R2 Server Manager

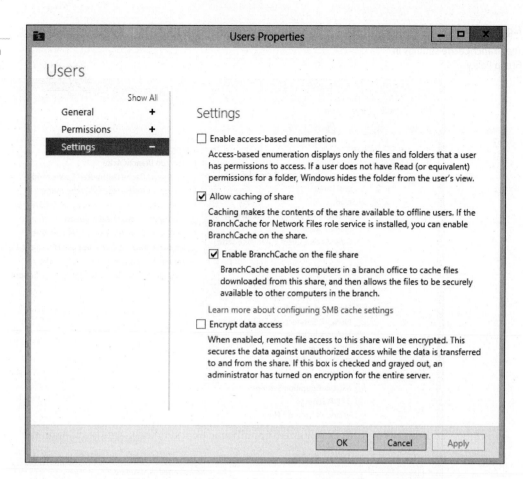

CONFIGURING BRANCHCACHE CLIENTS

BranchCache clients can be computers running Windows 8, Windows 8.1, Windows 7, Windows Server 2012 R2, Windows Server 2012, or Windows Server 2008 R2. BranchCache is installed by default in Windows 8.1, Windows 8 and Windows 7. To use a computer running Windows Server 2012 R2, Windows Server 2012, or Windows Server 2008 R2 as a BranchCache client, you must install the BranchCache feature.

To configure BranchCache clients, you must configure the appropriate Group Policy settings, found in the Computer Configuration\Policies\Administrative Templates\Network\ BranchCache node of a GPO or in Local Computer Policy, as shown in Figure 16-3.

Figure 16-3

The *BranchCache* settings in
Group Policy

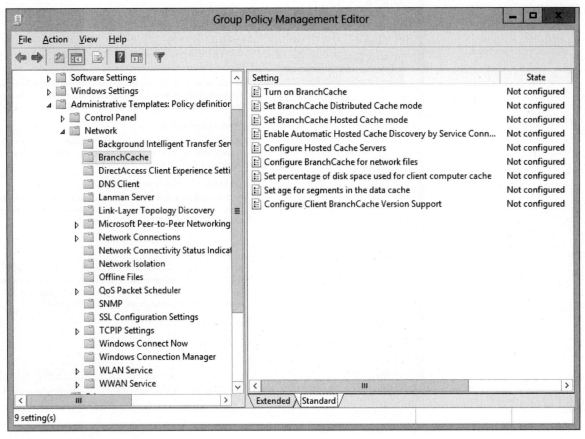

CONFIGURING A HOSTED CACHE MODE SERVER

To use hosted cache mode on your branch office network, you must have a server running
Windows Server 2012 R2, Windows Server 2012, or Windows Server 2008 R2 with the
BranchCache feature installed. You must also configure the *Turn on BranchCache* and *Set
BranchCache Hosted Cache mode* Group Policy settings.

The hosted cache mode server must also have a digital certificate issued by a certification
authority (CA) that the BranchCache clients trust. You can install an internal CA on the
network and use it to issue the certificate, or obtain a certificate from a commercial,
third-party CA.

Once you have obtained the certificate, you must use the Certificates snap-in on the
hosted cache server to import it. Finally, you must link the certificate to the
BranchCache service by opening an elevated command prompt and typing the following
command, replacing the thumbprint variable with the thumbprint value from the certificate you imported.

```
netsh http add sslcert ipport=0.0.0.0:443
certhash=thumbprint appid={d673f5ee-a714-454d-8de2-492e4c1bd8f8}
```

■ Using Remote Network Connections

<table>
<tr>
<td>

↓
<u>**THE BOTTOM LINE**</u>

</td>
<td>

Windows supports two types of remote client connections: dial-up, which typically uses standard asynchronous modems and telephone lines, and virtual private networking, which uses the Internet as the medium connecting the client to the remote access server. In addition, Windows 8.1 includes support for a new type of remote connection called DirectAccess, which eliminates the need to manually establish a connection to a remote server.

</td>
</tr>
</table>

While new technologies such as BranchCache aid technical specialists in maintaining permanent or semi-permanent links between remote sites, they do not address the other type of remote user: the traveling or telecommuting worker that must connect to the company network from a remote site. These workers do not have permanent connections, so they cannot log on to the network in the usual manner. However, Windows provides a number of remote solutions that enable these users to access network resources from any location with a telephone line or an Internet connection.

Remote network access is a client/server application, so administrators must plan and implement a server infrastructure at the network site before Windows clients can connect to it. The first step in planning a Remote Access solution for an enterprise network is to decide which connection type you plan to use. To use dial-up connections, you must equip your servers with at least one modem and telephone line. For a single-user connection, as for an administrator dialing in from home, a standard off-the-shelf modem is suitable. For multiple connections, there are modular rack-mounted modems available that enable you to connect dozens of users at once, if necessary.

In today's networking world, however, hardware and telephone costs and the near-ubiquity of high-speed Internet connections have caused dial-up remote connections to be almost entirely replaced by virtual private network (VPN) connections.

Understanding Virtual Private Networking

> Virtual private network connections violate standard networking concepts to provide security for private connections transmitted over the public Internet.

A dial-up connection is a dedicated link between the two modems that remains in place during the entire session, as shown in Figure 16-4. The client and the server establish a ***Point-to-Point Protocol (PPP)*** connection, during which the server authenticates the client and the computers negotiate a set of communication parameters they have in common. PPP takes the place of the Ethernet protocol at the data-link layer, by encapsulating the datagrams created by the Internet Protocol (IP) at the network layer, to prepare them for their transmission. PPP is much simpler than Ethernet because the two computers are using a dedicated connection, and there is no need to address each packet to a particular destination, as they must do on a local area network (LAN).

Figure 16-4

A dial-up remote access connection

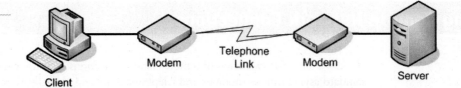

In a ***virtual private network (VPN)*** connection, the remote client and the remote access server are both connected to the Internet, using local service providers, as shown in Figure 16-5. This eliminates the expense of long distance telephone charges common to dial-up connections, as well as the additional hardware expense, since both computers most likely have Internet connections already. The client establishes a connection to the server using the Internet as a network medium and, after authentication, the server grants the client access to the network.

Figure 16-5

A VPN remote access connection

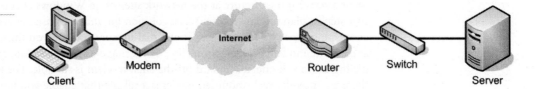

While it is theoretically possible for someone to tap into the telephone line used by a dial-up connection, intercept the analog signals exchanged by the two modems, convert them into digital data packets, and access the data, it is not likely to occur and remote connections are almost never compromised in this manner. Therefore, the data transmitted during a dial-up connection is considered to be relatively secure.

A VPN is another matter, however, because the client and the server transmit their data over the Internet, which makes the data packets accessible to anyone with the equipment needed to capture them. For this reason, VPN clients and servers use a specialized protocol when establishing a connection, which encapsulates their data packets inside another packet, a process called ***tunneling***. The VPN protocol establishes a virtual connection, or tunnel, between the client and the server, which encrypts data encapsulated inside.

In the tunneling process, the two computers establish a PPP connection, just as they would in a dial-up connection, but instead of transmitting the PPP packets over the Internet as they are, they encapsulate the packets again using one of the VPN protocols supported by the Windows operating systems. As shown in Figure 16-6, the original PPP data packet generated by the computer consists of an network layer IP datagram, encapsulated within a data-link layer PPP frame. The system then encapsulates the entire frame in another IP datagram, which the VPN protocol encrypts and encapsulates one more time, for transmission over the network.

Figure 16-6

VPN protocol encapsulation

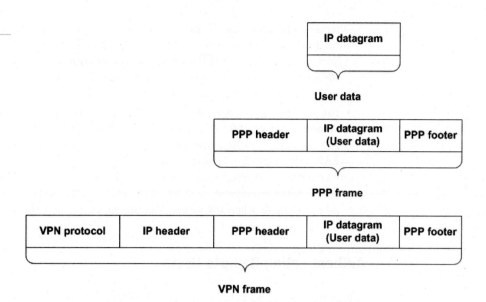

Having a data-link layer frame inside an network layer datagram is a violation of the Open System Interconnection (OSI) reference model's most basic principles, but this is what makes tunneling an effective carrier mechanism for private data transmitted over a public network. Intruders can intercept the transmitted packets, but they cannot decrypt the inner PPP frame, which prevents them from obtaining any of the information inside

The VPN protocols that Windows 8.1 supports are as follows:

- ***Point-to-Point Tunneling Protocol (PPTP)*** – The oldest and least secure of the VPN protocols, PPTP takes advantage of the authentication, compression, and encryption mechanisms of PPP, tunneling the PPP frame within a Generic Routing Encapsulation (GRE) header and encrypting it with Microsoft Point-to-Point Encryption (MPPE), using encryption keys generated during the authentication process. PPTP therefore can provide data protection, but not other services, such as packet origin identification or data integrity checking. For authentication, PPTP supports only the ***Microsoft Challenge Handshake Authentication Protocol*** version 1 (MS-CHAP v1), Microsoft Challenge Handshake Authentication Protocol version 2 (MS-CHAP v2), ***Extensible Authentication Protocol (EAP), or Protected Extensible Authentication Protocol (PEAP)***. Although it can use them (with EAP), one of the advantages of PPTP is that it does not require the use of certificates. In most cases, organizations use PPTP as a fallback protocol for clients running non-Windows operating systems.

- ***Layer 2 Tunneling Protocol (L2TP)*** – L2TP relies on the IP security extensions (IPsec) for encryption, and as a result performs a double encapsulation. The system adds an L2DP header to the PPP frame and packages it with the User Datagram Protocol (UDP). Then it encapsulates the UDP datagram with the IPsec Encapsulating Security Payload (ESP) protocol, encrypting the contents using the Data Encryption Standard (DES) or Triple DES (3DES) algorithm, with encryption keys generated during IPsec's Internet Key Exchange (IKE) negotiation process. L2TP/IPsec can use certificates or preshared keys for authentication, although administrators typically use the latter only for testing. The end result is that the L2TP/IPsec combination provides a more complete set of services than PPTP, including packet origin identification, data integrity checking, and replay protection. For VPN connections involving Windows clients, L2TP/IPsec is the preferred protocol.

- ***Secure Socket Tunneling Protocol (SSTP)*** – Introduced in Windows Server 2008 and supported only by clients running Windows Vista SP1 or later, SSTP encapsulates PPP traffic using the Secure Sockets Layer (SSL) protocol supported by virtually all Web servers. The advantage of this is that administrators do not have to open an additional external firewall port in the server, as SSTP uses the same TCP port 443 as Secure Sockets Layer (SSL). SSTP uses certificates for authentication, with the EAP-TLS authentication protocol, and in addition to data encryption, provides integrity checking and enhanced key negotiation services.

- *Internet Key Exchange, Version 2 (IKEv2)* – First introduced in Windows 7 and Windows Server 2008 R2, IKEv2 uses TCP port 500 and provides support for IPv6 and the new VPN Reconnect feature, as well as authentication by EAP, using PEAP, EAP-MSCHAPv2, or smart cards. IKEv2 does not support the older authentication mechanisms, however, such as PAP and CHAP. By default, Windows 8.1 computers use IKEv2 when attempting to connect to remote access servers, only falling back to the other protocols when the server does not support it as well.

Authenticating Remote Users

> Windows remote access connections use an authentication system that is entirely separate from the Kerberos authentication system that clients on the local network use. However, authentication is even more important for remote access clients than for local ones, because of the increased likelihood of intrusion.

CERTIFICATION READY
Configure remote authentication
Objective 5.1

CERTIFICATION READY
Configure virtual private network (VPN) connections and authentication
Objective 5.1

All remote access connections, whether dial-up or VPN, use PPP to package their data, and the PPP connection establishment process includes a sequence in which the client and the server negotiate the use of a specific authentication protocol. In this sequence, each computer sends a list of the authentication protocols it supports to the other, and the two then agree to use the strongest protocol they have in common.

In Windows 8.1, you configure the authentication method a VPN connection uses on the Security tab of the connection's Properties sheet, as shown in Figure 16-7. The options are as follows:

- **Use Extensible Authentication Protocol (EAP)** – EAP is a shell protocol that provides a framework for the use of various types of authentication mechanisms. The primary advantage of EAP is that it enables a computer to use mechanisms other than passwords for authentication, including public key certificates and smart cards, as well as providing an extensible environment for third-party authentication mechanisms. Windows 8.1 supports three types of EAP-based authentication Protected EAP (PEAP), *Secure Password (EAP-MSCHAPv2)*, and Smart Card or other certificate. EAP-MSCHAPv2, the default selection for new connections and the strongest password-based mechanism in Windows 8.1, requires a certificate only at the server. The Smart Card or other certificates option requires the clients, as well as the server, to have a certificate, stored either on a smart card or in the computer's certificate store.

- **Allow these protocols** – Provides support for the Password Authentication Protocol (PAP), Challenge Handshake Authentication Protocol (CHAP), and Microsoft Challenge Handshake Authentication Protocol Version 2 (MSCHAPv2), which are included to provide support for downlevel clients. These protocols apply only to PPTP, L2TP, and SSTP connections; IKEv2 connections must use EAP-MSCHAPv2 or a certificate.

Figure 16-7

The *Security* tab of a connection's *Properties* sheet

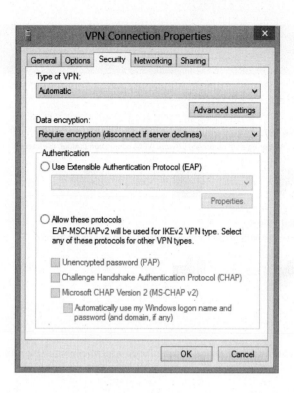

Creating a VPN Connection

To connect a computer running Windows 8.1 to a remote access server, you must create a new VPN or dial-up connection.

CERTIFICATION READY
Configure virtual private network (VPN) connections and authentication
Objective 5.1

In Windows 8.1, the Network Connections window contains a connection for every network interface adapter installed in the computer. The Windows installation program creates these connections automatically, but to connect to a dial-up or VPN server, you must create additional connections manually.

To create a VPN connection, use the following procedure.

CREATE A VPN CONNECTION

GET READY. Log on to Windows 8.1 using an account with administrative privileges and then perform the following steps:

1. Open the Windows Control Panel and then click **Network and Internet > Network and Sharing Center**.

   The *Network and Sharing Center* control panel appears.

2. Click **Set up a new connection or network**.

   The *Set Up a Connection or Network* wizard appears, displaying the *Choose a connection option* page.

3. Click **Connect to a workplace** and then click **Next**.

   The *How do you want to connect?* page appears, as shown in Figure 16-8.

Figure 16-8

The *How do you want to connect?* page

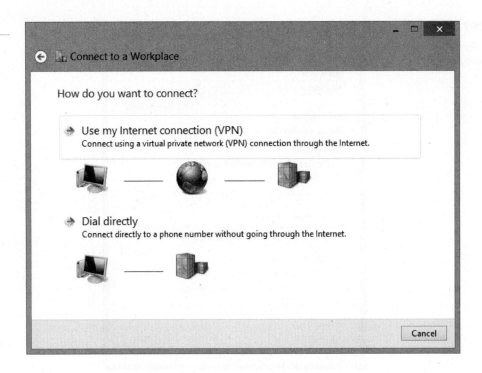

4. Click **Use my Internet connection (VPN)**.

   The *Type the Internet address to connect to* page appears, as shown in Figure 16-9.

Figure 16-9

The *Type the Internet address to connect to* page

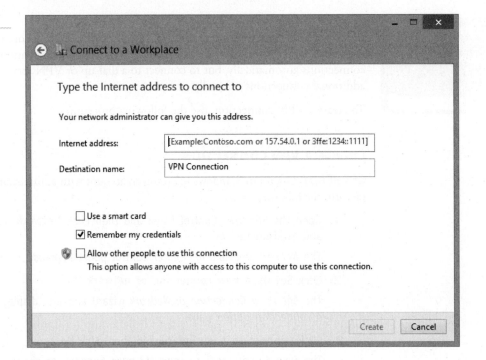

TAKE NOTE *

The process of configuring a dial-up connection is essentially similar to that of creating a VPN connection, except that for a dial-up, you must specify a phone number to call and configure other dialing criteria.

5. In the *Internet address* text box, type the fully-qualified domain name or IP address of the remote server to which you want to connect.

6. In the *Destination name* text box, type a descriptive name for the connection.

7. Click **Create**.

   The connection you created appears in the Networks display in the right fly-out pane.

Once you have created the connection, you can open the Network Connections window, right-click the icon and select Properties to display the connection's Properties sheet. From here, you can reconfigure the options you just set in the wizard, plus configure all of the other settings for the connection, such as the VPN and authentication protocols it should use.

To activate the connection, you select it in the Networks display, and a Network Authentication pane appears, as shown in Figure 16-10. After supplying credentials appropriate for the VPN server, the system establishes the connection between the two.

Figure 16-10

The *Network Authentication* pane

CERTIFICATION READY
Enable VPN reconnect
Objective 5.1

USING VPN RECONNECT

When a VPN connection is interrupted for any reason, it has always been necessary for the user to manually re-establish the connection. In recent years, the growing use of wireless Internet connections in public places has made this more of a problem. When a connection is interrupted, or a user moves from one access point to another, reconnecting to a VPN server can be an irritating chore.

Windows 8.1 includes a feature called ***VPN Reconnect***, based on the IKEv2 Mobility and Multihoming (MOBIKE) protocol, which enables a computer to reconnect to a VPN server automatically, after an interruption as long as eight hours. VPN only works with connections that use the IKEv2 protocol, which means that the client must be running Windows 8 or Windows 8.1 and the remote access server must be running at least Windows Server 2008 R2.

To configure VPN Reconnect, you open the Properties sheet for a VPN connection, click the Security tab, and click Advanced settings. In the Advanced Properties dialog box that appears, click the IKEv2 tab and select the Mobility checkbox, as shown in Figure 16-11. The default network outage time is 30 minutes, but you can configure it to be as short as 5 minutes or as long as 8 hours.

Figure 16-11

Enabling VPN Reconnect

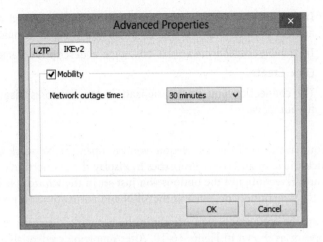

Creating a Broadband Connection

While many Internet Service Providers (ISPs) offer broadband services that provide "always on" connections to the Internet, some still offer metered connections that require users to log on and log off. Windows 8.1 provides wizard options that enable you to create a broadband connection that you can activate and deactivate at will.

To create a broadband connection to the Internet, use the following procedure.

 CREATE A BROADBAND CONNECTION

GET READY. Connect your computer to the modem or other hardware providing access to your ISP's network and log on to Windows 8.1 using an account with administrative privileges. Then perform the following steps:

1. Open the Windows control Panel and then click **Network and Internet** > **Network and Sharing Center**.

   The *Network and Sharing Center* control panel appears.

2. Click **Set up a new connection or network**.

   The *Set Up a Connection or Network* wizard appears, displaying the *Choose a connection option* page.

3. Click **Connect to the Internet**, and then click **Next**.

   The *How do you want to connect?* page appears.

4. Click **Broadband (PPPoE)**.

   The *Type the information from your Internet Service Provider (ISP)* page appears, as shown in Figure 16-12.

Figure 16-12

The *Type the information from your Internet Service Provider (ISP)* page

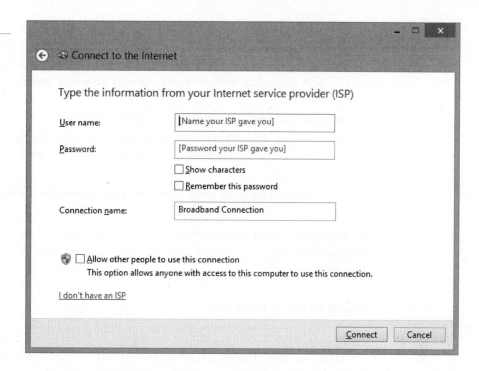

5. In the *User name* and *Password* text boxes, type the credentials provided by your ISP.

6. In the *Connection name* text box, type a descriptive name for the connection.

7. Click **Connect**.

   The wizard attempts to connect to the ISP's network and creates the connection. A *The connection to the Internet is ready to use* page appears.

8. Click **Close**.

   The wizard adds the connection you created to the Networks display in the right fly-out pane.

Using Broadband Tethering

> Broadband tethering is a new Windows 8.1 feature that enables a portable computer with a mobile broadband connection to function as a wireless "hot spot," sharing its Internet connection with other devices.

CERTIFICATION READY
Configure broadband tethering
Objective 5.1

Configuring broadband tethering is simply a matter of sharing your existing connection. To enable broadband tethering, use the following procedure.

 CONFIGURE BROADBAND TETHERING

GET READY. Connect your portable computer to the modem or other hardware providing broadband access to your ISP's network and log on to Windows 8.1 using an account with administrative privileges.

1. Open the Charms bar on the right side of the Windows Start screen and click Settings.

2. On the Settings screen, click Change PC settings.

3. On the PC Settings screen, click Network.

4. On the Network screen, under Mobile Broadband, select your connection.

5. On the screen named for your connection, click the *Share this connection* slider to turn it on, The network name, network password, and number of connected users appears.

6. Click Edit. An Edit network info screen appears.

7. Specify a different network name and password, if desired. These are the credentials that users will need to access your shared wireless broadband connection.

8. Click Save.

9. Click the back arrow twice to return to the PC settings screen.

At this point, wireless users will be able to select your connection, using the network name you specified, and connect using the password. Up to ten users can access the shared connection simultaneously.

Using Remote Desktop

In Lesson 12, "Configuring Remote Management", you learned how you can use Remote Desktop to connect to computers on the network and administer them from any location. It is also possible to use this Remote Desktop technology to provide clients with access to network computers and individual applications, even when the clients are at a remote location.

CERTIFICATION READY
Configure Remote
Desktop settings
Objective 5.1

Windows Server 2012 R2 includes a role called Remote Desktop Services, which provides clients with access to server resources in a variety of ways. The Remote Desktop Session Host role service functions much like the Remote Desktop Services service in Windows 8.1, except that it can provide multiple (licensed) users with access to the server desktop.

To provide remote clients with this type of access, using their standard Internet connections, there is a role service called Remote Desktop Gateway. Users at remote sites can use the standard Remote Desktop Connection client included with Windows 8.1 to connect to the gateway, and the gateway provides access to the Remote Desktop server.

TAKE NOTE *

Prior to Windows Server 2008 R2, Remote Desktop Services was known as Terminal Services, and the Remote Desktop Gateway as the Terminal Services Gateway. The services are essentially the same; only the names have been changed.

To access Remote Desktop Services using an Internet connection, you must open the Remote Desktop Connection client, click the Options arrow, click the Advanced tab, and then click Settings to display the RD Server Gateway Settings dialog box. Here, you specify the name or address of the Remote Desktop Gateway server and specify how you intend to log on.

Another new feature introduced in Windows Server 2008 is RemoteApp, which enables clients to access individual applications running on a Remote Desktop server. Unlike the standard Remote Desktop session, which creates a full-featured desktop at the client, RemoteApp enables servers to publish applications that appear on the client in separate windows, no different in appearance from applications running on the local computer.

Using DirectAccess

> **DirectAccess** is a feature in Windows 8.1 and Windows Server 2012 R2 that enables remote users to automatically connect to the company network whenever they have Internet access.

For many end-users, the entire concept of network computing is difficult to comprehend. There are people who don't know which resources are on their local drives and which are on network servers, and what's more, they don't care. They just want to be able to turn the machine on and know that it will work.

This issue can be particularly vexing for users that are traveling or working from home, and don't have immediate access to technical support. A VPN connection can provide them with access to the company network, but they have to remember to initiate the connection first. And if the connection should fail while they are working, they have to re-establish it, a process that can take several minutes each time a failure occurs.

Windows 8.1 and Windows Server 2012 R2 include a remote access solution called DirectAccess, which addresses these problems by enabling clients to remain connected to their host networks whenever they have access to the Internet, reconnecting automatically whenever it is necessary.

Designed as a replacement for VPNs, DirectAccess eliminates the need for client users to manually establish wide area connections to their networks. As soon as the client computer accesses the Internet, the system automatically initiates the connection to the network. If the client becomes disconnected from the Internet, such as when the user wanders out of range of a WiFi hot spot, DirectAccess re-establishes the network connection as soon as the client regains access to the Internet.

DirectAccess provides many other benefits to users and administrators, including the following:

- **Bidirectional** – Network administrators can initiate connections to client computers, to install updates and perform maintenance tasks.
- **Encrypted** – All intranet traffic between DirectAccess clients and servers is encrypted using the IPsec protocols.
- **Authenticated** – DirectAccess clients perform both a computer authentication and a user authentication, and support the use of smart cards or biometric devices, such as fingerprint scanners.
- **Authorized** – Administrators can grant DirectAccess clients full intranet access or limit them to specific resources.
- **Verified** – Administrators can use Network Access Protection (NAP) and Network Policy Server (NPS) to screen clients for the latest updates before allowing them access to the network.

SKILL SUMMARY

IN THIS LESSON, YOU LEARNED:

- BranchCache is a feature in Windows 8.1 and Windows Server 2012 R2 that enables networks with computers at remote locations to conserve bandwidth by storing frequently-accessed files on local drives.

- Windows 8.1 includes remote access client capabilities that enable users to connect to a network using dial-up or virtual private network (VPN) connections.

- In a virtual private network (VPN) connection, the remote client and the remote access server are both connected to the Internet, using local service providers. The client establishes a connection to the server using the Internet as a network medium and, after authentication, the server grants the client access to the network.

- Windows 8.1 and Windows Server 2012 R2 include a remote access solution called DirectAccess, which enables clients to remain connected to their host networks whenever they have access to the Internet.

■ Knowledge Assessment

Multiple Choice

Select one or more correct answers for each of the following questions.

1. Which of the following operating systems cannot use BranchCache? (Choose all that apply.)
   a. Windows Vista
   b. Windows Server 2008
   c. Windows Server 2008 R2
   d. Windows 7

2. BranchCache is a client/server application that supports which of the following two operational modes?
   a. Content Server cache mode
   b. Workstation cache mode
   c. Distributed cache mode
   d. Hosted cache mode

3. Which of the following is the most secure password-based authentication protocol supported by the VPN client in Windows 7?
   a. EAP (PEAP)
   b. EAP-MSCHAPv2
   c. CHAP
   d. POP

4. Which of the following IPv6/IPv4 transition technologies takes the form of a hardware device?
   a. ISATAP
   b. 6to4
   c. NAT-PT
   d. Teredo

5. What is the main advantage of using DirectAccess instead of VPN connections? (Choose all that apply.)
   a. Users don't have to manually connect to the remote network.
   b. DirectAccess uses IPv4 rather than IPv6.
   c. DirectAccess supports more operating systems than VPNs.
   d. DirectAccess connections are unidirectional.

6. Which of the following protocols does a dial-up client use to connect to a remote access server?
   a. PPTP
   b. L2TP
   c. PPP
   d. IPsec

Best Answer

Choose the letter that corresponds to the best answer. More than one answer choice may achieve the goal. Select the BEST answer.

1. Which of the following is the best remote access solution for users that have a minimal understanding of how networks operate?
   a. Dial-up access
   b. Metered broadband
   c. Virtual private network
   d. DirectAccess

2. Which of the following is the best remote access solution for network administrators who are looking for the simplest possible client configuration procedure?
   a. Dial-up access
   b. Metered broadband
   c. Virtual private network
   d. DirectAccess

3. Which of the following is the best remote access solution for network administrators who are servicing clients that will be traveling in a country that blocks all access to the Internet?
   a. Dial-up access
   b. Metered broadband
   c. Virtual private network
   d. DirectAccess

Build a List

1. Place the following steps of the broadband tethering configuration process in the correct order:
   _____ a) Click Settings.
   _____ b) Edit the network name and password.
   _____ c) Open the charms bar.
   _____ d) Select a mobile broadband connection
   _____ e) Click PPC Settings.
   _____ f) Click Network.
   _____ g) Turn on connection sharing.

Scenario 16-1: Deploying BranchCache

Ralph is an IT director who is trying to reduce the enormous WAN costs incurred by his network. Towards this end, he is using BranchCache in hosted cache mode in each of his company's five branch offices. Workers in the branches must frequently access case log files stored on servers at the company headquarters, update them with new information, and save them back to the server.

The content servers at the headquarters are all running Windows Server 2012 R2 and the BranchCache clients are a mixture of Windows 7 and Windows 8.1. Each branch office also has a hosted cache server running Windows Server 2008 R2.

After installing the required roles and features on the servers, and after configuring the appropriate Group Policy settings, Ralph has only noticed a slight reduction in WAN traffic. Describe two ways that Ralph can modify the installation to reduce the WAN traffic further.

Configuring Mobility Options

70-687 EXAM OBJECTIVE

Objective 5.2 – Configure mobility options. This objective may include but is not limited to: configure offline file policies; configure power policies; configure Windows To Go; configure sync options; configure Wi-Fi direct.

LESSON HEADING	EXAM OBJECTIVE
Using Windows Mobility Controls	
Opening Windows Mobility Center	
Configuring Mobile Display Options	
Configuring Presentation Settings	
Configuring Power Options	Configure power policies
Synchronizing Data	Configure offline file policies Configure sync options
Using Wi-Fi Direct	Configure Wi-Fi Direct
Configuring Windows To Go	Configure Windows To Go

KEY TERMS

Offline Files

Sync Center

transparent caching

Windows Mobility Center

Wi-Fi Direct

■ Using Windows Mobility Controls

THE BOTTOM LINE

As the computer market continues its trend towards smaller, more portable devices, the Windows Mobility Center becomes an increasingly important tool to many more users, providing convenient access to Windows 8.1's most frequently used mobile configuration settings.

Windows 8.1 includes a number of special tools designed specifically for mobile PCs, including smartphones, tablets, and all classes of laptop computers. Some of these tools take advantage of features that are unique to mobile computers, whereas others simply consolidate frequently used settings into a single interface.

Opening Windows Mobility Center

Windows Mobility Center provides users with quick access to the configuration settings most commonly adjusted by mobile computer users.

Windows Mobility Center is a shell application. It performs no special functions of its own; it simply provides a central point of access for many of the configuration settings that mobile computer users need frequently. These settings are located in various Control Panel applets, but placing them in a single window enables users to make adjustments quickly and easily. This is particularly beneficial to business users that give presentations with their portable computers.

To open the Windows Mobility Center on a Windows 8.1 mobile computer, open the Control Panel and click Hardware and Sound > Windows Mobility Center to display the window shown in Figure 17-1. You can also press the WIN+X key combination and select Mobility Center from the context menu that appears.

Figure 17-1

The Windows Mobility Center

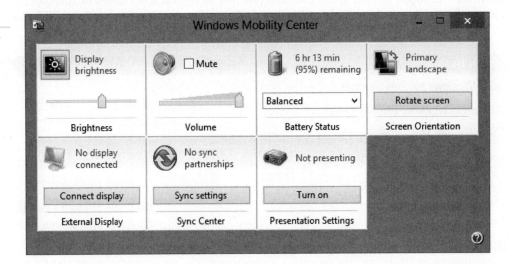

TAKE NOTE*

Windows 8.1 identifies mobile devices during the operating system installation and configures them to display the Windows Mobility Center and the controls specific to the hardware in the machine. Therefore, the Windows Mobility Center icon will not appear in a desktop computer's Control Panel.

The Windows Mobility Center window is divided into as many as eight tiles. The tiles that appear and the controls in them depend on the type of computer you are using, its hardware components, and the software supplied by the computer's manufacturer. You can modify configuration settings by using the controls that appear in the Windows Mobility Center window or by clicking the icon in one of the tiles to open the corresponding Control Panel applet.

The eight tiles that can appear in the Windows Mobility Center are as follows:

- **Brightness** – Enables the user to adjust the brightness of the computer's display.
- **Volume** – Enables the user to adjust the volume of the computer's speakers, or mute them completely.
- **Battery Status** – Displays the computer's current power status (AC or battery) and the battery's charge, as well as enabling the user to select one of the computer's power plans.
- **Wireless Network** – Displays the status of the computer's wireless network connection and enables the user to turn the wireless network adapter on or off.
- **Screen Orientation** – On a tablet PC, enables the user to toggle the computer's display orientation between portrait and landscape.
- **External Display** – Enables the user to connect an external display to the computer and modify the display settings.
- **Sync Center** – Enables the user to set up a sync partnership, start a sync event, or monitor the status of a sync event in progress.

- **Presentation Settings** – When turned on, prevents presentations from being interrupted by screen savers, alarms, and attempts to put the computer to sleep. This tile also enables the user to adjust the settings most often used during a presentation, such as the screen saver, the speaker volume, and the desktop background.

Configuring Mobile Display Options

To accommodate presentation audiences and other situations, mobile users are likely to adjust their display settings more frequently than desktop users.

One of the biggest benefits of mobile computing is the ability to collaborate with other users, bringing your data and your applications with you. Many portable computers have the capability to connect an external display device, making it possible for a group of users to view the desktop without having to crowd around a single small screen. Many people use this external display capability to give lectures, presentations, or demonstrations, using a variety of external display technologies.

Administrators should be familiar with the computer capabilities, configuration settings, and controls used to manage the display options, as discussed in the following settings.

CONNECTING AN EXTERNAL DISPLAY

In most cases, the ability to connect an external display to a portable computer depends on the system's hardware and software. Many portables include an external video port, such as a VGA (Video Graphics Array), DVI (Digital Visual Interface), S-Video, High-Definition Multimedia Interface (HDMI), or DisplayPort connector, which enables you to attach an external display to the computer, and video drivers that enable you to configure the properties of each display separately.

At its simplest, an external display can be a standard desktop monitor—analog or digital, LCD or CRT—connected to the portable device and configured to mirror the image on the device's own display. If the computer has an HDMI, DisplayPort, or S-Video jack, it is also possible to connect a similarly equipped television set. The user can then work with the computer in the normal manner, and a group of observers can follow the user's action on the external monitor. However, for more elaborate presentations or large audiences, many users employ a display projector, which is a device that uses computer display technology to project an image on a large screen or wall.

Installing the hardware is simply a matter of connecting the external display to the computer using whatever port is provided. VGA and DVI ports are designed for computer monitors. CRTs and lower-end LCD monitors use the standard 15-pin VGA port, while many LCD monitors use the 29-pin DVI connector. However, some DVI monitors come with an adapter that enables you to plug them into a computer with only a VGA port. Many of the small form-factor portable computers now on the market, such as tablets and ultrabooks, are equipped with HDMI or DisplayPort connectors, which are smaller than DVI and VGA connectors and can carry audio as well as video signals.

Portable computers that have a port for an external monitor typically have a video adapter that is capable of supporting two display configurations. This adapter, plus the device driver that goes with it, enables you to configure the displays using different resolutions, if necessary, and to choose how to use the two displays.

CONFIGURING MULTIPLE DISPLAYS

Windows 8.1 provides two ways to control the second display. Typically, when you plug a second display into a port, and the system is able to detect it, the current display is mirrored on the secondary device. To modify this default configuration, you can open the Windows Mobility Center and, in the Display tile, click or tap the Disconnect Display button. This causes a fly-out Second Screen menu to appear on the right side of the screen, as shown in Figure 17-2.

TAKE NOTE

Original equipment manufacturers (OEMs) can also modify the default Windows Mobility Center display, to add their own tiles controlling model-specific hardware and software features.

Figure 17-2

The *Second Screen* menu

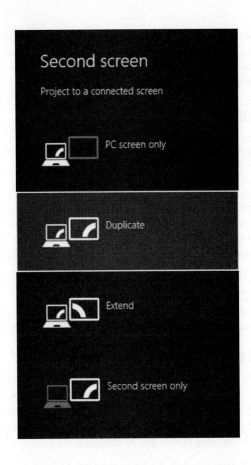

From this menu, you can select whether the system should use one display or the other, mirror the same content on both displays, or extend the interface to encompass both displays. With these options, the user can allow an audience to see the same content he or she is seeing on the device, or play a video or slide show on the secondary display while reading from notes or other documents shown on the primary.

The other method for controlling the displays is to open the Display control panel and click **Adjust resolution** to open the Screen Resolution dialog box, as shown in Figure 17-3. You can also open this dialog box by clicking or tapping the icon in the Display tile of the Windows Mobility Center.

Figure 17-3

Mirrored displays in the *Screen Resolution* dialog box

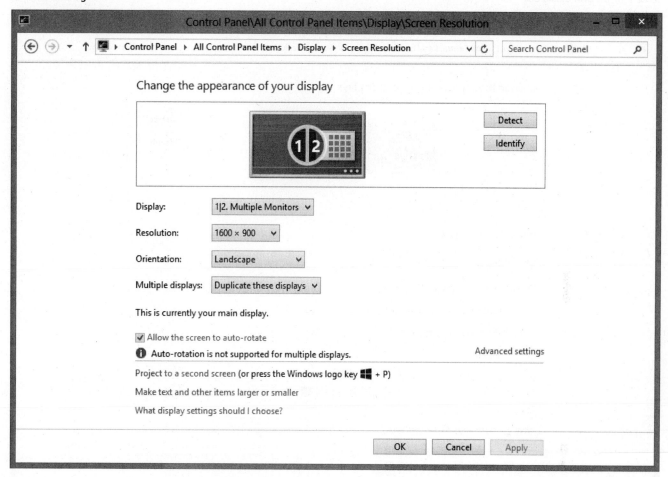

When the system is configured to mirror the displays, they must use the same resolution, and other settings, so any changes you make to the display configuration apply to both. However, if you opt to extend the screen to the second display, using either the Second Screen menu or by selecting Extend these displays in the Multiple Monitors drop down list of the Screen Resolution dialog box, the two displays appear as separate entities, as shown in Figure 17-4.

Figure 17-4

An extended display in the
Screen Resolution dialog box

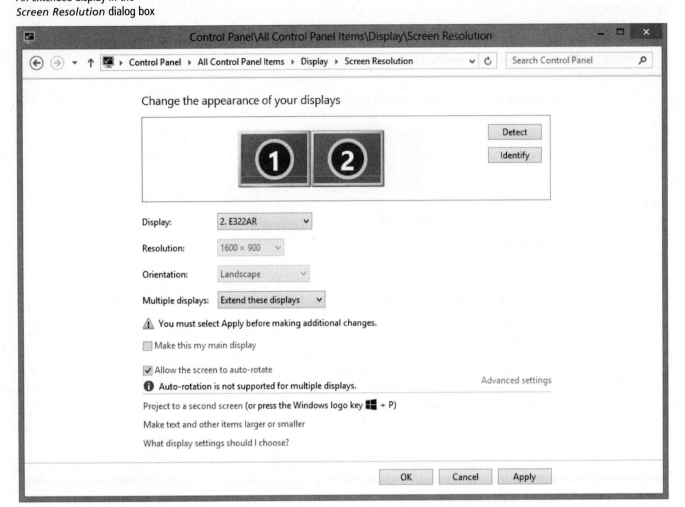

In this arrangement, you can configure the displays independently. When you select one of the displays, by clicking or tapping one of the numbered icons, or by selecting from the Display drop down list, you can specify a resolution and orientation that will apply to the selected display only.

USING A DISPLAY PROJECTOR

For presentations to larger audiences, many portable computer users prefer to use a display projector as an external display, instead of a standard monitor. A display projector is a device that works much like a monitor, except that instead of creating an image on an LED, LCD, or plasma display, it projects a live image of the computer's desktop onto a screen.

Most display projectors can connect to a computer's video port, just like a regular monitor. Some have HDMI or DisplayPort connects that provide access to an audio system as well. Some of the more advanced (and expensive) models can even connect directly to a network, either wired or wireless, enabling any computer on the network to send its desktop display to the projector.

Unlike external monitors, projectors are designed to mirror the computer's desktop, not extend it. Portable computers with external monitor ports typically have some sort of keyboard mechanism that enables you to select whether the computer should send the desktop to the internal display, the projector, or both. However, Windows 8.1 simplifies this selection process by displaying a dialog box when you connect a projector, asking you which display(s) you want to use.

Network projectors are a different situation, because they do not connect directly to the video display adapter, and they are not automatically detectible by Windows 8.1. Instead of simply directing the monitor signal out through a port, the computer uses the Remote Desktop Protocol (RDP) to transmit the monitor signals over the network to the projector device, which has an embedded Windows operating system built into it.

One of the first obstacles to using a network projector with Windows 8.1 is that Windows Firewall, by default, blocks the port used for RDP traffic. To simplify the process of configuring the necessary firewall exceptions and locating the projector on the network, Windows 8.1 provides the Connect to a Network Projector Wizard.

Unlike Windows 7, the Connect to a Network Projector Wizard is not installed with Windows 8.1 by default. It is instead provided as a feature, which you must add before you can run it.

To install and run the Connect to a Network Projector Wizard, use the following procedure.

 INSTALL AND RUN THE CONNECT TO A NETWORK PROJECTOR WIZARD

GET READY. Connect the projector to the network and configure it according to the manufacturer's instructions. Then, log on to Windows 8.1 and perform the following steps:

1. Open the Control Panel and click or tap **Programs > Programs and Features > Turn Windows features on or off**.

   The *Windows Features* dialog box appears.

2. Select the *Network Projection* checkbox and then click **OK**.

   The system installs the selected feature.

3. Click **Close**.

4. On the **Start** screen, type **connect** to perform and search and click or tap the **Connect to a Network Projector** tile.

   The Connect to a Network Projector Wizard appears, displaying the *Windows Firewall is blocking the network projector from communicating with your computer* page.

5. Click **Allow the network projector to communicate with my computer** to create exceptions in the Windows Firewall that will permit communications with the projector.

   The *How do you want to connect to a network projector?* page appears, as shown in Figure 17-5.

Figure 17-5

The *How do you want to connect to a network projector?* page

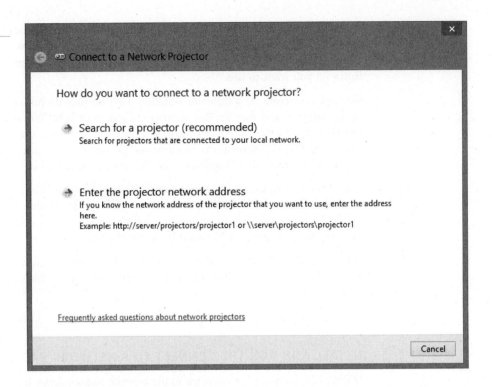

6. Click **Search for a projector (recommended)**.

   The wizard searches for a projector on the network and prompts you for a password if one is required.

7. You can also click **Enter the projector network address** to display the *Enter the network address of a network projector* page, in which you can manually supply the printer's network address and password.

8. Click **Connect** to establish the connection to the projector.

Configuring Presentation Settings

> The Presentation Settings dialog box provides quick access to the most common adjustments performed by presenters.

The designers of Windows 8.1 have attempted to anticipate the needs of many types of computer users. For people that use their mobile computers to give presentations to an audience, few things are more unwelcome than an unexpected system event, such as an error message or a screen saver kicking in. Depending on the audience and the type of presentation, the result of problems like these can range from simple embarrassment to lost sales.

Windows 8.1 includes a dialog box that bundles together the configuration settings that users most often adjust before giving a presentation, and makes it possible to activate all of the settings with a single switch.

To configure the presentation settings for a computer, use the following procedure.

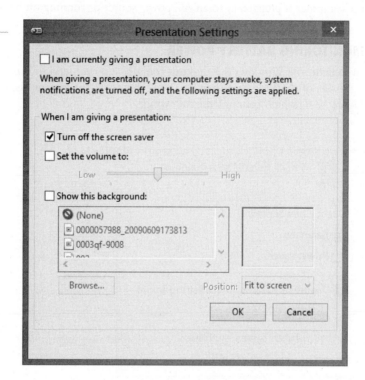

CONFIGURE PRESENTATION SETTINGS

GET READY. Log on to Windows 8.1 using an account with administrative privileges and then perform the following steps:

1. Open **Windows Mobility Center** and then click the icon in the **Presentation Settings** tile.

   The Presentation Settings dialog box appears, as shown in Figure 17-6.

Figure 17-6

The *Presentation Settings* dialog box

2. Use the controls to turn off the screen saver, adjust the speaker volume, or display an alternate desktop background when the Presentation Settings feature

3. Click **OK** to save your settings.

In addition to the settings in the dialog box, activating the Presentation Settings feature prevents the computer from displaying system notification messages or going to sleep. To activate the Presentation Settings feature, use one of the following procedures:

- Open the Presentation Settings dialog box, select the *I am currently giving a presentation* checkbox, and click **OK**.
- Open Windows Mobility Center and in the Presentation Settings tile, click **Turn on**.

Configuring Power Options

Windows 8.1 enables you to fine-tune the power consumption of a mobile computer by configuring individual components to operate at lower power levels.

Power conservation is a critical issue for portable computer users who rely on batteries, particularly when using the computer for a presentation or other business critical function.

CERTIFICATION READY
Configure power policies
Objective 5.2

Running out of power in the middle of a demonstration could be disastrous, so it is important for users to be aware of the computer's power level and its power consumption.

To conserve battery power as much as possible, virtually all portable devices made today include the hardware and firmware elements needed to dynamically adjust the power consumption of individual components. Some computer components, such as processors and LCD panels, can operate at various power levels, while other devices can be shut down completely when not in use. Windows 8.1 includes extensive controls called power plans that enable you to create power usage profiles for a portable computer and assign different profiles depending on whether the computer is plugged in to an AC power source or running on batteries.

MONITORING BATTERY POWER

By default, the Windows 8.1 desktop contains a power icon in the notification area on the right side of the Taskbar. When you click that icon, the system displays a tile like that in Figure 17-7, which contains the following:

Figure 17-7

The *Power* tile in the notification area

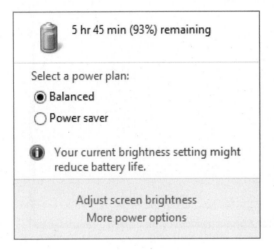

- An icon indicating whether the computer is currently using AC or battery power
- When running on battery power, the percentage of the battery charge remaining and the amount of time left until the battery is drained
- The power plan currently in use and options to select an alternative power plan
- Links to the Power Options control panel

You can also right-click the icon to open the Windows Mobility Center or the Power Options control panel.

TAKE NOTE *

The Power Options control panel does not display the High Performance plan by default. You must click the *Show additional plans* down arrow for it to appear.

WORKING WITH POWER PLANS

Power management is the process of balancing conservation versus performance. Windows 8.1 includes extensive power management capabilities, including support for the Advanced Configuration and Power Interface (ACPI) and the ability to configure power settings in three ways, using graphical control panel settings, Group Policy, or the command prompt.

The Power Options control panel is the primary interactive power configuration interface. From this control panel you can select the power plan that the computer should use; modify the settings for the default power plans; and create new, custom power plans of your own.

A power plan is a combination of power management settings that provides a balance between power consumption and system performance. Windows 8.1 includes three default power plans: Balanced (recommended), Power saver, and High performance, as shown in Figure 17-8.

Figure 17-8

The *Power Options* control panel

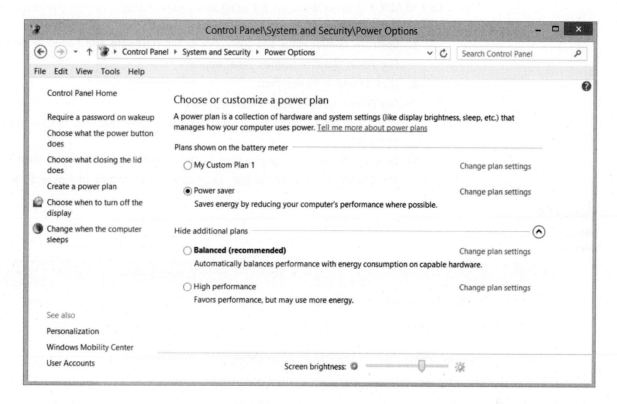

To select one of the default power plans, you can use any of the following procedures.

- Open the Windows Mobility Center and, in the Battery Status tile, select one of the plans from the dropdown list.
- Open the Control Panel and click or tap **Hardware and Sound** > **Power Options**, and select the radio button for the desired plan.
- Click the power icon in the notification area, and then select one of the plans from the menu that appears.

On portable systems, each power plan consists of two sets of settings, one for when the computer is plugged into an AC power source and one for when the computer is running on battery power.

All of the plans are more conservative when the computer is running on battery power, and the differences between the plan settings are incremental. There is, however, no way for the operating system to know exactly what effect the various power settings will have on a specific computer.

The LCD panel on a laptop with a large, widescreen display will obviously use more power than one with a smaller display, so turning the display off will conserve more battery power. In the same way, hard disk drives, processors, and other components can vary greatly in their power consumption levels. It is up to the user to determine what effect each of the power plans has on a specific computer.

Using the Power Options control panel, you can modify any of the individual settings in a power plan, or you can create a new power plan of your own. To create a custom power plan, use the following procedure:

 CREATE A CUSTOM POWER PLAN

GET READY. Log on to Windows 8.1 using an account with administrative privileges and then perform the following steps:

1. Open the Control Panel and then click or tap **Hardware and Sound** > **Power Options**. The *Power Options* control panel appears.

2. Click **Create a Power Plan**. The *Create a Power Plan* wizard appears.

3. Select the radio button for the default power plan that will be the basis for your new plan.

4. Type a name for your power plan in the *Plan name* text box and then click **Next**. The *Change settings for the plan* page appears, as shown in Figure 17-9.

Figure 17-9

The *Change settings for the plan* page

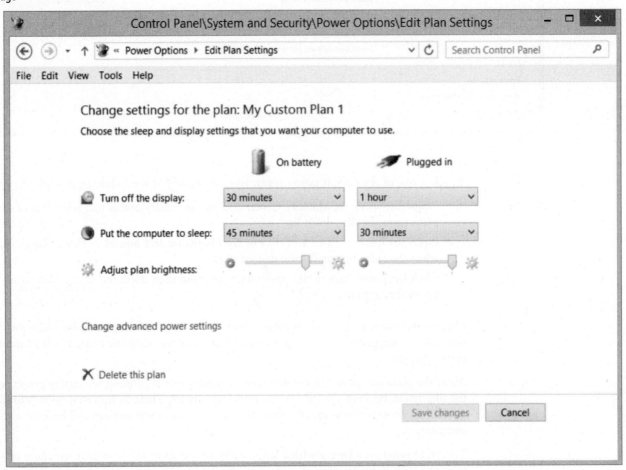

5. Modify the display and sleep settings as desired for the *On battery* and *Plugged in* power states and then click **Create**.

The *Choose or customize a power plan* page appears, with the new plan you created listed as one of the options.

6. Click the **Change plan settings** link for the plan you created.

The *Change settings for the plan* page appears again.

7. Click **Change advanced power settings**.

The *Advanced settings* page appears, as shown in Figure 17-10.

Figure 17-10

The *Advanced settings* page

8. Modify any of the settings as desired and then click **OK**.

9. Click **Save Changes** to close the *Change settings for the plan* page.

CONFIGURING POWER POLICIES

It is also possible for administrators to configure workstation power options using Group Policy. The Computer Configuration\Policies\Administrative Templates\System\Power Management container in every GPO, as shown in Figure 17-11, contains settings that duplicate all of the controls in the Power Options control panel.

Figure 17-11

Power Management settings
in a GPO

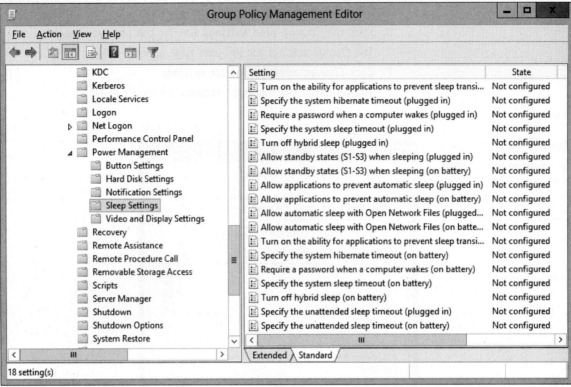

There are a few Power Management settings in Group Policy that you cannot configure through the Control Panel. In the Sleep Settings container, the following six settings appear:

- Allow applications to prevent automatic sleep (plugged in)
- Allow applications to prevent automatic sleep (on battery)
- Allow automatic sleep with Open Network Files (plugged in)
- Allow automatic sleep with Open Network Files (on battery)
- Turn on the ability for applications to prevent sleep transition (plugged in)
- Turn on the ability for applications to prevent sleep transition (on battery)

These settings enable you to control whether a workstation can go to sleep when applications are active or network files open.

USING POWERCFG.EXE

Powercfg.exe is the command line program for the Windows 8.1 power management system. As the most comprehensive power management interface, Powercfg.exe can configure settings that are not available from the Control Panel or in Group Policy.

One of the most valuable capabilities of Powercfg.exe is the ability to export entire power management plans to a file, and then import them on another computer.

To export a power plan, use the following procedure.

EXPORT A POWER PLAN

GET READY. Log on to Windows 8 using an account with administrative privileges and then perform the following steps:

1. Open a Command Prompt window with administrative privileges.
2. In the Command Prompt window, execute the **powercfg.exe –list** command (see Figure 17-12).

   The program displays the power plans on the computer.

Figure 17-12

Power plans listed by Powercfg.exe

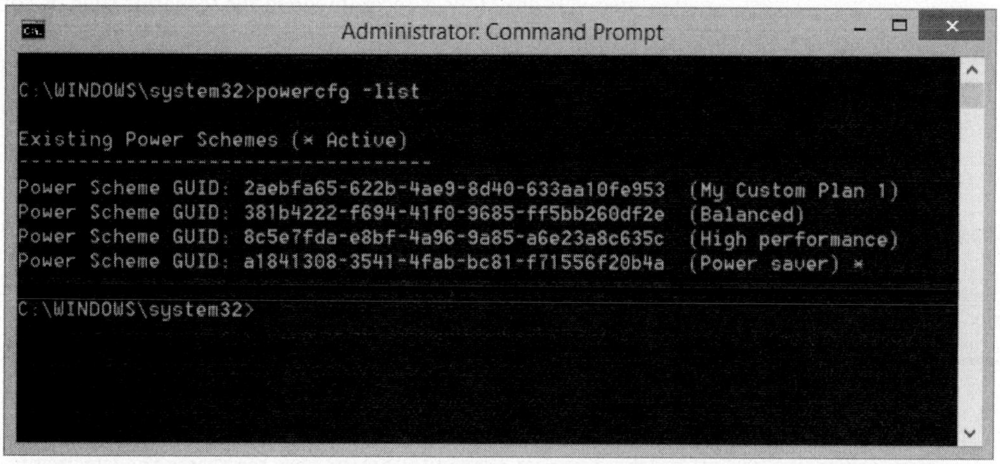

```
Administrator: Command Prompt                           _  □  ×

C:\WINDOWS\system32>powercfg -list

Existing Power Schemes (* Active)
---------------------------------------
Power Scheme GUID: 2aebfa65-622b-4ae9-8d40-633aa10fe953  (My Custom Plan 1)
Power Scheme GUID: 381b4222-f694-41f0-9685-ff5bb260df2e  (Balanced)
Power Scheme GUID: 8c5e7fda-e8bf-4a96-9a85-a6e23a8c635c  (High performance)
Power Scheme GUID: a1841308-3541-4fab-bc81-f71556f20b4a  (Power saver) *

C:\WINDOWS\system32>
```

3. Execute the following command (where *GUID* is the GUID value for the plan you want to export, as displayed in the list):

   ```
   powercfg.exe -export power.pow GUID
   ```

4. **Close** the *Command Prompt* window.

After transferring the file to another computer, you can import it using the following command.
```
powercfg.exe -import power.pow
```

Synchronizing Data

> Mobile devices enable users to take their data with them wherever they go, but this creates a version control problem.

Mobile computer users often connect to a network when they are in the office, and then take their computers with them when they go home or travel on business. Once the computer disconnects from the network, however, access to the network drives and the files they contain is interrupted. Fortunately, Windows 8.1 includes the ability to store copies of network files on the local drive for use when the computer is disconnected. This feature is called Offline Files. Windows 8.1 also makes it possible to maintain copies of files on handheld devices, such as smartphones and tablets running Windows.

The key to this offline files capability is the synchronization process that occurs when the computer or other device reconnects to the network. Simply copying the files to the mobile device is not enough. Users would have to remember to copy their revised documents back to the network drive after reconnecting. Synchronization is a process in which Windows 8.1 compares the offline version of a file with the network version, and makes sure that the most recent revisions are present in both places.

Windows 8.1 supports two types of synchronization, as follows:

- **One-way synchronization** – Data moves in one direction only, from the source to the destination. The system replicates any changes users make to the source files to the destination, but changes to the destination files are not replicated to the source. This is recommended for scenarios such as synchronizing music files on a computer with a portable music player.

- **Two-way synchronization** – Data moves in both directions. Changes users make to either copy of the files are replicated to the other system. In the event that both copies have changed, the system prompts the user to resolve the conflict by selecting one of the two versions. This is recommended for scenarios such as copying network-based document files to a mobile system for offline use.

The following sections describe the tools and procedures you can use to ensure that mobile computers synchronize their data reliably.

USING OFFLINE FILES

Offline Files is a form of fault tolerance that individual users can employ to maintain access to their server files, even in the event of a network service failure. Windows 8.1 workstations copy server-based folders that users designate for offline use to the local drive, and the users work with the copies, which remain accessible whether the computer is connected to the network or not.

CERTIFICATION READY
Configure offline file policies
Objective 5.2

If the network connection fails, or the user disconnects a portable computer, access to the offline files continues uninterrupted. When the computer reconnects to the network, a synchronization procedure occurs that replicates the files between server and workstation in whichever direction is necessary. If there is a version conflict, such as when users have modified both copies of a file, the system prompts the user to specify which copy to retain.

To synchronize a Windows 8.1 computer with a network folder you simply browse to the folder using File Explorer, right-click the folder name, and select Always Available Offline from the context menu. Windows 8.1 then establishes the partnership and copies the contents of the selected folder to the local hard drive.

Although it is an effective fault tolerance mechanism, primary control of offline files rests with the user, which makes it a less suitable solution for an enterprise network than other measures, such as File Redirection.

Configuring Share Caching

Administrators can configure shares to prevent users from saving offline copies. When you create a share using the Advanced Sharing dialog box, clicking Caching opens the Offline Settings dialog box, as shown in Figure 17-13. Here you can specify which files and programs users are permitted to select for storage in the Offline Files cache.

Figure 17-13

The *Offline Settings* dialog box

Configuring Offline File Policies

Administrators can use Group Policy to configure Offline Files behavior on Windows 8.1 workstations. The Computer Configuration\Policies\Administrative Templates\Network\ Offline Files container in every Group Policy object (GPO) has 28 policy settings, as shown in Figure 17-14.

Figure 17-14

The *Offline Files* Group Policy settings

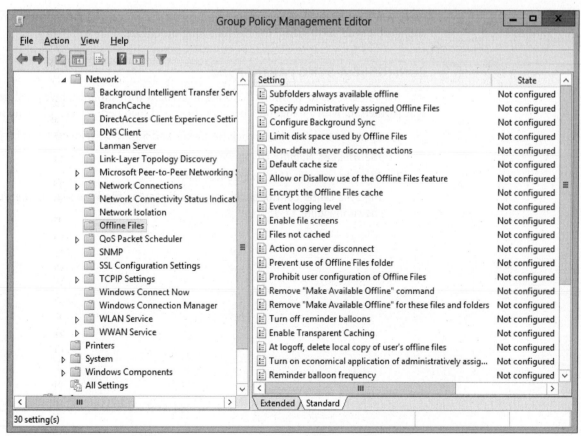

Using these settings, administrators can control whether workstations are permitted to use offline files, how much disk space to allocate to the offline files cache, whether to encrypt the contents of the cache, and when synchronization events should occur.

Using Transparent Caching

The Enable Transparent Caching policy setting causes Windows 8.1 to save copies of files users access from remote servers on a local drive, whether or not the files are configured as offline files. Unlike offline files, the cached files do not remain available when the computer is disconnected from the network, but they do provide the users with faster repeat access, while conserving network bandwidth.

Transparent caching is functionally similar to the BranchCache feature discussed in Lesson 16, "Configuring Remote Connections," except that each Windows 8.1 workstation has exclusive use of its own cache; it does not share the cached files with other clients.

Windows 8.1 decides whether to cache a file based on the network latency value for the connection between the workstation and the server. Transparent caching is designed primarily for clients and servers connected by relatively slow wide area network (WAN) connections. The network latency value is the round time transmission time between the client and the server. The default value for the policy setting is 32,000 milliseconds, or 32 seconds.

USING SYNC CENTER

Sync Center is an application that functions as a central control panel for all of a Windows 8 computer's synchronization partnerships, including those with network drives and mobile devices. Sync partnerships are pairs of folders or devices that are configured to synchronize their data on a regular basis. You can use Sync Center to establish synchronization partnerships, schedule synchronizations, monitor synchronization events, and manage synchronization conflicts.

CERTIFICATION READY
Configure sync options
Objective 5.2

Once you have established the partnership, you can configure its synchronization schedule. To configure a sync partnership, use the following procedure.

CONFIGURE A SYNC PARTNERSHIP

GET READY. Log on to Windows 8.1 using an account with administrative privileges, create a sync partnership with a folder on a network drive, and then perform the following steps:

1. Open **Control Panel** and click **Hardware and Sound** > **Windows Mobility Center**. The *Windows Mobility Center* window appears.

2. Click the icon in the *Sync Center* pane. The *Sync Center* control panel appears, displaying the *View sync partnerships* page, as shown in Figure 17-15.

Figure 17-15

The *Sync Center* control panel

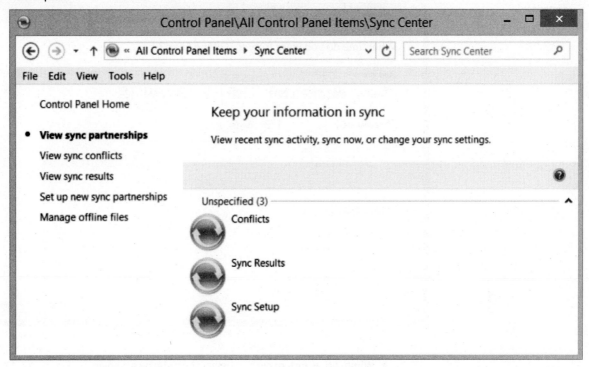

3. Select the Offline Files partnership and then click Schedule.

   The *Offline Files Sync Schedule* wizard appears, displaying the *Which items do you want to sync on this schedule?* page.

4. Select the network folder whose synchronization you want to schedule and then click Next.

   The *When do you want this sync to begin?* page appears.

5. Select one of the following options, configure its properties, and then click Next.

   • **At a scheduled time** – Using the interface shown in Figure 17-16, specify a date and time for the synchronization and a repeat interval. You can also click **More Options** to specify conditions under which the scheduled synchronization should or should not occur.

Figure 17-16

The *Sync Center Scheduled time* interface

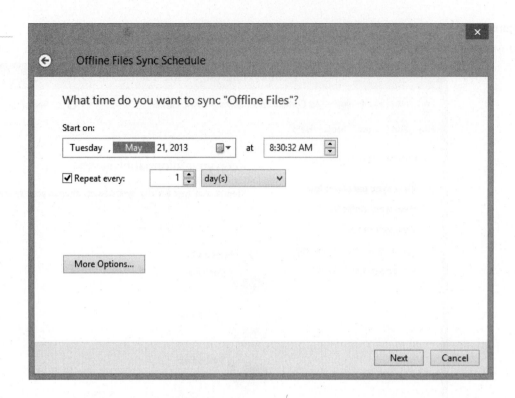

• **When an event occurs** – Using the interface shown in Figure 17-17, select an event or action that you want to trigger a synchronization, such as logging on to Windows or when the system has been idle for specified amount of time.

Figure 17-17

The *Sync Center Event or Action* interface

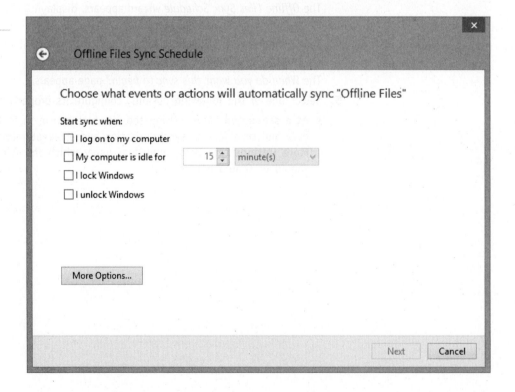

6. Specify a name for the schedule and then click **Save Schedule**.

CONFIGURING SYNC OPTIONS

The Offline Files and Sync Center features have been part of Windows for several versions, but in Windows 8.1 you can sync settings across-multiple Windows 8.1 systems.

When you specify a Microsoft account during the initial Windows 8.1 operating system setup, you are able to store your computer settings with the account on the Internet. These settings can include colors, backgrounds, desktop configuration, ease of access and language preferences, application settings, browser favorites, and even passwords. When you log on from another computer running Windows 8.1 using the same Microsoft account, you can download the settings you stored, effectively syncing your environment among multiple computers.

To control what settings the system should sync, open the Charms bar, click **Settings**, and then click **Change PC Settings**. On the PC Settings screen, click OneDrive and select **Sync settings**, to display the screen shown in Figure 17-18. From this page, you can toggle the sync function and select the individual settings that you want to sync to your Microsoft account.

Figure 17-18

The *Sync your settings* screen

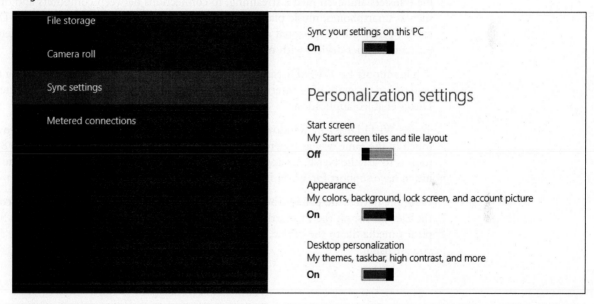

Before Windows 8.1 will actually sync your settings, you must designate the computer as trusted by responding to an email message that the computer sends to your Microsoft account. This confirms that you are in control both of the computer and the account.

Using Wi-Fi Direct

 THE BOTTOM LINE Wireless networking based on the IEEE 802.11 standards supports two communications modes: ad hoc and infrastructure.

CERTIFICATION READY
Configure Wi-Fi Direct
Objective 5.2

Most Wi-Fi networks are based on the infrastructure model, in which the wireless devices all connect to a central access point, which enables them to communicate with each other. Many of the broadband routers intended for the home and small business markets include a Wi-Fi access point, which provides network access to all wireless devices within proximity of the router.

An ad hoc wireless network, by contrast, consists of only two devices, which connect directly to each other, without the need for an intermediate access point. *Wi-Fi Direct* is a Microsoft implementation of ad hoc wireless networking, which enables a computer running Windows 8.1 to establish a connection to another wireless device.

Potential applications for Wi-Fi Direct range from computer-to-computer connections, for file transfers and even media streaming, to connections between computers and other devices, such as smartphones, music players, and the like. It is even proposed that Wi-Fi Direct could replace Bluetooth for personal networking connections, eliminating the need to equip computers and other devices with multiple radio transceivers.

While support for Wi-Fi Direct is built into Windows 8.1, it exists primarily as a series of application programming interfaces (APIs) with which software developers can create Wi-Fi Direct-enabled applications.

To use Wi-Fi Direct in Windows 8.1, you must first create a pairing between two devices, much in the same way as Bluetooth, but the only way to do that with Windows 8.1 native tools is to use the Netsh.exe application from the command line. Only one of the two devices has to have support for Wi-Fi Direct.

Once the devices are paired, the device you added appears on the Windows 8.1 computer in the Devices list on the PC Settings page. If appropriate, you can use the Play To function to push a media file to the device, or connect to it in other ways, depending on the application you are using.

Configuring Windows To Go

 THE BOTTOM LINE Windows To Go is a feature in Windows 8.1 that takes mobility to an entirely new level. With Windows To Go, you can take your workstation with you, while leaving your computer at home.

Windows To Go is essentially a way to install Windows 8.1 onto a removable USB drive. You can then plug the drive into another computer – even one that doesn't have Windows 8.1 installed – and boot Windows 8.1 from the portable drive. Once Windows 8.1 is running from the portable drive, the computer's own drives are inaccessible and the user has access to all of the applications and files on the portable drive.

CERTIFICATION READY
Configure Windows
To Go
Objective 5.2

For more information on how to configure Windows To Go, see Lesson 2, "Installing Windows 8.1."

SKILL SUMMARY

IN THIS LESSON, YOU LEARNED:

- Windows Mobility Center is a shell application that provides a central point of access for many of the configuration settings that mobile computer users need frequently.

- Most laptop computers have the capability to connect an external display device, making it possible for a group of users to view the desktop without having to crowd around a single screen.

- To conserve battery power as much as possible, virtually all laptops include the hardware and firmware elements needed to dynamically adjust the power consumption of individual components.

- Windows 8.1 includes a dialog box that bundles together the configuration settings that users most often adjust before giving a presentation and make it possible to activate all of the settings with a single switch.

- Windows 8.1 includes the ability to store copies of network files on the local drive, for use when the computer is disconnected.

- Sync Center is an application that functions as a central control panel for all of a Windows 8.1 computer's synchronization partnerships, including those with network drives and mobile devices.

■ Knowledge Assessment

Multiple Choice

Select one or more correct answers for each of the following questions.

1. Which of the following Second Screen settings must you select to create a display on two monitors using a different resolution for each one?
   a. PC screen only
   b. Duplicate
   c. Extend
   d. Second screen only

2. Which of the following tools can you use to import and export power management plans in Windows 8.1?
   a. Powercfg.exe and Group Policy
   b. The Power Options control panel only
   c. Powercg.exe only
   d. The Power Options control panel and Group Policy

3. Transparent caching saves temporary copies of files based on which of the following criteria?
   a. Number of requests for the file
   b. User time limits
   c. File size
   d. Network roundtrip latency

4. Which of the following Windows 8.1 utilities can you use to create a Wi-Fi Direct device pair?
   a. Nslookup.exe
   b. Netsh.exe
   c. Net.exe
   d. Netstat.exe

5. Which of the following commands will display the power profiles on a computer running Windows 8.1, along with their GUIDs?
   a. `powercfg.exe`
   b. `powercfg.exe -GUID`
   c. `powercfg.exe -list`
   d. `powercfg.exe -profile`

6. Which of the following settings is affected by default when you turn on the Windows 8.1 Presentation Settings option?
   a. Screen saver
   b. Volume
   c. Sleep
   d. Background

7. Which of the following tasks must you complete before you can sync your passwords and settings with other computers running Windows 8.1? (Choose all that apply.)
   a. Create a local user account.
   b. Log on using a Microsoft account.
   c. Join an Active Directory Domain Services domain.
   d. Verify that your computer is trusted.

8. The Windows 8.1 Mobility Center Window is divided into as many as eight tiles. Which tile would be accessed to configure settings that control attempts to put the computer to sleep?
   a. Sync Center
   b. Screen Orientation
   c. Presentation Settings
   d. External Display

9. Which of the following are ways that you can use to configure how Windows 8.1 works with multiple displays? Select all that apply.
   a. Windows Mobility Center > Display Tile > click the disconnect Display button.
   b. Open the Display control panel and click Adjust resolution
   c. Windows Mobility Center > Sync Center
   d. Windows Mobility Center > Screen Orientation

10. Wi-Fi Direct is a new Microsoft implementation for what type of wireless networking?
    a. Infrastructure model wireless networks
    b. Ad hoc wireless networks
    c. Workgroup-based networks
    d. Domain-based networks

Best Answer

Choose the letter that corresponds to the best answer. More than one answer choice may achieve the goal. Select the BEST answer.

1. Several new Windows 8.1 mobile computers have been purchased. Unfortunately, there is no way for the operating system to know exactly what effect the default power settings will have on a specific computer. What is the best approach to use to ensure you maintain a balance between power consumption and system performance on these new systems?
   a. Select the Power Saver Power Plan.
   b. Select the Balanced Power Plan.
   c. Select the High Performance Power Plan.
   d. Test each of the default Power Plans and then create a custom plan to meet your specific needs.

2. Which of the following is the best approach to use when connecting a new Windows 8.1 mobile computer to a network projector while avoiding problems with the Windows Firewall?
   a. Install the software that comes with the network projector and configure your Windows 8.1 Firewall settings manually.
   b. Install the Connect to a Network Projector Wizard feature and disable your Windows Firewall.
   c. Install the Connect to a Network Projector Wizard feature and let it determine the appropriate exceptions for the Windows Firewall.
   d. Install the Connect to a Network Projector Wizard feature.

3. Of the following tools, which provides you with the most comprehensive power management interface for configuring power policies?
   a. Control Panel
   b. Group Policy
   c. Windows Mobility Center
   d. Powercfg.exe

4. The company would like to provide users with access to their files while using their mobile devices. They want to conserve bandwidth and provide users with faster repeat access to the files while still allowing them to access the files when disconnected from the network. Which technology best fits this need?
   a. Transparent caching combined with offline files and two-way synchronization
   b. Share caching
   c. Transparent caching combined with offline files
   d. Share caching with offline files

5. The company wants to implement Windows 8.1 features that will support users who copy network-based document files to a mobile system. These features should ensure that if two users are working on the same file offline, when they reconnect, they have the option of resolving the conflict between the two versions. Which of the following features would best support that goal?
   a. Offline files with two-way synchronization
   b. Offline files with one-way synchronization
   c. Transparent caching, offline files and one-way synchronization
   d. Transparent caching, offline files and two-way synchronization

Matching and Identification

Complete the following exercise by matching the terms with their corresponding definitions.

_____ **a)** Windows Mobility Center
_____ **b)** Offline files
_____ **c)** Sync Center
_____ **d)** Wi-Fi Direct
_____ **e)** Transparent caching
_____ **f)** One-way synchronization
_____ **g)** Two-way synchronization
_____ **h)** Infrastructure model
_____ **i)** Ad hoc wireless networking
_____ **j)** Windows To Go

1. Designed for clients connected by relatively slow WAN connections.
2. Data moves from source to destination only.
3. A shell application that provides central point of access for mobile configuration settings.
4. Wireless devices connection to a central access point.
5. Allows you to install Windows 8.1 on a removable USB drive.
6. Allows users to access server files even in the event of network service failure.
7. Changes users make to either copy of a file is replicated to the other system. Data moves in both directions.
8. Microsoft implementation of ad hoc wireless networking.
9. Consists of only two wireless devices that connect directly to each other.
10. Functions as a central control panel for synchronization partnerships.

Build a List

1. In order of first to last, specify the correct order of steps to create a custom Power Plan.
_____ Click **Create a power plan**.
_____ Type a name for your power plan in the *Plan name* text box and then click **Next**.
_____ Select the radio button for the default power plan that will be the basis for your new plan.
_____ Click **Change advanced power settings**.
_____ Click the **Change plan settings** link for the plan you created.
_____ Modify the display and sleep settings as desired for the *On battery* and *Plugged in* power states and then click **Create**.
_____ Modify any of the settings as desired and then click **OK**.
_____ Click **Save Changes** to close the *Change settings for the plan* page.
_____ Open the **Control Panel** and then click or tap **Hardware and Sound > Power Options**.

2. Specify the correct order of steps to configure a sync partnership.
_____ Select the network folder whose synchronization you want to schedule and then click **Next**.
_____ Open **Control Panel** and click **Hardware and Sound > Windows Mobility Center**.
_____ Click the icon in the Sync Center pane. The *Sync Center* control panel appears, displaying the *View sync partnerships* page.
_____ Select the **Offline Files** partnership and then click **Schedule**.
_____ Select one of the following options, configure its properties, and (**at a scheduled time or when an event occurs**, then click **Next**.
_____ Specify a name for the schedule and then click **Save Schedule**.

3. Specify the correct order of steps to export a Power Plan.

_____ Close the *Command Prompt* window.

_____ In the Command Prompt window, execute the **powercfg.exe –list** command.

_____ Open a Command Prompt window with administrative privileges.

_____ Execute the following command (where *GUID* is the GUID value for the plan you want to export, as displayed in the list **powercfg.exe -export power.pow GUID.**

■ Business Case Scenarios

Scenario 17-1: Troubleshooting Network Projectors

A new network projector has recently been added to the company's network. A Windows 8.1 computer was connected to the network projector last week and several training presentations were given successfully. For some reason, another Windows 8.1 computer that is being used for training presentations this week cannot access the projector. What could be causing the problem?

Scenario 17-2: Configuring Multiple Displays

A user connected a second display to their mobile computer. The current display was then mirrored on the secondary device. The user would like to extend their current display instead of mirroring it. Can this be accomplished? If so, explain how it would be done.

18 LESSON

Configuring Security for Mobile Devices

70-687 EXAM OBJECTIVE

Objective 5.3 – Configure security for mobile devices. This objective may include but is not limited to: configure BitLocker and BitLocker To Go; configure startup key storage.

LESSON HEADING	EXAM OBJECTIVE
Securing Your Mobile Devices	
Configuring BitLocker	Configure BitLocker and BitLocker To Go
Understanding BitLocker Requirements	Configure startup key storage
Enabling BitLocker on Operating System Drives	
Configuring BitLocker To Go	Configure BitLocker and BitLocker To Go

KEY TERMS

BitLocker Drive Encryption

BitLocker To Go

Encrypting File System (EFS)

hardware-based encryption

Network Unlock

Personal Identification Number (PIN)

recovery key

Secure Digital (SD) cards

software-based encryption

startup key

Trusted Platform Module (TPM)

■ Securing Your Mobile Devices

THE BOTTOM LINE

As more employees use mobile devices to get their work done, administrators will need to ensure they have the technology and security in place to protect against the lost/theft of those devices while at the same time protecting against the accidental release of Personally Identifiable Information (PII) through location-aware apps.

With an increasing number of employees bringing their smartphones, tablets, and laptop devices into corporate network environments, balancing access with protection is critical for today's network administrators. Rather than focusing on banning the devices, you should educate users on how to keep their mobile devices secure, set security policies, and make sure you have the technology in place to manage them. There are a variety of threats to mobile devices. These include theft, loss, intercepting the wireless communications, and malicious software to name just a few.

In this lesson, you learn about the features in Windows 8.1 that you can use to prevent the loss of sensitive information when a computer/device is lost or stolen, policies that can be configured to protect your system, and how to keep your computer's boot environment safe from modification. You also learn how to configure Windows 8.1 to control whether or not you want to reveal your location to Windows Apps.

Configuring BitLocker

> BitLocker Drive Encryption is designed to protect the sensitive data stored on your hard drives even in situations when they are stolen and moved to another computer.

Encrypting File System (EFS) enables users to protect specific files and folders, so that no one else can access them. *BitLocker Drive Encryption*, on the other hand, is a feature available in Windows 8.1 Pro, Windows 8.1 Enterprise, and in all editions of Windows Server 2012 R2 that makes it possible to protect files by encrypting an entire volume or drive.

BitLocker Drive Encryption is designed to protect against brute force attacks to gain access to the drive or situations where someone tries to install and access the drive from another computer. This feature can further enhance security by checking the integrity of boot files when a *Trusted Platform Module (TPM)* chip is available on the system. The TPM is a dedicated cryptographic processor chip that the system uses to store the BitLocker encryption keys.

Although Windows 7 required you to configure BitLocker after the operating system was installed, Windows 8.1 supports the ability to enable BitLocker before you deploy the operating system. It also introduces two new options for encrypting your disk:

- **Encrypt used disk space only** – This option encrypts only the part of your drive that currently has data stored on it.
- **Encrypt the entire drive** – This option encrypts the full volume and offers more security. It encrypts areas of the disk that contain data that has been deleted but may still be retrievable from the drive.

You can configure Group Policy to specify the encryption option you want to use on each type of drive: fixed data drives, operating system drives, and removable data drives. If you do not configure and link a Group Policy Object (GPO), users will be able to choose the encryption type they want to use after BitLocker is enabled on their drive.

In Windows 8.1, you must be a member of the Administrators group to configure BitLocker, but non-administrative users can change the BitLocker *Personal Identification Number (PIN)* or password for the operating system and fixed data volumes by default. The PIN is any 4–20 digit number you choose, which is stored on your computer and must be entered each time you start the system. Although this can reduce help desk calls, you should consider either disabling this option through Group Policy or configure a policy that forces users to create complex passwords that are not easily guessed.

BitLocker supports manufacturer drives that provide *hardware-based encryption* capabilities. Although *software-based encryption* relies on the computer's resources and processor to encrypt data, hardware-based encryption uses its own dedicated processor that is located on the encrypted drive.

CERTIFICATION READY
Configure BitLocker and BitLocker To Go
Objective 5.3

Windows Server 2012 R2 includes a BitLocker feature called **Network Unlock**. This feature automatically unlocks an operating system volume at reboot if the computer is connected to a domain. Prior to the introduction of this feature, users needed to enter their PIN. For administrators, Network Unlock enables them to perform unattended installations and software upgrades without visiting each machine and unlocking it after a reboot.

Unlike EFS, BitLocker is not designed to protect files for specific users, so that other users cannot access them. Instead, BitLocker protects entire volumes and drives from being compromised by unauthorized persons. For example, if someone alters the server's boot components after stealing the hard drive and installing it into another computer, BitLocker will lock the protected volumes, preventing access. When the system boots successfully under normal conditions, the BitLocker volumes are accessible to anyone.

BitLocker is not designed to replace EFS or NTFS permissions. You must still protect your files and folders using these standard Windows 8.1 tools. Instead of being a replacement, consider BitLocker an additional layer of security and protection for your Windows 8.1 and Windows Server 2012 systems.

Understanding BitLocker Requirements

To use BitLocker, you need to understand how startup and recovery keys are used and what to do if you lose them.

The first time you enable BitLocker on a drive, you create a **startup key**. The startup key is used to encrypt/decrypt the drive. It can be stored on a USB drive or on a TPM chip. If the key is stored on a USB drive, you must insert the drive each time you start the computer and then enter the key.

If the startup key is stored on a TPM chip and the computer has a system BIOS that is compatible with its use, the key is automatically retrieved for you during startup.

TAKE NOTE ✱

The TPM chip enables BitLocker to enhance security by checking the validity of not only the encrypted volume, but your boot files, boot manager, and operating system files to make sure they have not been tampered with while the operating system was offline.

CERTIFICATION READY
Configure startup key storage
Objective 5.3

An alternative to the startup key is to use a PIN. The startup key or PIN can be changed through the BitLocker Drive Encryption control panel application after BitLocker is enabled. You can also make additional copies of the startup key to use in case the original is lost.

If you lose the startup key, move the drive to another system, or the system is compromised, you will need to use a **recovery key** to gain access to the drive. The recovery key is a 48-digit number that can be stored on a USB drive, a folder on another drive, or a hard-copy printout. If you save the recovery key to a USB drive, it will also include a machine-readable version that you can read by just inserting the drive; otherwise, you need to type in the number to recover the system.

TAKE NOTE ✱

You can determine whether you have a TPM chip by pressing the *Windows logo key* + *R* and typing tpm.msc. This opens the Trusted Platform Module (TPM) console on a Windows 8.1 computer. If the TPM chip does not appear in the console, you should also check to make sure it is enabled through the computer's BIOS.

BitLocker has five authentication methods to choose from during startup to provide additional protection for your encrypted data. These methods, in descending order from most to least secure, are as follows:

- **TPM + startup PIN + startup key** – The system stores the BitLocker volume encryption key on the TPM chip, but an administrator must supply a PIN and insert a USB flash drive containing a startup key before the system can unlock the BitLocker volume and complete the system boot sequence.

- **TPM + startup key** – The system stores the BitLocker volume encryption key on the TPM chip, but an administrator must insert a USB flash drive containing a startup key before the system can unlock the BitLocker volume and complete the system boot sequence.

- **TPM + startup PIN** – The system stores the BitLocker volume encryption key on the TPM chip, but an administrator must supply a PIN before the system can unlock the BitLocker volume and complete the system boot sequence.

- **Startup key only** – The BitLocker configuration process stores a startup key on a USB flash drive, which the administrator must insert each time the system boots. This mode does not require the server to have a TPM chip, but it must have a system BIOS that supports access to the USB flash drive before the operating system loads.

- **TPM only** – The system stores the BitLocker volume encryption key on the TPM chip, and accesses it automatically when the chip has determined that the boot environment is unmodified. This unlocks the protected volume and the computer continues to boot. No administrative interaction is required during the system boot sequence.

Enabling BitLocker on Operating System Drives

Enabling BitLocker to protect your operating system drive requires that your system meet certain requirements.

When you encrypt the drive where the Windows operating system is installed, BitLocker must store the startup key on a separate piece of hardware. The key can be stored on a TPM version 1.2 (or later) microchip or on a removable USB flash drive.

When you start a computer with a TPM that has BitLocker enabled, the TPM will check the operating system to make sure it has not been tampered with while the operating system was offline. If it detects any tampering with the boot files or drive, it will lock the system partition until a recovery key is entered to unlock it.

To support BitLocker Drive Encryption on the drive that contains your operating system, you need the following:

- **Two partitions** – BitLocker holds files needed to start your computer on one partition. This is called the *system partition* and needs to be a minimum of 100 MB in size. This partition is not encrypted. The second partition, encrypted by BitLocker, holds the operating system. This allows BitLocker to protect the operating system and the information in the encrypted drive and to perform its pre-startup authentication steps and verify system integrity.

- **NTFS** – The partitions must be formatted with NTFS to support the BitLocker feature. NTFS is a file system used to store and retrieve files on hard disks. It also provides improvements over older file systems (FAT, FAT32) in the areas of security and performance.

- **TPM Compatible BIOS** – Your BIOS must be compatible with TPM version 1.2 or 2.0; otherwise, the BIOS firmware must be able to read from a USB drive that contains the startup key on boot to enable BitLocker on an operating system drive. BitLocker needs the startup key from either the TPM or the USB flash drive before it can unlock the protected drive. If a USB drive is used on a non-TPM system, BitLocker will not be able to verify the integrity of the system.

If you attempt to enable BitLocker using the BitLocker Drive Encryption control panel for your operating system drive on a computer that does not have a compatible TPM, you will receive a message that states, "This device can't use a Trusted Platform Module." When this happens, you need to configure the *Allow BitLocker without a compatible TPM* option in the *Require additional authentication at startup* policy for operating system volumes before you can enable BitLocker.

To configure this policy for a single computer, use the Local Group Policy editor (gpedit.msc). To apply this policy across your domain, use the Group Policy Management Console (gpmc.msc).

Using the Group Policy Management Console, you find the *Require additional authentication at startup* policy in the following location:

Computer Configuration > Policies > Administrative Templates > Windows Components > BitLocker Drive Encryption > Operating System Drives

From there, select *Allow BitLocker without a compatible TPM*, as shown in Figure 18-1.

Figure 18-1

Configuring BitLocker to run a startup key and a startup PIN

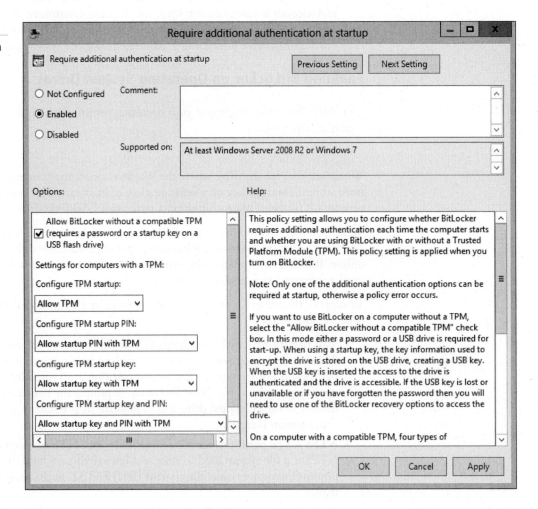

TURN ON BITLOCKER AND ENCRYPT THE OPERATING SYSTEM DRIVE

GET READY. Log on to Windows 8.1 using an account with administrative privileges.

> **TAKE NOTE** *
>
> To complete this exercise, your Windows 8.1 computer must be on a domain where the *Require additional authentication at startup* Group Policy option has been configured as discussed previously.

1. Open the Windows Control Panel and select **System and Security** > **BitLocker Drive Encryption**. The BitLocker Drive Encryption control panel application appears, as shown in Figure 18-2.

Figure 18-2

Reviewing the BitLocker Drive Encryption control panel

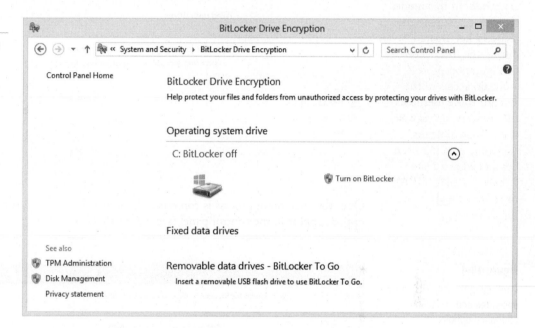

> **TAKE NOTE** *
>
> You should save the key in additional locations such as a folder on another computer or print out the key to have it in more than one location before you click **Next.**

2. For the drive that contains your operating system, click **Turn on BitLocker**.
3. When prompted to choose how you will unlock your drive at startup, click **Enter a password**.
4. Type a password, reenter it to confirm it, and then click **Next** to continue.
5. When prompted to back up your recovery key, click **Save to a USB flash drive**.
6. Insert your USB device, select it from the list provided, and then click **Save**.
7. After saving your recovery key, click **Next**.
8. Make sure the **Run BitLocker system check** is selected and then click **Continue**.
9. Click **Restart Now**.
10. To unlock the drive, type the password you specified and press **Enter**.
11. Log on to the computer.
12. Open the Control Panel and select **System and Security** > **BitLocker Drive**. You should now see that the encryption is in process (*BitLocker Encrypting*), as shown in Figure 18-3.

Figure 18-3

Reviewing the status of the encryption process

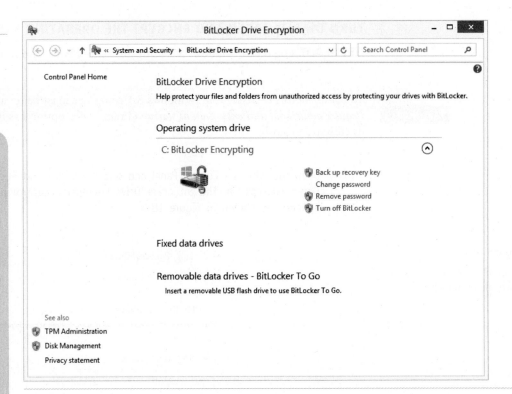

TAKE NOTE *

If a user loses the startup key and/or startup PIN needed to boot a system with BitLocker enabled, the system enters recovery mode. In this mode, the user can supply the recovery key created during the BitLocker configuration process and gain access to the system. If the user loses the recovery key as well, it is still possible for someone, who has been designated as a Data Recovery Agent (DRA), to recover the data on the drive.

Once the encryption process is complete, the status changes to BitLocker on, and additional options appear in the control panel (see Figure 18-4).

Figure 18-4

Confirming the drive has been encrypted and reviewing additional options

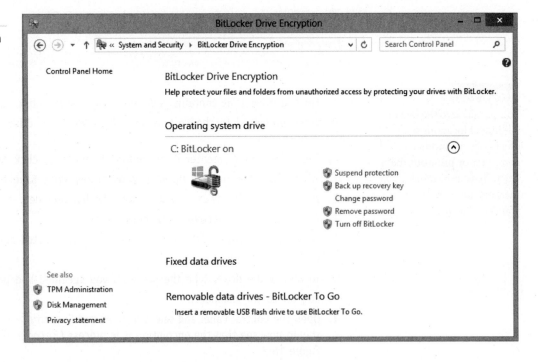

These options are as follows:

- **Suspend protection** – Use this option if you want to temporarily suspend BitLocker. This enables you to install new software, update your PC's firmware, hardware, or operating system. After the system is rebooted, BitLocker automatically re-enables itself on the drive.
- **Back up recovery key** – This option enables you to save your recovery key to a USB flash drive, save to a file, or print out the key.
- **Change password** – This option enables you to change the startup password after confirming your old password.
- **Remove password** – If you select this option, you will be prompted to add another unlocking method before removing the current option.
- **Turn off BitLocker** – This option turns off BitLocker on the drive.

Configuring BitLocker To Go

> BitLocker To Go is a feature in Windows 8.1 that enables you to take advantage of BitLocker Encryption to protect your removable USB devices (flash drives and external hard disks).

BitLocker To Go is BitLocker Drive Encryption on removable data drives. This includes *Secure Digital (SD) cards*, USB flash drives, and external hard disk drives. These drives can be formatted with NTFS, FAT16, FAT32, or exFAT file systems. SD cards are non-volatile memory cards used in mobile phones, digital cameras, and tablet computers (e.g., Microsoft's Surface RT).

CERTIFICATION READY
Configure BitLocker and
BitLocker To Go
Objective 5.3

Once encrypted, you must use a password or a smart card with PIN to unlock the drive. If needed, an administrator can configure the drive to be automatically unlocked on a computer for a specific user.

BitLocker To Go enables you to use the encrypted device on other computers without performing an elaborate recovery process. Because the system is not using the removable drive as a boot device, a TPM chip is not required.

To use BitLocker To Go, insert the removable drive and open the BitLocker Drive Encryption control panel application. The device appears in the interface, with a *Turn on BitLocker* link (see Figure 18-5) just like that of the computer's hard disk drive.

Figure 18-5

Reviewing removable data drives

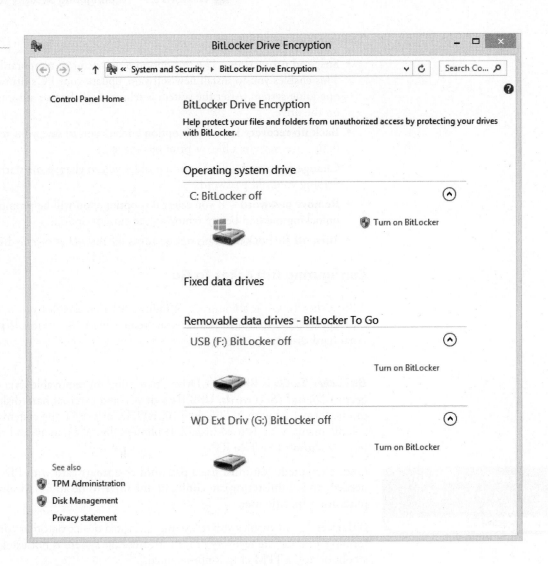

BitLocker Drive Encryption

« System and Security ▸ BitLocker Drive Encryption

Search Co...

Control Panel Home

BitLocker Drive Encryption

Help protect your files and folders from unauthorized access by protecting your drives with BitLocker.

Operating system drive

C: BitLocker off

🛡 Turn on BitLocker

Fixed data drives

Removable data drives - BitLocker To Go

USB (F:) BitLocker off

Turn on BitLocker

WD Ext Driv (G:) BitLocker off

Turn on BitLocker

See also

TPM Administration

Disk Management

Privacy statement

➡ ENABLE BITLOCKER TO GO ON A REMOVABLE DRIVE

GET READY. To enable BitLocker To Go on a removable drive, perform the following steps:

1. Open the Control Panel and select **System and Security > BitLocker Drive Encryption**.
2. Click **Turn on BitLocker** for the removable drive you want to protect.
3. Choose how you want to unlock the drive. The options include using a password or using a smart card to unlock the drive.
4. Choose where to back up the recovery key. The options include saving to your Microsoft account, saving to a file, or printing the recovery key.
5. Choose how much of the drive to encrypt. The options include used disk space only or the entire drive.
6. Start encrypting the drive.

CONTROLLING BITLOCKER TO GO BEHAVIOR

To control BitLocker To Go behavior for Windows 8.1 computers in a domain, you need to use the Group Policy Management Console to create a policy, link it to the appropriate domain, site, or organizational unit (OU) in the Active Directory Domain Services domain, and then edit the *Removable Data Drives* policies, located in the Computer Configuration\Policies\Administrative Templates\Windows Components\BitLocker Drive Encryption container.

These policy settings are as follows:

- **Control use of BitLocker on removable drives** – Specifies whether users are permitted to add BitLocker encryption to removable drives and whether they can remove BitLocker from drives that are already encrypted.
- **Configure use of smart cards on removable data drives** – Specifies whether users can or must use a smart card to access a removable drive.
- **Deny write access to removable drives not protected by BitLocker** – Prevents users from saving data to removable drives that are not encrypted using BitLocker.
- **Configure use of hardware-based encryption for removable data drives** – Specifies options that control whether BitLocker software-based encryption is used instead of hardware-based encryption on computers that do not support hardware-based encryption. It also enables you to specify which encryption algorithms can be used with hardware-based encryption.
- **Allow access to BitLocker-protected removable data drives from earlier versions of Windows** – Specifies whether FAT-formatted removable BitLocker drives are accessible from previous Windows versions.
- **Configure use of passwords for removable data drives** – Specifies whether removable BitLocker drives must be password-protected.
- **Choose how BitLocker-protected removable drives can be recovered** – Specifies whether DRAs can access the data on removable BitLocker drives.

SKILL SUMMARY

IN THIS LESSON, YOU LEARNED:

- BitLocker Drive Encryption and BitLocker To Go are features available in Windows 8.1 to protect your drive and volumes using encryption.
- BitLocker Drive Encryption can be used to encrypt used disk space only or the entire drive.
- BitLocker Drive Encryption can be used with fixed data drives, operating system drives, and removable drives.
- There are five authentication methods that can be used to provide additional protection for your encrypted drive: TPM+startup PIN+startup key, TPM+startup key, TPM+startup PIN, startup key only, and TPM only.
- To support BitLocker Drive Encryption on the drive that contains the operating system, you need two partitions, formatted with NTFS, a TPM compatible BIOS or BIOS firmware that supports booting from a USB flash drive.
- The Local Group Policy editor can be used to manage BitLocker policies on a local machine whereas the Group Policy Management console is used to create policies that are enforced across the entire organization.
- BitLocker To Go is BitLocker Drive Encryption for removable data drives. To unlock removable data drives, you need to use either a password or a smart card with a PIN.

Knowledge Assessment

Multiple Choice

Select the correct answer for each of the following questions.

1. Which of the following can be used to protect files after someone has successfully booted into a shared Windows 8.1 computer and logged in using an authorized user account? (Select all that apply.)
   a. BitLocker Drive Encryption
   b. BitLocker To Go
   c. NTFS
   d. EFS

2. What is a 4–18 digit number that you create when enabling BitLocker, which must be entered each time you start your system? (Select all that apply.)
   a. Startup key
   b. PIN
   c. Recovery key
   d. PII

3. To support BitLocker Drive Encryption on the drive that contains your operating system, you need which of the following?
   a. Two partitions
   b. EFS
   c. TPM Compatible BIOS or BIOS firmware that can read from a USB drive on startup
   d. NTFS

4. Which of the following is the least secure authentication method?
   a. TPM only
   b. TPM + startup key
   c. TPM + startup PIN
   d. TPM + startup PIN + startup key

5. Which key is used to encrypt/decrypt the drive and must be entered each time you boot your computer?
   a. Startup key
   b. Recovery key
   c. Personal key
   d. TPM key

6. What user account can be authorized to recover BitLocker drives for an entire organization?
   a. Domain administrator
   b. Enterprise administrator
   c. Data recovery assistance
   d. Data Recovery Agent

Best Answer

Choose the letter that corresponds to the best answer. More than one answer choice may achieve the goal. Select the BEST answer.

1. It is a Sunday afternoon and after arriving home from lunch with a friend, you discover your Windows 8.1 mobile device was stolen. It was configured to connect to your company's Active Directory domain. What is the quickest way to protect sensitive information on the device?
   a. Enable BitLocker Drive Encryption.
   b. Contact your company's network administrator.

   c. Call the police and report the theft.
   d. Connect using your Outlook Web app from another device and perform a remote wipe on your device.

2. With BitLocker To Go enabled on a data volume for additional protection, to disable it because there is no longer any sensitive data stored on the volume, what tool would you use?
   a. Local Group Policy editor
   b. Group Policy Management console
   c. Control Panel > Manage BitLocker
   d. Delete and reformat the volume

3. To use BitLocker to encrypt the drive that contains your operating system, which of the following drives supports this goal?
   a. 50 MB boot partition
   b. 50 MB system partition
   c. 200 MB boot partition
   d. 200 MB system partition

4. Which of the following represents the most secure authentication option?
   a. TPM only
   b. Startup key only
   c. TPM + startup key
   d. TPM + startup PIN

5. To disable the locating settings for all users in your Active Directory domain, which option enables you to do this with the least administrative effort?
   a. gpedit.msc
   b. gpmc.msc
   c. Windows 8 Control panel
   d. Windows Store

Matching and Identification

1. Match the following terms with their corresponding definitions.
   _____ **a)** Recovery key
   _____ **b)** BitLocker To Go
   _____ **c)** BitLocker Drive Encryption
   _____ **d)** Personal Identification Number (PIN)
   _____ **e)** Trusted Platform Module (TPM)

   1. Encryption feature designed to protect removable USB devices.
   2. A 48-digit number used when you lose/forget your startup key.
   3. A 4–20 digit number you create and enter each time you start.
   4. Dedicated cryptographic processor chip that the system uses to store BitLocker Drive Encryption keys.
   5. Used to encrypt entire volumes and drives.

Build a List

1. In order of first to last, specify the six steps used to encrypt a removable drive using BitLocker To Go.
   _____ Type BitLocker Drive Encryption from the Windows 8.1 start menu and select it from the results list.
   _____ Choose how you want to unlock the drive.
   _____ Start encrypting the drive.
   _____ Choose where to back up the recovery key.
   _____ Select Turn on BitLocker for the removable drive.
   _____ Choose how much of the drive to encrypt.

Business Case Scenarios

Scenario 18-1: Encrypting an Operating System Drive

Amanda Killingsworth is the network administrator for a small company that upgraded its Windows 7 mobile devices to Windows 8.1 for its sales staff. It also upgraded its Exchange server to Exchange Server 2013 and can use the Microsoft Outlook Web app. The sales staff travels a lot for the company and has in the past, left the devices at the airport. In a few cases, the devices have been stolen. What recommendations would you make to protect the sensitive data based on what you know about the network?

Scenario 18-2: Troubleshooting BitLocker Drive Encryption

You attempt to enable BitLocker Drive Encryption to protect the operating system drive on a Windows 8.1 computer but are unable to complete the process. What could be contributing to the problem?

Configuring and Managing Updates

OBJECTIVE 6.1 LESSON TO OBJECTIVE MAPPING

Objective 6.1 – Configure and manage updates. This objective may include but is not limited to: configure update settings; configure Windows Update policies; manage update history; roll back updates; update Windows Store apps.

LESSON HEADING	EXAM OBJECTIVE
Configuring Update Settings	
Checking for Updates	Configure update settings
Using the Windows Update Control Panel	
Hiding and Restoring Updates	
Configuring Windows Update Policies	
Configuring Update Policies	Configure Windows Update policies
Viewing Update History	Manage update history
Rolling Back Updates	Roll back updates
Updating Windows Store Apps	Update Windows Store apps

KEY TERMS

critical updates

important updates

optional updates

recommended updates

security updates

Service Packs

■ Configuring Update Settings

↓
THE BOTTOM LINE
Microsoft routinely issues patches, service packs, and drivers to Microsoft software products in the form of Microsoft and Windows Updates. Through end-user interaction or system administration, personal and enterprise computers running Microsoft operating systems, signed drivers, and applications are patched and secured against the latest vulnerabilities, security risks, and threats.

Why do users need to run updates on their computers? The answer is to protect, secure, improve, and enhance their experiences. Throughout the lifetime of Microsoft operating systems, signed drivers, and applications, new vulnerabilities are found, exploited, and used against end users. If a vulnerability is found in the "wild" or if a vulnerability is reverse-engineered by a malicious user, that user could potentially gain unauthorized access to a user's computer. To combat these vulnerabilities, Microsoft routinely releases new patches, enabling users to download and install them so they can protect their systems.

The second Tuesday of every month, sometimes known as "Patch Tuesday," is typically release day for all tested and signed patches from Microsoft. Microsoft is not strictly limited to issuing patches on the second Tuesday alone; for example, if a zero-day exploit is found, an update might be released as soon as possible. Along with Patch Tuesday, the day after is often considered "Exploit Wednesday." The day after patches are released, malicious users have been known to reverse engineer the patch, discovering the exploit it fixes and then preparing an attack targeted at users who have not yet patched their systems. Allowing updates to download and install automatically can therefore save a lot of headaches for the end user.

Checking for Updates

It is important to routinely check for updates and to also ensure that systems are configured to automatically download and install updates for all of your Microsoft products. Keeping your system up-to-date with the latest patches protects it from the latest threats.

To protect a Windows 8.1 operating system, you can download Windows updates from the *Update and recovery* screen, accessible through *PC Settings*. Clicking *Choose how updates get installed*, as shown in Figure 19-1, provides you with the ability to control when the system downloads and installs updates.

Figure 19-1

The *Choose how updates get installed* screen

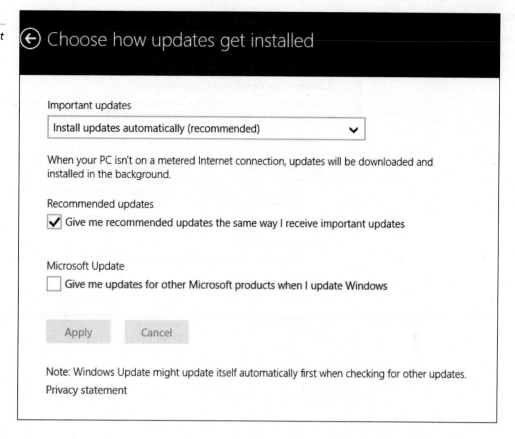

◉ Choose how updates get installed

Important updates

| Install updates automatically (recommended) ⌄ |

When your PC isn't on a metered Internet connection, updates will be downloaded and installed in the background.

Recommended updates
☑ Give me recommended updates the same way I receive important updates

Microsoft Update
☐ Give me updates for other Microsoft products when I update Windows

[Apply]   [Cancel]

Note: Windows Update might update itself automatically first when checking for other updates.
Privacy statement

CERTIFICATION READY
Configure update settings
Objective 6.1

There are several categories of updates provided by Microsoft; each category prioritizes the updates based on importance and recommended use by the end user.

- *Important updates* can be configured to be installed automatically; they typically include updates that fix or improve security, privacy, and reliability within the OS or application.
- *Recommended updates* can be configured to install automatically; they typically manage non-critical problems that might enhance end-user usability.
- *Optional updates* must be installed manually; they might include updates, drivers, and software not typically installed with the operating system.
- *Security updates*—rated as critical, important, moderate or low—are released to fix product-specific security-related vulnerabilities.
- *Critical updates* fix critical, non-security related "bugs."
- *Service Packs* are cumulative packages of updates and patches released for a system or application over a period of time.

Using the Windows Update Control Panel

Windows Update functions are also available through the traditional Windows Update control panel.

When you click *Change settings* in the Windows Update control panel, the *Choose your Windows Update settings* page appears, as shown in Figure 19-2. For users that require different download and installation options, update settings are configurable based on the end-user requirements.

Figure 19-2

The Choose your Windows
Update settings page

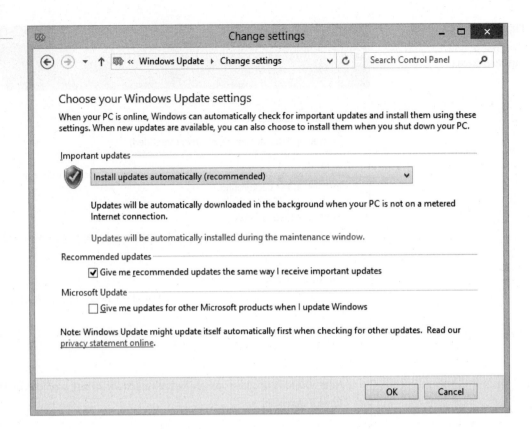

The installation options for important updates are as follows:

- **Install updates automatically (recommended):** When configured, Windows update will automatically download and install all of the important updates on the system.
- **Download updates but let me choose whether to install them:** When configured, Windows Update will automatically download important updates and notify the end user that it is ready for installation. For users in a heavy production environment where downloads can happen in the background, but where resources must be fully allocated to production tasks, the installation can take place at user discretion.
- **Check for updates but let me choose whether to download and install them:** When configured, Windows Update will not automatically download or install updates. The user will be notified of available download. Once the user downloads the updates, he will then be notified again when the recently downloaded updates are ready for install.
- **Never check for updates (not recommended):** When configured, Windows update will never automatically check for updates or notify the user. All update checks must be initiated by the end user. The user must then follow up with the download and installation tasks to perform all updates.

You can choose to install recommended updates in the same way as your important updates, which provides a more streamlined approach to downloading and installing all updates automatically. You can also chose to install updates for other Microsoft products as well.

There is also an option to check for updates for other Microsoft products. When you click the *Find out more* link on the Windows Update control panel, you are redirected to an external Microsoft site where you must agree to a Terms of Use agreement before installing the Microsoft Update service. This service searches for additional updates for other Microsoft products like Office, SQL Server, Exchange Server, and Visual Studio.

TAKE NOTE *

If update settings are configured by your system administrator, some options might be disabled for end-user configuration.

CHANGE UPDATE SETTINGS FROM THE CONTROL PANEL

GET READY. Log into a Windows 8.1 machine and then perform the following steps to change the Windows Update settings from the Control Panel:

> **TAKE NOTE** ☆
> If the Windows 8.1 computer you are configuring is on a domain that has implemented an intranet Windows Update server, some selections might be greyed out.

1. From the Windows 8.1 start menu, type Control Panel and then select it from the results list.

    The *Control Panel* window appears.
2. In the *Control Panel* window, click System and Security.
3. To display the *Windows Update configuration* window, click Windows Update.
4. Click Change settings. The *Choose your Windows Update settings* window appears.
5. From the drop-down selection under important updates, select one of the installation options.
6. Select the Give me recommended updates the same way I receive important updates check box and the Give me updates for other Microsoft products when I update Windows check box, if desired.
7. Click OK.

Hiding and Restoring Updates

> Occasionally, there are updates that are available that you do not want to be reminded of or that you do not want to install until you are ready to install them yourself. Hiding them from view eliminates the need to manually remove the update when you are selecting updates for installation in Windows Update.

If an update is hidden from view, you can easily make it visible again, which then enables you to install it.

 HIDE AND RESTORE UPDATES

GET READY. To perform this task, you must have a Windows 8.1 computer that is connected to the Internet and has an update available for installation. Then perform the following steps:

1. From the Windows 8.1 Start menu, type Control Panel and then select it from the results list.

    The *Control Panel* window appears.
2. In the *Control Panel* window, click System and Security.
3. Click Windows Update to display the *Windows Update* control panel.
4. If no updates are displayed for download, click Check for updates and then select the link indicating an update is available.

    The *Select the updates you want to install* window appears.
5. Right-click the update you want to hide and select Hide update.

    The update is now grey and will be hidden from future update selections.
6. Click the back arrow to return to the *Windows Update* page.
7. Click Restore hidden updates.

    The *Restore hidden updates* window appears.

8. Select the check box next to the update you want to restore and then click the **Restore** button.

   The updates now are restored and available for installation. You are returned to the *Windows Update* window.

9. Close the *Windows Update* window.

Configuring Windows Update Policies

↓
THE BOTTOM LINE Since Windows 2000, administrators have been able to configure Windows Update using Group Policy.

You can configure group policies on a local system by using the Local Group Policy Editor on that computer. In an enterprise environment, you can create Group Policy Objects (GPOs) and apply them to a site, a domain, or an organizational unit. By linking a GPO to an AD DS object, you deploy all of the policy settings in the GPO to the computers and users contained in the object.

Configuring Update Policies

CERTIFICATION READY
Configure Windows
Update policies
Objective 6.1

To view the configurable Windows Update policy settings, launch the Local Group Policy Editor or open a GPO in the Group Policy Management Editor and navigate to the Computer Configuration\Policies\Administrative Templates\Windows Components\ Windows Update folder, as shown in Figure 19-3.

Figure 19-3

Navigating to Windows
Update policies

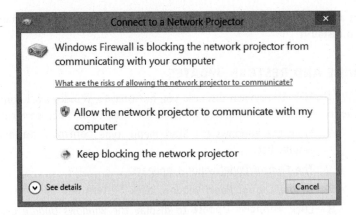

Each policy setting provides details about its function and how it reacts when enabled, disabled, or not configured. It is important to understand the client reaction before configuring any Windows Update policy setting, because any misconfiguration or unintended setting change can result in unforeseen downtime and possible data loss. When configuring Windows Update settings in an enterprise environment, you must understand the consequences of forced system restarts, application installations, and driver updates which are deployed to managed devices during production hours.

The following sections explain the functions of the Windows Update policy settings.

CONFIGURING THE INSTALL UPDATES AND SHUT DOWN DIALOG BOX POLICY

The *Do not display Install Updates and Shut Down option in Shut Down Windows dialog box* policy removes, or keeps in place, the Install Updates and Shut Down option when shutting down the system.

The following options are configurable within this policy setting:

- **Enabled:** When enabled, the *Install Updates and Shut Down* selection is removed from the *Shut Down Windows* dialog box, even when updates are available for installation on the system.

- **Disabled:** When disabled, if updates are available for installation on the system, the *Install Updates and Shut Down* selection is available to choose in the *Shut Down Windows* dialog box.

- **Not Configured:** When not configured, if updates are available for installation on the system, the *Install Updates and Shut Down* selection is available to choose in the *Shut Down Windows* dialog box.

CONFIGURING THE DEFAULT OPTION TO INSTALL UPDATES AND SHUT DOWN DIALOG BOX POLICY

The *Do not adjust default option to Install Updates and Shut Down in Shut Down Windows dialog box* policy enables the users to maintain their default shut down selections when shutting down from the Shut Down Windows dialog box.

The following options are configurable within this policy setting:

- **Enabled:** When enabled, the user's last shut down selection (Log Off, Shut Down, Restart, Hibernate, and so on) remains the default selection when the next system shut down is initiated from the *Shut Down Windows* dialog box.

- **Disabled:** When disabled, the *Install Updates and Shut Down* selection becomes the default selection when the next system shut down is initiated from the *Shut Down Windows* dialog box.

- **Not Configured:** When not configured, the *Install Updates and Shut Down* selection becomes the default selection when the next system shut down is initiated from the *Shut Down Windows* dialog box.

This policy has no effect if the *Do not display 'Install Updates and Shut Down' option in Shut Down Windows dialog box* is enabled.

CONFIGURING THE WAKE UP TO INSTALL SCHEDULED UPDATES POLICY

Windows computers that are in hibernation can be configured to wake from hibernation, install updates, and return to hibernation once the update installations have completed. The *Enabling Windows Update Power Management to automatically wake up the system to install scheduled updates* policy can wake the system up to perform scheduled updates.

The following options are configurable within this policy setting:

- **Enabled:** When enabled, Windows Update will wake up a system that is hibernating—using the Windows Power Management feature—to install updates that are scheduled for installation.

- **Disabled:** When disabled, Windows Update will not wake up a system that is hibernating in order to install scheduled updates.

- **Not Configured:** When not configured, Windows Update will not wake up a system that is hibernating in order to install scheduled updates.

If a hibernating system is running on battery power on wake up, updates will not be installed. Instead, the system will automatically return to hibernation after two minutes.

Windows Update brings only a computer out of hibernation if there are updates to be installed.

CONFIGURING THE AUTOMATIC UPDATES POLICY

One of the required policies for system wide control of Automatic Updates, the *Configure Automatic Updates* policy sets the method of downloading and installing Automatic Updates.

The following options are configurable within this policy setting:

- **Enabled:** When enabled, you must select one of the following additional options.
- **Notify for download and notify for install:** Requires user intervention to both download and install available updates. When updates are made available for download, the end-user is notified. The end-user must then initiate the download of available updates. Once the updates have been downloaded, Windows Update will again notify the end-user and require that she initiate the installation of the recently downloaded updates. This option requires the most user interaction and might leave critical systems at risk if updates are not installed on a regular schedule.
- **Auto download and notify for install:** Configured as the default setting, Windows Update will automatically download updates in the background without user intervention. Once the updates have been downloaded and are ready for installation, the user will be notified that there are updates ready for installation. The user is then given the opportunity to select and install the queued updates.
- **Auto download and schedule install:** Requires the least amount of end-user interaction and administrative effort. This selection enables a system administrator to fully automate the update installation by downloading and installing the updates in the background. If no schedule is selected, the system automatically installs updates every day at 3:00 AM.
  - o **Scheduled install day:**
    - 0 – Every day
    - 1 – Every Sunday
    - 2 – Every Monday
    - 3 – Every Tuesday
    - 4 – Every Wednesday
    - 5 – Every Thursday
    - 6 – Every Friday
    - 7 – Every Saturday
  - o **Scheduled install time:** Defined by hour, the selection list ranges from 00:00–23:00.

TAKE NOTE *

Scheduling for Windows 8, Windows 8.1, and Windows RT devices are not affected by this defined schedule; you must configure them using Computer Configuration\Policies\Administrative Templates\Windows Components\Maintenance Scheduler\Automatic Maintenance Activation Boundary. If a schedule is not defined in either location, Windows 8, Windows 8.1, and Windows RT devices will install updates every day at 3:00 AM.

- **Allow local admin to choose setting:** Local administrators to the system are allowed to choose their own download and installation settings; they will not be allowed to disable Automatic Updates.
- **Disabled:** When disabled, all update downloads and installations require the end user to manually initiate the process.
- **Not Configured:** When not configured, the end user can configure Automatic Updates from within the Control Panel.

CONFIGURING THE INTRANET MICROSOFT UPDATE SERVICE LOCATION POLICY

The *Specify intranet Microsoft Update service location* policy enables administrators to configure devices meeting the scope of the policy to receive updates from an intranet Windows System Update Services (WSUS) or System Center Configuration Manager (SCCM) server.

The following options are configurable within this policy setting:

- **Enabled:** When enabled, the device within the scope of the policy will detect and download selected updates from the specified intranet WSUS or SCCM server. Additionally, the *Set the intranet update service for detecting updates* option and the *Set the intranet statistics server* option require the fully qualified domain name (FQDN) and the port of the WSUS or SCCM server issuing the updates.
- **Disabled:** When disabled, clients will receive their updates from the Internet, not from an intranet server.
- **Not Configured:** When not configured, clients will receive their updates from the Internet, not from an intranet server.

CONFIGURING THE AUTOMATIC UPDATES DETECTION FREQUENCY POLICY

The *Automatic Updates detection frequency* policy controls how often the system will check for new updates to download and install.

The following options are configurable within this policy setting:

- **Enabled:** When enabled, Windows will check for updates at a configured time interval between 1 and 22 hours. The wait time uses the interval selected minus 0% to 20% of the hours configured.
- **Disabled:** When disabled, Windows will use the default interval of 22 hours.
- **Not Configured:** When not configured, Windows will use the default interval of 22 hours.

CONFIGURING THE NON-ADMINISTRATOR UPDATE NOTIFICATION POLICY

Enabled by default on Windows 8.1 devices, the *Allow non-administrators to receive update notifications* policy enables non-administrators to receive update notifications.

The following options are configurable within this policy setting:

- **Enabled:** When enabled, non-administrators will receive update notifications and are allowed to install the updates for which a notification was received.
- **Disabled:** When disabled, only users with elevated permissions will receive notifications and be able to install updates.
- **Not Configured:** When not configured, systems running Windows 7, Windows 8, and Windows 8.1 already permit non-administrators to be notified and to install updates.

CONFIGURING THE SOFTWARE NOTIFICATIONS POLICY

The *Turn on Software Notifications* policy notifies the end user of pending optional or featured updates are waiting for download or installation.

The following options are configurable within this policy setting:

- **Enabled:** When enabled, users will receive notifications when optional or featured software applications are available from Microsoft.
- **Disabled:** When disabled, users will not receive notifications when optional or featured software applications are available from Microsoft.
- **Not Configured:** When not configured, users will not receive notifications when optional or featured software applications are available from Microsoft.

CONFIGURING THE IMMEDIATE INSTALLATION OF AUTOMATIC UPDATES POLICY

The *Allow Automatic Updates immediate installation* policy triggers the system to install updates once they have been downloaded and prepared for installation.

The following options are configurable within this policy setting:

- **Enabled:** When enabled, Automatic Updates will be installed once they have been downloaded and queued for installation.
- **Disabled:** When disabled, Automatic Updates will not be installed immediately.
- **Not Configured:** When not configured, Automatic Updates will not be installed immediately.

CONFIGURING THE RECOMMENDED UPDATES THROUGH AUTOMATIC UPDATES POLICY

The *Turn on recommended updates via Automatic Updates* policy enables automatic installation of both important and recommended updates.

The following options are configurable within this policy setting:

- **Enabled:** When enabled, recommended updates and important updates will be received and installed.
- **Disabled:** When disabled, only important updates will be received and installed.
- **Not Configured:** When not configured, only important updates will be received and installed.

CONFIGURING THE NO AUTO-RESTART WITH LOGGED ON USERS POLICY

Configuring the *No auto-restart with logged on users for scheduled automatic updates installations* policy prevents a system from rebooting immediately after an update has installed if a user is logged in.

The following options are configurable within this policy setting:

- **Enabled:** When enabled, systems that have recently download and installed Automatic Updates, requiring a restart, will not be forced to restart immediately after installation. Automatic Updates will notify the end user to restart when convenient.
- **Disabled:** When disabled, systems that have recently downloaded and installed Automatic Updates, requiring a restart, will notify the end user that the system will restart in 5 minutes.
- **Not Configured:** When not configured, systems that have recently downloaded and installed Automatic Updates, requiring a restart, will notify the end user that the system will restart in 5 minutes.

WARNING When this policy is set to Disabled or Not Configured, systems with logged on users will restart 5 minutes after the installation. Users might lose unsaved data if the computer restarts without their knowledge.

CONFIGURING THE RE-PROMPT FOR RESTART WITH SCHEDULED UPDATES POLICY

The *Re-prompt for restart with scheduled installations* policy re-prompts users to restart at a specified interval. If the end user postpones a restart after automatic updates have been installed, the re-prompt for restart policy will notify the end user at the time specified.

The following options are configurable within this policy setting:

- **Enabled:** When enabled and an installation has been postponed, this setting will notify the end user to restart at the specified minute interval. The interval range must be between 1–1440 minutes.
- **Disabled:** When disabled, and an installation has been postponed, this setting will notify the end user to restart after 10 minutes.
- **Not Configured:** When not configured, and an installation has been postponed, this setting will notify the end user to restart after 10 minutes.

CONFIGURING THE DELAY RESTART FOR SCHEDULED INSTALLATIONS POLICY

An administrator can modify the *Delay Restart for scheduled installations* policy to allow additional time for the user to finish work before the restart is initiated.

The following options are configurable within this policy setting:

- **Enabled:** When enabled, a scheduled restart will occur after the specified minutes are reached. The minimum time allowed is 1 minute and the maximum time allowed is 30 minutes.
- **Disabled:** When disabled, a schedule restart will occur after 15 minutes.
- **Not Configured:** When not configured, a schedule restart will occur after 15 minutes.

CONFIGURING THE RESCHEDULE AUTOMATIC UPDATES SCHEDULED INSTALLATIONS POLICY

If a scheduled Automatic Update was not performed, the amount of time to wait for the next attempt at installation can be rescheduled to happen at next startup. This is configured through the *Reschedule Automatic Updates scheduled installations* policy.

The following options are configurable within this policy setting:

- **Enabled:** When enabled, once the wait time configured is reached, a scheduled installation will take place to install the updates that were missed earlier. The minimum time allowed is 1 minute and the maximum time allowed is 60 minutes.
- **Disabled:** When disabled, missed scheduled updates will be installed at the next scheduled update.
- **Not Configured:** When not configured, missed scheduled updates will be installed one minute after the computer has restarted.

CONFIGURING THE ENABLE CLIENT-SIDE TARGETING POLICY

You can configure the group names to be sent to an intranet WSUS or SCCM server using the *Enable client-side targeting* policy.

The following options are configurable within this policy setting:

- **Enabled:** When enabled, the configured target group will be sent to the intranet server.
- **Disabled:** When disabled, no target group information is sent to the intranet server.
- **Not Configured:** When not configured, no target group information is sent to the intranet server.

CONFIGURING THE ALLOW SIGNED UPDATES FROM AN INTRANET MICROSOFT UPDATE SERVICE LOCATION POLICY

Microsoft, by default, only allows the installation of updates that are signed by Microsoft. By configuring the *Allowed signed updates from an intranet Microsoft update service location* policy, an administrator can permit the installation of trusted updates that are not signed by Microsoft.

The following options are configurable within this policy setting:

- **Enabled:** When enabled, updates from non-Microsoft companies that are supplied by an intranet Windows Update server will be accepted if they are signed with a certificate found in the Trusted Publishers certificate store. Updates signed by Microsoft will also be installed.

- **Disabled:** When disabled, only updates delivered from the intranet Microsoft update server that are signed by Microsoft will be installed.

- **Not Configured:** When not configured, only updates delivered from the intranet Microsoft update server that are signed by Microsoft will be installed.

■ Viewing Update History

THE BOTTOM LINE

All of the updates installed on a Windows 8.1 system are listed in the *View update history* window.

CERTIFICATION READY
Manage update history
Objective 6.1

Viewing the update history can assist in troubleshooting failed updates, finding an update that could potentially be causing problems, or even help when verifying a required patch is installed prior to a software installation.

The View update history window also provides detailed information about the functions of installed updates, such as what security issues they address.

 REVIEW THE UPDATE HISTORY

GET READY. To review the update history of your system, log on to Windows 8.1 and then perform the following steps:

1. From the Windows 8.1 Start screen, type **Control Panel** and then select it from the results list.
   The *Control Panel* window appears.

2. Click **System and Security**.

3. Click **Windows Update** to display the *Windows Update configuration* window.

4. Click **View update history**.
   The *View update history* window appears.

5. Review the update history of your Windows 8.1 computer.

6. Double-click on an update.
   A *Windows Update* window appears, containing additional details about the update.

7. Click **Close**.

8. Click **OK** to close the *View update history* window.

9. Close the *Windows Update* window.

Rolling Back Updates

THE BOTTOM LINE

Microsoft routinely tests updates before deploying them to the mass market of Windows users. Unfortunately, there are times that a released update might conflict with a third-party application or program installed on the system. Rolling back updates enables the user to uninstall a previously installed update to the point before its original installation.

CERTIFICATION READY
Roll back updates
Objective 6.1

There are several ways to roll back an update to return a system to its previous state, including the following:

- You can perform a system restore to a time before the problematic update was installed.
- You can manually uninstall the update to return the component to its previous version. Uninstalling an update might also return a system to an operable state if a recently released update has prevented it from running properly.
- As indicated earlier, you can view updates based on their installation dates. If a system was working properly before certain updates were installed, you can review the update history and begin troubleshooting the problems by uninstalling the most recently installed updates.

 UNINSTALL AN INSTALLED UPDATE

GET READY. To uninstall an update, log onto Windows 8.1 and perform the following steps:

1. From the Windows 8.1 Start screen, type Control Panel and then select it from the results list.

   The *Control Panel* window appears.

2. Click System and Security.

3. Click Windows Update to display the *Windows Update configuration* window.

4. Click Installed Updates.

   The *Installed Updates* window appears.

5. Select the update you want to uninstall andthen from the toolbar above the list, click Uninstall.

   The *Uninstall* dialog box appears.

TAKE NOTE
You can also uninstall an update by right-clicking the update and selecting *Uninstall.*

6. Click Uninstall.

7. You might be prompted to reboot your machine after the update uninstall has completed. If prompted, you can click Yes to reboot or No to reboot at a later time.

Updating Windows Store Apps

THE BOTTOM LINE

On a daily basis, Microsoft checks to see whether there are any updates for the apps you've previously downloaded from the Windows Store. If any are found, a number indicator appears on the Store tile.

CERTIFICATION READY
Update Windows Store
Apps
Objective 6.1

To see the actual apps requiring updates, click the *Store* tile and select the *Updates* link. By default, all updates are selected automatically and clicking *Install* starts the update process, as shown in Figure 19-4. If for some reason you don't want to update all your apps at one time, you can click or touch each app to exclude it.

Figure 19-4

Managing update options

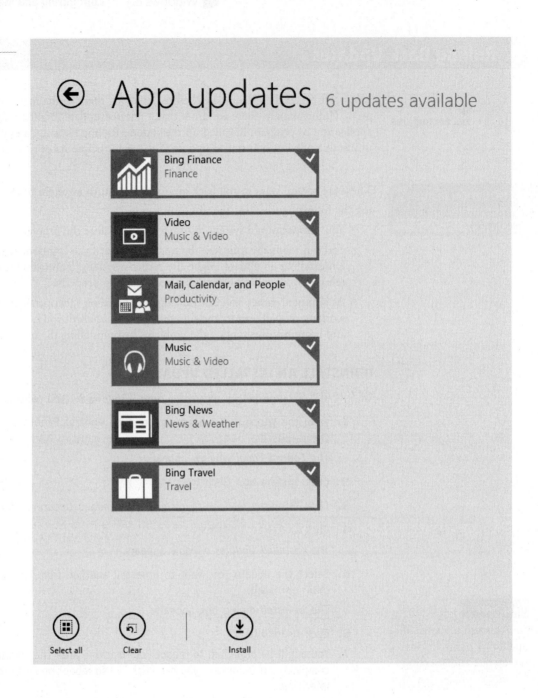

By default, Windows 8.1 is configured to download Windows app updates (but not install them) automatically in the background when your device is idle. If you don't want this to occur, you need to either change the appropriate setting on the Windows 8.1 device or use Group Policy to control the setting.

On a Windows 8.1 device, you can turn off the automatic download updates for apps by performing the steps in the following exercise.

DISABLE AUTOMATIC UPDATE DOWNLOADS

GET READY. To disable the automatic download updates for apps, perform the following steps:

1. Click the **Store** tile to open the Windows Store page.

2. Move your mouse to the upper-right corner and then click **Settings**.

3. Click **App Updates**.

4. Move the slider to the left to set it to **No**, as shown in Figure 19-5.

Figure 19-5

Turning off app updates on
Windows 8.1

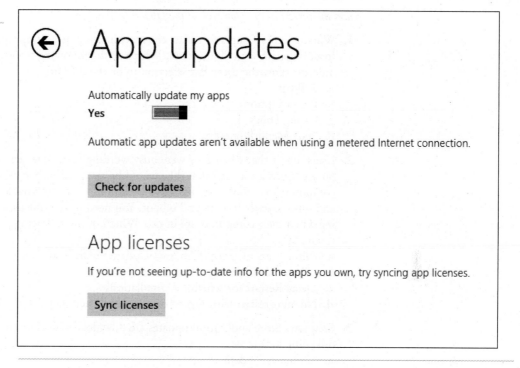

To change the setting through Group Policy, you can use either the *Local Group Policy editor (gpedit.msc)* or the *Group Policy Management console (gpmc.msc)*. Browse to the Computer Configuration\Policies\Administrative Templates\Windows Components\Store node and enable the *Turn off automatic download of updates* policy.

SKILL SUMMARY

IN THIS LESSON, YOU LEARNED:

- You perform updates on a Windows 8.1 system to enhance, improve, secure, and protect end users from threats.

- It is important to keep a system up-to-date with the lastest patches, service packs, and updates. You can configure automatic updates to require minimal user intertaction during downloading and installation.

- You can configure the download, installation, timing, and user interaction of updates using local or domain Group Policy settings.

- The update history lists recently installed updates, along with their statuses, dates of installation, and other more detailed information.

- If an updated is causing problems, you can easily roll back an installed Windows update to a previous version.

- Windows Store apps must be updated through the Windows Store.

Knowledge Assessment

Multiple Choice

Select the correct answer for each of the following questions.

1. When a user attempts to restart the machine, the default option in the Start screen is to Install Updates and Shut Down. Which of the following features can be changed in order to allow the user's last selection to be the default?
   a. Taskbar
   b. Power Options
   c. Group Policy
   d. Start Menu Properties

2. Users report that when they were busy working on a time-sensitive project, their computers issued a warning that they would be restarted in five minutes in order for the computers to complete an update installation. Users are unable to cancel the warnings and must save their work and reboot. You need to prevent users' computers from rebooting when their computers are in use. Which of the following policy settings should be modified?
   a. Allow users to cancel Windows Update restart initiation
   b. Client-side targeting
   c. Delay Restart for scheduled installations
   d. No auto-restart with logged on users for scheduled automatic updates installations

3. Windows Store application updates are downloaded and installed from which of the following locations?
   a. Windows Update
   b. Microsoft Update
   c. App Update
   d. Windows Store

4. To ensure that all computers can receive Automatic Updates even if the computers are in hibernation, which of the following policies should be changed?
   a. Enabling Windows Update Power Management to automatically wake up the system to install scheduled updates
   b. Configure Automatic Updates
   c. Automatic Updates detection frequency
   d. Allow Automatic Updates immediate installation

5. To prevent an update from appearing in the *Updates ready to install* list on the three computers in your office, which of the following actions should you take?
   a. Do not display 'Install Updates and Shut Down' option in Shut Down Windows dialog box
   b. Allow non-administrators to receive update notifications
   c. Manually hide the updates
   d. Uncheck the update from the list of available updates

6. After running Windows Updates, a critical application no longer runs properly. You have determined that an update is causing the problem. Which of the following actions should be your first troubleshooting step? (The solution must minimize the amount of system downtime.)
   a. Uninstall recently installed updates
   b. Perform a system rollback
   c. Perform a system restore
   d. Hide recently installed updates

7. To receive recommended updates the same way you receive important updates, which of the following Windows Update settings will implement this option?
   a. View update history
   b. Properties
   c. Change settings
   d. Check online for updates from Microsoft Update

8. The success or failure status of installed updates can be viewed in which of the following locations?
   a. View update history
   b. Installed Updates
   c. Microsoft Store
   d. Check for updates

9. Which of the following is the recommended Windows Update setting for downloading and installing updates?
   a. Download updates but let me choose whether to install them
   b. Check for updates but let me choose whether to download and install them
   c. Never check for updates
   d. Install updates automatically

10. Which of the following updates must be selected and installed manually in Windows Update?
    a. Featured updates
    b. Optional updates
    c. Recommended updates
    d. Important updates

Best Answer

Choose the letter that corresponds to the best answer. More than one answer choice may achieve the goal. Select the BEST answer.

1. Which of the following policy settings allows certain updates to be applied to a specific group of computers?
   a. Local Group Policy editor
   b. Client Side Targeting
   c. Group Policy editor
   d. Windows Domain Groups

2. Users are not receiving notifications that updates are available for download or install. Which of the following options should be configured?
   a. Give me recommended updates the same way I receive important updates
   b. Grant the user elevated privileges
   c. Configure Automatic Updates
   d. Allow non-administrators to receive update notifications

3. The details of an update and the applications it affects can be quickly viewed in which of the following locations?
   a. View update history
   b. Installed Updates
   c. Add/Remove Programs
   d. TechNet

4. Which of the following options can be configured so you can postpone an update until you are ready to install it at a later time?
   a. Hide update
   b. Ignore update
   c. Remove update from list
   d. Rollback update

5. Windows Server Update Service (WSUS) and System Center Configuration Manager (SCCM) are considered which type of Microsoft update service location?
   a. Internet
   b. Intranet
   c. Server-side target
   d. Client-site target

Matching and Identification

1. Match the following terms with their corresponding definitions.
   _____ a) Critical updates
   _____ b) Group policies
   _____ c) Important updates
   _____ d) Microsoft updates
   _____ e) Optional updates
   _____ f) Recommended updates
   _____ g) Security updates
   _____ h) Service packs
   _____ i) Update settings
   _____ j) Update history
   1. A cumulative collection of updates released over a period of time.
   2. All updates that have been installed on the system, sortable by status, importance, and date installed.
   3. Requiring additional components, these updates include Office products.
   4. Improves security, privacy, and reliability within the OS or application.
   5. Rated as critical, important, moderate, or low, these are released to fix product-specific security related vulnerabilities that might affect end-user or enterprise systems.
   6. Used to configure a large group of computers to receive the same updates.
   7. Modifying these will change the download and notification settings.
   8. Takes care of non-critical problems that might enhance end-user usability with the software.
   9. These updates and features must be manually installed.
   10. Fixes non-security related bugs.

Build a List

1. In order of first to last, specify the order of precedence for downloading and installing updates for other Microsoft Products.
   _____ Accept the Terms of Use.
   _____ Open **System and Security**.
   _____ Click **Install**.
   _____ Open **Windows Update**.
   _____ Click **Find out more**.
   _____ Open **Control Panel**.

2. In order of first to last, specify the steps in navigating to the Windows Update Policies.

_____ Expand Administrative Templates.

_____ Open Local Group Policy Editor.

_____ Expand Windows Components.

_____ Expand Computer Configuration.

_____ Select Windows Update.

3. In order of first to last, specify the steps in uninstalling a recently installed update.

_____ Open Installed Updates.

_____ Open System and Security.

_____ Open Windows Update.

_____ Open Control Panel.

_____ Select the update for uninstallation.

_____ Right-click and select Uninstall.

■ Business Case Scenario

Scenario 19-1: Configuring Updates for an Enterprise

You have been hired on as a consultant for a local call center that has a local datacenter with 25 fully redundant, virtualized Windows Server 2012 R2 servers, 200 phone operators on staff, and 125 desktops running Windows 8.1 Enterprise. The call center runs 24 hours a day, 7 days per week. You have been tasked with finding a solution to update all 150 systems without noticeable downtime. What solution and policies should be included in the plan of action to configure updates for this enterprise? Can any other solutions be used?

20 LESSON

Managing Local Storage

70-687 EXAM OBJECTIVE

Objective 6.2 – Manage local storage. This objective may include but is not limited to: manage disk volumes and file systems; manage storage spaces.

LESSON HEADING	EXAM OBJECTIVE
Working with Disks	
Understanding Partition Styles	
Understanding Disk Types	
Understanding Volume Types	
Understanding File Systems	
Using the Disk Management Snap-in	Manage disk volumes and file systems
Using Storage Spaces	Manage storage spaces
Using Diskpart.exe	
Using Disk Tools	

KEY TERMS

basic disk

Diskpart.exe

dynamic disk

exFAT

FAT

FAT32

GUID (globally unique identifier) partition table (GPT)

master boot record (MBR)

mirrored volume

simple volume

spanned volume

striped volume

■ Working with Disks

THE BOTTOM LINE

Hard disks are nearly always the primary storage medium in a computer running Windows 8.1, but in many cases, administrators must prepare a hard disk to store data by performing certain tasks before the computer can use it. After you prepare the hard disk, you can keep the data stored on the disk secure with tools and features provided by Windows 8.1.

When you install Windows 8.1 on a computer, the setup program automatically performs all of the preparation tasks for the hard disks in the computer. However, adding another disk is a common upgrade, and after you install the hardware, you must perform the following tasks before the user can begin storing data on it:

- **Select a partitioning style** – In Windows 8.1, two hard disk partition styles are available for both x86- and x64-based computers. The *master boot record (MBR)* partition style has been around as long as Windows, and is still the default partition style. *GUID (globally unique identifier) partition table (GPT)* has been around for a while also, but no x86 version of Windows prior to Vista supports it. (Windows XP Professional x64 Edition does support GPT.) You must choose one of these partition styles for a drive; you cannot use both.

- **Select a disk type** – Two disk types are available in Windows 8.1: basic disks and dynamic disks. Both the MBR and the GPT partition styles support basic and dynamic disks. You cannot use both types on the same disk drive. You have to decide which is best for the computer.

- **Divide the disk into partitions or volumes** – Although many professionals use the terms partition and volume interchangeably, it is correct to refer to creating partitions on basic disks, and volumes on dynamic disks.

- **Format the volumes with a file system** – Because of the high capacities of the hard drives on the market today, NTFS is the preferred file system for Windows 8.1. However, the FAT (File Allocation Table) file system is also available, in the form of FAT32 and exFAT.

The following sections examine these tasks in more detail.

Understanding Partition Styles

The term partition style refers to the method that Windows operating systems use to organize partitions on the disk.

There are two hard disk partition styles that you can use in Windows 8.1:

- **MBR** – This is the default partition style for x86-based and x64-based computers.
- **GPT** – First introduced in Windows Vista, you can now use the GPT partition style on x86-, as well as x64-based, Windows 8.1 computers.

Before Windows Vista, all x86-based computers used the MBR partition style only. Computers based on the x64 platform used either the MBR or GPT partition style, as long as the GPT disk was not the boot disk.

MBR uses a partition table to point to the locations of the partitions on the disk. Windows selected this style automatically on x86-based workstation computers because, prior to Windows Vista, this was the only style available to them. The MBR disk partitioning style supports volumes up to 2 terabytes in size, and up to either four primary partitions or three primary partitions and one extended partition. Data critical to platform operations is stored in hidden (unpartitioned) sectors.

Keep in mind, however, that unless the computer's architecture provides support for an Extensible Firmware Interface (EFI)-based boot partition, it is not possible to boot from GPT disks. In this case, the operating system must reside on an MBR disk, and GPT must reside on an entirely separate, non-bootable disk, used for data storage only.

One of the ways that GPT differs from MBR is that data critical to platform operation is stored in partitions rather than in hidden sectors. Additionally, GPT partitioned disks use redundant primary and backup partition tables for improved integrity. Although GPT specifications permit an unlimited number of partitions, the Windows implementation is restricted to 128 partitions per disk. The GPT disk partitioning style supports volumes up to 18 exabytes in size (1 exabyte = 1 billion gigabytes, or 2^{60} bytes).

➕ **MORE INFORMATION**

As far as the Windows 8.1 disk management tools are concerned, there is no difference between creating partitions or volumes in MBR and in GPT. You create partitions and volumes for both by using the same tools in the same ways.

Understanding Disk Types

Windows 8.1 supports two disk types: basic disks and dynamic disks.

Most Windows computers use basic disks, because they are the easiest to manage. A **basic disk** uses primary partitions, extended partitions, and logical drives to organize data. A primary partition appears to the operating system as though it is a physically separate disk and can host an operating system. A primary partition that hosts an operating system is marked as the *active partition*.

During the Windows 8.1 operating system installation, the setup program creates a *system partition* and a *boot partition*. The system partition contains hardware-related files that the computer uses to start. The boot partition contains the operating system files, which are stored in the Windows folder. In Windows 8.1, the system partition is the active partition, which the computer uses when starting.

When you use the Disk Management snap-in to work with basic disks using the MBR partition style, you can create up to three primary partitions. The fourth partition you create must be an extended partition, after which you can create as many logical drives as you need from the space in the extended partition. You can format and assign drive letters to logical drives, but they cannot host an operating system. Table 20-1 compares some of the characteristics of primary and extended partitions.

Table 20-1

Comparison of Primary and Extended Partitions

PRIMARY PARTITIONS	EXTENDED PARTITIONS
A primary partition functions as if it is a physically separate disk and can host an operating system.	Extended partitions cannot host an operating system.
A primary partition can be marked as an active partition. You can have only one active partition per hard disk. The system BIOS looks to the active partition for the boot files it uses to start the operating system.	You cannot mark an extended partition as an active partition.
You can create up to four primary partitions or three primary partitions and one extended partition	A basic disk can contain only one extended partition, but an unlimited number of logical partitions.
You format each primary partition and assign a unique drive letter.	You do not format the extended partition itself, but the logical drives it contains. You assign a unique drive letter to each of the logical drives.

When you use DiskPart, a command-line utility included with Windows 8.1, to manage a basic disk, you can create up to four primary partitions or three primary partitions and one extended partition.

TAKE NOTE*

> The DiskPart command-line utility contains a superset of the commands that the Disk Management snap-in supports. In other words, DiskPart can do everything Disk Management can do, and more.
>
> The Disk Management snap-in prohibits you from unintentionally performing actions that may result in data loss. DiskPart does not have the built-in protections that Disk Management possesses, and so does not prohibit you from performing such actions. For this reason, Microsoft recommends that only advanced personnel use DiskPart and that they use it infrequently and with due caution, because unlike Disk Management, DiskPart provides absolute control over partitions and volumes.

The alternative to using a basic disk is to convert it to a ***dynamic disk***. The process of converting a basic disk to a dynamic disk creates a single partition that occupies the entire disk. You can then create an unlimited number of volumes out of the space in that partition. The advantage of using dynamic disks is that they support several different types of volumes, as described in the next section.

Understanding Volume Types

> Dynamic disks can support five types of volumes: simple, spanned, striped, mirrored, and RAID-5 (Redundant Array of Independent Disks, level 5). Windows 8.1 only supports four of these volume types, however: simple, spanned, striped, and mirrored.

A dynamic disk is able to contain an unlimited number of volumes that function like primary partitions on a basic disk. However, you cannot access a dynamic disk from any operating system instance other than the one that converted it from basic to dynamic, which means you cannot use dynamic disks on multiboot systems.

When you create a volume on a dynamic disk in Windows 8.1, you can choose from the following four volume types:

- ***Simple volume*** – Consists of space from a single disk. Once you have created a simple volume, you can later extend it to multiple disks to create a spanned or striped volume, as long as it is not a system volume or boot volume. Windows 8.1 supports simple volumes on both basic and dynamic disks.

- ***Spanned volume*** – Consists of space from at least two, to a maximum of 32, physical disks, all of which must be dynamic disks. A spanned volume is essentially a method for combining the space from multiple dynamic disks into a single large volume. Windows 8.1 writes to the spanned volume by filling all of the space on the first disk, and then filling each of the additional disks in turn. You can extend a spanned volume at any time by adding additional disk space. Creating a spanned volume does not increase the read/write performance, nor does it provide fault tolerance. In fact, if a single physical disk in the spanned volume fails, all of the data in the entire volume is lost.

- ***Striped volume*** – Consists of space from at least two, to a maximum of 32, physical disks, all of which must be dynamic disks. The difference between a striped volume and a spanned volume is that in a striped volume, the system writes data one stripe at a time to each successive disk in the volume. Striping provides improved performance because each disk drive in the array has time to seek the location of its next stripe while the other drives are writing.

Striped volumes do not provide fault tolerance, and you cannot extend them after creation. If a single physical disk in the striped volume fails, all of the data in the entire volume is lost.

- *Mirrored volume* – Consists of an equal amount of space from two disks, both of which must be dynamic disks. In a mirrored volume, each disk holds an identical copy of the data written to the volume as a fault tolerance measure. If one disk fails, the data remains accessible from the second disk. Because of the data redundancy, a mirrored volume only provides half as much storage space as any of the other volume types.

TAKE NOTE *

The disk volume limitations described here are those of Windows 8.1 itself. It is also possible to implement these disk technologies using third party hardware and software products that have their own capabilities and limitations. For example, while Windows 8.1 does not support software RAID-5; there are many disk adapter products on the market that enable you to create RAID volumes of various types on computers running Windows 8.1.

The type of volume you choose for a Windows 8.1 computer depends on the user's needs. While standalone systems for home or small business users might benefit from striped, spanned, or mirrored volumes, for most Windows 8.1 workstations in an enterprise environment, simple volumes are adequate. If the client's computer stores data that requires additional performance or protection against failure, other volume types can fill the bill.

Understanding File Systems

To organize and store data or programs on a hard drive, you must install a file system. A file system is the underlying disk drive structure that enables you to store information on your computer. You install file systems by formatting a partition or volume on the hard disk.

In Windows 8.1, there are two basic file system options to choose from: NTFS and FAT. *NTFS* is the preferred file system for Windows 8.1, its main benefits being improved support for larger hard drives and better security in the form of encryption and permissions that restrict access by unauthorized users.

Because the FAT file systems lack the security that NTFS provides, any user who gains access to your computer can read any file without restriction. Additionally, most of the various FAT file systems have disk size limitations that render them impractical.

The FAT file systems that Windows 8.1 supports are as follows:

- *FAT* – The original 16-bit FAT file system for hard disks, also known as FAT16, is limited to partitions no larger than 4 GB, which makes it virtually useless for today's computers.

- *FAT32* – Using the 32-bit version of FAT, called FAT32, Windows 8.1 can create partitions up to 32 GB in size, with individual files up to 4 GB. Although these limits at one time seemed outlandishly large, they make FAT32 an impractical file system solution on computers today. The 32 GB maximum partition size is a deliberate restriction in Windows 8.1, not an inherent limitation of FAT32. In fact, Windows 8.1 can access FAT32 partitions up to 2 TB in size; it just can't create them. This limitation is intended to prevent Windows performance degradation caused by large FAT32 partitions.

- *exFAT* – Introduced in Windows Vista SP1, the Extended File Allocation Table (exFAT) file system, also known as FAT64, is a 64-bit FAT implementation that is intended primarily for large USB flash drives. The theoretical limitations of exFAT are partitions and files of up to 64 zettabytes in size. (1 zettabyte equals 1 billion terabytes or 10^{21} bytes.) The recommended maximum size for an exFAT partition in Windows 8.1 is 512 TB. The exFAT file system does not support the encryption and permission features found in NTFS, and is therefore not recommended for use on Windows 8.1 hard disks.

When you create or format a partition or volume using the Disk Management snap-in, the interface displays only the file system options that are available to you, based on the size of the partition or volume. Because of these size limitations, the only viable reason for using any of the FAT file systems on Windows 8.1 hard disks is the need to multiboot the computer with an operating system that does not support NTFS.

Using the Disk Management Snap-in

Disk Management is the primary Windows 8.1 graphical utility for creating and manipulating hard disk partitions and volumes.

Disk Management is a Microsoft Management Console (MMC) snap-in that you use to perform disk-related tasks, such as the following:

- Initializing disks.
- Selecting a partition style.
- Converting basic disks to dynamic disks.
- Creating partitions and volumes.
- Extending, shrinking, and deleting volumes.
- Formatting partitions and volumes.
- Assigning and changing driver letters and paths.
- Examining and managing physical disk properties, such as disk quotas, folder sharing and error-checking.

TAKE NOTE✱

You can also use command-line utilities, such as the DiskPart.exe program and Windows Powershell cmdlets, to perform Disk Management tasks.

OPENING THE DISK MANAGEMENT SNAP-IN

The Disk Management snap-in is a graphical tool you use to manage hard disks.

To access the Disk Management Snap-in, use the following procedure:

➔ OPEN THE DISK MANAGEMENT SNAP-IN

GET READY. Log on to Windows 8.1 using an account with Administrator privileges, and then perform the following steps:

1. On the Windows desktop, right-click the Start button and click **Control Panel**.
   The *Control Panel* window appears.
2. Click **System and Security**, and then, in the *Administrative Tools* category, click **Create and Format Hard Disk Partitions**.
   The Disk Management window appears.

The Disk Management console is divided into two customizable panes: the Top view and the Bottom view, which display disk and volume information, respectively. Although Disk Management can display only two views at any one time, three views are available:

- **Disk List** – As shown in Figure 20-1, this view provides a summary about the physical drives in the computer. This information includes the disk number; disk type, such as basic or DVD; disk capacity; size of unallocated space; the status of the disk device, such as online, offline, or no media; the device interface, such as small computer system interface (SCSI) and integrated device electronics (IDE); and the partition style, such as MBR or GPT.

Figure 20-1

Disk Management's Disk
List view

Disk	Type	Capacity	Unallocated Space	Status	Device Type	Partition Styl
Disk 0	Basic	127.00 GB	1 MB	Online	ATA	MBR
Disk 1	Basic	40.00 GB	40.00 GB	Online	SCSI	MBR
Disk 2	Basic	40.00 GB	40.00 GB	Online	SCSI	MBR
Disk 3	Basic	40.00 GB	40.00 GB	Online	SCSI	MBR
CD-ROM 0	DVD	3.25 GB	0 MB	Online	ATAPI	MBR

- **Volume List** – As shown in Figure 20-2, this view provides a more detailed summary of all the drives on the computer. This information includes the volume name; the volume layout, such as simple; the disk type, such as basic or dynamic; the file system in use, such as NTFS or CDFS; the hard disk status, such as healthy, failed, or formatting; the disk capacity and available free space; the percentage of the hard disk that is free; whether the hard disk is fault tolerant; and the disk overhead percentage.

Figure 20-2

Disk Management's Volume
List view

Volume	Layout	Type	File System	Status	Capacity	Free Space	% Free
(C:)	Simple	Basic	NTFS	Healthy (Boot, Page File, Crash Dump, ...	126.66 GB	97.08 GB	77 %
15.0.4420.1017 (D:)	Simple	Basic	UDF	Healthy (Primary Partition)	769 MB	0 MB	0 %
DATA (E:)	Simple	Basic	FAT32	Healthy (Primary Partition)	19.99 GB	19.99 GB	100 %
System Reserved	Simple	Basic	NTFS	Healthy (System, Active, Primary Partit...	350 MB	109 MB	31 %

- **Graphical View** – As shown in Figure 20-3, this view displays a graphical representation of all the physical disks, partitions, volumes, and logical drives available on the computer. The graphical view is divided into two columns: the disk status column (located on the

Figure 20-3

Disk Management's
Graphical View

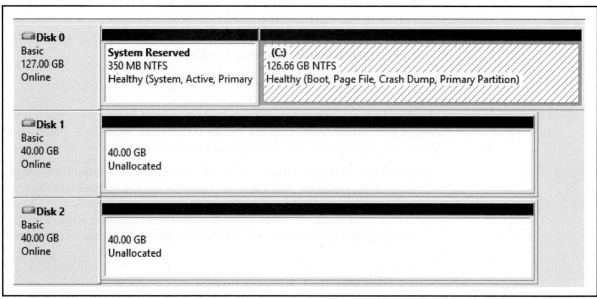

left) and the volume status column (located on the right). The information displayed in these columns and the commands available in the context menu produced by right-clicking them, are shown in Table 20-2.

Table 20-2

Disk Management Graphical View Information

	DISK STATUS COLUMN	VOLUME STATUS COLUMN
Information displayed	• Disk number • Disk type • Disk capacity • Disk status	• Volume name • Volume size • File system • Volume status
Context menu commands	• Convert a basic disk to a dynamic disk • Convert an MBR disk to a GPT disk • Create a new spanned, striped, or mirrored volume • Take the disk offline • Open the disk's Properties sheet	For a mounted partition or volume: • Mark a basic disk as active • Change the drive letter and paths • Format the partition or volume • Extend the volume • Shrink the volume • Add a mirror • Delete the volume • Open the volume's Properties sheet For unallocated space: • Create a new simple volume • Create a new spanned volume • Create a new striped volume • Create a new mirrored volume • Open the disk's Properties sheet

By default, the Top view pane depicts the Volume List view, and the Bottom view pane depicts the Graphical View. You can change the views of both the Top view and Bottom view to suit your purposes by clicking the View menu, selecting either Top or Bottom, and then selecting the desired view. You can hide the Bottom view by clicking the Hidden menu option.

TAKE NOTE You can circumvent using Control Panel to access the Disk Management console by using the Windows 8.1 Search feature, or by opening a File Explorer window, right-clicking Computer, and then selecting Manage from the context menu. In the Computer Management console that appears, select Disk Management. You can also right-click the Start button or press the WIN1X key combination and select Disk Management from the resulting context menu.

ADDING A NEW DISK

To add a new secondary disk, shut down your computer and install or attach the new physical disk per the manufacturer's instructions. Use the following procedure to initialize the new disk:

 ADD A NEW DISK

GET READY. Log on to Windows 8.1 using an account with Administrator privileges, and then perform the following steps:

1. Open the **Disk Management** snap-in.

   If the disk does not have a disk signature, the console automatically displays the *Initialize Disk* dialog box, as shown in Figure 20-4.

Figure 20-4

The *Initialize Disk* dialog box

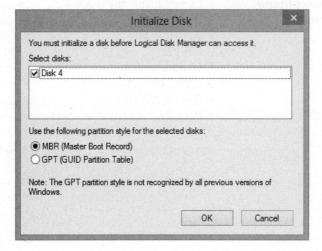

2. Select the partition style you want to use for the disk and then click **OK**.

   The disk is ready to be partitioned.

WARNING Converting the disk partition style is a destructive process. You can only perform the conversion on an unallocated disk, so if the disk you want to convert contains data, you must back up the disk, verify the back up, and then delete all existing partitions or volumes, before you begin the process.

CHANGING THE PARTITION STYLE

Disk Management has most likely selected the MBR partition style by default. You can quickly check which partition style the hard disk is assigned by right-clicking the disk status column in the Graphical view. If the context menu contains the Convert to GPT Disk menu item, the disk is using the MBR partition style.

You can also check the volume's information by opening the *Properties* sheet for disk and clicking the Volumes tab. This tab displays information such as disk type, disk status and partition style.

To convert the partition style for a disk, use the following procedure:

 CONVERT THE DISK PARTITION STYLE

GET READY. Log on to Windows 8.1 using an account with Administrator privileges, and then perform the following steps:

1. Open the **Disk Management** snap-in.

2. In *Disk List* view, right-click the disk you need to convert and, from the context menu, select **Convert to GPT Disk** or **Convert to MBR Disk**.

   The system then proceeds with the conversion. The length of time this process takes depends on the size of the hard disk.

CONVERTING A BASIC DISK TO A DYNAMIC DISK

When you create a striped, spanned, or mirrored volume on a basic disk, the Disk Management snap-in automatically converts the basic disk (and any additional disks needed to create the volume) to a dynamic one. Therefore, it usually is not necessary to manually convert disks yourself. However, you can convert a basic disk to a dynamic disk at any time, without affecting the data stored on it. Before you convert a basic disk to a dynamic disk, you must be aware of the following conditions:

- Make sure that you have enough hard disk space available for the conversion. The basic-to-dynamic conversion will fail if the hard drive does not have at least 1 MB of free space at the end of the disk. The Disk Management console reserves this free space when creating partitions and volumes, but you cannot presume that other disk management tools you might use will also preserve that space.

- You should not convert a basic disk to a dynamic disk if you are multibooting the computer. If you convert to a dynamic disk, you will not be able to start installed operating systems from any volume on the disk, except the current boot volume.

- You cannot convert removable media to dynamic disks. You can configure them only as basic disks with primary partitions.

- You cannot convert drives that use an allocation unit size (sector size) greater than 512 bytes unless you reformat the drive with a smaller sector size before the conversion.

- Once you change a basic disk to a dynamic disk, the only way you can change it back again is to back up the entire disk and delete the dynamic disk volumes. When you delete the last volume, the dynamic disk automatically reverts back to a basic disk.

To manually convert a basic disk to a dynamic disk, use the following procedure:

 ## CONVERT A BASIC DISK TO A DYNAMIC DISK

GET READY. Log on to Windows 8.1 using an account with Administrator privileges, and then perform the following steps:

1. Open the **Disk Management** snap-in.

2. In *Disk List* view, right-click the basic disk that you want to convert and, from the context menu, select **Convert to Dynamic Disk**.

   The Convert to Dynamic Disk dialog box appears, as shown in Figure 20-5.

Figure 20-5

The *Convert to Dynamic Disk* dialog box

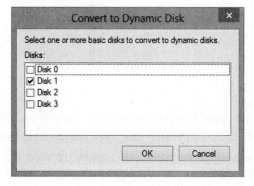

3. Select the checkboxes for the disks you want to convert and then click **OK**.

   If the disks you selected do not contain formatted partitions, clicking **OK** immediately converts the disks, and you do not need to follow the remaining steps.

If the disks you are converting to dynamic disks do have formatted partitions, clicking **OK** displays the Disks to Convert dialog box, as shown in Figure 20-6, which means that you need to follow the remaining steps to complete the disk conversion.

Figure 20-6

The *Disks to Convert* dialog box

4. The *Disks to Convert* dialog box lists the disks you chose for conversion for your confirmation. In the *Will Convert* column, check the value. It should be set to *Yes* for each of the disks that you are converting. If any of the disks have the value *No*, they might not meet Windows conversion criteria.

5. Click **Details**.

   The Convert Details dialog box appears, as shown in Figure 20-7. This dialog box lists the partitions on the selected drives that Disk Management will convert.

Figure 20-7

The *Convert Details* dialog box

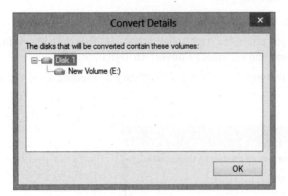

6. When you are ready to continue with the conversion, click **OK**.

7. On the *Disks to Convert* dialog box, click **Convert** to start the conversion.

   A Disk Management information box appears, to warn you that once you convert the disks to dynamic disks, you will not be able to boot installed operating system from any volume other than the current boot volume.

8. Click **Yes** to continue.

   Disk Management completes the conversion. If a selected drive contains the boot partition, the system partition, or a partition that is in use, Disk Management prompts you to restart the computer.

When you convert from a basic disk to a dynamic disk, Disk Management performs the following tasks.

- Basic disk partitions are converted to dynamic disk volumes of equal size.
- Basic disk primary partitions and logical drives in the extended partition are converted to simple volumes.
- Any free space in a basic disk extended partition is marked as unallocated.

CREATING PARTITIONS AND VOLUMES

The Disk Management console creates both partitions and volumes with one set of dialog boxes and wizards. To create a new partition on a basic disk, or a new volume on a dynamic disk, use the following procedure:

TAKE NOTE *

Technically speaking, the Disk Management snap-in creates partitions on basic disks and volumes on dynamic disks. However, in recent Windows versions, including Windows 8.1, the interface tends to use the terms interchangeably. In most instances, the snap-in refers to volumes on both basic and dynamic disks, but it still uses the term partition when referring to formatting and making a partition active.

 CREATE A VOLUME

GET READY. Log on to Windows 8.1 using an account with Administrator privileges, and then perform the following steps:

CERTIFICATION READY
Manage disk volumes and file systems
Objective 6.2

1. Open the **Disk Management** snap-in.
2. In the *Graphical* view, right-click the unallocated area on the volume status column for the disk on which you want to create a volume and, from the context menu, select **New Simple Volume**.

   The *New Simple Volume Wizard* appears.
3. Click **Next** to bypass the Welcome page.

   The Specify Volume Size page appears, as shown in Figure 20-8.

Figure 20-8

The *Specify Volume Size* page

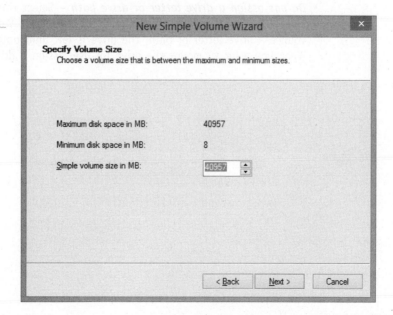

New Simple Volume Wizard	×

Specify Volume Size
Choose a volume size that is between the maximum and minimum sizes.

Maximum disk space in MB:	40957
Minimum disk space in MB:	8
Simple volume size in MB:	40957

[< Back] [Next >] [Cancel]

4. In the *Simple Volume Size in MB* spin box, specify the size for the new volume, within the maximum and minimum limits stated on the page, and then click Next.

The *Assign Drive Letter or Path* page appears, as shown in Figure 20-9.

Figure 20-9

The *Assign Drive Letter or Path* page

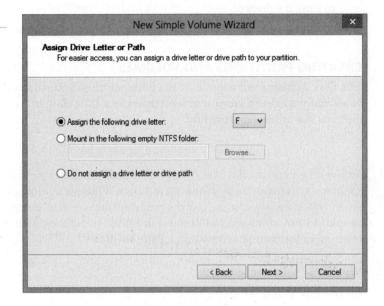

5. Configure one of the following three options and then click Next.

The Format Partition page appears, as shown in Figure 20-10.

- *Assign the following drive letter* – If you select this option, click the associated drop-down list for a list of available drive letters, and then select the desired letter you want to assign to the drive.

- *Mount in the following empty NTFS folder* – If you select this option, you are required to either type the path to an existing NTFS folder, or click Browse to search for or create a new folder. The entire contents of the new drive will appear in the folder you specify.

- *Do not assign a drive letter or drive path* – Select this option if you want to create the partition, but are not ready to use it yet. When you do not assign a volume a drive letter or path, the drive is left unmounted and inaccessible. When you want to mount the drive for use, assign a drive letter or path to it.

Figure 20-10

The *Format Partition* page

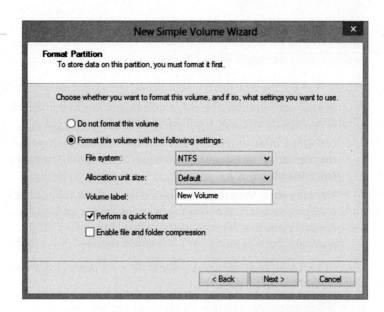

6. Specify whether and how the wizard should format the volume. If you do not want to format the volume at this time, select the Do not format this volume option. If you do want to format the volume, select the Format this volume with the following settings option and then configure the associated options, which are as follows. Then click Next.

The *Completing the New Simple Volume Wizard* page appears.

- *File system* – Select the desired file system: NTFS, FAT, FAT32, or exFAT. The options that appear in the drop-down list are based on the size of the partition or volume you are creating.

- *Allocation unit size* – Specify the file system's cluster size. The cluster size specifies the size of the basic unit that the system will use to allocate disk space. The system calculates the default allocation unit size based on the size of the volume. You can override this value by clicking on the associated drop-down list and then selecting one of the values in the list. For example, if your client uses consistently small files, you may want to set the allocation unit size to a smaller cluster size.

- *Volume label* – Specify a name for the partition or volume. The default name is New Volume, but you can change to name to anything you want.

- *Perform a quick format* – When selected, the wizard formats the disk without checking for errors. This is certainly a faster formatting method, but it is not the Microsoft recommended method. When you check for errors, the system looks for and marks bad sectors on the disk so that the system will not use them.

- *Enable file and folder compression* – When selected, file and folder compression for the disk is turned on. This option is available for the NTFS file system only.

7. Review the settings to confirm your options, and then click Finish.

The wizard creates the volume according to your specifications.

EXTENDING AND SHRINKING VOLUMES

The ability to shrink and extend volumes was first introduced in Windows Vista. (And you could extend volumes in Windows XP, too.) To extend or shrink a partition or volume, you simply right-click a partition or volume and select Extend Volume or Shrink Volume from the context menu, or from the Action menu.

TAKE NOTE*

You must be a member of the Backup Operator or the Administrators group to extend or shrink any partition or volume.

Windows 8.1 extends existing primary partitions, logical drives, and simple volumes by expanding them into adjacent unallocated space on the same disk. When you extend a simple volume across multiple disks, the simple volume becomes a spanned volume. You cannot extend striped volumes.

To extend a partition on a basic disk, the system must meet the following requirements:

- A basic partition must be either unformatted or formatted with the NTFS file system.

- If you extend a logical drive, the console first consumes the contiguous free space remaining in the extended partition. If you attempt to extend the logical drive beyond the confines of its extended partition, the extended partition expands to any unallocated space left on the disk.

- You can extend the partition of logical drives, boot volumes, or system volumes only into contiguous space, and only if the hard disk can be upgraded into a dynamic disk. The operating system will permit you to extend other types of basic volumes into noncontiguous space, but will prompt you to convert the basic disk to a dynamic disk.

To extend a simple or spanned volume on a dynamic disk, the system must meet these requirements:

- When extending a simple volume, you can only use the available space on the same disk, if the volume is to remain simple.

- You can extend a simple volume across additional disks if it is not a system volume or a boot volume. However, once you expand a simple volume to another disk, it is no longer a simple volume but becomes a spanned volume.

- You can extend a simple or spanned volume if it does not have a file system (a raw volume) or if you formatted it using the NTFS file system. (You cannot extend FAT volumes.)

When shrinking partitions or volumes, the Disk Management console frees up space at the end of the volume, relocating the existing volume's files, if necessary. The console then converts that free space to new unallocated space on the disk. To shrink a basic disk partition or any kind of dynamic disk volume except for a striped volume, the system must meet the following requirements.

- The existing partition or volume must not be full and must contain the specified amount of available free space for shrinking.

- The partition or volume must not be a raw partition (one without a file system). Shrinking a raw partition that contains data mighty destroy the data.

- You can shrink a partition or volume only if you formatted it using the NTFS file system. (You cannot shrink FAT volumes.)

CREATING SPANNED, STRIPED, AND MIRRORED VOLUMES

Spanned, striped, or mirrored volumes require dynamic disks. When you create a spanned, striped, or mirrored volume, you create a single dynamic volume that extends across multiple physical disks.

To create a spanned, striped, or mirrored volume, use the following procedure:

 CREATE A SPANNED OR STRIPED VOLUME

GET READY. Log on to Windows 8.1 using an account with Administrator privileges, and then perform the following steps:

1. Open the **Disk Management** snap-in.

2. In the *Graphical* view, right-click an unallocated area on a disk and, from the context menu, select **New Spanned Volume**, **New Striped Volume**, or **New Mirrored Volume**.

   A wizard appears, named for the volume type.

3. Click **Next** to bypass the *Welcome* page.

   The *Select Disks* page appears.

4. On the *Select Disks* page, under the *Available standard* list box, select each disk you want to use in the volume and then click **Add**. For a spanned or striped volume, you can add up to 31 additional disks; for a mirrored volume, you can add only one.

5. Specify the space you want to use on each disk by selecting the disk in the *Selected standard* list box, and then, using the *Select The Amount Of Space In MB* spin box, specify the amount of disk space that you want to include in the volume. For spanned or striped volumes, you can use different amounts of space on each drive. For mirrored volumes, you must use the same amount of space on both disks. Then click **Next**.

   The *Assign Drive Letter or Path* page appears.

6. Specify whether you want to assign a drive letter or path and then click **Next**.

   The *Format Partition* page appears.

7. Specify whether or how you want to format the volume and then click **Next**.

   The *Completing* page appears.

8. Review the settings to confirm your options, and then click **Finish**. If one or more of the disks you selected is a basic disk, a *Disk Management* message box appears, informing you that the wizard will convert the basic disk(s) to dynamic disk(s). Click **Yes** to continue.

   The wizard creates the volume according to your specifications.

Once the wizard has created the volume, it appears in the Graphical view with a single color on each of the disks contributing to the volume space, as shown in Figure 20-11.

Figure 20-11

A spanned volume in the *Disk Management* snap-in

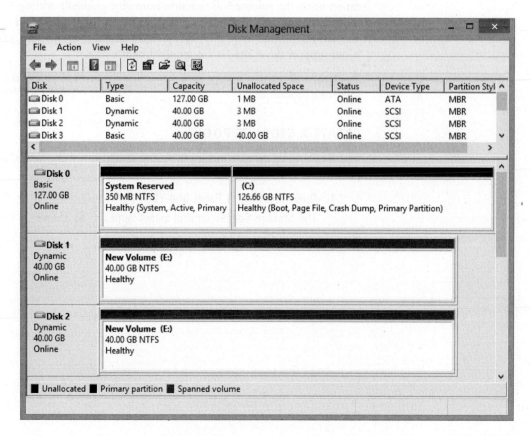

Using Storage Spaces

Windows 8.1 includes a new disk virtualization technology called *Storage Spaces*, which enables a computer to concatenate storage space from individual physical disks and use that space to create a virtual disk.

CERTIFICATION READY
Manage storage spaces
Objective 6.2

This type of virtualization is a feature often found in SAN and NAS technologies, which require a substantial investment in specialized hardware and administrative skill. Storage Space provides similar capabilities, using standard direct-attached disk drives or simple external arrays.

Storage Spaces uses unallocated disk space to create storage pools. A *storage pool* can span multiple drives invisibly, providing an accumulated storage resource that you can expand or reduce as needed by adding disks to or removing them from the pool.

When you create a storage pool, it appears to the operating system as a single volume, called a storage space, even if it consists of many physical disks. Storage spaces can also provide fault tolerance by using the physical disks in the storage pool to hold mirrored or parity data.

Storage spaces can also be thinly provisioned, meaning that while you specify a maximum size for the disk, it starts out small and grows as you add data to it. You can therefore create a virtual disk with a maximum size that is larger than that of your storage space.

For example, if you plan to allocate a maximum of 10 TB for your database files, you can create a thin 10 TB storage pool, even if you only have physical disks totaling 2 TB. The application using the volume will function normally, gradually adding data until the storage pool is nearly consumed, at which point the system notifies you to add more space to the pool. You can then install more physical storage and add it to the pool, gradually expanding it until it can support the entire 10 TB required by the disk.

To create and manage storage spaces, you use the Storage Spaces control panel, as in the following procedure.

CREATE A STORAGE POOL

GET READY. Log on to Windows 8.1 using an account with Administrator privileges, and then perform the following steps:

1. Open the Control Panel and click System & Security > Storage Spaces.
   The Storage Spaces control panel appears, as shown in Figure 20-12.

Figure 20-12

The *Storage Spaces*
control panel

2. Click **Create a new pool and storage space.**

   The *Create a Storage Pool Wizard* appears, displaying the *Select drives to create a storage pool* page, as shown in Figure 20-13.

Figure 20-13

The *Select drives to create a storage pool* page

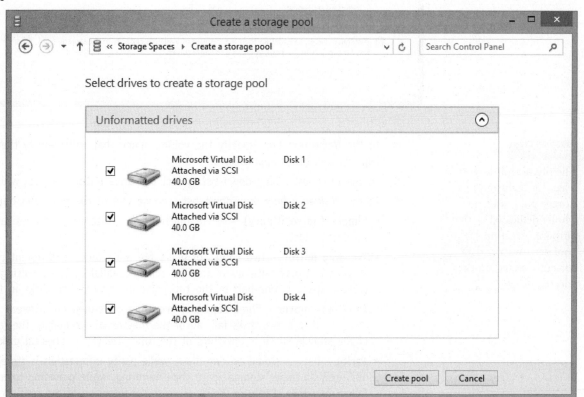

3. Select the checkboxes for the disks you want to include in the storage pool and then click **Create pool**.

The *Enter a name, resiliency type, and size for the storage space* page appears, as shown in Figure 20-14.

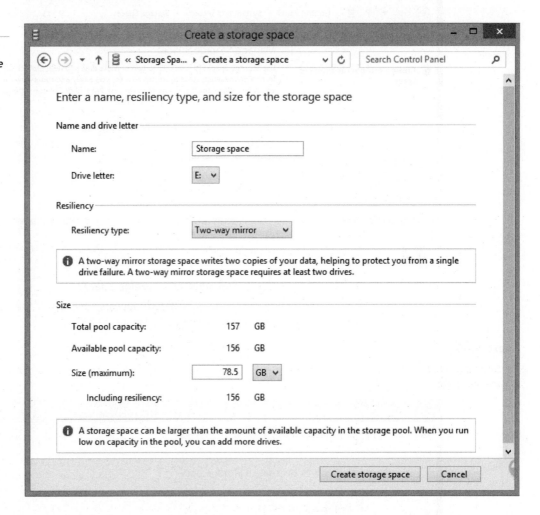

4. In the *Name* text box, specify the volume name that will identify the pool in File Explorer and other applications.

5. In the *Drive letter* drop-down list, select the drive letter the pool will use.

6. In the *Resiliency type* drop-down list, choose one of the following options:
   - **Simple (no resiliency)** – No redundant data is stored. If a physical disk fails, its data is lost.
   - **Two-way mirror** – Two copies of every file are stored on different physical disks, so that if a disk fails, all of its files remain available. The resulting size of the storage space is one-half of the total size of the physical disks in the pool.
   - **Three-way mirror** – Three copies of every file are stored on different physical disks, so that if two disks fail, all of the files remain available. The resulting size of the storage space is one-third of the total size of the physical disks in the pool
   - **Parity** – Data is stored on two disks, while parity information is stored on the third. This yields a larger storage space than mirroring, while providing tolerance for a failed disk drive. Parity is the most processor-intensive of the resiliency options.

TAKE NOTE*

The physical disks you select for inclusion in a storage pool must be wholly dedicated to that purpose. Creating the pool destroys any data currently stored on the selected disks.

7. In the *Size (maximum)* text box, specify the ultimate maximum size of the storage space (which can be larger than the currently available physical disk space).

8. Click Create storage space.

The storage space and the pool appear in the Storage Spaces control panel, as shown in Figure 20-15.

Figure 20-15

The *Storage Spaces* control panel, with a storage pool

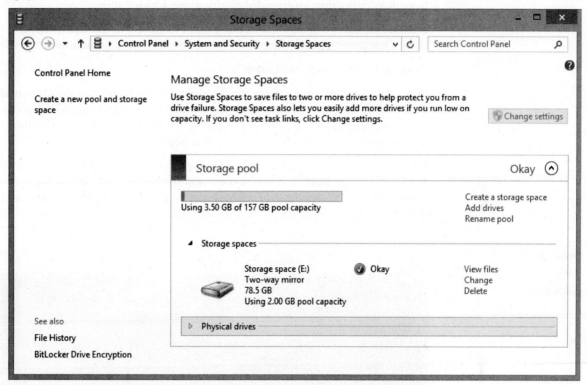

9. Close the *Storage Spaces* control panel.

The storage space is now ready for use an appears like a regular volume in File Explorer, the Disk Management snap-in, and other applications.

+ MORE INFORMATION

Parity is a mathematical algorithm that some disk storage technologies use to provide data redundancy in their disk write operations. To calculate the parity information for a drive array, the system takes the values for the same data bit at a specific location on each drive in the array and adds them together to determine whether the total is odd or even. The system then uses the resulting total to calculate a value for a parity bit corresponding to those data bits. The system then repeats the process for every bit location on the drives. If one drive is lost due to a hardware failure, the system can restore each lost data bit by calculating its value using the remaining data bits and the parity bit.

For example, in an array with five disks, suppose the first four disks have the values 1, 1, 0, and 1 for their first bit. The total of the four bits is 3, an odd number, so the system sets the first bit of the fifth disk, the parity disk, to 0, indicating an odd result for the total of the bits on the other four disks. Suppose then that one disk fails. If the parity disk fails, no actual data is lost, so data I/O can proceed normally. If one of the four data disks is lost, the total of the first bits in the remaining three disks will be either odd or even. If the total is even, because we know the parity bit is odd, the bit in the missing disk must have been a 1. If the total is odd, the bit in the missing disk must have been a 0. After the failed disk hardware is replaced, the system can use this information to reconstruct the lost data.

Using Diskpart.exe

In addition to the graphical interface in the Disk Management snap-in, Windows 8.1 also includes a command line tool called ***Diskpart.exe***, which you can use to manage disks.

Diskpart.exe is a powerful utility that can perform any task the Disk Management snap-in can and more. For example, Diskpart enables you to create a fourth primary partition on a basic disk, rather than an extended partition and a logical disk.

Diskpart.exe has two operational modes, a script mode and an interactive mode. If you choose to create Diskpart scripts, you can run them from the command prompt using the following syntax:

`Diskpart.exe /s scriptname`

When you run Diskpart.exe from the Windows 8.1 command prompt without any parameters, a DISKPART> prompt appears, from which you can execute additional commands. The typical working method is to shift the focus of the program to the specific object you want to manage, and then execute commands on that object.

For example, the `list disk` command displays a list of the disk drives in the system, as shown in Figure 20-16. The `select disk 1` command then shifts the focus to Disk 1. Any disk-specific commands you execute the program will now apply to Disk 1. The `create partition primary size=10000` command therefore creates a new 10 GB primary partition on Disk 1.

Figure 20-16

Shifting object focus in Diskpart.exe

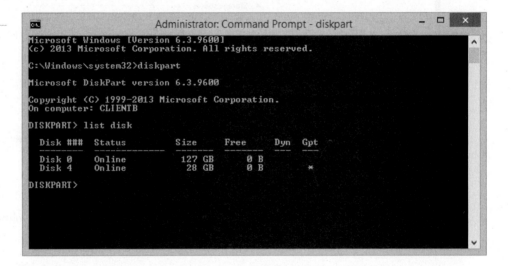

Using Disk Tools

Windows 8.1 provides a selection of tools that you can use to free up disk space, defragment volumes, and check disks for errors. These tools are simple and safe enough for most end-users and still powerful enough for administrators.

The Windows 8.1 disk tools are all accessible from each volume's Properties sheet. You can therefore access the tools from any File Explorer window or from the Disk Management snap-in.

USING DISK CLEANUP

When a disk starts to run low on storage space, it is often possible to reclaim space occupied by unnecessary files, such as temporary files, setup logs, and files in the Recycle Bin. Windows 8.1 refers to the process of deleting these files as cleaning up a disk.

TAKE NOTE*

Unlike the Disk Management snap-in, the Diskpart.exe program is particular about disk terminology. When you are working with a basic disk, for example, you can only create partitions, not volumes, unless you convert the basic disk to a dynamic disk first.

To clean up a Windows 8.1 volume, use the following procedure.

⊙ CLEAN UP A VOLUME

GET READY. Log on to Windows 8.1 using an account with Administrator privileges and then perform the following steps:

1. Open the **Disk Management** snap-in.

2. In the *Graphical* view, right-click a volume and, from the context menu, select **Properties**.

   The Properties sheet for the volume appears.

3. On the *General* tab, click **Disk Cleanup**. After a scan of the volume, the Disk Cleanup dialog box appears, as shown in Figure 20-17.

   The dialog box lists the types of files that are available for cleanup and specifies the amount of disk space you can reclaim.

Figure 20-17

The *Disk Cleanup* dialog box

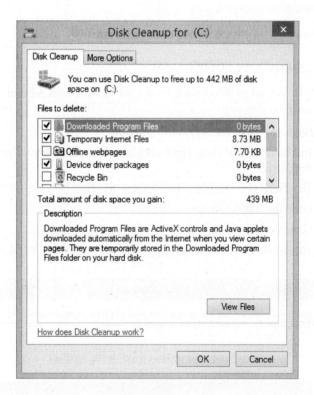

4. Select the checkboxes for the files you want to delete and then click **OK**.

   A *Disk Cleanup* message box appears.

5. Click **Delete Files** to confirm that you want to delete the selected files.

   Disk Cleanup deletes the selected files.

6. Click **OK** to close the volume's *Properties* sheet.

Once you delete files using the Disk Cleanup tool, you cannot reclaim them from the Recycle Bin.

DEFRAGMENTING DISKS

Hard disk drives write data in clusters, units of a standard size designated when you format the disk. Initially, when you save a file to a hard disk, the drive writes it to contiguous clusters, that is, a sequence of clusters that are all next to each other. Over time, however, as files are written and rewritten to the disk, the contiguous spaces grow smaller, and the drive is forced to split files into clusters located at different places on the disk. This process is called fragmentation.

Fragmentation reduces the efficiency of the disk because it forces the drive to relocate its heads many times to read a single file. The effect is the same as if you were forced to read a book with pages not in numerical order. You would spend a lot of time looking for each page and less time actually reading.

Windows 8.1 includes a tool that enables you to defragment your volumes by recopying fragmented files to contiguous space on the disk.

WARNING It is strongly recommended that you perform a full backup of your volumes before you defragment them. While the Windows 8.1 Disk Defragmenter is a reliable tool, defragmentation is a hardware-intensive process, and drive failures can conceivably occur.

To defragment a volume, use the following procedure.

DEFRAGMENT A VOLUME

GET READY. Log on to Windows 8.1 using an account with Administrator privileges and then perform the following steps

1. Open the **Disk Management** snap-in.
2. In the *Graphical* view, right-click a volume and, from the context menu, select **Properties**.

   The *Properties* sheet for the volume appears.
3. Click the **Tools** tab.
4. Click **Optimize**.

   The *Optimize Drives* dialog box appears, as shown in Figure 20-18.

Figure 20-18

The *Optimize Drives* dialog box

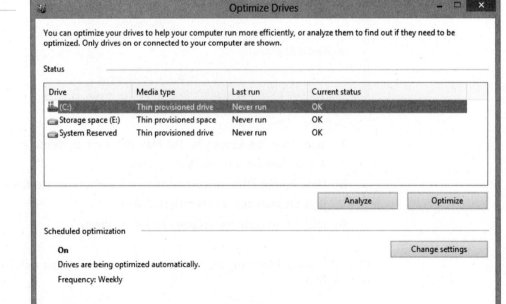

5. In the *Current Status* box, select the volume you want to work with and then click **Analyze**.

   The *Current Status* box displays the percent of the volume that is fragmented.

6. In the *Current Status* box, select the volume you want to work with and then click **Optimize**.

   The Disk Defragmenter manipulates the files on the volume to eliminate as much fragmentation as possible. When the process is completed, the *Current Status* box displays the new fragmentation percentage for the volume.

7. Click **Close** to close the *Optimize Drives* dialog box.

8. Click **OK** to close the volume's *Properties* dialog box.

The time required for the defragmentation process depends on the size of the volume, the number of files stored there, the amount of free space, and the degree to which the volume is fragmented. The process can easily take several hours. In addition to the graphical interface, it is also possible to defragment disks from the command prompt, using the Defrag.exe program. This enables you to incorporate defragmentation into scripts. The syntax for the command line interface is as follows:

```
Defrag.exe volume [/C][/E
volumes][/A][/X][/T][/H][/M][/U][/V]
```

- *volume* – Specifies the drive letter or mount point of the volume to defragment.
- /C – Defragments all local volumes on the computer.
- E *volumes* – Defragments all local volumes on the computer except those you specify.
- /A – Displays a fragmentation analysis for the volume without performing a defragmentation.
- /X – Consolidates the free space on the volume.
- /T – Tracks the operation currently in progress.
- /H – Runs the operation at normal priority, instead of the default low priority.
- /M – Defragments multiple volumes simultaneously.
- /U – Displays the progress of the operation currently in progress.
- /V – Displays information in verbose mode, with additional detail and statistics.

CHECKING FOR DISK ERRORS

Windows 8.1 includes a tool that can check disks for errors and, in many cases, repair them. If, for example, one of a system's volumes is unavailable for defragmentation, it could be due to errors that you must repair first.

To check a volume for errors, use the following procedure.

 CHECK FOR DISK ERRORS

GET READY. Log on to Windows 8.1 using an account with Administrator privileges and then perform the following steps:

1. Open the **Disk Management** snap-in.

2. In the *Graphical* view, right-click a volume and, from the context menu, select **Properties**.

   The *Properties* sheet for the volume appears.

3. Click the **Tools** tab.

4. Click **Check now**.

   If the system has not experienced any errors from that drive, a *You don't need to scan this drive* page appears.

5. Click Scan drive.

The system scans the selected disk and generates a result page.

6. Click Close.

You can also use the Chkdsk.exe utility to check for disk errors from the command prompt. For example, to check the C: drive for errors, search for bad sectors, and fix any errors found, you can use the following command:

Chkdsk.exe C: /f /r

SKILL SUMMARY

IN THIS LESSON, YOU LEARNED:

- There are two hard disk partition styles that you can use in Windows 8.1: MBR and GPT.

- Windows 8.1 supports two disk types: basic disks and dynamic disks.

- Basic disks can have up to four partitions: three primary partitions and the fourth usually being an extended partition, on which you can create multiple logical drives.

- Windows 8.1 supports four types of dynamic volumes: simple, spanned, striped, and mirrored.

- You use the Disk Management snap-in for MMC to manage disks.

- Windows 8.1 includes a new disk virtualization technology called Storage Spaces, which enables a server to concatenate storage space from individual physical disks and allocate it to create virtual disks of any size.

■ Knowledge Assessment

Multiple Choice

Select one or more correct answers for each of the following questions.

1. Which of the following statements are true of striped volumes? (Choose all that apply.)
   a. Striped volumes provide enhanced performance over simple volumes.
   b. Striped volumes provide greater fault tolerance than simple volumes.
   c. You can extend striped volumes after creation.
   d. If a single physical disk in the striped volume fails, all of the data in the entire volume is lost.

2. Which of the following are requirements for extending a volume on a dynamic disk? (Choose all that apply.)
   a. If you want to extend a simple volume, you can use only the available space on the same disk, if the volume is to remain simple.
   b. The volume must have a file system before you can extend a simple or spanned volume.
   c. You can extend a simple or spanned volume if you formatted it using the FAT or FAT32 file systems.
   d. You can extend a simple volume across additional disks if it is not a system volume or a boot volume.

3. Which of the following are not true in reference to converting a basic disk to a dynamic disk?
   a. You cannot convert a basic disk to a dynamic disk if you need to dual boot the computer.
   b. You cannot convert drives with volumes that use an allocation unit size greater than 512 bytes.
   c. A boot partition or system partition on a basic disk cannot be extended into a striped or spanned volume, even if you convert the disk to a dynamic disk.
   d. The conversion will fail if the hard drive does not have at least 1 MB of free space at the end of the disk.

4. Which of the following volume types supported by Windows 8.1 provide fault tolerance?
   a. Striped
   b. Spanned
   c. Mirrored
   d. None of the above

5. Which of the following are true statements regarding Storage Spaces? Select all that apply.
   a. Uses unallocated disk space to create storage pools
   b. Appears as a single volume called a storage volume
   c. Can be thinly provisioned
   d. Appears as a single volume called a provisioned volume

6. Which of the following commands is used to switch the focus from disk 1 to disk 2 using the Diskpart.exe tool?
   a. list disk
   b. select disk 2
   c. select disk 1 > 2
   d. diskpart.exe /select disk 1

7. Which of the following can impact the time it takes to complete the defragmentation process? Select all that apply.
   a. Volume size
   b. Number of files stored on a volume
   c. Amount of free space
   d. Degree to which the volume is fragmented

8. What are the maximum number of partitions available on a basic disk?
   a. 1 primary and 1 extended
   b. 2 primary and 1 extended
   c. 3 primary and 1 extended
   d. 4 primary and 1 extended

9. Which of the following are true statements regarding disks in Windows 8.1? Select all that apply.
   a. Boot partition contains the operating system files
   b. System partition contains the operating files
   c. System partition is the active partition
   d. Boot partition is the active partition

10. Which of the following operating systems support MBR and GPT partition styles? Select all that apply.
    a. Windows 8.1 x86-based
    b. Windows XP x64-based
    c. Windows XP x86-based
    d. Windows Server 2012 x64-based

Best Answer

Choose the letter that corresponds to the best answer. More than one answer choice may achieve the goal. Select the BEST answer.

1. Which of the following resiliency options provides the most protection to a storage space?
   a. Simple
   b. Two-way mirror
   c. Three-way mirror
   d. Parity

2. In Windows 8.1, there are four volume types to choose from. If the goal is to take advantage of dynamic disk features, protect the computer against single disk failure and the loss of storage space is not a major concern, which volume type would best fit the need?
   a. Striped volume
   b. Mirrored volume
   c. Spanned volume.
   d. Simple volume.

3. Windows 8.1 supports FAT, FAT32, exFAT, and NTFS file systems. Which of the following best reflects a viable reason to use a FAT file system instead of NTFS?
   a. The need to share files over the network
   b. The need to create partitions up to 32GB in size
   c. The need to use diagnostic utilities that only run on FAT systems.
   d. To support a multi-boot system with a non-Windows operating system

4. A user would like to perform basic disk maintenance on their computer. Of the tools available, which is likely to cause the most damage if used in the hands of a novice?
   a. Disk Management console
   b. Disk Cleanup
   c. Chkdsk.exe
   d. Diskpart.exe

5. A user indicates they would like to convert their basic disk to a dynamic disk to take advantage of the simple, striped, spanned, and volume mirror capabilities. Of the disks listed, which is most likely to support the conversion from basic to dynamic with the least amount of administrative effort?
   a. 1 MB free space at end of disk, non-multi-boot system, allocation unit size 512.
   b. 1 MB free space at end of disk, non-multi-boot system, allocation unit size >512
   c. 5 MB free space at end of disk, multi-boot system, allocation unit size 512
   d. 5 MB free space at end of disk, multi-boot system, allocation unit size >512

6. In Windows 8.1, Storage Spaces uses unallocated space to create storage pools. While creating a new storage pool, the option to select the type of resiliency must be chosen. If you have five hard disks in the pool, what resiliency type would provide the best choice in regard to protecting against disk failure?
   a. Simple
   b. Two-way mirror
   c. Three-way mirror
   d. Parity

Matching and Identification

Complete the following exercise by matching the terms with their corresponding definitions.

_____ **a)** Passphrase
_____ **b)** Location-aware printing
_____ **c)** Mobile broadband network
_____ **d)** Adhoc mode
_____ **e)** Infrastructure mode
_____ **f)** Denial of service
_____ **g)** WEP
_____ **h)** Shared secret
_____ **i)** WPA2-Enterprise
_____ **j)** WPA2-Personal

1. Configures wireless adapter to connect through a WAP.
2. Prevents legitimate users from communicating with a WAP.
3. Words and characters used to authenticate a wireless connection.
4. A security setting used to encrypt network traffic before it is sent in WEP.
5. Also known as WPA-PSK or pre-shared key mode.
6. Feature that allows you to set default printer for each network you connect to.
7. Wireless security protocol that uses a shared key to encrypt traffic.
8. Configures wireless adapter to connect to other wireless computers bypassing the WAP.
9. Also known as WPA-802.1x or WPA-RADIUS.
10. Provide high-speed access through portable devices; requires data plan.

Build a List

1. Order the steps to create a storage pool.
   _____ Select a fault tolerance option for the storage space.
   _____ Create the storage pool.
   _____ Launch The Create a Storage Pool Wizard.
   _____ Specify a name for the storage space.
   _____ Open the Storage Spaces control panel.
   _____ Create the storage space.
   _____ Select the disks to add to the storage pool.
   _____ Select a drive letter for the storage space.

2. In order of first to last, specify the correct order of steps to convert a basic disk to a dynamic disk.
   _____ In *Disk List* view, right-click the basic disk that you want to convert and, from the context menu, select **Convert to Dynamic Disk**.
   _____ Select the checkboxes for the disks you want to convert and then click **OK**.
   _____ Click **Details**. The *Convert Details* dialog box appears,
   _____ Click **Yes** to continue. Disk Management completes the conversion.
   _____ On the *Disks to Convert* dialog box, click **Convert** to start the conversion.
   _____ When you are ready to continue with the conversion, click **OK**.
   _____ The *Disks to Convert* dialog box lists the disks you chose for conversion for your confirmation.
   _____ Open the **Disk Management** snap-in.

3. Specify the correct order of steps to create a spanned or striped volume.
   _____ Click **Next** to bypass the *Welcome* page.
   _____ Specify the space you want to use on each disk by selecting the disk in the Selected standard list box, and then, using the *Select The Amount Of Space In MB* spin box, specify the amount of disk space that you want to include in the volume. Click Next.

_____ On the *Select Disks* page, under the *Available standard* list box, select each disk you want to use in the volume and then click Add.

_____ In the *Graphical* view, right-click an unallocated area on a disk and, from the context menu, select New Spanned Volume, New Striped Volume, or New Mirrored Volume.

_____ Open the Disk Management snap-in.

_____ Review the settings to confirm your options, and then click Finish. If one or more of the disks you selected is a basic disk, a *Disk Management* message box appears, informing you that the wizard will convert the basic disk(s) to dynamic disk(s). Click Yes to continue.

_____ Specify whether or how you want to format the volume and then click Next. The *Completing* page appears.

_____ Specify whether you want to assign a drive letter or path and then click Next. The *Format Partition* page appears.

4. Specify the correct order of steps to create a volume.

_____ Specify whether and how the wizard should format the volume.

_____ Open the Disk Management snap-in.

_____ Configure one of the following three options (Assign the following drive letter, Mount in the following empty folder, or Do not assign a drive letter or drive path) and then click Next.

_____ In the *Graphical* view, right-click the unallocated area on the volume status column for the disk on which you want to create a volume and, from the context menu, select New Simple Volume.

_____ In the *Simple Volume Size in MB* spin box, specify the size for the new volume, within the maximum and minimum limits stated on the page, and then click Next.

_____ Review the settings to confirm your options, and then click Finish.

_____ Click Next to bypass the Welcome page. The *Specify Volume Size* page appears.

■ Business Case Scenarios

Scenario 20-1: Creating Volumes on Dynamic Disks

Maria has 3 hard disks on her computer. Using the Disk Management tool, she created a striped volume. What are advantages and disadvantages of her choice of volume type?

Scenario 20-2: Converting Disk Partition Styles

Elliot, the junior administrator for the company, is currently reviewing a Windows 8.1 x86 system. After opening Disk Management and right-clicking the disk status column in the Graphical view, he notices the context menu contains the *Convert to GTP Disk* menu item. What does this mean and what are the implications of performing the conversion?

Monitoring System Performance

70-687 EXAM OBJECTIVE

Objective 6.3 – Monitor system performance. This objective may include but is not limited to: configure and analyze event logs; configure event subscriptions; configure Task Manager; monitor system resources; optimize networking performance; configure indexing options.

LESSON HEADING	EXAM OBJECTIVE
Monitoring and Diagnosing Performance	
Using Event Viewer	Configure and analyze event logs Configure event subscriptions
Using the Performance Monitor Console	Monitor system resources
Managing Performance	
Working with Processes	
Using Task Manager	Configure Task Manager
Using Resource Monitor	
Viewing System Configuration Details	
Adjusting Performance Settings	
Configuring Index Settings	Configure indexing options
Troubleshooting Windows 8.1	
Using the Windows Memory Diagnostic Tool	
Using the Windows Network Diagnostic Tool	Optimize networking performance
Viewing Problem Reports	

KEY TERMS

baseline	Get-WinEvent	Reliability Access Component Agent (RACAgent)
Clear-Eventlog	instance	Reliability Monitor
collectors	intelligent network	sources
custom view	log	subscriptions
data collector set	performance counters	System Configuration tool (msconfig.exe)
diacritic	performance object	
events	process trees	

■ Monitoring and Diagnosing Performance

THE BOTTOM LINE

For a computer to perform well, all of its components must be individually efficient. Windows 8.1 includes a variety of tools that enable you to locate components whose performance is below par.

A computer's level of performance is based on a combination of factors, any of which can function as a bottleneck that slows down the entire system. For example, a Windows 8.1 computer might have an extremely fast processor, but if it is lacking in memory, it will have to page data to the swap file on the hard drive more often, slowing down the system. In the same way, a computer might have a fast processor and plenty of memory, but if its hard drive is slow, the faster components can't run at peak efficiency.

TAKE NOTE*

Windows 8.1 includes an array of tools for monitoring and managing system performance that may be used by either standard users or administrators, as well as tool specifically designed for use by account holders with specific administrative rights. Further, the enhanced security of Windows 8.1 requires that some operations may only be performed using the local administrative account.

Windows 8.1 also includes Windows PowerShell 4.0, which has been enhanced to enable greater system diagnostic, management, and configuration capabilities.

Hardware problems are not the only cause of performance degradations. Software incompatibilities and resource depletion can also affect performance. In essence, the task of optimizing the performance of a Windows 8.1 computer consists of locating the bottlenecks and eliminating them. This might require a hardware upgrade or a reexamination of the computer's suitability to its role. Whatever the solution, the first step in determining what factors are negatively affecting the computer's performance is to quantify that performance and monitor its fluctuations.

The following sections examine some of the tools provided by Windows 8.1, which enable you to gather information about the computer's ongoing performance levels.

Using Event Viewer

Beginning in Windows Vista, the Event Viewer console has been enhanced to provide easier access to a more comprehensive array of event logs.

Software developers commonly use logs as a means of tracking the activities of particular algorithms, routines, and applications. A *log* is a list of events, which can track the activity of the software, document errors, and provide analytical information to administrators. Logs are traditionally text files, but the Windows operating systems have long used a graphical application called *Event Viewer* to display the log information gathered by the operating system.

CERTIFICATION READY
Configure and analyze
event logs
Objective 6.3

Windows has maintained the same three basic logs throughout several versions: a System log, a Security log, and an Application log. Recent versions have added a Setup log, and servers performing certain roles have additional logs, such as those tracking DNS and File Replication activities. The format of these logs has remained consistent, although the Event Viewer has undergone some changes. In Windows Server 2003 and Windows XP, Event Viewer first took the form of an MMC snap-in, rather than an independent application.

In Windows Vista and Windows Server 2008, Microsoft gave the Windows event engine its most comprehensive overhaul in many years. Windows Eventing 6.0 includes the following enhancements:

- A three pane display: Log List | Event Viewer | Actions.
- A new, XML-based log format.
- The addition of a Setup log documenting the operating system's installation and configuration history.
- New logs for key applications and services, including DFS Replication and the Key Management Service.
- Individual logs for Windows components.
- Enhanced querying capabilities that simplify the process of locating specific events, including the creation of Custom Views that may be saved, exported, or imported.
- The ability to create subscriptions that enable administrators to collect and store specific types of events from other computers on the network.

LAUNCHING THE EVENT VIEWER CONSOLE

The primary function of the Windows Eventing engine is to record information about system activities as they occur and package that information in individual units called *events*. The application you use to view the events is an MMC snap-in called *Event Viewer*. As with all MMC snap-ins, you can launch the Event Viewer console from the Start screen in a variety of ways, including the following:

- Search for **ev** and then select Event Viewer
- Type MMC, launch MMC.exe, and then add the Event Viewer snap-in.
- Open the Control Panel and click System and Security > Administrative Tools > Event Viewer
- Open the Computer Management console and then expand the Event Viewer node

USING THE OVERVIEW AND SUMMARY DISPLAY

Figure 21-1

The *Overview and Summary* screen in the *Event Viewer* console

When the Event Viewer console appears, you see the Overview and Summary display shown in Figure 21-1.

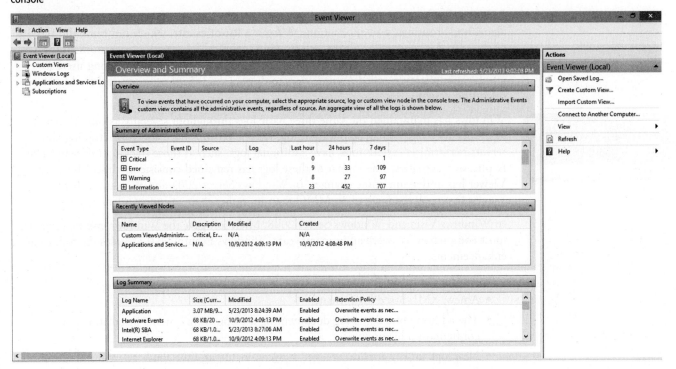

The Summary of Administrative Events displays the total number of events recorded in the last hour, day, and week, sorted by event type. This panel serves as a source for a quick diagnostic or performance check of your system health. When you expand an event type, the list is broken down by event ID.

When you double-click one of the event IDs, the console creates a filtered custom view that displays only the events having that ID.

VIEWING WINDOWS LOGS

When you expand the Windows Logs folder, you see the following logs:

- **Application** – Contains information about specific programs running on the computer, as determined by the application developer.

- **Security** – Contains information about security-related events, such as failed logons, attempts to access protected resources, and success or failure of audited events. The events recorded in this log are determined by audit policies, which you can enable using either local computer policies or Group Policy.

- **Setup** – Contains information about the operating system installation and setup history.

- **System** – Contains information about events generated by the operating system, such as services and device drivers. For example, a failure of a service to start or a driver to load during system startup is recorded in the System log.
- **Forwarded Events** – Contains events received from other computers on the network via subscriptions.

> The Administrative Events log under Custom Views is the fastest means to identify potential system or performance problems that may be recorded from the more than 200 logs available for review in Windows 8.1.

Selecting one of the logs causes a list of the events it contains to appear in the details pane, in reverse chronological order, as shown in Figure 21-2.

Figure 21-2

Contents of a log in the *Event Viewer* console

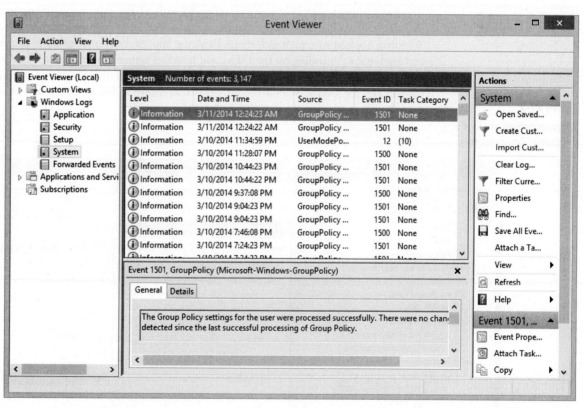

The Windows event logs contain different types of events, which are identified by icons. The five event types are as follows:

- **Information** – An event that describes a change in the state of a component or process as part of a normal operation.
- **Error** – An event that warns of a problem that is not likely to affect the performance of the component or process where the problem occurred, but that could affect the performance of other components or processes on the system.

- **Warning** – An event that warns of a service degradation or an occurrence that can potentially cause a service degradation in the near future, unless you take steps to prevent it.
- **Critical** – An event that warns that an incident resulting in a catastrophic loss of functionality or data in a component or process has occurred.
- **Verbose** – Provides verbose status, such as progress or success messages.

When you select one of the events in the list of events, its properties appear in the preview pane at the bottom of the list. You can also double-click an event to display a separate Event Properties dialog box.

VIEWING COMPONENT LOGS

The Event Viewer console contains a great deal of information, and one of the traditional problems for system administrators and desktop technicians is finding the events they need in a large mixture of results. Windows Eventing includes several innovations that can help in this regard.

One of these innovations is the addition of component-specific logs that enable you to examine the events for a particular operating system component or application. Any component that is capable of recording events in the System log or Application log can also record events in a separate log dedicated solely to that component.

The Event Viewer console comes preconfigured with a large collection of component logs for Windows 8.1. When you expand the Applications and Services Logs folder, you see logs for Windows applications, such as Internet Explorer. You might also see other vendor-specific logs and log folders depending on the OEM and installed system components. When you further expand the Microsoft and its child Windows folder, you will discover more than 200 folders that contain logs for specific Windows components, as shown in Figure 21-3. Each of these components has its own separate log, called a ***channel***.

Figure 21-3

Windows component logs in the *Event Viewer* console

In many cases, the events in the component logs are non-administrative, meaning that they are not indicative of problems or errors. The components continue to save the administrative events to the System log or Application log. The events in the component logs are:

- **Admin** – Information, warning, error, and critical event status.
- **Operational** – Operational status and configuration issues that might lead to problem cause identification.
- **Analytical and Debug** – These component logs are intended more for use in troubleshooting long-term problems and for software developers seeking debugging information. They need to be enabled by selecting the View > Show Analytical and Debug logs in the Action pane of the Event Viewer.

SCHEDULING A TASK TO RUN IN RESPONSE TO AN EVENT

Event Viewer offers the opportunity to associate an event with the Task Scheduler. Navigate to the Event Viewer log, which contains an event that you want to monitor. Select the event and right-click to Attach Task to This Event.

Identify the event source by providing the Log File, Source, and Event ID. You can then associate one of three Actions with the event:

- Start a Program.
- Send an email.
- Display a Message.

You can perform all three Actions by repeating the process and selecting each action during one pass through the process.

CREATING CUSTOM VIEWS

Another means of locating and isolating information about specific events is to use custom views. A ***custom view*** is essentially a filtered version of a particular log, configured to display only certain events. The Event Viewer console has a Custom Views folder in which you can create filtered views and save them for later use.

To create a custom view, use the following procedure.

 CREATE A CUSTOM VIEW

GET READY. Log on to Windows 8.1 and then perform the following steps:

1. Open Control Panel and click System and Security > Administrative Tools > Event Viewer.

   The *Event Viewer* console appears.

2. Right-click the Custom Views folder and then, from the context menu, select Create Custom View.

   The *Create Custom View* dialog box appears, as shown in Figure 21-4.

Figure 21-4

The *Create Custom View* dialog box

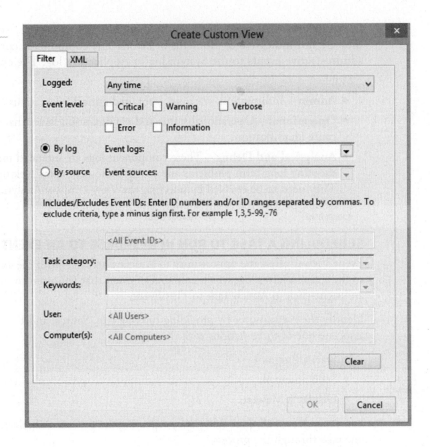

3. From the *Logged* drop-down list, select the time interval from which you want to display events.

4. In the *Event level* area, select the check boxes for the types of events you want to display.

5. From the *By log* drop-down list, select the log(s) from which you want to display events. Alternatively, from the *By source* list, select the source(s) from which you want to display events.

6. Optionally, you can specify event ID numbers, task categories, keywords, and user credentials to narrow your search.

7. Click **OK**.

The *Save Filter to Custom View* dialog box appears.

8. In the *Name* text box, type a name for the view, a description if desired, and select the folder in which you want to create your custom view.

9. Click **OK**.

The console adds your view to the folder you selected and displays the view in the detail pane.

SUBSCRIBING TO EVENTS

The Event Viewer console can provide an enormous amount of information about a Windows 8.1 computer. For a technical specialist supporting hundreds of workstations, quickly isolating relevant information can be a challenge. Using the Microsoft Management Console and adding the Event View snap-in, rather than selecting the local computer, you can remotely manage another computer's Event Viewer, using the interface shown in Figure 21-5.

Figure 21-5

The *Event Viewer* snap-in

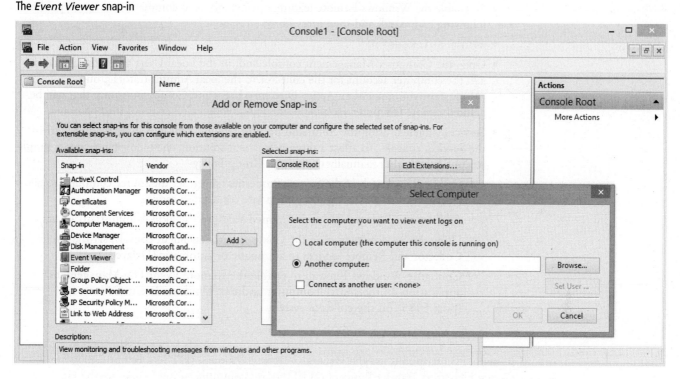

You can use the Event Viewer console on one computer to connect to another computer and display its logs. Although this saves some travel time, it is hardly practical to check logs for hundreds of computers on a regular basis.

The Windows 8.1 Event Viewer console provides a better solution for enterprise administrators in the form of subscriptions. ***Subscriptions*** enable administrators to receive events from other computers (called ***sources***) in the Event Viewer console on their own computers (called ***collectors***). Windows Eventing supports two types of subscriptions, as follows:

CERTIFICATION READY
Configure event
subscriptions
Objective 6.3

- **Collector initiated** – The collector computer retrieves events from the source computer. This type of subscription is intended for smaller networks, because you must configure each of the computers manually.

- **Source computer initiated** – The source computer sends events to the collector computer. Designed for larger networks, this type of subscription uses Group Policy settings to configure the source computers. Another advantage is the creation of a subscription that can be used to add computers at a later time (such as when you add new systems to the domain).

You create subscriptions in the local Event Viewer console. Before you can configure a subscription and event collection, you must configure both the source and collector systems to run the appropriate services required for remote communication and administration. Source computers require the *Windows Remote Management* service and collectors need the Windows Event Collector service. To configure the computers, use the following procedures.

On the collector computer:

- To start and autoconfigure the Windows Event Collector Service, open an elevated command prompt, type the following command, and then press *Enter*:
- `wecutil qc`

On each source computer:

- To enable the Windows Remote feature, open an elevated command prompt, type the following command, and then press *Enter*:
- `winrm quickconfig`
- Open the Computer Management console and, in the Local Users and Groups snap-in, add the computer account for the collector to the local Administrators group. (Alternately, you can add an Active Directory Users and Computers group that will be granted remote computer access.)
- Services launched using the command prompt sequence can be set for manual start in the Services console. To affect a more permanent solution, the following elements should be configured either manually or through Group Policy:
    - On the Remote tab of the System Properties sheet, set the source computer to allow remote connections using the appropriate connection service.
    - Add the computer or users to be granted access to the local Administrators group.
    - Using the Services snap-in in the Computer Management console, set the Event Collector and Remote services to automatic or automatic (Delayed) start.
    - Configure Windows Firewall to enable the Remote Event Log Management application on the source computer and the Windows Event Collector (port 5985) on the collector system.

TAKE NOTE * Event log subscriptions use the Hypertext Transfer Protocol (HTTP), or optionally, the Secure Hypertext Transfer Protocol (HTTPS), for communications. These are the same protocols used by Internet web servers and browsers, so most computers are configured to allow them through their firewalls. However, if you experience communication problems, make sure that the firewalls on the collector and all source computers are configured to allow traffic on TCP port 80 for HTTP or TCP port 443 for HTTPS in addition to specific firewall rules enabling the relevant remote applications.

Once you complete these tasks, you can proceed to create a subscription in the Event Viewer console on the collector computer, using the following procedure.

⊙ CREATE AN EVENT SUBSCRIPTION

GET READY. Log on to the Windows 8.1 computer you have configured as the collector and then perform the following steps:

1. Open **Control Panel** and click **System and Security > Administrative Tools > Event Viewer**.

   The *Event Viewer* console appears.

2. Right-click the **Subscriptions** node and, from the context menu, select **Create Subscription**.

   The Subscription Properties dialog box appears, as shown in Figure 21-6.

Figure 21-6

The *Subscription Properties* dialog box

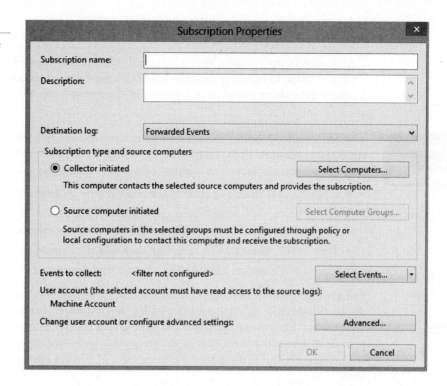

3. In the *Subscription Name* text box, type a name for the subscription.

4. Select one of the following subscription type options:

   - **Collector initiated** – If you choose this option, you must click **Select Computers** to display the *Computers* dialog box, in which you must specify the name of all the source computers from which you want to receive events.

   - **Source computer initiated** – If you choose this option, you must click **Select Computer** groups to display the *Computer Groups* dialog box, in which you can specify the names of source computers or the names of security groups into which you will add the computers from which you want to receive events.

5. Click **Select Events**. The *Query Filter* dialog box appears.

6. Use the controls to select the events you want the source computers to forward and then click **OK**.

7. Click **Advanced** to set delivery optimization settings or use **HTTPS** for additional security.

8. Click **OK** to create the subscription.

After creating a source computer initiated subscription, you must configure the source computers to forward their events by configuring a Group Policy setting called *Configure Target Subscription Manager*. This setting is found in the Computer Configuration\Policies\Administrative Templates\Windows Components\Event Forwarding folder of all local and AD DS GPOs.

USING WINDOWS POWERSHELL 4.0 TO ENUMERATE EVENT LOGS

Windows 8.1 offers you the option to use Windows PowerShell to manage event logs using the *Get-WinEvent* and *Clear-Eventlog* cmdlets.

A simple Windows PowerShell script to view Event Viewer logs follows:

```
Clear-Host
Get-WinEvent –Listlog * | Format-Table LogName
```

You can also use the –LogName parameter rather than the –Listlog parameter.

Using the Performance Monitor Console

A computer's performance level is constantly changing as it performs different combinations of tasks. Monitoring the performance of the various components over a period of time is the only way to get a true picture of the system's capabilities.

CERTIFICATION READY
Monitor system resources
Objective 6.3

The Performance Monitor console enables you to view information about your computer on a continuous, real-time basis. Like Event Viewer, the Performance Monitor console is an MMC snap-in that you can launch in a variety of ways, including the following:

- Open *Control Panel* and click *System and Security > Administrative Tools > Performance Monitor*.
- On the Start Screen, type *Perfmon*. Select the *Perfmon.exe* tile.
- Type MMC, launch MMC.exe, and then add the Performance Monitor snap-in.
- Open the Computer Management console and then select Performance.

Performance Monitor initially provides a high-level system summary, and it can measure and display hundreds of different statistics (called ***performance counters***) in a variety of ways. Performance Monitor can display a real-time graph, capture information for later graphic display, or analyze and present data in an interpreted, formatted report. You can either use pre-built diagnostic and performance measurements, or create a custom evaluation set of your own.

When you expand the Performance Monitor option in the left tools pane, the detail pane displays a real-time line graph for the % Processor Time performance counter.

ADDING COUNTERS

The performance counter that appears in Performance Monitor by default is a useful gauge of the computer's performance, but the snap-in includes hundreds of other counters that you can add to the display. To add counters to the Performance Monitor display, click the *Add* button in the toolbar, or press *Ctrl+I* to display the Add Counters dialog box.

TAKE NOTE *

Unlike most MMC snap-ins, Performance Monitor does not insert its most commonly used functions into the MMC console's Action menu. The only methods for accessing Performance Monitor functions are the toolbar buttons, hotkey combinations, and the context menu that appears when you right-click the display.

In this dialog box, specify the following four pieces of information to add a counter to the display:

- ***Computer*** – The name of the computer you want to monitor with the selected counter. Unlike most MMC snap-ins, you cannot redirect the entire focus of Performance Monitor to another computer on the network. Instead, you specify a computer name for each counter you add to the display. This enables you to create a display showing counters for various computers on the network, such as a single graph of processor activity for all of your workstations.

TAKE NOTE * You must have remote permissions, the appropriate remote service features started, and the related firewall ports enabled on both the source and collector systems to remotely gather Performance Monitor information.

- **Performance object** – A category representing a specific hardware or software component in the computer. Click the down arrow on a performance object to display a selection of performance counters related to that component.
- **Performance counter** – A statistic representing a specific aspect of the selected performance object's activities.
- **Instance** – An element representing a specific occurrence of the selected performance counter. For example, on a computer with two network interface adapters, each counter in the Network Interface performance object would have two instances, one for each adapter, enabling you to track the performance of the two adapters individually. Some counters also have instances such as Total or Average, enabling you to track the performance of all instances combined or the median value of all instances.

Once you select a computer name, a performance object, a performance counter in that object, and an instance of that counter, click Add to add the counter to the Added Counters list. The dialog box remains open so that you can add more counters. Click *OK* when you are finished to update the graph with your selected counters.

TAKE NOTE * Select the *Show description* check box to display a detailed explanation of the selected performance counter.

The performance objects, performance counters, and instances that appear in the *Add Counters* dialog box depend on the computer's hardware configuration, the software installed on the computer, and the computer's role on the network.

MODIFYING THE GRAPH VIEW

Once you select multiple performance objects and add them to the active Performance Monitor, the tool will display a real-time graph similar to Figure 21-7.

Figure 21-7

Performance Monitor
real-time display

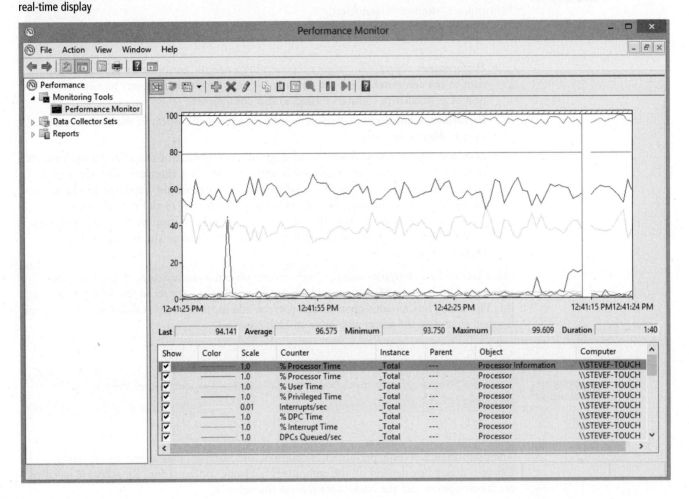

The legend beneath the Performance Monitor graph specifies the line color for the counter, the scale of values for the counter, and other identifying information. When you select a counter in the legend, its current values appear in numerical form at the bottom of the graph. Click the *Highlight* button in the toolbar (or press *Ctrl+H*) to change the selected counter to a broad line that is easier to distinguish in the graph.

If your computer is otherwise idle, you will probably notice that the line in the default graph is hovering near the bottom of the scale, making it difficult to see its value. You can address this problem by modifying the scale of the graph's Y (that is, vertical) axis. Click the *Properties* button in the toolbar (or press *Ctrl+Q*) to display the Performance Monitor Properties sheet and then click the *Graph* tab. In the *Vertical scale* box, you can reduce the maximum value for the Y axis, thereby using more of the graph to display the counter data.

Within the General tab of the Performance Monitor Properties sheet you can also modify the sample rate of the graph. By default, the graph updates the counter values every one second, but you can increase this value to display data for a longer period of time on a single page of the graph. This can make it easier to detect long-term trends in counter values.

TAKE NOTE* The *Performance Monitor Properties* sheet contains several other controls that you can use to modify the appearance of the graph. For example, on the Graph tab, you can add axis titles and gridlines, and in the Appearance tab, you can control the graph's background and select a different text font.

USING OTHER VIEWS

In addition to the line graph, Performance Monitor has two other views of the same data: a histogram view and a report view. You can change the display to one of these views by clicking the *Change Graph Type* toolbar button. You can also use *Ctrl+G* to scroll through the three report views. The histogram view is a bar graph with a separate vertical bar for each counter, as shown in Figure 21-8. In this view, it is easier to monitor large numbers of counters, because the lines do not overlap.

Figure 21-8

The *Performance Monitor* histogram view

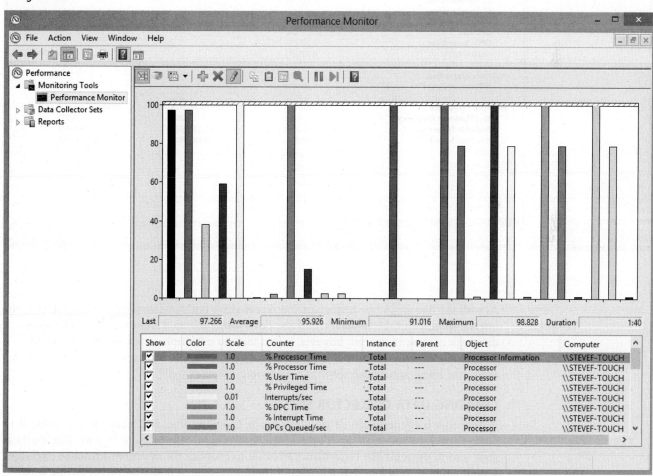

The report view (see Figure 21-9) displays the numerical value for each of the performance counters.

Figure 21-9

The *Performance Monitor*
report view

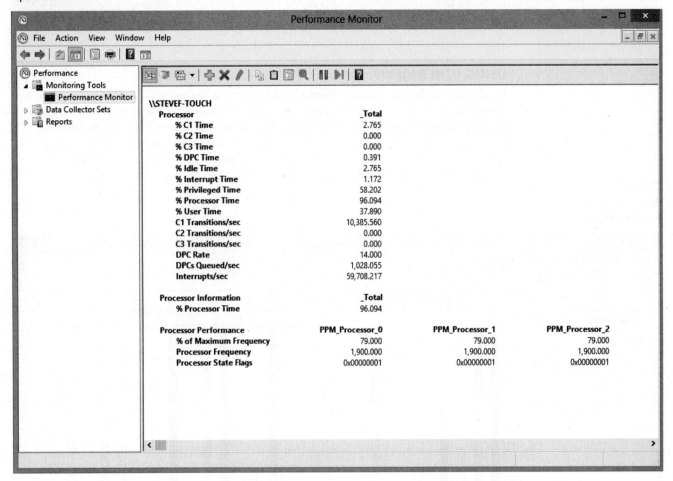

As with the line graph, the histogram and report views both update their counter values at the interval specified in the General tab of the *Performance Monitor Properties* sheet. The main drawback of these two views, however, is that they do not display a history of the counter values, only the current value. Each new sampling overwrites the previous one in the display, unlike the line graph, which displays the previous values as well.

CREATING DATA COLLECTOR SETS

Performance bottlenecks can develop over a long period of time, and it can often be difficult to detect them by observing a server's performance levels at a singular point in time. It is always a good idea to use tools like Performance Monitor to establish the operational baseline levels for a workstation. A *baseline* is simply a set of readings, captured under normal operating conditions, which you can save and compare to readings taken at a later time. By comparing the baseline readings to the workstation's current readings at regular intervals, you might possibly detect trends that eventually affect the computer's performance.

To capture counter statistics in the Performance Monitor console for later review, you must create a *data collector set*, using the following procedure.

CREATE A DATA COLLECTOR SET

GET READY. Log on to Windows 8.1 and then perform the following steps:

1. Open the *Performance Monitor* console.

2. Expand the **Data Collector Sets** folder. Then right-click the **User Defined** folder and, from the context menu, select **New > Data Collector Set**.

   The *Create New Data Collector Set* wizard appears, displaying the *How would you like to create this new data collector set?* page.

3. In the *Name* text box, type a name for the data collector set. Then, select the **Create manually (Advanced)** option and then click **Next**.

   The *What type of data do you want to include?* page appears.

4. Select the **Performance counter** check box and then click **Next**.

   The *Which performance counters would you like to log?* page appears.

5. Click **Add**. The standard *Add Counters* dialog box appears. Select the counters you want to log in the usual manner and then click **OK**.

   The counters appear in the *Performance counters* box.

> **TAKE NOTE** * You can also use the *Create New Data Collector Set* wizard to create performance counter alerts, which monitor the values of specific counters and perform a task, such as sending an email to an administrator, when the counters reach a specific value.

> **TAKE NOTE** *
> The default location is %systemdrive%\ Perflogs\Admin\ .)

6. Select the interval at which you want the system to collect samples and then click **Next**. The *Where would you like the data to be saved?* page appears.

7. Type the name of or browse to the folder where you want to store the data collector set and then click **Next**.

   The *Create the data collector set?* page appears.

8. If the account you are currently using does not have the privileges needed to gather the log information, click **Change** to display a *Performance Monitor* dialog box in which you can supply alternative credentials.

9. Select one of the following options:

   - **Open properties for this data collector set** – Saves the data collector set to the specified location and opens its Properties sheet for further modifications.

   - **Start this data collector set now** – Saves the data collector set to the specified location and starts collecting data immediately.

   - **Save and close** – Saves the data collector set to the specified location and closes the wizard.

10. Click **Finish**. The new data collector set appears in the *User Defined* folder.

11. Select the new data collector set and then click **Start** in the toolbar.

    The console begins collecting data until you click **Stop**.

Once you capture data using the collector set, you can display the data by double-clicking the *Performance Monitor* file in the folder you specified during its creation. This opens a Performance Monitor window containing a graph of the collected data, as shown in Figure 21-10, instead of real-time activity.

Figure 21-10

Performance Monitor information collected using a data collector set

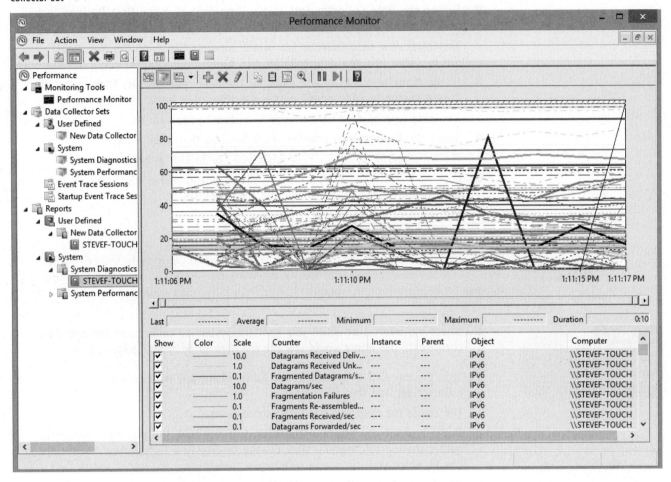

You can also choose to look at a formatted report generated by an analysis of the results, or the folder containing all of the XML components generating during the report generation period. To access these alternatives, right-click on the report or select *View* from the toolbar.

By repeating this process at a later time and comparing the information in the two data collector sets, you can often detect performance trends that indicate the presence of bottlenecks.

CREATING A SYSTEM DIAGNOSTICS REPORT

In addition to its user-configurable capabilities, Performance Monitor also includes preset system diagnostics, system performance, Event Trace Session, and Startup Event Session collector sets. The System Diagnostic and System Performance collector set can be found by expanding the Data Collector Sets\System node, selecting a report, and then clicking the *Start* button in the toolbar.

After allowing the program about 60 seconds to gather data, browse to the Reports\System\ System Diagnostics node to view the report. The same View options exist for pre-configured reports as for user-generated collector sets.

Using Reliability Monitor

Reliability Monitor is a stability-tracking tool that extends the capabilities of the Event Viewer, enhancing both baseline comparison and problem resolution. You can launch the Reliability Monitor in several ways:

- At the Start screen, type *Reliability Monitor.*
- Open *Control Panel* and click *System and Security > Action Center > Maintenance > View Reliability History.*

Reliability Monitor gathers information using a hidden scheduled task called ***Reliability Access Component Agent (RACAgent).*** The agent collects data from the event logs every hour and updates the Reliability Monitor display every 24 hours, as shown in Figure 21-11.

Figure 21-11

The *Reliability Monitor* window

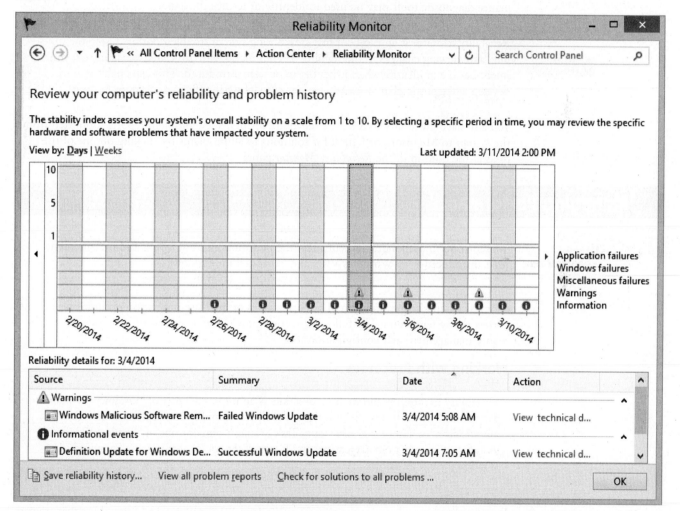

The stability index is a number from 0 to 10 (with 0 representing the least and 10 the most stability) that is calculated using information about the following types of events:

- **Software (Un)Installs** – Includes software installations, uninstallations, updates, and configurations for the operating system, applications, and device drivers.
- **Application Failures** – Includes application hangs, crashes, and terminations of non-responding applications.
- **Hardware Failures** – Includes disk and memory failures.

- **Windows Failures** – Includes boot failures, operating system crashes, and sleep failures.
- **Miscellaneous Failures** – Includes unrequested system shutdowns.
- **System Clock Changes** – Includes all significant clock time changes. This entry appears only when a significant clock time change has occurred recently.

Pertinent events appear in the System Stability Chart as data points. Clicking one of the points displays information about it in the System Stability Report.

The Reliability Monitor snap-in doesn't actually do anything except present event log information in a different way. It is not possible to configure the snap-in or alter the criteria it uses to evaluate a computer's reliability. If you ever notice that the stability index has decreased, you should check the events listed below the data point of instability. These events, or those listed on immediately preceding dates might be the cause for the value decline. Evaluate the nature of the event report to decide whether more detailed event log or additional performance diagnostic tools may be used to identify or resolve the issue.

TAKE NOTE*

> Reliability Monitor is an excellent first stop during system troubleshooting. Using the timeline, and viewing changes to the stability baseline along with associated event entries, you might be able to identify when issues began or were introduced. This can enable you to develop a diagnostic plan or identify an appropriate Restore Point for system recovery.

You also have the ability to Save the reliability history, View problem reports submitted from the system to Microsoft, or Check for solutions to all problems by clicking on one of the links at the bottom of the *Reliability Monitor* panel.

■ Managing Performance

↓ THE BOTTOM LINE

Windows 8.1 incorporates and enhances the performance monitoring and measurement tools introduced with Windows Vista and expanded in Windows 7.

Monitoring and diagnosing system performance is of little use unless you optimize settings or correct the system issues. The following section provides an overview of Windows 8.1 performance management and configuration tools.

Working with Processes

> The ability to monitor and manage processes is an important part of Windows 8.1 maintenance, and Microsoft provides a variety of tools that simplify configuration identification, modification, or automated correction. Task Manager remains one of the most significant tools for active system management, and is one of the tools most notably enhanced in Windows 8 and Windows 8.1.

Every application and service running on a Windows 8.1 computer, including those that are part of the operating system, generate processes, individual tasks that contribute to the overall performance of the system. When performance degrades, the most common method of troubleshooting is to examine the processes running on the computer and the system resources they are consuming. Task Manager remains the most prominent process analysis tool.

One of the challenges historically associated with use of the Task Manager has been the ability to identify process relationships called ***process trees***. The revised layout and presentation of Task Manager now groups processes together according to the process tree of which they are a member, and further groups the trees together based on the services or application features that they provide.

Because enhanced tools like Performance Monitor require advanced skillsets and elevated permissions, Task Manager is the tool most often recommended to the standard user for symptom or cause identification.

Using Task Manager

Task Manager is a graphical tool that has the ability to monitor, diagnose, and enhance system performance.

To access Task Manager, use one of the following procedures.

- Press CTL+ALT+DEL or CTRL+SHIFT+ESC and select Task Manager from the list of available options.
- On the Windows desktop, right-click the taskbar and select *Task manager*.
- On the Start screen, type *Taskmgr*, to raise the Task Manager tile.

USING WINDOWS TASK MANAGER

Once you launch Task Manager, click the More Details down arrow to enhance the display. In this mode, Task Manager displays the following tabs:

- **Processes** – Actually process trees, listed in groups that identify the process group or application with which they are associated, that you can expand as in Figure 21-12 to

CERTIFICATION READY
Configure Task Manager
Objective 6.3

Figure 21-12

The *Processes* tab

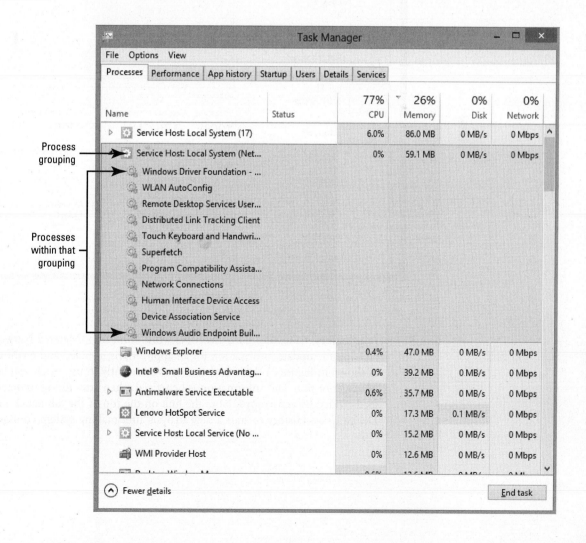

reveal all the processes within the group. Note that each Service Host set is also clearly identified.

- **Performance** – Real-time performance for system components including CPU, Memory, each disk volume, Bluetooth, Wi-Fi, and each Network Interface adapter. By clicking on the component in the left panel, real-time graphics are displayed at the top of the right panel along with configuration and statistical information in report format at the bottom of the right panel, as shown in Figure 21-13.

Figure 21-13

The *Performance* tab

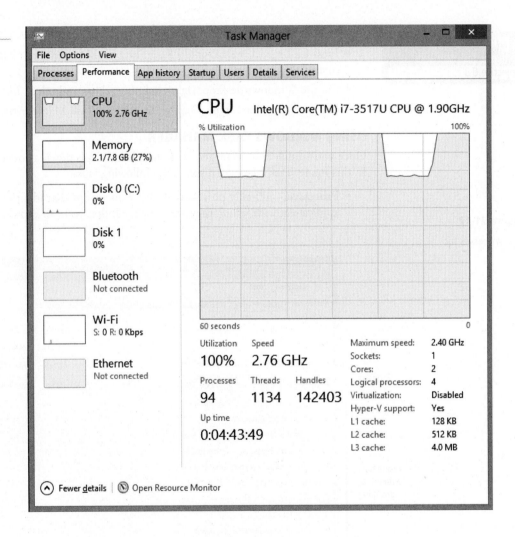

- **App history** – Provides CPU time, Network utilization, Metered Network Utilization, and app tile update information for all applications installed and enabled on the system, as shown in Figure 21-14, whether they are currently in use when you launch Task Manager or not. This information is beneficial when attempting to determine the system load created by active apps. Note the link on the top of the tab panel that enables you to Delete Usage History to start a new analysis after making system configuration changes.

Figure 21-14

The *App history* tab

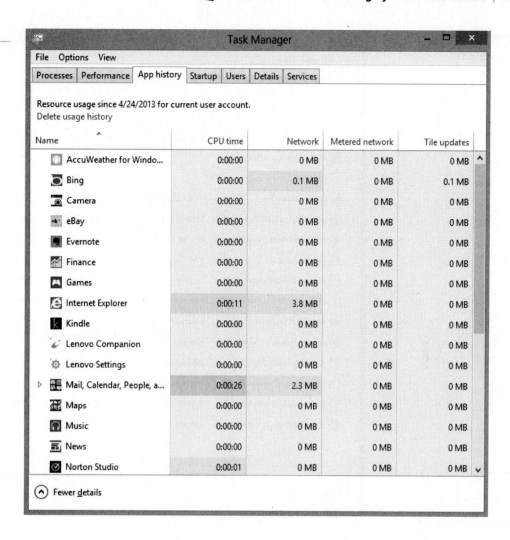

- **Startup** – Identifies all the system components that are launched upon system start, as shown in Figure 21-15. You can expand applications with multiple components to review the subcomponents or multiple instances. You can highlight and right-click on an application to disable its launch at startup, or select an application and use the Disable/Enable toggle button at the bottom right of the panel.

Figure 21-15

The *Startup* tab

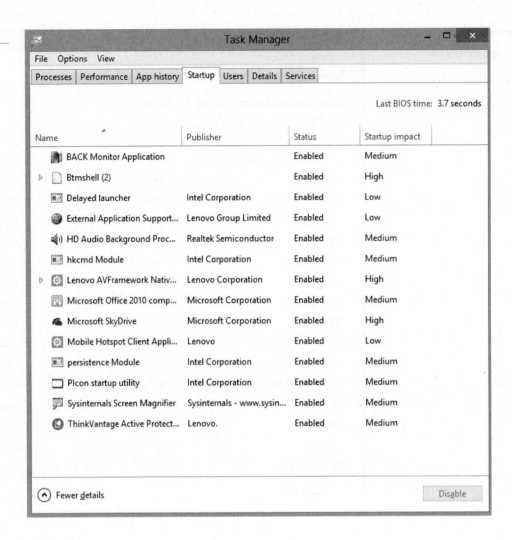

- **Users** – Identifies all users locally or remotely connected to the system. The example shown in Figure 21-16 expands the active user, identifying his active processes. After selecting a specific user, you can disconnect the session by using the *Disconnect* button at the bottom of the panel. The active user will be prompted for confirmation before the disconnect request is completed. This prevents the active user from accidentally disconnecting himself or remote support personnel.

Figure 21-16

The *Users* tab

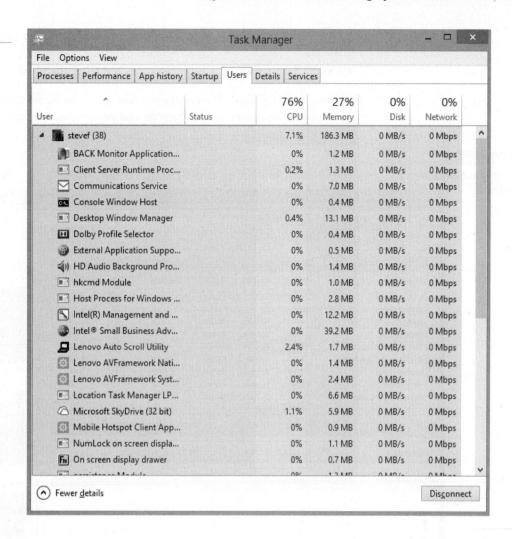

- **Details** – Displays the same information as the Processes tab, albeit with an updated format. Right-clicking on a process enables you to manage the process with End Task, End process tree, Set Priority, Set Affinity, Analyze wait chain, UAC virtualization, Create Dump File, Open File location, Search online, Properties, and Go To Services commands. These options provide diagnostic or performance enhancement settings. The Set **Affinity** capability enables you to assign a process to one or more specific processors in a multi-processor or multi-core system, providing customized processing capabilities.

- **Services** – Displays all of the enabled services for the current instance of the system. Right-clicking enables you to stop or start services, though not the ability to configure service properties. A link at the bottom of the panel enables a user with elevated privileges to launch the Services Management snap-in if there is a need to modify service start up properties.

Using Resource Monitor

Resource Monitor is a Performance tool that extends the capabilities of the Task Manager.

The Resource Monitor can be launched several ways.

- In Task Manager, select the *Performance* tab and click the *Open Resource Monitor* link at the bottom.

- Open the *Control Panel* and click *System and Security > Administrative Tools > Resource Monitor.*
- On the Start screen, type *perfmon.exe /res* and select the tile that appears.

When you launch *Resource Monitor* the window shown in Figure 21-17 appears, displaying a more comprehensive breakdown of process and performance statistics.

Figure 21-17

The *Resource Monitor* window

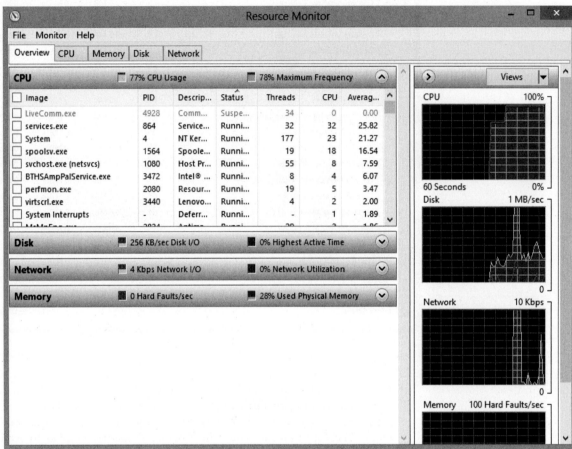

On the Overview tab, there are four real-time line graphs (CPU, Disk, Network, and Memory) that display information about the main system hardware components. Each of the four components also has a separate, expandable section listed below the Overview tab that display more detailed information in text form, such as the resources used by individual applications and processes. Clicking the CPU, Memory, Disk or Network tabs provides even greater analytical detail relative to the hardware component selected. All information is associated with the process using the hardware component.

You can use the check box to the left of each process to select one or more processes for more specific analysis. Once one or more processes are selected, both the graphical and numerical analysis information focuses solely on the selected process. Selections you make in the Overview tab are carried into the other tabs to simplify the task of researching system performance or analyzing process dependencies.

Examining the resources utilized by specific applications and processes over time can help you to determine ways to improve the performance of a computer. For example, if all of the system's physical memory is frequently being utilized, then the system is probably slowed by large amount of paging to disk. Increasing the amount of physical memory or reducing the application load will probably improve the overall performance level of the computer.

TAKE NOTE*

The Network tab and related sub-sections operate much like a Network analyzer. On this page, it is possible to monitor active network traffic, connections, listening services and ports, and performance. When testing network, firewall, or connection security settings, Resource monitor is an extremely powerful aid.

Given the emphasis on security layering that includes elements such as service hardening, Group Policy enforcement, and firewall configuration Resource Monitor can assist with analysis and testing of multiple security components. The Network tab is particularly useful for identifying active TCP/IP connections including process IDs, local and remote addresses and ports, listening ports, and associated network traffic.

Viewing System Configuration Details

The *System Configuration tool (Msconfig.exe)* is designed to support system boot and startup options without the need to use the Boot Control Database, recovery environment, or BCDEdit. You can use this tool to configure custom and diagnostic boot settings so that the user or technician does not have to tap the F8 key during boot.

Tapping the F8 key to access the recovery environment in Windows 8.1 can be problematic. Fast boot and system load processes, accelerated by UEFI-based systems, can make it nearly impossible to interrupt a boot process to enter the Recovery Environment. If the user or technician does not possess an independent boot medium, such as a Windows PE recovery disk or memory device, then the MSConfig tool provides a means to set the system to reboot into the alternate recovery diagnostic environments.

When you start the System Configuration tool, you see the General tab, in which you can temporarily set the system's default startup sequence to a diagnostic or selective mode. These modes can help you to identify programs loading at startup that are slowing the system down.

The Boot tab (see Figure 21-18) enables you to manage the boot mode for the system, including selection of alternate boot partitions on a multi-boot system, and the various Windows RE and Safe Mode boot options typically accessed through the F8 key. The Services tab enables you to enable or disable selected system Services for diagnostic purposes without making permanent changes through the Services snap-in.

Figure 21-18

The *Boot* tab in the *System Configuration* tool

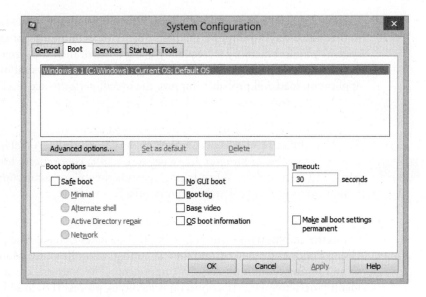

TAKE NOTE *

You can launch MSConfig from within the Windows 8.1 Recovery Environment. This enables you to reconfigure the boot process while performing diagnostic or recovery work.

Adjusting Performance Settings

Adjusting advanced performance settings in Windows 8.1 can be more important than in previous Windows operating systems. The graphics requirements and virtual memory (pagefile.sys) size can dramatically impact Windows 8.1 performance.

You can navigate to the Performance Options dialog box (see Figure 21-19) in several ways, all of which require elevated privilege.

- On the Start screen, type *Adjust Visual*, and then select the *Adjust the appearance and performance of Windows* tile.
- Open the System Properties sheet and, on the Advanced tab, in the Performance box, click Settings.

Figure 21-19

The *Performance Options* dialog box

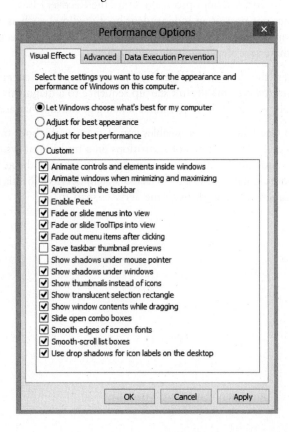

On the Visual Effects tab you can enable Windows 8.1 to choose what's best for your system, adjust for best appearance (effectively turning on all graphics effects), adjust for best performance (turning off all graphics effects and limiting some Windows 8.1 functionality), or customize your effects selection. Disabling some or all of the visual effects can significantly enhance the system's overall performance.

On the Advanced tab, you can configure the system processor to allocate more resources to running programs or background services. Clicking the Change button opens the Virtual Memory dialog box, which enables you to choose the paging file size.

A paging file is an area of disk space that Windows uses to store data that overflows from system memory. This virtual memory enables Windows to run programs that utilize more memory than is available in the system, but at the cost of reduced performance. This is because memory I/O is inherently faster than disk I/O.

In most cases, you should allow Windows 8.1 to automatically manage the paging file size. On a workstation in which memory is the performance bottleneck, you might be able to tweak performance by increasing the size of the paging file. Microsoft recommends you maintain sufficient available, contiguous drive space on your OS drive to support a virtual memory file twice the size of installed RAM.

Configuring Index Settings

CERTIFICATION READY
Configure indexing options
Objective 6.3

The Indexing Options control panel (see Figure 21-20) enables you to modify indexed locations, and to launch an automated troubleshooter by selecting the *Troubleshoot search and indexing* link.

Figure 21-20

The *Indexing Options* panel

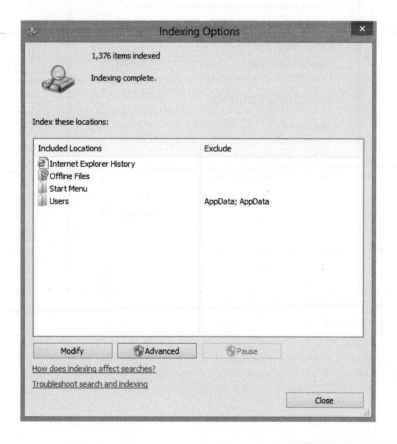

The Advanced button opens the Advanced Options dialog box, as shown in see Figure 21-21. The advanced options include the following:

- The ability to index encrypted files, but only when they are opened by the file owner or an account with equivalent permissions and access to the file encryption key (FEK).

- Treating similar words with diacritics as similar words. A ***diacritic*** is a vowel or consonant utilizing accent marks that may alter pronunciation or interpretation within select language sets. The default is for diacritic indexing to be disabled. Enabling diacritics can enhance searches for some language sets although it might decrease performance and will decidedly increase the index file size.

- Delete and rebuild the index. This can enhance system performance if the index becomes excessively large over time. An index file rebuild might require days to complete, and will dramatically limit the ability of Windows 8.1 auto-search features until the index file is fully rebuilt. Exercise caution when selecting this option.

- Relocate the index file. This option enables you to relocate the index file to an alternate drive, although the drive must be available during system operation, so you cannot use network and removable drive locations.

Figure 21-21

The *Advanced Options* dialog box

■ Troubleshooting Windows 8.1

THE BOTTOM LINE

Configuration and diagnostics tools are of little importance unless system technicians can use the information to enhance system performance and repair problems. Windows 8.1 continues the evolution of Microsoft automated problem detection, repair and reporting features introduced with the Windows Vista platform.

Standard diagnostic tools are now available both from within the Recovery Environment and Windows 8.1 operating system environment.

Windows 8.1 includes automated troubleshooters that enable standard users to diagnose and repair many common system problems. Some of the troubleshooters require elevated rights to correct a problem, though they will minimally diagnose and report symptoms or root causes that enable technical support personnel to focus quickly upon appropriate courses of action.

Using the Windows Memory Diagnostic Tool

The Windows 8.1 memory diagnostic tool performs extensive memory testing during a system reboot.

The Windows 8.1 memory diagnostic tool can detect, and based upon installed RAM features, sometimes effect a repair of system memory. Because of the comprehensive nature of the tool, it can only run during a system reboot or from the Windows Recovery Environment. To launch the Memory Diagnostic, follow the ensuing procedure:

- On the Start screen, type memory and select the Windows Memory Diagnostic tile.
- Open Control Panel and select System and Security > Administrative Tools > Windows Memory Diagnostic.
- Select the Memory Diagnostic after booting into the Windows 8.1 Recovery Environment.

The Windows Memory Diagnostic scheduler panel offers the ability to restart the system immediately and check for problems, or to schedule the tool for execution upon the next system restart. The tool operates using a character-based interface, as shown in Figure 21-22.

Figure 21-22

The Windows Memory Diagnostic tool

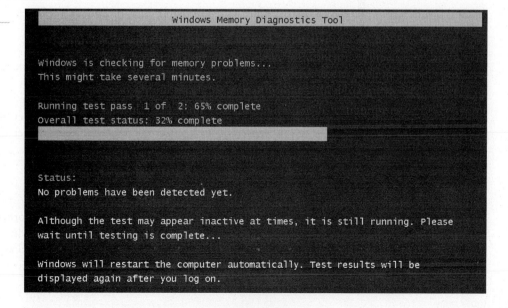

Using the Windows Network Diagnostic Tool

The Windows Network Diagnostic tool is one of several automated troubleshooting tools built into Windows 8.1 that provide network diagnostics and repair capability.

The Windows Network Diagnostic tool is an expansion of the basic network troubleshooting capabilities built into Windows 7. Windows 8.1 uses an ***intelligent network*** management system to detect, monitor, control, and attempt to automatically connect or repair both wired and wireless network connections. The Windows 8.1 Network Diagnostics tool automatically launches if the computer experiences network connectivity issues during system operation. Alternately, you can click on the red "X" that appears on broken network connections or network connected drives to launch the tool. You can also manually launch the tool to run diagnostics at any time in one of the following ways:

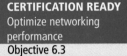

CERTIFICATION READY
Optimize networking performance
Objective 6.3

- Open the *Control Panel* and click *Network and Internet > Network and Sharing Center > Troubleshoot Problems*. This launches the list of Network and Internet troubleshooters shown in Figure 21-23.

Figure 21-23

The *Windows Network Diagnostic* Tool

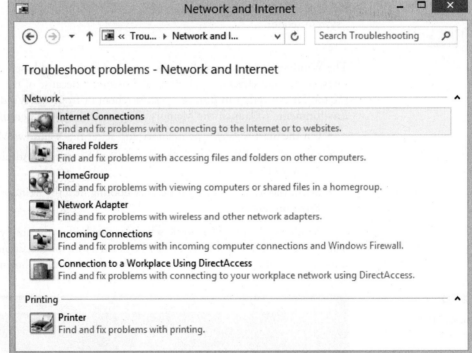

- From the Start Screen, type *networking* and then from the Settings search results, select *Find and fix networking and connection problems*. The Internet Connections troubleshooter appears.

Viewing Problem Reports

Action Center provides access to many of the user-enabled performance and diagnostic tools discussed in this lesson. Additionally, Action Center provides access to any problems reported to Microsoft during automated testing scenarios as well as recommended solutions provided by Microsoft, based upon your Problem Reporting history.

To access the Action Center control panel, shown in Figure 21-24 do one of the following:

- Select the Action Center icon in the notification area on the Desktop,
- On the Start screen, type **Action** and select the *Action Center tile*.
- Open the *Control Panel* and click *System and Security > Action Center*.

Figure 21-24

The *Action Center* panel

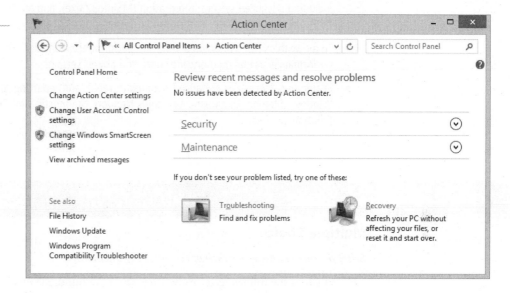

From the Action Center control panel, you can perform the following:

- Select *Troubleshooting* to access a list of Windows 8.1 troubleshooters, including Programs, Hardware and Sound, Network and Internet, and System and Security diagnostics tools.
- Select *View Archived Messages* to view messages associated with problem reports automatically sent to Microsoft. Should a problem be reported to Microsoft, and a possible resolution be available from Microsoft, clicking on the report provides instructions for problem resolution or redirection to a Microsoft site proving potential Knowledge Base patches or updates.

From within Action Center, you can also select *Change Action Center settings* and from among the options at the bottom of the panel select *Problem Reporting Settings* to set preferences for forwarding troubleshooter problem reports to Microsoft.

SKILL SUMMARY

IN THIS LESSON, YOU LEARNED:

- Windows uses a graphical application called *Event Viewer* to display the log information gathered by the operating system.

- The Performance Monitor enables you to view real-time, detailed system information, filter the information for problem isolation, or capture the data for later analysis. Performance Monitor provides line graphs, histograms, or interpretive reports to aid in results analysis.

- Reliability Monitor automatically tracks events that can have a negative effect on system stability and uses them to calculate a stability index.

(continued)

- The Task Manager provides both aggregate and detailed views for processes, process sets, hardware, software, and network resources.

- Resource Monitor expands Task Manager capabilities by providing more detailed analysis and graphics for CPU, Memory, Disk, and Network operations.

- Windows 8.1 provides a comprehensive set of informational and configuration tools including advanced system information (MSInfo32.exe), and startup configuration details (MSConfig.exe) available to the standard user.

- To aid with overall Windows 8.1 system performance, consider adjusting specific visual performance, virtual memory, indexing, and power settings.

- Windows 8.1 provides enhanced diagnostic, repair and reporting tools including the Windows Memory Diagnostic, Windows Network Diagnostic, and Problem Reporting and Solutions tool sets.

■ Knowledge Assessment

Multiple Choice

Select the correct answer for each of the following questions.

1. Which of the following terms best describes the hundreds of statistics that Performance Monitor can display?
   a. Performance objects
   b. Performance counters
   c. Instances
   d. Histograms

2. Which of the following is NOT one of the graphs found in Resource Monitor?
   a. CPU
   b. Disk
   c. Display
   d. Memory

3. Which of the following Event Viewer logs contains no events until you configure auditing policies?
   a. Application
   b. Security
   c. Setup
   d. System

4. When setting Visual Effects, which of the following is NOT an option offered by the interface?
   a. Best Appearance
   b. Custom
   c. Fast Boot
   d. Let Windows choose

5. In Event Viewer, what is the term used for the Windows component logs in the Applications and Services Logs folder?
   a. Instances
   b. Events
   c. Subscriptions
   d. Channels

6. In Task Manager, which tab enables you to set processor affinity?
   a. Performance
   b. Processes
   c. App History
   d. Details

7. Which of the following tools allows you to view configuration settings without making changes?
   a. MSConfig
   b. Task manager
   c. MSInfo32
   d. Windows Experience Index

8. In an event-forwarding situation, the source computers must have which of the following services running?
   a. Windows Event Collector
   b. Secure Hypertext Transfer Protocol
   c. Background Intelligent Transfer Service
   d. Windows Remote Management

9. A user has reported a history of system issues. Which tool would be the best researching the problem?
   a. Event Viewer
   b. Reliability Monitor
   c. Resource Monitor
   d. Task Manager

10. Which of the following is the primary function of the System Configuration tool?
    a. To configure and troubleshoot the Windows 7 startup process.
    b. To configure display and virtual memory settings.
    c. To configure services.
    d. To monitor CPU, Disk, Network, and Memory activity in real time.

Best Answer

Choose the letter that corresponds to the best answer. More than one answer choice may achieve the goal. Select the BEST answer.

1. Which of the following approaches would provide the best and most efficient method of analyzing event logs on twenty Windows 8.1 computers located on the same network?
   a. Use Event Viewer on each computer to analyze its logs.
   b. Use Event Viewer and create a custom view on each computer to analyze its logs.
   c. Use the Microsoft Management console and add the Event Viewer snap-in for each of the 20 computers.
   d. Create Subscriptions in the Event Viewer on the administrator's computer.

2. A standard user wants to be able to monitor the processes running on their computer. Of the tools listed, which would work best while keeping in mind elevated permission and skill sets needed to setup and gather the required information?
   a. Performance Monitor
   b. Reliability Monitor snap-in
   c. Task Manager
   d. Resource Monitor

3. A Windows 8.1 computer is not providing the high level of performance a user expected. The user indicates the hard drive light is blinking a lot when they are working on the computer. Which of the following would represent the most cost effective approach to solve this type of problem?
   a. Increase the physical memory.
   b. Increase the physical memory and add a larger hard disk.
   c. Increase the physical memory and install a faster processor.
   d. Install a faster processor.

4. A help desk employee needs to collect hardware, component and software information from standard users while providing phone support. Which is the best tool for collecting this type of information quickly?
   a. Task Manager
   b. System Information Tool
   c. Performance Monitor
   d. Resource Monitor

Matching and Identification

1. Match the following terms with their corresponding definitions.
   _____ a) Diacritic
   _____ b) Affinity
   _____ c) Performance counter
   _____ d) Data collector set
   _____ e) Collector
   _____ f) Performance object
   _____ g) Reliability Monitor
   _____ h) Events
   _____ i) Process tree
   1. Stability tracking tool
   2. Captured activity for process ID units
   3. Process relationship
   4. Processor association
   5. Captures performance counter data
   6. Performance Monitor statistic
   7. Recipient of forwarded events
   8. Vocabulary accent
   9. Performance Monitor category

Build a List

1. Specify the correct order of steps to create a custom view in Event Viewer.
   _____ From the *Logged* drop-down list, select the time interval from which you want to display events.
   _____ From the *By log* drop-down list, select the log(s) from which you want to display events.
   _____ In the *Event level* area, select the check boxes for the types of events you want to display.
   _____ Right-click the **Custom Views** folder and then, from the context menu, select **Create Custom View**.
   _____ In the Start screen, launch **Control Panel** > **System and Security** > **Administrative Tools** > **Event Viewer**.
   _____ Click **OK**. The console adds your view to the folder you selected and displays the view in the detail pane.

_____ In the *Name* text box, type a name for the view, a description if desired, and select the folder in which you want to create your custom view.

_____ Click **OK.** The *Save Filter to Custom View* dialog box appears.

2. Specify the correct order of steps to create an event subscription.

_____ Click **OK** to create the subscription.

_____ Use the controls to select the events you want the source computers to forward and then click **OK.**

_____ In the Start screen, launch **Control Panel** > **System and Security** > **Administrative Tools** > **Event Viewer.**

_____ Click **Select Events.** The *Query Filter* dialog box appears.

_____ Right-click the **Subscriptions** node and, from the context menu, select **Create Subscription.**

_____ Select one of the following subscription type options: **Collector initiated** or **Source computer initiated.**

_____ Click **Advanced** to set delivery optimization settings or use **HTTPS** for additional security.

_____ In the *Subscription Name* text box, type a name for the subscription.

■ Business Case Scenarios

Scenario 21-1: Using the Window Network Diagnostic Tool

A standard user is experiencing Internet connectivity issues. You have advised the user to run the Windows Network Diagnostic tool to repair the problem, to no effect. Diagnostics identify problems resolving host names and accessing specific services on remote computers. Explain what might be limiting the automated repairs associated with the Windows Network Diagnostic tool.

Scenario 21-2: Setting Up an Event Collector

A remote engineering system fails intermittently. The helpdesk attempts to create an event collector to monitor specific incidents occurring on the remote system, The remote system is visible across the network, and you confirm that you can telnet to the system. An event subscription exists in the collector computer; the remote system recently rebooted, yet there are no events in the Forwarded Events log. Explain some of the steps that you might take to affect a working solution.

22

LESSON

Configuring System Recovery

70-687 EXAM OBJECTIVE

Objective 7.1 – Configure system recovery. This objective may include but is not limited to: configure a recovery drive; configure system restore; perform a driver rollback; perform a refresh or recycle; configure restore points.

LESSON HEADING	EXAM OBJECTIVE
Performing System Recovery of Windows 8.1	
Creating a Windows 8.1 Recovery drive	Configure a recovery drive
Using System Restore	Configure restore points
Performing a Complete Restore	Configure system restore
Performing Driver Rollbacks	Perform a driver rollback
Using PC Refresh and PC Reset	Perform a refresh or recycle

KEY TERMS

driver roll back

PC Refresh

PC Reset

recimg.exe

restore points

system image

System Restore

■ Performing System Recovery of Windows 8.1

THE BOTTOM LINE

The ability to isolate problems, select the right tool(s) to resolve them and return a system to a functional state quickly is a key skill that all administrators need.

You just completed a new install of an application, updated a device driver for an existing piece of hardware, or removed a service that you think you no longer needed. In most situations, all will go well and you can expect Windows 8.1 to perform as expected. At some point in the future, at the most inopportune time, your Windows 8.1 system will fail to run the way you expect it to. When this happens, you will need to have the tools and experience to return the system to a functional state as quickly as possible.

In this lesson, you learn about the tools available with Windows 8.1 and how they can help you return your Windows 8.1 system to a functional state.

Creating a Windows 8.1 Recovery Drive

In the event that a fault occurs in Windows 8.1 that prevents the system from booting, it is still possible to start the computer and access the recovery tools in the Windows Recovery Environment (Windows RE). However, to do this, you must create a Windows 8.1 recovery drive before the problem occurs.

To create a recovery drive in Windows 8 or Windows 8.1, you can use either a writable optical disk or a USB flash drive.

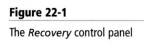

CERTIFICATION READY
Configure a recovery drive
Objective 7.1

If your computer is an original equipment manufacturer (OEM) product that includes a recovery partition containing the Windows 8.1 installation files, you can also create a recovery drive that includes those files, enabling you to use the disk to perform a complete reset of the computer,

To create a Windows 8.1 recovery drive, use the following procedure.

CREATE A RECOVERY DRIVE

GET READY. Log on to Windows 8.1 using an account with administrative privileges and then perform the following steps:

1. Open the **Control Panel** and, in the *View by* drop-down list, click **Large icons**.

   The *Control Panel* interface displays individual icons for each of the available applications.

2. Click **Recovery**.

   The *Recovery* control panel appears, as shown in Figure 22-1.

Figure 22-1

The *Recovery* control panel

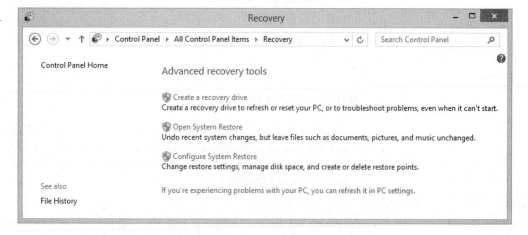

3. Click **Create a recovery drive**.

   The *Recovery Drive Wizard* appears, displaying the *Create a recovery drive* page.

4. To create a USB recovery drive, insert a flash drive with a capacity of at least 256 MB into a USB slot.

5. If your computer has a recovery partition that you want to include on the recovery drive, select the *Copy the recovery partition from the PC to the recovery drive* checkbox and then click **Next**.

   The *Select the USB flash drive* page appears, as shown in Figure 22-2.

Figure 22-2

The *Select the USB flash drive* page

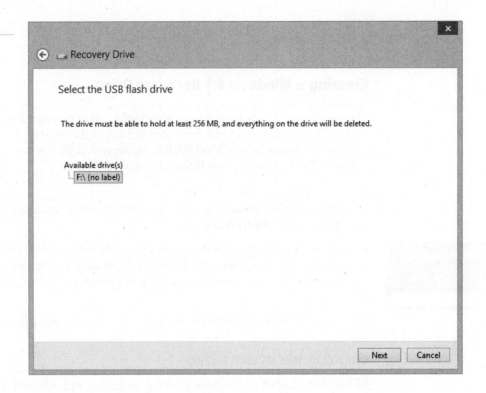

6. From the *Available drives* list, select the USB drive you want to use and then click Next.

   The *Create the recovery drive* page appears.

7. Click Create.

   The wizard creates the recovery drive and the *The recovery drive is ready* page appears.

8. Click Finish.

9. Close the *Recovery* control panel.

Using System Restore

Installing a new program or driver can sometimes make Windows 8.1 crash or function in a way you never expected. If this happens, you will want to return the PC's system files and programs to a time when things were working while not affecting your personal documents or other data.

Windows 8.1 *System Restore* is a recovery option for your computer that saves information about your drives, registry settings, programs, and files in the form of *restore points*. You use the restore points to return these items to an earlier state without impacting your personal files. You should create restore points prior to performing any major system event such as the installation of a program.

CREATING A SYSTEM RESTORE POINT

CERTIFICATION READY
Configure restore points
Objective 7.1

Windows 8.1, by default, automatically creates restore points every seven days if you have not created one during that time period. You can also create restore points manually anytime you choose, using the following procedure.

CREATE A SYSTEM RESTORE POINT

GET READY. To create a system restore point, log on to Windows 8.1 using an account with administrative privileges and, perform the following steps:

1. On the Start screen, type Create and select Create a Restore Point. The System Properties sheet appears, with the System Protection tab selected. System Restore.

2. On the *System Protection* tab, click Configure. The System Protection for Local Disk (C:) dialog box appears, as shown in Figure 22-3.

Figure 22-3

Setting disk space usage

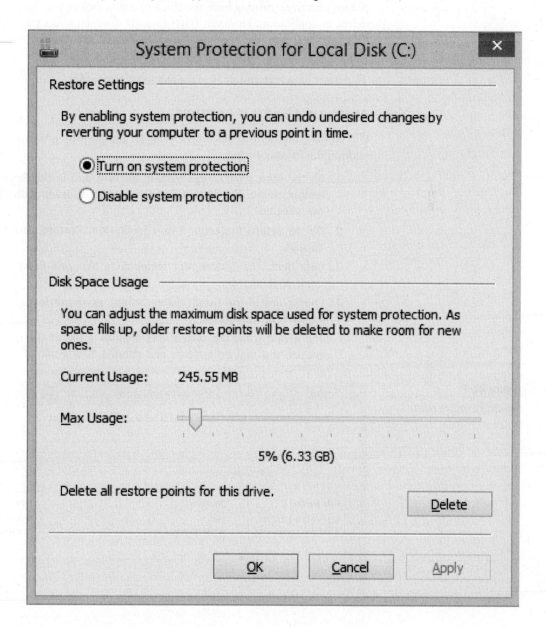

3. Confirm that the *Turn on system protection* option is selected, and under *Disk Space Usage*, drag the slider to set the maximum disk space you want to use for system protection, then click OK.

   As the amount of drive space is filled up, the system will delete the oldest restore points to make room for new ones.

4. Click Create. The *Create a restore point* dialog box appears.

5. Type a name for the restore point and click **Create**. The system creates the restore point and a System Protection message box appears.

6. Click **Close**.

7. Click **OK** to close the *System Properties* sheet.

PERFORMING A SYSTEM RESTORE

Using the system restore points you have created, you can restore the system to one of those points, effectively turning back the clock to a time before you installed a problematic update, driver, or application. However, system restore does not affect your documents, pictures, or other personal data. For example, a file you deleted after the restore point would still be deleted after you perform the restore.

To perform a system restore, use the following procedure.

 PERFORM A SYSTEM RESTORE

GET READY. Log on to Windows 8.1 using an account with administrative privileges and perform the following steps:

1. On the Start screen, type **System Restore** and in the *Results* list, click **Create a restore point**. The System Properties sheet appears, with the System Protection tab selected.

2. On the System Protection tab, click **System Restore**. The System Restore wizard appears.

3. Click **Next**. The *Restore your computer to the state it was in before the selected event* page appears.

4. Choose one of the listed restore points, as shown in Figure 22-4, and click **Scan for affected programs**.

   The wizard scans the system and displays a list of the updates, drivers, and applications that will be restored and deleted as a result of the restore process.

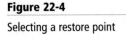

Figure 22-4

Selecting a restore point

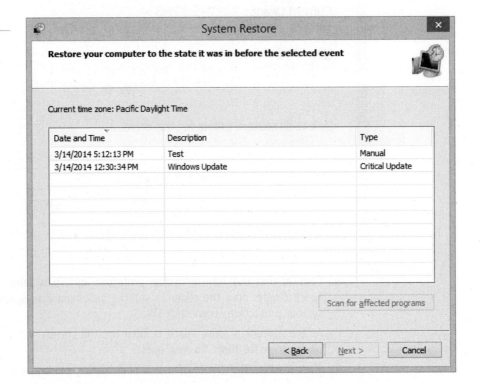

TAKE NOTE *

If you changed your Windows password, you should also create a password reset disk. To do this, type **create** on the Start screen and select *Create a password reset* disk.

5. Click **Close** to dismiss the list and then click **Next**. The *Confirm your restore point* page appears.

6. Click **Finish**.

7. Click **Yes** to begin the system restore process.

   Windows restarts the computer, restores your files and settings, restores the registry, and removes any temporary files as part of the restore process.

8. Log on to Windows 8.1 when the restore process is completed.

Performing a Complete Restore

> If you experience a crash of your Windows 8.1 system and your hard drive is no longer functional, you can perform a complete restore from a system image you have prepared previously.

To prepare for a complete restore, you will need to create a ***system image*** of your computer. The system image is an exact copy of the drives required for Windows to run. This includes the Windows 8.1 operating system, system settings, programs and files. When you restore from an image, it is a complete restore of entire drives; therefore, you cannot choose individual items for restoration.

In Windows 8, the option to create a system image could be found in the Windows 7 File Recovery application. That application is not included with Windows 8.1, but the Create a System Image wizard remains accessible. You can create a system image on a hard disk formatted with NTFS, on a USB flash drive, on one or more writable optical disks, or on a shared network folder.

CERTIFICATION READY
Configure system restore
Objective 7.1

 CREATE A WINDOWS 8.1 SYSTEM IMAGE

GET READY. Log on to Windows 8.1 using an account with administrative privileges and perform the following steps:

1. Open Windows Control Panel and select System and Security > File History. The File History control panel appears.

2. Click System Image Backup. The Create a System Image Wizard appears, displaying the *Where do you want to save the backup?* page, as show in Figure 22-5.

Figure 22-5

The *Where do you want to save the backup?* page

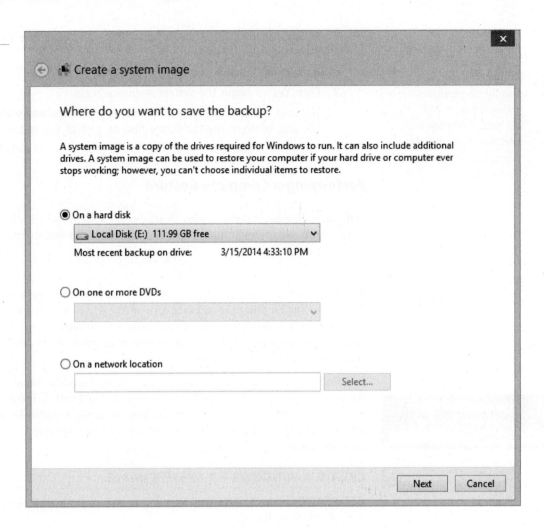

Create a system image

Where do you want to save the backup?

A system image is a copy of the drives required for Windows to run. It can also include additional drives. A system image can be used to restore your computer if your hard drive or computer ever stops working; however, you can't choose individual items to restore.

⦿ On a hard disk

🖴 Local Disk (E:) 111.99 GB free ⌄

Most recent backup on drive: 3/15/2014 4:33:10 PM

○ On one or more DVDs

○ On a network location

         Select...

Next   Cancel

3. Select one of the three storage options and choose a hard disk, DVD, or network location. If necessary, you can supply the credentials needed to access the network.

4. Click Next. The *Confirm your backup settings* page appears.

5. Click Start backup.

    Windows 8.1 saves the system image backup to the location you specified.

6. Click Close.

 PERFORM A COMPLETE SYSTEM RESTORE

GET READY. Log on to Windows 8.1 using an account with adminisrative privileges and perform the following steps:

1. Open the PC Settings screen and click Update and Recovery. The Update and Recovery screen appears.

2. Click Recovery.

3. Under Advanced startup, click Restart now. The *Choose an option* screen appears, as shown in Figure 22-6.

Figure 22-6

The *Choose an option* screen

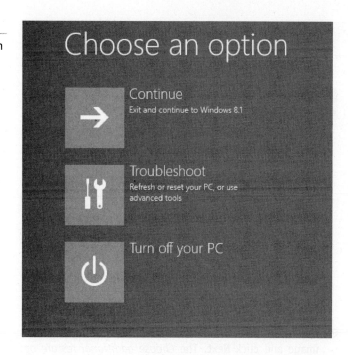

4. Click Troubleshoot. The Troubleshoot page appears.
5. Click Advanced options. The *Advanced options* screen appears, as shown in Figure 22-7.

Figure 22-7

The *Advanced options* screen

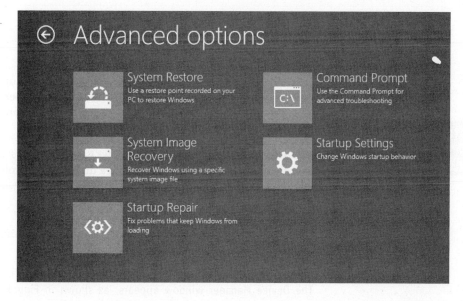

6. Click System Image Recovery. The computer restarts and the *System Image Recovery* screen appears.
7. Select an account and supply the appropriate password. Then click Continue. The Re-image Your Computer Wizard appears, as shown in Figure 22-8.

Figure 22-8

The Re-image Your Computer
Wizard

8. Choose whether to use the latest available system image or browse to a previous image and click Next. The *Choose additional restore options* page appears.

9. Configure the available options, if necessary, and click Next.

10. Review the selected re-imaging parameters and click Finish.

11. Click Yes to confirm your selection. The system restores the image and restarts.

Performing Driver Rollbacks

When installing a device driver for a new piece of hardware or updating and existing driver, you may discover your system is no longer functioning properly. If this occurs, you can quickly recover your system by rolling it back to the previous device driver.

CERTIFICATION READY
Perform a driver rollback
Objective 7.1

Driver rollback is a recovery feature in Windows 8.1 that enables you to reinstall the last device driver that was functioning. To roll back a driver, use the following procedure.

 ROLL BACK A DRIVER

GET READY. Log on to Windows 8.1 using an account with administrative privileges and perform the following steps:

1. On the Start screen, type Device Manager and select the Device Manage tile. The Device Manager window appears, as shown in Figure 22-9.

Figure 22-9

The Device Manager window

2. Expand the categories as needed to locate the device using the driver you want to roll back.
3. Right-click the device and choose **Properties**. The device's Properties sheet appears.
4. Click the **Driver** tab.
5. Click **Roll Back Driver**. An Update Driver Warning message appears.
6. Click **Yes**. The system installs the previous version of the driver.
7. Restart the computer (if necessary).

Using PC Refresh and PC Reset

Over time as you add/remove applications and make changes to your system, you may find it no longer functions quite as well as it used to. If this happens, you can use the PC Reset and PC Refresh options to return your system to a functioning state.

PC Reset is a tool that you use when you need to return your PC back to the original state it was in when you purchased it or first installed Windows 8.1. The tool removes any custom settings you have made, erases your personal data, and removes the Windows and desktop apps from the computer. This is basically a full reinstall of the Windows 8.1 operating system minus the need to answer the setup questions.

CERTIFICATION READY
Perform a refresh or recycle
Objective 7.1

For a less intrusive approach, you can perform a *PC Refresh*. A PC Refresh enables you to retain your personal data, your Windows Store apps, your basic configuration settings, such as mapped drives, and drive letter assignments, and your personalization settings. The BitLocker and BitLocker To Go also remain intact. A PC Refresh does not retain your PC settings, file associations, display settings, or desktop applications. If you have desktop applications installed, whether from disk or a website, the system creates an HTML file on your desktop following the PC Refresh that contains information about the application's name, along with a link to the manufacturer's website. To perform a PC Reset, use the following procedure.

PERFORM A PC RESET

GET READY. Log on to Windows 8.1 using an account with administrative privileges and perform the following steps:

1. Open the PC Settings screen and click Update and Recovery. The Update and Recovery screen appears.
2. Click Recovery.
3. Under *Remove everything and reinstall Windows*, click Get started. The *Reset your PC* screen appears, as shown in Figure 22-10.

Figure 22-10

The Reset your PC screen

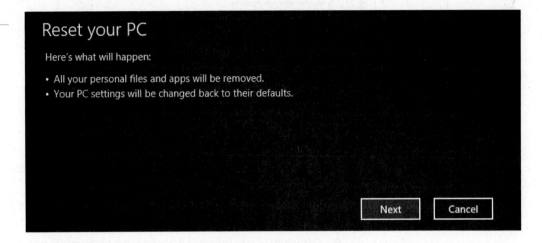

4. Click Next. A *Do you want to fully clean your drive?* screen appears.
5. Click **Just remove my files**. The *Ready to reset your PC* screen appears.

> **+ MORE INFORMATION**
>
> This process formats the drive. If you are not keeping the computer and the drive contains sensitive information, select *Fully clean the drive*. This will write random patterns to each sector on the drive, adding an additional level of protection.

6. Click **Reset**. The system restarts and reinstalls Windows, after which the standard initial configuration screens appear.

To perform a PC Refresh, use the following procedure.

PERFORM A PC REFRESH

GET READY. Log on to Windows 8.1 using an account with administrative privileges and perform the following steps:

1. Open the PC Settings screen and click Update and Recovery. The Update and Recovery screen appears.
2. Click Recovery.
3. Under *Refresh your PC without affecting your files*, click Get started. The *Refresh your PC* screen appears, as shown in Figure 22-11.

Figure 22-11

The Refresh your PC screen

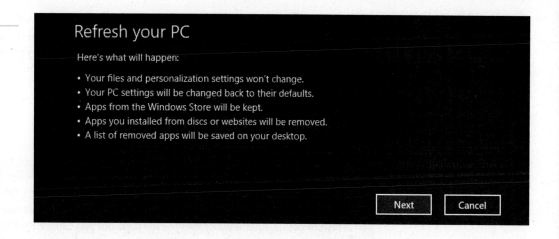

4. Click Next. The *Apps you'll need to reinstall* screen appears, listing any desktop application installed on the computer.
5. Click Next. The *Ready to refresh your PC* screen appears.
6. Click Refresh. The system restarts and performs the refresh.
7. Log on to Windows 8.1, using the same administrative account.
8. On the Windows desktop, double-click the Removed Apps icon. An *Apps removed while refreshing your PC* home page appears, as shown in Figure 22-12.

Figure 22-12

The *Apps removed while refreshing your PC* home page

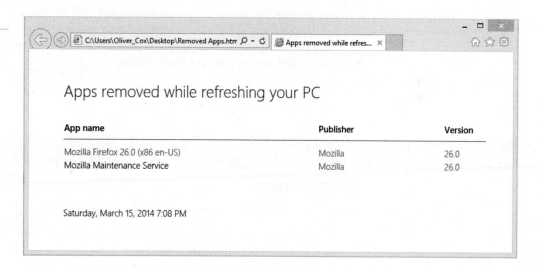

+ MORE INFORMATION

Clicking on an app name will take you to the manufacturer's website where you can download and reinstall the app.

9. Reinstall any applications that you need.
10. Delete the Removed Apps link.

If you want to keep your settings and desktop applications, you can use a utility called *Recimg.exe*. Recimg.exe captures an image of your PC after you install the applications and make any personal customizations, and stores it in a folder you specify. The next time you perform a PC Refresh, the system uses image and retains your settings and desktop applications.

SKILL SUMMARY

IN THIS LESSON, YOU LEARNED:

- Windows 8.1 System Restore is a recovery option that that saves information about your drives, registry settings, programs and files in the form of restore points. Windows creates restore points automatically every seven days but you can create them manually as well.

- To perform a complete system restore, you will need to create a system image. The system image is an exact copy of the drives required to run Windows 8.1.

- When installing a device driver for a new piece of hardware, you have the option to perform a driver roll back. This reinstalls the last device driver that was functioning.

- A PC Reset returns your PC back to the original state it was in when you purchased it. This removes any custom settings, erases your personal data and removes both Windows and desktop apps from the computer.

- A PC Refresh is less destructive, compared to a PC Reset. It enables you to retain your personal data, Windows Store apps, basic settings, custom personalization settings, BitLocker, and wireless settings.

- Recimg.exe can be used to capture an image of your PC after you have installed Windows and desktop applications and customized the system to your liking. The image is placed in a folder you specify and the next time you run a PC Refresh, the system uses the image and retains your settings and desktop apps.

■ Knowledge Assessment

Multiple Choice

Select one or more correct answers for each of the following questions.

1. Which of the following are true regarding system restore points? (Choose all that apply.)
   a. Create them on a monthly basis.
   b. Create them prior to performing a major system event.
   c. Windows 8.1 creates them every 7 days if one has not been created during that time period.
   d. Windows 8.1 creates them every 3 days if one has not been created during that time period.

2. You want to boot into Safe Mode on Windows 8.1. Which of the following could you use? (Choose all that apply.)
   a. Click **Change PC Settings** > **General** > **Click Restart Now** under Advanced Startup
   b. Press **F8** during startup
   c. Press **F9** during startup
   d. Type **shutdown /r /o** in the Run dialog box.

3. Which of the following tools would you use to create a system image that can be used for PC Refresh?
   a. Windows 8 File Recovery
   b. File History
   c. Reimg.exe
   d. Recimg.exe

4. Which option would you recommend to make sure your Windows 8.1 desktop applications are not lost during a restore?
   a. PC Reset
   b. PC Refresh with recimg.exe
   c. PC Reset with recimg.exe
   d. PC Refresh with recoverimg.exe

5. Which of the following will create an HTML file on your desktop that contains links to web sites for your desktop?
   a. PC Reset
   b. Recimg.exe
   c. PC Refresh
   d. PC Reset with recimg.exe

6. What entity is responsible for making sure driver files for Windows 8 are compatible with the operating system and will not impact the stability of the operating system?
   a. Microsoft
   b. Windows Hardware Quality Labs
   c. Windows Software Quality Labs
   d. Windows Quality Driver Labs

Best Answer

Choose the letter that corresponds to the best answer. More than one answer choice may achieve the goal. Select the BEST answer.

1. A user calls the help desk and indicates their Windows 8 computer is failing right after they enter their logon credentials. Other complaints from users indicate the problem is related to a new program that is in the Startup Group. Which option is the best approach to use to resolve the problem in the most efficient way?
   a. Use a system restore point to return the system to a previous point in time that it was functioning.
   b. Perform a Complete Restore.
   c. Boot into Safe Mode and use the Task Manager to disable the new program.
   d. PC Reset.

2. A user wants to be able to restore desktop applications on a Windows 8.1 computer should a problem occur in the future. Which combination of tools will make the process as simple as possible and require the least amount of administrative effort?
   a. Create an image with the Recovery Drive Wizard.
   b. Run Recimg.exe and use PC Refresh to restore.
   c. Run a PC Reset.
   d. Run Recimg.exe only.

3. A user is unable to log into a Windows 8.1 client computer. Which option will provide access as quickly as possible, to begin the troubleshooting process?
   a. Boot from a Windows 8.1 Recovery drive.
   b. Select the **Windows logo key + I**.
   c. Select the **Windows logo key + R** and type **shutdown /r /o**.
   d. Restart and press **F8**.

4. A user makes major changes to a Windows 8.1 client computer every two days. How frequently should the user create a system restore point?
   a. Every 2 days.
   b. Let Windows 8.1 create it automatically based on its default schedule.
   c. Every 5 days.
   d. Every day.

5. A user has just completed a PC Refresh on a Windows 8.1 computer. What is the best way to reinstall the desktop applications that were removed during the refresh?
   a. Refer to your notes on what was original installed on the computer.
   b. Contact your system administrator to see if they can provide a software inventory of what was on the system prior to the refresh.
   c. Refer to the HTML file on the desktop that was created as part of the refresh process.
   d. Ask the user of the computer what was original installed on their system.

Matching and Identification

Complete the following exercise by matching the terms with their corresponding definitions.

_____ a) Recimg.exe
_____ b) PC Reset
_____ c) PC Refresh
_____ d) Restore point
_____ e) Driver Rollback
_____ f) Registry

1. Used in combination with PC Refresh to restore your settings and traditional applications.
2. Should be created prior to performing any major system event. Allow you to return to a point in time.
3. Used to return your system to the state it was in when you purchased it or first set it up.
4. A database used by Windows to store information on services, installed programs and their settings, user profiles and system hardware.
5. Creates an HTML file on your desktop after it completes the restore process
6. Allows you to reinstall the last device driver that was functioning.

Build a List

1. In order of first to last, specify the six steps used to roll back a device driver:
   _____ Press the **Windows logo key** + **w** and then type **Device Manager**.
   _____ Right-click the device and then choose **Properties**.
   _____ Log into the Windows 8.1 computer with administrative credentials
   _____ Expand the category of devices and locate the device that uses the driver you want to roll back.
   _____ Click the **Drivers** tab.
   _____ Click **Roll Back Driver**.

■ Business Case Scenarios

Scenario 22-1: Troubleshooting a Device Driver Roll Back

A Windows 8.1 client computer is having problems with an HP LaserJet printer. The device driver is rolled back to see if this resolves the problem. After accessing the properties for the device, the option to roll back the device is greyed out. What could be causing this problem?

Scenario 22-2: Restoring the Missing Apps

Tom receives a call while working on the help desk from a Windows 8.1 user. The user informs Tom that Elliot, one of the junior administrators, just repaired his computer but he can no longer find some of the applications that were once installed on the computer. After talking to the junior administrator, Tom discovers that Elliot used the PC Refresh option. How should Tom respond to the user?

23 | LESSON

Configuring File Recovery

70-687 EXAM OBJECTIVE

Objective 7.2 – Configure file recovery. This objective may include but is not limited to: restore previous versions of files and folders; configure File History; recover files from OneDrive.

TECHNOLOGY SKILL	OBJECTIVE DOMAIN
Recovering Windows 8.1 Files	
Configuring Files History	Configure File History
Restoring Files and Folders	Restore previous versions of files and folders
Configuring File Restore Points	
Recovering Files from OneDrive	Recover files from OneDrive

KEY TERMS

File History

volume shadow copies

◼ Recovering Windows 8.1 Files

THE BOTTOM LINE

The capability to recover files and folders when they become corrupt or accidentally deleted has been available in versions of Windows for a long time. The primary method of file recovery on a computer running Windows 8.1 is the Windows 8.1 *File History* feature. File History is not intended to be a replacement for an enterprise-wide backup solution; however, it is quick, convenient, and easy to use.

➕ MORE INFORMATION

Since Windows Server 2003, Windows users have used *volume shadow copies* of their files to save and recover data. This feature was also available in Windows XP, Vista, and all versions of Windows 7, and was called Previous Versions. In Windows 8.1, it is renamed File History.

Configuring File History

File History is available on all versions of Windows 8.1 and simply requires you to switch it on and configure it.

CERTIFICATION READY
Configure File History
Objective 7.2

File History ensures that accidental deletion or corruption does not permanently prevent you from accessing your files. In addition, it is possible to retrieve a version you created at an earlier point in time. If you make changes that you need to remove, File History enables you to restore the previous version of a file, either to its original location, overwriting the original, or to an alternate folder.

To configure File History, use the following procedure.

 CONFIGURE FILE HISTORY

GET READY. Log on to the Windows 8.1 computer using an account with administrative privileges. To configure the File History feature, perform the following steps:

1. Open the Control Panel and click **System and Security** > **File History**. The File History control panel appears, as shown in Figure 23-1.

Figure 23-1

The File History control panel

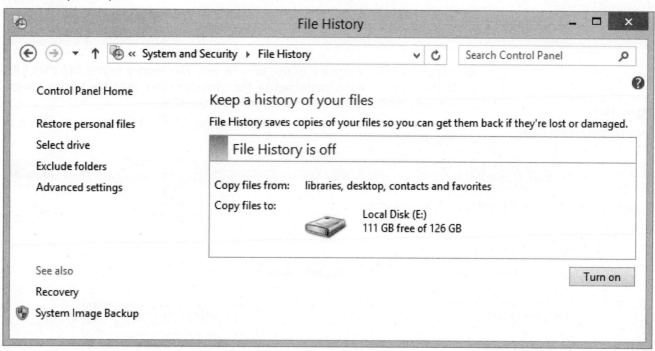

2. Click **Select Drive**, and the *Select a File History drive* dialog box appears, as shown in Figure 23-2.

Figure 23-2

The *Select a File History drive*
dialog box

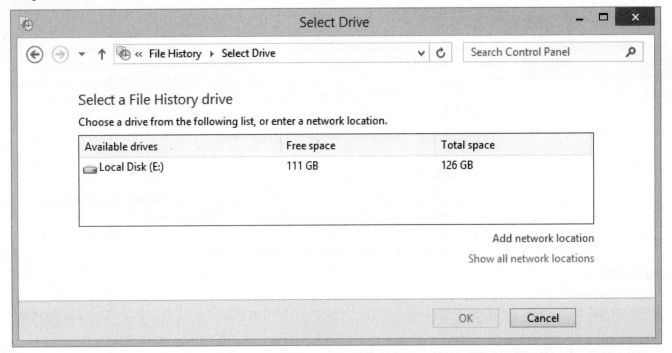

3. Select the drive you want to use to save your File History copies and click OK. If there are no drives connected to the computer other than the system drive, the only available option is Add a Network Location.

Figure 23-3

The *Advanced Settings* dialog
box

4. Click Advanced Settings. The Advanced Settings dialog box appears, as shown in Figure 23-3.

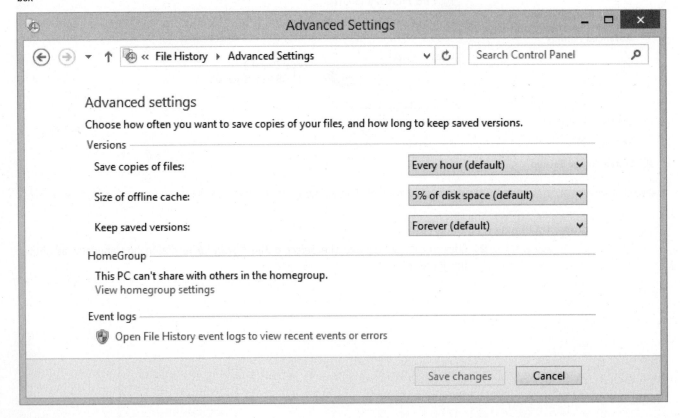

5. Select values for the following File History settings:
   - **Save copies of files** – Specify how often File History should create copies of your files
   - **Size of offline cache** – Specify how much of the disk's storage space File History should use for file copies
   - **Keep saved versions** – Specify how long File history should retain copies of your files
6. Click Save Changes.
7. Back on the File History control panel, click Turn on. File History begins saving copies of your files.

Restoring Files and Folders

Having configured File History, all your previous versions are now available to recover should the current versions become corrupted or should you accidentally delete them.

CERTIFICATION READY
Restore previous versions
of files and folders
Objective 7.2

Once you have identified the need to restore files from a previous point in time, File History enables you to safely recover those important files and folders, which may have become lost or corrupt.

To restore files using File History, use the following procedure.

 RESTORE FILES AND FOLDERS

GET READY. Log on to the Windows 8.1 computer with administrative privileges. To restore files and folders from your File History drive, perform the following steps:

1. On the Start screen, type Restore and select Restore your files with File History. The Home-File History window appears, as shown in Figure 23-4.

Figure 23-4

The Home-File History window

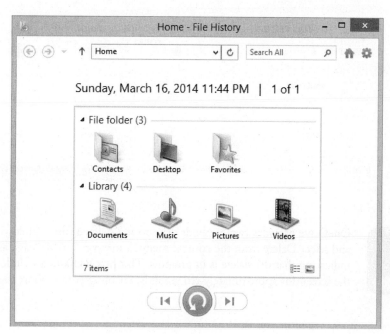

2. Select the file or folder you want to restore and then click the green restore button at the bottom of the window. The system restores the selected file or folder to its original location. If you right-click the file or folder, you can restore it to an alternative location or preview the file before restoring it.

Recovering Files from OneDrive

> Microsoft's OneDrive service provides every holder of a Microsoft account with free storage space in its Internet-based cloud. OneDrive also includes a Recycle Bin feature that enables you to restore files that you have accidentally deleted.

OneDrive (formerly known as SkyDrive) storage is accessible through a Windows app that is built in to Windows 8.1, or you can access it through Microsoft's OneDrive website, as shown in Figure 23-5.

Figure 23-5

OneDrive storage

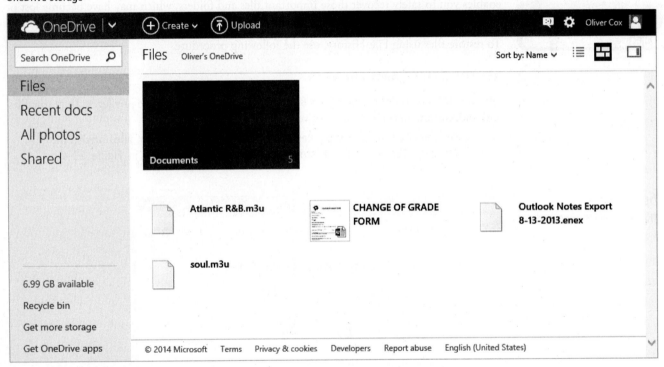

OneDrive provides two methods of restoring deleted files. When you right-click a file or folder and select Delete from the context menu, a message box appears, as shown in Figure 23-6, indicating that the delete is in progress. This box includes an Undo button, and it remains on the screen for approximately ten seconds, enabling you to abort the delete, if you prefer.

CERTIFICATION READY
Recover files from OneDrive
Objective 7.2

Figure 23-6

The OneDrive file delete
message box

Deleting Atlantic R&B from Oliver's

OneDrive

☐ Atlantic R&B

Undo

TAKE NOTE*

The OneDrive Recycle
Bin is located in the
cloud and has no con-
nection to the Windows
Recycle Bin on your
local drive.

Once the file or folder is deleted, OneDrive moves it to the Recycle Bin folder. You can view
your deleted files and folders by clicking the Recycle Bin link, as shown in Figure 23-7. To
restore files or folders in the Recycle Bin, you select their checkboxes, right-click, and choose
Restore from the context menu. OneDrive then restores the selected files or folders to their
original locations.

Figure 23-7

The OneDrive Recycle Bin

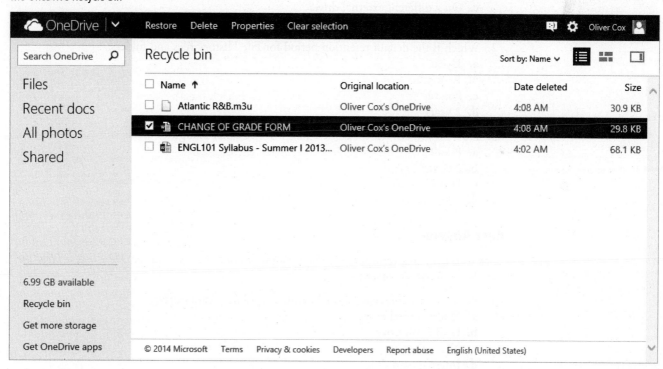

OneDrive retains the files and folders in its Recycle Bin for up to 30 days, after which it
begins permanently deleting the oldest ones. If, however, your available OneDrive storage
space reaches 10 percent, the system begins deleting files and folders, regardless of their ages.

SKILL SUMMARY

IN THIS LESSON, YOU LEARNED:

- The primary method of file recovery on a computer running Windows 8.1 is the Windows 8.1 File History feature.

- OneDrive includes a Recycle Bin feature that enables you to restore files that you have accidentally deleted.

- How to restore files in OneDrive.

Knowledge Assessment

Multiple Choice

1. Where is the File History stored if the File History drive is offline?
   a. Nowhere. File History is off.
   b. On a network share.
   c. On a different external drive.
   d. System drive cache.

2. Which is the default retention period for File History files and folders?
   a. 1 year
   b. 1 month
   c. Forever
   d. 2 years

3. How do you advertise a File History drive to other computer users?
   a. Email
   b. Network share
   c. HomeGroup
   d. File transfer

Best Answer

Choose the letter that corresponds to the best answer. More than one answer choice may achieve the goal. Select the BEST answer.

1. Which of the following should be used as a File History drive?
   a. External hard disk
   b. USB Flash drive
   c. Network share
   d. Internal hard disk

2. Which method should be used to preserve files and folders in Windows?
   a. System Recovery
   b. System Protection
   c. Previous versions
   d. File History

3. What percentage of your system drive should be reserved for an offline cache (when the File History drive is not available)?
   a. 1%
   b. 10%
   c. 20%
   d. 5%

Matching and Identification

1. Identify which of the following tasks you can accomplish with File History in Windows 8.1.
   _____ Create a recovery disk.
   _____ NTBackup.exe.
   _____ Create a File History Drive.
   _____ Backup the system state.
   _____ Restore Files and Folders.
   _____ Preview a file.
   _____ Create file restore points.

Build a list

1. Specify the correct order of steps necessary to recover files using file history. (Not all steps will be used.)
   _____ Enter Restore files at the start screen.
   _____ Choose settings.
   _____ Run System Recovery.
   _____ Select the relevant files.
   _____ Create a File History drive.
   _____ Restore files.
   _____ Select Restore my files.

■ Business Case Scenarios

Scenario 23-1: Choosing How to Preserve Files

To ensure that a user does not lose her important documents and files on a Windows 8.1 PC, what should you choose to do?

Scenario 23-2: Recovering Files

A Windows 8.1 user needs help. The user has encountered file corruption in some important work documents. How would you assist him?

Appendix A
Exam 70-687
Configuring Windows 8.1

EXAM OBJECTIVE	OBJECTIVE NUMBER	LESSON NUMBER
Install and Upgrade to Windows 8.1		
Evaluate Hardware Readiness and Compatibility	1.1	1
Install Windows 8.1	1.2	2
Migrate and Configure User Data	1.3	3
Configure Hardware and Applications		
Configure Devices and Device Drivers	2.1	4
Install and Configure Desktop Apps and Windows Store Apps	2.2	5
Control Access to Local Hardware and Applications	2.3	6
Configure Internet Explorer 11 and Internet Explorer for the Desktop	2.4	7
Configure Hyper-V	2.5	8
Configure Network Connectivity		
Configure IP Settings	3.1	9
Configure Networking Settings	3.2	10
Configure and Maintain Network Security	3.3	11
Configure Remote Management	3.4	12
Configure Access to Resources		
Configure Shared Resources	4.1	13
Configure File and Folder Access	4.2	14
Configure Authentication and Authorization	4.3	15
Configure Remote Access and Mobility		
Configure Remote Connections	5.1	16
Configure Mobility Options	5.2	17
Configure Security for Mobile Devices	5.3	18
Monitor and Maintain Windows Clients		
Configure and Manage Updates	6.1	19
Manage Local Storage	6.2	20
Monitor System Performance	6.3	21
Configure Backup and Recovery Options		
Configure System Recovery	7.1	22
Configure File Recovery	7.2	23

Note: Page numbers followed by f and t indicates figure and table respectively.